International Law in the 21st Century

NEW MILLENNIUM BOOKS
IN INTERNATIONAL STUDIES

Series Editors
Deborah J. Gerner, University of Kansas
Eric Selbin, Southwestern University and Umeå University

NEW MILLENNIUM BOOKS issue out of the unique position of the global system at the beginning of a new millennium in which our understandings about war, peace, terrorism, identity, sovereignty, security, and sustainability—whether economic, environmental, or ethical—are likely to be challenged. In the new millennium of international relations, new theories, new actors, and new policies and processes are all bound to be engaged. Books in the series will be of three types: compact core texts, supplementary texts, and readers.

Titles in the Series

International Law in the 21st Century
Christopher C. Joyner

Military–Civilian Interactions: Humanitarian Crises and the Responsibility to Protect, Second Edition
Thomas G. Weiss

Globalization and Belonging: The Politics of Identity in a Changing World
Sheila Croucher

The Global New Deal: Economic and Social Human Rights in World Politics
William F. Felice

The New Foreign Policy: U.S. and Comparative Foreign Policy
in the 21st Century
Laura Neack

Global Backlash: Citizen Initiatives for a Just World Economy
Edited by Robin Broad

Negotiating a Complex World: An Introduction to
International Negotiation
Brigid Starkey, Mark A. Boyer, and Jonathan Wilkenfeld
(new edition forthcoming)

Forthcoming in the Series

Liberals and Criminals: IPE in the New Millennium
H. Richard Friman

Law in International Politics: Key Issues and Incidents
B. Welling Hall

Global Politics as If People Mattered
Mary Ann Tétreault and Ronnie D. Lipschutz

The Peace Puzzle: Ending Violent Conflict in the 21st Century
George A. Lopez

Elusive Security: State, International, and Human Security in the 21st Century
Laura Neack

Political Violence
Philip A. Schrodt

International Law in the 21st Century

Rules for Global Governance

Christopher C. Joyner
Georgetown University

ROWMAN & LITTLEFIELD PUBLISHERS, INC.
Lanham • Boulder • New York • Toronto • Oxford

For my students
past, present, and future

ROWMAN & LITTLEFIELD PUBLISHERS, INC.

Published in the United States of America
by Rowman & Littlefield Publishers, Inc.
A wholly owned subsidiary of The Rowman & Littlefield Publishing Group, Inc.
4501 Forbes Boulevard, Suite 200, Lanham, MD 20706
www.rowmanlittlefield.com

P.O. Box 317, Oxford OX2 9RU, UK

Copyright © 2005 by Rowman & Littlefield Publishers, Inc.

British Library Cataloguing in Publication Information Available

Library of Congress Cataloging-in-Publication Data

Joyner, Christopher C.
  International law in the 21st century : rules for global governance / Christopher C.
Joyner.
    p.   cm.—(New Millennium books in international studies)
  Includes bibliographical references and index.
  ISBN 0-7425-0008-X (cloth : alk. paper)—ISBN 0-7425-0009-8 (pbk. : alk. paper)
  1. International law.   2. Globalization.   I. Title: International law in the twenty-first
century.   II. Title.   III. Series: New Millennium books in international studies
KZ3410.J69 2005
341'.09'05—dc22   2004016705

Printed in the United States of America

∞ ™ The paper used in this publication meets the minimum requirements of American National
Standard for Information Sciences—Permanence of Paper for Printed Library Materials, ANSI/
NISO Z39.48-1992.

Brief Contents

Preface   xv

Acknowledgments   xix

PART I: CONCEPTS AND PRINCIPLES

1. The Nature of International Legal Rules   3

2. The International Legal Community   23

3. The State   41

4. The Individual   61

PART II: FUNCTIONS AND PROCESSES

5. International Organizations   85

6. Agreements and Disputes   105

PART III: CHALLENGES AND RESPONSE

7. International Criminal Law   133

8. Use of Force Law   161

9. International Environmental Law   197

10. Global Commons Law   223

11. International Economic Law   253

PART IV: CONCLUSION

12. Looking Back to See Ahead: Globalization and Challenges to the
    International Legal Order   287

Notes   297

Glossary   333

Index   343

About the Author   361

Detailed Contents

Preface   xv

Acknowledgments   xix

PART I: CONCEPTS AND PRINCIPLES

1. The Nature of International Legal Rules   3
  Conceptual Foundations   5
  The Quest for Order   6
  The Nature of Legal Rules   7
  Making International Legal Rules   9
  Sources of International Rules   10
    Formal Agreements   11
      Treaties   11
      International Conventions   11
    Custom   11
    General Principles of Law   13
    Judicial Decisions and Scholarly Writings   14
  Historical Development of International Law   14
  Schools of Legal Thought   15
  Conclusion   21

2. The International Legal Community   23
  International Actors   25
    Sovereign States   25
    Transnational Actors   25
    Nonstate Actors   27
    Terrorist Groups   27
    Regimes   27
    Individuals   28
  Classification of States   28
  Sovereignty and States   33
  Sovereignty and Territory   35
  Legal Relations between States   36
  Law and the Community of States   37
  Dualism versus Monism   38

Doctrine of Incorporation   39
Conclusion   39

3. The State   41
  The State as Territory   43
    Acquisition of Territory   43
    Loss of Territory   45
  Self-Determination   46
  Recognition   47
  Rights and Duties of States   49
    Rights of States   50
    Duties of States   53
  State Responsibility   55
  Extinction   56
    Succession   56
  Conclusion   58

4. The Individual   61
  Nationality   63
    Acquisition of Nationality   63
    Statelessness   64
    Loss of Nationality   64
  Jurisdiction over Aliens   64
    Asylum   65
    Extradition   66
    The Case of Pinochet   68
    Special Provisions   69
  Individual Human Rights   69
    Collective Human Rights   72
    Implementation of Human Rights   75
    Regional Human Rights Systems   78
  The Role of the Nongovernmental Organization   80
  Conclusion   81

PART II: FUNCTIONS AND PROCESSES

5. International Organizations   85
  The Role of International Organizations   86
    International Organization Legal Rules   86
    Forms of International Organization Law   87
    International Organizations as Constitutional Lawgivers   88
      International Courts   88
    International Organizations as Prescriptive Lawgivers   90
      The Security Council   91
      The UN General Assembly   93
      The European Union   95
      The Organization of American States   95
    International Organizations as Administrative Lawgivers   96
      The Secretariat   96
      The Trusteeship Council   97

International Organizations and Socioeconomic Concerns | 98
Specialized Agencies | 99
Future Trends of International Organizations | 102
Conclusion | 104

6. Agreements and Disputes | 105
International Agreements | 106
Formulation of Treaties | 109
Treaty Interpretation | 113
Validity of Treaties | 115
Treaty Termination | 116
Conclusion on International Agreements | 118
Peaceful Settlement of Disputes | 119
The Nature of Disputes | 120
The Obligation to Settle Disputes | 121
Processes of Dispute Settlement | 123
Institutions for Dispute Settlement | 124
Regional Courts | 128
Conclusion | 130

PART III: CHALLENGES AND RESPONSE

7. International Criminal Law | 133
The Nature of International Criminal Law | 134
Crimes Committed by Private Persons | 136
Slavery | 136
Piracy | 137
Threats to Maritime Navigation | 138
Aerial Hijacking | 138
Hostage Taking | 139
Kidnapping of Diplomats | 140
International Drug Offenses | 140
Unlawful Use of International Mail | 141
Counterfeiting and Fraudulent Documentation | 141
Unlawful Acts against the Environment | 141
Crimes Committed by Governments | 141
Apartheid | 142
Aggression | 142
Crimes Committed during Armed Conflict | 143
Grave Breaches | 143
Violations of the Laws or Customs of War | 144
Genocide | 145
Crimes against Humanity | 146
State Responsibility for Criminal Offenses | 147
The Duty of Accountability | 148
Enforcement through State Jurisdiction | 149
Enforcement through Tribunals | 151
The Nuremberg Trials | 151

The Tribunal for the Former Yugoslavia   153
The Tribunal for Rwanda   154
The Permanent International Criminal Court   155
Truth Commissions   159
Conclusion   159

8. Use of Force Law   161
Law before the UN Charter   162
Prohibition on the Use of Force   165
Self-Defense   168
Collective Self-Defense   173
Other Justifications for the Use of Force   173
Internal Conflicts   173
Protection of Nationals Abroad   176
Humanitarian Intervention   176
Collective Security   179
Coercive Self-Help Short of War   180
Economic Coercion   181
The Security Council and the Use of Force   183
Peace Operations   188
The General Assembly   189
Regional Organizations   189
Weapons of Mass Destruction   190
Weapons Reduction   191
Weapons Nonproliferation   192
Nuclear-Free Zones   193
Testing   193
The Legality of Nuclear Weapons   194
Conclusion   194

9. International Environmental Law   197
Formulation of Environmental Law   198
The UN Environmental Programme   200
Other Concerned Organizations   201
Conference Diplomacy   203
Legal Sources of Environmental Protection   205
Judicial Cases   205
Normative Principles   206
International Agreements   209
Soft Law   211
Pollution Control Regimes   212
Riparian Law   213
The Law of the Sea   214
Regional Agreements   214
Dumping of Hazardous Wastes   214
Natural Resource Management   216
The Changing Nature of International Environmental Law   219
Conclusion   220

10. Global Commons Law   223
Regime Formation in the Global Commons   225

Common-Space Resource Regimes　　227
   The Oceans　　228
   Antarctica　　236
   The Atmosphere　　239
   Outer Space　　243
Regime Compliance and Enforcement　　246
Conclusion　　250

11. International Economic Law　　253
   The Bretton Woods System　　255
     New International Economic Order　　255
     World Trade Organization　　256
     International Financial Regulation　　261
     International Sale of Goods　　265
       Carriage of Goods　　266
     Intellectual Property Rights　　267
     Foreign Investment　　269
   Regional Organizations　　273
     European Union　　273
     North American Free Trade Agreement　　276
     The Andean Group　　278
     Association of South East Asian Nations　　279
   International Commodity Agreements　　280
   Conclusion　　282

PART IV: CONCLUSION

12. Looking Back to See Ahead: Globalization and Challenges to the
International Legal Order　　287
   The Process of Globalization　　288
     The Economic Dimension　　288
     The Cultural Dimension　　289
     The Political Dimension　　291
   Conclusion　　292

Notes　　297

Glossary　　333

Index　　343

About the Author　　361

Preface

History reveals that human societies can enjoy peaceful, orderly progress but only under the rule of law. Conflict breeds chaos; law produces order. So, too, it is in international society. In an increasingly complicated interdependent, multistate system, the rule of law becomes an ever more essential condition if conflict and confrontation between states are to be avoided and if cooperation and conciliation are to be fostered. Thus, a critical need emerges to regularize state behavior by creating norms and rules that guide and indeed govern relations among states. This highlights a core aim of this text—namely, to examine the basic principles, processes, and institutions that have been developed by states to encourage and facilitate orderly behavior within the international community.

Governments operate internationally through regular ways and permissible means of conduct, most often according to accepted rules of international behavior that have been created by states. Fundamental to the foundation for international cooperation and prosperity are rules of the international game, often referred to as international law. Given the rapidly growing role of legal rules in foreign affairs, students of international relations must understand the principles, concepts, content, and institutions that form these contemporary international rules, as well as the contemporary global issues that challenge their successful operation. This need points toward a fundamental purpose of this work.

In recent decades enormous changes have occurred in the nature of the world's society. Greater internationalization of law has become more necessary as internationalization of life has grown more complicated. While international law today is in no sense complete, its rapid expansion into a credible world system of rules is undeniable. This text aims to underscore this important realization, particularly as it relates to the raft of various interstate relations brought about by the complex forces of independence and globalization.

Similarly, this volume examines international law as a multifaceted process of international relations. It strives to explain and clarify how international law functions to make relations between governments not only possible but also productive as cooperative endeavors—not necessarily in the quest for a unified world order but rather to produce an orderly world in which the principal actors may engage in transnational activities guided by the rule of law.

Many traditional international law texts assume a case method approach by resorting to the use of international and national court decisions to illustrate principles and precepts of international law. Other works treat international legal rules in terms of their traditional framework and relevance for international relations but leave legal considerations a discipline distinct from international politics. This volume seeks to explain how international law and world politics are intimately interwoven such that special rules are constantly being created to deal with emerging problems of international affairs. By doing so, international legal rules can be seen for what they actually do—namely, to provide the institutional means for meeting human needs. By examining international law through the lens of international politics, the student can come to appreciate international legal rules as constructive means, rather than merely dubious nuances, in the relations among states. International law can thus be viewed as a nexus of pragmatic norms, principles, and rules that provide a juridical framework for governments, international organizations, and other multilateral associations to obtain rights and benefits for mutual security and diverse opportunities within the interstate society. By the same token, international law furnishes approved assurances for individuals to attain fundamental values and freedoms as well as protections of security within states. In these ways, this volume proffers insight into how international politics is made to fashion international legal rules and into how the ways and means of those rules operate to promote cooperation and conciliation in international relations between states.

There is no question that international politics and international law are inextricably intertwined. The relations among states occur through the interaction of a system of legal rules and norms to guide government conduct. Simply put, international norms flow from political roots. Consequently, this book endeavors to emphasize the need for and the functions of international rules in the new century to provide fresh insights into the ways that international law must adapt in the future to meet the dynamic challenges of new technologies, globalization, and interdependence.

A related purpose of this book is to investigate the constraints that sustain the normative structure of the international legal system. While self-interest usually is cited as a key in gauging the actions of states, it has become increasingly clear in the 21st century that interstate behavior is regularly guided by normative considerations. Governments usually make policy decisions based on what is perceived as best for their national interest, within the context of what is the proper conduct to follow as set out by internationally agreed-on rules. Thus, not all state behavior is, or ought to be, viewed as motivated by considerations of power.

Contemporary international law contains universal elements that are more pervasive today than in the past because they have been created by virtually all states. The interstate system in the early 21st century is far more complex than those of previous centuries.

The early 20th century saw the breakup of the European balance of power system, the ensuing demise of colonialism, the rise of a vocal majority group of developing states, the onslaught and end of Cold War tensions between the United States and the Soviet Union, and the collapse of that relatively stable bipolar system. More states today create international law than ever before. The development of universally applicable rules for interstate relations has become increasingly necessary to deal with the dynamic twin forces of economic interdependence and globalization that have come to mark international relations in the 21st century.

In these regards, students must understand the political constraints that impinge on the reach of international legal rules and the ways that normative constraints limit choices of political behavior. Consequently, another objective of this study is to furnish students with an appreciation of how international law operates as interstate rules in the interstate system and how political constraints affect the scope and substance of international law.

This volume has as its central concern the relationship of international law to its political roots. When the study of international affairs becomes indifferent to the role of rules and norms in the political intercourse between states, that discipline becomes an incomplete study of world events. Governments are not only interest dependent for their foreign policies, but they also interact according to rules, guidelines, and normative considerations. Thus, the conduct of interstate relations is neither capricious nor whimsical. Foreign policies of governments are purposefully thought out and intentionally designed. Likewise, international legal rules provide the blueprint—and the means—for allowing those policies to work in international relations. This point is manifest: The rules for interstate conduct are real and relevant. More significantly for the study of international relations, governments realize this fact and act accordingly.

In the end, these facts are unmistakable: International legal rules function and international legal institutions operate within political contexts. While international contexts vary in time, geography, and circumstances, they are inevitably affected by social, economic, and cultural factors. The need for and evolution of international legal rules, how they are interpreted, and the means in which they are applied will also vary according to those international contexts, which points toward the ultimate theme of this volume, which is thus: International legal rules are constructed by governments to serve as the means through which common regional and global problems might be addressed and resolved to satisfactory ends. Governments working alone or in groups cannot resolve large-scale regional or global threats to their common existence. Cooperation is critical. International legal rules provide the pragmatic instruments for that cooperative enterprise by offering the means for just and lasting solutions to meet those ends.

Christopher C. Joyner
Oakton, Virginia

Acknowledgments

Volumes of this length and breadth are rarely done without considerable influence from friends, colleagues, and professional institutions, and this one is no exception. The structure of this work originates from the public international law course that I have taught over the past three decades to students at Muhlenberg College, the University of Virginia, George Washington University, Dartmouth College, and Georgetown University. The course, like this text, strives to explain concepts and principles of international law and illustrates how they relate to contemporary issues of international law and politics. Similarly, much is made of real-world examples in both the course and this text to add credibility to the conceptual facets of international law.

This work has greatly benefited from the suggestions and valuable comments of colleagues and friends over the years. A number of colleagues read various chapters at different stages of the writing. Special appreciation is owed to my friend and colleague at Georgetown University, Professor Anthony Clarke Arend, who read and commented on the first chapter concerning international legal rules and subsequently made insightful observations about the legal implications for the use of force, which eventually found their way into chapter 8. Professor David Forsythe of the University of Nebraska at Lincoln constructively critiqued the chapter on human rights and the individual and made suggestions that greatly improved its tone and substantive content. Professor John King Gamble of Penn State read the chapter on international agreements and offered a number of extremely helpful ideas that became integrated into the final product. Colonel Jeffery Walker, a former judge advocate general air force officer and my teaching assistant at Georgetown University in 2004, added substantially to clarifying and elucidating points on the ways and means international law relates to the use of force in international relations, as reflected in chapter 8. Finally, Paul R. Williams, professor of international law at American University, proffered a number of valuable observations concerning state recognition and succession. His suggestions were extremely helpful in enabling me to interpret how mere academic explanations of the functions of these legal processes are translated into actual policy decisions in the real world of interstate relations.

I am greatly indebted to these and other friends in the international law profession who have been supportive and encouraging for this project over the seven years that it has taken me to bring it to fruition. Charlotte Ku, Executive Director of the American Society of International Law, encouraged my involvement in the society's activities over the past two decades. Boleslaw Boczek, professor of international law in the Political Science Department at Kent State University, was instrumental for two decades in compelling me to think about international legal issues in general and common space regimes in particular, especially the legal interrelationship between Antarctica and the law of the sea. His views and encouragement continue to affect my appreciation for roles that international legal rules play in the real world, as seen in chapter 10. John Norton Moore, Walter Brown Professor of International Law at the University of Virginia, likewise greatly influenced my appreciation for the law of the sea. In the late 1980s and throughout the 1990s, Professor Moore and I annually debated in summer seminars the legal merits of the secret war in Central America, which greatly added to my realization of the need to regulate more effectively the use of force, in international relations and within the internal affairs of states. Nico Schrijver, professor of international law at Vrije Universiteit in Amsterdam, became a fast friend as we served together on the board of the Academic Council on the United Nations System during the late 1990s. He taught me that the European perspective of international law turned on a deep respect and admiration for the stability and order that law brings to interstate relations, as opposed to the mere political gains that might be won or lost by a government engaging in a binding legal commitment. Finally, my appreciation of the importance of international criminal law grew mainly out of opportunities afforded to me by M. Cherif Bassiouni, professor of law at DePaul University. Professor Bassiouni furnished me with numerous invitations to attend conferences and workshops dedicated to exploring the nature of international crimes, the content of international criminal law, and the evolving onset of an international criminal court. For all these insights, which are incorporated into chapter 7, I am extremely grateful.

A special group of graduate students at Georgetown University also contributed to the production phases of this volume. Tanja Flanigan, my teaching assistant in 2000, proved to be an outstanding editor in rearranging sections of chapters, tightening up my sentence structure, and generally making the first six chapters of this work more articulate. Tereza Slepickova ably assisted me in the composition of the glossary, and Ashley Thomas facilitated the final phase of the work's composition by integrating the volume into a coherent, paginated whole. For all their efforts I am genuinely appreciative.

Several academic colleagues have been constant sources of encouragement over the years. My involvement in the International Studies Association since 1972 generated great supportive friendships, among them Professors Charles Kegley Jr., Roger Coate, and Jerel Rosati of the University of South Carolina; Eugene Wittkopf of Louisiana State University; Marvin Soroos of North Carolina State University; Karen Mingst of the University of Kentucky; Mickey East from George Washington University; and Larry Taulbee of Emory University. All of them played special roles in my intellectual development. Olav Stokke, Davor Vidas, and Willy Ostreng of the Fridtjof Nansen Institute in Oslo, Norway, as well as Professor Donald Rothwell of the University of Sydney School of Law and Dr. Richard Herr of the University of Tasmania, were all critical forces during the 1990s in shaping my appreciation for the ways in which international legal rules have been constructed for governing the south polar region. Here at Georgetown University, Professors Robert Lieber, George Shambaugh, Charles E. Pirtle, and the late Joseph Lepgold challenged my views on contemporary international law and at times forced me to rethink how and why legal rules work. For all their insights and intellectual provocation I am truly grateful. Other friends outside the world of academia reinforced encouragement over the years, especially William Stern, Ann Partridge Johnson, Drew Thomas, and Stewart Marshall III. Last but certainly not least, a sincere debt of personal gratitude is owed to my family—Nancy, Kristin, and Clayton—who put up with my impatience and preoccupations over the years that the project endured. In the end, however, while I am genuinely appreciative for the influence and wisdom of colleagues, friends, and family alike, the fact remains that I alone am responsible for any shortcomings of fact and conclusion, as well as errors of commission and omission that appear in this work.

Finally, I cannot omit paying tribute to my editor at Roman & Littlefield, Jennifer Knerr. She recruited my commitment to this project, nurtured my progress, and gently prodded when too many outside forces distracted me from moving on with this work. It was her unflagging patience and cheerful alacrity that served as preeminent incentives for the eventual completion of this text. Many editors would have given up on me long ago, but not Jennifer. For that I shall always be grateful, especially as students use this work in learning more about international legal rules in the 21st century.

I

Concepts and Principles

1

The Nature of International Legal Rules

- ❦ Conceptual Foundations
- ❦ The Quest for Order
- ❦ The Nature of Legal Rules
- ❦ Making International Legal Rules
- ❦ Sources of International Rules
- ❦ Historical Development of International Law
- ❦ Schools of Legal Thought
- ❦ Conclusion

On December 5, 2003, U.S. deputy defense secretary Paul Wolfowitz issued a directive that favored sixty-three U.S. coalition allies for contracts to reconstruct Iraq. The directive limited bidders to firms from the United States, Iraq, coalition partners, and other countries that sent troops to Iraq. It asserted that restricting contract bids was "necessary for the protection of the essential security interests of the United States." This Department of Defense order would prevent companies from states that objected to the Iraq war—notably, Canada, China, France, Germany, and Russia— from bidding on $18.6 billion in reconstruction contracts because their governments opposed the U.S.-led war. The Pentagon's decision to ban war critics from contracts opened diplomatic wounds, as it was widely viewed as the most substantive retaliation to date by the Bush administration against U.S. allies who opposed the U.S. decision to go to war in Iraq to oust Saddam Hussein's regime. The European Union (EU) announced on December 12 that it would try to determine whether the twenty-six contracts listed on the Pentagon's website justified an exemption from World Trade Organization (WTO) procurement rules on the basis of national security. Popular reaction in EU states was predictably vehement and negative, and the criticism from German chancellor Gerhard Schroeder was particularly strong. He maintained that the reconstruction of Iraq was "everybody's business" and that it made little sense to discuss who could take part and who could not. Germany called the decision "unacceptable," and Canada's deputy prime minister, John Manley, averred that the decision would make it difficult for Canada to donate further money for the reconstruction of Iraq. (Canadian officials said they had already contributed $225 million to the rebuilding effort.) On December 12, the European Commission and France threatened to take legal action over the decision of the U.S. government to *award Iraq reconstruction contracts to only those countries with troops in Iraq. A spokesman for the European Commission said on December 13 that contracts should be awarded on the basis of international law and WTO rules. Regarding legal action under WTO rules, it remained unclear how successful a European appeal might be. Experts pointed out that Iraq is not a member of the WTO, and any challenge would therefore be difficult. In addition, WTO rules do permit discrimination on the grounds of national security, a point the United States invoked when making the announcement concerning contracts. Perhaps most telling was the reaction of President George W. Bush when he defended his policy and pooh-poohed European threats of legal action. President Bush said that the policy would stand despite growing complaints from allies and from many of his own officials who were angered at how the Pentagon handled the decision. "It's very simple," he told reporters following a cabinet meeting. "Our people risk their lives. Friendly coalition folks risk their lives. And therefore the contracting is going to reflect that. And that's what U.S. taxpayers expect." The timing of the directive appeared especially unfortunate, as it came while President Bush's special envoy, former secretary of state James Baker III, prepared to travel to France, Germany, and Russia in an effort to persuade those governments to restructure Iraq's outstanding $120 billion debt. The president said that one way those countries could contribute was "through debt restructuring," but he indicated that this would not make any difference in the awarding of U.S. contracts. When asked about comments by German chancellor Schroeder that international law should apply in the tendering of contracts, President Bush replied: "International law? I better call my lawyer. He didn't bring that up to me."*

Public international law refers to the body of rules and norms that governs the interaction between states as well as between other international persons.[1] In this regard, *international law* consists of rules that are generally recognized as binding the members of the international community in their relations with one another. A rule in this sense is a prescribed guide for conduct or action—an accepted precept or doctrine for regulating international relations. International law is largely made by states, and it reflects their will and consent. Being consensual and conventional, international law provides the rules of conduct for regulating the intercourse of states. Like domestic law, or *municipal law*, international law is generally and habitually, though not always, observed by governments in their relations with one another.

Public international law should be distinguished from international ethics or morality as well as from international comity and diplomacy. *International ethics* and morality are concerned with principles that aim to govern international relations from the higher reach of conscience, justice, or humanity, such as those undergirding contemporary *human rights* law. Absent standards of international morality, international law could not exist. Many of its principles—for example, respect for treaties, nonintervention, good neighborliness—remain conditions essential to friendly and stable state relations. Though sometimes used as pretexts, various ideas and sentiments of humanitarian concern constitute the real motives for certain international law—for instance, the legal rules regulating the laws of armed conflict; treatment of prisoners of war; and prohibitions against crimes against humanity, genocide, and acts of torture. While international law might be predicated on a sense of justice and equity, international morality is not synonymous with international law. Still, during the last half of the 20th century, the former moved closer to the latter, as numerous international agreements were promulgated concerning the protection of innocent persons and respect for their human rights and personal dignity. These agreements might include the various conventions negotiated in recent decades to condemn and prohibit racial discrimination and apartheid, discrimination against women, mistreatment of children, and the abrogation of civil and political rights.

International comity concerns rules of courtesy, etiquette, and goodwill that ought to be observed by governments in their dealings with one another on grounds of convenience, honor, and reciprocity. Included among these is the extradition of alleged criminals in the absence of an express agreement; the observation of special diplomatic protocols and ceremonies; and the good faith and credit given in each state to the public acts, records, and judicial proceedings of other states. For example, the status of marriage, birth, and trials in one state is usually recognized as valid in other states. *Diplomacy* relates to the aims of national policy and the conduct by a government of its foreign affairs. Acts of diplomacy are often motivated by considerations of expediency or national interest rather than by those of courtesy, justice, and humanity.

Beyond the well-cultivated field of international law lies the vast realm of national policy where motives of interest and expediency prevail over the ideals of law and justice. The aims and means that govern international relations in interstate diplomacy should be in line with established customs and norms of international law but can be aloof from, and sometimes even antithetical to, recognized rules and principles. Thus, interstate law leaves little choice of policy options. The purpose of legal checks and normative standards is to determine where national policy ends and where international order begins.

CONCEPTUAL FOUNDATIONS

Is international law true law? Criticisms of international rules as real law tend to cluster under three main headings. First is the argument that international law lacks positive authority or command. It does not conform to the definition of law as a rule laid down by a sovereign sufficiently powerful to compel compliance; that is, it lacks the general command of a sovereign or legislative body with the power to enforce its decisions. Second is the assertion that no legal duty or obligation exists to compel states to obey international law, since no courts or judicial tribunals exist to interpret or enforce this so-called law. The premise here is that legal rules without a judiciary are not rules at all; at best, they are guidelines for those states that might wish to comply. Third is the charge that international law lacks sufficient sanction or physical power to compel states to obey its rules. Since there are no penalties prescribed for disobedience or violations, international law can at best be moral suasion. The conclusion is that international law is not really jurisprudence but rather a branch of international ethics, or "positive morality."[2] Though perhaps appealing to skeptics, this reasoning is flawed, as demonstrated by the nature of international legal rules in the real world.

Law essentially embodies customs, principles, and norms that function as rules to regulate conduct by persons in their mutual relations as members of a political community. For such rules to qualify as law, they must be generally recognized as binding and enforceable by an external power or appropriate sanction, though not necessarily accompanied by the threat or use of physical coercion to deal with violations. That is, assurances for securing compliance with these rules need not be predicated on the assertion of force or the promise of swift, certain punishment of wrongdoers. In the international dimension, guarantees of law for regulating states remain primarily couched in international public opinion and the political will of governments to make the law work in their national interest.[3]

It is obvious that the processes of governance in the international system are more primitive than comparable processes within states. International relations are largely decentralized among states. Political and legal institutions created to prescribe, apply, and enforce community values and policies tend to be fused and not easily distinguishable. There is no world executive, world legislature, or universal tribunal. While assertions about law made in international organizations can serve important functions and contribute to international order, rarely are they authoritatively controlling over the conduct of member states. Such international assertions differ markedly in form, content, and impact from those made in a domestic context.

Yet, it is shortsighted to conclude that international law, in the absence of a world government or a universal legislature, lacks a determinate lawgiver or sovereign authority. States are the principal lawgivers, and their roles in multilateral organizations and in global conferences bear witness to the growing importance of international agreements as acts tantamount to international legislation. For example, international agreements concerning global climate change, the laws of war, aircraft hijacking, ozone depletion, and the law of the sea all came about as products of prominent global conferences. Admittedly, governments of states may refuse to sign or ratify instruments produced by international organizations or conferences, and they will likewise not be bound by them; but binding interstate relationships are created nonetheless, with an obligational basis universally recognized as sufficient to make those agreements regarded as law for states that become parties.

If physical sanction or the threat of ensured coercion is considered an essential facet of law, then international law must be regarded as a legal system of imperfect obligation. But recourse to war is not the principal sanction of international law, nor is the use of armed force to guarantee obedience or expedite justice considered necessary and proper for the operation of international legal rules. Under contemporary international law, war can be justified by a state only in self-defense or as a last resort used after every other means for obtaining justice or redress has failed. That said, international law is not wholly without judicial sanction. In recent decades the corpus of international legal rules has been frequently administered and interpreted by a raft of judicial proceedings, including numerous courts of arbitration, courts for human rights violations, and regional tribunals to adjudicate war crimes and acts of genocide. There is also the International Court of Justice (ICJ), which since 1947 has adjudicated more than one hundred cases involving bilateral disputes between member states of the United Nations.

It is important to realize that no single state can change international law and that no statutes of one or two or a dozen states can create universal obligations for all states. International law rests on the common consent of states. International legal rules obtain their normative force not because any superior power or world government prescribes them but because they have been generally accepted by states as rules of conduct, with the expectation that states will follow suit. International law is regarded by many states as part of their municipal law, as its rules have been variously integrated into domestic regulations.

THE QUEST FOR ORDER

The foundation of the rules for regulating interstate relations rests on the innate or inherent need that humans have for order in society so that they might meet specific needs and protect fundamental interests. While people struggle to coexist in their natural environment and sometimes come into conflict with one another, they remain social and political creatures who realize that mutual cooperation and organization are as essential to human survival and progress as fighting, rivalry, and competition. Throughout history, people have sought mutual aid and collaboration within their societies and have developed a sense of interdependence toward those ends. Over the past two centuries this sense of interdependence has progressively expanded to encompass relations between states, as well as more intense affairs within them.

States are guided in their international relations by utilitarian motives. In other words, engagement in international relations allows states the opportunities to satisfy national interests and collective needs. As these needs become increasingly varied and complex in the 21st century, the imperative intensifies for greater mutual interdependence and collaboration among states and other international actors. States will engage in those international activities that they perceive as best serving their national interests. As a consequence, motives of utility and a sense of international common interest contribute to governments' accepting the necessity to conform to legal rules and principles designed to regulate the conduct of their activities.

THE NATURE OF LEGAL RULES

An order closely related to the functioning of formal and authoritative rules exists in the international political system. These rules are motivated and sustained by genuine national interests of states in restraining certain types of international actions, even though such restraints apply to their own conduct as well as to other states. To appreciate the substance of such constraining rules, it is useful to examine the incentives for the establishment of those rules, the means by which they are formulated, the ways in which they operate effectively, and the functions they serve. By doing so, we gain greater prediction into the ways and circumstances under which such rules function, as well as what their realistic potential might be as normative factors for constraining the international conduct of states.[4]

As a communication process, order entails information. Since the international system is dynamic, information required for ordering the system must relate to the present and future condition of the system. A lack of order often stems from uncertainty about the future conduct of others. Decisions are not based primarily on past events that are done and cannot be changed, nor are they predicated on the present, because events are ongoing and in the process of being made. Rather, decision makers need knowledge about the current state of affairs to make informed decisions. A government's decisions are intended to preclude unwanted future effects and to facilitate desired future ends and objectives. International law, framed by legal rules for state conduct, remains the principal channel for furnishing those expectations about future state behavior, and interstate diplomacy is the means through which governments communicate those expectations.

This notion of legal rule may give rise to misconceptions. As a legal element, a rule is not intended to describe behavioral regularity. Rather, a rule is at once a prescription of and proscription for behavior. As a prescription, the rule describes the necessary link between cause and effect; as a proscription, the rule operates as an ancillary motive for action. Legal rules convey instructions for behavior that is either required or prohibited; they define permissible behavior. This feature may explain why legal rules do not give way to easy prediction in international relations. Since international rules often leave broad scope for preferred actions, rule-conforming conduct can be neither definitive nor determinate. Given the contingent character of international legal rules and the inherent risk of their breach, the possibility of sanctions is usually implicit in the concept of legal rule. Whether sanctions will be invoked is not susceptible to prediction, yet the expectation of sanctions might be incentive enough to foster conformity with an international legal rule.

International legal rules serve to avoid unwanted collisions by setting areas of state behavior in which governments can operate freely and responsibly without encroaching on the rights of others. In short, legal rules limit a state's actions, guide its actions, schedule its actions, and signal disapproval of its actions. As the body of rules, norms, and principles for interstate relations, international law assists governments in coordinating their behavior by creating reliable mutual expectations. Thus, international legal rules of necessity must be articulate and intelligible since a legal rule's potency lies precisely in its effectiveness of being able to dissuade an undesirable action by some other state.

International legal rules give rise to law among states, and the law tends to codify the legal rules to guide state behavior. Legal rules clarify and sustain established patterns of behavior that are generally accepted by states. Rules that fail to reflect common political sense and the distribution of power risk falling into disregard and disuse. Similarly, the power and capability of states work to enforce and define the scope of international legal rules. To the extent that governments are able to manage their relations predictably through such legal rules of conduct—and not by erratic, capricious behavior—the international system will operate in a situation of relative order.

Nevertheless, a recurrent international event or pattern of state behavior does not necessarily indicate an operative legal rule. That conduct may simply reflect a government's policy position, political view, or a domestic norm that is applied abroad. Likewise, the consistent refusal by a government to engage in some action may be attributable to its lack of capability or political will. Explaining the actual reasons motivating a government's adherence to a legal rule can be more difficult than mere observation of interstate behavior. While a state acts to observe legal rules, that action does not reflect the rule itself. A state's policy declaration merely indicates that legal rules exist. The policies of a state impart vital information about the parameters of jurisdiction and intimate national aims and objectives. But policies are the results of decisions; they are not rules or norms themselves. National policies derive their legal meaning from acceptability under international practice.

Certain patterns of evidence suggest that legal rules for interstate conduct exist. In the first instance, international criticism of a government's deviation from a legal rule and the probable implementation of sanctions by another government clearly signify that something is amiss. Second, legal rules can come with the codification of legal materials. Treaties and other international agreements legally substantiate international concurrence on the permissibility or impermissibility of state conduct. Governments might refer to these materials to legitimize particular acts or to impugn the acts of other states. Warnings or declarations by governments can signal reaffirmation of the legal rule or indicate displeasure against its possible violation. Third, consistently repeated behavior by states can imply that a legal rule exists. In fact, legal rules are fixed by the accepted regularity of state behavior. By the same token, constant and repeated disregard of a legal rule can lead to its falling into disuse, or the legal condition of desuetude. For example, consider the widespread disregard by governments during World War I of the prohibition against dropping explosives from aircraft onto ground troops. The governments' continual doing so eventually led to the erosion of that prohibition, the legal acceptability of bombing as a permissible tactic of war, and the need to create new law to regulate use of that tactic.

MAKING INTERNATIONAL LEGAL RULES

For modern international law to be appreciated, it must be seen within its larger institutional context, especially in terms of how its rules are created, applied, and administered. International legal rules do not come from a single sovereign, and the international legal order is not hierarchical, as it is often viewed to be in domestic government. There is no world executive, no world legislature, and no world court—no supranational authority even approaching the semblance of a world government. International society can be conceived as being horizontally structured, populated primarily by states, which as actors are imbued with formally equal legal authority.

Contemporary international law supplies the process through which various policies are transformed into effective community prescriptions. If law is associated with a body of principles or rules administered by someone deemed to be authoritative, then questions arise about who may prescribe these principles or who may invoke them and with what expectations of behavior. The answers are found in the process of making international legal rules.

Some prefatory observations seem appropriate. First, states do not make international legal rules. People do. Government officials make foreign policy decisions, of which the construction of and agreement with international legal rules are part. In a real sense, individual decision makers are the only true actors in international relations since every foreign policy event results from decisions taken by individuals. The creation of international legal rules is the presumed product of rationality, to the extent that government officials are able to assess the implications of a legal rule for their state's national interest and decide that it best serves them in their international relations with other states. A government's concurrence with a legal rule depends on the domestic dynamics of its bureaucratic agencies and the ability to resolve interagency tensions in the formulation of foreign policy.

Second, international rule making should not depart radically from international expectations produced by the shared norms and accepted customs of states. The main limits of international judicial lawmaking are political, and the critical tolerance given the international political system comes down to the agreed-on rules that maintain norm stability. A diplomat entrusted with negotiations is the representative of certain national interests that he or she strives to promote and protect by establishing favorable rules. National interests may be disguised or subsumed by appeals to wider community interests, or they may be subordinated to longer-term interests of the international system on the basis of his or her values. But the diplomat negotiating an international agreement operates under no obligation to make decisions according to prevailing norms. The diplomat is not formally bound by past precedent nor by the facts of a situation nor by the need to ensure justice. The range of policy options is more extensive, and proposals are more susceptible to political considerations. Implementing political solutions for international problems can become transformed into legal rules through treaties, customs, practices, and principles. Put tersely, making international legal rules is an inherently political process.

Third, in making international rules, the political process becomes a contest to determine which values and conceptions of national interests will prevail. Such a political process involves the need to grapple with international norms, jurisdictional competencies, and decision-making authorities. There is the need to determine who gets what, when, and from whom. Hence, the international lawmaker strives to influence the distribution of rewards and authority in the international society and in a manner that does not upset existing values and expectations of those governments participating in the rule-making process.

Finally, the functions customarily assigned to international law remain dependent on and closely related to international political institutions, and the relationship of international legal processes to political processes comes mainly as a function of those institutional arrangements. Those institutional arrangements can survive only so long as they are politically tolerable. To the degree that these institutions can be adapted to orderly change, a durable system of international law will exist. To the degree that such adaptation fails, international change is more likely to be unpredictable, uncontrollable, and prone to the use of violence.

International lawmaking does exist, though it is not possible to remove all political discretion and policy choice from that process. Society has a general interest in maintaining a system that acts according to relatively clear and known standards, that is not unduly susceptible to local or temporary pressures, and that is insulated from immediate political considerations. But the complexity of contemporary international society, the rapidity of change within it, and the profound impact that change can have on all states require a more abstract, generalized legal structure that allows for greater license in fitting legal premises to political facts.

In the international system, formal authority must be legitimized in some way. The rules that are formally prescribed and enforced constitute the international legal system. Rules make the law, which involves establishment of formal authority upheld and acknowledged by accepted doctrine. But international legal rules are not force, and force is not law. For force to be used lawfully, it must be subjected to the tests of acceptance and recognized authority. For legal rules to have force, they must be acknowledged by members of the international society as being legitimate and authoritative. These are the critical challenges that international rule making confronts.

Governments acknowledge the obligatory character of international law as a body of rules, but they have traditionally reserved the right to determine for themselves what the rules are, when they should be applied to what specific circumstances, and how they should be managed. The contemporary interstate system does lack a world government, but it is not anarchic in the sense of being lawless or without order. Government officials do not possess unlimited discretion to act willfully or capriciously without regard for international rules or norms. Several considerations dissuade governments from doing this. For one, there is the general realization that order and stability are desirable in the conduct of foreign relations. Similarly, there exists the preference for predictability in gauging state behavior and the fact that many rules carry reciprocal advantages. Finally, there is a desire not to offend other states, whether motivated by the desire to foster better relations or avoid the imposition of punitive sanctions.

At any given time in the international legal system a considerable consensus exists among governments on the applicable legal rules and their interpretation for how a state should conduct its foreign policy. Most governments are satisfied most of the time with the substance, protections, and functions of international law. Where change is desired but frustrated, political controversy can erupt and governmental institutions might be challenged.

SOURCES OF INTERNATIONAL RULES

International law has its roots in the society that it governs. The modern rules for international relations have undergone a process of evolution as old as the state system itself, dating back in origin to the Treaty of Westphalia in 1648. Over the past four centuries, specific *sources of international law* have been created that are widely acknowledged and accepted by the international community.

Formal Agreements

Paramount among the sources of international law are international *treaties* and *conventions*. These black-letter agreements—normally written and expressly agreed to by parties participating in special negotiations—become legally binding, but only on those governments that adhere to them. Such instruments cannot be enforced against those who do not become a party to them or who assume the role of being only limited parties.

Treaties

In general, there are two forms of international agreements. The first is the contract treaty, which is usually bilateral in nature and concerns problems of particular interest to the participating states. Bilateral trade agreements, treaties of friendship navigation and commerce, and extradition treaties typify contract treaty relationships.

International Conventions

A second form of agreement is the international convention, which constitutes a multilateral agreement that establishes international rules and norms for the conduct of states in their mutual relations. Conventions tend to attract several states as parties, as they are concerned with major issues of broad international interest. When a multilateral instrument is seen to be of such importance and universal interest that it is able to attract parties from the majority of states, that agreement is called a "law-making convention." As the international community has expanded and as transnational problems have increasingly evolved into serious global concerns, the number and scope of such lawmaking conventions have grown. Examples of such lawmaking agreements include the 1982 UN Convention on the Law of the Sea, the 1949 Geneva Conventions on the Laws of War, the 1966 International Covenant on Civil and Political Rights, and the 1991 Convention on Chemical Weapons.

Formal agreements make rules explicit, and multilateral instruments often codify past practices. Treaty agreements serve the useful function of making international rules certain, uniform, and stable. In addition, a treaty serves as an effective means for implementing international law nationally. Treaties also serve to secure foreign policy goals for states. This feat can be accomplished by regulating matters previously uncontrolled by international rules or through consolidating support for a particular view of a customary norm, the meaning of which has been blurred by conflicting interpretations or varying policy assertions.

Custom

A second major source of international legal rules is custom. During the 18th and 19th centuries, when international interactions were less complex than those today, states adopted in their mutual relations certain standard practices that evolved into obligatory rules. Through widespread adherence and repeated use, certain practices by governments became accepted as law, with normatively binding constraints. To establish the normative nature of a customary practice now, however, the belief must dictate that such a practice is required or permitted under international legal rules. The belief that such a requirement exists is called *opinio juris (sive necessitatis)*, which asserts the psychological conviction that a special norm has emerged that carries within it the perception by states of a legal obligation to adhere to that practice.

In international law, as in other affairs, certain patterns of behavior that are repeatedly done the same way over a long period without challenge tend to be accepted as the proper way, giving rise to a general usage based on custom. For example, suppose that several governments adopt some particular course of conduct out of necessity or convenience. Initially, its observance by governments is discretionary. But as time passes, adherence to the usage is repeated time and time again, and it becomes stronger as more governments practice it more often. Occasionally, the practice may be violated, but it is generally observed. At some point, usage of that practice will command a consensus among states. It is then that the practice passes from usage into custom, a rule of conduct grounded in international approval. The extraterritorial rights and privileges extended by states to foreign diplomats who are lawfully within their borders arose from the force of custom. Likewise, several notions in the evolution of ocean law—including the three-mile territorial sea limit, the definition of piracy, and allocation of the spoils of war—arose from customary state practice. But custom is not mere frequency of behavior or habitual conduct. For custom to rise to the threshold of being considered international law, the society of states must consent to regard that practice as obligatory.[5] It is unnecessary and indeed impractical to establish compliance by all states concerned as evidence that the customary norm exists.

A number of problems appear when relying on custom as a source of international law in the 21st century. First, in the conduct of states, it is sometimes difficult to substantiate precisely what the customary practice is. Not all states practice the same customary conduct, all the time, under similar circumstances. Second, there is the problem of determining at what stage custom can be said to have become authoritative and controlling, the necessary attributes for a legal rule to be in effect. International law does not set an explicit period for the maturation of a customary rule. By its slow, ponderous nature, customary development of a rule by many actors involves an unwieldy, uncoordinated, and unstructured process. What governments do under which circumstances, and when and where they perform such actions, will not be consistent for all states participating in international relations.[6] A third difficulty with custom as a source of contemporary international rules is the rapid advancement of modern technologies. Custom, by its very nature, implies a gradual process of performance, acceptance, and adherence. In the post–industrial age, technological developments do not permit such a gradual process to function satisfactorily. There is the constant need for creating new legal rules to regulate the accelerating pace of new technological advancements that transcend national borders. One only has to think of the vast number of international satellite broadcasts, the information revolution in Internet capabilities, and the tremendous growth of transborder financial flows to appreciate the profound implications presented by new technologies and to realize that a gradual process of customary legal development cannot satisfactorily cope with rapid, pervasive technological globalization.

A fourth problem is the question of who is bound by customary law. To be bound by international custom, a state does not have to be a party to the development of that customary practice. This has been clearly evidenced since the 1960s when numerous colonial territories secured their independence and were recognized as new members of the society of states and became subject to customary international law by virtue of attaining statehood. However, if a state were to persistently object to a particular practice during the period that the practice was being formed into customary law, and if that state claimed the right for itself not to be obligated to that practice, then international law permits that state to opt out. Known as the persistent objector rule, this caveat is sometimes regarded as a weakness or a loophole in the utility of custom as a source for general international law. An example of the persistent objector rule can be seen in the practice of certain Latin American states—for example, Chile, Ecuador, and Peru—who had persistently refused to accept the legitimacy of the customary development of a three-mile territorial sea based on the distance that a cannon in the 18th century could fire seaward. These states, and a number of others, choose instead to extend their territorial claims in the early 1950s out to two hundred nautical miles.

General Principles of Law

The third major source of international legal rules is the "general principles of law recognized by civilized nations." International law concerns the rights of actors and the protection of those rights. There is a substantive law, which sets forth and explains the rights of those actors; and an adjectival law, which describes the procedure by which redress might be obtained when those rights are violated. General principles are usually drawn from the experience of municipal law and are often applied to clarify and interpret law when it is obscure, ambiguous, or polemical.

A number of *general principles of international law* have been recognized by states in their dealings with one another; among them are the following:

1. A sovereign is subject to the law. The sovereign state is not above the rule of law, and as such, political leaders of states are subjects of only limited authority.
2. The right of self-defense by a state is limited. For self-defense to be exercised lawfully, there must be reasonable apprehension of the danger, with a proportionate amount of force used to meet that danger.
3. The state must abide by its international treaties. The obligation to abide by international agreements is among the most universally accepted general principles of law, and it represents the foundation for relations between states in the international legal system (see chapter 6).[7]
4. Unjustified harm done to a neighboring state is a legal wrong. If such harm is done, some form of restitution must be made to the victim state.
5. International disputes should be settled peacefully. If bilateral negotiations are not successful, then states should resort to intercession by a third party (see the discussion on dispute settlement in chapter 6, p. 119).[8]
6. Specific rights acquired by states are to be protected under the law. States are entitled to due process in their public and private dealings, particularly in terms of international economic relations.
7. Consultation should be undertaken by one government with another before taking action that affects the latter's interests. This is not merely a matter of diplomatic courtesy or political convenience; it is essential for maintaining good neighborliness and mutual respect.

Numerous other principles of law emerged in the last half of the 20th century as guideposts for state behavior. These more specific principles of law embody rules concerning the permissibility of certain state actions under various circumstances. These include legal principles pertaining to self-determination, equality, nondiscrimination, decolonization, nonintervention, nonaggression, the common heritage of mankind, permanent sovereignty over natural resources, and self-defense (each treated more fully throughout the text).

In any event, general principles of law remain burdened with the difficulty of being framed as sources of law in terms of morality and justice. Morality and justice remain highly subjective concepts, susceptible to disparate interpretations. As a consequence, general principles in their application may be vulnerable to vagaries perceived in the situation or in the particular context in which they are set. What is moral and just to one government might not be moral and just to another. Greater complications arise if economic ideologies or political motives are mixed into the principle's intent or application.

Judicial Decisions and Scholarly Writings

A fourth source of modern international law has twin dimensions and is deemed to be secondary and indirect when compared with treaties, custom, and general principles. This source encompasses, first, judicial decisions of courts—national and international—and, second, the teachings and writings of the most highly qualified jurists and publicists. Two points are notable here. The first is that for international law, court decisions are regarded mainly as guidelines; tribunals cannot set precedents. There is no *stare decisis* in the law of nations. Accordingly, a decision by a national court or international tribunal, including the International Court of Justice, cannot be held as binding authority for determining subsequent court decisions. While important, judicial decisions and arbitral awards should not be overrated as sources of general international law. Each case is decided on its own merits, and the decision affects only those states involved in the case.

The second point is that, while writings of scholars and jurists supply a rich inventory of opinions on the law, they carry no binding legal authority. Though perhaps useful as analytical commentators on what the law is, or should be, legal *publicists* cannot cement legal concepts into place that can obligate national governments. Text writers and the analytical deductions of other scholars cannot create or codify international legal rules. As sources of law, these writers are relevant to the extent that governments may adopt their suggestions and interpretations in the application of international legal rules to foreign policy.

A number of other sources contribute to the evolution and codification of international legal rules. Resolutions of international organizations assist in clarifying and reifying the substantive content of international law, as their adoption by state representatives reflects what governments consider binding norms, or at least the preferred direction in which international rules should be directed. Perhaps most significant here are resolutions adopted by various UN-affiliated bodies, especially the *General Assembly*. General Assembly resolutions, though mere recommendations and not legally binding under UN Charter law, often provide the impetus necessary for creating new legal rules. Such was the case for resolutions over the past half-century that crystallized norms leading to the codification of numerous international conventions on issues as diverse as the need to prevent genocide, outlaw torture, and halt racial and gender discrimination, to the creation of special international regimes to manage activities in outer space, the oceans (including the deep seabed), and the earth's environment.

HISTORICAL DEVELOPMENT OF INTERNATIONAL LAW

International law in the 21st century emerged from historical experience. The body of international law developed when mutual rights and obligations between social groups and institutions in a society coincided and when legal rules became the means for maintaining balance between various participants in that society. In this sense, two elements proved essential for establishing an international legal community. First, there was the geographical situation. Sovereign states are geographically bound into coexistence, which furnishes the fundamental necessity for international law. Second, governments became mutually aware that rules are useful and necessary for creating expectations about other states' behavior and that they provide the psychological element underpinning orderly international legal relations. In other words, rules provide expectations. If all governments follow the same rules in their relations, they would then know what to expect from each other in the course of their international dealings.

Present-day international law grew from the convergence of two factors: first, the development of certain theories and principles concerning international conduct; and, second, the evolution of various international practices or custom recognized as obligatory behavior by governments. During its formative period, international law was primarily developed by scholars and jurists who relied on the synthesis of great ideas and theoretical considerations rather than on any accumulated body of state behavior in international relations. Once the fundamental concepts and principles of international law were firmly established and recognized in state conduct, theory gave way to practical considerations. It then became the main function of the juridical commentators and analysts to interpret and apply the law in conformity with its most authoritative evidence and uses.

Modern international law is often affirmed as the product of modern European civilization. While that is true, traces of international legal rules can be seen in the practice of ancient civilizations as well. The Egyptian Pharaohs entered into treaties of alliance, peace, extradition, and the treatment of envoys with neighboring kings as early as the 14th century BC, as did the Hebrew kings. Similarly, the Assyrian, Babylonian, Hindu, and early Chinese civilizations practiced rules of warfare and diplomacy not unlike those of modern times. The seafaring principalities of India established legal rules for ocean navigation and regional commerce. The Greeks, because they were introverted in their foreign relations, were said to have contributed little to the principles of modern international law. Even so, the Greek system of independent city-states bore a close resemblance to the contemporary nation-state system as treaties conducted relations between city-states. Indeed, the Aetolian and Achaean leagues of the 3rd century BC represented early organizational efforts at international cooperation and facilitated the development of arbitration as a dispute settlement technique.[9] In addition, the influence of Greek philosophy, especially from the Stoics, was important for introducing the notion of natural law that became adapted as an important element in the Roman system of jurisprudence.

The Romans developed the notion of *jus gentium* (law of nations), which was Roman civil law applied to foreigners and the outside world. Philosophically, *jus gentium* advocated that there are common legal institutions and principles found everywhere, which constitute a universal law for all peoples. This notion became closely associated with natural law and served as a cardinal principle undergirding the purpose of modern international law.[10]

SCHOOLS OF LEGAL THOUGHT

Throughout history, authorities have disputed the meaning and scope of international law. Opinion divides mainly along two lines of thought. On the one hand is the *naturalist school of thought*, which is concerned with the rules and principles that ought to be observed in international relations. On the other hand is the *positivist school of thought*, which is interested in only those norms and regulations that are observed and grounded in lawmaking treaties and in other interstate agreements.

Many early writers were concerned mainly with the law as it ought to be. Their fundamental purpose was to seek out axiomatic truths thought to be reposed in the law of nature. During the Middle Ages, the concept of natural law further developed as the church integrated it into a doctrinal system. The law of nature increasingly became identified with the law of God and was modified by the impact of Christian theology. Three key points are relevant here. First, international law was regarded as part of a universal law of nature in which international legal order was not distinguished from national order. The collapse of the religiously ordered political system called into question fundamental political conditions. By what right and authority did monarchs rule? What obligations did sovereigns owe the church, God, and their subjects? Thus began a search for universal principles on which to base human relationships and law. Of particular note is the sense of ethical jurisprudence that pervaded Spanish scholars of the 16th century. The fundamental tenet was that relations among polities were governed by principles of justice and that such principles were perpetual, immutable, and universal principles of natural law. Second, domestic law was mostly predicated on custom and common conceptions of morality. Law was not viewed as an artificial creation of government or courts, consciously designed to implement community values. Legal processes were neither formalized nor bureaucratic. Law was decentralized, localized, and grounded in popular feelings of right and wrong. It was a natural morality, intended to comply with the natural order of social affairs. Third, there was little appreciation for law and policy when such was related to foreign affairs. Law and policy were interlinked, blurring the distinction between the "ought" and the "is" of political power. The sovereign authority made decisions on the basis of what it believed the law should be, presumably through the prisms of justice, reason, and morality. The law of nations became viewed as part of the law of nature, based on necessity and reason. Such views were reflected in the writers of the day whose intellectual discourse helped to shape the philosophical development of the law of nations.

The intellectual seeds of international law germinated in the 16th century. Among the early natural law writers, Francisco de Vitoria (1480–1546), a professor of theology at the University of Salamanca, examined the question of just war and the bases for Spanish authority in the Americas. His works have special relevance for international law. De Vitoria argued that all men were free under the law of nature and that imperial claims to domination were invalid. The pope, he asserted, was neither the civil nor the spiritual overlord of nonbelievers; and in his treatise *De Indis,* de Vitoria averred that just war could not be waged against Indians simply because they refused to accept papal authority. Moreover, the mere discovery of Indian lands in the New World could not confer a valid title, because only lands without an owner could be claimed through discovery.[11]

Another Spanish theological scholar, Francisco Suarez (1548–1617), at the University of Coimbra, argued that *jus gentium* was a body of law applicable between polities, not a natural law common to all of them. While individual territories might be independent, they required a body of rules to govern their interrelations.[12] Suarez became the first thinker to posit the notion of a society or community of sovereign polities, linked together by a body of law applying to their mutual relations.

The founder of the pure law of nature school was Samuel Pufendorf, the world's first professor of international law, who taught at the University of Heidelberg. Pufendorf argued that the law of nations was part of the law of nature, and he denied that customary state practice or treaties could ever be sources of international law. In an even more striking proposition, he advocated that during war, no mercy should be shown, because that would only delay return of a natural condition of peace. For the same reason, he asserted that there should be no laws of war, since they would interfere with the design of nature.[13]

The person most critical in the development of modern international law was Huigh Cornets de Groot (1583–1645), better known as Hugo Grotius. A Dutch theologian, Grotius combined objective reasoning with empirical observation and emphasized the actual practice of states in their foreign dealings and the decisions of the courts in Europe. These acts, he believed, furnished convincing evidence that rules of natural law existed. The widespread agreement over a particular rule in itself clearly indicated that such a rule existed in natural law and thus should exist for the law of nations.

In his principal work *De Jure Belli ac Pacis Libri Tres* (Three Books on the Law of War and Peace; 1625), Grotius assumed that there was a universal, immutable law of nature (*jus naturale*) based on right reason and human sociality. He claimed that the law of nations received its authority and sanction from the law of nature. There was an essential morality and divine justice in the nature of things, and nations as well as persons ought to be governed by this universal principle. Relations between polities, though subject to the law of nature, were also governed by *jus gentium*, the law of peoples, which had been established by the consent of the community of nations.[14]

Certain fundamental facets underlying the Grotian system—especially the doctrines of legal equality, territorial sovereignty, and independence of states—remain cardinal principles of international law today. These principles were recognized in the Peace of Westphalia and became the very foundation for the new order of Europe that was established in 1648 by the treaties of Osnabrück and Münster.[15] Though the principles of sovereignty and territoriality were more fully developed by his successors, Grotius planted the seeds for their exposition and thus contributed to the dogma of supreme power or sovereignty of states as philosophers elaborated it during the 17th and 18th centuries. These developments gave rise to a logic underpinning the doctrine of the fundamental rights and duties of states. If states are sovereign and independent, they must be equal before the law and thus entitled to equal protection in the exercise of their rights and equally bound to fulfill their obligations. This logic underpinned the Grotian notion of *pacta sunt servanda*—the legal principle that treaties made in good faith are binding—which he asserted should be the basis of international treaty law, and which he drew from the domestic law of contracts. In another work, Grotius contended that the ocean is by nature incapable of being appropriated or occupied and should therefore be free for use by all peoples.[16] This principle gave rise to the modern doctrine of the freedom of the seas. For all his contributions, Grotius is usually remembered as the "father of modern international law."

The Grotians, or the eclectic school, occupied a middle ground between the naturalists and positivists, though they preserved the distinction between the law of nature and the positive, or voluntary, law of nations based on custom and consent. Among the eclectics, two figures stand out. Christian von Wolff (1679–1754), a German philosopher, contended that the foundation for international community should come as a world superstate (*civitas maxima*), having authority over the component member states.[17] This notion of world government found little support among his contemporaries. More lasting were the views of Emmerich de Vattel (1714–1767), a Swiss diplomat. His major work, *Le droit des gens*,[18] was designed as a practical manual for statesmen. In his writings, Vattel suggested that two kinds of law, voluntary and necessary, comprised the law of nations. Custom and treaties formed voluntary law, and natural law formed the essence of necessary law. Vattel specifically rejected Wolff's fiction of a superstate as the foundation of international law.

Instead, he accepted the doctrine of a state of nature, especially with regard to the ratio-nale of equality of states, as articulated in 18th-century natural law. Since states were composed of men, and because all men were by nature free and equal, it followed that sovereign states should be regarded as free persons living together in a state of nature.[19]

A combination of forces coincided to undermine the relevance of natural law for interna-tional rules. Trust in a universal order of states contributed to the erosion of natural law as a guiding legal philosophy. Burgeoning nationalism personified by the American and French revolutions articulated fundamental principles of human rights and liberties and intro-duced the political system of democracy that came to epitomize Western thought and action. Political, economic, and social changes gave rise to imperialism, national socialism, and communism. The upshot of all these developments was that positivism as a legal phi-losophy became popular and thus found its way into international legal philosophy.

Several scholars contributed to elaborating the theory and nature of international legal positivism that dominated 18th- and 19th-century European thinking and the purposeful development of international legal rules. The positive, or historical, school of international jurists emphasized the importance of custom and treaties as sources of international law. Among the early positivists was Alberico Gentilis (1552–1608), a professor of civil law at Oxford who posited that positive law (*jus voluntarium*) was determined by general con-sent. Rather than use abstract reasoning and systematic exposition, Gentilis used historical examples to support his points of law.[20] Another positivist was John Selden, commis-sioned by the British crown to attack Grotius's views on freedom of the *high seas*. To rebut Grotius, Selden contended that portions of the sea had been lawfully appropriated by England.[21] Richard Zouche (1590–1660), a professor of civil law at Oxford, published the first manual of international law in 1650.[22] He believed that precedents set by the inter-course among states furnished the substance of international law. Zouche was also the first writer to clearly divide the law of war from the law of peace, with greater prominence given to the latter.

The 18th century produced three leading positivists. The principal figure among them was Cornelius van Bynkershoek (1673–1743), a celebrated Dutch jurist on the Supreme Court of Holland who asserted that the bases of international law were customs and trea-ties commonly consented to by various states. As customs change, so should the law of nations.[23] While Bynkershoek contributed much to fashioning the legal rules of neutrality and blockade during belligerency, he is best remembered for suggesting the "cannon shot rule" to determine the breadth of territorial waters offshore coastal states. This proposi-tion held that territorial dominion should extend seaward only as far as a cannon on shore could carry, and it became the basis for the three-nautical-mile limit for the territorial sea, which became almost universally accepted over the next two centuries.[24]

A second positivist, John Jacob Moser (1701–1785), was a prolific German scholar who authored some five hundred volumes on international law and foreign relations. His trea-tise *Volkerrecht* emphasized that the practice of states determines their international rela-tions and that the law of nations was based in the experience of men and nations, as demonstrated by historical facts and precedents.[25] A contemporary German scholar, Georg Friedrich von Martens (1756–1821), published his most important work, *Precis du droit des gens moderne de l'Europe*, in 1788. This volume, generally regarded as the first systematic manual on positive international law, is notable for its clear exposition of the fundamental rights and duties of states.[26]

These writers contributed much intellectually to crystallize international law in theory and in real-world application. Nevertheless, certain political developments in the 19th century transformed the law of nations from the quest for a universal system of justice into the set of particular rules for governing the relations of states. For one, the growth of nationalism and the tendency to regard the state as the embodiment of social solidarity pushed natural law farther from the legal realm. The rise of Hegelian philosophy brought with it belief in the sense of "state will"—that as the preeminent social organization in fact, the state could be subjected to law only by its own consent.

The development of democracy in the 19th century also contributed to the growth of international legal rules. Increased participation in politics, as well as popular demands for equal states and recognition, led to greater efforts by various groups to control or influence government. Law became a distinct, conscious process that could be made, modified, or nullified as customs changed and as old norms were called into question. The old way associated with a stable community concerned with stable ideas set in traditional situations was no longer sufficient to meet the rapidly changing forces of industrialization and social mobility. Codifications of national law led to new legislative initiatives that sought to separate law from justice and create new policies based on new norms stemming from the popular will. New institutions of popular government arose to promote public policy. Law became the rational instrument for implementing that policy.

At the same time, the rise of positivist thought helped to distinguish international law from municipal law. A universal legal system did not exist. Commercial law became "nationalized" into private international law, separate and distinct from public international law, or the law of nations. Positivism also served to narrow the range of international practice that might qualify as law. The reluctance to depend on ethical jurisprudence led positivists to take a more critical view of custom as a source of law. That states had acted similarly in the past was no longer a sufficient rationale to constitute the creation of a legal norm. Instead, positivism insisted that for custom to become law it had to reflect a widespread acknowledgment among states that the norm was legally binding. Fundamental to positivism was the notion that law is a matter of formal political consensus and not a set of universal moral principles assigned to the international arena. Morality and ethics were not irrelevant but merely subservient to rationality and common sense.[27]

The Congress of Vienna in 1815 marked formal recognition of the political system that dominated world politics for a century. The rules of international law were made to fit the conditions of Europe, and the interests of Europe created those same rules. The substance and growth of international law became tied to the states that formed Europe.

During the 19th century, three assumptions about world politics and international relations became prominent. First, the state was the only important actor in world politics. Second, international stability depended on the state's remaining sovereign and independent. Third, economic interdependence, largely because of increasing specialization of productivity, was not an issue of prominent international concern, since economics lay outside the political arena. By the end of the 20th century, profound international development had erased all such presumptions. The two Hague peace conferences in 1899 and 1907, both of which had the objective to replace force and war with reason and law, ushered in the critical transition to the era of modern international law. Here the effort was to regulate war and settle disputes, principally through diplomacy and arbitration. The first Hague peace conference, attended by twenty-eight states, formulated three conventions on the pacific settlement of international disputes, the law and customs of war on land, and rules concerning maritime warfare; it also created the Permanent Court of Arbitration. The second Hague peace conference, attended by forty-four states, concluded thirteen conventions and one declaration and made profound contributions in placing legal limitations on war.

In their mutual relations, the states of Europe in the early 20th century had to emphasize the cardinal legal principles of sovereignty, independence, and formal equality. These became keystones for justifying and maintaining the balance of power alignment that had earmarked the latter decades of the 19th century. But these same standards did not apply to other parts of the world. The search for markets and political influence led to European colonization throughout developed societies in Asia and Africa and prompted the United States to interfere in affairs throughout Latin America and the Caribbean.

The development of international law after World War I became intertwined with the efforts of the League of Nations to promote peace and cooperation through international organization as well as to foster international disarmament among major military powers. The League successfully assisted in the settlement of some thirty international disputes and convened conferences to deal with important legal questions concerning narcotics traffic, slavery, disarmament, and the law of the sea. The League attempted to realize the ideal that national might should be subordinated to collective international right, codified in the rule of law. But it was not to be, as the onslaught of the Second World War destroyed that international order and created the need for a new international system governed by new legal rules.

From World War II to the end of the Cold War, the United States and the Soviet Union vied for a Third World majority, and international law became the political instrument of rival superpower ideologies. During this era of colonial empire breakup and Cold War competition, much law relating to self-determination, nondiscrimination, and human rights was developed. Since 1990, the international community has witnessed the collapse of communism, the rise of ethnonationalism, the spread of profound civil violence, and the intensification of globalized industrialization. All these developments have made necessary the establishment and enforcement of more universal legal principles designed to protect humankind from itself.

Looking backward, the scope and substance of international law expanded tremendously during the 20th century. This proliferation of legal rules, greatly facilitated by the activities of the United Nations, came in response to the creation of more than 150 new states, the development of powerful new technologies that produce transnational impacts, the rise of severe global problems that require international solution, and the profound growth of world interdependence. Much new law was needed to deal with these conditions; much new law was created in response; and much new law remains to be implemented.

An international political system based on the old adage that "all must hang together lest each one hang separately" presently generates strong incentives for international cooperation among national governments. It is clear that new institutions and common policies must be devised for redressing contemporary global problems, including those involving military conflict, economic development, transborder monetary exchange, conservation and resource protection, and human rights deprivation. Save for various international organizations and selected ad hoc conference efforts, the responsibility of reducing common policies into common international law is still left to national decision makers.

It is wrong to assert that national policies with significant international impacts are not regulated by international prescriptions and are remanded exclusively to policymakers as national decisions. In a political world greatly influenced by international economic considerations, national policymakers strive to avoid conflict to mitigate adverse impacts on their national economies. International law facilitates these efforts as it provides the ways and means necessary to align consonant national policies with consonant international laws. Key to these efforts is the obligation of governments to act "reasonably" with respect to international legal doctrine by drawing on the experience of other states involved in similar situations.

The process of taking effective decisions to govern transnational events describes the essence of international law. By the early 21st century, this process has already been subjected to effective restraints that limit the freedom of national decision makers and promote policy choices compatible with an international political system comprising associated states who share a common set of fundamental rights and duties. The role of government officials becomes to distill from common international experience and shared values those general principles of law that, if adopted, can make for more consonant national decisions.

CONCLUSION

The contemporary system of international legal rules has its roots in the Treaty of Westphalia of 1648, which ended the Thirty Years' War and marked the formal recognition of states as sovereign, independent political units. But the main thrust of international law today emerges as the product of 19th-century European experience, as elaborated through 20th-century global developments. As broadly conceived today, international law remains a body of rules binding on states in their relationships with one another. These rules have emerged from the raft of formal agreements made by states; the customary practice of states; the general principles of law accepted by states; and, to a lesser extent, various court decisions and scholarly writings interpreting those rules. All states by their governments' choosing are bound by most of these rules, which entail reciprocal rights and duties.

Importantly, the rules of international law are not static; they are dynamic. All or some of the member states can change them through various means, so long as these changes do not infringe on those states that choose not to accept them. As evidenced in modern times, the rules of international law originate in the needs of the international community, as determined through consent of the member states. To the extent that modern international legal rules become broadly codified, that process occurs mainly through governments of states negotiating multilateral agreements.

The flow of decisions from governments that invoke legal rules furnishes the substance of international law in the 21st century. International law remains in a process of change and adaptation to circumstances worldwide. As states become more dependent on each other for common values and shared interests, matters arise for mutual regulation and formal codification. In the absence of developed supranational legislative institutions, legal rules must be prescribed, modified, adjusted, and applied by the ponderous process of negotiating international agreements or by individual state practice. Consequently, international rules can remain fluid in international legal discourse until crystallized by formal treaty agreement or subjected to the political strains and tensions of state practice.

In the 21st century, certain criticisms persist about the content, means, and effects of international legal rules. It is sometimes said that national sovereignty dictates the parameters of international law, with governments of states free to decide what constitutes international legal rules, how those rules should be interpreted, and in which situations those rules should apply. Such a perspective invites the belief that states apply international law only when they want to do so, in whichever situations are deemed most suitable to their national interests. But governments do not act arbitrarily and without regard to international legal prescriptions. The fact is that governments are not free to make foreign policy decisions in the absence of legal consequences. The substance supporting this conclusion forms the next chapter.

2

The International Legal Community

     Q International Actors
     Q Classification of States
     Q Sovereignty and States
     Q Sovereignty and Territory
     Q Legal Relations between States
     Q Law and the Community of States
     Q Dualism versus Monism
     Q Doctrine of Incorporation
     Q Conclusion

A March 2004 report by the U.S. Census Bureau estimates that the world's popula-
tion will reach 9.1 billion by 2050, a nearly 50 percent increase from the 6.2 billion
in 2002. Even so, the population growth rate among the 193 states that form the
international community is slowing significantly because of fewer births and because
of more deaths attributable to AIDS. The bureau report estimates that world popula-
tion growth will slow to 0.42 percent by midcentury, compared with 1.2 percent
from 2001 to 2002—a level far below the peak growth of 2.2 percent between 1963
and 1964. Bureau officials caution that these projections are based on two vari-
ables—namely, fertility rates in developing countries and the death toll from AIDS.
Birth rates have declined in the United States and European states, and the report's
projections assume they will drop below two children per woman by midcentury.
Yet, fertility rates remain high in India, in parts of Africa, and in other developing
countries where contraception is often not available. The bureau's report reckons
that at least one hundred million women in the developing world prefer fewer chil-
dren but are not using contraception. Family-planning education is made difficult
because of the remoteness of villages in many countries. At the same time, the impact
of AIDS has been drastic, killing off more than twenty million people since the epi-
demic began in the early 1980s. An estimated forty million people now live with
HIV—many of them in Asia, Latin America, and sub-Saharan Africa—and it is antici-
pated that most of them will die within the next decade. This trend could be reversed,
however, if AIDS education programs were expanded. The Census Bureau also pro-
jects an increase in the number of the world's elder population, with an estimated
17 percent of people expected to be above the age of sixty-five by 2050, compared

with 7 percent in 2002. Also in March 2004, the UN Population Division reported that by 2007, more people will be living in cities than in rural areas, marking a historic demographic shift. The report, World Urbanization Prospects: The 2003 Revision, *discovered that while 48 percent of the global population lived in urban areas in 2003, this number is expected to exceed the 50 percent mark by 2007, marking the first time in history that urban residents will exceed the rural population. The report estimates that the world's urban population will rise from 3 billion in 2003 to 5 billion by 2030 and that the rural population will decline from 3.3 billion to 3.2 billion. The UN Population Division report predicts that over the next eleven years Tokyo will maintain its current position as the world's most populous city, increasing its population from thiry-five million in 2003 to thirty-six million in 2015. The second and third places will be the Indian cities of Mumbai, with 22.6 million, and New Delhi, at 20.9 million. The next two on the list are Mexico City with 20.6 million and Sao Paulo at 20 million. The UN Population Division simultaneously released its* World Population Policies 2003, *which identifies high mortality rates as the most significant concern in developing countries, whereas low fertility and declining population typify developed countries. The report states that over 90 percent of countries support providing contraceptives and that developed and developing countries share the desire to lower immigration.*

States have been regarded as the major actors with rights and duties in international relations since the Peace of Westphalia in 1648. But this fact does not give an accurate or complete picture of either the scope or process of international law in contemporary world affairs. To appreciate the situation in the 21st century, one must consider other actors who operate in the international arena and affect the development of international rules.

Various categories of actors participate in today's interdependent world of complex transactions and global telecommunications. These actors are subjects of international law—that is, they possess *international legal personality,* or the legal capacity that conveys certain entitlements and obligations arising from international legal rules. States are foremost among these participants, but also included are international organizations, transnational groups, multinational corporations, private associations, and even the individual person. The interaction of these various actors in the world community has necessitated vast and often rapid changes in international legal rules to keep pace with the needs of governments and business enterprises whose commerce, transportation, and information issues demand the order and regularized behavior that only law can provide.

The system of rules for organizing international relations presupposes a common set of values and norms that reflects a sense of coexistence. But within this system there is no central authority. There is no sovereign executive who issues commands, nor a world government that makes laws, nor an international police officer who ensures justice and upholds order for members of the society. The rules of international relations are made, applied, and enforced by the actors themselves. Consequently, in international relations, the authority structure runs horizontally. That is, the actors interact in relatively regular ways, although there are leaders and followers. Interactions among actors are based more on learned rules, norms, and personal influence than on the ability of any individual or collective under constitutional mandates or statutory obligations to command or impose sanctions for noncompliance.

INTERNATIONAL ACTORS

Different types of actors, operating at different levels, participate in the international community. National, transnational, and certain nonstate actors exert notable influence within the international system. To varying degrees, all have been made persons or subjects with legal status, personality, rights, and duties under international law.

Sovereign States

States are national actors and are the principal persons under international law.[1] Essential conditions and characteristics distinguish a state from other international actors. A state possesses a definite territory on which a population is permanently settled and organized for political purposes. To qualify for statehood, a polity must have a population that is significant and permanent. An uninhabited island or the continent of Antarctica has territory, but neither qualifies as a state without a permanently settled population. The operation of a government is necessary for the ensurance of internal stability and for the fulfillment of international obligations. While international law does not favor any particular form of government, there must be at a minimum some authority that exercises governmental functions and is capable of representing that entity in foreign relations. A government serves as the mechanism for making and enforcing laws, and the condition of *sovereignty* permits the polity to be independent from external control and to possess the autonomous power to enforce laws within the state's jurisdiction. The premier role that states play in the international system derives from their legal condition of sovereignty, their status of commanding people's political loyalty, and their control of the preponderance of economic and military influence in foreign relations.

As an important caveat, the terms *nation* and *state* are often used interchangeably, though they are quite distinct conceptually. A *state* is a political unit defined in terms of having a distinct territory with recognized borders, a permanent population, an autonomous government that exercises effective control of the territory and its inhabitants, and a capacity to enter into relations with other states. The first three qualities are literal and realistic. The fourth condition is normative and posits a legal, rather than an actual, prerequisite to statehood. In any event, a polity cannot qualify as a state unless it has the competence to conduct international relations with other states as well as the political, technical, and financial capabilities to do so. The United States, Argentina, Germany, and Kenya are states. Hong Kong, Kurdistan, Northern Ireland, and the Falkland Islands are not, as they all lack the qualities of sovereignty and independence to engage in foreign relations. In contrast, a *nation* comprises a particular people who share a common ethnic and cultural identity, common historical background, common language, and often, a common religion. The nation promotes an emotional relationship through which the individual acquires a sense of cultural identity. The Palestinians, Kurds, Jews, Japanese, and Sami are examples of nations. Even so, nations normally do not enjoy the special status of statehood, since they lack the essential qualities of territory and sovereign independence.

Transnational Actors

Transnational actors are international organizations that serve as centralizing forces in the international system. These are usually referred to as *intergovernmental organizations* (IGOs) and comprise member states that send delegates to represent their interests and policies. Often there is a permanent staff working at a headquarters with employees whose loyalty is to the organization rather than to their state of nationality. The purposes of these organizations transcend any individual state, and they often seek to foster cooperation among member countries to produce specific policies aimed at addressing common problems. An IGO has legal capacity and personality accrued from rights and duties given to it by the formal international agreement negotiated as its charter (which governs its activities). Other legal capacities may be given to it by subsequent agreements. The value of IGOs as lawmakers and problem solvers in modern international relations is consequential. Accordingly, it is not surprising that as new problems arose internationally during the 20th century, the number of all types of IGOs expanded impressively, from 176 in 1909 to more than 6,415 as of 2004.[2]

The United Nations (UN) is the premier general-purpose IGO with supranational features. Every state in the international community—except for Taiwan and the Holy See (the Vatican)—are members of the United Nations. When combined with its main organs and numerous specialized agencies, commissions, and multilateral programs, the United Nations forms an international system that produces far-reaching impacts on rule creation for international relations as well as for implementing multilateral policies intended to remedy serious global problems.

The functional agencies of the United Nations are IGOs, as are regional organizations. Each UN agency has its own separate charter, membership, and legal competencies to make international rules, although each performs specialized tasks for managing and coordinating various multilateral activities. For example, the International Civil Aviation Organization schedules all world aircraft flight patterns; the International Telecommunications Union orchestrates global broadcast frequencies; the International Atomic Energy Agency monitors all its 127 member states' use of nuclear power; and the International Maritime Organization establishes international safety and navigation standards for shipping on the oceans. Regional organizations are multipurpose, structured institutions usually having combined military, political, economic, and social goals that are formally created by treaty agreements with a specific geographic regional focus. The Organization of American States, the Organization of African Unity, the Association of South-East Asian Nations, and the European Union (EU) are representative examples of such multilateral transnational regional actors. Of these, the EU is the most advanced in its institutional organization. It attained a high degree of economic integration by establishing rules that eliminate barriers to trade, investment, and movement of labor and by establishing a quasi government with limited decision-making authority, which in some cases supercedes the sovereignty of member states. Perhaps most intriguing, the member states of the EU have developed a special legal system that is unique and pertinent to their regional activities (see chapter 5). Transnational actors are noteworthy for international law in two particular ways. First, intergovernmental organizations are competent to and often do create new international legal rules for their members. These rules are codified through treaty agreements into international law, which limits certain activities of member states in their mutual relations. Second, with regard to international nongovernmental organizations (INGOs), these organizations can be powerful influences on the substance and strength of new legal rules as they are being negotiated. Nongovernmental organizations serve as pressure groups for influencing the content of new law made in international conferences, for setting the scope of its application in national debates, and for confirming the degree to which it will be enforced on the relevant states. In a real sense, INGOs serve as salient lobby agents for various international legal issues that are taken up for negotiation by states and intergovernmental organizations.

Nonstate Actors

Nonstate actors include INGOs, which are issue-oriented private groups and enterprises that operate internationally. The Roman Catholic Church, Greenpeace International, the Antarctic and Southern Ocean Coalition, and Amnesty International are representative examples of INGOs. The number of all types of INGOs has proliferated, from around 37 in 1900 to nearly 43,958 as of 2004.[3] In addition to the public INGOs, a second type of nonstate actor is the transnational business enterprise, more commonly called the multinational corporation. The tremendous expansion of international trade and commerce since 1960 produced the rise of huge multinational firms with branch subsidiaries in many states. Corporations are currently the major commercial vehicles through which rights and duties under international economic law are asserted. Many of these corporate organizations amass gross products larger than the domestic products of most states, and this economic might gives them substantial influence in international relations. In 2004, there are at least five hundred thousand multinational corporations and their foreign affiliates operating internationally, with their transactions governed by a special system of international legal rules, the substance and scope of which is addressed in chapter 11.

Terrorist Groups

In the aftermath of the September 11, 2001, bombing of the World Trade Center and the Pentagon, the transnational activities of terrorist groups have attracted extraordinary international concern. The State Department's *Patterns of Global Terrorism* estimated in 2004 that at least 350 transnational terrorist groups and individuals were operating in the United States, among them thirty-six groups designated as foreign terrorist organizations.[4] Clearly there are international connections among terrorist groups, including financial support for their operations, transportation of their members, Internet and cell phone communications, and purchasing of weapons. Religion is a powerful transnational force fostering state-sponsored terrorist operations abroad. Iran, perhaps the chief exporter of terrorism, is well known to direct violent activities against targets in Bahrain, Kuwait, Saudi Arabia, and Iraq. The principal terrorist group operating today, al Qaeda, consists of a global network of semipermanent cells comprising trained militants who are established in at least seventy-six states. In fact, since September 11, more than thirty-three hundred al Qaeda operatives from forty-seven countries have been arrested in ninety-seven countries.[5]

Regimes

The international system is earmarked by special transnational, legally grounded relationships called regimes. As defined by international relations theorists, a regime involves ''a set of implicit or explicit principles, norms, rules, and decision-making procedures around which actors' expectations converge in a given area of international relations.''[6] Regimes have evolved directly in response to serious global concerns, such as the use of the oceans, protection of the environment, governance of Antarctica, protection of human rights, the conduct of warfare, and the nonproliferation of nuclear weapons. In practice, regimes comprise rules of international law, international agreements, international organizations, and patterns of compliant conduct by states and other participants acting in international relations. Like international rules, regimes aim to create expectations of behavior for international actors, and by collectively doing so, they coordinate the cooperative regulation of activities of states in the area of concern. Regimes are usually organized around a central framework treaty, with attendant agreements and rules adopted to deal with new concerns as they arise.

Individuals

Under traditional international legal theory, individual persons were treated as objects of law, rather than as subjects. That is, persons had no rights or duties, as they were the responsibility of states. In recent years, this view has been overturned. The rise of human rights law has elevated the individual human being to the level of a subject entitled to protection under the rule of international law. The law of human rights pertains to people, not governments; persons may receive legal remedies before international tribunals, and individuals may be liable for offenses against the law of nations, such as piracy, war crimes, crimes against humanity, and genocide. In the 21st century, the individual person no longer is deemed to be solely the sovereign prerogative of the state of which he or she is a national. Rather, the international legal protection runs deeper: The individual enjoys certain fundamental protections and civic responsibilities that may not be abrogated by governments.

CLASSIFICATION OF STATES

Notwithstanding the proliferation of modern transnational actors, the most important participants in international relations remain states, or more accurately, the governments of states. States alone are fully sovereign and independent, and they all enjoy full international personality. Not all national entities qualify as states, however. Some polities exhibit traits of statehood but lack essential qualities. The lack of internal stability and governmental control during the 1990s so seriously undermined the credibility of Somalia and Afghanistan that they were labeled "failed states." Similarly, the presence of territory, population, and an effective government do not perforce demonstrate the presence of a state. Puerto Rico, Guam, and the Virgin Islands have these three features of statehood but are not states under international law. They lack the fourth essential ingredient, sovereign independence, since they remain, by their own electoral choice, territories of the United States. Unless the people under a government living in a defined territory possess independence—the ability to govern and regulate their internal and external affairs without outside interference or control—that polity cannot properly claim to be a state.

In addition to sovereign states, several other types of polities have been established, some with legal personality, others without. In some cases, so-called composite international persons, or *unions,* have been created. This kind of polity occurs when two or more independent states become linked together such that they act internationally as a single person. Two varieties of such composite units exist today: the real union and the federal state.

The *real union* results when two independent states become linked by treaty under the same ruler or government and thereafter function internationally as a single actor. A real union is not a unitary state actor. It is a composite of two separate states acting as a single international person. Normally under the treaty or constitution consolidating the arrangement, each member of the union retains internal sovereignty and its own constitution, but there are common ministers or joint councils who advise the sovereign on matters affecting the interests of the union, including issues of war and peace, finances, control of the armed forces, and the conduct of foreign affairs. The component states are pledged to peace with each other and must concur on any extradition or commerce treaties concluded with other states. Modern history has recorded a number of prominent real unions, including Austria and Hungary from 1867 to 1918, Denmark and Iceland from 1918 to 1944, Sweden and Norway from 1814 to 1905, and the union of Tanganyika and Zanzibar to form Tanzania in 1964. More recently, a real union was temporarily formed by the merger in 1990 of North and South Yemen, which was dissolved to create the Republic of Yemen in 1991.

The *federal state* arrangement is a permanent union of previously independent polities with its own constitution, central government organs, and specified powers over the citizens in the separate member polities. While member entities possess inherent nondelegated powers of their own, the central government can deal directly with individual citizens and fix the extent and scope of its power and jurisdiction. The federal state alone is able to declare war, make peace, and conclude international military or commercial agreements, though federal constitutional provisions can authorize limited international activities by member polities. The federal union is fully sovereign and independent as an international actor and is considered a complete international person, with *de jure* international personality. Representative examples of federal states include the United States since 1789; Switzerland, 1848; Germany, 1871; Mexico, 1857; Brazil, 1891; Canada, 1919; and the Soviet Union, 1922.

Certain forms of pseudo-unions have also developed that have not acquired legal personality. The two most prominent of these are the personal union and the confederation. A *personal union* occurs when several states become joined by possessing the same ruler or sovereign. The relationship does not constitute a composite state, nor does it create a real international personality. Each state retains its own sovereignty, and each remains a distinct, separate subject of international of law. Examples are the union of Great Britain and Hanover, 1714–1937; Belgium and the Congo Free State, 1885–1908; and the members of the British Commonwealth of Nations in their relationship to Great Britain since 1931.[7]

A *confederation* is a permanent association of states joined by treaty or compact for purposes of common defense and general welfare. A central government exists with powers of its own, especially for the conduct of foreign affairs; but each state otherwise remains sovereign and independent and enjoys its own international personality. A member state may conclude treaties with other countries, maintain its own diplomatic representation abroad, engage in commercial relations, and act as a sovereign polity in virtually all respects. The central organ of the confederacy is a congress formed of delegates from each of the member states. This central government does not deal directly with individual citizens but operates through the member states themselves. As such, the confederation is not considered to be an international person. Moreover, history reveals this type of governmental arrangement to be unsatisfactory as a governing organization, as confederations have collapsed and been replaced, usually by a federal state system. Among modern confederacies, the most prominent have included the United States, 1778–1787; the German Confederation, 1815–1866; the Swiss confederation, 1291–1798; and the Confederation of Senegambia (joining Senegal and the Gambia), 1982–1989. An exceptional modern confederation is that of the United Arab Emirates (UAE). Created by treaty in 1971 by seven sheikdoms in the Persian Gulf, the UAE is now recognized as a sovereign state: it participates in international affairs, and it holds membership in the United Nations and in a number of its specialized agencies.

Some states have been admitted into the international community with certain qualifications attached to their legal status. In this sense, they differ in some ways from the normal condition of statehood. One such category contains the so-called *neutralized states*. This is not synonymous with the status of neutrality, which a state voluntarily adopts as its status at the beginning of an international armed conflict between other states or even in peacetime. Rather, a neutralized state accepts the status of neutrality imposed on it by a group of outside powers. Neutralized states may be compelled to resist entering into alliances with other states that might require its participation in future conflicts; in turn, the powers mandating that neutrality will be obligated to respect that status. There are only a few such neutralized states, and only one, Switzerland (since 1815), survives today. The others include Laos, 1962–1974; Belgium, 1919–1940; and Austria, 1955–1992.[8]

Another category contains certain *conditional states*—that is, countries who are admitted into the international community under formal agreements to adhere to special rules or fulfill certain obligations imposed by other states as the price for admission. Such conditions were not regarded as impositions on the sovereignty of the state in question, since they were contained in the text of treaties entered into freely by the concerned state. For example, in 1878 the Congress of Berlin made the admission of Montenegro contingent on special obligations for religious and racial tolerance, maintenance of fortifications, and freedom of transit across the country. When the new countries of Poland, Czechoslovakia, and Yugoslavia were admitted in 1919 under the Treaty of Versailles, special conditions were set in that instrument regarding the treatment of minority groups. In a 1955 treaty involving the United States, the Soviet Union, the United Kingdom, France, and Austria, an independent Austrian state was reestablished under several conditions, including provisions granting equal human rights and prohibitions on political or economic union with Germany and on the acquisition of certain types of weapons.[9]

The Cold War era produced a new phenomenon, the *divided state,* which was separated into two entities, each with an operative government and each recognized by other governments as an independent state. Among these divided states are the two Germanys, the Federal Republic of Germany and the German Democratic Republic; the two Koreas, the Republic of Korea (South) and the Peoples' Republic of Korea (North); the two Chinas, the Peoples' Republic of China and the Republic of China (Taiwan); the two Vietnams, the Democratic Republic of Vietnam (North) and the Republic of Vietnam (South); and the two Yemens. Over the past three decades, three of these divided states have become reunified: Vietnam in 1976 after the North conquered the South and formed the Socialist Republic of Vietnam; Germany in 1990 through a one-thousand-page bilateral treaty agreement detailing the particulars of reunification,[10] augmented by a multilateral accord containing a German renunciation of war and a pledge to recognize Poland's 1945 western borders; and North and South Yemen by treaty in 1990 to form the Republic of Yemen. Both China and Korea remain divided states.

The *State of the Vatican City* is also a member of the international community. In 1929, the Lateran Treaty established the Vatican as a sovereign independent state occupying 109 acres in Rome. This agreement, which was incorporated into the Italian constitution of 1947, also provides that the pope is pledged to perpetual neutrality and may intervene into international affairs as a mediator only on request. The Holy See, despite being the world's smallest sovereign state, has become more active in international relations and currently maintains diplomatic relations with more than 125 states. In 1965, the Vatican embassy negotiated a cease-fire in the Dominican Republic that facilitated withdrawal of U.S. troops. In 1990, Panama's strongman, Manuel Noriega, sought refuge in the residence of the papal nuncio shortly after the U.S. invasion of Panama. The Vatican's role was instrumental in persuading Noriega to surrender to U.S. forces, which had surrounded the embassy. The Holy See gained international attention in 1994 during the UN Conference on Population, in Cairo, Egypt, as the Vatican joined forces with Islamic states such as Libya and Iran to oppose multilateral birth control policies that included abortion as an option of choice.

In classical international law, the four smallest countries in Europe are known as the "dwarf states," which represent anomalous legacies of the past. The principality of Andorra, only 174 square miles in area and situated in the Pyrenees between Spain and France, was a medieval relic coruled by France and the bishop of Urgel in Spain from 1278 to 1993. Andorran voters chose to end that feudal system in 1993 by adopting parliamentary democracy and control over their own foreign policy. Liechtenstein, bounded by Austria and Switzerland and only sixty-two square miles in area, is a constitutional monarchy that thrives on banking and on being an international corporate haven. Monaco, a tiny principality (1.21 square miles) located on the Mediterranean coast of France, is known for tourism and its famous Monte Carlo casino. San Marino, located in north central Italy on the slopes of Mount Titano and only twenty-three square miles in area, is the oldest republic in the world, reputedly founded in the 4th century AD. These little countries, long secluded from world affairs, opted during the 1990s to become more active participants in international activities. All of them joined the United Nations and several specialized agencies during the 1990s, and all have sent delegates to a number of international conferences and have ratified an impressive number of multilateral conventions.

The process of decolonization created several small, thinly populated polities, mostly from island groups that attained independence during the 1960s and 1970s. Among such *ministates,* or *microstates,* are the Maldive Islands (116 square miles, 300,220 population), Kiribati (277 square miles, 85,500 population), Grenada (131 square miles, 97,000 population), Dominica (290 square miles, 65,000 population), Palau (177 square miles, 18,500 population), Tuvalu (10 square miles, 10,600 population), and Nauru (8 square miles, 10,600 population). All of these polities enjoy the status of being internationally recognized as sovereign states in the world community, and all have become members of the United Nations.

A relatively recent category of international actor is that of the *associated state.* This modern concept refers to a polity that delegates special governmental functions (usually related to foreign affairs or defense) to a "principal state" while retaining its international status, which distinguishes it from the unpopular protectorate condition of the colonial era. The associated state is regarded as a subject of international law. Modern examples include the Federated States of Micronesia, the Commonwealth of the Northern Marianas, the Republic of the Marshall Islands, and the Republic of Palau, all of which were formerly part of the United States UN Strategic Trust Territory of the Pacific and are now members of the United Nations.[11]

Finally, it should be noted that the East European *satellite states* during the Cold War (including Czechoslovakia, East Germany, Hungary, Poland, Rumania, and Bulgaria) were viewed as legally independent of external control but were often subjected to various pressures from the Soviet Union that greatly impinged on their freedom to act in foreign affairs. Even so, these states were regarded as lawful polities, recognized as full members of the international community.

There are also nonsovereign entities in the international system that do not enjoy international personality. These include the member states of a federal union; nomads, pirates, and tribes that lack sufficient political organization and the necessary qualities of states; social groups, political parties, and nationalities that, while having important influences on international relations, do not enjoy de facto international legal personality. Commercial multinational corporations exercise tremendous economic and political power trans-nationally, but they are actually corporate creatures registered in a state, bound by that state's laws and regulations. Though corporations are subject to *private international law* through which they engage in contractual arrangements with other corporations and governments, they are not subjects of public international law. Colonies and provinces, which have territory and population, also lack international personality in that they are not self-governing territories.

So-called subservient states were mandates of the League of Nations (1921–1945) and were trusteeships of the United Nations (1945–1994). Article 22 of the League of Nations Covenant created a system of mandates whereby a system of international supervision was established for certain colonies and territories formerly under German or Turkish sovereignty. The intention here was that the well-being and political development of these areas would be entrusted to more advanced states, subject to the supervision of the League of Nations. Since these territories were at varying stages of political development, they were divided into three categories. Class A mandates were parts of the former Ottoman Empire and were deemed to be so sufficiently developed that they were provisionally recognized as states. Class B mandates consisted of former German colonies in Africa and were administered from neighboring colonies of the mandatory power. The Class C mandates included the former German South-West Africa and all former German colonies in the Pacific. These areas—because of small populations, remote locations, and relative political backwardness—were administered under the laws of the mandatory power as integral portions of their territory.

The onslaught of the Second World War, coupled with the collapse of the League of Nations, interrupted the process of preparing independence for the mandated territories. As a result, with the exception of South-West Africa during 1946–1947, the remaining mandates were placed under a special *trusteeship system* of the United Nations through bilateral agreements between the UN and designated former mandatory powers. South Africa, which had legally supervised South-West Africa as a league mandatory power, refused to relinquish control to the United Nations and indicated its intention to annex the territory. In addition, the United States was given administrative control over certain former Japanese islands (the Northern Marianas, the Marshall Islands, Micronesia, and Palau) as a special strategic trust territory under the UN Security Council. The trusteeship process worked successfully as all the affected territories either attained sovereign independence or were assimilated into other states. In 1990, the achievement of independence by Namibia ended the struggle with South Africa over the territory of South-West Africa. The final trust territory to achieve independence was Palau in 1994.

Dependent or semisovereign states have also existed. These polities retained certain measures of sovereignty and international personality, even though their foreign and internal affairs remained controlled or managed by some other state. In terms of foreign relations, the superior state controlled important facets of external sovereignty, such as diplomatic rights of legation and treaty making. This relationship proved anomalous, difficult to maintain, and usually ended in annexation or independence. Two classes of semisovereign states are notable, the first being *vassal states,* which owed allegiance to the suzerain state. The former term, derived from feudalism, described the relationship of service and protection between vassal and lord, and it characterized the legal condition in the Ottoman Empire with certain tributary states, such as Rumania, Serbia, and Bulgaria in the 19th and early 20th centuries. Vassal states theoretically possessed only rights and privileges granted to it by the suzerain, but in fact, they often functioned independently.

Such relationships are no longer found in international law, as they are considered illicit vestiges of colonialism.

A second form of semisovereign polity was the international *protectorate*. This situation occurred when a weak or dependent state was placed through treaty or mutual consent under the legal protection of a more powerful state. The protecting state functioned as a trustee, like a guardian toward a ward. The main duty of the foreign power was protection, an international responsibility that conveyed the right to intervene in the internal and external affairs of the protected state. Internationally, protectorates were more dependent on the superior state than states were in a vassal relationship. In the early 20th century, various protectorates of Great Britain included the Malay states, Uganda, and Zanzibar. In the case of France, protectorate status was arranged for Tunis, Cambodia, and Morocco—likewise the case of Cuba under the United States from 1898 to 1939. Most protectorates operated within the framework of colonialism, and most lost their legitimacy during the era of decolonization in the 1950s. No formally declared protectorates exist today, though the term's relevance for the "associated state" relationship is still mentioned.

Still another special nonsovereign arrangement found in international law is the *condominium*, which is a territory jointly governed by two or more states. Several examples of condominiums existed during the last century, among them the New Hebrides (now independent as Vanuatu), governed by Great Britain and France, 1906–1980; the Anglo-Egyptian Sudan, 1889–1956 (now independent as the Sudan); and Tangier, governed by Great Britain, France, Spain, Portugal, Belgium, the Netherlands, and Italy, 1923–1956 (now incorporated into Morocco). The only surviving condominium is the Ile des Faisans (Island of Pheasants), located near the mouth of the Bidassoa River, which forms the common frontier between Spain and France for seven miles in the Bay of Biscay. Condominia are not full members of the international community, mainly because they play little role in international relations, have no governments of their own, and lack the necessary legal ingredient of sovereign independence.

SOVEREIGNTY AND STATES

Independent states remain the necessary and primary subjects of the international legal community. The governments of states determine the political shape, norms, and rules for relationships in the international community. Of considerable importance, they have not forfeited that power in creating other institutions for the international community. Moreover, only states are capable of creating law in the international realm and of constituting secondary subjects of international law.

The state has evolved into the core actor and subject of international law mainly out of practical necessity. International rules cannot be made enforceable unless governments enforce them within their own territory, through their own laws, on their own nationals, or impose them forcibly on other states, whether alone or in concert with other governments. This is the case because national governments have obtained a near monopoly of legal, political, and judicial power within their territories that permits them to enforce international norms at the domestic level as well as assert foreign policies aimed at attaining national and international objectives.

The concept of state sovereignty has produced unfortunate ramifications for the development of international legal rules. The notion of sovereignty confronts scholars with a profound dilemma of interstate relations. How can law be binding on sovereign actors, who by the very fact that they are sovereign cannot be bound by any law? The "natural and inalienable rights of man" principle that was so cherished by Enlightenment philosophers has been transmuted to the international realm over the past two hundred years into the correlative principle of "the fundamental rights of states." This concept of sovereignty, derived from 18th-century rationalism and reinterpreted by 19th-century conservatism, became more effective as it presumed that international relations operated in a fixed order of nature, with the state at the center of the universe.

In this same vein, realist political scientists currently suggest the theory of indivisible sovereignty. According to this view, sovereignty cannot be divided. The sovereignty of a state is a quality that is present and absolute, nondivisible, and not quantifiable. A state must be fully sovereign; otherwise, it is not a true state. Such a view reinforces the traditional notion of external sovereignty, which asserts that no restrictions can be subjected on states in their mutual relations.

There exists also within international legal theory a profound contradiction that impedes the development of international law. This is a fundamental problem that undercuts the possibility for a society of states to be effectively governed by an agreed-on system of law that is capable of providing security for all peoples. This difficulty emanates from the fact that the doctrine of state sovereignty constitutes a pivotal proposition in international law theory. Even in the UN Charter, the "organization is based on the principle of the sovereign equality of all its Members,"[12] and nothing contained in the Charter "shall authorize the United Nations to intervene in matters, which are essentially within the domestic jurisdiction of any state or shall require the Members to submit such matters to settlement under the present Charter."[13] It is generally recognized that any so-called fully sovereign state may through its treaty-making capacity voluntarily impose limitations on the exercise of its sovereignty. However, the extent of sovereignty or independence that a state can exercise may not be so much the product of law as it is the result of that state's military or technological capability.

The proposition that all states are equal derives from the doctrine of sovereignty. Equality is conceived as a natural right of states. Just as humans are free and equal in the state of nature, so too are states free and equal in their international relations. While this doctrine of equality may appear plausible in legal theory and be particularly appealing for its democratic tendency, it is a fallacy in actual fact. States are inherently not equal. They are unequal not only in geographic size, quantity, and quality of population; abundance of natural resources, industry, and technological capability; and availability of military power but also in terms of their legal obligations and capacity to adhere to, or comply with, the law. States, like people, are relative to one another. They enjoy neither the same status nor equal treatment under international law. As of 2004 there are 191 members of the United Nations, but it remains acutely recognized that the five permanent members of the Security Council who have the power of veto are "more equal" than all the others.

Regrettably, this notion of sovereign state rights has proved a highly disruptive and disintegrative force in modern international relations. Sovereignty, while implying freedom to do whatever one wishes to do, actually breeds irresponsibility and an excuse for violating international rules. A fundamental difficulty for contemporary international law stems from the fact that states were historically regarded as sovereign in their external or international relations as in the policies they exercised within their respective territorial jurisdictions. The theory of sovereignty that arose in early 17th-century Europe was concerned mainly with internal affairs of the state. Its purpose was to replace the anarchy that had characterized the Middle Ages with greater social, political, and economic order through the centralized rule of an absolute monarch, the so-called sovereign. Since then, the attraction for these conditions of internal absolutism has disintegrated as new political theories of constitutionalism, federalism, and pluralism took root and were promoted by political philosophers and the public alike. Moreover, in its external facets, the concept of sovereignty has collapsed even further in the modern age under the compelling forces associated with increasing interdependence and globalization. The confusion surrounding sovereignty stems largely from attempts to adjust old theory to new facts. The classic concept of sovereignty, with its attendant corollary advocating the equality of all states, hardly resembles the political and economic realities of the early 21st century. The predominant behavior of states in the international community clearly indicates that they are interdependent and that numerous rules and norms govern their conduct. International obligations cannot be avoided by a state's invocation of its own constitutional law. The need for limitations on state sovereignty is widely and consistently recognized by their governments to bolster international cooperation through the rule of interstate law.

SOVEREIGNTY AND TERRITORY

Sovereignty ranks among the most confounding concepts in international relations, and it often suggests dual meanings. Sovereignty may be used as a synonym for being independent, especially to signify that the government officials in one state are free from the control of government officials in other states. But sovereignty also suggests the notion that within a specified area, the prescription and enforcement of legal rules are vested exclusively in the government officials of the state that claims that territory. This is usually called territorial sovereignty.

Sovereignty over territory and population was traditionally regarded as a claim by a state to absolute and unfettered formal authority within that state's territory. This claim did not derive from any outside source and could not be subjected to external controls imposed by other states. The very essence of sovereignty is seen as freedom from external control. States that are not free of such external control are not considered fully sovereign in their international relations. Prevailing opinion holds that states should not obstruct another state in the exercise of its governmental functions within its own territory, nor should they engage in international affairs on its behalf. Such actions are inconsistent with the latter state's sovereignty.

In the era when states were regarded as the only participants in international affairs, a state had to retain independence over its internal governmental processes. This quality of independence was usually associated with the concept of sovereignty. In modern affairs, there is less need for such a high degree of exclusive and segregated authority. Absolute independence and freedom from interference in a state's internal affairs are no longer essential for political or military security. In fact, such protective isolation is no longer possible for any state in today's increasingly complex, interdependent world, which has become characterized by profound commercial globalization and multifaceted forms of massive transborder data flow. The more transactions that cross international boundaries, the more interdependent peoples everywhere become. Consequently, there is less effective operational scope for exercising exclusive formal authority. Moreover, numerous new political actors have been created to facilitate these integrative processes: universal organizations such as the United Nations and its functional agencies (e.g., the International Atomic Energy Agency, the International Telecommunications Union, and the International Civil Aviation Organization), as well as regional arrangements such as the European Union, Association of Southeast Asian Nations, and the North American Free Trade

Agreement. States have entered into legal relationships with one another to form new organizations having supranational authority that lawfully affects the internal affairs of member states. These new intergovernmental agencies can adopt (with member state consent) policies and measures that legally restrict the absolute control a government might exercise in its external foreign relations with other states.

Sovereignty refers to formal authority, though not necessarily to effective control. The point is sometimes made that a state gives up a portion of its sovereign authority by its commitment to a treaty or by its participation in an international organization. In terms of legal obligation, the point is valid. By such participation, a government limits its state's formal authority to unilaterally prescribe and enforce certain decisions that affect its welfare. But it should be noted that the state also gains from these relationships, as it consolidates access to new resources and legal opportunities and as it increases its role over other decisions affecting its national interests.

Is the European Union a sovereign polity? To the extent (1) that the EU exercises exclusive and ultimate authority over certain important governmental functions within the territory covered by its treaty of unification, (2) that it can enter into binding relations with other states and organizations external to the union, and (3) that it possesses immunities and rights normally accorded to sovereign polities, it is certainly a sovereign entity. But if sovereignty is thought to mean exclusive control and jurisdiction over territory, then the European Union cannot be considered sovereign. While it has grown profoundly in its legal and political reach over the activities of member states, the EU remains more a functional authority than a territorial authority. Yet, if the past is a prologue and if the EU continues to expand its scope of authority over European affairs, its policies will certainly and pervasively affect the internal affairs of its member states.

LEGAL RELATIONS BETWEEN STATES

In domestic society, governments can enforce contracts, deter citizens from breaking rules, and use their monopoly of legally sanctioned force to uphold the system of law. The operation of municipal police forces and judiciaries underscore these domestic capabilities. The lack of these governmental capabilities is what realists have in mind when they describe the international system as being anarchic. The international system has no formal authority structures to enforce rules and ensure compliance with norms of conduct. The power of one state is countered only by the power of other states; thus, they rely on self-help to enforce rules and norms of international law.[14]

Despite its condition of anarchy, the international system is far from being chaotic. Nearly all interactions among states closely adhere to international rules that were created to produce expectations of what conduct by a government is considered proper and therefore permissible. To keep pace with rapid technological developments in international relations, the legal rules among states must remain in constant flux. International law cannot be static; it must be dynamic. Otherwise, the accelerated pace of transnational technological development will leave international law even further behind. While these normative rules change over time, those fundamental to making the international system function remain intact after three centuries.

International law emerged through the transformation of the hierarchy of medieval society into a group of independent states. The critical feature in the evolving state system was that legal obedience to a superior sovereign was replaced by rules to be observed by polities perceived as equal under the law. In the past, a vertical legal relationship had existed between the superior sovereign with jurisdiction over lower persons in the domestic sphere. No legitimate authority was created to ensure observance by a state of the duties created by this body of rules. As individual polities in the international arena, legal relations between states became cast as a horizontal scheme. The sole sanction to a breach of these rules was self-help, through the reaction by the state injured by the act of another. The fundamental norm for coexistence came down to the need for sovereign states to observe the same rules in their relations with other states that they expected to be applied to themselves.

The point here is that states are not wholly sovereign actors. Sovereignty may be conceived as an aggregate of powers, some of which may be subtracted without destroying the state. In an interdependent society, no state can be wholly independent. States rely on each other, as well as on other international actors, for their mutual survival. This is clearly realized in the global process of international trade and commerce, which is made possible only though the enactment of international legal rules. The very existence of interstate legal rules that are binding on national governments lends a certain primacy to international law and denigrates the claim on the part of states to having absolute sovereignty in the arena of external relations. External sovereignty in the 21st century finds little esteem as a fixed and irreducible quantity. Rather, external sovereignty should be measured more properly as a variable dependent on the potential of a state's power.

LAW AND THE COMMUNITY OF STATES

A critical question confronting law and politics in the modern era concerns the extent to which sovereignty, viewed through the domestic law of a state, can be reconciled with the development and function of international law and organization. The fact is that at the basis of community lies the controlling notion of active organization to preserve peace and order. Without such a notion, there can be no community of individuals or states. But attaining and maintaining the sense of international legal community is not easy. Sovereign states sometimes act as if they were fully autonomous and independent, even to the point that they feel unaccountable for their foreign policy actions. Internally, states set their own limits for their scope of domestic power and jurisdiction through their own laws and government. A similar attitude holds for international affairs. Governments are free to make whatever foreign policy they desire, so long as it best suits their long-term national interests.

These attitudes mirror the realist political-science position. Realists assert that the iron-clad law of international politics holds that legal obligations must yield to the national interests of a state. Foreign policy should not be evaluated within the terms of international law or abstract standards of morality. Such a view denies the existence of a world community and the validity of international law as binding legal rules. Legal rules for international relations can be better understood and appreciated by realizing that they arise chiefly as a result of events, rather than as a cause. The law among states is a social science that derives its validity from a dominant consensus among states. International legal rules are undergirded not by pillars of support from a few national polities; rather, their lines of force and obligations stem from the center of international social gravity—that is, from the conduct and behavior of all states themselves. Consequently, international rules serve as the foundation that lends structure, equilibrium, and order to the process of interstate politics. In this way legal rules contribute to making international relations a community experience. At the same time, there must be order for international rules to take root and grow. A simple proposition emerges in this regard: international rules are effective in direct proportion to the degree that a sense of community is present and practiced by states.

External sovereignty comes down to the self-control exercised by a state in its foreign affairs. Still, the degree of external sovereignty held by a state is not absolute; it is limited in various ways. First, various norms, principles, and customs have evolved into international legal rules to which states have obligated themselves. The government of a state is responsible for its violation of these rules. Second, states have limited their sovereignty through conventional interstate law—that is, by the law of treaties. When states pledge to abide by the terms of international agreements, they perforce limit their willingness to engage in acts that contravene those provisions. A state is held responsible for any breach of its express agreements. Third, there are special treaties of alliance, guarantee, and protection by which a state obligates itself to give aid to another state or to assist in maintaining certain conditions or states of affairs. These obligations assume priority over what options a state might have in various situations. Fourth, states undertake membership in international organizations in which members enjoy equal rights and are reciprocally bound by various duties toward other members set out in that contractual relationship. In any event, the external sovereignty and independence of states in contemporary international relations must be understood in an absolute and unrestricted sense.

Since the international political system is in constant flux, the international legal community formed by this society must adapt to these changes. States in contemporary times must produce new rules and practices that can generate or solidify new law. This situation can be clearly seen in changing economic conditions; growing world commerce leading to the creation of new trade law and new international institutions (the *General Agreement on Tariffs and Trade* and its *World Trade Organization*); the advance of new technologies having profound transnational repercussions (the Internet and satellite communication); and the global rush to industrialization, which has produced serious problems for the planet's environmental condition (global warming and ozone depletion). The international legal community must create binding legal rules and principles to deal with these new challenges, which might literally threaten the very survival of humankind.

DUALISM VERSUS MONISM

The intellectual debate between the *dualists* and the *monists* should be mentioned within the context of the actors and their legal rules in the modern international community. These two schools of legal theory concerning the distinction between the law of states and municipal law matured last century but remain polemical today. On the one hand, the dualists contend that international law and municipal law differ in certain respects. In terms of sources, international legal rules look to treaties and state practice that evolve in the society of states, whereas for municipal law the sources of authority are found in customs and legislation that have been approved and enacted by a recognized lawmaking authority within the state's jurisdiction.

In terms of subjects, international rules regulate relations among states in an international society, whereas municipal law is concerned with individual citizens in their relations to one another and to the state. While no central executive authority exists in international law to compel the observance of legal rules, individual citizens under municipal law are subjected by the rules and power of the government. Dualists therefore argue that international law cannot ever function as the law of the land for a state except through municipal custom or statutory enactment. There cannot be self-executing treaties, since enabling legislation is required to activate provisions of an international agreement on persons and corporations in a state.[15]

Monistic theorists differ on this point. They do not admit any essential difference between the subjects of international and municipal law. They contend that for both legal systems, it is the individual person who ultimately remains the subject of legal regulation. Both interstate and municipal law regulate human conduct. Governments of states are formed of humans who create the legal rules that aim to promote order in domestic and interstate societies. Thus, interstate law shares the same creators and aspirations as municipal law. As such, interstate law is not without commanding authority and should be considered intimately part of the same juristic conception as municipal law. In sum, the doctrine of monism asserts that the sum of legal principles—national and international—constitutes a single body of rules on the individual.[16]

DOCTRINE OF INCORPORATION

The notion of community permeates the debate between the dualists and the monists. The doctrine that international legal rules are part of a state's law of the land enjoys considerable support in the history of Anglo-American jurisprudence.[17] Respect for the doctrine of incorporation, which held that international law was an integral part of municipal law, underwent profound change in the 19th century. In the 1700s, such juridical constructs of international law were dominated by natural law and generally accepted in legal theory. But by the 1850s, positivism became firmly rooted in jurisprudential thought, and the underpinnings for law were regarded as being sanctioned by consent. Thus, in the absence of a specific statute, executive decision, or judicial precedent, the municipal law governing a state's role in international matters should be derived from the implied or express consent of its government.

It is true that in recent decades the doctrine of incorporation might have lost some of its sway under the impact of modern nationalism. Nevertheless, international legal rules operate within the channels of municipal law, as evidenced in the juristic practice of states, including that of the United States. In this sense, international law evolved as part of the law of the land and was affirmed as a principle of positive law. In that same respect international law contributes to the sense of a world community comprising various actors that voluntarily obligate themselves to being subject to international legal rules.

CONCLUSION

The Treaty of Westphalia in 1648 ushered in the state system that continues to dominate international relations in the 21st century. The modern state still possesses sovereignty and a high degree of political authority organized for public ends. Sovereignty reflects a state's independence and, at least theoretically, its equality under international law with other states. But a state's sovereignty in its foreign relations is not unbounded. States have adopted in their common interest stipulated restraints on their freedom to act internationally in an interdependent world. These limitations flow from the raft of rules that have been agreed to by every state via bilateral treaties, through multilateral conventions, and in international organizations that commit governments to abide by obligations that affect the direction of their foreign policy actions.

The nature of the world community affects the impact that international legal rules have on its subjects. In the current international system, states function in an environment that helps determine their actions. Nonetheless, states remain the key actors in making, breaking, and enforcing international rules. A state legally, economically, and politically affects the international system, and the international system legally, economically, and politically affects every state. While the impact of the system on a state's policy varies according to specific issues and circumstances, international rules still furnish regulatory guideposts for national foreign policy actions. To be sure, a state may decide to ignore or disobey the rules. Such a violation of international rules should not be inferred as meaning that no rules exist. Rather, it should be seen more properly as a comment on the government of that state and its willingness to disregard the lawful restraints contained in that rule.

While the sovereign state remains the key political unit, the structure of modern international society is distinguished in several ways from the past. For one, the number of legitimate actors in the international community has grown profoundly, with 193 states today, nearly quadruple the number of original UN members after the Second World War. Most new states are medium or small actors at various stages of economic and social development. Likewise, international organizations have proliferated in disparate forms in modern international society. Though rarely universal, membership in intergovernmental organizations can be multilateral, regional, or selective in scope. Moreover, most organizations retain their own legal personality and are capable of acting through their own organs as subjects of international law. The point here is that international relations today are strongly influenced by the presence and activities of permanent multilateral organizations, nearly all of which have been created by formal international treaty agreements. Thus membership in international organizations requires that states assume certain duties and obligations, which entails a willingness to accept permanent restrictions on their freedom of action as related to various competencies of the organization. Such a situation works to diminish the substance of a state's sovereign prerogatives in many dimensions of its international activities.

Notwithstanding these legal attributes, the interstate system during the early 21st century is passing through a period of stress and crisis. The conflict between forces of ethnonationalism and those of transnational unitarianism is real and fundamental to current international relations. Ethnic and tribal tensions within states are disintegrating societies, and evidence is mounting of global economic, social, and political interdependence in the aftermath of the Cold War. Religious ideologies exacerbate the conflict even more. Consequently, the ways in which these divergent forces are resolved will determine the character of the international system in the coming century, which constitutes a centrally important problem to international law and politics. A paradoxical situation thus has evolved in recent years. While increased interdependence of states will require more international rules and organizations to function effectively, the psychological attitude and willingness of governments necessary for such cooperation remain wanting. The society of states, still the essential arbiter of effective legal rules, remains in a primitive condition of development. The key lies in the respect that governments give to the fundamental rights and duties agreed on for fostering more communal international relations. We now turn to these rights and duties of states and to their attendant responsibilities in the next chapter.

3

The State

- ❦ The State as Territory
- ❦ Self-Determination
- ❦ Recognition
- ❦ Rights and Duties of States
- ❦ State Responsibility
- ❦ Extinction
- ❦ Conclusion

The old adage that "good fences make good neighbors" does not always ring true. In 2003 the government of Israel began construction on a security barrier consisting of walls, razor wire, and trenches and running through the West Bank. The Palestine Centre in Washington, D.C., asserts that the fence—really, a barrier—will stretch for about 650 kilometers, about twice the actual length of the 1967 "Green Line" that defines the West Bank. The extra length is needed to accommodate the zigzags that encompass individual Israeli settlements near the border areas. The Israeli government contends that the barrier is necessary to stop suicide bombers from infiltrating into Israeli territory. Critics assert that, if constructed, the barrier should be erected along the Green Line demarcation that separates Israel and the Palestinian territory prior to the 1967 six-day Middle East war and that it not cut into and encircle Palestinian population areas. Critics, including the United States and the European Union, object that the barrier violates the human rights of Palestinians and breaches international law. The legal implications of the security fence constitute a serious issue. On December 8, 2003, the General Assembly voted 90–8 to request an advisory opinion from the International Court of Justice (ICJ) in The Hague on the barrier Israel is building in occupied Palestinian territories. The resolution requests an opinion on "the legal consequences arising from the construction of the wall . . . considering the rules and principles of international law." The vote, with seventy-four countries abstaining, indicated that the assembly is deeply divided over bringing the issue, which many countries view as a political issue, before the world's leading multilateral forum. Israel, the United States, Australia, and five small Pacific island states voted against the resolution, while the abstainers included Russia, European Union countries, and several Latin American countries. The United States had already vetoed the proposal in the Security Council in October 2003, but governments resurrected the idea in the General Assembly, where the veto is not an option. The ICJ heard oral arguments on the case in February 2004 and issued its decision on July 9, 2004. By a vote of 14–1, the Court concluded that Israel's barrier was unlawful because it "severely impedes the exercise of the Palestinian people to its right of self-determination." Associated with the security fence is a concurrent web of projects around Jerusalem, including the linking of thirteen nearby Jewish settlements with the city, which in effect redraws the map of the sacred city to a point that it is viewed as an attempt to break Palestinian religious, economic, political, and cultural ties; preempt negotiations over Jerusalem's final status; and preclude the chance of the city becoming capital of a future Palestinian state. While Israel denies this charge, Palestinian critics complain that Jerusalem is the most visible example of Israel's settlement of besieging and caging Palestinian communities and controlling their exits and entrances with settlements, roads, and fences to divide Palestinian neighborhoods and separate Jerusalem from the West Bank. Palestinians complain that building the barrier amounts to the enslavement of the whole Palestinian people by confining them to cantons. The wall is not a means of achieving security but is actually a massive war crime. The Israeli government, however, maintains that the security fence is a temporary, necessary, and nonviolent measure. It is not to be construed as a border and has no political significance. The purpose of the barrier is simply to eliminate the prospects of terrorism by reducing the capacity of Palestinian terrorists to infiltrate and perpetrate acts of terror. While Israeli prime minister Ariel Sharon vowed that Israel will "make every effort to minimize its infringement on the daily life of the Palestinian population," the fence would turn about 55 percent of the present West Bank into permanent Israeli territory. From the view of Palestinians, the barrier and the so-called access roads for Israelis would splinter the remaining Palestinian enclaves into isolated "Bantustans" which would not be politically or economically viable as a sovereign independent state.

International society is constantly changing. New actors appear and disappear. Polities break apart, and new entities are created. Intergovernmental organizations grow in number to deal with emerging transnational issues. Other nonstate actors proliferate and continue to alter the international landscape. Even so, states remain the preeminent actors in contemporary international relations. As the touchstone for formulating and implementing legal rules, the state enjoys being the entity longest contemplated as a person in international law and is still widely viewed as the most important legal actor. Quite accurately, "the law of nations" today essentially remains the law for the states.

States are organic creatures: they are born, they live, and they die. But states are also anthropomorphic creations. They are founded and fashioned by humans, used by humans for their own social and political purposes, and ended by humans. Modern international law adapts to the progressive existence of states by establishing rules that condition the creation, existence, and death of statehood. This is not to say that international rules deal comprehensively with the origins, existence, or maturity of states, for they do not. It is impractical to set rigid rules that determine the lawfulness of an independent political community's existence. The state, which remains a historical and geopolitical reality, functions more as the creator of law than as a creature of law. On a general level it is possible to determine the rules that govern formal acknowledgment by the international community that an entity qualifies for admission into the interstate society. Most salient among these legal rules are the essential characteristics usually accepted for defining a state—namely, an entity's occupying a clearly defined territory; possessing a permanent population; operating an effective governmental capacity, internally and externally; and having the capacity to engage in international relations, including the ability to fulfill international legal obligations.

THE STATE AS TERRITORY

The foundation for international law is grounded in geographical considerations. That is, states occupy definite portions of the earth's surface, within which their governments exercise jurisdiction over persons and property to the exclusion of other states. Such authoritative jurisdiction by a government over its claimed bounded space is described as the exercise of territorial sovereignty. It is a relationship not merely of persons to persons, nor of one state to another. Rather, it is more akin to the rightful ownership of property in municipal law, with the government of a state acting as the sovereign over its claimed territory.

The extent of a state's territory consists of land, water, and air. The land domain consists of all land and islands possessed by a state, including the subsoil beneath its land and water surface to an indefinite depth. The territorial waters of a state extend seaward to twelve nautical miles from the coastal *baseline*, with sovereign possession attached to the water column, living and nonliving natural resources, and the seabed. States enjoy exclusive sovereignty in the airspace above their land and water territory. The frontiers or boundaries of a state are critical features for demarcating the extent of territorial jurisdiction, and they must be accurately drawn and definitely ascertained to avoid international disputes and conflicts. This is especially true for land-based borders. Natural features—such as forests, mountains, and valleys—provide some frontiers. Most boundaries are artificial calculations, necessarily fixed by treaties that usually follow mathematical lines jointly surveyed on the basis of latitude and longitude by the affected governments. For navigable rivers, which are commonly used for demarcating international boundaries, the legal rule dictates that the boundary line follow the middle of the *thalweg*, or the navigable channel through which the strongest current flows downstream. If the river is not navigable, the older, Grotian rule applies in which the boundary runs down the middle of the stream. For states separated by lakes or landlocked seas, boundary lines are often drawn in the middle of such water bodies, though sometimes boundary commissions are arranged to survey boundary lines based on special natural considerations. Such appears to be the case for boundary lines in the Great Lakes (separating the United States and Canada), Lake Constance and Lake Geneva (separating Switzerland and France), and Lake Victoria in central Africa (separating Uganda, Tanzania, and Kenya). Notwithstanding boundary demarcation, all littoral states enjoy common use of the water.

Acquisition of Territory

In what ways can spatial sovereignty be obtained over territory? The historical practice of states illustrates a number of ways, all but one of which remain accepted as legitimate in contemporary international law.[1] Original title to territory may be obtained through three forms of acquisition—occupation, accretion, and prescription—and in each case, the territory may be acquired only if it is not already under the jurisdiction of another state. In the early development of international legal rules, an act of *discovery* was considered sufficient to convey a claim of lawful title, a practice that was increasingly challenged in the 17th century with the belief that the original discovery of some land could furnish only inchoate, or imperfect, temporary title. For such a claim to be perfected as lawful, it must be followed by effective *occupation*—that is, permanent settlement of that land demonstrated by a minimum of authoritative control. That is the rule today. Occupation establishes the permanent presence of the claimant state, in which resides a population under the effective control and administration of a government.[2]

Accretion is a minor way of acquiring territory. It consists of a state's territory becoming larger through the action of nearby rivers or oceans when gradual alluvial deposits add new land formations to the mouths of rivers and lakes or along the seacoasts of the littoral state. The following legal rule generally applies: an accessory annexed to a principal becomes part of the principal and thus property of the principal's owner. Soil added to a riverbank becomes an addition to the territory of that riparian state. Similarly, islands that are built up within a state's territorial waters not only become the property of that coastal state but can also cause the outward extension of the marine frontier for demarcating the baseline for which territorial sea is determined.[3]

Another form of obtaining original title to territory is *prescription*, which refers to the continued occupation or possession of land over a prolonged period, provided that such possession is uninterrupted and uncontested.[4] This notion presupposes the existence of a prior sovereign whose control over the territory lapses, either through the failure to occupy that land effectively or on account of abandonment or wrongful claim. Assuming that the original title lapsed, the "squatter" claimant may acquire title to the territory. Prescription remains controversial as a means of acquiring title to territory, largely because international law does not set specific time limits for the possessor to perfect the effectiveness of a claimed occupation. The issue of whether one state can acquire title to territory despite an earlier recognized title by another state is much debated in international law, the gravity of which is well illustrated by the war in 1982 between Argentina and the United Kingdom over the disputed Falkland Islands/Islas Malvinas in the south Atlantic.[5] Also troubling is the fact that universal agreement does not exist on the legal propriety of this means of territorial acquisition.

Sovereign title to territory may be derived from other states. Historically, the most common way is through voluntary *cession*. This involves a legal process that consists of the formal transfer by treaty of territory from one state to another. The grantee's right to claim title to the ceded territory is derived from the treaty agreement. Such a treaty of cession usually contains stipulations respecting the rights and duties of allegiance or nationality, the proportionate share of public debt assumed by the annexing or ceding state, and any special conditions attached to the cession.[6] When territory is ceded by one state to another, the ceding state has the power to transfer the allegiance of the inhabitants, and the acquiring state is obligated to confer nationality on those persons, though it is not necessarily required to give them political rights as citizens. The practice of holding plebiscites to determine whether a transfer of territory accords with the will of the majority of inhabitants would seem desirable as a rule, as in the case of East Timor in 1999.[7]

Cession can take different forms. A popular means has been through a treaty of sale, which involves the sovereign owner deeding a piece of territory to another state. Much of the United States' territory was acquired in this manner, through such well-known acquisitions as the Louisiana Purchase (from France in 1803), the Florida Purchase (Spain, 1819), the Gadsden Purchase (Mexico, 1853), the Alaska Purchase (Russia, 1867), and the Virgin Islands (Denmark, 1916).

Another form of cession involves the exchange of territory by states, in effect a land swap. A pertinent example of this occurred along the Gulf of Acaba when Jordan and

Saudi Arabia traded small patches of land in 1971. A more modern form of cession has been by gift, as one government gives a tract of territory to another state.

Cession also occurs by coercive means. In the past, such involuntary cession was commonly accomplished through *conquest*, which involves the incorporation of foreign territory under the jurisdiction of a conquering or occupying state after the former is subjugated by armed force. Historical practice regarded conquest as lawful if the incorporation was followed by an official act of specific intention, such as a treaty or decree of annexation, and if the receiving power could demonstrate its ability to maintain permanent possession. The legal effects of conquest on the native people of a conquered territory followed the rules for succession of states, especially in that the annexing sovereign did not acquire any special rights over the lives and property of his new subjects.[8]

Events during the 20th century transformed attitudes toward the lawfulness of conquest. The establishment of the League of Nations signaled serious doubts about the legality of conquest. In the League's Covenant, article 10 carried the implied obligation of member states to deny legal recognition to territories seized from other members.[9] Less than a decade later, the Kellogg-Briand Pact of 1928, which outlawed aggressive war as an instrument of national policy, directly impugned the lawfulness of a state to use force to annex foreign territory.[10] Following Japan's conquest of Manchuria in 1931 and the subsequent establishment of the puppet state of Manchuko, U.S. Secretary of State Henry Stimson issued a pronouncement that strongly condemned Japan's actions and denied the legal validity of the acquisition of territory by use of force.[11] The League Assembly later endorsed this so-called *Stimson doctrine of nonrecognition* against Japan in 1932.[12] The international community's reaction to Italy's invasion of Ethiopia in 1935; Germany's subjugation of the Rhineland in 1938; and the Soviet Union's conquest of Latvia, Lithuania, and Estonia in 1940 underscored the pervasive attitude of impermissibility toward the acquisition of territory through the use of force.

The UN Charter invalidates any pretense that would regard conquest as a lawful means for acquiring title to territory. The relevant provisions of the Charter, especially article 2, paragraph 4, make it abundantly clear from the legal perspective that the threat or use of force against the territorial integrity or political independence of another state is prohibited, save in situations of national self-defense or where the Security Council decides to take a specific action.[13] Iraq's conquest of Kuwait in August 1990 and the adverse reaction by the international community in the Gulf War of early 1991 highlights the unacceptability of subjugation in modern practice. Similarly, Israel's seizure and military occupation of the West Bank and Golan Heights in June 1967 remains unrecognized by the international community as a lawful claim to title, even though Israel formally annexed the Golan in 1981. The bottom line in contemporary international law is clear: the so-called right of conquest is no longer permissible as a means of acquiring title to territory, since subjugation involves an unjust use of force and deprives a people of any opportunity to fulfill their self-determination.[14]

Loss of Territory

Just as title to territory can be gained by states, it can also be lost. There are several ways that a state may lose territory today: through physical loss, prescription, conquest, cession, and dereliction. Of these, two deserve special comment. First, while territory may be enlarged by accretion, it may also be diminished through physical means, such as earthquakes, volcanoes, and the shift of a riverbed. Such violent changes, known as *avulsion*, can cause the emergence of new land or alterations in the shape of existing land.[15] Such changes, because they are so sudden and extensive, are generally viewed as not altering the previous location of an international land boundary, although the disappearance of an island near the coast through volcanic action can require new baselines to be drawn for determining the extent of coastal jurisdiction offshore. Second, there is the notion of dereliction, which resembles the process of abandonment. The owner state completely leaves a territory with the intention of withdrawing from it forever, thus relinquishing sovereignty over it. Dereliction requires, first, that the territory actually be abandoned and, second, that the owner demonstrate genuine intention to relinquish its sovereign claim. In effect, dereliction is necessary before the process of prescription can lawfully occur. For example, in the 1968 Ram of Kutch arbitration ruling, it was held that Pakistan implicitly relinquished its title to a region on the common border with India. For over a century, Pakistan's predecessors did not object to assertions of sovereignty by the British and by India and thus did not openly challenge India's exercise of sovereignty in the disputed area.[16] If a dispute arises over the sovereign ownership of some territory, the critical question becomes, Which claimant state possesses the superior title to that land?[17] The proliferation of states since decolonization has not lessened the number or the intensity of territorial disputes between states. Several contentious claims over territory remain serious obstacles to friendly relations between states. Among those currently outstanding are sovereignty disputes concerning the Spratlys group in the South China Sea (involving China, Vietnam, the Philippines, Malaysia, Taiwan, and Brunei); the Kurile Islands (between Russia and Japan); the Falkland Islands/Islas Malvinas (between the United Kingdom and Argentina); the annexations of East Jerusalem and the Golan Heights by Israel (among Israel, the Palestinians, and Syria); the status of the Western Sahara (involving Morocco, Mauritania, and Spain); and the territory of Kashmir (between India and Pakistan). Numerous conflicts persist over boundary demarcation as well—for example, those concerning the border regions between India and China, Iran and Iraq, Ethiopia and Eritrea, Azerbaijan and Armenia over Nagorno-Karabagh, and Ukraine and Russia over the Crimea.

SELF-DETERMINATION

The legal principle of *self-determination,* which involves a people's right to choose how they will organize and govern their society, is fundamental but much misunderstood as the justification for establishment of a state.[18] Some peoples might prefer not to have independence and self-governance as an independent state. For example, Puerto Rico has remained part of the United States for more than a century, while still exercising a form of autonomy that is not full statehood. As a rule of international law, the right of self-determination was formally articulated as early as 1919 in Woodrow Wilson's "Fourteen Points" and in the 1948 Universal Declaration of Human Rights.[19] Self-determination embraces the right of a people organized in an established territory to determine for themselves their collective political destiny. The era of decolonization transformed self-determination into a dynamic concept in international relations. Self-determination was formalized as a legal precept in the 1960 UN Declaration on the Granting of Independence to Colonial Countries and in the two 1966 UN Covenants on Human Rights.[20] Moreover, the International Court of Justice endorsed the right in its 1975 Advisory Opinion on the Western Sahara.[21]

The legal precept of self-determination suggests that every people possesses a right to its own nation-state. Yet, while great rhetorical and sentimental appeal resides in this principle, it appears to contradict another equally respected principle of international law—an existing state's right to territorial integrity. Put tersely, one people's right to self-determination may well mean that another people's right to territorial integrity is threatened or violated.[22] That realization cannot be cast aside when considering the balance between justice and peace in today's international system.[23]

RECOGNITION

The existence of states provides the basis of the contemporary international legal order. But what should determine the lawful existence of a state or even a government? State practice has devised special rules and procedures for this purpose, albeit governments perform them unilaterally and discretionarily. This process of formally acknowledging the legal existence of a state or government in international relations is called *recognition.*

In a legal system as individualistic as international law, rights and responsibilities cannot be created for a subject of the law unless that subject has been publicly acknowledged. A state can exist independent of recognition, but some form of recognition is necessary to secure the admission of that polity into the international community. Governments of states have complete discretion in granting recognition as subjects of international law to other entities. They are limited primarily by their interest or willingness to establish direct contact with an independent territorial group that demonstrates signs of permanency. Recognition thus remains an executive act. Recognition attaches certain legal consequences to an existing set of facts, as applied to either a state or government that claims to be the lawful representative of a state. The recognition of a state defines its membership in the world community and supports its claim as a separate judicial personality—that is, as an international person. Also important is the fact that recognition carries with it entitlement to the rights and privileges held by states under international law. Recognition assumes that the recognized state is capable and willing to not only claim the benefits of international law but to also abide by its rules. The overarching purpose of recognition, then, is to allow the recognized state to participate in the mutual and reciprocal giving and taking that form the essential conditions of interstate relations.[24]

The act of recognition amounts to a state's becoming accepted into the international community, whether explicitly or implicitly. Recognition is explicit when the government of the recognizing state issues a formal statement. A new state may be recognized implicitly by an established state through the conclusion of a treaty; through the sending or receiving of diplomatic agents; by saluting its flag; or by establishing official relations, such as proffering the intention to treat the entity as an international person. The critical ingredient remains a clear indication of intent to recognize the state or new government; otherwise, the quality of the implicit recognition will be deemed as lacking.

Formal recognition can take various forms. It may be official and collective, as in the case of Austria in 1955 when it was admitted to full statehood (in exchange for its neutrality) through a treaty agreement between the United States and the Soviet Union that correlatively resulted in the admission of fifteen states into the United Nations.[25] It may also be conditional, as in the case of Belgium, Yugoslavia, and Czechoslovakia, which were created after the First World War. Belgium's recognition by the Allied powers was conditioned on its remaining neutral, while Yugoslavia and Czechoslovakia were admitted to statehood on the condition that they assimilate various minorities into newly created states after the war. Although the tacit and the express recognition binds only the recognizing state, the acknowledgment is often taken to be a certificate of admission into the international community.

There is no legal right of admission into the international community, nor is there a legal duty for governments to recognize other polities. Similarly, there is no legal right or duty to be recognized, although a new polity that fully satisfies the criteria for independent statehood has a strong moral claim to being able to engage in diplomatic intercourse with the international community. However, it remains for other governments to recognize that polity on the basis of their individual perceptions of that polity's capabilities.

Recognition was traditionally accorded to states and governments and could be done either in a de facto or a de jure manner. De facto recognition entails a provisional recognition of the government of a state. By extending de facto recognition, the recognizing government is indicating a desire to enter into relations with the target government on a temporary, or less than inclusive, diplomatic basis. The suggestion is that conditions must be met by, or circumstances must be clarified in, the newly recognized government before full recognition will be granted.[26] De jure recognition carries the full range of diplomatic rights and duties associated with complete recognition of a government. As such, de jure recognition conveys uncontested legality to the recipient government, meaning full and permanent recognition. The type of government may well be a serious issue at stake. For example, the British government in 1921 granted de facto recognition to the Soviet government and then extended de jure recognition in 1924. The United States, however, refused to recognize the Soviet government until 1933, at which time it was granted de jure recognition.[27]

Historically, when a new government in a state came into existence by violent or questionable means, other governments were confronted with the legal dilemma of deciding whether to recognize the new government. Recognition signifies a willingness to deal with that government as the lawful representative of the state. Often, a refusal to recognize a new government was done by some governments not on the basis of objective criteria but rather to demonstrate political or ideological disapproval of it. In this context, recognition of a foreign government was sometimes mistakenly interpreted as implying approval of that government, even when the recognizing state did not intend as much. To avoid such misinterpretations, the prevalent practice today has become to officially recognize (or not recognize) states, but not governments. Known as the *Estrada Doctrine*, this policy was first articulated in 1930 by Genaro Estrada, Mexico's secretary of foreign relations. The legal significance of this policy is clear: politics can be diminished in the process. Recognition of a polity can be affirmed more on the basis of objective tests for statehood: Does the government have authoritative control over the machinery of government? Does it have popular support? The Estrada Doctrine does not abolish recognition of governments; rather, implicit recognition substitutes for formal recognition.[28] Many governments today apply this policy in their recognition practice—for instance, Spain, France, the United States, and the United Kingdom.

Two theories of recognition prevail in modern international law. First, there is the *constitutive theory of recognition*, which suggests that recognition is a law-creative action. It is the act of recognition that endows a polity with the legal status of statehood and infuses a government with the legal capacity to engage in international diplomatic relations. In the constitutive theory, recognition becomes a formal legal act intended to attach the prescribed legal consequences of statehood on some new polity. It is not supposed to be political in nature or in consequence.[29] Second, there is the *declaratory theory of recognition*, which maintains that statehood or governmental authority exists separately from the act of recognition by some state. The existence of a state is based in fact; it is not dependent on formal acknowledgment by some other government. The declaratory theory asserts that recognition by a government merely acknowledges a factual situation: the existence of a state. The act of recognition does not create the legal existence of that state.[30]

While recognition remains a process essential for international relations, neither theory satisfactorily explains the legal condition of a polity before the moment of formal recognition. Of greater substantive concern is whether standards of recognition are more political than legal. If formal recognition of a state by some government depends on the former polity fulfilling requisite qualifications that define a state—that is, it must have territory with recognized borders, a population, a responsible government, and the qualities of being sovereign and independent—then there should not be any real question over the status of that polity. If an entity fully meets those qualifications, then government officials in other states should deem it acceptable for recognition as a state. Such is not always the case, as political considerations of governments sometimes preempt perceptible reality. During the Cold War, the United States refused to recognize the legitimacy of several communist states, including the Democratic Republic of Germany (until 1973), the People's Republic of China (until 1978), Vietnam (until 1995), and the Democratic Republic of Korea. Many states also refused to recognize the Hanoi-installed government of Kampuchea (Cambodia), which had seized power while Prince Sihanouk's UN-recognized government was in exile. Similarly, the United States refused to recognize the government in Haiti imposed by military coup in 1991 that overthrew the democratically elected government of a former Catholic priest, Henri Aristide.

The contemporary practice of governments identifies three key so-called objective interrogatory tests for determining whether a polity should be recognized as a state. First, does the new government exercise de facto control over its country's administrative machinery? Second, is there any resistance in the country to the new government's authority? Third, does the government have the support of a substantial amount of public opinion in the country? The fundamental consideration for recognizing statehood remains whether a polity qualifies as a state by being a bounded territory that is inhabited by people and administered by a government that can operate independently in international relations. If so, it merits recognition.

Once recognized, a state assumes its central role as actor and as subject of international law largely out of practical necessity. International norms cannot be upheld unless governments either enforce such norms within their own territory, through their own laws, and on their own nationals, or impose them forcibly on other states by acting alone or in concert with other governments. This is the case because national governments have obtained a monopoly of legal, political, and judicial power within their territories that permits them to enforce international norms at the domestic level and to undertake foreign policies to attain various national and international objectives.

RIGHTS AND DUTIES OF STATES

The state exists socially and survives changes in its decision-makers, as well as transitions in governments themselves. The state, as an international social actor, is made subject to certain international rights and obligations, not unlike the individual person in a society who has rights and obligations stemming from his/her particular roles in the social system. The customary practice of states, bolstered by special international conventions, has codified these rights and duties into acknowledged legal obligations today, and governments are expected to abide by them.[31]

There exist certain essential rights of states that undergird the positive legal rules and customs of international relations. These rights (to which are attached corresponding duties) were formerly identified with natural rights and formed what was described earlier as the so-called law of nature. Today, they assume a broader and deeper significance than the ordinary positive rules of international law. While neither absolute nor unchallengeable, these rights are controlling, fundamental principles grounded in conditions essential to state coexistence and modern international relations. To a considerable extent, they furnish the ultimate basis or source of contemporary international legal rules.

Rights of States

Fundamental among the rights of states are independence, equality, sovereign territorial jurisdiction, and self-protection (often expressed as self-defense). Paramount among these state rights is the right of existence, which involves self-preservation and self-defense. The right of self-preservation takes priority over all other rights and duties, and it far exceeds the ordinary notion of a right. It is the principle that underlies all positive rules and customs and evokes the basic instinct of all living organisms. If a state does not exist, there is no reason for it to expect entitlement to other rights and duties. The legal ability of a state to preserve itself is essential to its maintaining existence.

A state clearly has the right to take actions deemed necessary for its own security and defense. It has no right, however, to mobilize its forces on border regions or to make gestures that might be threatening to the safety and existence of another state. A state may take measures to prevent acts of propaganda or espionage from being launched from its soil against another state, and the duty obtains for a government to refrain from such propaganda or espionage in its own foreign affairs. Similarly, a state is obligated not to permit organized conspiracies or military actions from being directed against a friendly state from its territory. A state is also obliged to observe strict and impartial neutrality toward other states that are engaged in belligerent conflict.

The right of self-preservation includes the right of a state to protect the corporate integrity and inviolability of its territory with the corresponding duty of respecting that of other states. To protect and preserve corporate integrity in extreme cases of necessity, the violation of territorial sovereignty of another state might be justifiable under the concept of anticipatory self-defense.

A second fundamental right of states is that of sovereign decision making. By virtue of being a state, a polity is entitled to assert a certain measure of freedom in its international affairs. States have the right to make choices and decisions in their foreign policies, which presumably are designed to reflect their perceived interests in various issues. Voluntary consent is key to national sovereignty. This right produces the corresponding duties of respecting the independence (external sovereignty) and autonomy (internal sovereignty) of other states, which flow from the freedom necessary for a state to conduct its foreign relations. Independence is neither absolute nor unlimited. It remains a question of degree, linked to the amount of freedom needed by a state to conduct its own foreign affairs. Several rights of states flow from sovereignty and independence. States have the right to establish and change their own form of government, to adopt their own constitution and laws, and to select their own rulers. With the right of independence also comes the aforementioned right of self-determination. Peoples have the right to determine for themselves their own political institutions and their own destiny. But in the early 21st century, this right is becoming considerably more complicated, as ethnic groups, tribal units, and national minorities are increasingly clamoring for their own states.[32] A state has the right to negotiate and conclude treaties and to maintain diplomatic intercourse with other members of the international community. States can make and change their own internal laws, rules, and regulations, including those affecting immigration. States have the right to exercise exclusive jurisdiction over all persons on property within their territory and may exercise limited jurisdiction over their nationals traveling abroad. A state has jurisdiction over all of its vessels on the high seas and in the high skies.

One of the oldest rights that sovereign states enjoy is that of equality before the law. All fully independent or sovereign states—however weak or powerful, small or large—are entitled to equal protection in the appreciation of these rights under national law. This principle of equality, which is almost universally acknowledged, stems from the fundamental rights derived from sovereign independence. That is, states are recognized as equal members of the international community only when they are independent, meaning free of external political control and able to decide state action in international affairs. The right of equality under international law is recognized regardless of a state's size, population, political importance, governmental organization, or ideological predisposition.

But what is the meaning of equality under international law? Sovereign equality does not mean that all states are equal in power, wealth, or capability. Rather, equality suggests that all states have equivalent standing in terms of their rights, duties, and treatment in interstate dealings. Each state possesses similar equal status as a subject of international legal rules. States are juridically equal. They enjoy the same rights and possess equal legal capacity in the exercise of those rights.[33] Once recognized as a state having collective legal rights and duties toward other states, other community members who grant such recognition will view those rights and duties reciprocally. Equality connotes that no one state may claim jurisdiction over another state. This means that a state cannot normally be sued in the courts of another state or taxed by the latter without its consent. The state accepts as valid the official acts of other states when those acts take place in each respective state's territory. It seems obvious that no consensual legal system could exist without due regard for the principle of equality embedded in its reciprocal relationships.

A fourth fundamental right of states is the right of respect. By virtue of formal recognition as a state, an entity is entitled to international respect. Fundamental to the right of respect is the subsidiary right of sovereign immunity.[34] That is, the independence from external control represents a central right of the modern state. The state possesses exclusive territorial jurisdiction over its own acts. States enjoy immunity from suits in the courts of another state. Under traditional international law, the doctrine of *absolute sovereign immunity* prevailed: a foreign sovereign could not, without consent, be made a defendant in the courts of another state. The modernized theory of state immunity is more restrictive, as it applies to sovereign or public acts of a state and not necessarily to so-called private acts that a state might sponsor or condone. The principle of *sovereign immunity* embraces the individual head of state (*personal immunity*) and the government of a foreign sovereign (*state immunity*).

Under the rules of modern international law, sovereigns and heads of state traveling or residing abroad enjoy inviolability and absolute immunity from local criminal and police jurisdiction. Foreign sovereigns also enjoy certain fiscal immunities, such as freedom from direct personal taxes and customs duties. These immunities extend to the family residence and visiting quarters when sovereigns are abroad. Sovereigns who have left office do not have a right to such immunities, although they may enjoy them as a matter of courtesy.

The question of state immunity is more important and more complicated. That a state cannot be held liable without its own consent has long been a fundamental principle of international law. Under the traditional theory of absolute immunity, a state was exempted under all circumstances from the jurisdiction of other states. Its government could not be sued abroad without its consent; its public property could not be seized or attached; its public vessels could not be boarded, arrested, or sued; nor could any land or property owned by a foreign state be taxed in any other country.[35]

International legal rules require each state to respect the validity of the public acts of other states, in that the courts of one state will not pass judgment on the lawfulness or the constitutionality of the acts of a foreign sovereign done under its own law. In the United States this is the so-called *act of state doctrine*.[36] In *Banco Nacional de Cuba v. Sabbatino*, the U.S. Supreme Court held that the act of state doctrine is not a formal, inflexible rule of international law. Rather, it held that U.S. courts would not examine the validity of an act of expropriation within another state's territory by a foreign sovereign government in the absence of a treaty or some controlling legal principle.[37] In reaction, Congress in 1964 passed the Hickenlooper Amendment to the Foreign Assistance Act of 1961, which provided that no courts in the United States could decide on grounds of the federal act of state doctrine to determine the merits of implementing principles of international law in a case in which a claim of property was asserted, based on confiscation after January 1, 1959, by an act in violation of the principles of international law.[38] While the Department of State strongly objected to the Hickenlooper Amendment, that act of Congress has had little impact since then on the determination of a foreign government's immunity from suit in U.S. courts.

In recent years new problems have arisen over state immunity. The proliferation of government-owned enterprises in international commerce necessitated greater clarification of the status of foreign corporations and their formal protections under international law. Key issues turned on the nature and purpose of the sovereign activity and on the distinction between public and private acts of governments. Regarding the seizure of government property, it is a rule of international law that a foreign sovereign cannot be deprived of its property by the courts of another state.[39] The general rule holds that the real property of a foreign government located in another state enjoys immunity from suit and seizure.[40]

In recent decades, the view favoring more restricted sovereign immunity for foreign governments has gained credibility and greater international acceptance. For the United States, this trend was initiated in 1952 when the acting legal adviser to the Department of State, Jack B. Tate, wrote a letter to the acting attorney general in which he argued for a restrictive theory of immunity by the U.S. government.[41] The rationale was that since several states had adopted the restrictive theory, U.S. courts should deny immunity to the private activities of foreign sovereigns.

The modern sovereign immunity policy of the United States is set by the Foreign Sovereign Immunities Act (FSIA) of 1976,[42] which accomplishes several objectives. For one, it vests decisions on sovereign immunity questions exclusively in courts, thus eliminating political institutions such as the Department of State from the decision. The FSIA codifies the *restrictive theory of sovereign immunity*, as it limits the immunity to public acts and excludes commercial or private acts. The FSIA also gives U.S. citizens a remedy to satisfy legal judgments against a foreign state, whereas before they had no avenue of redress.[43] More emphatically, in 1996 Congress added an exception to the FSIA that permitted U.S. citizens to bring federal suit against seven designated terrorist states—Cuba, Iraq, Iran, Libya, North Korea, Sudan, and Syria—seeking damages resulting from torture, extrajudicial killing, aircraft sabotage, or hostage taking in a foreign land perpetrated by an national agent performing these crimes as official duties.[44]

A fifth right of states is the right to *commercial intercourse*. States have the right to engage in mutual trade relations. This right has evolved from the increasing interdependence and globalization of the world marketplace. In the 21st century, the right to conduct commerce has become less of a legal right and more of a necessary condition for modern state progress and development. Yet, an intentional breach of economic relations by one state stands as a clear affront to the affected state, and the imposition of economic sanctions may be deemed an unfriendly and perhaps hostile act. Commercial discrimination and undue restrictions on free trade violate the rules of contemporary international law and contravene the fundamental basis for commercial transactions under the General Agreement on Tariffs and Trade and the World Trade Organization arrangement. The right to engage in commercial relations cannot help but become more salient and fundamental to the economic security and survival of states in coming decades.

One caveat: International organizations entail composite actors in diplomatic and legal intercourse. Unlike states, international organizations are not original persons subject to international legal rules. They are derivative subjects of the law, created by states for states.[45] Yet, as distinct subjects of international law, international organizations have legal rights as well. The treaty that creates each international organization binds its legal personality. The instrument of its incorporation defines and shapes the international organization's constitution and delegates the authority of these international agencies over their member polities.

In this regard, it is important to consider the relationship of the UN Charter to the municipal legislation of member states. Can the UN Charter, as a multilateral convention, supersede conflicting domestic legislation of member states? The answer is no. An international treaty, even as part of the supreme law of the land, does not automatically supersede municipal laws that might be inconsistent with it, unless the treaty is self-executing.[46] States comprise international organizations, and the governments of the former determine the extent to which legal commitments of the latter will bind them in a given circumstance.

Duties of States

For states to coexist in an international community, the rules for international relations have coalesced into certain duties to which states are obliged to abide. Among those important are the following: to refrain from intervening into the affairs of other states, to settle international disputes peacefully, to refrain from the threat or use of force, and to carry out treaty obligations in good faith.

The paramount duty of states in the 21st century remains the legal obligation to abstain from *intervention* into the affairs of other states, especially when it involves the use of military force. States are obligated to respect the territorial integrity and political independence of all other states. In so doing, states are obliged not to intervene in the internal or external affairs of other states, especially by forcible means. The issue of armed intervention has become a preeminent consideration in modern international relations, not only during the Cold War era, but even more so in the years following. In this context, intervention may be defined as the dictatorial interference by one state into the affairs of another state. The rule of nonintervention poses great difficulty and complexity for international law, given that a profound conflict exists between the political theory and fundamental legal principle of nonintervention and actual state practice. As a rule of customary law codified and reaffirmed in several legal instruments, states are prohibited from militarily intervening into the affairs of other states.[47] But as a fact of international relations, governments all too frequently use armed force against their neighbors.

The post-Westphalian system of international law rests on the doctrine of legal equality and independence of sovereign states. This doctrine presupposes the freedom of action by a sovereign with its own sphere of jurisdiction and the noninterference in internal or external affairs of any other sovereign. Nonintervention arises as a necessary corollary of the equality and independence of sovereign states, and it must be regarded as a fundamental principle of international law. Not surprisingly, the tendency among publicists is to accept the principle of nonintervention as the proper and normal rule of international relations. But the rules of international law are supposed to rest on state practice as well as on fundamental principles, on the actual conduct of governments as well as on theoretical precepts. When examining the actual practice of states, one can find numerous examples of armed intervention based on all sorts of grounds and pretexts. A legitimate question might therefore arise about the viability of this rule of nonintervention in actual conduct of states: If the prohibition against intervention is violated so frequently, does it retain legal merit as an operative norm under contemporary international law?

Armed interventions occur for several reasons and can be based on numerous grounds, such as those for self-preservation, for national policy or state interest, or to end human rights atrocities. Opinion remains divided on what constitutes legal or justifiable grounds for intervention or, indeed, for whether any such right to intervene even exists. Perhaps the strongest agreement centers on the admissibility of intervention for the sake of self-preservation, which is less a legal rule than a fundamental right that underlies positive law and custom. To justify intervention on this ground, the danger to a state must be direct and immediate, not merely contingent or remote. The great difficulty here is that preservation may be used as a pretext for intervention.

There are notable exceptions to the rule of nonintervention. Such grounds for permissible intervention are referred to as *intervention by right* and are intended to provide lawful opportunities to right particular wrongs. The right to intervene may be granted by treaty to protect the lives and property of nationals of the intervening state. Such an intervention should be diplomatic in nature, and forcible means should never be employed save as a last resort.

International practice admits other exceptions to the rule of nonintervention on moral or humanitarian grounds. Forcible interference may be justified in extreme cases—for example, when great evils are being perpetrated, when gross crimes against humanity are being committed, or when the danger of racial extermination is actually possible. Yet intervention, like war, amounts to the exercise of high sovereign political power. The government that intervenes carries out a political act, sometimes for self-interested political purposes often guised in international legal rules. To prevent such cases from being used as mere pretexts, intervention on humanitarian grounds should be collective in character, where several states participate or where one state acts as the agent of a number of other states.

States also have the duty to abstain from so-called *subversive intervention*—that is, to refrain from engaging in propaganda, information warfare, or legislative action designed or intended to foster rebellion, sedition, or treason against the government of another state. Subversive intervention may also involve the use of communications and cyber-attack techniques by one state aimed to disrupt or undermine the existing political authority structure of another state. Though a clear violation of international law, practices of subversive intervention often occur. The increasing interdependence of world society has closely integrated the political, economic, social, and cultural interests of states. The pervasive reach of computer technology through the Internet has made national borders nonexistent. Hence, the problem of coping with subversive intervention is made complicated by the desire to respect a given state's freedom of expression and by the technological difficulty of preventing the transboundary flow of propaganda and, more ominously, computer-generated viruses that might disrupt banks, public utilities, government facilities, as well as national security installations.

A number of other legal duties retain relevance for states in the 21st century. For example, there is the duty of states to prevent the counterfeiting within its territorial jurisdiction of coins, currencies, postage stamps, and securities of some other state.[48] Another duty is the need of governments to refrain from fomenting civil strife in the territory of another state. A state should not permit its soil to be used as the staging ground for insurrections or guerilla raids aimed at overthrowing a neighboring government. In addition, another obligation is to settle international disputes peacefully.[49] Several techniques have been devised to lessen tensions and resolve disputes in interstate relations; among them are negotiation, conciliation, mediation, good offices, arbitration, and adjudication. States share a critical duty to fulfill in good faith those obligations arising from treaties and other sources of international law. This embodies one of the oldest principles of international law, *pacta sunt servanda*, which means that treaties must be observed in good faith. As world interdependence and economic globalization have accelerated in recent decades, this duty of adhering to contractual obligations has evolved into an essential condition of the contemporary international legal order.

Finally, states incur the modern duty to ensure that no activities within their jurisdiction cause harm or injury to the territory of a neighboring state or to common space areas beyond the limits of national jurisdiction.[50] Since the Stockholm Conference on the Environment in 1972, more than five hundred international agreements have been negotiated, adopted, and implemented to create and substantiate the particular obligations of states regarding the need to halt transnational pollution and international dumping, as well as to conserve and protect natural living resources, the atmosphere, the oceans, and the polar regions from manmade activities (see chapter 10). This duty to preserve and protect the global environment has been starkly realized over the past three decades in the emergence of an array of rules, principles, and agreements that now form the branch of international environmental law (see chapter 9).[51]

STATE RESPONSIBILITY

State responsibility means that a state is held internationally accountable for the failure to observe its international obligations as well as for any violations of the rights of other members of the international community. Such a failure or violation is termed an international delict, or delinquency. Realist theorists suggest that the quality of sovereignty authorizes the state to be the sole judge of its international responsibilities, especially given that there exists no international judiciary or police force. Yet, that assertion cannot extricate a state from being legally accountable for its actions. A state is directly responsible for its own actions and for the acts of its officials or agents when carried out under its authority. State acts that violate international legal rules or cause injury to another state constitute international delinquencies, whether committed willfully or as a consequence of culpable negligence. Such acts should be condemned; the government responsible should tender an apology; the agents should be punished; and in cases of material damage, appropriate indemnity or reparations should be made. A state is also directly responsible for maintaining the orderly and law-abiding conduct of persons residing in its jurisdiction, who are subject to its laws. States are legally bound to use reasonable due diligence to prevent injurious acts against other states—whether by nationals or by foreigners operating from its territory. Likewise, states are responsible for ensuring that aliens within their own jurisdiction are given legal protection and means of redress as well as a measure of justice similar to that given to its own citizens. In other words, aliens are entitled to seek redress through municipal tribunals in a state for grievances caused by that government or nationals of that state.

The state remains the sole judge of civil privileges enjoyed by aliens. A state bears no obligation to extend to aliens the enjoyment of civil and private acts or to guarantee them equal treatment in securing economic or social opportunities. Educational, economic, and cultural rights and privileges granted to aliens stem from international agreements, by the principle of reciprocity, or via simple courtesy. The principal demand of aliens under the rules of international law turns on the protection of life and property, coupled with the lawful access to administrative authority and local courts for ensuring these activities. The assumption generally made implies that an alien is a citizen or national of another state whose government is interested in protecting that alien's personal and property rights. The implication here suggests that a state has the duty to protect its nationals abroad, although the extension of any diplomatic protection or prosecution of claims remains primarily a matter of discretion within each government. What becomes clear is that modern international law asserts that a state can be held responsible for acts by its public officials or agents who injure aliens. This reflects the principle of imputability—that is, legal attribution of some act by a natural person attaches to a state, whereby the act is considered done by the state. Hence, through imputability, a state becomes responsible for an act committed by its government officials.

The setting up of mixed commissions for the adjudication of claims by a state for injuries to their nationals in other states embodies a principal example of this kind of process. These mechanisms afford a salient example of the effectiveness of international law as the protector of the weak and as the balancer for conflicting interests. Today, a number of these commissions are in operation—among them, the Iran Claims Commission and the Kuwaiti Claims Commission (from the 1991 Gulf War).

EXTINCTION

States do not live in perpetuity. They die. In international law, the end of a state is known as *extinction*. A state ceases to exist when it loses the essential characteristics of being a state. States are extinguished through voluntary incorporation, forcible annexation, division into several states, or through union with other states.

The recognition of a state's extinction through merger, division, or cession acknowledges an accomplished fact. Extinction occurs after resistance to the situation has ceased or after the government of the extinct polity ceases to function. A reasonable time should be permitted to lapse for the recognizing state to judge the evidence and stability of the new condition of affairs or to determine the capacity of the new state or states to carry out their international obligations. Such recognition is generally tacit.

States that become wholly extinct lose all international personality, and their rights and obligations devolve to the annexing or incorporating state. Whether any agreements or promises made by the incorporating government to the annexed state are observed remains more a matter of conscience and moral duty than a formal legal obligation.

Succession

Once a state passes away, questions arise over the disposition of its legal obligations and material assets. The process of transferring sovereignty over a territory from one subject of international law to another is called *succession*.[52] When one state takes the place of another and assumes prominent exercise of all its sovereign territorial rights, power, and duties, universal succession is said to occur. This succession becomes universal in the case of total absorption, whether through voluntary agreement, division of a state into several international persons, or the union of several states into a single international person. The forcible annexation, subjugation, or division of a state into several parts of existing states is no longer considered permissible under contemporary international law.

Some cases of succession may be only piecemeal. Partial succession can occur under several circumstances, such as when a state acquires a portion of territory of another state through cession or conquest; when a new state is formed as a consequence of a successful revolt or a declaration of independence; when a fully sovereign state loses a portion of its external sovereignty or independence by being incorporated into a confederacy or federal union; or when a member of a federal union becomes a separate, fully sovereign state.

Legal consequences flow from the process of succession. In the case of a state's total extinction, absorption, and incorporation by another state, the critical legal question is the extent to which the absorbing state succeeds to rights and obligations of the extinguished state. If third-party states have claims against the latter, the settlement of those claims falls to the successor government. Citizens of the defunct polity retain no appeal under international law against actions taken by the absorbing state, since their former country lost its international personality and is no longer a subject of international law. Any claim by or against those citizens involving their former government becomes a domestic question for the absorbing state. The new sovereign determines the extent to which it will be bound by the extinct state's obligations toward its newly acquired citizens. Finally, extinction of the legal personality of a state abrogates all political and military treaties between that extinct polity and other states party to those agreements.

Even though no rules of international law bind them to do so, governments of successor states are generally willing to assume contractual obligations of extinct states with respect to third states or citizens of other states. No common state practice legally binds states, however, regarding debts contracted by the predecessor state. The debts owed by citizens of the latter state become domestic matters to be handled by the absorbing state.

Regarding the legal effects of partial succession, public- and private-property rights are usually settled through an instrument that transfers title and territory to the new owner. Under partial succession, the public property of a predecessor state that is located in a successor state normally passes to the latter. When Czechoslovakia partitioned itself into the Czech Republic and the Republic of Slovakia, all immovable state property was allocated to each republic respectively—in other words, ownership depended on where a property was located. Movable property was apportioned on a two-to-one ratio. Similarly, state property that was held abroad—such as embassies, consulates, and cultural centers—was either divided between the two republics or sold, with proceeds split between the two republics.

While it seems reasonable that a successor state should assume responsibility for financial obligations—particularly public debts—of an extinguished state that it has subsumed, this is not an explicit rule of contemporary international law. The debts of a transferred area may or may not be assumed by the new sovereign. For example, in the 1919 Versailles Peace Treaty, which ended World War I, Germany was compelled to cede certain portions of territory to France—namely, Alsace Lorraine and the Saar Basin. The successor states assumed portions of the German debt, proportionate to each area transferred.[53] When the successor entity is a newly independent state (or an ex-colony or ex-protectorate), no state debt of the predecessor state normally passes to the new polity unless the agreement of transfer provides for otherwise. When two or more states unite to form a new successor state, the state debt of the predecessor states passes on to the new polity. The situation in 1990 involving reunification of the two Germanys is a case in point. When a state dissolves, becomes extinct, or parts of the predecessor state form two or more successor states, the state debt of the dissolved entity normally passes in equitable proportions to the successor states.[54] In the case of the former Soviet Union, the Russian Federation became solely responsible on November 23, 1990, for the enormous domestic and foreign indebtedness of the Soviet Union after the former Soviet republics jointly refused to assume any portions of that debt.

Acts of state succession can affect the status of treaty relationships. If a party to an international agreement alters its form of government or expands or contracts its geographical boundaries, the provisions of that treaty are usually not affected. Prior agreements remain in full force, so long as the territorial changes are not so profound as to impair the ability to the government of that state to function responsibly. In the case of universal succession, political treaties such as alliances become abrogated immediately, as do treaties of commerce, navigation, and extradition. Since the original contracting state disappears, so do the legal obligations owed it by other states.

If two or more states unite to form a single successor state, treaties in force for the merged polities usually continue in force for the successor state. This situation may be reversed if the new government and other treaty parties agree or if the application of a treaty to the merged successor state appears incompatible with the object or purpose of that instrument.

As in the case for partial succession, the universal successor acquires complete rights of sovereignty over territory absorbed by the government of the successor state. It may therefore make any changes in the law or political institutions of the extinguished state that it deems necessary or desirable. Contracts, franchises, and concessions to private companies and individuals are normally maintained. Under contemporary international law, rules and principles governing partial succession may be substantially modified by considerations of public policy and interest of the ceding and the absorbing states. In the case of partial succession, there is a continuity of state life and personality by the state that has lost the portion of its territory. In any event, private property rights, especially over land, usually remain officially unaffected by changes in territorial sovereignty. The rules of modern international law do not support the general confiscation or redistribution of private personal property when succession occurs. While people change their political allegiance and while their legal relations with a former sovereign are dissolved, their relations with one another in the area remain undisturbed.[55]

CONCLUSION

Over the past four centuries, legal rules have been secularized, nationalized, and politicized to define and accommodate the role of the state as the key actor in international relations. Under modern international law, the state is regarded as a defined territory inhabited by an association of people who are constituted as a political society subject to the authority of a sovereign government. That government has the power, capability, and means to maintain the political organization of the association, to protect the rights of its people, to conduct relations with other states, and to assume legal responsibility for its actions. The state has become central to international law simply because the state became central to the international political system.

Governments of states make international rules; they break international rules; and they are expected to enforce international rules. In any event, these international rules set the legal parameters within which states coexist and conduct their foreign relations. In this respect, governments have agreed to legal rules that authoritatively set out how territory may be acquired by states; to the criteria under which new polities should be acknowledged as acceptable states; and to the conditions and legal implications of states passing away from the scene. Similarly, legal rules have evolved in the form of rights and duties to direct the conduct of governments toward greater order and less conflict in interstate relations. States have legal rights to exist; to be respected as sovereign, independent polities; and to use self-defense if necessary to protect their territorial integrity. No less important, states remain obligated to perform certain corresponding duties, preeminent among which is to refrain from armed intervention in the affairs of other states. States are also expected to settle their disputes peacefully, to abide by international agreements made in good faith, and to abstain from polluting the air and water beyond their national jurisdiction.

In the end, governments are responsible for their state acts. It is true that sovereignty was long used as a shield to protect governments from external criticism and international sanctions. But in the 21st century, national sovereignty is increasingly perceived for what it is rather than for what it was. The condition of sovereignty exists as a right enjoyed by states; it cannot be a license for their governments to violate international legal rules with impunity. Sovereignty survives as a principle of international law, but it does not convey absolute legal authority to governments to conduct their foreign or domestic affairs in any manner they see fit. On the contrary, international rules were expressly formulated to permit only certain conduct by governments. This trend toward more restrictions on national sovereignty is becoming more evident, particularly as the individual person has emerged over the last half-century as a legitimate subject under international law. Importantly, as demonstrated in recent years, states are formally according the individual numerous special rights and protections that their governments are supposed to safeguard, not abuse. Though the state remains the preeminent international personality, it can no longer be regarded as being sovereign above all international legal rules. The legal status of the sovereign state is being perceptibly altered by the rise of new legal rights for nonstate actors, especially the individual person. It is to these legal considerations that we now turn.

4

The Individual

- ❧ Nationality
- ❧ Jurisdiction over Aliens
- ❧ Individual Human Rights
- ❧ The Role of the Nongovernmental Organization
- ❧ Conclusion

On December 13, 2003, U.S. forces in Iraq captured former Iraqi leader Saddam Hussein. On January 9, the United States officially announced that Saddam was a prisoner of war (POW) under the 1949 Geneva Conventions. That decision raises a number of key questions concerning the status of Saddam under international humanitarian law. For one, is Saddam Hussein entitled to POW status? The answer here is yes. The Geneva Conventions apply to international armed conflicts and a resultant occupation, both of which apply to the case of Iraq during 2003–2004. Under article 4 of the Third Geneva Convention, Saddam may be given POW status because of his military status and his role as a combatant in the conflict. Second, how will the POW status affect his treatment while in American custody? Most international legal commentators believe that the POW status will not greatly affect the way in which Saddam Hussein is treated. The Third Geneva Convention provides detailed rules for the humane treatment of POWs, including protections against compelling a prisoner to give more than his name, rank, serial number, and date of birth. As nationals of the detaining state, U.S. military interrogators may not use force or torture on a captured belligerent to compel him or her to give information. Moreover, the International Committee of the Red Cross is specially empowered under the Geneva Conventions to have unobstructed, multiple access to Saddam (and any other POWs) while in detention. Third, can Saddam be tried for past war crimes and other past offenses? The answer here is yes. The Geneva Conventions do not preclude Saddam Hussein from being tried for past war crimes, genocide, crimes against humanity, and any other violations of the law. The Third Geneva Convention in article 129 provides that all persons implicated in war crimes must be prosecuted for those acts. In Saddam's case, this would include war crimes committed in the war between Iran and Iraq during 1980–1988 and the 1991 Gulf War. He could also be prosecuted for crimes against humanity and for genocide, such as gassing the Iraqi Kurds in 1988, the massive killings of Shiites who rebelled in the south in 1991, and the brutal repression of the Marsh Arabs. If the United States directly prosecutes Saddam for war crimes, he must be tried—per the Third Geneva Convention—before a court martial or a federal court. He could not be lawfully tried before a commission similar to those being convened to try "unprivileged combatant" detainees in Guantanamo Bay. The United States could turn Saddam over for trial to another competent government—such as Iraq—so long as it was a party to the Geneva Conventions. Finally, will a special tribunal created by the Iraqi Governing Council under authority of the Coalition Provisional Authority lawfully be able to try Saddam under international law? The reaction is mixed. Many human rights experts are concerned that the statute of the special Iraqi tribunal lacks guarantees to ensure that competent judges and prosecutors experienced in human rights cases will be available. The statute also does not ensure that guilt must be proven beyond a reasonable doubt, a fundamental right under article 14 of the International Covenant of Civil and Political Rights, nor does it prevent the death penalty. Finally, the statute affirms that Iraqi criminal law and procedure will furnish the legal foundation for individual criminal responsibility and liability for punishment not otherwise specified within the statute. This is troubling because contemporary Iraqi law permits coerced confessions and the exclusion of counsel during interrogation under certain circumstances.

The status of the individual, be that person a head of state or a common peasant, has risen appreciably in modern international law. While the Statute of the International Court of Justice recognizes only states as parties to international legal agreements, the UN Charter and other international instruments clearly indicate that individuals are now accorded a prominent position as subjects, rather than as objects, of international legal rules. In this regard, a state's rights of independence and territorial supremacy provide for rights over internal affairs and external freedoms from outside interference. Governments retain supreme authority over all persons and private property within their territory. The state decides who its citizens are, who may enter its territory, and the conditions under which its aliens may reside or work. Yet, the rights of territorial supremacy and political independence are not absolute, as they have become subject to limitations imposed by international law on how governments treat their nationals. This is reflected in the contemporary legal rules regarding the nationality of individuals, the treatment of aliens, extradition law, and rules for asylum. Most emphatically, restrictions on state actions are now realized in the infusion of human rights protections and rules for international criminal jurisdiction that have rapidly evolved during the past three decades. All these concerns, however, are enmeshed in questions of state jurisdiction and how that authority squares with basic principles of state sovereignty, the equality of states, and noninterference in domestic affairs.

The place of the individual person under modern international law is secured through the jurisdiction of a state. *Jurisdiction* refers to the state's scope of legal authority and translates into the legal capacity of a government to prescribe, enforce, and adjudicate rules of law for individuals within its state's boundaries. Jurisdiction remains a vital core feature of state sovereignty. It refers to the limits within which authority is exercised and how the exercise of that authority can change or end legal relationships and implement obligations for persons within states, whether among themselves or with their national institutions. A state's legislature has authority to enact laws governing the conduct of persons within its borders. The executive branch retains the authority to enforce laws against persons who violate a state's legal rules. The courts of a state possess the authority to adjudicate civil and criminal cases against persons under the laws of that state. Persons who breach international legal rules to which their governments have obligated themselves can be held accountable under domestic law for those violations.

NATIONALITY

The relationship between the individual person and international legal rules is traditionally forged through the link of *nationality*.[1] Nationality in its political guise refers to the status of a person bound by the tie of allegiance to a state and who is therefore entitled to the protection of that state.[2] Though nationality remains of great significance internationally, each state may prescribe for itself the laws and conditions under which a person may acquire or lose the nationality of that state.[3] Similarly, the municipal laws of each state determine the nationality of juridical persons (e.g., business corporations), though the place of incorporation and control of interests usually remain the standard determinants.

Acquisition of Nationality

Nationality is acquired mainly through birth, although a person may also acquire the nationality of another state through naturalization or through other means in accordance with the latter's nationality laws. The principal rules for determining nationality by birth apply through *jus soli* (the law of soil or place) and *jus sanguinis* (the law of blood). Customary international law holds that an individual born on the soil of a particular state to parents who are nationals of that state is a national of the state in question. Under *jus soli*, as practiced by the United States and most Latin American states, the legal rule goes further. Mere birth on the soil of a state is sufficient to create the bond of nationality, regardless of the nationality of the parents.[4] For example, if a child were to be born to a French couple visiting the United States on holiday, that child would be a U.S. national under U.S. law. General agreement based on comity exists that the rule of *jus soli* does not apply to children born of foreign heads of states or of foreign diplomats visiting or posted abroad.

The civil-law principle of *jus sanguinis*, practiced by most European states and countries decolonized from European control, declares that a child's nationality follows that of its parents, regardless of the place of birth. Given the divergent practices of *jus sanguinis* and *jus soli*, a person may be born of double nationality, commonly called dual citizenship. For example, a child born of French parents within United States territory will be a national of France under the rule of *jus sanguinis* and of the United States under the principle of *jus soli*. A person may even obtain quadruple nationality if, for instance, he or she is born of a Chinese father and a Turkish mother on board a British ship anchored in a U.S. port. Obviously such cases of multiple nationalities can present considerable difficulty for the persons and governments concerned, particularly regarding military service, voting privileges, and diplomatic protection.

Naturalization functions as a voluntary means by which an alien may become a national of some state through a certain legal process in accordance with its municipal laws. A naturalized citizen is generally entitled to the same rights and privileges as a native-born national of that state. Special consideration usually accrues from a government to an alien applying for naturalization if the person has been in active service to that state. Conversely, in considering candidates for naturalization, some governments discriminate against persons from Asian or African ancestry, and they may impose other reasons for rejection—for example, educational deficiencies, criminal records, health impairments, physical or mental defects, antithetical political opinions, or membership in undesirable political groups. Naturalization may more broadly include such means of acquiring nationality as marriage, adoption, security of domicile, or active service in a foreign government. The change of nationality of the population in a certain territory as the result of cession or annexation is actually a form of collective, or mass, naturalization.[5]

Statelessness

A person can acquire *statelessness* through deprivation of his nationality by the state of his birth, the revocation of this naturalization status, or other causes. Sometimes a child might be stateless at the time of birth, such as when born to parents who are themselves stateless or if a foundling and thus born to parents whose nationalities are unknown.

Statelessness produces unfortunate consequences, and certain international legal measures, albeit limited, have been taken to mitigate that condition. The Universal Declaration of Human Rights of 1948 emphatically asserts in its article 15 the right of nationality for every person against arbitrary deprivation, and a number of international instruments have been adopted to specifically ensure the rights and protections afforded by nationality.[6] Certain measures to remedy statelessness are included in the Convention Relating to the International Status of Refugees of 1933 and the Convention Relating to the Status of Refugees of 1951.[7] Most significantly, these principles were incorporated into the Convention Relating to the Status of Stateless Persons of September 28, 1954,[8] and the Convention on the Reduction of Statelessness of August 30, 1961.[9] Even so, these international conventions have attracted only a few parties, rendering the scope of legal protection for refugees relatively constricted.

Loss of Nationality

A person may lose his or her nationality by voluntary act or by order of a government. The act by which a person renounces original nationality and acquires the nationality of a new state is called *expatriation*. Should a government deprive an individual of nationality, the process called *denationalization,* or expatriation, is said to occur. Each state establishes its own rules and determines what acts or reasons might result in the loss of nationality to its native-born or naturalized citizens. Acts that warrant loss of nationality vary among countries, although most governments include voting in foreign elections, service in the armed forces of another state, acceptance of a government office normally reserved for citizens of a foreign state, desertion in time of war, treason, and renunciation of nationality either through naturalization abroad or through a formal declaration registered with an embassy or legation of that person's own state. Importantly, the 1951 Convention Relating to the Status of Refugees, the 1954 Convention Relating to the Status of Stateless Persons, and the 1961 Convention on the Reduction of Statelessness suggest that every person has the right to a nationality, though at times mass deprivation of nationality has occurred when a government denationalizes a large number of its nationals abroad who are deemed to be undesirable elements.[10]

JURISDICTION OVER ALIENS

States are not obligated under international law to admit aliens into their territory. A state may exclude all aliens or certain undesirable persons, but discrimination against the admission of any particular races or nationalities undoubtedly can create political repercussions. That said, determination of who may be admitted comes through national statutes. The enactment of immigration laws lies within the competence of a state's legislature, which generally authorizes an immigration office to execute and administer this process. Determination of questions of fact by the proper administrative authorities remains controlling in the absence of any abuse of discretion. Once admitted into the state, an alien receives entitlement to the equal protection of the laws of that country. By the same token, the government of a state retains the sovereign right to expel or deport any alien whose entry is found to be illegal or whose presence is deemed to be prejudicial to the security or interests of that state. Generally speaking, an alien cannot be prevented from voluntary departure if he has paid all taxes and fulfilled all other obligations required by the state during his stay or visit.

The rights and duties of aliens depend on the laws and regulations of different states. While political rights are generally reserved for citizens, aliens usually receive entitlement to civil privileges, subject to certain restrictions, such as where land may be purchased, what professions may be practiced, or what investments may be made in defense-related industries. Such restrictions must not be applied to any group on the bases of racial, religious, national, or ethnic grounds. Since aliens are entitled to the protection of the states in which they reside, they are obligated to pay taxes and to perform other duties required by law. Whether aliens are exempted from military service of the state of domicile depends on the prevailing laws of that state and its treaties with their home states.

During the era of colonialism in the late 19th and early 20th centuries, there arose a special weighted system of extraterritorial jurisdiction imposed by Western powers on certain Asian and African countries. Known as *capitulations*, the practice occurred in Turkey, Japan, Egypt, Morocco, Thailand, and China; and it exempted West European resident aliens from the local jurisdiction of such countries. Instead, Western nationals who were arrested as aliens in any of the aforementioned countries were tried in the host country by his or her respective government's consular officials. Such an intrusion on national sovereignty was justified on grounds of the fundamental differences in civil and criminal codes as well as the judicial systems in those countries from Western states. Even so, states that enjoyed this privilege of special extraterritorial jurisdiction in developing states never reciprocated for nationals from the capitulating foreign state. While a Brit arrested in Turkey for stealing would be tried in the British consulate under British law, a Turk arrested in England for the same crime would be tried by a British court, under British law. Consequently, by the 1930s, the system of capitulations was recognized as being inherently unfair and inequitable, and the treaty relationships were dissolved on the basis of being fundamentally unequal treaties.[11]

Asylum

Asylum refers to formal sanctuary offered to fugitives who are accused of political offenses or who are victims of persecution in another state. So long as the person remains in the territory of the state granting asylum, the police power of the seeking state remains ineffective—that is, unless the fugitive is handed over, a situation known as *refoulement*. If the asylum grantee were to travel to another state, however, the risk of being extradited would reappear, as would be the case when a grantee is expelled at a later date.

The right of asylum in international relations, like the right of expatriation, is often regarded as if it were the right of an individual. That view is mistaken. Insofar as this so-called right of asylum exists, it belongs to the state, without any corresponding duty.

Asylum, then, refers to the granting of safe haven or refuge by a government to aliens who are political offenders or even to ordinary criminals, in the absence of extradition treaties. A state is privileged, but not obliged, to grant asylum to any particular person in the absence of treaty obligations. Under the modern law of states, an individual does not have a right to asylum in the sense that any particular state must receive him or her. But past experience and humanitarian considerations suggest that every government should be under an obligation to grant temporary refuge to persons fleeing from persecution in their own state. In the end, however, asylum can be given for various reasons at the option of a state.

The critical question then becomes, which persons should be granted political asylum? The criteria regarding who should qualify for a grant of asylum is contained in article 1-A (2) of the 1951 Geneva Convention on the Status of Refugees, which defines a *refugee* as a person who "owing to well-founded fear of being persecuted for reasons of race, religion, nationality, membership of a particular social group or political opinion, is outside the country of his nationality and is unable or owing to such fear unwilling to avail himself of the protection of that country; or who, not having a nationality and being outside the country of his habitual residence as a result of such events, is unable or, owing to such fear, unwilling to return to it." Most democratic states are willing to grant asylum, provided that those persons seeking refuge satisfy the host authorities that they are indeed political or racial victims of persecution. There are limitations to this 1951 Geneva Convention approach, however. In recent years, large groups of persons fleeing political turmoil and civil conflict (such as in the cases of Bosnia, Burundi, Rwanda, and Kosovo) have been granted temporary asylum in neighboring countries, as opposed to individuals being singled out for persecution and treated accordingly as a refugee by a receiving government. Still, once asylum is granted, demand for extradition from the refugee's government will be denied on grounds of the commission of political offenses. There is no duty for a government to return a refugee to the country from which he or she fled. The absence of a duty in such cases accords with the well-established practice of providing in extradition treaties that political offenders shall not be surrendered.[12]

Political asylum is not grounded in merely legal considerations. Defining a political offense is subjective and imprecise, especially when the act committed is criminal but has political or ideological motivations. A political crime is one that is politically motivated and carries a political purpose. To the extent that guidelines are available for granting asylum, they are contained in the UN General Assembly's Declaration on Asylum in 1967, but these are only hortatory and nonspecific in content.[13] Importantly, article 14 (1) of the Universal Declaration of Human Rights provides for the right of an individual to seek territorial asylum. Nonetheless, it remains the prerogative of a government to grant that request.

Extradition

Fugitive criminals or persons accused of criminal offenses in one country who flee into another may be delivered by the government of the latter to the authorities of the former, per the demand of the government of the state in whose territory the crime was committed. This formal procedure of surrendering a fugitive is known as *extradition* and normally is legally ensured by means of bilateral treaty relations between states. There does not exist, however, any generally recognized international legal rule that mandates that, in the absence of a treaty obligation, a criminal must be surrendered by one sovereign on the request of another. Even so, it is in the interest of civil society and the international community that all persons guilty of serious crimes be extradited for arraignment and trial to the place where the crime has been committed.

Extradition furnishes a formal means of penetrating the cloak of sovereignty that a state offers an individual from the police power of the fugitive's own state, since the latter's authority does not extend into the jurisdiction of another state. An attempt to inject that authority would constitute unlawful interference into the domestic affairs of the state and a violation of that state's sovereignty. Resort to extradition procedures alleviates this conundrum.

Four steps generally form the extradition process. Suppose a crime occurs in one state and the offender flees to another country. Some time later, the presence of this offender is discovered, and local law enforcement officials notify the government of the state where the crime originally took place. A decision is made to go forward with extradition proceedings, which initiates the first step: a request is presented from the seeking state to the host state through diplomatic channels, asking for extradition of the alleged fugitive. On receipt of an extradition request, the next step begins. The government of the host state undertakes an investigation to determine if extradition is warranted back to the seeking state. Evidence is furnished by the law enforcement officials of the seeking state in an effort to make a compelling case to the host government for extradition. The criteria for this determination vary, but normally if there is sufficient evidence for local police to make an arrest in the host state, then extradition is likely to be granted. If sufficient evidence exists, the third step involves the arrest and detention of the fugitive, who is detained until law enforcement agents from the requesting state arrive. Finally, the agents from the requesting state will take the suspect into custody and return him or her for trial. While these steps make the extradition process appear neat and clear-cut, the bilateral proceedings are often tedious and protracted, largely on account of political complications and recourse by the fugitive to appeal the extradition order.

Several customary rules of extradition are often observed by governments. For one, states generally refuse to extradite their own nationals, though the United States and the United Kingdom take exception to this practice. Likewise, just as a government, unless bound by treaty, may refuse extradition at its discretion, so may it grant extradition at its discretion, unless restrained by municipal law. Extradition remains essentially an executive act, though at times a national judiciary may decide the legal or technical points involved. Reciprocity is the cardinal principle of extradition treaties, which historically include a list of crimes for which extradition might be performed. No person may be tried for offenses not included in the extradition treaty or not described in the extradition proceedings. In the more modern extradition treaty, specific crimes are not enumerated. Rather, the treaty has a blanket provision providing that extradition may be performed if both states recognize the same crime. It is likewise not permissible to convict and punish a person for a crime that is different from that asserted at the time of extradition. Extradition may be refused if the offender's act does not constitute the same crime in the state where he or she is found.[14]

An important exception to criminal acts susceptible to extradition is the *political offense*. The practice of harboring political offenders became a legal principle in early 19th-century Europe, and it is now a near-universal rule followed by governments. In recent decades, however, difficulties have arisen in distinguishing a political offense from an ordinary crime because they have become so mixed in nature. Would assassination of a political leader by a lone gunman be a political crime? Would "terrorist acts," such as bombing a military barracks or a government-owned television station, constitute a "political offense" if done by a national liberation group struggling to gain self-determination? Or should those acts be considered criminal offenses whose perpetrators are subject to extradition if apprehended in a foreign state? Throughout the past century, it became accepted practice that political crimes should not be limited to specific offenses committed against the state but should include all offenses with political motives or purposes, whether committed by one person or by a group. But this view opened the door to widespread abuse in the 1970s and 1980s, as members of known terrorist organizations were often granted safe haven by certain Middle Eastern governments or as magistrates in Western states refused to extradite on the basis of the political offenses exception.[15]

The Case of Pinochet

The case of General Augusto Pinochet, the former president of Chile, well illustrates the political and legal complications associated with extradition. In October 1998, Pinochet traveled to Great Britain. On October 16, Baltasar Garzón, a judge investigating cases of Spanish nationals who were tortured in Chile during the 1970s, requested British authorities to arrest the former dictator. He was arrested that night in London. Spain later formally sought Pinochet's extradition, as did Belgium, France, and Switzerland. The charges against Pinochet included the abduction, torture, disappearance, and execution of thousands of political opponents. Pinochet challenged his arrest on the ground that he enjoyed *diplomatic immunity* from arrest and extradition as a former head of state. The House of Lords, Britain's highest court, twice rejected Pinochet's claim of immunity. In its first judgment, which was later annulled, the Lords ruled that although a former head of state enjoys immunity for acts committed in his functions as head of state, international crimes such as torture and crimes against humanity were not "functions" of a head of state. In the second, more limited judgment, the Lords held that once Britain and Chile had ratified the United Nations Convention against Torture, Pinochet could not claim immunity for torture. A British magistrate then determined that Pinochet could be extradited to Spain on charges of torture and conspiracy to commit torture. In March 2000, however, after medical tests reportedly revealed that Pinochet no longer had the mental capacity to stand trial, he was released and he returned home to Chile.

The most striking feature of the Pinochet case was that a Spanish judge had the authority to order Pinochet's arrest and request extradition for crimes committed mostly in Chile and mostly against Chileans. This authority derives from the principle of *universal jurisdiction,* which asserts that every state has an interest in bringing to justice the perpetrators of particular crimes of international concern, no matter where the crime was committed and regardless of the nationality of the perpetrators or their victims. The Spanish court's action and the United Kingdom's decision to initiate extradition proceedings reflect a new international determination to end impunity for crimes against humanity. No less significant, Pinochet's arrest and detention in London significantly advanced human rights internationally and in Chile.[16]

Abuse of the political offense exception might also be curtailed by applying the principle of *aut dedere aut judicare,* which requires a state that denies an extradition request to pursue the allegations itself. In other words, a government must either extradite or prosecute persons accused of an offense. Nonetheless, unless a state obliges itself through formal agreement to this practice, alleged criminals might purposefully evade deserved punishment.[17] Even where violent acts fall within the prescribed jurisdiction of an international convention, the principle of *aut dedere aut judicare* only obligates the home state to submit the case to the proper domestic authorities. Nothing requires the government to actually try the case.[18] The real possibility exists that in such cases official investigations in the home state might turn up "insufficient evidence" on which to indict the suspects.

Special Provisions

To preclude a government's evasion of prosecuting a criminal offender by political chicanery, states have sought to negotiate special provisions into salient international agreements that codify the obligation to extradite or prosecute. Certain conventions include notable *aut dedere aut judicare* provisions that require contracting parties to extradite or prosecute accused offenders—for example, the 1970 Convention on the Suppression of Unlawful Seizure of Aircraft (Hague Convention),[19] the 1971 Montreal Convention for the Suppression of Unlawful Acts against the Safety of Civil Aviation,[20] the 1979 Convention against Torture,[21] the 1988 Convention on the Suppression of Unlawful Acts against the Safety of Maritime Navigation,[22] and the 1999 UN Convention on Suppression of Financing Terrorism.[23] Not only do these provisions ensure that suspected persons are more ably prosecuted, but they also diminish the possibility that some government might invoke the political offense exclusion. The political offense exception is intended to protect persons from being persecuted for their political beliefs. It is not intended to be a loophole for violent offenders evading criminal prosecution. These international conventions help to close that loophole for several important unlawful acts, many of which are associated with terrorist violence.[24]

INDIVIDUAL HUMAN RIGHTS

Intolerance and the resultant abuse of people are ancient and persistent. Discrimination and brutality are global and pervasive. Whether the issue is race, religion, ethnicity, gender, age, or some other characteristic, few human traits have escaped being targets of discrimination and abuse somewhere in the world. In this respect, attitudes on racial or other forms of demographic superiority have played powerful, destructive roles in history. Consequently, many social divisions and problems today remain legacies of intolerance and racism that, when combined with political and economic nationalism, are used by leaders to rationalize oppression against selected groups of their citizens. Racist views of social history, such as that of Italy's fascism and Nazi Germany's national socialism, were transformed into brutally repressive ideologies that proclaimed war and conquest as the natural order of things, substantiating the survival of the fittest in foreign policy. Such forms of social Darwinism were all too often translated into genocidal attacks against selected groups—in particular, Jews, gypsies, homosexuals, the aged, and the infirm. Protection of those persecuted peoples remained muted by considerations of national sovereignty. Under traditional international law, the governments of states retained supreme authority over their internal affairs. International legal rules were to be applied to a state's foreign affairs, not its domestic matters. The near-universal belief held that a state's treatment of its people fell beyond the province of international concern inasmuch as the individual, alone or collectively, was deemed merely an object, and not a subject, of international legal rules.

This situation changed profoundly in the last half of the 20th century as statesmen and stateswomen became more cognizant of the need to safeguard the minimal rights of the individual. The manifold changes in territorial ownership in Europe after the First World War highlighted the need to guarantee rights that protected minorities, given the rise in nationalistic sentiments and the very real danger that racial, ethnic, linguistic, and religious minorities in those new territories might be oppressed and subjugated by their new governments. Consequently, a number of treaties were concluded between the Allied powers and such countries as Czechoslovakia, Austria, Greece, Bulgaria, Hungary, Poland, Rumania, Turkey, and Yugoslavia, in which those governments pledged just and equal treatment for their minority groups.[25] These legal obligations were subsequently reaffirmed by various resolutions adopted by the League of Nations and by cases addressed by the Permanent Court of International Justice.[26]

The devastation of the Second World War, the pervasive atrocities by the Nazis against the Jews and other peoples during the Holocaust, and the violence inflicted by the Germans and Japanese on occupied populations became catalysts precipitating a strong movement after the war for the international protection of fundamental human rights. In the last half-century, respect for human rights has been codified into treaty law, the law of international organizations, and general international law. That most governments have committed themselves to be bound by most of these legal rules is a sea change in international law, one affirming that the relationship between the state and its persons is no longer exclusive to the domestic sphere. The individual has been transformed from an object of state sovereignty into a subject of international law with defined rights, duties, and protections in the international community. Put tersely, the state remains the principal international legal actor. Its agents or other persons who violate human rights are now subject to international legal rules, although individuals who are victims of human rights abuse remain objects of the law and must seek legal redress through judicial organs of the state.

Human rights have not arrived full-panoplied as a set of legal rules on the international stage. Like all law, human rights law evolved through a pattern of development, which occurred though progressive stages. The rules of human rights law initially emerge by being articulated as internationally perceived common values. Next they are declared in an international document as fulfilling certain fundamental needs and interests that benefit people in the international community. These rights then are articulated in a prescriptive form, by an international institution that either prepares a multilateral instrument or elaborates an international convention. Once made available for international consideration, they become codified into legally binding commitments when the instrument is ratified by a requisite number of states and enters into force. In the final two stages, means for enforcement are agreed on, usually by national governments through their own domestic means, and processes are established to criminalize a violation, which usually requires the development of international penal proscriptions.[27]

These developments proceed out of the general conviction that persons should and must be internationally protected. Given the gross humiliation of human dignity during the Second World War and by many tyrannical regimes since, the demand for legal protection of the individual becomes urgent and imperative. Although the United Nations was created to be a collective security arrangement, a state's treatment of its own citizens now officially appears as a subject of international concern—a point on which the UN Charter is unequivocal. Members of the organization pledge to affirm faith in the dignity and worth of the human person and to accept as one of the United Nations' fundamental purposes the promotion and encouragement of respect for human rights and fundamental freedoms for all without discrimination.[28] The respect for human rights and freedoms is repeatedly asserted in the UN Charter. ''We the Peoples of the United Nations,'' according to the preamble, are determined ''to reaffirm faith in the fundamental human rights and to promote social progress and better standards of life in larger freedom.'' Among the chief purposes and principles of the United Nations is that of achieving "international cooperation in promoting and encouraging respect for human rights and for fundamental freedoms without distinction as to race, sex, language, or religion."[29] Again, article 55 reasserts that "universal respect for, and observance of, human rights and fundamental freedoms for all" are necessary for international cooperation.

The elucidation and development of human rights through the United Nations mark a watershed event. The bedrock of UN activity—the Universal Declaration of Human Rights—launched a revolution in human rights law. Adopted by the General Assembly in December 1948, the Universal Declaration is the first international statement to use the term *human rights* and is heralded by human rights organizations as the fundamental statement on international human rights norms. This document—which consists of thirty articles—contains a list of civil, political, and social rights that represent the threshold of transition of the individual's place in international law. However, the Universal Declaration is not a law-making instrument; it is a General Assembly resolution that possesses hortatory force but no legally binding authority. Formal legal obligations arise only when a government becomes party to some instrument containing specific rights and duties. Some legal commentators have argued that its provisions embody general principles of law or that the instrument has acquired the status of customary international law.[30] State practice, however, makes such conclusions difficult to accept on the whole. Importantly, some rights specifically listed in the Universal Declaration—such as those to life, liberty, and security of person as well as the freedoms from torture, slavery, and murder—have evolved into accepted norms of modern customary international law.

The conception of human rights as international legal rules may be conveniently viewed in terms of three generations of rights. The first generation is concerned with safeguarding the individual's liberty and protecting his or her rights from the government. To this end, the International Covenant on Civil and Political Rights, which has been in force since 1976, details the basic civil and political rights of states and individuals.[31] Peoples are guaranteed the fundamental right to self-determination, the right to own and dispose of their property freely, and the right not to be deprived of their means of subsistence. Likewise, the rights stipulated for individuals are fundamental for a civil society. They include, among others, the right to life; the right to liberty and freedom of movement; the right to equality before the law; the right to presumption of innocence until proven guilty; the right to be recognized as a person before the law; the right to privacy; the freedom of thought, conscience, and religion; the freedom of opinion and expression; and the freedom of assembly and association. There is the profound objective of preserving and protecting human dignity and personal security, as the covenant prohibits torture and inhuman or degrading treatment, as well as slavery or involuntary servitude, arbitrary arrest and detention, and debtors' prisons. It forbids propaganda advocating war or hatred based on race, religion, national origin, or language. The Covenant also provides for the right of people to choose freely whom they will marry, and it guarantees the rights of children. It prohibits discrimination based on race, sex, color, national origin, or language; it restricts the death penalty to only the most serious crimes and forbids the punishment entirely for persons less than eighteen years of age. To facilitate implementation, the instrument establishes the UN Human Rights Committee, which reviews reports submitted by state parties on human rights conditions in their countries.

Second-generation human rights are associated with various democratic socialist movements that operated in the 20th century to ensure that public benefits meet the basic needs for all persons. The underlying ambition here is the equality of human beings. In other words, individuals are entitled to certain minimum standards of economic and social opportunities, and the state should contribute to those ends. The second generation of human rights is designed to facilitate that end: it is the International Covenant on Economic, Social, and Cultural Rights—in force since 1976—which furnishes a catalogue of second generation basic economic, social, and cultural rights to which individuals are entitled.[32] Recognized as paramount among these are the rights to employment, social security, an adequate standard of living, and education, as well as the rights to participate in cultural life and to be a beneficiary of scientific progress. The instrument does not merely list these rights but describes and defines them in considerable detail. In addition, the instrument forbids the exploitation of children and requires that all party states cooperate to end world hunger. State parties under this covenant are obligated to send periodic reports to the UN Economic and Social Council, although since 1985 a special committee of independent experts has functioned to review those reports.

A third generation of human rights, called new solidarity rights, evolved in the last half of the 20th century to promote various rights to which all persons by virtue of being part of humanity are entitled. Among these core rights, which instill the notion of solidarity, are the rights to international peace, a healthy environment, development, disaster relief, and a share in the common heritage of mankind. While no single international instrument embraces all these aspirations, a number of special agreements make major contributions to those ends. Included among these multilateral accords are the 1959 Treaty on Antarctica, the 1967 Outer Space Treaty, and the 1982 Convention on the Law of the Sea, the 1992 Climate Change Convention, and the 1992 Convention on Biological Diversity.

The Universal Declaration of Human Rights was essentially codified into legal rules by the International Covenant on Civil and Political Rights and the International Covenant on Economic, Social, and Cultural Rights. Both of these latter agreements transformed into binding treaty obligations the principles in the Universal Declaration, which can be applied to the legal order of states. Since these three instruments furnish the essence and foundation of modern human rights law, they are often collectively referred to as the *International Bill of Human Rights*.[33] Yet, the absence of effective enforcement machinery or sanctions, other than world opinion, limits the impact of the two covenants. Both legal instruments are non-self-executing, which requires that governments devise special national implementing legislation to integrate the documents' specific provisions into municipal law. The instruments' effectiveness in protecting human rights depends on the willingness of individual governments to implement such provisions domestically.

Chief among the accomplishments of these international human rights agreements is their application to all persons under the jurisdiction of contracting parties. No longer is it undue intervention into the internal affairs of a state for a contracting party to complain that some other contracting party is mistreating its nationals below the guaranteed standards in these instruments to which they are lawfully obligated. Any alleged breach of its obligations may be referred to a competent organ, as expressly provided for in the instrument, or to the International Commission of Human Rights.

Collective Human Rights

Evil and inhumanity to innocent people know no limits. This realization, as tragically demonstrated by the extermination practices of the Third Reich, prompted the international community to fashion international legal rules for the physical protection of people as a group. These rights are intended to be universal and are nonderogative—that is, they are immune from suspension or compromise by governments.

Coming specifically in response to the horrors of the Holocaust, the Convention on the

Prevention and Punishment of the Crime of Genocide was adopted by the UN General Assembly in late 1948.[34] This instrument declares that genocide, whether committed in peacetime or war, is a crime under international law that is a grave offense against the law of states and for which the individual perpetrator is punishable. The convention defines *genocide* as the commission of certain enumerated acts "with the intent to destroy, in whole or in part, a national, ethnical, racial, or religious group, as such."[35] The acts constituting genocide include killing members of a group; causing serious bodily or mental harm to members of a group; deliberately inflicting on a group conditions of life calculated to bring about its physical destruction in whole or in part; imposing measures intended to prevent births within a group; or forcibly transferring children of a group to another group. To be guilty of the crime of genocide, an individual must have committed one of these acts with the specific intent of destroying in whole or in part a national, ethnic, racial, or religious group. The Genocide Convention does not establish an international criminal court but would have established "a competent tribunal of the State in the territory of which the act [of genocide] is committed."[36]

The Genocide Convention pronounces as possible offenses the conspiracy, incitement, directing, planning, attempts, and complicity to commit genocide, as well as acts of genocide themselves. Important to note, the plea of obedience to superior orders is not acceptable as a mitigating factor for commission of the crime, since heads of state, public officials, and private individuals are equally punishable. (Obedience to superior orders can be held as a mitigating factor in determining the punishment for an offender, however.) Nor can genocide be considered a political offense excluded from extradition. Parties are obliged to honor extradition requests. The convention demonstrates the growing area of international criminal law that directly affects individuals, not just states. Even so, the convention is weakened by a lack of international enforcement mechanisms and the large number of reservations that governments have attached to their acceptance of the convention.

Besides the critical need of a group to protect itself against physical attacks on its very existence as a specific entity, groups must be protected from discriminatory treatment as such.[37] During the era of decolonization in the 1960s and 1970s, a particularly odious form of human rights degradation was legally exposed and condemned. Adopted by the UN General Assembly in 1965, the International Convention on the Elimination of All Forms of Racial Discrimination entered into force in 1969 and prohibits preferential or discriminatory acts based on race, color, ancestry, nationality, ethic origin.[38] The convention guarantees protection from racial discrimination in those rights set out in both the International Covenant on Civil and Political Rights and the International Covenant on Economic, Social, and Cultural Rights; and it further condemns racial segregation, apartheid policies, and groups espousing theories of racial superiority. The convention establishes a Committee on Elimination of Racial Discrimination, which is authorized to handle complaints and disputes by states. This convention reflects the efforts of the United Nations to implement humanitarian goals set out in the Universal Declaration of Human Rights.

Slavery or *slave-related practices* were among the earliest abrogations of human rights to be expressly condemned as international criminal offenses for which individuals may be held legally accountable. Such acts of enslavement refer to the status or condition of a person over whom the power of ownership is exercised. The concept of slave-related practices includes debt bondage, serfdom, martial bondage, slave labor, and sexual bondage.[39]

As a by-product of colonialism, the international community registered its disgust with racial bigotry and purposeful segregation. In this regard, *apartheid,* or the intentional separation of peoples in a society on the basis of race, is condemned as an international offense against fundamental human rights. Apartheid involves acts that are expressly intended to establish and maintain systematic domination over a racial group of persons. Such acts of apartheid are manifold and include physical injury, killing, torture, arbitrary arrest, and imprisonment; denial of participation in the political, economic, social, or cultural life of the country; and the physical and legislative separation of the group from the rest of society. To address these concerns, the International Convention on the Suppression and Punishment of the Crime of Apartheid was adopted by the United Nations General Assembly on November 30, 1973; within three years, it had attracted the sufficient number of state ratifications for it to enter into force.[40] The convention proclaims apartheid to be a crime against humanity and declares that all inhuman acts attributable to the policies and practices of apartheid crimes violate the principles of international law.[41] Liability for committing the crime of apartheid extends not only to individuals, members of organizations and institutions, and representatives of the state who commit the offense but also to all persons who "directly abet, encourage, or co-operate in its commission," regardless of where they are at the time.[42] Resort to universal jurisdiction is sanctioned, as a person charged with the offense may be tried by any state party and by any international tribunal having jurisdiction accepted by the states who are party to the convention. To implement the convention, periodic reports are required from state parties, which are reviewed by a special "Group of Three" appointed by the chairman of the UN Commission on Human Rights. The findings of the Group of Three are then reported to the commission.

The unequal status and discriminatory treatment of women have arisen as particular human rights concerns over the past half-century, and international legal rules have been created to redress those inequities. An early achievement came with the Convention on the Political Rights of Women,[43] adopted in 1953 by the United Nations General Assembly. This convention guarantees to women equal voting rights and the right to seek and hold public office. However, the major international instrument concerning the position of women is the 1979 Convention on the Elimination of All Forms of Discrimination against Women (CEDAW), in force since 1981.[44] The convention seeks to do away with discrimination against women and obligates parties to condemn such discrimination.[45] States are also obliged "to embody the principle of equality in their national constitutions or other appropriate legislation" and to adopt laws or other measures, "including sanctions where appropriate, prohibiting discrimination against women."[46] Finally, CEDAW requires state parties to take measures in the political, social, economic, and cultural realms to advance the enjoyment of equal rights by women.[47] Implementation of the instrument is facilitated through periodic reports relating to legislative, juridical, or administrative measures adopted by state parties to give effect to the convention. These reports are reviewed by the Special Committee on the Elimination of Discrimination against Women, which has the power of international shame, but not sanction, against governments who derogate from CEDAW's obligations.

Children have also emerged as a specific concern of international human rights protection. Legal standards concerning children were codified in 1989 by the Convention on the Rights of the Child.[48] This instrument unequivocally spells out the rights to which every child is entitled, regardless of where or to whom it is born and regardless of its sex, religion, or social origin. The protections in the Convention on the Rights of the Child strive to reinforce fundamental human dignity, as they underscore the role of the family in society, seek respect for the child as a person, endorse the principle of nondiscrimination, and establish clear obligations for parties to bring their national legislation into line with the convention's provisions. This convention creates a treaty-monitoring body of experts, the Committee on the Rights of the Child, which has the authority to recommend domestic policy changes based on information submitted to it in reports by state parties.

The crime of *torture* refers to any conduct by which severe physical or mental pain is inflicted on a person at the instigation of, or under the responsibility of, a public official to obtain information or a confession; to humiliate or denigrate a person; or to inflict unlawful, inhuman, cruel, or degrading punishment. To provide legal redress for such offenses, the Convention against Torture and Other Cruel, Inhuman, or Degrading Treatment was adopted by the UN General Assembly on December 10, 1984, and entered into force on June 28, 1987.[49] Evolving out of a General Assembly declaration in 1975, this instrument aims to prevent and punish acts of torture committed by government officials or others acting in an official capacity. The convention defines torture as "any act by which severe pain or suffering, whether physical or mental, is intensely inflicted on a person" for the purpose of "obtaining from him or a third person information or a confession."[50] Contracting states undertake to adopt effective legislative, administrative, judicial, or other measures to prevent torture in any territory under their jurisdiction.[51] No exceptional circumstances may justify torture, and no orders from superior officers or a public authority may be invoked to justify the use of torture. The Torture Convention establishes a reporting system, a Special Committee Against Torture, as well as an optional interstate-complaints and individual-petitions system, albeit no specific enforcement measures or sanctions are mandated for parties to take against delict governments.

Implementation of Human Rights

Since 1945, the United Nations system has generated a wide range of human rights standards and norms for the protection of the individual person under modern international law. Critical questions remain, however. First, in what ways can these standards and norms be implemented? Second, to what degree has protection of these rights been made effective? To some extent, the answers lie in political bodies of the United Nations and in special expert institutions created by the various legal instruments. But in the main, the answers rest with the governments of states themselves.

The General Assembly has the authority under article 13 of the UN Charter to initiate studies and make recommendations concerning human rights. Human rights issues regularly appear on its agenda and are often discussed in the Assembly's Third Committee (Social, Humanitarian, and Cultural Committee) and the Sixth Committee (Legal). The Assembly has also established a number of subsidiary organs that deal with human rights concerns—namely, the Special Committee on Decolonization, the Special Committee against Apartheid, and the UN Council for Namibia. The Economic and Social Council (ECOSOC) may make recommendations on human rights, draft conventions for assembly action, and call international conferences on human rights matters.

The UN Commission on Human Rights, originally established as a subsidiary organ of ECOSOC in 1946, has emerged as a respected vehicle for examining evidence of a state's gross violation of human rights and making recommendations to ECOSOC. This authority led the commission to assume a public debate function, as it established working groups that have focused on specific situations in South Africa and Chile and on the topics of disappearances and the right to development. In addition, special rapporteurs were appointed by the commission to treat human rights situations in specific countries, such as for Afghanistan, Cuba, El Salvador, Guatemala, Iran, and Iraq. Likewise, special rapporteurs were appointed to deal with particular issue areas of human rights concern, such as summary executions, the use of torture, the resort to mercenaries, and the sale of children.

UN organs have also established expert bodies that study and assess human rights conditions. The Subcommission on Prevention of Discrimination and Protection of Minorities, set up by the Commission on Human Rights in 1947, established several working groups to examine select human rights situations, such as the contemporary forms of slavery, the rights of indigenous populations, and the administration of justice during detention. In 1985 ECOSOC created a special Committee on Economic, Social, and Cultural Rights (hereafter, the Economic Rights Committee), which began operation two years later. Unlike other expert human rights committees, the Economic Rights Committee is neither autonomous nor responsible to the state parties. It reports to ECOSOC, a main organ of the United Nations. Moreover, while its purpose is to facilitate and enhance implementation of the International Covenant on Economic, Social, and Cultural Rights, several factors combine to make widespread implementation of this instrument problematic, if not unlikely, in the foreseeable future. Among these obstacles are the vagueness of many principles contained in the covenant; the lack of legal texts and judicial decisions for guidance; and the ambivalence that many states have in accepting economic, social, and cultural matters as attaining the threshold of fundamental human rights. Important also is that each government will have to offer considerable economic and technical resources, as well as a reordering of social and educational priorities, to ensure enjoyment of the "progressive" rights advocated in this document.[52] The Economic Rights Committee makes few decisions, though since 1990 it has periodically issued general comments on various economic and societal facets of human rights. Included among the topics addressed as general comments are international technical measures; the obligatory effects of the covenant on contracting parties; the right to adequate housing; the rights of persons with disabilities; and the economic, social, and cultural rights of older persons. Importantly, the Economic Rights Committee may not consider petitions from individuals or exercise competence to hear complaints between states.

The process of implementing human rights standards is sustained through expert bodies established by particular international conventions. These bodies are autonomous and not formally attached to the United Nations, though at times they are assisted and serviced by the UN Secretariat and the UN Center for Human Rights in Geneva. The first such organ created by UN treaty was the Committee on the Elimination of Racial Discrimination, established in 1965 under part II of the convention bearing the same name. Composed of eighteen experts of high standing elected by signatory states, this committee receives reports from state parties, and from these reports it makes suggestions and general recommendations to the General Assembly. The committee is empowered to seek additional information as a matter of urgency from state parties, as it did from Yugoslavia, Croatia, and Bosnia-Herzegovina from 1993 to 1995 as international concern escalated over the states' resident ethnic cleansing. There is also an interstate complaint procedure, in which one state party may bring a complaint against another state party, which the committee thus seeks to resolve. The committee meets twice annually and is authorized to interpret articles of the convention, adopt decisions, and submit general recommendations based on state reports that it receives.[53] The International Covenant on Civil and Political Rights, which entered into force in 1976, establishes under its part IV a special Human Rights Committee. This body consists of eighteen independent expert members elected by the parties to the covenant for four-year terms. The committee operates through consensus and as its main task receives and assesses reports submitted to it by state parties. These reports are supposed to provide information on what measures contracting governments have taken to give effect to the rights recognized in the Covenant. The committee may also seek additional information from states, as was done in 1992 for the Federal Republic of Yugoslavia, Croatia, and Bosnia-Herzegovina concerning measures necessary to prevent ethnic cleansing and arbitrary killings. The Human Rights Committee has adopted a variety of general comments that highlight certain human rights concerns, including among them are the right to life (1984), the rights of the child (1989), the concept of nondiscrimination (1989), self-determination and the rights of minorities (1995), and the impropriety of attaching reservations to human rights agreements (1994).

An Optional Protocol to the Covenant on Civil and Political Rights adds legal force to the Covenant, as it extends the authority of the Human Rights Committee to investigate and issue findings on alleged human rights violations by state parties.[54] The protocol provides the committee with the competence to receive and consider communications from individuals alleging violations by a state party to the protocol. The committee is not a court, however. Its decisions (which are called "final views") do not carry binding power based on the merits of a case, nor does the protocol contain enforcement mechanisms or even measures for sanctions. Nonetheless, these deficiencies do not detract from the case decisions to date that seriously test the ways and means that governments treat their nationals, be they laws pertaining to deportation of minorities, due process in capital offense cases, extradition procedures when confronting the death penalty, or whether a person in military detention had recourse to the courts.

A third body of experts is the Committee on the Elimination of Discrimination against Women, which was established when the Convention on the Elimination of All Forms of Discrimination against Women entered into force in 1981. The committee, formed by twenty-three experts, strives to implement the convention by examining reports submitted by state parties on measures taken to comply with the convention. The committee reports annually to the General Assembly through ECOSOC. Besides reviewing reports, the committee may make suggestions and issue general recommendations, which are intended to spotlight special measures. Such recommendations have addressed a variety of issues. Among them are the various needs to more fully advance women's integration into education, the economy, politics, and employment; to provide greater opportunity for women to participate in government service; to halt violence against women; to promote greater equality for women in marriage; and to eliminate female circumcision. Even so, certain deficiencies detract from the committee's effectiveness, most notably its limited time for meeting—only two weeks each year—and the inability of the committee to receive individual petitions or entertain interstate complaints. Specific conditions affecting women, however, have received heightened attention over the past decade in other UN human rights bodies and agencies, thereby affording greater scrutiny on the ways and means of eliminating discrimination against women. In these regards, the plight of young girls in developing countries falling into slavery and into child prostitution has taken on special concern in recent years.

The Convention against Torture and Other Cruel, Inhuman, or Degrading Treatment or Punishment entered into force in 1987. Part II of the convention provides for a Committee against Torture. The committee, composed of ten independent experts, is given the competence to hear interstate complaints and communications from individuals, although states must declare their willingness to accept that competence. The committee may invite governments to respond to reports of torture and to participate in examining the evidence. These proceedings are confidential, although findings can be published in the committee's annual report. Since 1990 a number of cases have been brought to the committee, many of which concern liability for acts of torture committed by military officials in Latin American states during the 1976–1985 period.[55] In addition a special rapporteur on torture was appointed in 1985 by the United Nations Commission on Human Rights, who is directed to work closely with the Committee against Torture in seeking credible evidence and reliable information on questions relevant to torture. The rapporteur produces an annual report for the commission.

The 1989 Convention on the Rights of the Child establishes a special committee whose purpose is to examine questions concerning the status and treatment of children in states party to the convention. The committee, formed by ten independent experts, began operation in 1991 with the competence to hear states' reports on issues affecting children. The committee produces a report every two years to the General Assembly through ECOSOC, and it also discusses issues on particular topics affecting the child, such as the plight of children in armed conflicts, the economic exploitation of children, and special concern over conditions affecting the "girl child" in developing societies. Though the committee's general reporting functions are notable, it lacks the authority to hear complaints by governments or individuals concerning the mistreatment of children by any government or in any particular state society. Nor is there any power to enforce or order sanctions as remedies for urgent action to protect children. The committee can use the state's reporting obligation to request from governments further clarification of situations and often issues special concluding observations in which the negative facets of targeted states' reports are evaluated and publicized.

The international law for human rights has evolved from the need to protect rights for the individual person to the need to protect rights of persons in groups. Legal rules for human rights today not only safeguard the rights of the individual but have also been formulated as collective rights. Yet, distinguishing between notions of individual and collective human rights is neither simple nor clear-cut. Some rights are clearly individual, such as the right to life, freedom from torture, freedom of religion, and freedom of expression. Some rights are clearly collective, such as the right to self-determination or the right of groups to be protected from genocide, racial discrimination, and religious persecution. Other rights constitute collective manifestations of individual rights, such as the need to protect the rights of children, women, or any particular racial group. It is important that the legitimate interests of the state, the individual, and the group be balanced to avoid impinging on the human rights of any person and to ensure more efficient functioning of the state in the protection of the human rights of persons within its jurisdiction. Thus, rules for human rights have proliferated over the past half-century, expressly with the purpose of protecting the personal dignity and physical security of the individual within the society of states. To this end, the reach of international criminal law has grown rapidly as well, especially by designating particular actions as offenses against modern international law and highlighting the need for holding accountable those persons responsible for such crimes. This theme will be more fully addressed in the next chapter.

Regional Human Rights Systems

The international protection of human rights has found serious consideration in regional dimensions as well. The European Convention for the Protection of Human Rights and Fundamental Freedoms was drawn up in 1950 within the Council of Europe,[56] with the express intention of establishing the collective enforcement of certain rights stipulated in the Universal Declaration of Human Rights. To this end, a catalogue of civil and political rights and freedoms are guaranteed by Western European contracting states to their citizens. Included among these are the rights to life and liberty; prohibitions of slavery and servitude; freedom from arbitrary arrest, imprisonment or exile; the right to a fair trial; and the freedoms of thought, speech, association, and religion. The European Convention furnishes the most ambitious transnational legal program dealing with human rights. Much of its success can be attributed to the cultural affinity that states share from being part of European civilization.

The European Convention provides for a separate European Commission of Human Rights (created in 1954) to receive, investigate, and instigate complaints pertaining to human rights disputes filed by signatory states or by individuals in individual petitions. The convention also establishes a European Court of Human Rights (ECHR), which began in 1959 to hear cases arising under the European Convention in Strasbourg, France. Forty-one European states are contracting parties to this treaty, making its jurisdiction effectively more extensive than that of the European Court of Justice. The European Court of Human Rights, however, provides judicial protection for the fundamental rights of the individual. It may thus hear cases that might not be heard under the laws of an aggrieved individual's home state. For example, in Great Britain there is no written constitution that enumerates the rights guaranteed for persons under the law. Great Britain's obligations to the preservation of human rights under the European Convention carry certain written guarantees that protect British citizens from any capricious acts of its government's agents. While no formal enforcement power is given to either the commission or the court, the pressure of adverse publicity leads governments to comply with its decisions.[57]

States contracting to the European Convention may litigate cases before the ECHR. While individual persons lack legal capacity to be parties, they can petition the European Commission of Human Rights to correct actions that allegedly fail to comply with the convention.

A regional system of human rights law was developed for application to states in the Americas. The Inter-American Commission on Human Rights was created in 1959, and the next year its statute was approved by the Organization of American States (OAS). In 1971, the commission was recognized as one of the principal organs of the OAS, and it became the foundation on which human rights law for the Americas was constructed. The commission is endowed with broad powers to promote the awareness and study of human rights among states in the region. Any person, group of persons, or nongovernmental entity legally recognized in an OAS member state may lodge petitions with the commission, alleging a violation of the convention by a state party. In that respect, the Inter-American Court declared that the commission has the authority to determine whether the domestic law of any state party violates the obligations assumed in ratifying the convention. If so, the commission may recommend that governments repeal the particular law in question.

Drafted by the OAS, the American Convention on Human Rights came into force 1978,[58] and the following year the Inter-American Court of Human Rights (IACHR) was established in San Jose, Costa Rica. This court functions principally to interpret the convention, though it hears claims from governments alleging that an individual's civil and political rights have been impinged on by some other state's action. Unlike the European regional system, however, individuals are not permitted to appear directly or indirectly before the IACHR. Only states may come before the court. Still, the place of the person as a subject of international law remains relevant. The court hears cases involving disputes between states when one government accuses another of violating freedoms of individuals that are guaranteed under the convention. The relevant states must consent to the jurisdiction of the court to resolve such disputes. While only a few OAS members accept the compulsory jurisdiction of the IACHR, the court by 2004 had rendered at least ninety-one decisions and judgments on cases involving alleged violations of human rights. In addition, advisory opinions may be issued by the IACHR to provided judicial guidance to member governments about certain practices that might violate the Inter-American Human Rights Convention. In this way, the court contributes to the ongoing development of regional law for the Americas concerning state compliance with provisions of that instrument. As of 2004, at least seventeen advisory opinions had been given by the IACHR on issues as diverse as judicial guarantees in states of emergency to restrictions to the death penalty and the legal nature of various parts of the American Convention on Human Rights.[59]

THE ROLE OF THE NONGOVERNMENTAL ORGANIZATION

The weakness of human rights law today lies in the content of the core treaties, which offer only weak enforcement provisions. Moreover, the rules for human rights suffer from the unwillingness of governments to enforce them within their own states, in particular against officials and military/security police within their own governments who perpetrate atrocities against fellow citizens. This situation has led many *nongovernmental organizations* (NGOs) to implement programs that monitor and report on human rights. Such efforts are meant to expose human rights violations and thus pressure governments into taking measures to halt the violations and punish the offenders.

Among these, Amnesty International (AI) is perhaps the best known. Since being founded in 1961, AI has worked worldwide through a mass membership by specifically targeting governments to release political prisoners and prisoners of conscience, as well as to halt torture and the use of the death penalty.[60] More recently established are a number of human rights groups based in the United States and comprised mainly of lawyers. Among these are the Lawyers Committee for Human Rights, Human Rights Watch, the International Human Rights Law Group, and the Minnesota Lawyers' International Human Rights Committee.[61]

Three long-standing human rights NGOs have played salient roles in dealing with human rights emergencies—the International Committee of the Red Cross (ICRC), the International Commission of Jurists (ICJ), and AI. The unique nature and considerable respect given the ICRC's entitlement to act under the Geneva Conventions of 1949 and the Additional Protocols of 1977 contribute to its success in being able to approach governments, as does its historical record of action for assisting civilian victims and prisoners of war.[62] The ICJ focuses on the rule of law and undertakes research missions, political trial observations, promotion of conferences and seminars, and, at times, governmental interventions. Many of its efforts are academic and aim to educate and inform various communities on human rights issues.[63] Finally, AI relies on grassroots organizations and mass media outreach, while also using legal and diplomatic channels to gather information and to pressure governments to change their human rights practices. AI's annual country reports provide an international catalogue for violations of individual human rights in every state.

In general, human rights–oriented NGOs take direct action to influence governments. They are not responding to national emergencies so much as they are to actual human rights abuses. It is important to remember that these NGOs vary in their approaches, and their abilities are bounded by their respective mandates, resources, expertise, and political orientation. In addition, human rights NGOs tend to implement a number of similar actions, such as pressuring for diplomatic missions and interventions; promoting public discussions; mobilizing public opinion; encouraging and supporting monitoring and investigations of abuses; and providing direct legal, humanitarian, and medical aid to victims. Notable also are the contributions of NGOs to human rights norms. For example, much of the modern law of war stems from efforts of the ICRC to establish the body of humanitarian norms in armed conflict that every state now recognizes. Furthermore, AI and the Lawyers Committee for Human Rights were leading campaigners in working to create an international criminal court capable of prosecuting persons for breaching international legal rules that prohibit war crimes, genocide, and crimes against humanity.

CONCLUSION

Over the last half of the 20th century, the advent of international human rights law produced an important socializing impact on the international community. Governments now realize that massive violations of human rights can carry a high political and economic price. Such knowledge affects their international behavior—not because they suddenly have become good or altruistic but because they have foreign investments, military aid, or international commercial stakes at risk or because their domestic political base might be severely weakened by international condemnation.

When international legal rules reflect the aspirations of the community and capture its imagination, they acquire a political and moral force whose impact cannot often be predicted. History teaches profound lessons about the power of ideas and the irony of hypocrisy, such that the human rights revolution for freedom and human dignity at times overshadows political realism, with its preponderant focus on military and economic power.

The preservation of human rights is not self-enforcing. The system of international legal rules has no central institutions of enforcement—there are presently no courts of general jurisdiction (though in the future, the permanent International Criminal Court may mark a turning point), no marshal service, no police force, and no armies to compel governments to comply with human rights obligations. The effective enforcement of human rights is generated by attitudes in governments concerning how self-interests are affected by public acts, institutions, or officials. The human rights situation comes down to this: the rule of law remains a dead letter unless supported by the values and expectations of the community as a whole, as interpreted and implemented by national governments. For three decades after the Second World War, international human rights and humanitarian law seemed moribund in practice and largely symbolic as norms. These rules embodied great goals of civilized peoples, but their many provisions appeared little more than lofty aspirations. Once these conventions were negotiated and entered into force, governments generally ignored them whenever they wanted. Abuses were common, condemnatory rhetoric was plentiful, effective sanctions were scant. As internal conflicts flared up—particularly in developing countries—the human rights of innocent peoples became victim to national power struggles and ethnic hatreds.

Today this appears less the case. Nongovernmental organizations have assumed the role of public human-rights watchdogs. They document and publicize abuses, proselytize for legal change, pressure governments, and arouse public opinion. More significantly, human rights NGOs now directly participate in international rule making. Some fifteen hundred NGOs have consultative status with the United Nations as official observers. Nearly 140 NGOs were accredited as observers to the June 1998 conference in Rome that agreed on a convention for a permanent International Criminal Court. NGOs became the principal advocates for the treaty banning antipersonnel land mines in 1997. A general attitude has emerged that human rights are real rights and that protection of them is a serious concern for most governments. During the last decade of the 20th century, the human tragedies in Somalia, Bosnia, Burundi, Rwanda, East Timor, and Kosovo pushed human rights to the forefront of international concern and underscored the necessity of protecting innocent peoples from their own governments or from internal anarchy. These are all important accomplishments, but much more remains to be done. The ongoing tragedy of the Congo remains a horrific case in point, as four million people, nearly all civilians, were killed in internal violence between 1998 and 2004.

The place and security of the individual person in the world community have benefited from the unprecedented modern development of international legal rules. The individual today holds a recognized status in international law. Persons are transnational actors with international rights, duties, and protections. They engage in all kinds of transborder activities governed by legal rules. In normal circumstances, the individual derives international legal personality from being a national of a state and subject to that state's jurisdiction, criminal processes, and diplomatic protection. It is the legal principle of nationality that establishes the legal privileges and duties of persons within their own state and within the scope of that state's legal obligations to international legal rules.

Yet, in no other realm of international law in the 21st century is the role of the individual more salient than in human rights. This expansion in protective legal rules flows from the ever-increasing sharing of fundamental values and expectations among governments. The international community is now seized with the realization that individuals must be protected from a variety of depredations, often committed in their own state by persons acting in an official capacity. Government policies are the preeminent cause of human rights violations today. Nonetheless, claims that national sovereignty excludes public scrutiny of a state's human rights practices are no longer accepted. Certain depredations become international concerns when committed through state policy due to the presumed international impact of such behavior. Collective action becomes necessary to protect persons against what are clearly seen to be policies that not only offend, but also threaten and harm, individuals who are now recognized actors within the world legal community.

The raft of international legal rules designed expressly to protect the rights of individual persons is impressive indeed. Far less impressive, however, is the enactment and enforcement of criminal proscriptions on the national level. This inadequacy does not come from any lack of significance attached to the right to be protected. Rather, it stems from the inability—or more accurately, the unwillingness—of governments to protect individuals under their jurisdiction. The upshot has been to transform a broad array of these protected rights into the status of internationally prohibited crimes, the prosecution of which the international community (as well as an individual government) acquires as a notable legal stake. (This process of international criminal law is addressed in chapter 7.)

The emergence of the conviction that certain principles of human rights must be observed has fostered new rules of general international law. Such rules stem from numerous international conventions in which states undertake obligations to implement these rules out of respect for human dignity. These undertakings by most governments substantiate the conclusion that new principles and rules are in force that meet with a consensus in international society and are obligatory even absent an express declaration that they merit full compliance. The critical transitional stage between public opinion and international legal rules in fashioning human rights law is the pervasive acceptance of such rights in multiple interstate agreements.

II

Functions and Processes

5

International Organizations

  ❧ The Role of International Organizations
  ❧ Future Trends of International Organizations
  ❧ Conclusion

The inviolability of UN headquarters is apparently not so inviolable when critical diplomatic situations are perceived by major powers. On February 12, 2004, Adolfo Aguilar Zinser, Mexico's former UN ambassador, revealed that the United States and the United Kingdom spied on UN delegations during 2003 when the Security Council was debating a resolution authorizing war against Iraq. The government of Chile, which then held one of ten rotating seats on the Security Council, averred (as did Mexico) that most of its UN mission telephones had been wiretapped in early 2003 during the prologue to war. Other states on the Security Council who might have been bugged include Guinea, Angola, Cameroon, and Pakistan. A former military translator, Katherine Gun, was accused in Great Britain of leaking a memo that said that the U.S. National Security Agency had initiated a "surge" of eavesdropping on six UN delegations with important swing votes in the Security Council. Gun, who was charged in the United Kingdom in a criminal case of violating British secrecy laws, confessed to leaking the January 31, 2003, memo because "it exposed serious illegality and wrongdoing on the part of the U.S. government, who attempted to subvert our own security services." The case against her was dismissed on February 25. The next day, Clare Short, a former member of Tony Blair's cabinet, publicly asserted in a BBC interview that she had seen transcripts that clearly indicated that British agents conducted surveillance on the office of UN Secretary-General Kofi Annan in New York during the intense diplomatic struggle over whether to invade Iraq. To exacerbate these revelations, Australian diplomat Richard Butler said on February 27 that his phones were routinely bugged during his tenure as chief UN weapons inspector for Iraq during the 1990s, and other sources indicated that the United States monitored former UN chief weapons inspector Hans Blix's mobile phone during his travels to Iraq. As expected, the United Nations reacted sharply to these allegations, asserting that any attempt by a government to eavesdrop on the Secretary-General's conversations would constitute a violation of international legal agreements that govern diplomatic relations. Foremost among these are the 1946 Convention on the Privileges and Immunities of the United Nations, the 1947 Headquarters

Agreement between the United Nations and the United States, and the 1961 Vienna Convention on Diplomatic Relations. These treaties ensure the inviolability of UN headquarters. "The premises of the United Nations shall be inviolable," declares article 3, section 9, of the 1947 agreement, which was ratified by both the United States and Great Britain. Moreover, it asserts that the United Nations' "property and assets . . . shall be immune" from any form of "interference, whether by executive, judicial or legislative action." If it is true that the United States and Great Britain conducted covert operations against these facilities, serious breaches of these international instruments were committed.

THE ROLE OF INTERNATIONAL ORGANIZATIONS

International organizations (IOs) function as intergovernmental political bodies and forums where representatives from states convene to discuss and negotiate issues involving their mutual political, social, and economic concerns. These multilateral bodies are sometimes viewed as arenas where governments in dispute trade accusations, where countries rhetorically lament and occasionally address disparities in socioeconomic situations, where states deliberate and discuss concerns over one another's conduct, and where parties discuss transnational problems and posit various solutions. From a cynical perspective, international organizations—the United Nations in particular—are often depicted as ineffective multilateral bureaucracies hobbled by waste, inefficiency, and mismanagement. Although a certain degree of truth resides in these impressions, none accurately reveals the whole picture, purposes, or activities of international organizations or their successes, nor do they suggest the broad truth that international organizations have emerged since World War II as the preeminent institutional source of international legal rules. In this regard, the United Nations system stands out as the main multilateral engine for creating international rules.

As formalized in their founding documents—usually called charters—the purposes of international organizations are to develop friendly relations among states; cooperate in solving international economic, social, cultural, and humanitarian problems; and promote respect for human rights and fundamental freedoms. To accomplish these objectives, member states resort to using these institutions and processes to make new international legal rules that address problems accrued from changing circumstances and political developments. This chapter examines the ways and means employed by IOs for creating international norms, rules, and processes that affect the behavior of states in their interstate relations. In so doing, the purposes and functions of these multilateral bodies as international lawmakers are evaluated, as are the institutions that perform those roles.

International Organization Legal Rules

International organizations play extensive, sophisticated roles as lawgivers to the international community. IOs create, amend, and implement international legal rules from a variety of sources for their member states. Yet, few observers truly appreciate or even acknowledge such contributions. IOs entail complex institutional arrangements, usually formed by several organs and agencies, many of which constantly remain engaged in making, codifying, and revising international legal rules. These rules are often pragmatic and highly utilitarian. They can be negotiated, adopted, adapted, and implemented more easily into the mainstream of international intercourse through the multilateral forums afforded by these organizations than they can by unilateral diplomacy and other such traditional means. This role of lawmaker often evolves into the creation of new legal norms—that is, those legal principles that are agreed on as "right" and proper actions, which have become binding on members of the international community and which serve to guide, control, and regulate proper and acceptable conduct among international actors.

Forms of International Organization Law

International organizations contribute substantially to international lawmaking by serving as sources, forums, and facilitators of the law-creating process. The rules, principles, and norms generated by multilateral bodies and processes primarily take the form of public international law, or, in other words, the law that concerns the structures, powers, and relations of international actors—most directly, its member states.

Rather than be merely procedural, public law created by IOs functions in mainly substantive ways. Legal rules created by IOs are chiefly designed to influence the essence and scope of the rights and obligations of member states, expressly to influence the conduct of interstate actions. In this regard, IO law can be broken down into three distinct forms. First, international organizations serve as a source of constitutional or regulatory law. The charter of an IO, in effect its constitution, embodies the fundamental law of the organization. The charter furnishes the body of rules and norms in accordance with which the powers of a multilateral body and its member states are exercised. The organization's charter strives to give lawful form to the institution, to set out the organization's legal structure, and to provide a legal framework through which the process of international organization might function authoritatively and effectively.

A second type of law created by IOs is prescriptive, or remedies, law. Such prescriptive law generally aims to lay down authoritative rules, set out written directives, or establish customary norms that must be followed. It consists of laws that impose obligations to do (or forbear from doing) certain things, the infraction of which is considered to be an offense not only against that IO but also against international society as a whole. Prescriptive laws may be backed up by punitive sanctions, which can be applied by the IO when certain charter norms and principles are egregiously breached.

Third, IOs supply a source for varieties of administrative law. International administrative law, as the name suggests, aims to manage or supervise the execution of international affairs. Such administrative law includes the rules and regulations governing the operation of the IO and its various agencies; the substantive and procedural rules that these agencies formulate and apply pursuant to their regulatory and other administrative functions; and relevant court decisions involving public agencies and states. Though little appreciated outside the organization itself, the body of law for administering internal IO affairs can be sophisticated and complex. This should not be surprising, however, since internal administrative law for the organization must oversee the operation of the organization, at home and in its activities abroad. For example, in the case of the United Nations, administrative law must cover its eight thousand permanent employees who work in more than forty agencies located in sixty-seven states. Comparatively, the European Union (EU) has 34,600 employees working to coordinate the application of law and policy in fifteen member states (and after 2004, at least twenty-five states).[1] The Organization of American States (OAS) has some six hundred employees who carry out its legal and functional matters in thirty-five member countries.

It is important to realize that these three forms of IO law are not exclusive to any organ or agency alone. Each body of an IO contains various rules and procedures that might be construed as being constitutional, prescriptive, and administrative in content. Moreover, most multilateral bodies have developed their own capabilities to generate new legal rules that might be construed as constitutional, prescriptive, and administrative in effect. The basic point here is that, in their various capacities, IOs act as international rule creators. Their potential as lawmakers is real and frequently realized. The kind of legal rule produced, however, remains dependent on the context, circumstances, and purposes of the law being created.

International Organizations as Constitutional Lawgivers

The charter of an international organization forms an instrument of international law.[2] As a multilateral agreement articulating principles and rules for the conduct of member states, an IO's charter becomes a viable contributor to the development of modern international law. These charters are significant for their profound influence on the dynamics of the international process for legal development. More than this, the lasting significance of a charter instrument lies in its scope and capacity for generating new legal principles and functional agencies, which in turn can produce further additions to international law.

The charter of an IO can establish a general, multipurpose organization or one dedicated to special tasks requiring mutual assistance.[3] It can also affirm the legally binding quality of key rules for member state conduct—among them, principles involving nonintervention, peaceful settlement of disputes, collaboration, the respect for various rights, the sovereign equality of states, and the duty of cooperation. But most charters go far beyond being statements of agreed principles and rules. They can actually authorize creation of an elaborate system of major organs and subsidiary agencies; numerous committees and commissions; and a nexus of cooperation between the central body and a network of specialized agencies, subsidiary organizations, and nongovernmental organizations throughout the world. The UN Charter, for instance, furnishes the fundamental constitutional law for operating the only general-purpose, universal organization in the world today, and for that reason, it holds a unique place among international legal instruments.

Each major organ in an IO significantly contributes to fashioning the rule of law among states. At the same time, IOs themselves remain products of international law. Their charters amount to legally binding multilateral agreements—international conventions—to which several member governments pledge their obligations with attendant rights and duties.[4] Perhaps the exemplar of this IO arrangement is the United Nations, which comprises six major organs: the General Assembly, the Security Council, the International Court of Justice, the Trusteeship Council, the Secretariat, and the Economic and Social Council. Each of these organs, to varying degrees, makes salient contributions to the international rule of law. As a constitutional instrument, the UN Charter legitimizes the authority, structure, and functions of these various UN components, a pattern that is generally replicated by analogous organs in other major multilateral organizations.

International Courts

Many IOs establish formal tribunals for resolving disputes among member states. For example, in the United Nations, the organ perhaps most visible for its role in affecting the international legal process is the International Court of Justice (ICJ). This court is the principal juridical arm of the United Nations, and its Statute remains an integral part of the Charter. By ratifying the Charter, governments perforce become obligated to accept the

ICJ's constitutional statute as well.[5] Through its deliberations, the ICJ clarifies the rule and role of international law between states. In the process, the court may interpret the legal implications of the UN Charter for the organization as well as for its membership. It also contributes to facilitating application of that constitutional law internationally.

The ICJ performs juridical duties independent of other UN organs and reaches decisions on the bases of international law, not international political considerations. Only governments of states may appear before such international tribunals, and decisions by these courts apply only to the governments involved. Importantly, international juridical decisions neither constitute nor rely on precedents, which traditionally bind a court's subsequent decisions. Generally speaking, international tribunals attached to IOs do not abide by the practice of *stare decisis;* rather, each decision rendered by a court is deliberated on an ad hoc basis, as determined by the facts of that particular case, without binding implications for future cases. Even so, international court decisions—especially those made by the ICJ—are widely recognized as important statements of existing international law, and they are often cited as authority to support fundamental principles or precepts of international legal development.

Decisions of the ICJ and most other international tribunals are final and binding, with no possibility of appeal. Such finality of a court's decision no doubt gives pause for governments and dissuades them from rushing to seek international juridical remedies for settling long-standing disputes. Persistent political stalemate has been viewed by governments as preferable to the possibility of losing in court. As a consequence, international tribunals in general—and the ICJ in particular—have assumed less than a notably active role in promoting an international juridical process. In the case of the ICJ, a total of one hundred cases have been submitted to the tribunal since 1946. Of those, the Court has rendered seventy-eight judgments on disputes concerning, among other issues, land frontiers and maritime boundaries; territorial sovereignty; the nonuse of force; noninterference in the internal affairs of states; diplomatic relations; hostage taking; the right of asylum; nationality; rights of passage; and economic rights. The ICJ has also rendered twenty-four advisory opinions since its creation, dealing with a variety of issues, such as admission to United Nations, reparation for injuries suffered in the service of the United Nations, the territorial status of South-West Africa (Namibia) and Western Sahara, judgments rendered by international administrative tribunals, the expenses of certain United Nations operations, the applicability of the United Nations Headquarters Agreement, the legality of the threat or use of nuclear weapons, and the legal consequences of Israel's constructing a barrier in the Palestinian-occupied territories.[6] In sum, that amounts to the Court's hearing an average of fewer than two cases each year. Yet, since 1993, the court has experienced a redirection in course by becoming especially active. As of late 2004, twenty-two cases are pending before the ICJ. This development suggests that governments are recognizing the value of impartial judicial settlement over the frustration produced by the protracted nonresolution of international disputes.[7]

The Court contributes directly and indirectly to international lawmaking. Many cases pertain to boundary disputes or disputes over jurisdiction in given areas—for example, offshore maritime claims and continental shelf delimitation. An ICJ decision determines the legal status of such territory. Hence, the Court furnishes a means for settling bilateral disputes lawfully, peacefully, with formal adversarial procedures. States are offered the opportunity to resolve their differences through the rule of law rather than through a resort to armed force. Importantly, each World Court decision directly contributes to the body of law regulating the specific behavior between the disputants. Moreover, certain principles set out in ICJ cases become adopted in state practice in general, which affects the application of international law beyond the scope of a particular case.

The United Nations recently expanded its juridical functions by creating *special international tribunals* that deal with violations of humanitarian law in the former Yugoslavia and in Rwanda. In 1993 the Security Council created the war crimes tribunal for the former Yugoslavia, a move that came in reaction to genocidal atrocities and ethnic cleansing perpetrated by Bosnian Serbs against Muslims in Bosnia-Herzegovina.[8] In the aftermath of eight hundred thousand Rwandans being massacred between April and July 1994, the Security Council acted similarly to set up a special tribunal to deal with persons accused of committing crimes against humanity and genocide in that tribally instigated bloodbath.[9] Both juridical bodies are ad hoc criminal courts created by Security Council resolutions. Modeled after the 1945 Nuremberg military tribunal, the decisions of both tribunals are legally binding. Unlike the ICJ, governments of states do not appear before these courts. Rather, these tribunals investigate, try, and prosecute individual persons who are accused of committing these heinous offenses. No death penalty can be imposed, however. While the jurisdiction and prosecutorial purpose of the Bosnian and the Rwandan tribunals are limited to criminal activities of individuals within those states, the success or failure of these courts will be viewed as indicators of the realistic prospects for success of the International Criminal Court activated in July 2002.

The European Union has also instituted a complex regional judicial system to rule on multilateral legal issues. Key to this process is the *Court of Justice of the European Communities*. Created in 1952 as the juridical institution of the EU, the Court of Justice ensures that community law is interpreted and applied in ways that are always identical for all EU member states, under all circumstances. Thousands of cases came before this tribunal over its first three decades. To cope with this influx and improve legal protections offered to European citizens, a Court of First Instance was created in 1989. This court is responsible for ruling on certain categories of cases in the first instance, particularly those relating to competition rules and actions brought by private individuals. Located in Luxembourg, the Court of Justice comprises fifteen judges—traditionally, one from each member state—who are appointed by joint agreement of member states' governments for a renewable term of six years. The main responsibility of the Court of Justice is to ensure that the law is observed in the interpretation and applications of the treaties establishing the European communities and of the provisions laid down by the competent community institutions. To be sure, the court has wide jurisdiction to hear various types of action and to give preliminary rulings.

A second court within the European Union is the *Court of Auditors*. Established in 1977 with the revision of the treaties' budgetary arrangements, this tribunal became a full-fledged institution with the implementation of the Treaty on European Union in 1993. Following the Treaty of Amsterdam in 1999, the Court of Auditors' auditing and investigative powers were broadened so that it could more effectively combat fraud against the community budget. Also seated in Luxembourg, this judicial body comprises fifteen members appointed by the Council for a renewable term of six years. The principal role of the Court of Auditors is to monitor the proper implementation of the EU budget.[10]

International Organizations as Prescriptive Lawgivers

International organizations contribute to international rule making by codifying certain principles of international law to regulate relations among states. Core among international legal instruments in this regard is the UN Charter, which sets out fundamental principles of contemporary international law. The two principal obligations considered most essential for states are, first, to refrain from the threat or use of force against other states or in any manner inconsistent with the purpose of the Charter, as contained in article 2 (4); and second, to settle disputes by peaceful means, as contained in article 33. These obligations are departures from international law's traditionally more permissive—or at least more ambiguous—attitude on the use of force. The charter aims to make those obligations universal among the UN membership, which today includes nearly all functioning states. While the means for enforcement and the degrees of state compliance with use-of-force provisions in the UN Charter are uneven and at times ineffective, these principles are still applied by the United Nations—in particular, by the Security Council—in considering disputes and in attempting to minimize interstate violence. Despite the remarkable growth in the number of states, increased frequency of state contact, and expanded sources of interstate tension over the past five decades, the scale and scope of international conflict has not approached the level of world war. While the United Nations' contribution to this trend is debatable, the prescriptive principles in the UN Charter clearly delineate the permissible legal parameters for using force in interstate relations.

The Security Council

Within the United Nations system—the core of international organizational activity—the chief responsibility for maintaining international peace and security falls to the Security Council. Per the UN Charter, the Security Council's main functions are to settle disputes peacefully (under Chapter VI) and to meet threats to or breaches of the peace with concerted action by the organization (Chapter VII). In carrying out these functions, the Security Council is empowered with the authority to make decisions binding on the entire UN membership. In accepting the Charter, each member state agrees that the Security Council may act on a state's behalf and that it will make decisions per its own discretion.[11] Legally, this means that certain Security Council resolutions are binding on all members of the United Nations, specifically those resolutions that contain action statements averring that "the Security Council decides that. . . ." Such resolutions are considered to be Security Council fiats, endowed with the binding force of legal obligation on member states as a whole.

Security Council resolutions that pertain to international disputes, threats to the peace, breaches of the peace, or acts of *aggression* are prescriptive and often carry the force of law, and members are expected to abide by those fiats. The scope of Security Council resolutions has been dramatized since 1990 by several *sanctions measures* enacted by the United Nations against transgressor states.[12] In the wake of the Cold War, Security Council policymakers viewed sanctions as more humane than military action but as a punitive instrument of international relations nonetheless. Throughout its history, the Security Council invoked collective sanctions as enforcement actions under Chapter VII only in fourteen cases: Afghanistan (1999–), Angola (1993–), Ethiopia and Eritrea (2000–2001), Haiti (1993–1994), Iraq (1990–2003), Liberia (1992–), Libya (1992–2003), Rwanda (1993–), Sierra Leone (1997–), Somalia (1992–), South Africa (1977–1994), Southern Rhodesia (1966–1979), Sudan (1996–2001), and the former Yugoslavia (1992–2002). As events and circumstances have changed, sanctions were fully lifted against Angola, Ethiopia and Eritrea, Haiti, South Africa, Southern Rhodesia, Sudan, and the former Yugoslavia. In the case of Libya, sanctions were lifted by the Security Council in September 2003 after Tripoli agreed to pay up to $10 million to each family of the 270 victims of the 1988 Lockerbie bombing. UN sanctions remain actively in force against Afghanistan, Liberia, Sierra Leone, Somalia, and Rwanda.

An important distinction exists between the obligation of a state to abide by a mandatory Security Council measure and that state's resultant compliance with it. Obligations flowing from certain Security Council resolutions are legally binding. They are deemed compulsory under international law. Yet, governments at times resist complying with those obligations. The reasons for such reluctance vary—from adverse international political pressure, to domestic economic considerations, to social or cultural inhibitions, and to perhaps even outright indifference. The fact remains, though, that the Security Council possesses the authority to create international law—to impose legally binding obligations acknowledged by all members—and that it has often done so over the past five decades. From its first meeting in 1945 through 2003, the Security Council has adopted over fifteen hundred resolutions, of which more than seven hundred qualify as binding law for the international community.[13] That is undoubtedly an impressive accomplishment, albeit one still underappreciated in the modern development of international law.

The *Council of the European Union*, the main decision-making body of the EU, contributes to multilateral rule making. As such, it embodies the member states, whose representatives convene regularly at the ministerial level. The Council exercises several key responsibilities that have prescriptive bearing on EU law. Foremost, it serves as the Union's legislative body; however, it fulfills its legislative power in concert with the European Parliament on a range of issues. The Council also concludes, on behalf of the EU, international agreements with one or more states or with international organizations; it takes the decisions necessary for framing and implementing the common foreign and security policy; and it coordinates the activities of member states and adopts measures pertaining to police and judicial cooperation in criminal matters. Finally, with respect to European rule making, the *European Commission* must be mentioned. This body, which is appointed by the fifteen member states after each commissioner is approved by the European Parliament, remains the driving force in the Union's institutional system. The Commission takes on several prescriptive functions, beginning with the right to initiate draft legislation and present legislative proposals to the parliament and to the council. Second, as the Union's executive body, the Commission is responsible for implementing the European legislation (directives, regulations, and decisions) as well as the budget and program adopted by parliament and the Council. Third, the Commission functions as the institutional guardian of EU treaties and, with the Court of Justice, seeks to ensure that European Community law is properly applied. Finally, the members of the Commission assume a direct role in international rule making, as they serve as international representatives of the Union to negotiate international agreements, most notably in the field of trade and multilateral cooperation.

Regarding law for the Americas, the *Permanent Council of the Organization of American States (OAS)* is empowered to consider, first, matters referred to it by its general assembly or by its ministers of foreign affairs; and, second, issues presented by the secretary-general, whether on hemispheric peace and security, or on the development of member states. The Permanent Council is composed of one representative from each member state and is delegated specific powers and functions, the most notable being the peaceful settlement of disputes and the Council's functions as the Organ of Consultation, per the Inter-American Treaty of Reciprocal Assistance. To facilitate its work, the Permanent Council may establish special committees and working groups. However, unlike the UN Security Council, it cannot issue legally binding decisions for the OAS membership.

The UN General Assembly

While the General Assembly might resemble a global parliament, it is clearly not a legislature per se. Save for budgetary and membership questions, the General Assembly lacks explicit authority to fashion, adopt, and implement binding legal norms or fiats on any of the United Nations membership without each government's sovereign consent. The authority to make or assert legal rules is not supplied to the General Assembly by the UN Charter, by any binding declaration, or by state practice. Still, the General Assembly does evoke a certain quasi-legislative capability that can directly influence the nature and substance of contemporary international law in several ways. As such, the General Assembly contributes to the body of prescriptive law furnished by the United Nations to the international community at large.

The lawful competence of the General Assembly to contemplate legal issues flows from the UN Charter. Article 10 gives the General Assembly the authority to discuss and adopt *resolutions*, which are in effect recommendations on any matter within the scope of the charter, either to the United Nations membership in general, or to the Security Council in particular.[14] The General Assembly is also responsible for initiating studies and making recommendations aimed at promoting international political cooperation and encouraging the progressive development of international law and its codification. Other General Assembly studies and recommendations relate to promoting international cooperation on economic, social, cultural, educational, and health matters, as well as efforts to secure human rights and fundamental freedoms without distinction as to race, sex, language, or religion.[15] Therefore, the General Assembly's power to recommend actions that enhance the norm-creating process of international law plainly serves a prescriptive purpose.

Formal consideration of international legal rules within the United Nations primarily falls to the General Assembly. In this regard, two principal bodies are used to encourage the progressive development and codification of the law of nations—namely, the *Sixth (Legal) Committee* of the General Assembly and the *International Law Commission*. The Sixth Committee is entrusted with the consideration of legal issues that are of concern to the Assembly. The Sixth Committee's current topics of concern include, among others, measures to eliminate terrorism, nonnavigational uses of international waters, activities of the UN Commission on International Trade Law, jurisdictional immunities of states and their property, and the safety and security of United Nations personnel.

The Sixth Committee makes its own reports on these topics. In addition, the Sixth Committee is responsible for examining reports on legal matters to the General Assembly from other UN bodies. The Sixth Committee, moreover, can draft texts of international conventions, which are then presented to member states in the General Assembly for approval. Perhaps most notable among the products of this drafting process is the 1948 Convention on the Prevention and Punishment of the Crime of Genocide.[16]

The International Law Commission (ILC), comprising thirty-four jurists, remains prominent in the General Assembly's efforts to promote the codification of international law. The ILC functions as a study and composition group to discuss, design, and draft international conventions. These conventions are then submitted for debate in the General Assembly and are usually presented to the international community for consideration as multilateral agreements.

While the ILC's "codification" endeavors are admirable, they are often criticized for being tedious and overly ponderous.[17] To complete many agreements, the treaty-drafting process alone often exceeds a decade, an excessively prolonged period for negotiating the text of an international instrument, given this era of globalization and spectacularly rapid scientific and technological advancement. By way of illustration, the question of state responsibility has preoccupied the ILC's attention since 1953, albeit with only mixed success at producing agreed-on conclusions on the law and its relevance for state behavior.[18] Similarly, the ILC considered and worked for nearly five decades on a Draft Code of Offenses Against the Peace and Security of Mankind,[19] as well as on a Draft Statute for an International Criminal Court (see chapter 7).[20] Still, the ILC has produced a number of successful draft instruments, among them the four 1958 Geneva Conventions on the Law of the Sea;[21] the 1961 Vienna Convention on Diplomatic Relations;[22] the 1969 Vienna Convention on the Law of Treaties;[23] and the 1973 Convention on the Prevention and Punishment of Crimes Against Internationally Protected Persons, Including Diplomatic Agents.[24] The ILC also produced the 1978 Convention on the Succession of States in Respect of Treaties,[25] as well as its companion instrument, the 1978 Convention on the Succession of States in Respect of State Property, Archives, and Debts,[26] although the latter is not yet in force.

Perhaps the General Assembly's most salient role in shaping prescriptive law derives from its right to formulate and adopt international resolutions, as delegated by article 10 in the Charter. From 1945 through the fifty-eighth session in 2004, the General Assembly adopted at least 11,359 resolutions, spanning a vast and varied range of international issues.[27] While this record of the General Assembly's formal concern, deliberation, and articulation of views is admittedly impressive, the fact remains that, except for budget and membership questions, General Assembly resolutions are *not* legally binding on member states. These resolutions are only recommendations—and thus only advisory and hortatory measures—without any specific legally binding authority attached. The General Assembly may draft, approve, and recommend international instruments for multilateral agreement. The Assembly cannot, however, compel them as binding obligations on member states. The General Assembly performs as a political organ in its deliberations. It was never intended to be a world legislature for authorizing resolute actions or for imposing legally binding remedies on its membership.

Although the legal status of General Assembly resolutions is unmistakably nonbinding, these instruments have frequently served as the genesis for subsequent multilateral treaties drafted and promulgated under UN auspices. General Assembly "declarations," largely because of their bold and assertive quality, contain the greatest likelihood of evolving into conventions adopted by the international community. Prominent among the many conventions dealing with the use of force that grew out of UN General Assembly declarations are the 1967 Outer Space Treaty,[28] the 1968 Treaty on the Nonproliferation of Nuclear Weapons,[29] and the 1971 Seabed Arms Control Treaty.[30] Also noteworthy is that practically all of the international law pertaining to outer space has evolved from resolutions deliberated on and produced by the General Assembly's Committee on the Peaceful Uses of Outer Space, which were then adopted by the General Assembly and which subsequently gave rise to appropriate international conventions.[31]

A vast number of agreements on human rights have also originated from General Assembly resolutions. The General Assembly's concern for human rights is long-standing and clearly evident in the Universal Declaration on Human Rights, adopted without formal opposition in 1948.[32] Similarly, General Assembly resolutions were instrumental catalysts for producing, in 1966, two cornerstones of modern human rights law: the International Covenant on Civil and Political Rights[33] and the International Covenant on Economic, Social, and Cultural Rights.[34] No less impressive, though, is the panoply of additional human rights law to which the General Assembly contributed over the past three decades. Promoted by General Assembly resolutions, major international conventions have been promulgated to prohibit all forms of racial discrimination,[35] suppress and punish the crime of *apartheid*,[36] eliminate discrimination against women,[37] protect the rights of the child,[38] prohibit hostage taking,[39] and outlaw torture.[40]

General Assembly resolutions have contributed to clearly defining certain general principles of international law for state practice. Indeed, perhaps the most detailed expression outlining the international legal obligations of states is supplied by General Assembly resolution 2625, the 1970 Declaration of Principles of Law Concerning Friendly Relations and Cooperation among States.[41] General Assembly resolutions articulate and reify important legal principles that strive to keep pace with the transforming character of the international system and the emergence since 1960 of nearly 140 new independent states. There is no doubt that resolutions adopted by the General Assembly substantially contribute to reaffirming the legitimate authority of nondiscrimination, nonaggression, self-determination, and decolonization as accredited principles of international law. Also significant is that General Assembly resolutions are used by developing countries as vehicles to introduce new concepts to the international community that eventually aim at attaining the status of general principles of international law. Outstanding among such precepts that have recently developed into legal principles are the common heritage of humankind,[42] the criminalization of apartheid,[43] and permanent sovereignty over natural resources.[44]

The United Nations' General Assembly is not a world legislature. As such, it cannot make international rules or statutes. It does not codify international laws or norms through its resolutions, even if they are adopted unanimously, repeatedly, or without any formal opposition. General Assembly resolutions are merely recommendations. But declarations by the General Assembly can function as instruments to distill and crystallize into tangible form the international community's consensus regarding a customary norm. Through such a distillation–crystallization procedure, the resolution is presented to the international community for its acceptance or rejection. State practice, then, becomes the main factor determining whether General Assembly resolutions give rise to new norms of international law or remain merely recommendations for action. Such new norms are subsequently codified into recognized principles of international law through the promulgation of special conventions adopted by the General Assembly and then ratified by the requisite number of parties.

The European Union

Within the European Community, the European Parliament functions as the regional legislature for nearly 375 million Europeans. Elected every five years by direct universal suffrage, the European Parliament has three essential functions. First, it shares with the Council of the European Union the power to legislate—that is, to adopt European laws (directives, regulations, and decisions). This involvement in the legislative process helps to ensure the democratic legitimacy of the legal texts adopted. Second, the Parliament shares budgetary authority with the Council and can therefore influence EU spending. At the end of the procedure, it adopts the budget in its entirety. Third, the Parliament exercises democratic supervision over the Commission and exercises political supervision over all the institutions.

The Organization of American States

The key agency in the Organization of American States (OAS) for sponsoring international legal instruments and formal declarations is the Secretariat for Legal Affairs and, within it, the Inter-American Juridical Committee and the Department of International Law. The Inter-American Juridical Committee advises the OAS on juridical matters and promotes the progressive development and codification of international law. The Department of International Law facilitates the work of the Juridical Committee. Importantly, since 1948 these agencies have facilitated the adoption and implementation of at least seventy-one binding legal instruments on those OAS members who ratify them. Included among these are conventions concerning territorial asylum, the rights and duties of states in civil strife, protection of human rights, the general rules of private international law, the prevention of torture, the adoption of minors, the international return of children, the protection of national archeological and historical heritage, mutual assistance in criminal matters, abolition of the death penalty, illicit trafficking in firearms and explosives, and the facilitation of disaster assistance.

International Organizations as Administrative Lawgivers

Administrative law is generally regarded as law concerning the powers and procedures of administrative agencies, especially law that governs judicial review of administrative action. Administrative law thus aims at several objectives: to resolve particular controversies over discretionary administrative powers; to search for means to obtain justice; to reconcile desires for freedom with demands for good governance; and to formulate policies that reflect the democratic will. In essence, then, administrative law within the UN system treats law that concerns powers, procedures, and judicial review that affect United Nations administrative agencies.

In these regards, the United Nations contributes to the formulation of international administrative law in three special ways: first, through the administrative duties and operation of the Secretariat in general, and of the Secretary-General in particular, as the coordinator of internal UN law and as a good officer for international dispute settlement; second, through the successful administrative experience of the Trusteeship Council in preparing non-self-governing territories for their eventual independence; and, third, through the Economic and Social Council and administration of its appended specialized agencies. Clearly, though, it is the Secretariat that performs the hallmark administrative legal function for the UN system.

The Secretariat

Administrative legal functions affecting the entire body of an IO are performed substantially by the secretariat. The role of the Secretariat in creating international law is multifaceted. Headed by a secretary-general, the Secretariat generally engages in promoting agreement among governments through quiet diplomacy, good offices, and reconciliation of national differences over international legal concerns. For example, establishing and maintaining UN peacekeeping missions require the UN Secretary-General to play a pivotal role as administrator and diplomat.

The Secretariat remains constantly involved in numerous international negotiations having legal purpose or intent. For example, peacekeeping, refugee relief, humanitarian aid programs, and technical assistance projects are all processed through and administered by offices in the Secretariat, with legal accountability devolving to the respective oversight agencies. Also of great significance, the Secretariat is responsible for planning and coordinating meetings and international conferences sponsored annually under the auspices of an international organization. These conferences, which nearly always involve scores of governments negotiating issues of international legal concern, can generate new "hard" international law in the form of binding international conventions negotiated and opened for signature.[45] Or, as is often the case of UN meetings, new "soft" international law is produced in the form of formal declarations, action plans, or conference statements.[46] While not legally binding, such instruments still retain normative value by demonstrating the range of international opinion, the strength of consensus on a particular issue, and the degree of influence a state has via its behavior.

A chief function of an IO secretariat is to facilitate resolution of controversies and disputes between governments of member states. In performing this role, secretariat personnel are often called on to serve as mediators, conciliators, or consensus builders—all processes that can contribute to the peaceful settlement of international disputes and hence the rule of law. By way of example, the UN Secretariat (and Secretary-General) actively worked to negotiate a cease-fire for the Iran–Iraq War (1988) as well as to end conflicts in Afghanistan (1989), Cyprus (1967), Namibia (1990), the Falkland Islands (1982), Lebanon (1982), Cambodia (1990), and the former Yugoslavia (1994). Through quiet diplomacy, the Secretary-General can play a pivotal role in international dispute settlement. By so doing, he contributes to peaceful relations between states and thereby permits international law to more effectively influence the mutual relations of the disputants.

As regards international law, the UN Secretariat serves as an officially designated world depository for international agreements. More than forty-five thousand international treaties, conventions, and other international instruments are registered with the UN Secretariat—a realization that highlights the scope and depth of international legal relations today. Further, the *United Nations Treaty Series* is an authoritative registry of international legal agreements, and for most governments that fact contributes to the authoritative legitimacy of those instruments.

As an administrative legal body, the Secretariat supplies information and advice to member governments on a variety of subjects. Such power of information can have substantial influence on shaping the attitudes of member states toward international legal questions and issues. It is not surprising, then, that the UN General Assembly often requests that the Secretary-General prepare reports, studies, or policy analyses of particular questions under consideration. Such reports carry the weight of institutional legitimacy and political impartiality.

The Secretariat is also responsible for administering the rule of law inside the organization. For example, in the case of the United Nations, there are more than eight thousand employees. Such a high degree of interpersonal contacts cannot help but create interpersonal conflicts, grievances, and at times even criminal activities among an IO's population. It falls to the Secretariat to administer internal law to settle grievances and criminal activities throughout the organization—law that ensures that due process is carried out, with hearings, prosecutions, and penalties imposed to fit the crime.

The Trusteeship Council

Unique to the United Nations, the Trusteeship Council was created as an original UN organ in the Charter to administer and supervise non-self-governing territories for which the United Nations was given responsibility after World War II.[47] In the five decades since the Trusteeship Council began functioning, all of these trusteeship territories either gained their independence or were assimilated into other states. The last remnant of the UN trusteeship system—the small island of Palau, which had been part of the United States Strategic Trust Territory in the Pacific—gained its independence in 1994 and is now a member state of the United Nations.[48] As a consequence, the Trusteeship Council by its very success has been rendered defunct, as its main purpose has been fully accomplished.

Though often slighted among UN institutions, the Trusteeship Council actually carried out a cardinal function of international law—the creation of new international legal actors. The Trusteeship Council was responsible for preparing, as new legal actors, former colonies and post–League of Nations mandates—that is, states with the capability of participating in the international legal system as independent, sovereign, self-governing polities. The Council successfully performed its mission, as patently evidenced by the impressive list of states that emerged as the direct result of its administrative legal oversight: Jordan, Israel, Syria, Cameroon, Rwanda, Burundi, Tanzania (with Zanzibar), Togo, Nauru, Papua New Guinea, Somalia, Namibia, the Marshall Islands, Micronesia, Northern Marianas, and Western Samoa—all were trust territories that attained independence under the administrative legal oversight of the Trusteeship Council.

International Organizations and Socioeconomic Concerns

Many IOs have a special body dedicated to formulating policy initiatives for alleviating economic and social problems. In the United Nations, for instance, there is the Economic and Social Council (ECOSOC). This body is composed of fifty-four members elected by the General Assembly, and it focuses its concern on international economic, social, cultural, educational, and health matters. ECOSOC consequently engages in a range of studies dealing with international legal issues including, *inter alia*, narcotic drug control, water use, trade, refugees, the environment, status of women, and so forth. Importantly, though, ECOSOC has the authority only to recommend. It reports and makes recommendations to the General Assembly. The real lawmaking significance of ECOSOC rests in its administrative links to the specialized agencies. It is through these sixteen functional agencies, as well as through the International Atomic Energy Agency and the General Agreement on Tariffs and Trade, that a vast amount of international law is proposed and codified for member states. In this regard, the ECOSOC acts as a coordinating agent for much of the UN system, with attendant administrative and oversight legal responsibilities.[49]

Under the European Union, the *Economic and Social Committee (ESC)* is the advisory body for ensuring that the various economic and social interest groups—for example, employers, trade unions, farmers, and consumers—are represented in the institutional framework of the European Union. The ESC, founded in 1957 by the Treaty of Rome, has evolved into a forum for dialogue and an institutional stage that allows groups involved in Europe's economic and social life the opportunity to be an integral part of the community's decision-making process. Through its opinions, the ESC contributes to defining and implementing EU policies, and functions as an institutional bridge between Europe and its citizens. When the Treaty of Maastricht entered into force in 1993, the ESC attained a status similar to that of the other institutions, especially with regard to its rules of procedure and budget. In 1997, the Treaty of Amsterdam significantly broadened the ESC's scope of action, especially in social matters. Regarding functions, the Economic and Social Committee has three roles. First, it advises the three main institutions—the Council of the European Union, the European Commission, and (since the Treaty of Amsterdam) the European Parliament. Second, it works to promote greater civil commitments to the European Union endeavor, with the aims of fostering more civic participation, leading to a more democratic society. Third, the ESC functions to enhance the role of civic groups and associations in non–European Community countries, which it does through public dialogues and discussions. In sum, the ESC advises only on economic and social concerns. It does not make new laws for the EU or for its member states.

In the Organization of American States (OAS), considerable effort focuses on providing technical support for economic integration efforts, working with the Inter-American Development Bank and the United Nations Economic Commission for Latin America and the Caribbean to create a Free Trade Area of the Americas agreement by 2005, as mandated under the Summit of the Americas process. The OAS pays special attention to ensure that the concerns of smaller economies are taken into account. Notwithstanding the value of these agencies, the principal organ for promoting social and economic development through the OAS structure is the *Inter-American Agency for Cooperation and Development (IACD)*. The IACD was established in early 2000 to promote new and more effective forms of cooperation among OAS member states and to enhance partnerships with the private sector and civil society. Headquartered in Washington, D.C., the agency is governed by a nine-member Management Board of officials selected from among the member states, as well as by an administrative arm—the Executive Secretariat for Integral Development. Together, the Board and the Secretariat manage all technical cooperation and training activities of the OAS.

The main aim of the IACD is to tap the considerable capabilities of OAS member states and legally forge new private- and public-sector partnerships to assist people in the Americas to overcome poverty, benefit from the digital revolution, and advance their economic and social development. A Special Multilateral Fund, composed of the annual voluntary contributions of member state governments, is the principal grant-making instrument of the Inter-American Council for Integral Development for technical cooperation projects. The fund provides grant financing for both multicountry and national projects in the areas of education, science and technology, environment, social and cultural development, economic integration and employment, and the strengthening of democracy. Since 1999 over $75 million in grant funding has been delivered to support more than four hundred projects through the fund. Significantly, each of these technical cooperation projects is the product of various international legal arrangements, formalized through special international legal agreements.

Specialized Agencies

For the United Nations, the importance of ECOSOC is amplified by the specialized agencies that operate within its jurisdictional purview. Significantly, each functional agency proceeds under its own international charter or constitution. In acting as an independent body, each agency has its own institutions, membership, rules, procedures, and lawmaking capability. Consequently, each agency functions lawfully as a separate administrative organization with responsibility over its own internal affairs and legal dealings. Some specialized agencies are technical organizations and convene their own meeting sessions, deliberate policies, take decisions, and negotiate and draft international legal agreements that address particular problems of concern. For each functional agency, however, the ability to create and administer international legal rules is essential. Some brief comment on the agencies reveals the broad scope and reach of their international lawmaking capacity.

The Food and Agriculture Organization (FAO) was established in 1945 to raise nutritional levels and living standards and to secure improvements in the production and distribution of food and agricultural products. With a membership of 187 states and one organization (the European Community), the FAO has negotiated numerous recommendations, codes, and institutional arrangements to deal with the changing place of food, fisheries, forests, and agriculture in international relations.[50]

The International Bank for Reconstruction and Development (or the World Bank) was established in 1945 to provide loans and technical assistance for economic development in developing countries.[51] The World Bank facilitates capital investment and cofinancing of projects from public and private sources. Bilateral lending agreements made between the World Bank and its membership of 184 states are legally binding and often place conditions on recipient states (see chapter 11).[52]

The International Development Association, created in 1960 and affiliated with the World Bank, provides funds for development on concessional terms to developing countries. Transactions between the association and recipient states are regarded as legally binding agreements.[53]

Established in 1956 as a separate legal entity, the International Finance Corporation strives to promote economic development by encouraging the growth of productive enterprise and private capital investment in developing countries.[54]

The International Civil Aviation Organization (ICAO), formally established in 1947, promotes standards and regulations for international civil aviation.[55] ICAO has accomplished much to produce standards for aircraft safety and operation measures, as well as to devise uniform regulations affecting meteorological services, air traffic control, communications, radio beacons, and search-and-rescue operations. In this way, ICAO contributes to simplifying customs, immigration and public health regulations as they apply to international air transport by its 188 contracting states. Among its array of international legal activities, ICAO has drafted more than fifty international air law agreements, among them the 1944 Warsaw Convention on International Civil Aviation, the 1963 Convention on Offences and Certain Other Acts Committed on Board Aircraft, the 1970 Convention for the Suppression of Unlawful Seizure of Aircraft, and the 1991 Convention on the Marking of Plastic Explosives for the Purpose of Detection.[56]

The International Fund for Agricultural Development since 1976 has worked to mobilize additional funds for agricultural development projects in developing countries through projects and programs that benefit the poorest rural populations.[57] As of 2005, at least 163 states are formally participating in the fund's activities.[58]

The International Labor Organization (ILO) promotes employment and improves living standards to obtain greater social justice. The ILO was created in 1919 as part of the League of Nations under the Treaty of Versailles and was incorporated into the United Nations in 1946.[59] With 177 member states, the ILO has promulgated at least 182 conventions and nearly two hundred formal recommendations over the past five decades. Significantly, governments have changed some 2,230 national laws and practices in response to concerns raised by ILO supervisory bodies.[60]

The International Maritime Organization (IMO), formerly known as the Inter-Governmental Maritime Consultative Organization, was established expressly to provide advisory and consultative assistance, as well as international cooperation, in maritime navigation.[61] Today considerable efforts are made by IMO's 164 member states and thirty-five participating intergovernmental organizations to promote the highest standards for safety and navigation, as well to devise and implement international restrictions on vessel-source pollution of the high seas. To those ends, since its inception in 1958, IMO has adopted more than fifty binding multilateral agreements, of which thirty-eight are still in force for those state parties.[62]

The International Monetary Fund (IMF) was established in 1945 to promote international monetary cooperation, expansion of trade, and currency and exchange stability.[63]

Much of the IMF's activity since 1990 has involved loans and the rescheduling of debt payments to member states, often with strict conditions of austerity and reform measures. Significantly, each international agreement made between the IMF and its 184 member states constitutes a set of specified binding legal obligations.[64]

The International Telecommunications Union (ITU), oldest among the specialized agencies, began in 1865 and was formally integrated into the UN system in 1947.[65] Its purposes are many: to establish international regulations for radio, telegraph, telephone, and space radio-communications, as well as to allocate radio frequencies among its 189 state parties and per its numerous ancillary agreements.[66]

The United Nations Educational, Scientific, and Cultural Organization (UNESCO) was established in 1945. As its lofty ambition, UNESCO seeks to promote collaboration among its 190 member states through education, science, and culture to further justice, the rule of law, and human rights and freedoms without distinction to race, sex, language, or religion.[67] Since its founding, UNESCO has promulgated hundreds of recommendations and resolutions, as well as twenty-two international standard-setting agreements, among them the 1952 Universal Copyright Convention, the 1954 Convention for the Protection of Cultural Property in the Event of Armed Conflict, the 1971 Ramsar Convention on Wetlands of International Importance Especially as Waterfowl Habitat, and the 2001 Convention on the Protection of the Underwater Cultural Heritage.

Since being established in 1985, the United Nations Industrial Development Organization (UNIDO) has designed and implemented programs to support and facilitate the industrialization of developing countries.[68] As of late 2004, 171 states serve as formal parties to UNIDO's development activities.[69]

The Universal Postal Union (UPU), established in 1874, became a specialized agency in 1947 and operates to facilitate reciprocal exchange of correspondence by setting uniform procedures and speeding up mailing procedures.[70] The UPU entails the largest physical distribution network in the world. More than six million postal employees work in over seven hundred thousand postal outlets to ensure that some 430 billion mail items are processed and delivered each year throughout the world. The UPU is truly universal, currently claiming 190 states as members, setting the rules for international mail exchanges, and making recommendations to coordinate mail flow and improve the quality of service for customers.[71]

The World Health Organization (WHO) was established in 1948 to aid the attainment by all peoples of the highest levels of health.[72] Much of WHO's efforts coordinate disease control and proffer medical assistance to needy states among its 192 members.[73] Since 1990, the WHO has focused considerable attention on controlling the spread of the AIDS virus, the deadly Ebola viruses, and the SARS (severe acute respiratory syndrome) pandemic, as well as drafting a Framework Convention on Tobacco Control.[74]

The World Intellectual Property Organization (WIPO) was created in 1970, although its origins trace back to the International Bureau of Paris Union (1883) and the Berne Union (1886).[75] WIPO seeks to promote international cooperation among its 181-member governments for the legal protection of *intellectual property*, which includes artistic and scientific works, sound recordings, broadcasts, inventions, trademarks, industrial designs, and company names.[76] Importantly, WIPO administers some twenty-three treaties in the field of intellectual property, including the Convention for the Protection of Literary and Artistic Works, the Hague Agreement Concerning the International Deposit of Industrial Designs, and the Strasbourg Agreement Concerning the International Patent Classification.

The World Meteorological Organization (WMO) aims to improve and coordinate international meteorological work.[77] WMO does so by promoting international exchange of weather reports and greater standardization of observations among its 187 member states. In addition, WMO coordinates global scientific activity to allow increasingly prompt and accurate weather information and other services for public, private, and commercial use, including international airline and shipping industries. As well, it offers special weather services to developing countries for their own economic needs.[78]

Though not a specialized agency, the International Atomic Energy Agency (IAEA) was established in 1956 to promote the peaceful uses of atomic energy and to ensure that its assistance is not used for military purposes.[79] The IAEA functions to foster scientific and technical cooperation in the peaceful use of nuclear technology. In so doing, it often serves as an enforcement agent to inspect facilities in its 137 member states to prevent proliferation of nuclear weapons.[80] The IAEA sponsored at least twenty binding international agreements, among them the Convention on Early Notification of a Nuclear Accident, the Convention on Assistance in the Case of a Nuclear Accident or Radiological Emergency, the Convention on Physical Protection of Nuclear Material, and the Vienna Convention on Civil Liability for Nuclear Damage.

Also outside the family of UN functional agencies, the *General Agreement on Tariffs and Trade (GATT)* was established in 1947 to set rules for world trade and to provide a multilateral forum for discussing trade-related issues.[81] GATT is not, however, a legally recognized international organization—that is, international law does not recognize GATT, although the organization does at times function as an international ad hoc agency. As revised in 1994 and now in force, GATT operates to facilitate negotiation of liberalized trade policies and resolution of trade disputes through the World Trade Organization.[82] Today, at least 148 states are legally bound to these new dispute-settlement provisions (see chapter 11).

FUTURE TRENDS OF INTERNATIONAL ORGANIZATIONS

The activities of international organizations clearly influenced the establishment of international legal order over the past five decades, and they no doubt will continue to do so. Regarding the progressive development of constitutional law, efforts by IOs will likely create a considerable body of soft law for guiding state behavior in global environmental matters. The likelihood is that the United Nations will serve as the proving ground for establishing certain concepts as general principles of law through the repeated adoption of resolutions by the General Assembly and by special ad hoc conferences. Among environmental concepts that seem ripe for such attention are the "polluter pays" principle, the principle of good neighborliness, and the notion of sustainable development. Governments have manifest national interests in protecting and conserving the earth's environment for future use, and IOs can be readily employed to formulate international legal norms toward those ends. Nonetheless, transforming these concepts from nonbinding soft law to principles of binding hard law is not tantamount to states accepting and implementing them. Such processes require much higher ambition.

One constitutional law consideration likely to confront the United Nations in the future is the composition of the Security Council. Political pressures are evident for the Security Council's membership to be expanded, in particular its number of permanent members. Candidates for permanent status have been suggested, ostensibly states that, since 1960, have acquired a certain preeminent status in the international community. Included in this group are Germany and Japan, as well as the developing countries Brazil, India, Indonesia, and Nigeria. The argument put forward is that the world community has changed appreciably since 1945, but the composition of the Security Council has not kept pace with those developments. Certain Great Powers are now not-so-great, and certain other states have ascended to power greatness. Hence, the conclusion follows that the time has come to alter the composition of the Security Council by adding more members with the veto power, a scenario made feasible by amendment of the UN Charter.

Whether such a change can take place depends on the political will of the present permanent members. Amendment of the Charter constitutes a substantive question. Accordingly, for such a change to pass, a two-thirds majority of the Security Council—that is, nine of fifteen votes—must be secured, in which no permanent member casts a negative vote. Whether such a majority can be secured seems dubious—particularly since, by doing so, the current Great Powers would be diluting their very power on the Council.

The future course of IO-derived prescriptive law for member states' conduct seems more problematic. In the area of prescriptive law, issues likely to command the future attention of the IOs—in particular, the UN Security Council—include imposing measures against governments who violate the nonproliferation of nuclear arms, setting stronger prohibitions against chemical and biological weapons, and fixing controls on the export of missile technology. No doubt, too, the Security Council will remain concerned with transnational terrorism as well as with threats to the peace and with breaches of peace. But the Council may well exercise more restraint in voting to authorize UN peacekeeping missions to resolve internal conflicts. Such missions are too financially costly for the United Nations: In late 2004, at least $ 2.48 billion remained unpaid by member states for peacekeeping efforts since 1990, a sum that threatens to bankrupt the entire UN organization. Even more ominous perhaps are the political costs associated with the loss of men, women, and national treasure, particularly by the Great Powers on the Security Council. The tensions in 2003 between the United States and France over the legal authority to invade Iraq may have seriously damaged the Security Council's ability to respond to future international crises. These developments erode the domestic backing necessary to portray UN support as being in the national interest of those states.

While IOs, especially the United Nations, will surely attempt to establish more prescriptive norms to meet new threats to the peace, the critical issue still hinges on compliance and enforcement. When certain governments fail or refuse to comply with punitive norms affecting peace and security, how should the United Nations react? The key, of course, lies in the composition and political will of the Security Council and the ability of the Great Powers to act resolutely and in concert to enforce sanctions against a state committing a threat to, or a breach of, the peace. If the past is prologue, reaction by the Security Council is likely to be calculated more on political considerations than as a resolute response to a grave breach of international law. Such is the price of having five potential vetoes on the Council.

A positive indication of the rule of law, especially regarding prescriptive law creation, is the increasing tendency of national governments to use international tribunals to punish individuals for committing genocidal atrocities and to utilize the International Court of Justice to resolve bilateral disputes between states. This trend seems likely to persist, so long as governments perceive that these tribunals act fairly and impartially in reaching decisions on cases.

Finally, the administrative law generated by IOs appears likely to expand as international trade and commerce continue to grow. Regional trade agreements and new common market arrangements will continue to evolve. The GATT, augmented by activities of its World Trade Organization and expanding international commercial dealings, will surely require readjustments and innovations in the formulation and implementation of new international legal rules to meet changing circumstances.

CONCLUSION

International organizations in general and the United Nations in particular contributed substantially to shaping the international legal order throughout the last half of the 20th century. The UN Charter provides a set of values for the international system in its preamble, where "the people" reaffirm their "faith in fundamental human rights" and "in the equal rights of men and women and of nations large and small," with the determination "to promote social progress and better standards of life in larger freedom." The fundamental "purposes and principles" in the Charter express international concern over the need to suppress acts of aggression and to support principles of international law, peaceful settlement, and international cooperation. In sum, the Charter codifies normative constructs into hard legal principles for directing interstate behavior. Even so, critical problems remain regarding the political will of states to mind and enforce those legal principles.

As a universal intergovernmental organization, the United Nations is likely to maintain its impressive record as the main seedbed for germinating new rules and norms of international law. The body provides a global forum for negotiating and drafting international agreements that address emerging problems of international law. It furnishes opportunities for governments to exchange ideas and positions on almost any issue affecting interstate relations, and it offers lawful channels for national governments to seek peaceful redress for any grievances that might be inflicted by some other government.

In the end, however, the contributions made by IOs to create legal rules for a just and lasting international order ultimately depend on the political will of their member states to accept and make those rules work. Put simply, states create legal rules through international organizations; states break these rules in spite of their commitments; and states often must enforce the law through multilateral organizations, especially the United Nations. But neither IOs nor the United Nations should be viewed as magic bullets capable of producing international justice and righteousness. Rather, these organizations constitute political bodies that operate through political means, often for political purposes. Hence, international law created through the United Nations and other international organizations can only be as strong as their member states are willing to make them—which is a powerful concept, given the Great Powers on the Security Council.

Legal rules developed through the United Nations system and other IOs are manifestly intended to function for the benefit of the member states. But these laws can only function with the genuine cooperation and diplomatic perseverance by the governments of those same states. For intergovernmental international organizations, as well as for each of the current 193 states in the world community, global cooperation will remain the predominant challenge in determining the effectiveness of the contemporary legal order in the years to come.

6

Agreements and Disputes

    ❦ International Agreements
    ❦ Peaceful Settlement of Disputes
    ❦ Conclusion

The UN Charter is the preeminent multilateral agreement negotiated since the end of the Second World War to found an international organization. But in the aftermath of the 2003 Iraq War and unilateral U.S. intervention, UN officials are seriously considering whether to permit the UN Charter to be radically changed to allow for preventive interventions; otherwise, the UN risks becoming a secondary player on the international scene. It appears clear that the need for Charter reform is real, since the UN framework of principles and practices concerning the use of force is being challenged as unsuitable and inadequate to meet the threats posed by terrorism and weapons of mass destruction as well as the constant tension between concern for human rights and the respect for sovereignty. The main question UN member states must answer is whether the traditional concept of self-defense is obsolete and needs to be redefined within the UN Charter to allow the preventive use of force. Does the world community share a moral responsibility or obligation to intervene into a state where massive human rights violations are occurring? If so, what should delineate the grounds for such an intervention? A high-level panel appointed in 2004 by UN Secretary-General Kofi Annan to study UN reform must resolve issues concerning how international cooperation can be strengthened to combat terrorism and the proliferation of weapons of mass destruction. The real challenge, however, lies in getting the 191 UN members to agree to those treaty changes that Annan recommends. In any event, the role of the United States will be crucial for a successful reform effort. Many American government officials believe that, as set out in the 1945 UN Charter, the Security Council has an anachronistic structure and that the best role for the world body lies in postconflict and in humanitarian situations. They further contend that unilateral action by the United States and other major powers seems likely in the face of continued UN "failures," such as the organization's handling of Bosnia, Iraq, Kosovo, and East Timor. It therefore becomes the duty of individual states to address those critical issues of terrorism and weapons of mass destruction, given the lack of consensus within the Security Council. In the same vein, U.S. officials argue that the United Nations must be more decisive in dealing with the questions of humanitarian interventions and human rights when governments are corrupt and when they violate the human rights of their citizens. The administration of George W. Bush signaled in 2004 its preference for a more certain model for conflict intervention that permits individual states to take the lead with the United Nations playing a vital and important follow-up role. Such a scenario was already played out successfully in East Timor and Sierra Leone, where Australia and the United Kingdom, respectively, took the initiative to intervene and were backed up with UN support. Moreover, preemptive and preventive attacks might be necessary to obviate possible threats to individual states' security interests. Yet, many other governments express concern that unless norms for preemptive or preventive war are enshrined in an amended UN Charter, international law will become little more than the rule of the strongest—in other words, U.S. might will make legal right. Consequently, the challenge for the United Nations lies in building an international consensus and in convincing governments that shared sovereignty is the basis for resolving issues. However, in the 21st century, where transnational terrorism and weapons of mass destruction pose grave threats to all states, sovereignty is something that seems jealously guarded and not easily shared.

Interstate relations in the early 21st century are marked by cooperation and conflict. Governments are willing to promote and protect their national interests by entering into interstate agreements that serve like-minded ends. This helps to explain why international legal agreements among governments have proliferated in quantity, number of parties, and jurisdictional scope over the last four decades. Today there are more legal agreements involving more states that govern more issues than ever before. By the same token, the ever-increasing process of global interdependence means that more states have more contact with one another, thus creating more opportunities for more confrontation and more serious conflict. The fact that conflict occurs between states means that special legal rules and means are needed to deal with disputes, either to prevent them or to settle them peacefully. Those rules and means do exist, and they are used to support special techniques for peaceful settlement of disputes. While the ambition of peaceful resolution of interstate conflict is not new, its expedition becomes acute in an era of complex political interdependence, accelerating economic globalization, and the proliferation of weapons of mass destruction.

INTERNATIONAL AGREEMENTS

International treaties and conventions are contract-like agreements between two or more states, usually negotiated for the purpose of creating, modifying, or extinguishing mutual rights and reciprocal obligations. An international agreement establishes a formal relationship between states or international organizations that is intended to be legally binding and governed by international legal rules.[1]

Legal rules governing international agreements grew in salience and scope over the last half-century, as conditions of state interdependence intensified and as treaties became essential for regular international intercourse. In fact, the multiparty agreement represents the closest and often the only approximation of international legislation governing the relations among states. In modern international law, several notable examples are evident. The UN Charter, with nearly all states as contracting parties, legislates the cardinal prohibition against the use of force between states.[2] A nexus of international agreements establishes a legal regime for human rights, as well as a system for establishing a system of international criminal law. Multipartite agreements, which are used to create a variety of international organizations and bodies—such as the specialized agencies in the United Nations, the Organization of American States, the European Union, and the North American Treaty Organization—serve as those bodies' constitutions. International agreements also set out a framework for regulating international commerce and financial transactions, as principally laid down by the 1994 General Agreement on Tariffs and Trade/World Trade Organization. Finally, multilateral agreements are increasingly used to codify and solidify customary legal rules regulating interstate conduct. The four 1949 Geneva Conventions on the Law of War, the 1961 Vienna Convention on Diplomatic Relations, the 1969 Vienna Convention on the Law of Treaties, and the 1982 UN Convention on Law of the Sea amply attest to that.

An international document does not have to be called a treaty to be a binding agreement under international law. In fact, the terminology used for international agreements varies, and one can think of several representative terms, such as *convention, concordat, pact, protocol, accord, charter, declaration, statute, act, covenant, exchange of notes, agreed minute,* and *memorandum of understanding.* But different names for international agreements are of little legal consequence. Certain terms might appear useful, but they are principally descriptive. What is important is the fact of agreement, indicated in appropriate negotiated form, by a head of state or by a properly authorized representative. By whatever name, the essential quality of the instrument is the agreement, grounded in absolute obligations that are realized and incurred by the parties. Though not designated as treaties, the status of these documents can be made legally binding and formally obligatory. Moreover, agreements contracted between international actors other than states, as well as those not done in written form, may also be legally binding, just as may oral agreements between official representatives of states.[3] Agreements between states and international organizations are to be regulated by a special treaty—the Convention on Treaties between States and International Organizations or between International Organizations, which was drawn up in 1986 but has yet to enter into force.[4] This point is critical: In a system of international legal rules that theoretically adopts a consensual approach and roots its law in the concurrence among states, formal agreements among states remain the principal source of legal obligation.

The practice of treaty making is ancient. The oldest known text dates back to an agreement of alliance between Ramses II of Egypt and Khetasar, King of the Hittites, in 1272 BC that contained provisions for mutual recognition and for the reciprocal extradition and humanitarian treatment of political refugees.[5] Such agreements constitute primary sources and evidence of modern international law. The negotiation of international agreements has become one of the cardinal functions of modern diplomacy. Indeed, the scope of treaty making has broadened so much that the contemporary inventory of treaties includes nearly every conceivable subject matter and that the great lawmaking treaties of the past half-century constitute in substance, if not in form, a species of international legislation.

Modern agreements come in many forms with a variety of contents. While no scientific classification of treaties is available, they can be appreciated in terms of their varied purposes and subject matters. Treaties exist of alliance, protection, guarantee, peace, neutrality, commerce, extradition, arbitration, environmental conservation, pollution prevention, copyright protection, monetary exchange, financial arrangement, consular conventions, and so forth.

International agreements take two basic forms. The most prevalent, the bilateral treaty, is a formal agreement between two states and is closely analogous to contracts between individuals in domestic legal systems. Normally, a bilateral treaty is concluded between two governments that desire to promote or regulate special interstate interests or matters. The other form of agreement is the multilateral (or multipartite) convention, which is negotiated by and involves more than two states. Military alliances traditionally take this form of international agreement, as exemplified by the 1948 North Atlantic Treaty Organization and the 1947 Rio Pact on Reciprocal Assistance. Other multilateral instruments serve states' interests concerning economic, environmental, and social matters; such agreements establish international regimes or administrative agencies to carry out policies commonly agreed on in the instrument. Still other international agreements have more pervasive legal reach in that they involve numerous parties. These are regarded as *lawmaking treaties* and are often designated as international conventions. Current examples of such lawmaking agreements include, among many others, the UN Charter, the 1949 Geneva Conventions on the Laws of War, the 1994 General Agreement on Tariffs and Trade/World Trade Organization, the 1982 Law of the Sea Convention, the ICAO conventions outlawing aircraft hijacking, and the 1989 International Convention on the Rights of the Child.

Contemporary legal rules provide for the regularity of state behavior in international relations. Patterns of diversified interstate intercourse are complex and complicated, and a single set of compatible rules facilitates management of relationships. To the extent that a multipartite convention is claimed by its parties to represent a codification of existing customary law or of general principles of law, more universal legal relations are established. For parties it becomes merely a restatement of legal rules already acknowledged; for nonparties, it might represent a salient consensus about what the customary legal rule is while imposing on them the onus of justifying conflictive practices in their foreign policies. Though not formally bound to the international agreement, nonparties remain obliged to the codified customary law.

Even absent the pull of custom, substantial agreement among states usually isolates a lone deviationist government. This is not to say that acceptance of an agreement by multiple states automatically leads to the codification of legal obligations for all states. But it does mean that the formal institutionalization of a set of legal rules by a considerable majority of states produces clear obligations for those governments, with pervasive legal weight and application throughout the international community. International agreements reify that process. The greater the number of states that resolutely agree with an international norm, the more likely that international norm is to be regarded within the international community.

The interstate agreement furnishes the closest international analogue to legislation, aside from select decisions taken by the UN Security Council. Yet, unlike the Security Council, such agreements are drawn up and approved through the consent of states. The legal glue that binds governments together in this formal relationship is the fundamental notion of *pacta sunt servanda*, the legal principle that asserts that agreements made in good faith shall be binding. Since states usually enter into treaties and conventions with the expectation that the provisions will directly affect the states' future affairs, it is reasonable that an agreement should not be considered inapplicable simply because future events do not comport fully with the expectations of one or more parties. The key point here is that an international agreement, whether labeled a treaty or something else, represents more than a contractual arrangement between governments. This can be more appreciated by viewing international agreements as the quasi-legislative cement that binds states into a systematic web of international legal rights and obligations.

Legal scholars view the law of treaties as deriving from general principles of contract formation and obligation common to domestic legal systems. The consensual approach to international legal rules promotes this analysis. So also does the fact that most international agreements are bilateral treaties between two states, as opposed to general legislation adopted by and for the entire international community. Nearly all treaty agreements contain the substance of mutual advantage and reciprocal rights, which foster a bargain-type arrangement resembling a contract. It is nonetheless sobering to realize that parties to all these interstate agreements are political entities, represented by governments who are subject to the pressures and changes of politics and who also serve as international legislators.

Formulation of Treaties

Treaties are born, they live, and they die. During a treaty's life span, it may undergo changes or alterations that can result from changes in the international political milieu or from new needs that the treaty might be able to serve.

International agreements do not just happen. They are made through a legal process. As affirmed through state practice and rules of diplomacy, the treaty-making process generally undergoes four stages, though these are not always separate and distinct. The first stage involves the diplomatic process of *negotiation*, which is carried out by authorized government agents. Diplomatic channels or special meetings of representatives may be used for bilateral agreements, although in the modern era it is more often that an international conference is convened by concerned states or by an international organization for multipartite accords. For agreements negotiated under the aegis of an intergovernmental organization, the text may be drafted by a body within that agency or by an international conference per the organization.

In modern states, the treaty-making power is vested mainly in the executive, though parliamentary and democratic trends point toward increasing participation of representative bodies. Governments are free to designate anyone to represent the state to conclude a treaty agreement, provided that the person is duly authorized to engage in such negotiations. Those representatives involved in treaty negotiations must be properly accredited under the rules of negotiation to engage in diplomatic responsibilities and must possess credentials from their government to that effect.[6]

The second stage involves *adoption* and *authentication*. Adoption involves the formal act of settling the form and content of a proposed agreement. Once the text of a treaty is negotiated and drafted into formal format, it may be adopted by the parties in any of several ways. For bilateral treaties, adoption comes through mutual consent. For agreements negotiated by a limited number of parties, adoption usually comes through unanimous consent. For multilateral agreements negotiated through an intergovernmental organization or at an international conference, adoption is done through voting rules or by decision of the agency competent to issue such rules.

Adoption of a final text by the negotiators is followed by its authentication, popularly referred to as *signature*. This procedure aims to affirm for parties involved in the negotiations the exact terms in a treaty text and to acknowledge their formal acceptance of those terms. Negotiators may merely initial the document on behalf of their governments; alternatively, it may be incorporated into the final act of the conference or adopted as a special resolution. Most often, though, negotiators just affix their signatures to the treaty in its final form. In this regard, only persons fully accredited by their government may sign, such as heads of state, ministers of foreign affairs, and representatives with plenary powers. While the act of signature does not obligate a state to the text, once a government signs an international agreement, it is obliged to refrain from any act that would defeat the instrument's object and purpose, at least until that government ratifies the agreement or makes the decision not to become party to it.[7]

Most modern international agreements become legally effective only after *ratification*, the third step in treaty making. Every state develops domestic procedures defining the treaty-ratification process, and although municipal laws vary considerably from state to state, some common features are present.[8] Ratification is usually held to be an executive act, taken by the head of state or government through which formal acceptance of the treaty is affirmed. Until this affirmation is consummated, an international agreement does not create legal obligations for a state, save for rare instances when an instrument becomes binding for parties on their signature alone. It remains for those parties to determine whether a nonratified agreement may be regarded as legally binding. In a related vein, the unconstitutional ratification of an agreement by one state should not be regarded as voiding the international obligations and responsibilities of the other ratifying parties. The latter states remain bound to their commitment, irrespective of the legitimacy of the former's act of ratification.[9] Similarly, partial or conditional ratification is not permissible, though states may legally refuse to ratify a treaty concluded by its properly accredited agents acting within their powers. A state that refuses to ratify on insufficient grounds or mere caprice would lose credit with the rest of the international community.

It must be realized, however, that ratification is not the final step for bringing a treaty into force. The concluding step actually entails reciprocal communication of the fact of ratification—generally termed, in a bilateral treaty, as the exchange of ratifications; or, in the case of multipartite agreement, the *deposit of ratifications* including an agreed-on depositary, which may be a single state or an international official such as the Secretary-General of the United Nations.

An important question relating to treaty making concerns the possibility of whether states not originally participating in the negotiation, signature, and ratification of an international agreement might be permitted at a later date to assume a treaty's legal obligations and privileges and thus become bound to its provisions. Such a formal act by a third party is called *accession* and is normally done in established multilateral agreements. Accession is possible only if provided for in the treaty or if consent for accession is given by treaty parties. For modern multilateral agreements—in particular, those negotiated under the auspices of the United Nations or its agencies—the opportunity for signature may be kept open for as long as two years, thus blurring the timely distinction between signature and accession.

On matters of common concern to governments, a variety of practices tends to promote uniformity, which suggests that certain legislation exists for the entire international community. The most forthright and direct is the multilateral convention, with multiple parties and provision for the adherence of still others. In an era of heightened globalization and interdependence, such an approach becomes obvious for dealing with transnational matters of mutual interest and serious concern. The manifest advantage is that of obtaining a uniform arrangement, with parties' accepting in each case the lowest common denominator of agreement possible to secure ratification. Yet, the search for unanimity or consensus tends to produce compromises that are not fully satisfactory to anyone, which makes for difficulties in convincing domestic politicians that the agreement is in the national interest and should be ratified.

Given these realities, it is hardly surprising that the ratification of bilateral and multilateral treaties might be rejected by states that are signatories. In normal circumstances, a state is not obligated to an international agreement until ratification takes place. It is therefore possible for a prospective party—that is, one who negotiates in good faith, duly signs the document, and transmits the instruments to the appropriate municipal organ for approval—to refuse to consent to ratification, in accordance with its constitutional provisions. For example, in the United States, the Senate is free to deny consent to a treaty negotiated by the executive branch in concert with other foreign governments. Under such conditions, the treaty is rendered unratified and becomes legally inoperable for the United States. Though rarely done, the Senate has opted for refusal over ratification for some significant agreements, including bilateral treaties with Great Britain and with Colombia over suppression of the slave trade (1824); with Denmark for the acquisition of Saint Thomas and Saint John islands (1867); and with Great Britain over the *Alabama* claims (1867). Of the vast number of multilateral instruments considered by the U.S. Senate, two main rejections stand out: the Treaty of Versailles,[10] which ended World War I and created the League of Nations (in 1919); and the Comprehensive Test Ban Treaty,[11] which prohibits the testing of nuclear weapons (in 1999).

Treaties may be modified by individual states during the process of adoption. These modifications, called *reservations*, are formal changes or amendments inserted into a treaty by one party as an implied or specified condition of ratification. A reservation allows a potential treaty party to unilaterally announce that certain provisions of a treaty will not apply to that state. A reasonable inference is that such an opportunity appears to transgress the intent of *pacta sunt servanda*—that is, that the state in question is not demonstrating the good faith expected during and after treaty negotiations. Even so, the applicable international legal rule holds that a reservation must be acceptable to other parties if the agreement is to enter into force and thus have reciprocal legal effects for all parties.

If the instrument is a bilateral agreement, few problems arise over the status of reservations. Put bluntly, either the party ratifies the original instrument with the attached reservation, or it refuses to do so, thus killing the agreement. While reservations are a manifestation of national sovereignty, they are not practicable in bilateral treaties, simply because if the two parties are unable to agree on a particular provision, then there is no agreement on that provision and thus no binding legal obligations.

Reservations pose considerable problems for multilateral agreements. Traditionally, reservations are permitted in international agreements, unless specifically prohibited by the treaty. The final clauses of a treaty should specify whether any reservations are permissible and, if so, which ones. If no such specification is made, then reservations not incompatible with the fundamental purposes of the treaty are permissible, per the 1969 Vienna Convention on the Law of Treaties.[12] Likewise, when a reservation is made, the traditional rule applies that all parties must accept said reservation. If a state accepts a reservation to a convention made by another state, then the reservation modifies the agreement for both states. But the reservation does not modify the terms of the agreement for other parties. Other states may still formally object to the reservation but may opt not to oppose the instrument's *entry into force*. In that case, those states may choose to recognize or not recognize the legal inclusion of the reserving state among parties to the agreement. In any case, they are not legally bound to a reservation by another government.[13]

Notwithstanding the possibilities of rejection or modification by some states, when a set of legal rules is articulated and ratified by a substantial number of states, the international community must take those rules seriously. Such rules establish contours for government policy actions, which are often quite difficult to renegotiate. It is usually much easier to secure agreement on well-delineated standards than to obtain agreement on changes in those standards, simply because efforts to change the agreement are likely to produce disagreement, factions, and antagonists on various positions. In international treaty making, state practice suggests that it is almost always easier to keep what you have, if that is relatively satisfactory, than to secure agreement on any particular changes or revisions in a legal instrument. By the same token, states share the common ambition of obtaining a workable set of rules that is consistent with their interests. From the view of various states, many sets of rules might be consistent with their particular interests. The key point here is to create the set of workable rules that is most common to most states—that is, to negotiate a workable treaty arrangement that tends to blend the interests of most states rather than to satisfy the particular interest of any single state. There may even be occasions when a third party feels compelled to abide by international agreements to which it is not formally a party. It might come to regard these rules as binding, due to its state interests or perhaps because of the possibility of retaliation by other states and the undesirable consequences of such retaliation.

States enjoy, by right of sovereignty, wide latitude in their international arrangements with one another, although informal restraints on their activities are commonplace. Indeed, governments are reluctant to make agreements with one another that might offend other states, contradict other legal arrangements to which they are bound, or require considerable renegotiation or revisions of existing legal agreements to ensure equality of treatment for all parties. In making international agreements, there exists in fact a so-called international interest that states recognize as always being present and that exerts pervasive influence on the direction of their individual foreign policies. This international interest may be formally acknowledged, as in the case of the UN Charter, which is now accepted by all states as being a formal restraint on the negotiation of bilateral arrangements that might conflict with it. There is a constitution-like quality here, in the sense of invalidating inconsistent bilateral accords made beforehand or afterward that impugn the Charter's provisions.

The main difficulty complicating the modern treaty process is not the fundamental precept that international agreements must be honored in good faith. Rather, problems arise with the processes of appraisal, modification, and termination. In a bilateral arrangement, an agreement that furnishes mutual advantages to parties and that may be terminated by either party on short notice generally functions satisfactorily, as the possibility of one party's being able to terminate the treaty can work as an incentive for both parties to discuss and modify problematic provisions. Obviously, agreements made for a long duration or agreements produced by coercion or oppressive negotiations are far less satisfactory, unless the political conditions causing the disagreement remain unchanged and thus force a better-than-nothing type arrangement. One only has to remember the fate of the Treaty of Versailles that ended the First World War to appreciate this truism. The point here is that international political circumstances do change, and agreements excessively onerous to a party will tend not to endure for that state under circumstances conducive to denunciation. The simple fact is that a government that perceives itself in a better position by being unbound to a treaty will not obligate itself to any agreement that it considers a detriment. Similarly, when considering the role of states as legislative participants in the international community, fellow states must exercise caution before approving a government's attempt to freeze the legal future to ensure its own relative political advantages. Interstate relations are dynamic and complex. Most states have a greater interest in preserving international order and discouraging violence. The legal position of a single state should not be deemed superior to other states merely because of that state's national capabilities or military might. Under the law of treaties, the set of legal rules accepted by a certain group of states is meant to apply equally to every state, irrespective of power or position.

Only in recent decades were serious efforts made to develop international codes for treaties and other interstate agreements. Two major conventions, drawn mainly from general principles derived from state practice, now furnish essential legal rules for the law governing interstate agreements. During the 1960s, the UN International Law Commission drafted convention articles containing legal rules for making and interpreting international agreements. This draft text became the focus of discussion at the UN Diplomatic Conference on the Law of Treaties held in Vienna in 1968 and was eventually incorporated into a formal international instrument, the Vienna Convention on the Law of Treaties, adopted by the conference in its second session in 1969. Most provisions in this convention are declaratory of customary international legal rules. The Vienna Convention, in its article 2 (1), defines a treaty as ''an international agreement concluded between states in written form and governed by international law, whether embodied in a single instrument or in two or more related instruments and whatever its particular designation.'' Thus, an instrument does not have to be called a treaty to be a binding document.

Some states have special domestic instruments that perform treaty-like functions. For example, *executive agreements* entail a unique practice by the United States in its relations with other states. An executive agreement may be concluded by the president or his agents but does not require the Senate's final advice or approval. It is a binding international obligation made by the executive branch, often based on prior authorization by Congress within limits set by Congress. Occasionally, however, executive agreements are concluded without congressional authority, within the power vested in the office of the president. If, however, an executive agreement is not authorized by previous legislation, or if it falls outside the ambit of presidential authority, then the agreement is null and void. Executive agreements are used for a variety of purposes. Though not well known, one important function of executive agreements seeks to settle claims of U.S. nationals against foreign governments. Other famous executive agreements include the Far Eastern Agreement signed at Yalta in February 1945, which included the controversial agreement of approving the veto within the Security Council, in exchange for the admission of two Soviet republics, Byelorussia and the Ukraine, to be admitted as sovereign states into the General Assembly; and the Paris Peace accords, which ended the Vietnam War in 1975.

Treaty Interpretation

There is little question that international legal rules are made precise in formal treaties. Where agreement on a mutually acceptable basis can be negotiated, treaties present certain advantages. For one, the explicit language of treaties, even if relatively general, tends to limit the discretion of national officials more so than repeated formulations by decision makers. Printed words, formally ratified by governments, are more tangible and realizable than vague and inferred state behavior. Another advantage is that treaties frequently involve codifications of past practices and thereby perform the useful function of making rules clear, certain, and stable. Of fundamental importance, though, is the notion that a treaty embodies a commitment by the parties to a distinct process of interpretation. This commitment is rooted in the fact that a treaty represents the product of consensual activity between two or more states, and its provisions reflect the collective expectations and interests of the parties. Given that parties to an agreement form its collective norm-creating body, the competence of authoritative interpretation is vested in their composite association, as opposed to in each state individually. Consequently, in entering into a treaty relationship, a state binds itself not only to the terms of the agreement but to a process of interpretation that involves all the contracting states. In interpreting a treaty text, the task becomes to ascertain what the text means to the parties collectively rather than to each state individually. However, the fact remains that controversy can arise regarding the interpretation of various provisions in an international instrument as well as whether it has been terminated or suspended.

The view that a state is bound by treaty-based legal rules as interpreted by its government stands at odds with the view that a state is bound by the same rules as some impartial observer interprets them. In the first case, the theoretical possibility is left open that governments may interpret international agreements arbitrarily and unreasonably. In fact, such extreme behavior rarely occurs. In the modern context of world politics, competing rules of treaty interpretation have emerged. One school of thought argues that the focus of interpretation should be on the meaning of the text. Since most treaties are negotiated by educated people, by the time a treaty is completed, ambiguities are largely eliminated and the text reflects the actual intention of parties. This view suggests rules of interpretation that severely restrict the types and occasions in which outside evidence might be used to improve the meaning of the treaty. A second school maintains that the intention of the parties is critical, and a broad array of evidence might be introduced to shed light on treaty's meaning.[14] In this regard, it becomes helpful to examine the *travaux preparatoires*—that is, the preparatory work that occurs during the negotiation phase of an agreement's text—when the ordinary meaning of a provision seems ambiguous or obscure.

Rules for treaty interpretation derive from general jurisprudence. Strictly speaking, such rules form no part of international law proper, and the contracting parties are free to apply any rules they agree on. Nonetheless, certain rules of interpretation are generally accepted. For instance, to ascertain the meaning of legal rules in a treaty, the fundamental objective is to determine the actual intent of the parties in negotiating the treaty text. In this respect, the language of a treaty should be interpreted according to its plain and reasonable sense. Ordinary words are to be interpreted in an everyday, ordinary sense and technical words in their technical sense. Interpretation should be balanced and should generally follow the spirit rather than the letter of the instrument. Likewise, words having more than one meaning should be interpreted in the general sense, rather than the technical, unless clearly used as such. If the meaning of a stipulation seems ambiguous, the most reasonable meaning is preferred over the least reasonable—likewise, the most adequate meaning to the purpose of the treaty and the meaning most consistent with recognized principles of international law. With regard to legal construction, the entire instrument should be viewed as a composite whole, and individual stipulations should be considered within its context. To interpret a provision out of the treaty's whole context is to disregard the true intent of the negotiators. Finally, situations might occur where conflicts arise between different treaties to which the same state is party or with different provisions in the same treaty. In the former instance, the treaty that is made most recently takes priority. In the latter case, legal rules that are specifically stipulated or permitted are considered to prevail over the more generalized provisions. Moreover, an imperative rule normally takes priority over a statement of general permission. In addition, treaties should be liberally construed to carry out the intent of the parties in order and thereby secure equality and reciprocity between them.

Parties comply with treaties for a variety of reasons. First, compliance is necessary to accomplish the objectives of a particular treaty as well as to reinforce the principle of the sanctity of treaty obligations. Further, compliance contributes to inhibiting noncompliant governments from becoming free riders regarding the restraint exercised by other states. That is, a noncompliant state might benefit from restraints shown by others, without having to assume the costs of compliance, which amounts to a form of unfair, unjustified legal competition. Finally, states tend to comply with treaties because of their vested interest in reciprocal compliance by other parties to the agreement. Reciprocity is important for making treaties functional. This is especially true for security-related agreements because the parties' mutual interests in preserving their national security extend beyond perceived advantages of the treaty itself.

Validity of Treaties

Article 26 of the Vienna Convention asserts that "every treaty in force is binding upon the parties to it and must be performed by them in good faith." This modern codification of the ancient principle of *pacta sunt servanda* obligates governments to comply with their international agreements. Yet certain conditions or circumstances may arise under which treaties are rendered invalid and are thereby nullified as international legal instruments.

The mere negotiation of documents between states does not ensure their validity under international law. An international agreement must adhere to a variety of essential conditions and special rules before it can obtain legal validity and thus become a legitimate international contractual instrument. For one, the parties to an agreement must be capable of contracting legal instruments. Fully sovereign states possess this contracting power; provinces or other municipal divisions within states do not. The United States, Canada, and France may engage in lawful treaty-making activities, whereas California, Saskatchewan, and Burgundy may not. Also important is that certain intergovernmental organizations are given the right to conclude valid international agreements with states and among themselves. Indeed, the vast array of international legal rules created during the past three decades largely comes as a product of UN organs and agencies.

As a second condition, the validity of an international document depends on the authority granted to the agents entrusted with its negotiation. Persons not authorized to negotiate on behalf of a government, or who exceed that authority, cannot create obligations for that government.

A third element of validity is freedom of consent. For a treaty to apply legally to a state, the state's government must give consent. In negotiating a treaty, the application of force, intimidation, or duress during the treaty-making process is not permissible and will invalidate the lawfulness of the treaty. Resort to pressure tactics can also invalidate the legitimacy of an international agreement. When done, one may reasonably question the validity of an international peace treaty and any allegations of psychological duress and political pressure that were placed on the vanquished state during the course of negotiations. Do these conditions invalidate that agreement? No, because the particular pressures and duress that accompany peace treaties do not overshadow the fact that the vanquished government still retains the ultimate option of consent. That government may still reject the treaty's conditions and attempt to renegotiate them into more favorable terms. It is different, however, in the case of personal duress or intimidation imposed against negotiators of a party. In such circumstances, a treaty is rendered invalid. While resorts to force or threats against governmental representatives are rare, one well-known case stands out. In March 1939, German chancellor Adolph Hitler summoned to Berlin the President of Czechoslovakia, Dr. Hacha, and his foreign minister, M. Chvalkovsky. In a formal meeting, they were subjected to excessive psychological pressure to sign a treaty giving Germany control over the Czech state. Hermann Goering and Joachim von Ribbentrop physically harassed the Czech leaders, even threatening to bomb Prague and other major cities in the country if they did not sign the treaty. Reports indicate that President Hacha actually fainted, only to be revived by an injection from Hitler's physician so that he might complete the treaty-making process.

Invalidation of an international agreement may also result if fraud occurs during the negotiation. The deliberate use of falsified maps, distorted or forged documents, and false statements by government representatives in drawing up the treaty might all be considered fraudulent means leading to a treaty agreement's invalidation. Similarly, a treaty can be voided if the agreement contains, or was created as the result of, a substantial error—even if the mistake was unintentional. For example, suppose that allegations are made regarding the accuracy of the latitudinal designations used to produce an agreement settling a border dispute between states. If proven, that agreement would be rendered null and void.[15] In addition, modern treaty law asserts that the corruption of a state agent may give rise to invalidation, a legal rule that calls into question the propriety and lawfulness of giving lavish gifts to diplomats when treaties are signed.

Finally, the treaty must not be in conflict with the acknowledged rules and principles of international law. For example, an international agreement would not be binding if its intent were to subjugate or partition a state, assert proprietary right over part of the high seas, or promote the slave trade. Most international legal commentators concur that an international agreement may be invalidated if its provisions contradict or violate customary international normative principles, or *jus cogens*. Briefly put, the concept of *jus cogens* embraces the notion that there exist certain peremptory norms that are accepted and recognized by the entire international community as norms of general international law from which no derogation is permitted.[16] While it remains difficult to specify what rules universally qualify as contemporary peremptory norms of international law, several are often cited as being of a *jus cogens* character. Among these are respect for the inviolability of diplomatic agents; respect for the prohibition on the aggressive use of force between states; respect for the self-determination of peoples; respect for fundamental human rights; respect for international status of the oceans, the air, and space beyond the limits of national jurisdiction; and respect for the basic rules governing armed conflict, especially those regarding humanitarian considerations.[17]

Treaty Termination

Treaties do not necessarily last forever. Some agreements expire; others can be terminated. Treaties can become extinct when their time limit expires or when, in the course of their existence, they can no longer perform per the specific purpose of the contract or are superceded by a subsequent agreement's entry into force. Treaties may be dissolved by mutual consent, express renunciation by a party, or a denunciation or withdrawal by notice in accordance with terms of the instrument.

A treaty relationship among states might be ended in several ways. Perhaps the most obvious occurs when an agreement contains specific terms for termination in its provisions. Usually, these include clauses that set a date for the agreement's expiration or that permit a party to denounce or renounce the agreement, effectively allowing a state to withdraw from its legal obligations.[18] Treaties may also be ended through the explicit or tacit agreement of the instrument's parties, who can terminate a treaty by expressly declaring that they are abrogating the treaty relationship. Or governments can end a treaty by implication—that is, by concluding a new agreement, the provisions of which supercede or replace those in the former document. Similarly, the overt noncompliance by all parties to an agreement will legally render the instrument a dead letter. The tacit agreement among parties to permit a treaty to lapse into nonobservance effectively terminates its legal relevance and does so with the consent of the affected states.

A principal international legal rule holds that a treaty relationship may be terminated when one party breaches the provisions of the agreement and the other party or parties then opt to consider the treaty abrogated by the violation. It is important to understand that violation of an international agreement does not render that treaty ipso facto null and void, nor does it automatically bring about an end to the legal relationship among the parties. The treaty relationship must be terminated by the aggrieved parties. It remains at their discretion to declare that the violation was so severe that they consider the treaty void and that they no longer want to be bound by the provisions in the instrument.

Another ground for treaty termination is the concept of *rebus sic stantibus*, known as the doctrine of changing circumstances. The presumption here suggests that international conditions have changed so profoundly since a treaty entered into force that the treaty at present would violate the original intentions of the parties to agreement. Contemporary international law supports the view that *rebus sic stantibus* is a valid principle of international law. The problem, though, comes not in validity of the concept but rather in its international application. As demonstrated by international practice, the clause *rebus sic stantibus* remains an implied condition for all treaty agreements. Herein lies the dangerous temptation that any party might resort to use this doctrine on the pretext that international conditions have changed since the treaty originally entered into force and that the agreement should therefore be voided. This kind of rationale makes *rebus sic stantibus* susceptible to abuse at the political convenience of one party who might find a treaty's legal obligations too restrictive. Thus, resort to this clause of changing circumstances comes only in exceptional circumstances. There is general agreement among states that a change in government or even in the form of government does not usually affect treaty obligations. Since considerable risk surrounds the abuse of this principle, it must be stressed that the principle of *rebus sic stantibus* implies that a complete change must happen in the state under which the treaty was formed. The change of circumstances must be such that it renders the execution of the treaty difficult or impossible or that it requires performance of obligations that were not foreseen by the contracting parties and, had they been foreseen, would never have been undertaken. Three examples illustrate these conditions. First, in 1941 the United States abrogated its legal obligations under the International Load Line Convention to accommodate shipping greater amounts of war materiel to Great Britain under the lend-lease program. The U.S. government decided that during wartime it was more urgent to supply Great Britain with war materiel by overloading ships than to comply with the convention's more restrictive load limits.[19] Second, in the early 1970s, a number of Middle Eastern oil-producing governments used *rebus sic stantibus* as a legal justification to substantiate their repudiation of oil concession agreements made during the 1930s with the major oil companies. Clearly, political conditions within those states and in relations between the governments and the companies had changed profoundly over the previous four decades. Thus these governments sought to nationalize those foreign corporate holdings and run their own domestic oil industries rather than have the corporations control them, as had been the earlier case. Finally, in 2002 the United States withdrew from its 1972 bilateral Antiballistic Missile Treaty with Russia. The rationale by the U.S. government for withdrawal was that the international threat environment had profoundly changed in the modern era of terrorism. Russia was not the main threat; certain rogue states were. Consequently, a national missile defense system, which would violate the antiballistic missile accord, is currently needed for national security. Hence, withdrawal had to occur.

Finally, treaties may also be rendered void if the onset of war occurs, if a subsequent change takes place in the status of a contracting party's international personality, if a treaty's terms are rendered inconsistent with subsequent international law, or if any of the implied conditions under which the instrument was negotiated are violated. Such implied conditions mean that the treaty should be observed in its essentials by all parties, that it remains consistent with the fundamental rights of independence and self-preservation, and that no vital change occurs in the circumstances or conditions under which the treaty was made.

Treaties are artifacts of political choice and societal existence. The process through which they are formulated aims to ensure that the final product will represent the accommodation of interests amongst negotiating states. Modern treaty making emerges as a creative enterprise through which governments weigh gains and losses of commitment and work to redefine and reinterpret their interests in light of the terms of agreement. Treaty making can be a learning process that enables governments not only to realize different conceptions of their national interests but also to discover how those interests evolve. In the end, states operate under a sense of obligation to conform their conduct to the appropriate governing norms. Accordingly, the fundamental principle that the exercise of governmental power is subject to legal rules contributes to the ethos of national compliance with international agreements.

It is not surprising that agreements between states reflect important distinctions. Some agreements are essentially contracts, as in the sale of military equipment, loan agreements, or other purchase arrangements. Some agreements entail property settlements, such as those that set national boundary lines or transfer territory. Still other treaties are designed as legislation regulating, for example, the ways that foreign policy may be conducted by states. Treaties of friendship, navigation, and commerce; the conclusion of a peace arrangement; and treaties of political or economic alliance reflect such regulations. Traditional discussions about treaties are usually concerned only with agreements to which states are parties. This flows from the belief that states are the only subjects of international law. Today that is no longer the case. Realization that individuals are also subjects of modern international law invites serious consideration of the possibilities of agreements between states and individuals. Moreover, the rapid development of international organizations with far-reaching activities and concerns—and with relationships to states as well as to other organizations and even individuals—necessitates consideration of all types of agreements involving these intergovernmental agencies.

Conclusion on International Agreements

Treaties are historically regarded as formal contracts between states, with respective rights and duties attached. Today, treaties are considered to be an important, if not the paramount, source of international law. They deal with issues involving a wide range of international relations. Treaties come in varied sizes and shapes. They may be bilateral or multilateral, simple or conditional, executed or executory. Treaties cover an array of subjects—commerce, friendship, extradition, peace, incorporation, sale, and so forth. Governments may formulate reservations to a treaty, although doing so generally weakens the instrument but still provides a means of obtaining a state's consent to oblige the many other treaty provisions.

Intergovernmental agreements are superior in several ways to other sources of international legal rules. Treaties provide a concrete manifestation of the law. International legal rules are formulated to regulate, and the fact that governments formally acquiesce to be bound to these rules as they are established, usually without protraction or unnecessary objections, ought not to be dismissed as irrelevant. Generally, the language is carefully drafted and subject to no more ambiguity in its interpretation than typical domestic legislation. The utility of the treaty-making process and the value of respecting, adhering to, and maintaining international agreements are realized by all states. All governments consider treaties far more than mere scraps of paper. States are strongly disposed to honor international agreements faithfully and to comply with their terms. It is in their national interest to do so, in terms of gaining benefits and of maintaining a respected international reputation. Perhaps most significant, states appreciate that international agreements contribute considerable stability and certainty to the conduct of international affairs. When a treaty exists and governments party to the treaty know what to expect from one another, then the chances escalate for predictable and regularized interstate behavior.

The profound proliferation in the number of states and other international actors since 1960, coupled with the heightened technical complexity of international relations and the increasing interdependence of intergovernmental activities, make the promulgation of multilateral agreements of greater necessity, but their acceptance increasingly difficult. International organizations consequently opt for greater use of international declarations, resolutions, codes, and guidelines to advance international legal intentions, since these "soft law" instruments indicate international commitment but do not require ratification. Such instruments are, without any argument, not legally binding.

Besides creating international obligations, a treaty acts as a domestic directive for guiding bureaucratic behavior. Government bureaucracies are notably status quo–oriented organizations, wherein caution and conservative approaches tend to overshadow creativity and adventurism in policymaking. Low-level bureaucrats do not typically consider violation of an international agreement among their policy options. In addition, a treaty inhibits not only conduct that is clearly prohibited by its terms but also activities that fall within gray zones of doubt. The bottom line simply means that when governments enter into an international agreement, they alter their behavior, their relationships, and their expectations of one another over time in accordance with a treaty's terms. Why? Because treaties provide the stability of expectations and the predictability on various international issues that governments need for foreign policymaking.

Finally, the existence of a legal text or a treaty-based norm furnishes evidence of a commitment to the relationship that is embodied in that agreement. The relationship entails, on one level, a set of shared understandings about the nature of relationships as represented by the international instrument. But the generalized interpretation of words in a treaty, and at times the elusiveness of their meaning, suggests that a state's obligation exceeds mere agreement to abide by the terms of an agreed-on text regulating substantive rules of behavior. It also signals a commitment by governments to a process of mutual understanding and relationship building. When carried out pervasively, this process contributes to the establishment of legal rules and a predictable international order in which states might operate with minimal confrontation and conflict.

PEACEFUL SETTLEMENT OF DISPUTES

A major function of international law is to deal with disputes between states, either by preventing them altogether or by providing means for their peaceful resolution. International differences may arise on various grounds that are broadly distinguished as either legal or political. Legal differences, or conflicts of rights, are disagreements that arise from controversies to which recognized legal rules or principles may be readily applied. Political differences, or conflicts of interests, are disagreements involving political, economic, or social interests to which applying such legal rules or principles becomes impractical. Nevertheless, the fact remains that legal and political differences cannot always be separated in practice, especially since international relations intermix so profusely and since legal claims are often made as pretexts for disguised political objectives. That said, the ways of settling international differences are generally described as peaceful/amicable and coercive/hostile. State practice suggests that peaceful means of settlement are more susceptible to resolving legal disputes than political differences. In this complex era of multifaceted global interdependence, it hardly seems surprising that the emphasis should be placed on reducing international differences and preventing conflicts rather than on their pacific settlement after they have arisen. To this end, a fundamental modern international legal rule maintains that states are obliged to exhaust all peaceful and amiable means of resolving differences before resorting to coercive or hostile means.

Yet, disputes in international relations are inevitable. Naturally, each state pursues its own interests, objectives, and values. But when states coexist and interact in a common societal framework, some of these interests, objectives, and values inevitably come into conflict. Each state will then seek ways of making its own interests prevail, a practice that can give rise to a dispute with other states who disagree with those policies.[20]

The Nature of Disputes

Two significant elements mark interstate disputes. First, a specific disagreement must exist between the parties. That is, there must be a well-defined subject matter so that at least the governments can articulate what the dispute concerns. Second, a dispute must involve conflicting claims or assertions. One party must actually assert or declare what it wants or what it feels entitled to with respect to the other state. Similarly, the other party must manifest its refusal or its conflicting claims with regards to the first party's allegations. In this respect, international disputes appear to evince a general life cycle or pattern of development. While it seems reasonable to suppose that not all disputes follow the same path of evolution, certain conditions generally indicate the life process of most disputes:

1. A government first perceives that it has been aggrieved or injured wrongly.
2. The government believes that some other government bears responsibility for the injury.
3. From that belief, the aggrieved government develops a sense of entitlement and redress.
4. The injured party then formulates a specific claim that is rejected by the perceived instigator government.

These phases do not provide answers for identifying what factors cause disputes, nor what conditions lead a government to react in one way or another in terms of claim and response, nor how the development of a dispute might be affected by third parties during the dispute resolution process. Even so, the concept of dispute as a process supplies insights for international affairs. It serves to distinguish the threshold at which a disagreement reaches such intensity that it strains and even threatens relations between the parties.

Disputes are more than complaints, grievances, or disagreements. The notion of dispute indicates that a disagreement reaches a point of sufficient definition and clarity where the use of certain established methods of dispute resolution might be appropriate. Thus, from the perspective of international legal rules, an interstate dispute appears as a disagreement between governments in which various well-known techniques—such as mediation, arbitration, or adjudication—might be helpful in resolving the conflict.

A plausible scenario might suggest that in such a dispute situation a more powerful state could simply impose its views or interests on the weaker party through coercion or force. Yet, that scenario does not often happen in international affairs. More typically, a state—especially if less powerful than the other party—will attempt to exert moral suasion on its adversary by asserting that its claim is justified, legitimate, or right under international law. Framing a demand in legal terms not only serves to bring moral and political pressure on the other party to accede to its demand, but it also provides a means to mobilize support at home by the state making the demand as well as to appeal to the international community for support of its claims. Regardless of its basis or rationale in policy, the feeling that a state's demands or claims in a dispute must be justified or legitimized by normative or legal principles is deeply ingrained in interstate behavior.

Certain factors should be noted about the nature of international disputes. One misconception alleges that disputes are inherently destructive episodes. The fact is that disputes stem from states' contradictory interactions, which in and of themselves are not negative. That is, disputes do not necessarily imply a failure or breakdown of legal order in international society. Admittedly, it can be argued that, without some conflict and disputes, international society would become static, producing a status quo without change or development. A second misconception suggests that disputes always perforce pose serious problems for relationships between states. In practice, however, nearly all interstate disputes are worked out through informal, routine negotiations between governments. International disputes become an international problem only when, and to the extent that, they disrupt or threaten to disrupt useful interstate relations or the general world community order and consequently may lead to armed conflict and excessive social costs. Third, it is often assumed that outbreak of an international dispute means that international legal rules failed to preserve cooperation. That view is simply not accurate. The fact that a dispute takes place does not necessarily mean that international legal rules have been breached by one party or the other. Rather, most disputes arise over differing interpretations of the facts or of the application of law to the circumstances of the dispute. Merely because a dispute exists does not automatically mean that international laws have been violated, a perception that people share about most disputes.

The Obligation to Settle Disputes

Every political system must find ways to identify and deal with disputes that pose serious social risks to the community. In domestic legal orders, many sophisticated techniques are available to identify and resolve disputes. Either party has recourse in seeking intervention by the state through the judicial system at various levels, or at times the state may intervene at its own discretion. In the society of states, however, the discretion of the international community or a third party to intervene assumes much greater limitations. Third-party intervention becomes considered proper and permissible only when all parties to the dispute consent or when the dispute escalates to the point where it threatens general international peace and security. In this latter case, if the dispute involves members of the United Nations, the Security Council may assert the prerogative to intervene.

Interestingly enough, the prevailing view in international law suggests that in the absence of a special agreement, states are under no legal obligation to settle their disputes. There is no international legal rule stipulating that states, absent special agreement, must submit their disputes to third parties for impartial settlement. Nor can any state be compelled to submit its disputes with other states to any form of peaceful settlement, unless under a particular treaty obligation to do so.[21]

International law requires that disputes between states be settled peacefully, and to this end, states party to the UN Charter have assumed broad treaty obligations. Article 1 (1) of the Charter provides that the first purpose of the United Nations is "to maintain international peace and security and to that end: . . . to bring about by peaceful means, and in conformity with the principles of justice and international law, adjustment or settlement of international disputes or situations which might lead to a breach of the peace." In these regards, the Charter mandates in article 2 (3) that "all Members shall settle their international disputes by peaceful means in such a manner that international peace and security, and justice, are not endangered." The Charter then stipulates in article 33 that member states must actively seek to settle by peaceful means any dispute of which the continuance is likely to endanger international peace. In addition, the parties may bring disputes to the attention of the Security Council or the General Assembly. The Security Council may then recommend appropriate procedures or measures of adjustment, including referral of a legal dispute to the International Court of Justice.

It is clear that the UN Charter establishes international obligations for its parties and special intervention powers of the organization for those disputes whose persistence "is likely to endanger the maintenance of international peace and security." But it is less clear whether member states are obligated to seek to settle all disputes, even those that are not likely to threaten international peace and security. The most sensible interpretation suggests that states should settle all their disputes peacefully, and the United Nations can assist toward that end.[22] But the organization has no general authority to intervene to bring about a settlement for disputes that do not involve coercion or pose a threat to international peace and security. The Security Council may determine what role is most appropriate for itself in the dispute settlement process. Thus, to evaluate potential threats to international peace and security, the Security Council may investigate any dispute or situation that may foster international friction or incite conflict.

Neither conventional nor customary international legal rules obligate all states to settle all their disputes all of the time. Many disputes between states are minor. Indeed, some might be better off left unresolved, and there is no practical way to enforce such an obligation. Yet a principle of customary law has emerged that requires that parties to a significant dispute make the effort to negotiate in good faith a settlement to that dispute. The obligation is not to obtain a settlement; rather, it is to undertake—in good faith—efforts to reach that end. A government that deliberately refuses to participate in good-faith negotiations to settle a significant dispute not only incurs the risk of being criticized and condemned by the international community but also invites negative inferences about the merits of its position in the dispute.

Many international disputes exist between many different states and involve many different issues and types of claims. For example, some disputes raise general issues over territorial claims, jurisdiction, diplomatic protection, treaty obligations, and oceanic jurisdiction, whereas others may be more particular and may focus on the expropriation of property, transnational pollution, interference with aircraft, or fishing rights. Some disputes are distinguished by their nature and involve disagreements over the facts of a case, the substance of applicable legal rules, what the law should be, the terms of some arrangement, and who should decide the outcome of such concerns. Determining the nature of a dispute may be difficult. Hence there can be added value in using an outside negotiator, mediator, or arbiter to ascertain where disagreement actually lies.

The quality of the relationship between the disputants may affect one's perception of the dispute. It can make a considerable difference in how the dispute is handled if the parties enjoy long-term consistent relations with each other, as opposed to having only infrequent contact. States that have long-term vested interests with each other seem less likely to disrupt their advantageous relationship over some issue and more willing to seek a negotiated settlement between themselves. However, when a long-term consistent relationship is interrupted by the emergence of a new, revolutionary regime in one of the parties, disputes can arise with a particularly nasty character. To appreciate this point, one needs only to think of the United States' recent experiences with Cuba, Libya, Iran, and Iraq.

Finally, disputes between states can be distinguished by their nature and by the perceived propriety of resorting to judicial settlement. In other words, does the dispute concern a legal issue, which would make it justiciable and thus appropriate for settlement though adjudication? Or, is the dispute rooted more in political or nonjusticiable issues, which would render it inappropriate for adjudication? For many governments, the most salient concerns here involve the preservation of national honor and the protection of national security or other perceived vital interests. The argument is made that such concerns should not be susceptible to adjudication as a dispute settlement technique, largely because in any case, disagreement will arise not only over what the law is but also what the law should be. Put tersely, disputes grounded in political concerns, especially those involving the use of force by one state against the other, are typically viewed by governments as being nonjusticiable in an international court. Such disputes are overtly susceptible to politicization and may thus be manipulated by considerations beyond the bounds of legal standards.[23]

Processes of Dispute Settlement

At least seven recognized peaceful methods are used for settling international differences. The first of these, *negotiation*, involves a process whereby the parties directly communicate and bargain with each other in an effort to agree on resolving the issue. Diplomacy is constantly used to alleviate friction and smooth over difficulties and thus seeks to effect compromises and settle claims. States are obligated under customary legal rules to try this method of settlement before resorting to use of force or coercive means for redress. By opting to use negotiation, parties retain most control over the process and outcome, thus making it the least risky way for governments to deal with differences. As such, negotiation is manifestly the predominant, preferred means for resolving international disputes. In addition, diplomatic negotiation places the onus of responsibility for resolving the dispute on the parties themselves, thus making any agreement reached freely done by the parties through accommodation and compromise. The resolution of several minor coastal boundary disputes between the United States and Canada since 1970 furnishes a useful example of successful bilateral negotiation.

A second technique, *good offices*, involves efforts by a third party to bring the disputants into communication with one another and facilitate their own negotiations. Good offices are really a form of intercession aimed at getting the parties to resume negotiations with one another. The third party—the good officer—meets with each disputant separately and suggests ways of bringing the states back to the bargaining table. There is no legal obligation for a government to offer good offices, nor are states obligated to accept good offices if proffered by another state. The good officer may also act as a messenger between the disputants to improve the political climate. Good offices are used only with the concurrence of both disputants and are especially useful in situations where the parties have broken off diplomatic relations. U.S. Secretary of State Alexander Haig attempted good offices in April 1982 between Great Britain and Argentina in an attempt to avert conflict over the Falkland Islands/Islas Malvinas, but he was not successful. Good offices were also used by former president Jimmy Carter in 1992 to bring representatives from Ethiopia and Eritrea to the Carter Center in Atlanta, Georgia, where they eventually worked out a peace plan to end the states' civil war. Likewise, in 1988 Secretary-General Perez de Cuellar offered to Iran and Iraq the United Nations in New York as a neutral site where they could negotiate a cease-fire to end their eight-year war.

In the third technique, *mediation*, a neutral third party (the mediator) actively participates in the dispute settlement process itself. Mediation may be undertaken by an individual, a government, a group of states, or an agency of an international organization. The mediator is expected to advance informal and nonbinding, but concrete, proposals for resolving substantive questions in the dispute. The mediator assists the parties directly, either jointly or separately. The advantage of using a mediator lies, first, in the impartial outsider's being able to sponsor proposals that might not have occurred to either disputant or, second, the opportunity for the parties to save face by accepting a neutrally sponsored proposal rather than one presented by an adversary to the dispute. Even so, the parties are under no legal obligation to accept the mediator's proposals, which serve only as advice and have no legally binding quality on any party to the dispute. As with good offices, the outcome of a successful mediation exercise comes in a negotiated agreement between the disputant parties. Not surprisingly, the critical ingredient in the mediation process is that the disputants must trust the integrity and neutrality of the mediator.

Modern examples of mediation are numerous. In 1905 the United States engaged in successful mediation efforts between Russia and Japan to end their war (for which Theodore Roosevelt's personal role earned the president the Nobel Peace Prize). During 1948–1949 the American diplomat Dr. Ralph Bunche undertook efforts to end the active hostilities between Israel and its Arab neighbors (for which he, too, won the Nobel Peace Prize). Perhaps best known among modern mediation attempts is that by President Jimmy Carter at Camp David in 1978 to bring about a peace treaty between Egypt and Israel (and for this mediation effort and others in Haiti and North Korea, President Carter won the Nobel Peace Prize in 2002). Pervasive hostilities in Central America during the 1980s prompted Costa Rica to put forward a peace proposal in 1987 (the Contadora Framework), which eventuated in bringing peace to Nicaragua, El Salvador, Guatemala, and Honduras (and for which Oscar Arias, serving as the key mediator, was awarded the Nobel Peace Prize). Finally, there were the intense personal efforts during 2000 by President William Clinton to mediate a final peace accord between Israel and the Palestinian Authority, which floundered largely on irreconcilability over the status of Jerusalem.

Institutions for Dispute Settlement

Commissions of *inquiry*, a fourth technique, involve a method of settlement in which the parties request or agree to the intervention of a third party, usually on a formal basis, for the purpose of finding out the facts underlying a dispute and, if agreed to by the parties, for suggesting terms toward a mutually agreeable settlement. The report of a commission of inquiry is nonbinding, although its findings and recommendations could have important influence on how the dispute is resolved.

The Hague Peace Conference of 1899 established commissions of inquiry as formal institutions in its Convention I for the Pacific Settlement of International Disputes. The second Hague Peace Conference of 1907 expanded the role of such commissions by setting out procedures for such commissions by prescribing meeting places, languages, and the selection of members to a commission. Recent examples of such commissions have been few, albeit notable. One well-publicized fact-finding mission was the effort of UN Secretary-General Kurt Waldheim in February 1980 to investigate grievances by the revolutionary government of Iran against the United States and the deposed Shah. That effort concluded unsuccessfully in March 1980 when the commissioners were not permitted to visit with any of the hostages being held in the U.S. embassy in Teheran. In 1988, the International Civil Aviation Organization convened a fact-finding investigation to determine the circumstances leading to the shoot-down of Iran Air Flight 655 by a U.S. warship in the Persian Gulf. In 1992–1993, the UN Security Council convened three such commissions to investigate reports that "ethnic cleansing" (genocidal atrocities) was being perpetrated by Serbs against Muslims in Bosnia. The commissions' discovery of mass graves and pervasive evidence of crimes against humanity was critical in the Security Council's decision to create a special war crimes tribunal for the former Yugoslavia that would prosecute and punish the alleged perpetrators of these offenses. Finally, the UN General Assembly in 1991 approved a Declaration on Fact-Finding by the United Nations in the Field of Maintenance of International Peace and Security.[24] As suggested by this document, inquiry in most cases is likely to be effective if it is structured and if neutral third parties are involved in the fact-finding process.

A fifth settlement procedure involves submitting a dispute to an already-established commission of *conciliation* to examine all aspects of a dispute and to suggest solutions to resolve differences between the parties. Conciliators may meet with the disputants separately or jointly, and the parties are free to accept or reject their findings and recommendations. Many important agreements after the Second World War contained provisions setting up commissions of conciliation—for example, the Pact of Bogota (1948), which established the Organization of American States. During the 1950s several disputes were submitted to such commissions, such as that between Denmark and Belgium in 1952, two disputes between France and Switzerland in 1955, and a conflict between Greece and Italy in 1956. Even so, conciliation is rarely used today, largely because governments prefer to use commissions of inquiry to find out facts, mediation to obtain third-party proposals for solutions, and even arbitration and adjudication to secure binding awards or judgments.

International *arbitration*, a sixth technique, involves the reference of a dispute, with consent of the parties, to an ad hoc panel for binding decision, usually on the basis of international legal rules. Parties frame a special agreement, the *compromis*, which defines the nature and limits of the issues to be arbitrated; the machinery and procedures of the panel, including the method of selecting the arbitrator or arbitrators; and the rules and principles that determine the decision. Parties are bound to submit in good faith to the award. Aside from treaty stipulations, however, there is no general legal obligation resting on states to resort to arbitration to settle their differences.[25]

It was with the *Alabama* claims case in 1871 that arbitration first became recognized as an important technique for maintaining international peace.[26] In this case, the United States won an award of $15.5 million in compensation for direct losses caused by Confederate cruisers illegally supplied to the South by British interests during the U.S. Civil War.

The widespread acceptance of arbitration came at the Hague Peace Conference of 1899, with the adoption of the Convention for the Pacific Settlement of International Disputes and its establishment of the Permanent Court of Arbitration. This agreement created a list of 150 named arbitrators, from which two could be selected, one by each disputant, to create an ad hoc arbitration tribunal who would then render binding decisions. Though not often used, this Hague court symbolizes the faith placed in arbitration as a dispute settlement process by political leaders and international lawyers.[27] Perhaps not surprisingly, then, resort to the process of arbitration has been extensive. Hundreds of compulsory arbitration agreements were concluded throughout the 20th century, handling thousands of claims. In fact, more than seventy thousand claims were dealt with by forty mixed arbitral tribunals after World War I to cover claims by nationals of the Allied powers against Germany, Italy, and Turkey. One famous case, the *Island of Palmas* arbitration of 1929 between the United States and the Netherlands, was decided by a sole arbiter from Switzerland. Some arbitrations have been ad hoc, such as the *Rann of Kutch* case over territory disputed by India and Pakistan (1968)[28] and the *Delimitation of the Continental Shelf* arbitration between the United Kingdom and France (1977).[29] The Beagle Channel dispute between Argentina and Chile was first decided in 1977 by an arbitral tribunal comprising five judges of the International Court of Justice. Argentina, however, rejected the decision as null and void, a rare instance of a party's refusing to accept an arbitral award after it has agreed to accept the process. Subsequently, the two countries consented to accept papal mediation, which led to an agreement by the pope to arbitrate and which culminated in a treaty-based award to Chile in December 1984.[30]

Special legal institutions have facilitated opportunities for arbitration. The Iran–United States Claims Tribunal was established in 1981 as an international arbitral body to settle the claims of U.S. nationals against the Iranian government and of Iranian nationals against the United States that arose out of the violations of property rights stemming from the circumstances surrounding the hostage crisis. Many of these claims concerned sales of materials that were either undelivered by U.S. corporations or not paid for by the new Iranian government. Since then, more than 2,000 claims have been settled, involving 600 awards and 130 decisions.[31]

In 1991 the UN Security Council established, under its Chapter VII authority, the UN Compensation Commission, headquartered in Geneva. It aims to process, determine, and arrange payment for any claims against Iraq arising out of the 1991 Persian Gulf War. Its chief purpose is to decide the validity of claims arising since August 2, 1990, the date of Iraq's invasion of Kuwait. Since its establishment, the commission has received approximately 2.65 million claims seeking compensation in excess of $348 billion. Nearly one hundred governments submitted claims for themselves or for their nationals and corporations. Over the past decade, the commission has resolved 2,602,722 claims, with compensation awards exceeding $48 billion as settlements for claims involving personal injury, death, or property damage resulting from the invasion.[32]

An increasingly salient form of arbitration is that concerning commercial arbitration between private persons or business enterprises. In this regard, one important tribunal is the International Court of Arbitration of the International Chamber of Commerce, a permanent arbitral organization based in Paris. Each year this tribunal receives some 350 cases, with a view to arbitrating business disputes of an international character. Other similar arbitral organizations include the London Court of International Arbitration, the Stockholm Chamber of Commerce Arbitration, and the World Trade Organization, about which much more will be said in our discussion of international economic law.

The United Nations Commission on International Trade Law developed the UNCITRAL

Arbitration Rules, which are widely used in international arbitration proceedings involving governments and corporations. The 1965 Convention on the Settlement of Investment Disputes between States and Nationals of Other States establishes a special Center for the Settlement of Investment Disputes under the auspices of the International Bank for Reconstruction and Development in Washington, D.C. This center provides an autonomous mechanism, free from national laws, to administer ad hoc arbitrations for legal disputes arising out of transnational investments, usually involving expropriation proceedings.

As a special arrangement, arbitration can be a flexible instrument when highly technical disputes necessitate specially qualified arbitrators. The ad hoc character of the tribunal permits the arbitrators to apply any principles recognized in the *compromis* that can circumvent or supercede existing legal principles, thus allowing the decision to be based on a mutually agreed-on framework. Even so, arbitration as a process suffers from certain frailties. For one, arbitration cannot take place unless the disputants give their mutual consent, and one will often refuse to do so for fear of not winning. In the main, arbitration works in a particular instance only if the conditions within and between the states are ripe for settlement. Arbitration facilitates the process of dispute settlement not because it compels governments to resolve their differences peacefully but because it provides a procedure through which the final details of a settlement can be worked out once those governments realize that it is in their mutual best interests to end the dispute.

Adjudication, or settlement through the judicial process, provides the seventh technique of peaceful dispute resolution and is a process specifically mentioned in article 33 of the UN Charter. It involves the reference of a dispute, by agreement or consent of the parties, to the International Court of Justice or some other standing and permanent judicial body for binding decision, usually on the basis of international legal rules. If the rules of the tribunal permit, the parties may at times agree to an advisory or nonbinding opinion (as opposed to a binding decision) or to a declaratory judgment that specifies what principles should be applied by the parties in the settlement of their dispute.[33] Jurisdiction in adjudication depends on the consent of the parties, which are legally bound to comply with the decision handed down by the tribunal. In addition, all parties are normally represented on the court, and the court is likely to be responsive to the desires of the parties regarding certain aspects of procedures in resolving the dispute.

The International Court of Justice (ICJ) was established in 1946 as the United Nations successor to the Permanent Court of International Justice, the judicial body affiliated with the League of Nations. The ICJ, popularly known as the World Court, functions on the legal bases of Chapter XIV of the Charter and the Statute of the court, which forms an integral part of the charter. All members of the United Nations are ipso facto parties to the Statute, but nonmembers may become parties as well if approved by the General Assembly and the Security Council.

The ICJ is composed of fifteen judges elected for nine years (five being elected every three years), with the possibility of being reelected by the General Assembly and the Security Council. Candidates for the court are nominated by national groups in states and are elected as individuals regardless of their nationality, although no two judges may be nationals from the same state. By tradition, the permanent members of the Security Council have judges elected to the Court, although China had no judge during the period of 1960–1984, due to the controversy over China's representation.

Given that the ICJ is a law-applying institution, it possesses certain advantages over other methods of dispute settlement. For one, the Court operates on a continual basis, so it is always prepared to deal with disputes. For another, it contributes to the development of a shared body of legal rules, substantive and procedural, through which differences between states can be resolved. In this regard, since 1946 the Court has delivered seventy-six judgments on disputes concerning, among other issues, land frontiers and maritime boundaries, territorial sovereignty, the nonuse of force, noninterference in the internal affairs of states, diplomatic relations, hostage taking, the right of asylum, nationality, guardianship, rights of passage, and economic rights. Importantly, nearly all these decisions have been accepted and implemented by the participating states. In fact, states are submitting cases to the ICJ more now than ever before, with twenty-four currently on the Court's docket. Moreover, the ICJ may give advisory opinions at the request of any of the five organs of the United Nations or the sixteen specialized agencies within the UN system. That competence can be used to advise the requesting organ about legal questions—as in the case put forward by the UN General Assembly on the legality of nuclear weapons—or to issue a legal opinion on the subject in question. Since 1946 the Court has rendered twenty-four advisory opinions on a variety of issues, such as admission to the United Nations, reparation for injuries suffered in the service of the United Nations, territorial status of South-West Africa (Namibia) and Western Sahara, judgments rendered by international administrative tribunals, expenses of certain United Nations operations, applicability of the United Nations Headquarters Agreement, and the legality of the threat or use of nuclear weapons.[34]

This is not to suggest that the ICJ is becoming widely popular for dispute resolution. Certain difficulties still encumber the ability of the ICJ to function as a true international tribunal. Most important is that states who are party to a dispute must be willing to submit to the authority of the Court. In that regard, there still exists a fundamental problem of mistrust. Not all states party to the UN Charter and the Statute of the ICJ are mandated to appear before the Court. Some, including the United States, have reserved the right to make final judgment on whether the case involves their domestic jurisdiction, which means that they can in effect refuse to accept jurisdiction (through the so-called 1946 Connally Amendment). The ICJ has only that jurisdiction that the governments are willing to grant to it in each case. Such a restrictive tendency has diminished the role that adjudication in general—and the World Court in particular—plays in resolving major political conflicts among states. Moreover, because jurisdiction in adjudication remains voluntary, governments of sovereign states are reluctant to submit to adjudication any political (nonjusticible) disputes when their perceived interests are at stake, especially if their case rests on shaky legal grounds. They prefer familiar techniques such as diplomatic negotiation to the less-flexible, more-final judicial determination. In sum, what contributes to the precarious condition of adjudication as an instrument for international dispute settlement is an uncertainty with legal rules, a dearth of legislative institutions with the authority to adjust legal rules to the changing international environment, and the lack of organized judicial procedures for the enforcement of judgments.

Regional Courts

Resort to institutions on the regional level for adjudicating disputes increased markedly during the 20th century. The first attempt came in 1907, with the establishment by treaty of the Central American Court of Justice, whose jurisdiction included cases between individuals and foreign states. This court was dissolved in 1918, however, in the belief that its regional role would be supplanted by the newly proposed Permanent Court of International Justice.[35]

The appeal of regional adjudication reappeared after the Second World War. In Western

Europe, the Court of Justice of the European Coal and Steel Community was created in 1952, with the broad jurisdiction to ensure observance of legal rules in the interpretation and application of treaties governing the European Communities (EC). This court was replaced by the European Court of Justice (ECJ) in 1973. Disputes may be brought before the ECJ by EC institutions, member states, national tribunals, and even individuals. Much of the court's attention is focused on resolving disputes between the national laws of member states and EC law. Like the ICJ, the ECJ can issue advisory opinions at the request of community organs or member states. Due to its unique nature, the ECJ not only functions as an international tribunal but also operates as a constitutional, administrative, and appeals court. Moreover, under the ECJ, individuals and corporations, as well as states, may participate in proceedings before the court, and national courts may also invoke the expertise of the ECJ.

Another contemporary regional judicial system is the Andean Court of Justice, created in 1983 by the Andean Pact countries. The Andean court, however, has not been much used, owing largely to economic and political priorities being placed on attaining a common market approach to regional integration, as opposed to juridical solution for regional concerns. Mention should be made that the League of Arab States has contemplated creation of an Arab Court of Justice since 1950, but the lack of resources and political commitment in the region has precluded its inception. Similarly, in 1964 the Organization of African Unity established—by protocol to the Charter of the Organization Unity—a Commission of Mediation, Conciliation, and Arbitration. Although this body was created to function as a quasi adjudicator, it has no mandatory jurisdiction over organization members, nor has it ever been used.

The modern trend suggests that governments prefer permanent regional judicial institutions over ad hoc tribunals. In theory, regional courts should be more viable mechanisms for resolving disputes than world courts. Even so, aside from Europe, states appear reluctant to use them. The success of a regional court depends on the political and economic solidarity of the member states, but governments still resist giving regional courts compulsory jurisdiction to adjudicate. Moreover, there are neither defined links nor hierarchies between global juridical institutions and regional courts. Regional courts operate independently from national courts and international courts and from one another, which can make coordination of juridical efforts difficult.

It is not surprising that certain criticisms tarnish the use of adjudication as a process for peacefully settling international disputes. First, in the application of international legal rules for resolving a dispute, the perception is that a tribunal automatically benefits the status quo powers, since the laws established by those states tend to serve and benefit those states. Second, certain disputes are by nature nonjusticiable. That is, they are not amenable to settlement in a court applying international legal rules, because they involve questions of vital or political interests. Third, and perhaps most telling, there is no enforcement capability to compel a state to honor an award—or decision, in the case of an international court—made against its perceived national interest. At times, when a state ''loses'' its case, it will object to carrying out the award to decision. The objector usually advances the doctrines of nullity or impossibility of performance, often asserting that the tribunal in question either exceeded the power granted to it or deviated from the rules of procedures in making the award or decision. A losing government might thus decline to honor the award or decision. In such a situation, what recourse does the winning state have when the loser refuses to comply with the decision? The former may resort to measures of self-help, short of war—for example, a diplomatic protest or economic sanctions. In the case of the ICJ, there is provision in the UN Charter in article 94 (2) for the aggrieved party to seek recourse to the Security Council, which may decide to take measures "to give effect to the judgment." Nonetheless, only one such incident has occurred in the history of the United Nations, and in that case the Security Council chose not to act.[36]

CONCLUSION

The techniques used to resolve international disputes peacefully are consensual, though consent on the use of any particular technique is usually obtained from governments in advance. Different types of disputes call for different methods of settlement. In some cases, it may be best to deal with situations on a pragmatic, ad hoc basis as they arise. In other cases, it may be sensible to have arrangements in place should the need arise to use them. The craft of effective dispute settlement in great measure involves, first, a determination of which method or combination of methods will be most useful in bringing about resolution of the particular dispute and, second, how and when such techniques should be employed.

While perhaps obvious, the various techniques for peaceful dispute resolution are not mutually exclusive, nor must they be used independently. In fact, in some cases, parties use multiple techniques to obtain the most productive results. Negotiation is always used in good offices and mediation, and sometimes the offer of good offices can eventuate into a critical mediation role for the third party, as happened to the United States during the 1990s in the Middle East peace process. Likewise, a fact-finding inquiry can produce important revelations that affect the course of dispute settlement, as occurred in 1992 with a special UN commission's investigation of ethnic-cleansing reports in Bosnia, which led in 1993 to the establishment of a special tribunal to prosecute persons accused of war crimes, crimes against humanity, and genocidal atrocities perpetrated as ethnic cleansing in the former Yugoslavia. Key characteristics for the success of all these dispute settlement techniques are their flexibility and adaptability to particular circumstances. Putting exact legal limits or strict procedural rules on their operation seems likely to gain little.

The fact remains that even the best dispute techniques or the best institutions cannot substitute for general attitudes of cooperation, accommodation, and good neighborliness between the governments involved or for their willingness to settle differences through peaceful means in good faith. No less relevant is the role of dispute avoidance. If governments can forestall disagreements and prevent disputes from occurring, then interstate relations will be more stable and orderly.

Peaceful means of settling disputes have long been a part of international practice, but before the 20th century, there were no legal rules restraining the use of force between states. The contemporary view on the question of peaceful settlement of disputes is embodied in the UN Charter. All members of the United Nations have the duty to settle disputes by peaceful means, a principle that has been integrated into the body of customary legal rules. Not only are states obligated to avoid use of force in dealing with their differences, but they are also obligated to strive proactively and perseveringly to resolve their disputes peacefully by means of their own choice.

In the final analysis, third-party dispute settlement techniques have enriched the environment for the international bargaining process, but they have neither halted war nor removed conflict from interstate affairs. Nevertheless, these techniques have been important in lessening the frequency and the intensity of international conflict and have furnished greater opportunities for peaceful collaboration and cooperation. Greater resort to them will mean more opportunities to resolve differences between states and to lessen interstate conflict.

III

Challenges and Response

7

International Criminal Law

   Q The Nature of International Criminal Law
   Q State Responsibility for Criminal Offenses
   Q The Permanent International Criminal Court
   Q Truth Commissions
   Q Conclusion

On January 29, 2004, the Chief Prosecutor for the International Criminal Court announced that the tribunal's first case would target the Ugandan rebel leaders who have kidnapped thousands of children over the past decade to serve as soldiers or sex slaves. The new permanent war crimes court obtained jurisdiction for the case when Ugandan president Yoweri Museveni lodged a formal complaint against the Lord's Resistance Army (LRA) with the Hague-based tribunal in December. The LRA includes remnants of a northern rebellion that was launched against Museveni, a southerner, when he won control of the country in 1986. Led by a mysterious former altar boy named Joseph Kony, the group seeks to replace Uganda's government with an administration based on the Ten Commandments. The LRA is accused of pillaging villages; summarily executing citizens; and hacking off limbs, ears, and lips of those suspected of aiding the central government. As many as twenty thousand children between the ages of eleven and fifteen have been abducted by the LRA in northern Uganda during its seventeen-year insurgency. While in captivity, the rebels have forced children to be soldiers, compelled them to kill their parents, and coerced them into becoming sex slaves. The conflict is blamed for the deaths of twenty-three thousand people, and nearly 1.5 million people in Uganda are living in camps without adequate sanitation, food, and water. Importantly, Uganda is one of ninety-two countries in 2004 who have ratified the 1998 Rome Statute that created the International Criminal Court (ICC). The Court can prosecute cases only if they are committed in the territory of, or by citizens of, countries that have ratified the treaty. Alternatively, a country that has not ratified the treaty could ask the Court to intervene in a conflict on its own territory, or the UN Security Council could request that the Court open a case. The ICC's Chief Prosecutor, Luis Moreno-Ocampo, asserted that the Court would begin collecting evidence concerning the LRA in the spring of 2004 and then seek to secure arrest warrants against those offending persons who will be prosecuted.

The international community is becoming increasingly interdependent and globalized as transnational activities of states and nonstate actors penetrate into the
territory and affairs of all states. International commercial transactions, global telecommunications, transborder data flow, computer Internet operations—these modern
activities are restrained neither by territorial borders, nor by well-defined boundaries of
legal rules. So long as these penetrations are constructive and positive for affected states,
then international legal rules will deem those activities permissible. But when governments or nationals undertake such activities and subsequently harm a government or
person of another state, issues of legal responsibility emerge and legal questions arise.
Who is to be held accountable for those injuries? Who should make restitution for the
harm done to the victim state or to the victimized nationals? Who should enforce the legal
rules to secure that restitution? These are not merely rhetorical questions. They beg real
answers to be addressed in the foreign policy actions of states.

The same challenges apply to gross violations of international human rights by governments or their agents. How should governments—particularly official decision makers
and individual offenders—be held accountable for human rights transgressions committed against their own citizens? Do governments have any special obligation or jurisdiction
in seeking to impose accountability against persons in other states for offenses defined by
the international community as international crimes? These issues pose serious challenges
for international law, particularly with regard to the legal principle of state responsibility
and the implications it presents for the legal rules embodying international criminal law.
Events during the 1990s prompted the creation of two ad hoc criminal courts: the International Criminal Tribunal for the Former Yugoslavia and the International Criminal Tribunal for Rwanda. These developments are of great consequence, for both of these special
courts strongly influenced the development and substance of international legal rules
affecting criminal conduct by individuals in the 21st century.

THE NATURE OF INTERNATIONAL CRIMINAL LAW

International criminal law consists of penal and procedural aspects of international law,
coupled with international procedural aspects of national law. Regarding the penal
dimension, the conventions, customs, and general principles establish certain offenses that
are international crimes and thus identify elements of criminal responsibility and means
of enforcement. Since the Nuremberg trials in 1945, the body of international criminal
legal rules has constantly expanded in scope, content, application, and enforcement. In
this process, the principle of individual criminal responsibility for conduct proscribed
under international law is reaffirmed.

International crimes are established through international legal rules, primarily through
conventions, but also through custom and general principles of law. Importantly, the
essence of international criminal legal rules is framed within the principles of legality.
These principles require that there be no crime without a law (*nullum crimen sine lege*), no
punishment without a law (*nulla poena sine lege*), and no ex post facto application of laws.[1]
Thus, under the rules of international criminal law, a crime must be sufficiently defined
and publicized such that persons realize a particular conduct is deemed to be criminal.
The prohibited conduct must be defined clearly and unambiguously as impermissible.
These principles are intended to foster fundamental justice, as they protect against arbitrary application and capricious abuse of legal rules. The policy intent is implicit, given

that these principles also enhance deterrence and thus increase compliance by governments with international criminal rules.

Two other general principles of law hold special relevance for international criminal legal rules. First, there is the concept of *jus cogens*, a peremptory norm of international law. *Jus cogens* refers to the legal status attained by certain international crimes. Norms that are *jus cogens* reflect compelling law and assume the highest hierarchical position among all legal rules and principles. As a consequence, *jus cogens* norms are deemed nonderogable—that is, they cannot be denied or suspended under any circumstances.[2] The implications of *jus cogens* assume those of a duty, not optional rights. International crimes that rise to the level of being *jus cogens* are nonderogable in time of war and peace. That is, such *jus cogens* norms may not be superceded by international agreements or policy decisions. Moreover, recognition that certain international crimes are *jus cogens* carries the duty to prosecute or extradite offenders, renders inapplicable statutes of limitation for such offenses, and activates application of universal jurisdiction in the apprehension of offenders. Among international crimes that rise to the level of *jus cogens* are aggression, genocide, crimes against humanity, piracy, slavery and slave-related practices, and torture. Legal foundations for this conclusion rest on international *opinio juris*, the psychological conviction that such behavior is required by international practice. This feeling is substantiated by the large number of states that have ratified conventions prohibiting these activities. These crimes are said to affect the interests of the entire international community because they threaten international peace and security and shock the very conscience of humanity. The second general principle, *obligatio erga omnes*, means an obligation that flows to all. Certain norms, because of their universal character, have universal application. Obligations that are derived from *jus cogens* crimes are therefore *erga omnes*, peremptory norms applicable to all persons.[3] Special human rights protections were intentionally incorporated into international criminal law, and repeated violations of life, liberty, personal integrity, and physical security led to the criminalization of those acts.

The body of law relating to international crimes falls roughly into two categories. First, there are those crimes that relate to the acts of private persons and that are usually perpetrated during peacetime. Some of these are crimes associated with acts of terrorism, which have become the focus of several recent multilateral instruments. These crimes are not usually committed directly by agents of a state, though governments may be complicitous by giving sanctuary to offenders who seek refuge from prosecution or extradition. Prototypical among such offenses is the centuries-old crime of piracy. Other offenses that fall under this category include activities that interfere with international civil aviation or international maritime navigation, that threaten diplomatically protected persons, or that involve hostage taking. Others have been subjected to international prohibitions in conventions because they involve traffic in illicit commodities—narcotics, slaves, women, children, and endangered species—or harm to a common good requiring international cooperation—such as overfishing, pollution of the sea by oil, interference with submarine cables, unlawful use of the mails, or counterfeiting currency.

The second category of international crimes applies to acts sponsored by governments or committed by public officials on behalf of a state. These are violations of international norms intended to restrain the conduct of state officials toward other persons. Such offenses may occur during armed conflict and may include conventional war crimes, crimes against the peace, crimes against humanity, and acts of aggression. The commission of genocide, support for apartheid, and the systematic use of torture by government agents also qualify as criminal offenses under this category. It is under this second category of crimes that governments that systemically violated human rights norms and violently victimized massive numbers of persons during the 20th century fall. We look first to international crimes committed by individuals in their private capacity.

Crimes Committed by Private Persons

Certain activities by individuals are deemed unlawful simply because they are perceived to be so evil that they shock the conscience of humankind. Among such international criminal offenses are slavery, piracy, threats to maritime navigation, threats to the safety of civil aviation, and hostage taking. Other individual crimes pose threats to the safety and security of various international services, such as trafficking in narcotics, endangering use of the international mail system, and counterfeiting currencies.

Slavery

Great Britain abolished slavery in 1807 and began the international movement to outlaw the slave trade through several bilateral treaties with like-minded states throughout the 19th century. A number of international conventions have been promulgated, beginning with the Convention of Saint-Germain-en-Laye of 1919, which provided for the total abolition of slavery and of the slave trade on land and sea. The 1926 Convention to Suppress the Slave-Trade and Slavery—coupled with its companion instrument, the 1956 Supplementary Convention on the Abolition of Slavery, the Slave Trade, and Institutions and Practices Similar to Slavery—furnish the core legal rules that prohibit slavery in contemporary international affairs.[4] The glaring weakness of these documents is their lack of viable enforcement provisions. Parties are expected to enforce the rules prohibiting slavery in their own states, but no sanctions are provided to punish parties or nonparty states that tolerate or engage in slave-related practices. Albeit when slavery occurs, it is often because governments acquiesce in those practices in their societies.

Slavery does not threaten world peace, nor it is necessarily transnational in character; yet, slavery shocks the conscience of the world community.[5] It contravenes the fundamental principle that every individual is entitled to be free and secure in his or her person. Concern over the unlawfulness of the slave trade is reiterated in article 99 of the 1982 Law of the Sea Convention, which asserts:

> Every State shall take effective measures to prevent and punish the transport of slaves in ships authorized to fly its flag, and to prevent the unlawful use of its flag for that purpose. Any slave taking refuge on board any ship, whatever its flag, shall ipso facto be free.

The same instrument reaffirms in article 110 the right of all public vessels to stop, visit, and search any merchant vessel on the high seas when there is reasonable ground for suspicion that the ship is engaged in the slave trade.

Although a crime under modern international law, slavery is still practiced in a number of states. For example, in Mauritania it is believed that at least one hundred thousand people are held as property, and another three hundred thousand "freed" slaves still serve their masters. More than 40 percent of the inhabitants remain in servitude or in a slavelike relationship with the Arab Berber population, about 30 percent of Mauritania's 2.5 million people. In the Sudan, the capture and trafficking of children still flourishes and is particularly active in southern Kordofan and Darfur. The Arab-dominated government periodically conducts raids on African villages in the south and abducts hundreds of young black Sudanese who are then sold into slavery in the north.[6] Increasing in modern times are certain slave-related practices that lack specific normative sanction and enforcement means in international criminal law. Such contemporary vagaries of slavery include the widespread traffic of women and children for sexual exploitation and the forced indentured servitude of persons in return for their unlawful entry into Western states.[7]

Piracy

Piracy is the oldest internationally recognized crime, and a pirate today is still considered an outlaw and enemy of all humankind (*hostis humani generis*). Piracy *jure gentium* (under the law of nations) is the first international crime warranting universal jurisdiction, a concept that permits any state to bring a pirate to justice at any time, anywhere.

The rules against piracy developed in the common interest of maritime states to protect their overseas trade. They were first codified in the 1958 Geneva Convention on the High Seas and subsequently incorporated nearly verbatim into the more comprehensive 1982 Law of the Sea Convention.[8] According to the modern definition, piracy refers to any illegal acts of violence, detention, or any act of depredation committed for private ends by the crew or the passengers of a private ship or private aircraft and directed (*a*) on the high seas or the exclusive economic zone beyond the territorial sea, against another ship or aircraft, or against persons or property on board such a ship or aircraft; or (*b*) against a ship, aircraft, persons or property in a place outside the jurisdiction of any state. Voluntary participation in the operation of a pirate ship or aircraft and in the incitment or facilitation of piratical acts are also considered to be piracy.[9]

A pirate craft carries the nationality of the state in which it is registered. In modern times, the failure of a ship or an aircraft to display a flag is not a sufficient condition to classify the vessel as piratical. If the vessel flies no flag or the flag of an unrecognized entity, or if the municipal laws of a state provide that piratical acts are grounds for denationalizing the status of a vessel, then that pirate ship or aircraft would be regarded as stateless by all governments. In any event, ships of any nationality that are reasonably suspected of piracy may be boarded, and if those suspicions prove justified, persons and property on board may be seized. The courts of the state whose ship seizes the pirate vessel may prosecute the pirates and determine what action should be taken with regard to the vessel and property on board.

Not everyone may enforce sanctions against piracy. Today, government vessels of any state may seize a pirate ship or aircraft on the high seas or at any place else beyond the territorial jurisdictions of another state, arrest the pirates, and seize the property on board. Private vessels, however, are not authorized to hunt down pirates; that duty belongs to the public warships of states.

Though piracy was largely eradicated by the 19th century, sporadic attacks on the high seas continue today. During the 1970s, hundreds of piratical attacks were reported to have occurred against the Vietnamese boat people in Southeast Asian waters. According to statistics compiled by the International Criminal Court's International Maritime Bureau, more than one thousand attacks occurred during the 1990s, and since 1995 some fifteen hundred crew members have been taken hostage, with two hundred among those being killed. Most of these attacks occur in the South China Sea and off the coast of Southeast Asia in the Gulf of Thailand, the Java Sea, and the Celebes Sea, though some are also reported around the Horn of Africa, Kenya, and along Brazil.[10]

Not all acts endangering the safety of ships are piracy under international law. For example, the seizure by Captain Galvao of a Portuguese vessel the *Santa Maria* in 1961 to dramatize his opposition to the Portuguese dictator Antonio Salazar does not meet the definitional criteria for piracy. Only one ship was involved, not two, and the takeover was not carried out for private ends—that is, with the intent to rob or plunder. Similarly, the impromptu seizure by five Palestinians of the Italian cruise ship *Achille Lauro* en route from Alexandria, Egypt, to Port Said in Mediterranean Sea in 1985 was not a true act of piracy, since it involved only one ship and since the action was taken by the Palestinians not for private gain but to avoid being handed over to Western authorities.[11]

Threats to Maritime Navigation

The *Achille Lauro* affair attracted worldwide interest, largely because it demonstrated the threat of contemporary terrorism to innocent persons traveling abroad. At the same time, the seizure of the Italian cruise ship highlighted the legal anomaly that no specific international crime fit the particulars of that incident. The episode did not qualify as piracy *jure gentium,* since neither the requirement for two ships nor that for private ends motivation was met. Nor was the situation an act of mutiny by crew or passengers. The *Achille Lauro* episode involved the violent takeover by five gunmen of a cruise ship and their forcing it to sail to another port. Reacting to this legal aberration, the International Maritime Organization, a functional United Nations agency, convened in a special diplomatic conference session in 1988 and codified a new international crime: "unlawful acts against the safety of maritime navigation on the high seas," as well as a related criminal offense pertaining to damaging the safety of platforms fixed on continental shelves.[12] Among the acts that qualify as a criminal offense are the threat or forcible seizure of a ship, the destruction of navigational facilities, engaging in conduct that places a ship in danger, and the injury or murder of a person on board during the commission of any of those acts. Importantly, the conventions that codify these activities as international crimes focus on the apprehension, conviction, and punishment of persons who commit them, especially through the obligation of each party to prosecute alleged offenders or extradite them to a state having jurisdiction under the convention.[13]

Aerial Hijacking

The progressive criminalization of aerial hijacking in international law reflects the pattern that, as more persons feel threatened by some criminal conduct, international instruments will be negotiated and, over time, greater specificity regarding their penal characteristics will emerge in convention provisions. During the 1960s and 1970s, a series of aircraft seizures highlighted the serious nature of aircraft hijacking. Between 1968 and 1982, 684 attempted aerial hijackings occurred, resulting in at least five hundred deaths and four hundred injuries. From 1968 through 1972, at least 168 skyjackings were instigated from the United States to Cuba. This concern prompted governments to take actions that eventuated in the creation of a new crime in international law. The crime of aerial hijacking—the unlawful seizure of aircraft in flight perpetrated by private individuals for personal reasons or political motives—emerged as an international criminal offense, because nearly all governments recognized the real dangers posed by such threats to the safety of aircraft and passengers and were willing to take appropriate legal and security measures.

The International Civil Aviation Organization (ICAO) spurred interest in the development of international legal rules to combat aircraft hijacking and unlawful acts against international air safety. In 1963, ICAO drafted the Tokyo Convention on Offenses and Certain Other Acts Committed on Board Aircraft.[14] This instrument treats the legal status of skyjackers incidentally, merely regarding them as offenders. But the growing number of aerial hijackings in the late 1960s convinced ICAO to draft a stronger legal document: the 1970 (Hague) Convention for the Suppression of Unlawful Seizure of Aircraft.[15] This agreement formally establishes aerial hijacking as a distinct international crime and removes from the receiving state that government's discretion regarding prosecution of an offender. Parties are duty bound to extradite or prosecute offenders, regardless of their motivation. In September 1971, ICAO convened a third diplomatic conference and concluded the Montreal Convention to Discourage Acts of Violence against Civil Aviation (the Montreal Aircraft Sabotage Convention).[16] This instrument stipulates as international criminal offenses other acts that threaten air transportation—such as placing explosives in aircraft, the destruction of aircraft in service, damage to airport navigation facilities, acts of violence against persons on board aircraft, and extortion hoaxes aboard an aircraft. In 1988, the Protocol for the Suppression of Unlawful Acts of Violence at Airports Serving International Civil Aviation was signed in Montreal, with the express purpose of strengthening enforcement provisions that contribute to the punishment of persons who attack public airport facilities.

The lessons derived from threats against aircraft and airport facilities are clear. International criminal law must evolve to establish the nature of a criminal activity and to institutionalize the lawful means to suppress it. Moreover, while essential for setting out the framework for multilateral law enforcement, international agreements alone cannot work as effective weapons against the threat of skyjackers. There must be genuine cooperation by all states to apprehend and prosecute offenders, as well as the political willingness by governments to uphold their international legal obligations by refusing refuge for offenders, regardless of the political circumstances. Finally, on the national level there must be stringent anti-skyjacking legislation and security measures enacted to deter and apprehend would-be offenders. While legal instruments clarify the nature of the international crime and identify the ways and means of dealing with offenders, the extent to which those instruments work effectively remains dependent on the degree to which national governments are willing to implement and enforce them.[17]

Hostage Taking

Criminal concern over the taking of hostages in peacetime does not stem from concerns over unlawful aircraft seizures or ship seajackings. Such hostage taking is recognized as a separate international crime in which the intention of the hostage takers is to bring pressure to bear on governments or to protect themselves from attack or reprisal. The need to criminalize such an offense internationally was spotlighted in 1979 by the takeover of the U.S. embassy by revolutionary students in Teheran, Iran.[18] The militant hostage takers seized fifty-three members of the American embassy staff and demanded the return of the shah of Iran (who had fled to the United States) to stand trial for crimes against the Iranian people. The Iranian government did nothing to prevent seizure of the embassy, nor did it make efforts to liberate the American hostages. On the contrary, the government approved of the hostage-taking action. In reaction, the Carter administration sought redress through the International Court of Justice. On November 29, 1979, the United States filed its application with the court in the Case Concerning United States Diplomatic and Consular Staff in Teheran (*United States v. Iran*), seeking an order of interim measures in connection with the seizure of its Teheran embassy and the taking of diplomatic hostages.[19] The court issued an order for interim measures on December 15, 1979, unanimously instructing Iran to give U.S. diplomatic personnel full protection, privileges, and immunities guaranteed under international law and to not put the hostages on trial. Iran ignored the order. On March 20, 1980, the United States presented its case before the court, and on May 24, 1980, the court handed down its judgment on the merits. The court found that Iran had violated its obligations under international conventions and general rules of international law, that Iran bore responsibility for the hostage taking, that normal diplomatic privileges had to be restored, and that no hostages were to be put on trial.[20] Largely in response to these events in Iran, the UN General Assembly drafted and approved, in December 1979, the International Convention against the Taking of Hostages, which entered into force in 1983.[21]

The taking of foreign hostages by Saddam Hussein's government in Iraq in 1990 was the largest such seizure in history. Two weeks after its invasion of Kuwait, Iraq announced on August 15, 1990, that it would hold all male foreigners from "aggressive nations" until the threat of war against Iraq abated. Some six hundred foreign nationals were then transported to various military or industrial facilities, where they were held as "human shields" to deter a U.S. attack. Intensive diplomatic negotiations involving the UN Security Council, Western governments, and Saddam Hussein over the following four months led to the selective release of more than a million foreign nationals from Iraq, including among them two thousand U.S. citizens, twenty-five hundred other Westerners, and thirty-two hundred Soviet citizens. There is no question that Iraq's 1990 hostage taking breached international law and served as a catalyst to underscore the relevance of hostage taking as a criminal act under the modern legal rules for states.

Kidnapping of Diplomats

A related modern crime is the threat and use of force against internationally protected persons, including diplomats. The incident that precipitated criminalization of this offense was the seizure and killing of eleven U.S. diplomats by Palestinian terrorists in Khartoum, Sudan, in 1971. While protection of diplomats is rooted in customary international law, the modern penal prohibition emerges from international conventional rules—in particular, the 1973 Convention on the Prevention and Punishment of International Crimes against Internationally Protected Persons, Including Diplomatic Agents, which entered into force in 1977.[22]

International Drug Offenses

The unlawful traffic of drugs and related drug offenses have been elevated to an international crime in modern times. The international community is clearly concerned with dangerous effects of drug traffic and drug use, and such activities are now criminalized internationally. While a number of specialized conventions aim to regulate the cultivation, manufacture, trade, and use of narcotic drugs, the main instrument for regulating unlawful traffic in drugs is the UN Convention against Illicit Traffic in Narcotic Drugs and Psychotropic Substances, adopted by an international conference in 1988 with direct penal intent.[23] This instrument enumerates offenses that are to be treated as crimes under the domestic laws of states party to the convention, with detailed provisions for international cooperation to bring international drug traffickers to justice. An innovation permits shipments of drugs to pass through states so that police agencies can trace shipments to their buyers. Each party is obliged to establish jurisdiction over offenses committed in its territory, on board a vessel flying its flag, or on an aircraft registered under its law at the time an offense is committed. Parties are further obliged to exchange criminal evidence and eliminate safe havens for drug offenders, and each enumerated offense is deemed to be extraditable under any extradition treaty existing between the parties.

Unlawful Use of International Mail

The unlawful use of international mail is prohibited to maintain the integrity of international postal systems. For protection against this crime to be realized, interstate cooperation in prosecuting or extraditing offenders is essential. Placement of hazardous materials into the mail system, while not a crime that shocks the conscience of the international community, is clearly an offense against the safe and secure postal activities embodied in the 189-member-state Universal Postal Union.[24]

Counterfeiting and Fraudulent Documentation

Governments have a clear interest in ensuring the stability of the international monetary system by protecting the value of currencies that operate in that system. This has led them to the international criminalization of activities involving the falsification of financial documents and the counterfeiting of currencies. To these ends, the international prohibition on counterfeiting proscribes the making, passing, buying, selling, or transporting of counterfeit currency. The national interest here is not one of being morally offended nor that of an act constituting a threat to world peace. Rather, the main interest for states is that of economic security and international necessity in maintaining the stability of the international monetary system. The principal instrument negotiated to curtail such criminal activities remains the 1929 International Convention for the Suppression of Counterfeiting Currency.[25]

Unlawful Acts against the Environment

Among the newest types of international crimes are activities that do serious harm or degradation to natural resources, endangered species, or common areas protected by various international agreements. Worldwide concern for the environment has led in recent years to the adoption of several international instruments that aim to protect the air, seas, rivers, land, and polar regions, as well as certain endangered animal species, such as whales, salmon, tuna, dolphins, polar bears, seals, and migratory birds. Individuals are prohibited by international agreements from overfishing and polluting the seas, and governments are generally responsible for ensuring that air pollution from their territory does not cause harm to other states or common areas beyond the limits of national jurisdiction.[26] While the criminal nature of damaging protected areas of the environment may not at present appear to threaten international peace or endanger national security, the potential long-term consequences remain legitimate concerns for future generations. Violations of resource conservation and antipollution rules, which are usually perpetrated by individuals in their private capacity, are becoming increasingly viewed as international criminal acts.

Crimes Committed by Governments

The 21st century witnessed the worst violence in human history, with the past fifty years being especially brutal. Since the end of the Second World War, more than 250 conflicts have erupted around the world, in which 90 million civilians, mostly women and children, have been killed and more than 170 million people were deprived of their rights, property, and human dignity.[27] The majority of these victims have simply been forgotten, and few of their perpetrators have been held accountable. But within the past decade some important developments have occurred—namely, the international criminalization of such acts, the foundation of judicial procedures and institutions for bringing offenders to justice, and the evolution of political will by governments to prosecute and punish those suspected of committing particularly heinous acts.

Most of these international crimes are committed with the sponsorship of governments or by public officials on behalf of a state. Among international crimes committed by agents of a state during armed conflict are aggression, war crimes, crimes against humanity, and genocide—all of which are considered grave violations against humanity. These acts are *jus cogens*, and the normative prohibitions against them apply to all persons. International legal rules impose clear obligations on governments to investigate and prosecute suspected violators of humanitarian law (the *laws of war*) and other high human rights crimes. International treaty instruments implement rules of international criminal law, as they prohibit certain offenses that contravene human rights norms and obligate governments to national or international prosecution of offenders. Government agents become subjects of international legal norms and are made liable for national or international prosecution for international crimes committed against innocent persons. Contrariwise, the victim remains an object of international law. Any redress sought by an individual against those agents for human rights violations must be done through the state, which represents the victim in international or national tribunals. Therefore, under international criminal law, individual victims do not have the legal or juridical authority to take criminal offenders to court. That duty belongs to the government of a state.

Apartheid

The intentional attempt by a government to establish and maintain domination by one race of persons over another race, known as apartheid, is conducted on a national level and usually affects just the citizens of the state where it is being practiced. But it reaches the level of an international crime because it transforms an intranational act or condition into a situation deemed offensive by international standards. Apartheid contravenes the presumptions that all persons are born free and equal in dignity and are entitled to certain fundamental human rights and freedoms as set out in the 1948 Universal Declaration of Human Rights. The unlawfulness of apartheid is affirmed and codified by two international instruments: the 1966 International Convention on the Elimination of All Forms of Racial Discrimination[28] and the 1973 International Convention on the Suppression and Punishment of the Crime of Apartheid.[29] While the practice and condemnation of apartheid appear only applicable to South Africa—a situation that has ended—the possibility that similar practices might evolve among settler regimes and occupied territories in other parts of the world sustains the relevance of the crime for modern international law.[30]

Aggression

No international convention specifically declares that aggression is a crime under international law. Even so, the concept of aggression embodies the prohibition against unlawful use of force and pursuit of an "unjust" war. The UN General Assembly in 1974 defined aggression in a consensus resolution as "the use of armed force by a State against the sovereignty, territorial integrity or political independence of another State, or in any other manner inconsistent with the Charter of the United Nations."[31] Acts considered to be aggressive include invasion or attack by the armed forces of a state against the territory of another state; military occupation or annexation of the territory of another state; bombardment or use of weapons against the territory of another state; blockade of another state's coasts or ports; attack by armed forces of one state against the military forces of another state; action by a state that allows its territory to be used by another state for committing an act of aggression against a third state; and the sending of armed bands or groups of irregulars or mercenaries to carry out acts of armed force against another state which are of such gravity as to constitute aggression. The General Assembly concluded that aggression represents "the most serious and dangerous form of the illegal use of force, being fraught, in the conditions created by the existence of all types of weapons of mass destruction, with the threat of a world conflict and all its catastrophic consequences."[32] This resolution is not a binding legal instrument. Its legal relevance relies not only on customary legal rules but on the willingness of states to abide by their UN Charter obligations. Though not formally linked to aggression, the charge of crimes against the peace is closely aligned with it. That offense was applied in the Nuremberg and Tokyo war crimes trials against persons thought responsible for initiating the Second World War. Of significant note, the 1998 Statute of the Permanent International Criminal Court would make aggression eligible for inclusion as a prosecutable offense under the Court, pending agreement on a resolute definition of the nature of such a criminal act.

Crimes Committed during Armed Conflict

The modern legal competence to deal with offenses in wartime evolves from the precedent set by the International Military Tribunal at Nuremberg,[33] the article 6 provisions of its charter,[34] and the Nuremberg trials that followed in 1945. This legal legacy is reaffirmed and strengthened in the statutes of two special international tribunals that were created during the 1990s by the Security Council to prosecute alleged offenders for high crimes and human rights violations in the former Yugoslavia and Rwanda. Thus, international codification and consensus since the Second World War confirm war crimes as international criminal acts and permit governments to identify and punish persons for those extraterritorial crimes wherever and whenever they are committed.[35]

Governments today allocate to special international institutions legal competence to deal with particular crimes during armed conflict designated as having an international character and perpetrated by certain persons during a specified period in a given territory. Persons may be prosecuted under contemporary international law for four groups of such criminal law offenses: grave breaches of the four Geneva Conventions of 1949;[36] violations of the laws or customs of war; acts of genocide;[37] and crimes against humanity.[38] These acts are stipulated by the international community as criminal offenses against all humankind, from which there should be no impunity.

Grave Breaches

The clearest articulation of grave breaches is found in the four Geneva Conventions of 1949—in particular, common articles 50, 51, 130, and 147, which prescribe minimum rules to noninternational situations of armed conflict.[39] Nonetheless, commission of a grave breach warrants individual criminal liability, and governments party to these conventions remain bound by the corresponding duty to prosecute accused offenders. Similarly, parties have the obligation to search for, prosecute, and punish perpetrators of grave breaches, unless parties opt to relinquish such persons for trial in another state.

The duty to prosecute grave breaches under the Geneva Conventions is limited to international conflicts, a requirement that derives from common article 2 of the four Geneva Conventions. More recently, the Statute of the International Criminal Tribunal for the Former Yugoslavia incorporates the essential language of this common "grave breaches" provision into its article 2 and gives that tribunal lawful authority to prosecute persons "committing or ordering to be committed" certain acts that rise to the level of war crimes under modern international humanitarian law. At present, commission by persons of any of the following acts is considered, without qualification, a war crime: willful killing; torture or inhuman treatment, including biological experiments; willfully causing of great suffering or serious injury to body or health; extensive destruction and appropriation of property, nonjustified by military necessity and carried out unlawfully and wantonly; compelling a prisoner of war or a civilian to serve in the forces of a hostile power; willfully depriving a prisoner of war or a civilian of the rights of fair and regular trial; unlawful deportation or transfer or unlawful confinement of a civilian; taking civilians as hostages.

Since the violence in Rwanda was more of an ethnic rampage than an internal war, the statute for the Rwanda tribunal does not address grave breaches per se. Rather, it refers to "violations of Article 3 common to the Geneva Conventions and of Additional Protocol II."[40] In this regard, violations as enumerated in article 4 of the Rwanda statute "include, but are not limited to" the following acts: violence to life, health, and physical or mental well-being of persons—in particular, murder as well as cruel treatment such as torture, mutilation, or any form of corporal punishment; collective punishments; taking of hostages; acts of terrorism; outrages against personal dignity—in particular, humiliating and degrading treatment, rape, enforced prostitution, and any form of indecent assault; pillage; the passing of sentences and the expediting of executions without previous judgment pronounced by a regularly constituted court, affording all the juridical guarantees that are recognized as indispensable by civilized peoples. A threat to commit any of these acts would amount to a grave breach as well.

The rules of contemporary international law assert that accused offenders of these grave breach prohibitions should be apprehended, prosecuted, and if convicted duly punished. Neither the Geneva Conventions nor the statutes of the International Criminal Tribunal for the Former Yugoslavia or the International Criminal Tribunal for Rwanda contain provisions that approve of, or guarantee impunity for, offenders under special conditions or circumstances. All of these instruments function with the intent to promote prosecution of alleged offenders, not absolve them of individual responsibility or accountability.

The Abu Ghraib prison scandal during 2004, which implicated 23 U.S. military intelligence personnel and four contractors, underscores this point. Among the abuses and acts of torture reportedly perpetrated by these Americans against Iraqis were forcing them into unlawful stress positions, compelling prisoners to perform humiliating and degrading acts, physically beating them, and using dogs to threaten prisoners during interrogations. Not only are these acts grave breaches under the 1949 Geneva Convention on Prisoners of War, they also violate the 1984 Convention against Torture.

Violations of the Laws or Customs of War

Another vital ingredient of international humanitarian law is the 1907 Hague Convention Respecting the Laws and Customs of War on Land, especially the regulations annexed thereto.[41] The relevance of these rules for contemporary international criminal law is underscored in the statute of the International Criminal Tribunal for the Former Yugoslavia, which upgrades these prohibitions into a modern context. The Statute's article 3 asserts that persons should be prosecuted for violating the laws or customs of war (as derived from the Hague Regulations), including, but not restricted to the following: employment of poisonous weapons or other weapons calculated to cause unnecessary suffering; wanton destruction of cities, towns, or villages or devastation not justified by military necessity; attack and bombardment, by whatever means, of undefended towns, villages, dwellings, and buildings; seizure of and destruction or willful damage done to institutions dedicated to religion, charity, education, and the arts and sciences, as well as to historic monuments and works of art and science; plunder of public or private property. These provisions originate from articles 23–28 of the 1907 Hague Regulations and are generally regarded today as violations of the laws of war under international humanitarian law. That is, although certain war crimes may not entail grave breaches or genocide, they may constitue serious depredations of human rights and thus legally obligate states to prosecute offenders.[42]

Genocide

The 1948 Convention on the Prevention and Punishment of Genocide, inspired by the horrors of the Holocaust, provides an absolute obligation to prosecute persons responsible for committing acts of genocide. As defined in article 2 of the convention, genocide is "the intent to destroy, in whole or in part, a national, ethnical, racial or religious group, as such" and includes any of the following acts: killing members of the group; causing serious bodily or mental harm to members of the group; deliberately inflicting on the group conditions of life calculated to bring about its physical destruction in whole or in part; imposing measures intended to prevent births within the group; and forcibly transferring children of the group to another group. These provisions enumerate various acts that qualify as war crimes prosecutable as acts of genocide under modern international law. The Genocide Convention stipulates in article 3 that certain specific actions shall be punishable: genocide; conspiracy to commit genocide; direct and public incitement to commit genocide; attempt to commit genocide; and complicity to commit genocide. The Genocide Convention mandates that persons accused of committing genocide be tried by a competent tribunal of the state in the territory in which the act was committed or by an acceptable international tribunal and that parties punish convicted offenders through "effective penalties."[43] The convention does not obligate parties to prosecute all offenders in their custody, nor does it explicitly call for the prosecution of all such offenders irrespective of their location. Under the Genocide Convention, parties are obligated only to exercise domestic jurisdiction pursuant to the territorial principle, with the possibility to try offenders by a competent tribunal of the state where the offense was committed, or by an international penal tribunal that may have jurisdiction.

Notwithstanding these qualifications, genocide remains a high crime under customary international law and gives rise to universal jurisdiction to the same degree as war crimes and crimes against humanity. Indeed, genocide was treated as an offense against the law of nations even before the Genocide Convention was drafted. The General Assembly adopted resolutions in 1946 that affirmed the Nuremberg principles and declared genocide to be an international crime.[44] Every state thus has the customary legal right to exercise universal jurisdiction to prosecute offenders for committing genocide, wherever it is committed and by whomever. The Genocide Convention does not derogate from that obligation. Parties to the antigenocide instrument have merely obligated themselves to prosecute offenses committed solely within their territory.

Crimes against Humanity

A customary obligation under international law has emerged since the Second World War to prohibit and prosecute crimes against humanity. These egregious international criminal acts are committed systematically on a massive scale. The rules of international law assert clear international jurisdiction over persons alleged to have committed crimes against humanity, and no statutory limitations are permissible.[45]

The criminalization of such acts originates in article 6 of the 1945 Nuremberg Charter. Crimes against humanity are directed at any civilian population and are prohibited in armed conflict, regardless of its international or internal character. The International Criminal Tribunal for the Former Yugoslavia statute stipulates these critical points in the modern context and enumerates eight categories of specific acts to be regarded as crimes against humanity: murder; extermination; enslavement; deportation; imprisonment; torture; rape; and persecution on political, racial, and religious grounds. A ninth category, "other inhumane acts," was included to make the list all-inclusive. Torture and rape, however, were not designated as crimes against humanity until the 1990s.

As previously mentioned, condemnation of acts of torture finds explicit expression in the 1984 Convention against Torture, which is now in force and accepted as a peremptory norm in human rights law. As defined in article 1, *torture* means

> any act by which severe pain or suffering, whether physical or mental, is intentionally inflicted on a person for such purposes as obtaining from him or a third person information or a confession, punishing him for an act he or a third person has committed or is suspected of having committed, or intimidating or coercing him or a third person, or for any reason based on discrimination or any kind, when such pain or suffering is inflicted by or at the instigation of or with the consent or acquiescence of a public official or other person acting in an official capacity. It does not include pain or suffering arising only from, inherent in or incidental to lawful sanctions.

Many of the most brutal atrocities committed against victims of human rights abuse include acts of torture under this definition, which has been elaborated by other international instruments prohibiting torture.[46]

The Torture Convention obligates each state party to ensure that all acts of torture are made criminal offenses under its domestic law and to establish its jurisdiction over the offense when, among other criteria, the alleged perpetrator or victim is a national of that state. Moreover, if a state does not extradite an alleged offender, that government is required to "submit the case to its competent authorities" for prosecution. In addition, the convention prohibits any "exceptional circumstances"—including conditions or threats of war, internal political stability, or public emergencies—from being used by a government to justify torture. Nor may an order from a superior officer or public authority be used to justify acts of torture.

The Torture Convention appears to suffer from certain weaknesses in its application, especially when compared with the Genocide Convention. The Genocide Convention explicitly asserts forthright duties mandating that offenders "shall be punished" and that persons accused of committing genocide "shall be tried by a competent tribunal of the State in the territory of which the act was committed" or by an acceptable international tribunal. Moreover, the state is required to "provide effective penalties" for persons found guilty of genocide. In contrast, the Torture Convention requires parties only to "submit" cases of alleged torture to their "competent authorities for the purpose of prosecution," and it makes acts of torture punishable simply by "appropriate penalties, which take into account their grave nature." Regrettably, the antitorture instrument fails to mandate explicitly that prosecution must occur for all alleged cases of torture or to stipulate that, without exception, severe penalties will be handed down for persons found guilty of a torture offense.

The crime of rape, the criminality of which was largely overlooked in past wars, took on urgency with the reported massive sexual assaults against women in Bosnia and Herzegovina during 1992 and 1993.[47] By designating rape as a specific crime against humanity, the gross criminality of the act is spotlighted as a grave violation of human rights—indeed, a war crime under international law—and international concern now directly focuses on the need to punish perpetrators. Yet the concept of crimes against humanity has yet to be legally codified into a special convention that outlines and details the explicit criminal nature of those offenses and the specific obligations of states in confronting perpetrators.

STATE RESPONSIBILITY FOR CRIMINAL OFFENSES

State responsibility entails the obligation of a state to make reparations for its failure to comply with an obligation under international law. State responsibility remains predicated on an act or omission that violates an international legal obligation resulting in injury to the claimant state. Though often associated with responsibilities to injuries aliens, state responsibility rests on substantive grounds of international law, including violation of the rule that prohibits the use of force in international relations. State responsibility can result from actions directly attributable to a government through its agents, in particular those carried out by its executive, legislative, or judicial organs. Traditionally, the individual has not been treated as a subject of international legal rules. In recent decades, however, certain crimes have become so egregious and internationally salient that their perpetrators are regarded as being subject to prosecution under the rules of international law. These persons can be pursued, indicted, arrested, tried, convicted, and punished in accordance with international criminal law.

The rules for international criminal law have several sources; chief among them are international and regional human rights rules and regional instruments on interstate cooperation in penal matters. While the application of international criminal rules in conventions is made binding only on parties to those conventions, some obligations have risen to the level of universal norms—such as the right to life, liberty, and security of the person; the right to equal protection under the law; and the right to be free from torture and cruel, inhuman, and degrading treatment or punishment.

The basis for, and elements of, a state's international criminal responsibility are established by international legal rules. The enforcement of international criminal law relies on domestic criminal justice systems. Enforcement of sanctions depends on the national law of the enforcing state, which is guided by international human rights norms and standards. In a real sense, national domestic law and international legal rules must function complementarily to make international criminal law viable and effective.

Two methods are used to enforce international criminal rules. The first and most common method of enforcing international criminal rules is through the voluntary cooperation of governments for the investigation, prosecution, trial, and punishment of individuals who are sought by national justice systems as accused offenders for the commission of international crimes. Cooperation among states in international penal matters may take various forms: use of extradition proceedings, transfer of criminal proceedings, international and regional treaty agreements, mutual recognition of foreign judgments, seizure of assets, bilateral treaties, and national legislation. The effectiveness of these cooperative means depends on the willingness of national governments to make them work.

The second method entails the establishment of a special international tribunal to enforce norms through the investigation, prosecution, adjudication, and sanction of accused offenders. The International Military Tribunal at Nuremberg, the International Military Tribunal for the Far East, the International Criminal Tribunal for the Former Yugoslavia, and the International Criminal Tribunal for Rwanda represent models of such bodies. These courts investigate and secure evidence, apprehend persons charged with offenses, and enforce orders and judgments. The creation of the permanent International Criminal Court in 1998 aims to provide a tribunal that complements national criminal jurisdiction. That is, the Court will prosecute persons accused of war crimes, genocide, and crimes against humanity when national governments opt not to prosecute and defer that responsibility to the Court instead.

International law in the 21st century recognizes that individuals are criminally responsible for their actions. It is more difficult to apply this same reasoning to the governments of states. While it is true that international legal rules assert that states are accountable for their wrongful conduct—which can result in the imposition of damages or other sanctions against them—the state as a legal abstraction cannot be brought before an international criminal court as an individual person can. The shield of sovereign impunity obstructs such criminal accountability, and the people of a polity should not be made to account for the actions of a relatively few officials and executors. Individuals in a state—be they government officials, military personnel, or private citizens—who transgress norms of international criminal law can be held accountable. It is the responsibility of states' governments to ensure that their nationals are held accountable for their actions and that accused offenders are investigated and prosecuted. If convicted, the offenders must be punished either by the prosecuting government or by some other acceptable tribunal, depending on the circumstances. Individual criminal responsibility holds the contemporary status of a general principle of law under the rules of national and international penal systems.[48]

The invocation of state responsibility can serve as a means for obtaining compensatory and punitive damages, as well as for deterring future violations of international criminal rules. This is not to assert that states are ipso facto criminally liable for the actions of their nationals. Rather, it is to suggest that the governments of states have the obligation to ensure that persons accused of international crimes are prosecuted for their offenses, regardless of their status as nationals or aliens. States are obliged to apply the rules and sanctions of international criminal justice to those persons who share in the responsibility of conspiring, planning, carrying out, aiding and abetting, or committing the proscribed conduct.

The Duty of Accountability

Fundamental to the punishment of high criminal offenses is the principle of individual criminal responsibility. For contemporary international law, a person who plans, instigates, orders, commits, or otherwise aids and abets in the planning, preparation, or execution of these acts shall be held individually responsible for the crime. International criminal law today thus confronts the principle that individuals may be held criminally liable under international law, even though their conduct might have been considered valid or even mandated by domestic law.

To enforce the laws of war and the prohibitions against genocide and crimes against humanity only against ordinary soldiers and officers of low- or midlevel rank is not enough. "Superior orders" is insufficient as a defense against a charge of violating high human rights crimes; justice still demands that culpability apply along the entire chain of command. Due obedience cannot exonerate a perpetrator from criminal responsibility. The soldier who pulls the trigger; the commander who gives the order or knows the crime is going to be committed and does not use his authority to stop it; the civilian decision maker who makes the policy generating the criminal act—all these persons are liable for criminal accountability for that offense. Accountability under international law thus reaches military elites and civilian government officials, as well as individual civilians and paramilitary forces who commit the acts.[49]

Enforcement through State Jurisdiction

Norms of international criminal law tend to be declarative, with the expectation that the legal rules are embodied in the national legislation through which it is to be enforced. Put another way, international criminal law proscriptions apply directly to individuals, though nearly all international criminal conventions rely on indirect enforcement. States are expected not only to enforce these provisions through the national criminal justice systems of state parties but also to cooperate in the prosecution and punishment of offenders.

International legal rules limit the ability of a state to apply its statutes extraterritorially. Traditionally, a state may not prosecute an individual seized beyond its borders unless it has lawful jurisdiction over the act committed by that person. Jurisdiction to prescribe must exist before the jurisdiction to adjudicate and enforce. *Extraterritorial jurisdiction* therefore involves two determinations: first, whether a domestic law exists that covers the offensive act; second, whether a sovereign state may, under international law, prescribe such conduct extraterritorially. In this connection, five fundamental principles and theoretical constructs under international law are generally available to a government for exercising prescriptive jurisdiction over persons: territoriality, nationality, the protective principle, passive personality, and universality theory.

The principal jurisdictional basis for states to prescribe rules over their nationals and their property rests on territoriality. International law permits a state to exercise jurisdiction to prescribe rules that apply to persons, their conduct, or their activities within its legal reach. Generally, a state has jurisdiction over all persons and property within its territory. States can pass legislation regulating the conduct or the status of persons within its territory or even conduct beyond its borders that can produce intended and substantial effects on its territory. This territorial principle of jurisdiction underpins the notion of national sovereignty in international law. Under this territorial notion, the state's jurisdictional authority derives from the presence of a person in the resident polity. It also allows a state to exercise its jurisdiction to subject persons or things to its judicial processes and to enforce its legal rules by using the government to induce or compel compliance with them.[50] A state may therefore regulate the actions of persons and may punish individuals who commit crimes within its borders. Of the jurisdictional principles, the territorial application is the most widely accepted and least disputed. It is key to the international application of a state's criminal law abroad, especially when a foreign event affects the state.

The territorial principle is further refined into subjective and objective territorial views. The notion of subjective territorial jurisdiction is used to justify legislation punishing criminal conduct that commences within a state and is completed abroad. A state retains the right to punish the perpetrator of a crime committed elsewhere when the intent to commit said crime was formulated within the state of origin. The objective territorial view includes offenses that commence outside a state's territory but are completed within it. Also known as the *effects doctrine*, objective territorial jurisdiction may be justified when certain crimes generate serious repercussions, or "effects," within the state.

A second basis for jurisdiction rests in the nationality of a person. The *nationality principle*, which is universally accepted in the international community, allows a state to prescribe laws that bind its nationals, regardless of where the national is or where the offense occurs. A state's jurisdiction effectively extends to its citizens and the actions they take beyond the territorial jurisdiction of the state. As mentioned earlier, the link between a state and its nationals generates reciprocal rights and obligations. The state is expected to protect its citizens when they are abroad, but when an individual's conduct harms the interests of his or her state, the state may punish the conduct regardless of where it occurred.

Third, jurisdiction may accrue from a government's perception of due harm to its state's national interests. This *protective principle* concerns acts abroad deemed prejudicial to the security interests of a state. Under the protective principle, a state may exercise jurisdiction over persons who commit certain acts outside its territory if such acts threaten the security, territorial integrity, or political independence of the state. Importantly, the protective principle allows states to prosecute nationals of other states for their conduct outside the offended state.

Jurisdiction can be asserted on grounds of the *passive personality principle*, which gives a state extraterritorial jurisdiction over offenses committed by foreigners against its nationals wherever the crime takes place. The passive personality notion implies that persons carry the protection of their state's law with them beyond the territorial jurisdiction of their own state. Under the passive personality principle, acts committed abroad by aliens against the nationals of a state convey jurisdiction to the host state. This assertion challenges the fundamental premise of sovereign jurisdiction of a state over its own territory, which obviously undercuts the fundamental principle of territorial sovereignty. The passive personality principle is not widely used, largely because it is controversial and often conflicts with the territorial principle.

Finally, there is the *principle of universal jurisdiction*, which recognizes that certain acts are so heinous and widely condemned that any state may prosecute an offender once custody is obtained. Such crimes—for example, piracy, slave trading, harming diplomats, hijacking aircraft, perpetrating war crimes, and committing genocide—are of universal concern to states, and their perpetrators are considered to be the enemies of all humankind. A person accused of such crimes can be arrested and tried by any state, any time, anywhere, without regard for the nationality of the accused. The principle of universal jurisdiction does not require establishment of any link between the criminal and the prosecuting state. All that is required is universal condemnation of the crime.

The principle of universal jurisdiction is codified in several modern international legal agreements designed to deter acts of criminal violence—namely, those conventions that prohibit piracy, threats to maritime safety, aircraft hijacking, torture, and genocide. Modern international legal rules recognize that the world community universally condemns such illicit behavior. Under these various instruments, offenders are effectively branded *hosti humani generis* (the enemies of humankind), and governments are given the duty to capture, prosecute, and punish any offender on behalf of the international community. Universal jurisdiction has thus emerged as a key principle for asserting jurisdiction over persons who violate international criminal law.[51]

Nevertheless, a state's jurisdiction can become a complex matter, not only because of domestic constitutional or legal issues, but also on account of conflict of law rules. This is particularly true when a state's concerns over individuals or juridical persons are projected into the international legal arena. There are occasions when a state might apply its internal criminal law to events that occur elsewhere but have an impact on that state. Similarly, no state is obliged to exercise jurisdiction, even if international legal rules would permit such action. Each state adopts its own domestic laws to indicate in which circumstances it will exercise jurisdiction over activities abroad. As such, a state can criminalize conduct that occurs beyond its borders and provide for prosecution if the offenders come within its territory. A state's assertion of its jurisdictional competence is in this way referred to as extraterritorial criminal jurisdiction, though the actual prosecution and punishment of the offender is done domestically. It is in this manner that national governments have attempted to enforce international criminal law, most often for those crimes committed by private persons.

Enforcement through Tribunals

State jurisdiction traditionally has proven inadequate to enforce rules of international criminal law. As a consequence, the international community has on occasion created special tribunals to address matters relating to international crimes, paying particular attention in modern times to those crimes committed by agents of the state. In this respect, since 1945 four prominent international criminal law tribunals have been established: the International Military Tribunal at Nuremberg; the International Criminal Tribunal for the Former Yugoslavia; the International Criminal Tribunal for Rwanda; and the permanent International Criminal Court.

The Nuremberg Trials

The Second World War wreaked havoc across Europe and cost the lives of millions of soldiers and civilians. But the greatest horror only became apparent in early 1945 when Allied troops began liberating concentration camps that had been set up throughout central Europe by the Nazi regime. Millions of civilians and prisoners of war had been seized by the Nazis and transported to the camps, where they were eventually killed. At least six million Jews and other minorities targeted by the Nazis—including gypsies, homosexuals, and ethnic Slavs—died in the camps. As the war in Europe was ending, the Allied governments agreed that it was necessary to punish those persons responsible for these atrocities. They set up an international military tribunal in the German city of Nuremberg and conducted trials of high-level German officials after the war. In addition, six organizations were indicted for their criminal purposes and activities before and during the war. The four principal allies—the United States, Great Britain, Soviet Union, and France—appointed judges to the tribunal and furnished prosecutors.

The first modern international war crimes trials began on November 20, 1945, as twenty-one Nazi German officials were tried on three basic charges. First, some defendants were charged with conspiring and ultimately launching "an aggressive war"—that is, committing "crimes against the peace." This charge was defined in the indictments as "the planning, preparation, initiation, and waging of wars of aggression, which were also wars in violation of international treaties, agreements, and assurances," including the Kellogg-Briand Pact of 1928.[52] A second charge was the commission of war crimes—that is, acts that violated the traditional concepts of the laws of war, including the use of slave labor, the bombing of civilian populations, and the issuing of reprisal orders that required fifty captured soldiers be shot for each German soldier killed by partisans. War crimes were defined in the tribunal's charter as "murder, ill-treatment or deportation to slave labor or for any other purpose of civilian population or in occupied territory, murder or ill-treatment of prisoners-of-war or persons on the seas, killing of hostages, plunder of public or private property, wanton destruction of cities, towns or villages or devastation not justified by military necessity."

The third count was that of committing crimes against humanity, which was aimed at defendants responsible for the death camps, concentration camps, and killing rampages on the Eastern front. These crimes were defined as "murder, extermination, enslavement, deportation, and other inhumane acts committed against any civilian population before or during the war, or persecution on political, racial, or religious grounds in execution of or in connection with any crimes within the jurisdiction of the International Military Tribunal, whether or not in violation of domestic law of the country where perpetrated."

The Nuremberg trials lasted eleven months. Of the twenty-one defendants in custody—one of the accused Nazis, Martin Bormann, could not be found and was indicted in absentia—eleven were sentenced to death, three were acquitted, and the rest received prison sentences. In November 1946 the sentences were carried out, and ten of the defendants were hanged. (Hermann Goring, who had been sentenced to die, committed suicide hours before his scheduled execution.) In addition to individuals, three organizations were found guilty of engaging in criminal activities: the SS, the gestapo, and the Corps of the Political Leaders of the Nazi Party.

Critics of the Nuremberg process argue that the trials represented victors' justice because they were imposed on the vanquished leadership at the end of the war. Moreover, the absence of neutral or German judges on the court made the tribunal appear as a form of revenge. In addition, defendants were being tried ex post facto—that is, for acts that were not criminal offenses when they were committed. It was the London Charter in 1945 that created the offenses of crimes against the peace and crimes against humanity. Critics also posit that no appeal was afforded to the defendants, even in the case of capital punishment verdicts, and that the Allied victors did not investigate war crimes attributed to members of their own armed forces. While these criticisms are fair, the fact remains that the offenses of the accused were so heinous, so contrary to human decency, that effective prosecution and punishment of their perpetrators were at minimum a necessity for the postwar order.

Prosecution of the Nazis represented an unprecedented effort to punish people accused of war crimes and crimes against humanity. For the first time, notions of collective guilt and conspiracy were used to justify international punishment. For the first time, an organized effort was made to apply principles of international law to punish persons responsible for gross violations of international norms. Nuremberg made clear that international legal rules applied to individuals as well as to governments of states. Crimes against international legal norms are committed by men and women, not by abstract political entities called states. Only through punishment of the persons responsible for those crimes could international law be enforced and could justice be served.

Closely associated with the Nuremberg tribunal was the International Military Tribunal for the Far East, established in Tokyo after the war and sometimes called the Tokyo War Crimes Trials. As in Nuremberg, a special charter defined the categories of crimes—

namely, crimes against the peace, war crimes, crimes against humanity, and conspiracy to commit those crimes. An eleven-judge tribunal was set up to prosecute Japanese officials and industrial leaders who had overseen the country's military aggression throughout Asia in World War II. The trials began on June 4, 1946, and judgments were handed down November 4, 1948. Of the twenty-eight defendants—of whom the most prominent was former prime minister Hideki Tojo, who ordered the attack on Pearl Harbor—seven were sentenced to death. The others received prison sentences.[53]

The trials at Nuremberg and Tokyo represent a milestone for international criminal law. Traditionally, enforcement of international humanitarian norms was left to states, who largely ignored them. For the first time, these tribunals provided the enforcement of international humanitarian law at the level of the individual criminal. Persons were punished for their crimes—severely.

The Tribunal for the Former Yugoslavia

Nearly forty-five years passed before the next serious international effort was made to prosecute perpetrators of massive violations of humanitarian law. The international reaction over the shocking extent of war crimes committed during 1991–1993 in the former Yugoslavia, especially through "ethnic cleansing," prompted the Security Council to create the International Criminal Tribunal for the Former Yugoslavia (ICTY). The way was paved for this court by a series of Security Council resolutions. In August 1992 Security Council resolution 771 held that persons who committed, or ordered the commission of, grave breaches of the 1949 Geneva Conventions for the Protection of War Victims were individually responsible for such acts. The resolution called on international humanitarian organizations to gather information relating to such breaches. In October 1992, Security Council resolution 780 requested the Secretary-General to establish an impartial commission of experts to examine the information submitted and to report to the Security Council its findings. The commission concluded that grave breaches of the Geneva Conventions were indeed committed on a massive scale in the territory of the former Yugoslavia. In response, the Security Council in February 1993 adopted resolution 808, which provided that an international tribunal be established for the prosecution of persons responsible for serious violations of international humanitarian law in the former Yugoslavia since 1991. In addition, it requested the Secretary-General to report on specific proposals for implementing this resolution. Finally, the Security Council on May 25, 1993, adopted resolution 827, which approved the report of the secretary-general and created the tribunal based on the statute annexed to his report.

The Tribunal can prosecute individuals for genocide, crimes against humanity, grave breaches of the Geneva Conventions, and violations of the laws and customs of war committed in the territory of the former Yugoslavia since 1991. In addition, the ICTY's chief prosecutor stated publicly in March 1998 that the Tribunal's jurisdiction extended to violence committed in Kosovo. The Tribunal is expected to prosecute leaders for command responsibility, and such suspects can be indicted for ordering, planning, conspiring, or failing to stop violations of which they should have been aware.

The Tribunal has primacy over national courts, in the former Yugoslavia and in the rest of the world. No persons may be tried twice for the same crime, either in the ICTY or in the ICTY and a national court. There may be no trials in absentia, and jurisdiction only covers natural persons. Prosecutions against juridical persons, such as organizations or associations, are not permitted.

The ICTY has three main components. First, there is the judges' chambers. The Tribunal has sixteen judges who are responsible for adopting and amending the rules of procedure and evidence, reviewing indictments, hearing cases, and rendering judgments. The judges are divided into three trial chambers of three judges each and one appeals chambers with seven judges. Judges serve terms of four years and are elected by the General Assembly from a list submitted by the Security Council. The President of the Tribunal serves as chief justice, presides over the appeals chamber, and has the authority to communicate with the Security Council when a state refuses to cooperate with the Tribunal.

The second part of the ICTY is the office of the prosecutor, which has responsibility for investigating alleged crimes, framing indictments, and prosecuting cases. The Chief Prosecutor, who is appointed for a four-year term by the Security Council, has principal responsibility for overseeing the investigation and prosecution of all cases.

A third component of the ICTY, the Registry, serves as administrative arm of the Tribunal. The Registry performs a variety of functions—among them, acquiring equipment, hiring personnel, and processing financial matters. The Registry also recommends protective measures for witnesses and furnishes counseling and support for victims and their families. Finally, people in the Registry assist the judges in preparing legal memoranda, developing directives for assigning counsel, and running the detention facility where the accused are held before and during trial.

Located in The Hague, the ICTY receives most of its funding from United Nations members states' assessed contributions. As of September 2004 at least 103 accused persons have appeared in proceedings before the tribunal, including more than twenty indicted for genocide. Sixty-one individuals have been tried, of whom forty-one were officially convicted and five were acquitted. Fifty-eight accused persons are in custody at the detention unit in The Hague, and at least twenty-one are still at large and for whom arrest warrants have been issued, among them Radovan Karadzic and Ratko Mladic.[54]

The Tribunal for Rwanda

The horrifying massacre of eight hundred thousand to one million Tutsis and moderate Hutus in Rwanda during April–June 1994 created an international outcry for punishing the perpetrators of the genocide. In response, the Security Council adopted resolution 935, which requested the Secretary-General to establish a Commission of Experts to examine evidence of serious violations of international humanitarian law in Rwanda and to report its findings to the Security Council. The Commission concluded that grave breaches of international humanitarian law were committed by both sides, but the overwhelming evidence revealed that genocide was perpetrated by Hutus against minority Tutsis. Determining that the situation in Rwanda constituted ''a threat to international peace and security'' under chapter 7 of the UN Charter, the Security Council adopted resolution 955 on November 8, 1994. This action established the International Criminal Tribunal for Rwanda (ICTR) to prosecute persons responsible for genocide and other serious violations of international humanitarian law in Rwanda (or by Rwandans in neighboring countries) in 1994. Located in Arusha, Tanzania, the Tribunal's work reaffirms the legal principle that individuals who violate fundamental norms of international humanitarian law can be held responsible by the international community.

The ICTR is governed by its statute, which is annexed to Security Council resolution 955. The rules of procedure and evidence, which the judges adopted in accordance with the statute, establish the framework necessary for a functioning judicial system. In regard to structure, the ICTR comprises three main parts. First are the chambers, which consist of fourteen judges who are responsible for issuing indictments as well as for hearing cases at the trial and the appellate level. The judges are divided into three trial chambers of three judges each and one seven-judge appellate chamber. The Tribunal is headed by a President, equivalent to a chief justice. The second part of the ICTR is the Office of the Prosecutor, which is responsible for investigations, framing indictments, and prosecuting the cases. The chief prosecutor for the ICTR is shared with the ICTY and is appointed by the Security Council for a four-year term. Third is the Registry, which serves as the administrative arm of the tribunal. The registry of the ICTR is also responsible for providing protective measures for witnesses, counseling and support for victims and their families, and the appointment of defense counsel for the accused.

The Rwanda Tribunal is empowered to prosecute individuals for genocide, violations of common article 3 of the 1949 Geneva Conventions, and crimes against humanity committed in Rwanda between January 1, 1994, and December 31, 1994. The ICTR retains primary jurisdiction over national courts, in Rwanda and throughout the world. Trials in absentia are not permitted, nor may a person be tried for the same crime twice, either before the Tribunal or a national court. The ICTR has jurisdiction only over natural persons. No prosecution may go forward against juridical persons such as organizations or associations.

The process of indictment and prosecution is international. Once indictments are handed down by the Tribunal, an arrest warrant is issued. Because the tribunal has no police authority, it is often not able to locate and apprehend persons indicted. The tribunal is thus dependent on international cooperation for the apprehension and surrender of accused offenders. As of late 2004, sixty-nine persons had been arrested, and twelve convicted. Among those found guilty was Jean Kambanda, the former prime minister of Rwanda, who is serving a life sentence in a Mali prison with five other convicted persons. At least fifty-six indicted persons are in the custody of the ICTR in Arusha, and of these, twenty are on trial. At the same time, the Rwandan government is conducting its own investigations and trials of persons suspected of committing crimes. More than 120,000 persons are in Rwandan jails awaiting trial, but with a domestic legal system virtually destroyed in the civil war, the Rwandan government has found it quite difficult to resolve most of these cases.[55]

The ICTR shares certain elements in common with the ICTY. For one, the Statute of the Rwanda Tribunal is similar to that of the ICTY, and the two tribunals share the same chief prosecutor and the same seven-judge appellate chamber. Each has separate registrars and deputy prosecutors, however, and neither the ICTY nor the ICTR is related in any way to the International Court of Justice, which is located in The Hague. Whereas the two regional criminal courts are concerned with the acts of individual persons, the ICJ's mandate and jurisdiction are limited to disputes between governments of states.

THE PERMANENT INTERNATIONAL CRIMINAL COURT

A functioning, permanent international criminal court fills a missing link in the international legal system. The International Court of Justice at The Hague handles only cases between states, not individuals. Without an international criminal court to enforce rules of individual accountability, acts of genocide and egregious violations of human rights often go unpunished. While ad hoc international tribunals were established to prosecute persons for massive criminal offenses in the former Yugoslavia and Rwanda, one only has to think of the numerous instances during the last thirty years in which crimes against humanity and war crimes were committed for which no individuals have been punished.

In Cambodia in the 1970s, more than two million people were killed by the Khmer Rouge. Since then, civil wars in Uganda, Mozambique, Liberia, El Salvador, the Congo, Sierra Leone, and around the Great Lakes region of Africa have led to the tremendous loss of civilian life, including as many as five million unarmed women and children. Of course, these cases represent only a fraction of the human rights depredations occurring worldwide.

As early as 1948, the UN General Assembly called for an international penal tribunal to try persons accused of genocide and asked the International Law Commission (ILC) to study the need for such a court. A draft statute was completed in 1951 and a revised statute in 1953, but the General Assembly decided to defer the matter, pending adoption of a definition of *aggression*. Thirty-six years later, in response to a request from Trinidad and Tobago, the General Assembly in 1989 asked the ILC to resume work on an international criminal court. The horrific experience with ethnic cleansing in the former Yugoslavia during 1992–1993 and the massive atrocities committed in Rwanda during 1994 became catalysts personifying the urgent need for an international criminal court. By 1994 the ILC had successfully completed work on a draft statute and submitted it to the General Assembly. To consider the major substantive issues arising from that draft statute, the General Assembly created the Ad Hoc Committee on the Establishment of an International Criminal Court, which convened twice in 1995. The ad hoc committee's report generated the creation of the Preparatory Committee on the Establishment of an International Criminal Court, which was charged with preparation of a widely acceptable consolidated draft text for submission to a diplomatic conference. The Preparatory Committee, which met from 1996 to 1998, convened in a final session in March–April 1998 and completed the drafting of the text.

The United Nations Diplomatic Conference on the Establishment of an International Criminal Court convened in Rome from June 15 to July 17, 1998. The Rome conference ended on July 18, 1998, with the adoption of an instrument—the Rome Statute, or Rome Treaty—to create the *International Criminal Court* (ICC). A total of 160 countries participated in the Rome conference. The ICC statute was adopted after a vote called by the United States. The text was approved 120–7, with twenty-one abstentions.[56] The aim of the Court is to bring to justice persons responsible for "the most serious crimes of international concern"—such as genocide, crimes against humanity and war crimes—when domestic criminal justice systems fail to do so. The ICC will have also jurisdiction over the crime of aggression, pending a formal definition. The Court will complement national judicial systems and will be able to assume jurisdiction only after it determines that a national system is unwilling or unable to do so. The treaty required sixty ratifications to enter into force, which occurred on July 1, 2002. By September 2004, at least 139 states had signed the treaty and 94 states ratified it—among them Australia, Canada, France, Germany, Italy, New Zealand, Norway, and the United Kingdom.[57]

The Rome Statute marks a historic achievement, as it establishes for the first time a universal framework to end impunity for the most serious crimes under international law. It includes many important elements advocated by like-minded governments and NGOs that were working for the creation of an independent and effective international judicial body. Under the Rome Statute, the ICC will be composed of a Presidency, the Chambers (including an appeals division, a trial division, and a pretrial division), the Office of the Prosecutor, and the Registry. On the Court will sit eighteen judges elected by the Assembly of States Parties for nonrenewable terms of nine years. The prosecutor and one or more deputy prosecutors will be elected in the same manner and under the same terms. The ICC will serve as a full-time judicial body.

The Statute gives the Court jurisdiction over three core crimes—genocide, crimes against humanity, and war crimes. The definition of genocide in the ICC statute was non-controversial and was extracted verbatim from the 1948 Genocide Convention. The statute codifies crimes against humanity in a multilateral treaty for the first time since Nuremberg. The ICC will have jurisdiction over crimes against humanity committed by official or nonstate actors in times of peace or armed conflict. Apart from acts recognized under the Nuremberg and Tokyo charters, and under the statutes of the ad hoc tribunals for the former Yugoslavia and Rwanda, the ICC will be authorized to prosecute new crimes against humanity, including forcible transfers of population; severe deprivation of physical liberty; sexual slavery; enforced prostitution; forced pregnancy; persecution on political, racial, national, ethnic, cultural, religious, gender, or other grounds that are universally recognized as impermissible under international law. The ICC will also be able to prosecute offenders who commit acts of apartheid and the enforced disappearance of persons. In addition, the definition of *torture* under the ICC statute now makes such acts prosecutable, regardless of whether they were committed by state officials or not.

Moreover, the Court will have jurisdiction over war crimes committed in international and in noninternational armed conflicts. The inclusion of internal armed conflicts within the Court's jurisdiction was vital, as most armed conflicts in the world today occur within national borders. The Statute thus marks a major step forward in that, for the first time, a prominent multilateral agreement unequivocally codifies offenses in internal conflicts as war crimes.

Widespread support existed at Rome for inclusion of aggression as a crime, but complicating the debate was disagreement over the act's definition and the proper role of the Security Council in determining whether the crime has been committed. In the end, inclusion of aggression as an offense has been put off until an acceptable definition can be produced.[58]

The court's ultimate independence and effectiveness hinge on whether the ICC prosecutor retains the authority to initiate proceedings on his or her own motion (*propio motu*) rather than depend on referrals by the Security Council or by state parties. Although such referrals are necessary mechanisms for triggering the Court's jurisdiction, they are not sufficient if the ICC is to be effective in punishing and deterring international crimes. The Security Council is a political body that has often been paralyzed by the veto power of its five permanent members. States are often reluctant to file complaints involving another state's nationals, especially if doing so might interfere with diplomatic or economic relations or might invite retaliatory complaints. As a consequence, an independent prosecutor is essential if cases are to be tried in situations of heinous criminal conduct where there is little political will to proceed.

The Rome Statute reflects a compromise between requiring the ICC to obtain Security Council permission to proceed and precluding the Security Council from any ability to stop investigations. The Security Council, acting pursuant to Chapter VII of the UN Charter, can require the Court to defer investigations or prosecutions for a renewable twelve-month period. This compromise provides more than enough scope for the Security Council to carry out its Chapter VII responsibilities. At the same time, it ensures that permanent members of the Security Council cannot use their veto power unilaterally to prevent investigations or prosecutions from going forward.

To uphold standards of international criminal justice, the ICC must ensure the application of all relevant international rules and standards of fair trial and due process. The Rome Statute incorporates the rights protected in the Universal Declaration of Human Rights, the International Covenant on Civil and Political Rights, and the Convention against Torture and Other Inhuman or Degrading Treatment or Punishment. Among the fundamental rights guaranteed by the treaty are the right to remain silent; the right to counsel; the right to the presence of attorney when being questioned; and the right to examine and have examined witnesses. Furthermore, all defendants are presumed innocent, with the prosecutor bearing the burden of proving guilt beyond reasonable doubt.

Many human rights organizations advocated the need for the ICC Statute to include explicit provisions on crimes of sexual and gender violence, provisions on the protection of children, redress to victims of crimes within the Court's jurisdiction, and adequate protection of victims and witnesses. The Rome Statute largely reflects these vital needs. For instance, article 7 stipulates that crimes against humanity and war crimes include conduct directed specifically at women, such as "rape, sexual slavery, enforced prostitution, forced pregnancy, enforced sterilization or any other form of sexual violence of comparable violence." Also deemed a war crime is the conscription or enlistment of children under the age of fifteen into national armed forces or the use of them to participate actively in hostilities in international armed conflict. The Court's Registry will include a victims and witnesses unit to provide protection, counseling, and other assistance, and the unit will include staff with expertise in trauma relating to crimes of sexual violence.

Member states of the United Nations are obligated to give to international tribunals created by the Security Council various forms of assistance—including, but not limited to, the arrest, detention, and surrender of accused offenders. This obligation derives from article 39 in Chapter VII of the UN Charter, which allocates to the Security Council broad responsibility "with respect to threats to the peace, breaches of the peace, and acts of aggression," with the specific authority to "decide what measures shall be taken . . . to maintain or restore international peace and security." The obligation to carry out these measures is explicitly stated in the UN Charter, which provides in article 48 that "the action required to carry out decisions of the Security Council for the maintenance of international peace and security shall be taken by all Members of the United Nations." The obligation of states to surrender alleged offenders to these ad hoc international criminal tribunals is articulated in paragraph 4 of UN Security Council resolution 827 (on Yugoslavia) and paragraph 2 of resolution 955 (on Rwanda), both of which provide that the Security Council

> decides that all States shall cooperate fully with the International Tribunal and its organs in accordance with the present resolution and the Statute of the International Tribunal and that consequently all States shall take any measures necessary under their domestic laws to implement the provisions of the present resolution and the Statute, including the obligation of States to comply with requests for assistance or orders issued by a Trial Chamber under Article 29 [for Rwanda, Article 28] of the Statute.[59]

Thus, all persons who participate in the planning, preparation, or execution of serious violations of international humanitarian law are implicated in the commission of the crime and are therefore individually responsible. Both tribunals also hold that principal responsibility for war crimes pursuant to orders falls to those in authority who gave the orders. No provisions are made for pardons, amnesties, or impunity laws. Alleged offenders will be tried for high crimes and will not be excused because of their political power or military rank.

While acknowledging these principles, the experience of the ICTY and the ICTR since 1993 reveals certain weaknesses of international tribunals. Both tribunals proved impotent to enforce arrest warrants and subpoenas. The exercise of such means of apprehension remains in the hands of occupant military forces and local security police. In addition, the tribunals' viability and success depend on constant political and financial support from the United Nations, particularly the Great Powers on the Security Council. Such dependency obviously invites the likelihood that political considerations will creep in and impair the prospects for effective, impartial tribunal operations. Moreover, the arrest of indicted persons ultimately depends on the genuine cooperation of the government in whose territory indicted persons are located, an order sometimes difficult to secure. Failure to apprehend indicted persons cannot help but undercut the credibility and effectiveness of both tribunals.

TRUTH COMMISSIONS

Truth commissions can be successful in fostering peace and national conciliation. Such commissions establish a historical record of the crimes and the context in which they were committed.[60] The South African Truth Commission is generally regarded to have been successful as an instrument of national reconciliation. Its purpose was to rescue South Africa from the denial and lies about its past, bestow dignity on those who had suffered, and extend a magnanimous offer of forgiveness to the perpetrators of horrible crimes. It granted amnesty to persons who fully disclosed their crimes during the period of apartheid, but only if the crime was not disproportionate to its political aim. When combined with prosecutions, the South African experience since 1995 proffers a unique model that worked successfully, owing to the right chemistry of conditions—peace, genuine political will, and a functioning local judicial system.[61] But other facts remain. First, truth commissions do not produce full justice, nor are they intended to do so. Second, a truth commission does not reveal the whole truth. Third, reconciliation will stay incomplete, as will the restitution for the crimes committed. Last, if a truth commission is to help heal a society of the pain and suffering brought about by internal war and violent ethnic strife, then forgiveness—not justice—is the price deemed necessary. This last point poses the crux of the dilemma: Should those who perpetrate the most terrible of crimes escape punishment at the price only of admitting their guilt and showing remorse? For the experience chosen by South Africa, the price of peace and reconciliation is "the truth" with amnesty. It is neither justice nor compensation for victims. How well forgiveness actually works as a strategy for fostering political stability will be realized only in the coming years.[62]

CONCLUSION

On December 10, 1948, the UN General Assembly adopted the Universal Declaration of Human Rights as the common standard to which all peoples and governments should strive. In an ideal world, the rights and conditions in the Universal Declaration would prevail. People would coexist peacefully, cooperate, and exercise due diligence through nondiscrimination in their everyday affairs. Miscreants would be apprehended, prosecuted, and punished in accord with the rules of national and international law. Prescriptions for justice would be overriding guidelines for, and considerations of, law and policy. Every responsible authority would be held accountable for acts or omissions. People would be punished for their unlawful actions.

But we do not live in an ideal world. In the world today there are 193 sovereign states, governed by human beings with political ambitions who perceive, formulate, and execute policies in the name of and under the guise of national interests. In the course of this governing process, the fundamental human rights of innocent persons are sometimes brutally victimized by individuals claiming to act in the name of the state. What makes this situation all the more repugnant is that in nearly all these cases the perpetrators can evade prosecution and punishment, even for the most horrendous of crimes. In cases of war crimes, crimes against humanity, and acts of genocide—crimes that have been deemed offenses against all humankind and the perpetrators of which are branded war criminals and enemies of all humankind—few of the guilty are charged, prosecuted, and punished. There has been little remedy for the victims or their family survivors.[63]

A clear duty exists for governments to prosecute and punish persons who commit the most serious human rights violations. This comes as the logical extension of individual responsibility in international humanitarian law concerning grave breaches, as first articulated normatively in the 1949 Geneva Conventions. International legal obligations to punish grave human rights violations curtail national discretion with regard to impunity; and impunity laws, such as amnesties, are legally limited in existing international criminal law. While sometimes politically convenient or expeditious, such laws may well be incompatible with international criminal legal rules. The international legality of such impunity laws depends on the prosecutorial performance of a state in any specific case.

Key concerns remain. Salient among these is how victims of serious human rights violations can enforce their rights to remedy by punishment of the perpetrator. Implementation of the doctrine of individual criminal responsibility, widely recognized since the Nuremberg trials, should compel individual offenders to accountability. Yet, the individual victim still lacks the fundamental right to initiate proceedings against an alleged perpetrator.

There also remain the critical duties of compliance and enforcement. The fact is that international criminal law is neither automatic nor self-enforcing. Governments must make compliance work by exercising the necessary political will to punish the guilty—whether it be the soldier in the field who pulls the trigger, the militiaman in the countryside who rapes and pillages, the officer who gave the orders to perpetrate unlawful acts, or the leader who made the decision for his armed forces to commit crimes against humanity. For international criminal rules to be meaningful, the governments of states must institute and implement national *and* international laws, must support and protect the national judiciary, and must uphold and carry out sentences against those who are convicted. To do otherwise is to emasculate the law and perpetrate impunity. Until the requisite political will is demonstrated, particularly by the Great Powers on the UN Security Council, the international legal rules to prohibit and punish war crimes, genocide, torture, and crimes against humanity will remain inert and ineffective. Regrettably, so too will the ability of states to afford victims adequate remedies for human rights offenses committed unjustly against them.

If the rules of international criminal law are to be relevant, they must be enforced. The final word on impunity comes down to the realization that high crimes that violate human rights are evil, vile, and impermissible. Such offenses must be not be allowed to escape punishment. There can be no peace without justice, and there can be no justice without accountability. The application of legal rules by governments must reflect these obligations if international criminal law is to exert real impact as a deterrent on would-be perpetrators. This will remain a prominent challenge for all states in the 21st century.

8

Use of Force Law

- Law before the UN Charter
- The Security Council and the Use of Force
- Peace Operations
- The General Assembly
- Regional Organizations
- Weapons of Mass Destruction
- Conclusion

On March 20, 2003, some 150,000 U.S.-led coalition forces invaded Iraq to over-throw the regime of Saddam Hussein. The principal legal rationale used by the Bush administration rested on the contention that Iraq possessed weapons of mass destruction and thus constituted a grave threat to the United States, as did the links between Saddam Hussein and certain terrorist groups. The United States asserted that ancillary legal grounds for its military action, even without the Security Council's explicit approval, stemmed from Security Council resolution 1441 (November 2002). This proviso stipulated that Iraq was in material breach for its past uncooperative behavior with UN resolutions and gave Saddam Hussein a final opportunity to either comply with onsite inspections for weapons of mass destruction or face "serious consequences." The American invasion amounted to those serious consequences. The war was short. By May 20, 2003, President Bush declared on the aircraft carrier USS Abraham Lincoln that the mission was accomplished: the brutal regime of Sad-dam Hussein had been toppled by coalition forces. In the aftermath of victory, a salient question persisted, however: Was this massive American military intervention lawful? The Security Council did not give formal approval for U.S. military action, nor can it be said convincingly that the United States acted in self-defense. While it is true that Saddam's government remained in violation of sixteen previous UN Security Council resolutions, it remains arguable whether that situation alone provided a sufficient threshold for the United States to launch an all-out war against Iraq. Moreover, the principal justifications originally given for the Iraq War have lost much of their legal potency. More than a year after the declared end of major hostilities, no weapons of mass destruction have been found. No significant link between Saddam Hussein and international terrorism has been discovered. Further, the political, economic, and security difficulties of establishing stable institutions in Iraq is making the country an increasingly unlikely staging ground for promoting democracy in the Middle East. As time passes, the Bush administration's dominant justification for the war is that Saddam Hussein was a tyrant and a massive human rights abuser who deserved to be overthrown—an argument suggesting that U.S. action constituted a humanitarian intervention. In 2004 the Bush administration cited this rationale not simply as a side benefit of the war but also as a prime justification for it. Other reasons are still regularly mentioned, but the humanitarian one has gained prominence. Yet, the critical question is not simply whether Saddam Hussein was a ruthless leader; he most certainly was. Rather, the question is whether the circumstances were present that would lawfully justify humanitarian intervention by the United States. Among most international legal experts, serious doubts persist that this was the case.

G overnments often use armed force against each other in their international rela- tions, and the price in human terms is excruciating. During the 20th century, at least 110 million people were killed in wars between states.[1] The rationale thus becomes clear for putting legal limits on the use of force in interstate relations. In the international system, the unrestricted use of force is not conducive to the security, stabil- ity, and good order of intercourse between states. In addition, it undermines the attain- ment of basic needs by most members of international society. When one considers the continuing development of evermore sophisticated weaponry and the massive destructive capability of modern military technology, placing restrictions on the use of force between states makes eminent sense. To this end, state representatives and diplomats throughout the past century invested intense efforts in crafting international legal rules that stipulate under what circumstances the use force is permissible and when it is prohibited. This effort at universal norm creation did not come about easily or quickly, nor has it proven to be wholly successful. Still, it evolved as a diplomatic process that coincided with the refinement of the modern state as the basic polity operating in the world political system.

The legal rules regulating the right to use *force* (*jus ad bellum*) may be considered from two vantage points. First, there are rules applied to individual states or specific groups of states (such as alliances) that act on their own initiative. These are usually viewed as rules for types of unilateral force. Second, there are rules that indicate when force may be used by a competent international organization, such as the United Nations. This form of force is usually designated as the collective use of force, since it stems from a collective decision made by a duly authorized intergovernmental body. In a real sense, the distinction between "unilateral" and the "collective use" of force does not amount to the numbers of actors involved. Rather it is distinguished by the purpose and authority attributed to that use of force.

LAW BEFORE THE UN CHARTER

Legal rules governing the international use of force developed as an evolving set of prohi- bitions. As early as the 4th century, theologians such as Saint Augustine began grappling with the notion of just war (*bellum justum*). This doctrine permitted the use of force when some polity deserved it—that is, when the cause was directed at a good end, when the prospects for victory were reasonably good, when innocent persons were protected from direct harm, and when the use of force was decided by a legitimate authority. Following the Treaty of Westphalia in 1648, such authority fell under the discretion of the state. Hugo

Grotius revised the just war theory that deemed war illegal unless it was undertaken for a "just cause." What a just cause entailed covered a variety of situations, but the term essentially implied retribution for a wrong done or for a right illegally denied. Consequently, certain situations justified (legitimized) the use of armed force. Among these were the necessity of self-defense, the enforcement of fundamental rights, the seeking of restitution for injury, and the punishment of a wrongdoer. To resort to war beyond these bounds was deemed unlawful. In a real sense, the just war doctrine established the foundation for modern international legal rules pertaining to the use of force.[2]

The rise of the state in 17th-century Europe refined the rules for using armed force, in context and in concept. If a government believed that it had just cause to pursue war against another state, that belief rendered its action legally proper, even absent any test for a just or righteous cause. No objective test was available for a state's right to use force. Consequently, state practice came to be regarded as the ultimate source of international legal rules—that is, legal positivism put into international practice. By the late 18th century, the sovereign right of a state to decide for itself whether and when it would resort to war had emerged as the prevailing doctrine. By the end of the 19th century, international legal rules were adopted governing the actual conduct of the fighting (*jus in bello*), but they did not prevent states from asserting the right to pursue war. Sovereignty gave to the state a unilateral right to make that decision for itself. International legal rules could regulate the conduct of war, but the decision to pursue armed conflict still resided within a state's government. The government was not bound by any corpus of international norms. This development proved crucial in the evolution of *jus ad bellum*. The attribution of unrestrained legal competence to governments precluded any need for express rights to be established regarding when, where, or how armed force should be used by states against one another.

The right to go to war, derived from just war theory and state practice, is firmly rooted in national sovereignty. This construct dominated international relations throughout the 19th century to the establishment of the League of Nations in 1919. During this period, governments began to categorize the use of force according to legal rationales in particular circumstances, such as self-defense, the rescue of a state's nationals, or in reprisal for injuries suffered. More significantly, governments tended to agree that resort to armed force for these purposes neither constituted a full state of war nor required states to invoke obligations to declare a formal condition of belligerency. Violence applied in these contexts amounted to lawful exercises of force short of war, which furnished the legal origins for similar principles today.

The Covenant of the League of Nations introduced formal restrictions on the sovereign right of states to use force.[3] Under the Covenant, use of armed force was lawful only if the procedural safeguards set out in articles 10–16 were followed. If these were observed, a state was entitled to seek its objectives through war. Nonetheless, the covenant produced two significant consequences. First, the right of self-defense surfaced as a genuine legal exception to the procedural restraints on a state's right to use force; that is, use of force by a state in self-defense became formally recognized in the Covenant as a lawful exception to the general prohibition on the use of force. Second, the notion of collective security framed in the Covenant emerged as a deterrent to potential aggressor states. Governments were obligated to avoid using force against one another under the Covenant except in cases of self-defense. But if they did, the Covenant provided, under article 16, that all other League members were duty bound to turn against the aggressor state. This is the first instance that such a collective security commitment was incorporated into a near-universal multilateral agreement. Indeed, article 16 of the Covenant even provides for the Council to instigate economic sanctions against a member state that transgressed its international obligations by using unlawful force against another state. While intended mainly to deter aggression by states, such sanctions were imposed by the League on one occasion: in 1936 against Mussolini's Italy for its invasion and conquest of Ethiopia. This sanction effort by the League of Nations failed for several reasons, among them the lack of an effective enforcement agency to monitor the sanctions operation, the absence of the United States as a member of the League, and the ongoing world economic depression. Even so, the important fact remains that punitive economic action was instigated against a malefactor member state and that action was implemented as actual policy as opposed to merely rhetorical condemnation.

Another significant development in the campaign to limit the use of force in international relations came in the previous decade. This was the Kellogg-Briand Treaty (or Pact of Paris), which was promulgated in 1928 and remains in force today with sixty-three states as parties.[4] This agreement represents the first attempt by governments to outlaw war as an instrument of national policy. Although lofty in its ambitions, the Kellogg-Briand Treaty heralded a landmark development in the law governing the use of force. It demonstrated that the international community can politically and legally agree on a general ban on war and formalize that agreement as a legally binding obligation. Still, the Pact proved to be fatally flawed on at least three counts: first, it contained no teeth in the form of enforcement powers; second, it failed to furnish any means of deterrence against potential aggressor governments; and third, it provided for no mandatory dispute settlement procedures among the parties. In addition, the ban applied to war only narrowly. It did not prohibit the broad use of force between states. Notwithstanding these deficiencies, the Kellogg-Briand Pact did stipulate a prohibition on the right to go to war and ensured that the right to use force in self-defense could develop as a distinct legal right. Although the Pact makes no specific reference to self-defense, its *travaux preparatoires* clearly suggest that this right was preserved, as the reality of such an exception was already presumed. Though disparaged by realist political scientists as demonstrating the idealistic nature of international law in halting interstate violence, the Kellogg-Briand pact remains a harbinger for formally outlawing acts of aggression and for punishing (through international criminal courts and other means) persons in government who promote those illegal ends.[5]

During the period after World War I, the right of states to use armed force was governed by a blend of customary and treaty law. While self-defense as a right contains ingredients of just war theory and principles common to all major legal systems, the use of force by states to attain national objectives was basically rejected, as governments became obliged to seek peaceful means to settle international disputes. The League of Nations Covenant sought to place limitations on a state's right to use force. The Kellogg-Briand Pact condemned recourse to war and renounced it as an instrument of national policy. Yet, states reserved the right to use force in self-defense. In matters of reprisal and the rescue or defense of its citizens abroad, states' limited use of force short of war was still viewed as legitimate.[6] With the creation of the United Nations in 1945, however, the international community moved to abandon the notion of permissible "just war" in favor of outlawing the use of force generally. This effort was motivated by humanitarian concerns in the aftermath of two world wars as well as by the realization that new military technology—particularly nuclear weapons—made war so destructive that no states' national interests would be served by a resort to modern, global armed conflict. In effect, the fear of a nuclear third world war overrode the desire for justice. Paradoxically, denunciation of the right to use force hinged on the same legal principles—sovereignty and respect for territorial integrity—that had supported and justified resort to force: because all states are sovereign and equal members of the international community, each state's sovereign right to independence and territorial integrity should be respected as a matter of law. Use of force is inimical to these rights and must therefore be prohibited.

The delegates who met in San Francisco to finalize the UN Charter in 1945 did not have to articulate in full the contemporary legal rules for restricting unilateral use of force by states. By the end of the Second World War, a web of customary and treaty law was already in place for regulating the use of armed force between states. This web became the foundation for the UN Charter's famous provisions banning the aggressive use of force. In fact, the adoption of the UN Charter boldly underscored these customary rules, as they became integrated into the modern international legal framework for the recourse to force by states. Importantly, in the 21st century these rules continue to affect interpretations of when, in which circumstances, and under what conditions the use of force is permissible and when it is prohibited. This is not surprising, since the UN Charter proclaims three principal goals: the preservation of the peace, the protection of human rights, and the promotion of self-determination. Interestingly enough, the Charter system creates a tension among these goals, with peace upheld as predominant. To be sure, justice, the pursuit of human rights, self-determination, economic development, and the correction of past wrongs still remain goals to be sought, but they must not come at the expense of peace. Thus, the Charter treats as its paramount objective the need to prevent interstate violence from occurring.

Prohibition on the Use of Force

Given the experience of two world wars, the framers of the Charter believed that armed force was too dangerous to be considered a legitimate means for altering the political or territorial status quo of the international community. Accordingly, the legal cornerstone for UN Charter law governing recourse to force is article 2, paragraph 4. This provision mandates in full that all members of the United Nations "shall refrain in their international relations from the threat or use of force against the territorial integrity or political independence of any state, or in any other manner inconsistent with the Purposes of the United Nations."

The fundamental intent of article 2(4) is that states are proscribed from using force against the "territorial integrity" or "political independence" of other states. As provided for elsewhere in the Charter, force is explicitly permitted only when undertaken for self-defense (per article 51) or if pursuant to a Security Council authorization (per article 42). Within the state, the right of the government to regulate the lives of its citizens is viewed by international law as a normal legitimate exercise of national sovereignty. In international relations, transnational intervention is usually seen as a violation of a state's sovereignty and territorial integrity. Thus under the Charter paradigm, nonintervention emerges as a principle of international law essential for fostering friendly relations among states.

Article 2 (4) constitutes a basic proscription on the use, and even the threat, of force that in some way violates the territory or independence of states or contravenes the purposes of the United Nations. The UN Charter goes further than any other binding modern legal document in asserting the unlawfulness of a state to use force in its interstate relations. Since 1945, this provision has been reaffirmed numerous times, most notably in a series of General Assembly resolutions and in several Security Council debates.[7] Moreover, the International Court of Justice in *Nicaragua v. United States* strongly asserted that the general ban on the use of force reflects the customary practice of states—in particular, the law of state responsibility.[8]

While article 2(4) might appear resolute in its prohibition on the use of force, its wording is not immune from ambiguity. Article 2 (4) prohibits the use of force "against the territorial integrity or political independence" of any state and "in any other manner inconsistent with the purposes" of the United Nations. One may interpret this phraseology to mean that the provision bans only that use of force that is actually directed against the territorial integrity or political independence of a state, or that runs contrary to the purposes of the United Nations. Put another way, if a state's use of force does not lead to the loss or permanent occupation of the territory of another state, or if it does not seek to overthrow the authority structure of a state, then does that force compromise the fundamental meaning of article 2 (4)?[9] The answer to that query remains unclear.

Critical in the verbal construction of article 2 (4) is the question of what exactly is meant by "force." Like every legal system, international law strives to prevent the use of violent measures to settle differences. By using the term *force*, article 2 (4) is generally interpreted to mean *armed force*—that is, the intentional use of military action by one state against another state. Such force may be direct, as in a deliberate attack by a state's regular armed forces against another state; or it may be indirect, as in the case where armed irregular groups such as guerrillas or partisans operate on one state's behalf against another state. Both uses of force are usually labeled under international law as acts of aggression, which of course means that the legal rule of nonintervention has been violated. This said, international law does not extend the formal concept of force to nonmilitary actions. Concepts such as economic aggression or cultural imperialism are not synonymous with unlawful armed intervention. While resort to economic coercion or subversive propaganda surely are unfriendly acts (which may or may not be unlawful), the prevailing view is that they fall outside the legal scope of "force" as used in article 2, paragraph 4 of the UN Charter. More emphatically, the meaning of "aggression" as formally defined by the General Assembly in its resolution 3314 (1974) is clearly limited to acts of armed force. In that resolution, aggression is defined as "the use of armed force by a State against the sovereignty, territorial integrity or political independence of another State, or in any other manner inconsistent with the Charter of the United Nations, as set out in this definition." This definition essentially reaffirms the ingredients of article 2 (4). Interestingly, though, the threat to use force is not included in the definition of aggression, and the force used must be armed force. Moreover, this definition of aggression includes the word *sovereignty*, presumably to eschew any argument based only on the "territorial integrity or political independence" of a state.[10]

While the UN definition of aggression was produced through consensus over ten years of deliberations by a special ad hoc General Assembly committee, it is generally viewed as being neither authoritative nor controlling. The definition of aggression that was adopted in 1974 as a resolution by the General Assembly is considered by most governments and legal scholars to be nonbinding. It is regarded as having only recommendatory character, and it is viewed more as a political statement than as a substantive legal definition for regulating state behavior.[11]

All governments acknowledge the fundamental importance attached to the general prohibition on the use of force between states. As a consequence, in every instance involving use of force in recent years, the governments employing violence acknowledged that contemporary international legal rules presume that use of force is unlawful. That said, this consensus neither, matched by agreement on the exact scope of the ban, nor the circumstances for resorting to self-defense under the charter. Often, aggressor governments attempt to mask their aggression by claiming a rightful cause, such as acting in self-defense; obtaining legitimate invitation; or upholding a noble cause, such as those on humanitarian grounds or to protect the human rights of oppressed minorities.

The debate over how broad the ban on the use of force should extend turns on how the relevant legal principles are interpreted.[12] One school of thought interprets the UN Charter strictly and asserts that this document radically transforms the right of states to use force. These *strict interpretationists* argue that article 2 (4) in the Charter establishes a total ban on the unilateral use of force. Any right of unilateral action by a government rests only in so far as the Charter explicitly preserves one. According to this strict view, the legal effects of article 2(4) forbid a state from employing force, save under specific exceptions articulated in the Charter itself. Thus, the right of self-defense under article 51 and the now-obsolete article 107 provision for taking action against ex-enemy states are considered the only permissible exceptions to the prohibition of unilateral use of force in article 2(4). Bluntly put, a state may use force only in self-defense, as provided for in article 51. The strict interpretation school contends that the maintenance of international peace and security is the paramount aim of international law. Consequently, the use of armed force is permissible only under the most exceptional of circumstances. The rationale for this conclusion seems evident: the destruction caused by the violence of one state using force against another state nearly always outweighs the evil it was intended to oppose. In addition, the strict interpretationists perceive that permissive opportunities to use force only invite abuse from more powerful states that seek to enhance their own interests at the expense of weaker states.[13]

A second school of thought interprets the Charter more liberally. These commentators argue that the instrument does not alter the general direction or purposes of international law. This *liberal school* presumes that in a decentralized, anarchic international society—that is, one not having a global police force or an international judiciary—self-help remains the governing principle for state conduct. Governments must enforce the law themselves and seek vindication for rights unlawfully denied. Therefore, armed force may be used by a state under certain conditions to correct unjust wrongs—not only in self-defense, but also to preserve human life in extraordinary circumstances. While self-defense remains the preeminent rationale for using force, these liberal interpretationists contend that, under certain extreme circumstances, resort to armed force should be permissible. This is especially so when innocent human life is at risk in other states: to rescue one's nationals, halt genocidal atrocities, or prevent pervasive crimes against humanity. These liberal scholars contend that a complete ban on the use of force weakens the state's ability to protect itself from unlawful international behavior and thus becomes an obstacle to halting gross injustices perpetrated by other governments on innocent victims.[14]

During the late years of the 20th century, the consensus among state representatives and commentators was that article 2(4) should not be interpreted so loosely as to facilitate its abuse by more powerful states. The common view was that legal emphasis should strengthen obligations to avoid using force rather than create loopholes that might permit more intentional violence. More recently, however, technological globalization and economic interdependence appear to be rendering national sovereignty more porous. When coupled with the pervasive rise and acceptance of human rights law, these realizations suggest that new norms may need to emerge in order to challenge such an all-encompassing prohibition. It seems appropriate that the right to use force remains limited. But the need to protect human rights and preserve international justice appears to be gaining momentum as lawful rationales for the use of armed force against authoritarian and corrupt regimes.

Self-Defense

The contemporary legal framework for the *principle of self-defense* by states is contained in Article 51 of the UN Charter. In full, this provision stipulates that

> Nothing in the present Charter shall impair the inherent right of individual or collective self-defence if an armed attack occurs against a Member of the United Nations, until the Security Council has taken measures necessary to maintain international peace and security. Measures taken by Members in the exercise of this right of self-defence shall be immediately reported to the Security Council and shall not in any way affect the authority and responsibility of the Security Council under the present Charter to take at any time such action as it deems necessary in order to maintain or restore international peace and security.

Under international law, a state traditionally reserved the sole right to determine whether such a degree of emergency exists to justify the employment of force in self-defense. In essence, article 51 imposes a limitation on that right. A state acting on the basis of self-judgment does so at its own risk; and its actions, at least in theory, are subject to scrutiny by the Security Council. Yet, use of the adjective "inherent" in article 51 clearly establishes a right of states to use force in self-defense. Further, article 51 does not imply an impairment of that right until the Security Council has acted. The right of self-defense does not flow from the Charter. Self-defense is a natural right (*droit naturel*, as in the authentic French text of article 51) or, in terminology more familiar to American ears, an inalienable right of all states that existed before the Charter's entry into legal force.

To be appreciated as a contemporary legal rule, the principle of self-defense must be considered within the context of the state's corresponding general duty to refrain from the use of force. This notion grew out of the Covenant of the League of Nations and the 1928 Kellogg-Briand Pact, reaching full fruition in the UN Charter. But the right of self-defense exists in some form within every legal system—consider that a homicide will be excused under U.S. law if reasonable grounds existed for the use of lethal force to defend oneself or others from a lethal attack or from imminent threat of death or grievous bodily harm. There is no disagreement that states may use force if attacked. However, what is more problematic is determining what constitutes an imminent threat of attack as grounds for a state's use of justifiable force.

In international law, the parameters of the right of self-defense were definitively drawn in the diplomatic correspondence between U.S. secretary of state Daniel Webster and British special ambassador Lord Ashburton over the now-famous sinking of the ship the *Caroline*.[15] During an armed insurrection in southern Canada in December 1837, British military forces seized the *Caroline* while anchored in an American port on the Niagara River and subsequently sent it over Niagara Falls. British forces attacked the *Caroline* because it had been used to ferry men and supplies across the river in support of the Canadian rebels. The diplomatic exchange arose over British efforts to secure from U.S. custody the release of a British national involved in the incident. Webster indicated that for British action to be lawful, Great Britain had to show "a necessity of self-defense, instant, overwhelming, leaving no choice of means and no moment for deliberation." Moreover, the British had to establish that after entering the United States, their troops "did nothing unreasonable or excessive; since the act justified by the necessity of self-defense must be limited by that necessity and kept clearly within it."[16] This view became the standard interpretation for the lawful exercise of force in anticipatory self-defense by a state. In essence, force may be used in self-defense if it is done in response to an immediate and pressing threat that cannot be avoided by alternative measures and if the force used is proportional to the danger presented. If, however, the crisis can be avoided by diplomatic negotiations or if the danger perceived is little more than a feeling or suspicion, then self-defense is not justified. Similarly, an attack on a naval vessel cannot be used as a pretext to occupy the territory of the offending state.[17]

A more intriguing question today is whether international law should be regarded as a "suicide pact" when it comes to self-defense. Plainly put, the credibility of international law in the early 21st century is being severely tested by rapidly evolving notions of *anticipatory self-defense*. If a government's intelligence service detects that a foreign army is massing along its border, does that state have to wait until it is actually attacked before taking measures to defend itself? Or does modern international law permit that government to exercise preemptive self-defense to protect itself before a military assault can strike? Though open to conjecture, the answer appears to be that if the threat is real, imminent, and overwhelming—consistent with the principles first set forth in the *Caroline* case—then resort to preemptive self-defense is lawful. For instance, heavy and persistent troop concentrations along a border with a neighboring state could trigger an anticipatory or preemptive use of force to meet the threat of attack before the latter actually occurred. This was the situation that justified the preemptive attack by Israel on Egypt and its Arab neighbors in the case of the Six Days' War of June 1967.[18] A second scenario may be less definitive in its legal conclusion. Assume that intelligence information indicates that a known terrorist group in State X is plotting an attack on State Y. It is also known that the government of State X is generally supportive of that terrorist group, or at least unwilling to eliminate it. Does State Y have the lawful right to defend itself preemptively by bombing or covertly attacking that terrorist group in State X before it can instigate a terrorist attack? Does it matter that State Y uses military force against individuals in State X without the approval of State X's government? Can the death and destruction caused by State Y's military intervention be justified as a lawful exercise in self-defense? Or does that armed force amount to an overt act of aggression that violates the territorial integrity and political independence of State X? As demonstrated by the United States' attack on Afghanistan in October 2001, these are real-world questions that demand real-world legal answers.

Legal commentators remain split on this issue. Nonetheless, in the aftermath of the terrorist attacks against the United States on September 11, 2001, the weight of authority seems to favor the permissibility of a preemptive response, providing that three conditions are met: first, the terrorist threat is real and genuine; second, the terrorist threat is immediate and imminent, allowing no time or available mechanism for negotiation or deliberation; third, the preemptive response taken is militarily necessary and proportional to the perceived threat. In any event, a critical concern over preemptive self-defense will remain. This is the overwhelming temptation by some governments to abuse the criteria required by misrepresenting facts and information to legitimize the case for preemptive action when the situation does not actually warrant it.[19]

It is important to realize that in mid-2002, the Bush administration sought to convert the principle of self-defense into a broad doctrine of anticipatory self-defense that might justify unilateral preemptive strikes against other states—in particular, Iraq. On June 1, 2002, at West Point, President Bush set forth "preemptive self-defense" as a new doctrine for U.S. security policy. The successful strategies of the Cold War era, he declared, are ill-suited to national defense in the 21st century. Deterrence and containment will not dissuade terrorists or dictators from possessing weapons of mass destruction. This reasoning may seem logical, but as a party to the UN Charter, the United States is like all member states and thus obligated to abide by the principles of international law that explicitly control under what conditions governments may lawfully resort to armed force abroad. All of these conditions require either a legitimate invocation of article 51 (self-defense) or the authority of the Security Council in the form of a resolution adopted under chapter 7 of the Charter, calling for a collective security action. President Bush's case for war with Iraq featured prominently in his administration's national security strategy, which was issued on September 20, 2002. It is true that preemptive self-defense—defined as the anticipatory use of force when confronting an immediate, imminent attack—has become more accepted as a legitimate response under modern international law. Yet, while recognized as a valid concept under international law, anticipatory self-defense is certainly not free from controversy. Furthermore, for such preemptive self-defense to be asserted lawfully, the threat must be real, immediate, and overwhelming; and it must leave no time for deliberation. In effect, if you see an armed attacker coming at you—really bearing down on you with malice in his eyes—you may defend yourself before the attack strikes your territory or people. Yet, while a doctrine of preemptive or anticipatory self-defense might be legally respected and accepted, the lawfulness of "preventive" attacks is far less certain.[20] An action taken as "preventive war" would permit one state (the United States) to attack another state (Iraq) when the latter's past practices and explicit statements suggest that one day it might conceivably pose a threat to the former state's national security. The problem with preventive attacks—in contrast to attacks in anticipatory or preemptive self-defense—is that the actual nature of the threat does not have to be imminent, immediate, or overwhelming. If adopted as a rationale for national security policy, a doctrine of preventive war would invite states to determine whether, when, and where some other government constituted a potential threat and would excuse an armed attack on the grounds that at some undefined later time the other government might strike the former state. Such a policy would be more speculative and presumptive. It would be based on acts that *might* occur. One can be sympathetic with the view that this position was motivated by the threats of terrorists, who are stealthy and cannot be easily deterred, as well as by the enormous dangers posed by weapons of mass destruction. Nonetheless, adoption of a policy doctrine by one government—particularly the sole remaining superpower—that accepts preventive wars could provide almost limitless rationales for other governments to embark on military actions against other states. Today's international system is characterized by the relative infrequency of interstate war. Developing and promoting doctrines that endorse preventive attacks might do much to unravel the international legal rules governing the use of force. In sum, the U.S. national security doctrine of engaging in preventive attacks seems gravely problematic at best.

As noted, the legal sweep of self-defense has changed over time. In recent decades, governments no longer perceive the customary right of self-defense to be a narrow exception to the general ban on the use of force. Instead, armed response taken in self-defense is broadly asserted as permissible in various situations, so long as some element of a state's safety or well-being is at risk. But herein lies the rub for many legal commentators. The customary right to use force in self-defense often exceeds the legal bounds of the right set out in article 51. In a number of contemporary situations nominally involving the use of force in self-defense, no direct attack has occurred against the responding state. Rather, action is taken preventively by a powerful state to avert some potential future attack, real or imagined, by a far less militarily capable adversary. This situation is well illustrated in the cases of Israel's destruction of Iraq's Osirik nuclear reactor in 1981 and the attack in March 2003 by the United States on Iraq to prevent Saddam Hussein from using weapons of mass destruction against the American homeland or other Western targets.

However, the more widely accepted and legally well-grounded idea of anticipatory self-defense provided the main legal justification for retaliation against nonstate actors following acts of terrorism against the United States. For example, in 1998 the United States launched cruise missile attacks against targets in Sudan and Afghanistan in response to the bombing of American embassies in Nairobi, Kenya, and Dar es Salaam, Tanzania. The stated intention was to destroy the al Qaeda groups believed responsible. Likewise, in late October 2001 and in retaliation for the al Qaeda–led attacks on the World Trade Center and the Pentagon on September 11, 2001, the United States launched a combined special forces and air assault against Afghanistan, the state that was giving al Qaeda sanctuary. The legal rationale for U.S. action was self-defense against reasonably anticipated future attacks by al Qaeda resulting from the Taliban government's unwillingness to intervene and to stop such activities from being planned and carried out from Afghanistan. Generally, the legal justifications offered by the United States to explain these aberrations were acceptable to the international community.

Under contemporary international legal rules, the right of a state to engage in self-defense appears permissible in the following circumstances:

1. when the action comes in response to, and is directed against, an ongoing armed attack on the state's territory—for example, by Kuwait against Iraq in August 1990;
2. when action comes in anticipation of an armed attack or a threat to a state's security so that the intended target state may strike first, with force—for example, by Israel to justify its air strike against Iraq's Osirak nuclear reactor in 1981; or
3. when the action comes in response to an attack against a state's interests—in particular, its territory, nationals, property, or rights guaranteed under international law.

If a state's assets are indeed threatened, then its government may use armed force to protect them—for example, the use of force by Israel against Uganda at Entebbe in 1976 or the military action by the United States against the Osama bin Laden terrorist organization in Afghanistan in 2001. Unfortunately, the manner in which UN Charter law interacts with preexisting customary law clouds the conditions within which self-defense is warranted as a legal right of states.

Controversy persists, however, over the circumstances under which self-defense may be lawfully used. One school of thought argues for a restrictive approach to the use of force and asserts that a broad right of self-defense is no longer permissible. Article 51 stipulates that "nothing shall impair the inherent right of individual or collective self-defense if an armed attack occurs against a member of the United Nations." But here tension arises with article 2 (4), which prohibits the use of all armed force. If articles 2 (4) and 51 are read in tandem, the suggested conclusion is that the only lawful right of self-defense available today is that defined in article 51. Traditional customary law becomes superceded by UN Charter law, leaving the practical result that a state may resort to self-defense only if "an armed attack occurs" against it, but not otherwise. Consequently, the restrictionists' interpretation of self-defense concludes that no lawful right exists to use force in anticipation of an attack, when there is a nonviolent threat, or to protect anything other than state territory.

A second approach views the *scope of self-defense* in broader terms. While doubt remains about how far the principle of self-defense may be stretched under contemporary international legal rules, state practice clearly indicates that UN Charter law will not work as a straight jacket for dictating how governments will respond when their national security is perceived to be at risk. The U.S. military invasion of Iraq in the spring of 2003 clearly spotlights this point. An argument can be made that the adoption of article 2 (4) did not completely curtail the right to use force, therefore preserving the customary right to use force in self-defense. In addition, some hold with the view that article 51 was never intended to be the definitive legal statement on the right of self-defense. To be sure, the *travaux preparatoires* of the San Francisco conference (that finalized the UN Charter) suggest that the inclusion of article 51 was done more to clarify the relationship between regional organizations and the Security Council than to clarify the nature of self-defense. Regional organizations may take armed action without Security Council authorization if it is a matter of self-defense, but they need the permission of the Security Council to take "enforcement" action.[21] The point is also often made that article 51 actually preserves the customary right of self-defense because of the reference therein to the "inherent" right. If interpreted as "preexisting in customary law," then self-defense can be considered to be an inalienable right of statehood. Finally, it should be noted that article 51 does not stipulate that self-defense is available only if an armed attack occurs. As seen in recent years, "an armed attack" may occur not only when troops cross a border but also when missiles are launched, or when aircraft are deployed on bombing runs, or when nonstate actors engage in transnational attacks. These arguments support the view that article 51 was never intended to constrict the right of self-defense that predated the charter. Similarly, in *Nicaragua v. U.S.*, the issue concerning the legitimacy of anticipatory self-defense was expressly reserved by the court, with the majority favoring the restrictive view.

The safest conclusion on self-defense is that the precise parameters of the concept remain open to debate among legal commentators. A rather broad right of self-defense appears evident under preserved customary law, but that conclusion runs counter to the interpretation of article 51 by many governments since 1945. Clearly, policy arguments supporting broader interpretation of the right of self-defense reflect the views of powerful states who wish to preserve their freedom of action in a rapidly globalizing international society, particularly since international law is such an imperfect system. The majority of states with less military capability argue for a narrower right of self-defense, one that may be exercised only if an armed attack occurs against a state's territory. Self-defense for them is an exceptional right to be used only in exceptional circumstances, which can be defined in relatively objective terms by an armed attack against state territory.

The question also arises regarding what constitutes an "armed attack" under international law. In *Nicaragua v. U.S.*, the International Court of Justice concurred that an armed attack included "not only action by the regular armed forces of a foreign State across an international border, but also 'the sending by or on behalf of a State of armed bands, groups, irregulars, or mercenaries, which carry out acts of armed force against another State of such gravity as to amount to an actual armed attack carried out by regular forces' or its substantial involvement therein.'"[22] But does one state commit an armed attack when it supplies assistance to armed bands operating inside another state? In the *Nicaragua* case, the court fell short of providing a definitive answer. The court's decision held that while the provision of weapons, finance, training facilities, and general encouragement for armed forces operating against another state entailed an unlawful use of force against that target state, this in itself did not rise to the level of "an armed attack" such as to legitimize the use of force in self-defense. The threatened state could use force in self-defense against the rebels operating within its territory. But in taking action against the supplier state, even though it was committing an unlawful use of force, the threatened state must remain restricted to responding with "proportionate countermeasures." It remains unclear, though, who should determine the limits of proportionality and what such countermeasures should be.

Collective Self-Defense

In an era of multilateral coalitions organized to deal with transgressors, it is important to realize that self-defense can occur by many states operating together. As preserved in article 51, force may be used lawfully if undertaken in collective self-defense under the same circumstances as individual self-defense—that is, in response to an armed attack or in the broader situations suggested by customary state practice. While not specifically defined in the Charter, collective self-defense implies the use of force in self-defense by two or more states, regardless of whether one state, some states, or all states in the group are attacked. This authorization to use collective force in self-defense furnishes the legal basis for post–World War II military alliances such as NATO. These treaty arrangements envision that all members of the alliance will use force in self-defense if any one of them is subjected to an unlawful use of force. In the case of a nonalliance situation, a victim state will generally request assistance from others, who may come to its collective self-defense under article 51 of the Charter. As a consequence, collective self-defense consists of concerted action taken by several states in response to an actual armed attack against any one state, as opposed to the joint exercise by states of their individual rights of self-defense.

Collective self-defense can also take the form of "coalitions of the willing." A case in point is the military invasion and occupation of Iraq in 2003, in which the United States, United Kingdom, Australia, Poland, and Spain joined to oust Saddam Hussein. Although there were several coalition partners, this was overwhelmingly a U.S. operation. The commanding officers and senior planners of the operation were American, as were the majority of troops, aircraft, munitions, and military equipment used in the fighting.

Other Justifications for the Use of Force

States sometimes claim that the use of force is lawful if it aims to achieve certain "legitimate" purposes. The critical consideration here is the notion of legitimacy and how it is produced. One common explanation is that a resort to force arose from the customary right of self-defense, which mirrors the right derived from the *Caroline* formula. Alternatively, a state might claim that some act of force was lawful on grounds that it does not violate article 2(4) when interpreted liberally. Finally, and perhaps most polemically, a government might claim that new customary rules have evolved since 1945 that permit the use of force for certain purposes under particular circumstances. This appears to be the case with the United States and its formulation in 2002 of the strategic doctrine of "preventive war."

Internal Conflicts

There is no argument that one government may lawfully request the deployment of another state's military forces in its territory. In 1958, Lebanon requested that the United States send military forces to protect itself from internal communist threats. The lawfulness of the situation was never in question. The criteria for legality here are that the legitimate government of a state, freely and without external pressure, makes an explicit request for military assistance to the legitimate government of another state. Likewise, many legal commentators hold that a state may seek to ensure the safety of its nationals by briefly invading another state, as in the case of the rescue mission by Israel at Entebbe in 1976 and as alleged by the United States when it invaded Grenada in 1983. Such interventions are supposed to be limited, however, and must not threaten the authority structure of the targeted state.

Normally under international law, a state's resort to armed intervention is not permissible. The general principle of nonintervention is controlling. No state has the right to intervene militarily into the affairs of another state. Each state retains the right to determine its own domestic policies for itself, and no state may intervene or interfere in that process in any way. Under international legal rules, a condition of internal war is considered lawful, irrespective of the kind of government in question. (This is not to say that domestic law cannot outlaw armed insurrection. Indeed, in most instances armed rebels who are captured are tried for common crimes such as murder and assault, as well as subversion or treason.) Put another way, military intervention by a state cannot be legally justified by an arbitrary desire—for example, to assist the "democratic" faction of a rebel group engaged in an insurgency in another state. Even so, two fundamental questions complicate the legal situation in modern internal wars. First, when exactly does an internal conflict rise to the level of a civil war such that the established government no longer retains legal competence to request external assistance to help quash the rebellion? Second, what can be said about the legal situation when the sides establish rival governments and each requests assistance from different outside states?

The first query is difficult to answer definitively. Generally, the authorities in a state are competent to request assistance from other states, excluding requests that would deprive indigenous peoples of their inherent protected rights, such as freedom from genocide. But at what point does an internal rebellion reach the level of an internationally recognized civil war, thereby abrogating the legal competence of the established authorities? Unfortunately, in most cases such questions of fact become susceptible to devolving into issues of interpretation. The civil war in one state—which requires that third parties not intervene—might be viewed as a mere insurrection in another state in which friendly states can lawfully take actions to help governments suppress the violence.

As to the second query, once a civil war is recognized internationally, modern legal rules assert that no state is permitted to respond to requests for military assistance from either party. If a state does, it will be using force unlawfully, as the former Soviet Union did when it intervened in Afghanistan in 1979 at the invitation of the allegedly legitimate government that it had installed illegitimately through an armed invasion and occupation. The Soviets engaged in other legally suspect foreign interventions during the Cold War years, such as their "invitation" into East Germany in 1953, Hungary in 1956, and Czechoslovakia in 1968. Not to be outdone, the United States undertook similar military adventures, including purported invitations to intervene in the Dominican Republic in 1965, Grenada in 1983, and Panama in 1989. Although each of these U.S. interventions produced positive political outcomes in the long term, the legitimacy of the invitations remains problematic.

During the 1960s and 1970s, much international attention focused on the use of force to achieve self-determination and to assist national liberation movements. The often-made argument asserted that such force was legitimate in that it furthered the principles of the UN Charter. Even so, the debate that emerged tended to generate more passion and heat than sensibility and light. Three key issues drive the legal debate. First, there is the nature of the relationship between the colonial government and the self-determination movement. May the colonial power use force to suppress a self-determination movement? Today, the answer to that query is no, as established authoritatively by the UN Security Council. When Indonesia sought in 1999 to use force to suppress the people of East Timor in their quest for independence, the Security Council responded with resolution 1264, authorizing member states to use "all necessary measures" to protect the rights of the Timorese. The clear message today is that all states, inclusive of the colonial power, have the duty to refrain from taking forcible action that deprives people of their right to self-determination, freedom, and independence. To do otherwise is to act counter to the principles and purposes of the UN Charter.

A second legal issue turns on the national liberation movement's right to use force to attain self-determination. Could national liberation movements lawfully use force to overthrow the colonial regime in power and thus achieve self-determination? Critical here is identification of which groups are authorized to use force. That is, what precisely determines the legitimate status of some faction as a national liberation movement, and does this status differ legally from that of an insurgent group within the traditional situation of a civil war? Resolute answers to these questions remain elusive. It seems evident, however, that so-called wars of national liberation, being fought for purposes of self-determination, were more so internal conflicts. They were not a form of belligerency waged across national borders by two entirely distinct legal persons subject to the international rules for the use of force. Perhaps the most satisfactory conclusion is the following syllogism. Modern international law does not prohibit internal conflicts; wars of national liberation and self-determination movements are forms of internal conflict; hence, the use of force to achieve self-determination may be considered a legal expression of popular revolt, subject to the rules of law accorded to civil wars. Thus, contemporary international rules do not classify the use of force by a national liberation movement as being unlawful.

A third complication flows directly from the first two. May an established state lawfully use interstate force to assist a national liberation movement's fight for self-determination? Such a right, for example, was claimed by India after its invasion of East Pakistan in 1971 to create Bangladesh. Yet, there is no generally accepted customary practice that would allow a government to give armed assistance to national liberation movements operating in another state. Nor can it be said that UN Charter law supports such aid being given. While some General Assembly resolutions suggest the propriety of assisting such groups, these resolutions are not legally binding. Moreover, they have been opposed by some of the most militarily powerful states, such as the United States, France, and United Kingdom. Still, if such a situation is genuinely regarded as an internal matter, states remain under the general obligations to not intervene and to abide by the rules in article 2 (4). Perhaps the most widely accepted view concerning the role of third parties' interfering in wars of national liberation is that in a movement's struggle for self-determination, a third party may give political or economic assistance but not military aid. The crisis in Bosnia-Herzegovina during the early 1990s tragically illustrates how excessive external interference from Serbia, Croatia, and Iran distorted and exacerbated an internal conflict principally aimed at self-determination. By 1994 the Security Council adopted mandatory resolutions that prohibited outside assistance from any party to the conflict, thereby reinforcing the obligation of nonintervention.

In sum, modern legal rules concerning a state's intervention into another state's internal conflict come down to this. States may intervene only to assist a foreign government that is experiencing low-intensity civil strife and only in cases where the government freely gives its explicit consent. With respect to providing force to facilitate a war of self-determination, the general legal rule asserts that foreign states may not give military assistance to rebels, since to do so would violate the prohibition on interference into the domestic affairs of other states. The rebels are expected to succeed or fail on their own abilities.

Protection of Nationals Abroad

Governments often claim the right to use force to protect their nationals abroad. This justification was used by Belgium in 1960 when it sent paratroopers into the Congo to protect its missionary workers from rampant violence in the newly independent state. Likewise, in June 1976 Israeli forces landed at Entebbe airport in Uganda to rescue Israelis who had been taken hostage by Palestinian commandos in an aircraft that was hijacked and forced to land there. The United States proffered the rescue of American nationals as the legal rationale for at least three missions since 1980. Among these were the invasion of Grenada in 1983 to rescue one thousand medical students believed to be in danger; its invasion of Panama in December 1989 following General Noriega's decision to annul the democratic elections just held there; and sending in U.S. Marines to protect Americans in Liberia in August 1990, a day after the rebel leader ordered the arrest all foreign nationals in the capital city of Monrovia.

Many international law commentators today are reluctant to concede the lawfulness of a state's using armed force to protect its nationals abroad. They see such permissiveness as an invitation to abuse a right to intervene.[23] This view is consistent with the two preeminent UN resolutions adopted concerning the use of force, the Declaration on the Inadmissibility of Intervention in Domestic Affairs of States (1965), and the Declaration of Principles of International Law (1970). Yet, state practice seems to suggest that, on occasion, resort to military force could be legally justified. Writers who view the use of force permissively—such as D. W. Bowett, Myers McDougal, and Michael Reisman—argue that such intervention can be a legitimate extension of self-defense.[24] That is, injury to a national within a foreign country whose government cannot or will not provide adequate protection becomes tantamount to injury to the state itself. In support of this view, general customary law suggests that four conditions must be met for the use of armed force to be lawful for this purpose:

1. The state in which the nationals are located must be unwilling or unable to protect them.
2. The nationals must be in grave danger or immediate life-threatening harm.
3. The use of force must come as the last resort.
4. The acting state must use only that force that is absolutely necessary and depart the territory of the target state as soon as it is practical.

In other words, continued occupation by an intervenor of the target state's territory without its government's consent (as the United States did during its interventions into Grenada and Panama) is generally considered to be impermissible. While imposing these conditions should be regarded as a positive development, certain problems arise from their inherently subjective interpretation. For instance, who determines if a host government is actually unwilling to help? Or if perceived "hostage" conditions are really life threatening? Or what measure of force may be absolutely necessary? These questions are not easily answered and will vary according to the particular circumstances of each case. Even so, such conditions are intended to be salient legal guideposts for curbing the depth and breadth of violence in situations where a government militarily intervenes to rescue its nationals in another state.

Humanitarian Intervention

Governments occasionally perpetrate mass human rights atrocities on thousands of their own citizens within their own borders. Most of these genocides are tribally or ideologically motivated and occur during periods of internal strife in African and Asian countries, such as those that occurred in the Central African Empire during 1976–1979; Cambodia, 1975–1979; Uganda, 1970–1977; Burundi and Rwanda, 1994; Sierra Leone, 1999; and the Congo, 1998–2003. Europe, too, has not proven immune, with large-scale genocidal ethnic pogroms in Bosnia, Croatia, and Kosovo occurring within the last fifteen years. Does international mortality and justice mandate that other governments accept the responsibility to stop these brutal massacres? Or does the principle of national sovereignty serve as a legal prophylactic to prevent other states from militarily intervening and violating territorial integrity of the perpetrating government?

Humanitarian intervention refers to an action in which a state or a group of states uses armed force to protect the inhabitants of another state from their own government's perpetuation of gross human rights abuses against them. The motivation for humanitarian intervention resembles the justification for protecting nationals abroad, although no necessary link—other than common humanity—unites the intervening state and the persons in danger. Principles of international morality and justice seem receptive to permitting such a general right to intervene forcibly for humanitarian purposes without the consent of the territorial sovereign or where a government is systematically murdering its own people. Such a claim was alleged by the United States and NATO to justify military action against Serbia (Yugoslavia) during 1999. This intervention was guided by two factors: first, the intervention was authorized by a competent international organization, NATO; second, the use of armed force only came when the Kosovar Albanians suffered extreme deprivation of human rights that amounted to genocide at the hands of Serb military and paramilitary forces.[25]

Setting aside considerations of morality and justice, state practice does not unequivocally support the existence of a right of humanitarian intervention, nor do contemporary legal rules endorse conditions for its lawful exercise. Even so, a number of actions occurred in modern times that were predicated on the assumed legitimacy of humanitarian intervention. For example, in December 1971 India intervened militarily in East Pakistan, an action partly justified by the eruption of a brutal civil war and the resulting exodus of some ten million Bengali refugees into northeastern India. Following twelve days of fighting, Pakistan surrendered, Eastern Pakistan seceded, and in its place the new state of Bangladesh was born. While India initially suggested in the UN Security Council that humanitarian intervention provided the legal rationale for its action, Indira Ghandi's government subsequently dropped that claim. Instead, the Indian government asserted that the preeminent legal justification for its invasion of East Pakistan was an act of self-defense, taken in response to the West Pakistani attacks that came against India two weeks before.

State practice does not deny the right of humanitarian intervention, nor does it create a legal obligation on all states to intervene. During the late 1960s, when the region of Biafra attempted to secede from Nigeria, the Nigerian army acted with such flagrant cruelty against Biafran civilians that it generated worldwide condemnation. Yet not a single government sought to intervene to protect the thousands of civilian Biafrans who were massacred. In 1977, Tanzania intervened into Uganda, following many years of tribal atrocities committed under the brutal regime of Idi Amin. Yet, Tanzania chose not to justify the overthrow of the Ugandan dictator on grounds of humanitarian intervention; instead, Tanzanian president Julius Nyerere based his government's action on a claim of self-defense against recurring transborder attacks by Ugandan forces. In 1978 when Vietnam invaded Cambodia and overthrew the Pol Pot regime—which had been responsible for killing between one million and three million Cambodians from 1972 through 1974—most governments condemned Hanoi's action, and few legal authorities supported Vietnam's claim of humanitarian intervention to halt the ongoing genocide.

More recently, in 1991 the United States and the United Kingdom used humanitarian intervention to justify the lawfulness of establishing and maintaining no-fly zones over northern and southern Iraq. These zones, however, were set up without explicit UN Security Council authorization to protect the Kurds in the north and the Shiites in the south from the excesses of the Iraqi government. Admittedly, humanitarian intentions may well have motivated these actions, which amounted to blatant interference with Iraqi national sovereignty. But such humanitarian motivations cannot give rise to a presumed legal right to act, particularly since the Security Council approved neither action.

Perhaps the most egregious example of international nonaction came in the case of the genocidal atrocities in Rwanda in 1994, in which eight hundred thousand people (mostly Tutsis) were massacred by their fellow Hutu countrymen. The tragedy was magnified as the world watched the massacres occur for one hundred days on CNN in the summer of 1994. Incredible as it may seem, and irrespective of humanitarian sympathies, not a single government nor the UN Security Council, Organization of African Unity, or NATO did anything to halt the genocidal carnage.

These mass tragedies aside, the lawfulness of humanitarian intervention remains contentious.[26] The essential problem lies with article 2 (4) and the fact that humanitarian intervention directly contravenes the fundamental intent of that provision—namely, to obligate governments to refrain from the threat or use of force against the territorial integrity or political independence of another state. No less important is the realization that to halt the violations of human rights, humanitarian intervention can lead to removal of the offending government or at least compromise its ability to function. Little doubt exists that either of these consequences jeopardizes the political independence of the target state, a situation that is viewed as impugning the legitimacy of such an action under article 2 (4) and undercutting the aims and purposes of the UN Charter. Of course, should a humanitarian crisis threaten international peace and security, the UN Security Council may sanction collective intervention. This was arguably the case in Somalia and in Haiti during the early 1990s, wherein the Security Council deemed as a threat the destabilizing effects of masses of refugees crossing borders and taking to rickety boats as a result of internal conditions.

In short, little evidence suggests that states in the early 21st century have accepted a lawful right of humanitarian intervention. The bottom line today is that states continue to value their sovereignty and political free will above the value they place on the protection of foreign peoples' human rights. Put bluntly, few governments are willing to risk their national blood or treasure to safeguard or rescue the lives of strangers in strange lands. That said, the use of force by NATO in Kosovo against Serbia and the internationally accepted establishment by the United States and United Kingdom of no-fly zones in Iraq may be harbingers in the formation of a new customary exception to article 2 (4).[27]

Still, the risks of accepting such a doctrine must not go unnoticed. Humanitarian intervention may serve as a legal cloak to mask ulterior political motives for undertaking military intervention into another state. The possibilities for abuse are real and evident. If such a legal right is evolving, it can only exist if based in treaty obligations or if demonstrated in state practice, supported by adequate *opinio juris*. Moralistic sentiments and ethical principles cannot produce a right or a norm simply because one ought to exist. For an international legal rule to emerge, the governments of states must accept the rule and demonstrate that acceptance in the conduct of their interstate relations.

Collective Security

In the aftermath of the Second World War, the United Nations reserved unto its Security Council the right to authorize use of armed force against states deemed delinquent of their international obligations. Such an action is often termed the *collective use of force,* or more properly *collective security.* Put simply, this is the multilateral use of force on behalf of the community at large, in contrast to an act done in pursuit of an individual state's own national interests. It is important to remember that the powers considered here are additional to any rights that states enjoy as individual members of the international community. That is, collective security undertaken by the United Nations under chapter 7 of the Charter is not legally synonymous with collective self-defense. Collective security is generally thought to consist of force used by members of an international organization (the United Nations) against a state that commits aggression against a member state. The aim is to preserve international peace and security through deterrence, but if that fails, all the organization's membership should come to the defense of the threatened state. *Collective self-defense*, however, suggests more of an alliance arrangement in which states are bound in a treaty relationship for their mutual defense, and an attack on one by an aggressor state will trigger a collective response in self-defense.

Two distinctions are useful here. First, the purposes of collective security and collective self-defense are not the same. Collective security aims to maintain general international peace and security. Collective self-defense entails an emergency response to an emergency situation, though the governments engaged in self-defense may continue the defense so long as the threat exists to the state or its territory remains occupied by the aggressor. Second, resort to the right of self-defense, whether exercised individually or collectively, does not depend on a decision of any international organization, including the Security Council of the United Nations. States may undertake that right at their own initiative, albeit an international arrangement often serves as the mechanism through which collective self-defense is undertaken. This appeared to be the case in the U.S. invasion of Grenada, in which the United States partially premised its intervention as lawful collective self-defense under the aegis of the Organization of Eastern Caribbean States, even though the United States was not a member. Similarly, collective self-defense during the Gulf War was the form of an armed response sanctioned by the UN Security Council and taken by a coalition of twenty-nine allied states against Iraq in 1991 to oust the country's forces from Kuwait. Likewise, collective self-defense through NATO was the legal premise put forward by the United States when it launched its attacks on the al Qaeda terrorist network in Afghanistan in late October 2001.

In the past, attacks by a nonstate actor were not deemed acts of war. Rather, they were considered to be violations of criminal law in the state where the act was perpetrated or breaches of various international agreements pertaining to certain international crimes. The al Qaeda attacks of September 11, 2001, amounted to the most massive attacks by a nonstate actor in history and are therefore *sui generis.* In addition, although the U.S. military response came more than a month after the September 11 attacks, the legal rationale asserted by the United States maintained that the situation amounted to a war on terrorism that was being undertaken by NATO in self-defense of its member states. Nevertheless, an important limitation in the UN Charter restricts collective (and individual) self-defense. Article 51 permits the inherent right of individual and collective self-defense to be exercised "until the Security Council has taken the measures necessary to restore international peace and security." While these situations are rare, the principle seems clear— the use of armed force in self-defense should end once the Security Council adopts its own measures to redress the situation.[28]

Coercive Self-Help Short of War

On certain occasions, governments unilaterally take coercive measures without belligerent intent to obtain redress or retaliate for injuries suffered from an offending state, to enforce legal rights, or to attain political or economic advantages. If tensions between states rise to the level of hostility, in most cases those states do not engage in immediate armed conflict. Governments often pursue a ladder of escalation in the use of coercive measures against one another. Under the contemporary system of international legal rules, such measures vary in form and intensity. Early on in the dispute, diplomatic protest and even the severance of diplomatic relations precede resort to other measures of coercion short of war. Retaliation may take the form of a relatively soft action that does not involve the use of armed force, or acts of armed reprisal might be taken in response to an unlawful act of the other state. Economic sanctions might be enacted to impose pressure on an offending state. Finally, resort to a blockade around the offending state's ports can occur to intensify economic and political pressures on that government.

Retorsion refers to a legal but deliberately unfriendly act that is directed by one state against another state in retaliation for an equally unfriendly but lawful act. The express purpose of retorsion is to compel the offending state to change its unfriendly conduct. Acts of retorsion involve lawful acts by all parties. Armed force is never used for retorsion, since it would then become an act of reprisal. While not necessary, acts of retorsion often assume the form of a similar unfriendly act done to the target state. Examples of acts of retorsion include the severance of diplomatic relations, as the United States did to Iran for allowing students to seize and take hostage the fifty-four U.S. diplomats in the U.S. embassy in 1979; the placing of restrictions on the movement of foreign diplomats and nationals or their expulsion, as the United States did to Soviet employees at the United Nations in New York City in 1980 in response to travel restrictions placed by the Soviets on U.S. diplomats in Moscow; the mutual expelling of diplomats or nationals from a host state, as in the case of Cuban and U.S. officials in May 2003; banning exports or placing quotas on specified imports, such as that done by the United States to Japanese automobiles during the 1980s; and restricting the fishing rights of an offending state in the retaliating state's waters, which was done by the United States to Japan in September 2000 for its refusal to comply with the International Whaling Commission's moratorium placed on harvesting whales.

Reprisals entail coercive measures short of war directed by one government against another state in retaliation for the commission of alleged unlawful acts. Reprisals are taken as retaliatory means against a state to compel that state to make satisfactory redress for an earlier unlawful act. Reprisals may be taken as acts not involving armed force, or they may be prosecuted as forms of armed actions against the offending state. Reprisals not using armed force are usually deemed permissible and can take a variety of forms, such as seizure of the offending state's property, freezing its financial assets, nonperformance of treaty obligations, or taking into custody nationals of the offending state. Yet, armed force is sometimes used for reprisal by a government that regards the use of violence as a proper procedure to vindicate rights unlawfully denied or to inflict retribution and punishment for injury or harm suffered. Such action amounts to vengeance or, in biblical terms, extracts "an eye for an eye and a tooth for a tooth." Prior to the UN Charter, the use of armed force in reprisal was regarded as lawful, so long as three criteria were met. First, an illegal act was committed by the offending state; second, an unsatisfied demand for redress was made; and third, the reprisal entailed a reasonably proportionate response to the injury suffered in the prior illegal act.[29] Reprisals were viewed as a means of securing satisfaction and redress in an international system that could not otherwise be provided. This is no longer the case.

Modern international legal rules hold that reprisals that use armed force violate the UN Charter's prohibition of the use of force. In fact, the 1970 Declaration on Principles of International Law Concerning Friendly Relations and Cooperation among States explicitly prohibits acts of reprisal involving armed force. It is not surprising, then, that reprisals taken with armed force are usually clothed in claims of self-defense. Notwithstanding that pretext, most commentators would agree that modern acts of reprisal would include the air strikes by the United States against Libya in 1986 in response to Muammar Quadaffi's alleged complicity in terrorist attacks against Americans; the bombing by the United States of Iraq in 1993 in retaliation for an alleged assassination attempt against former president Bush; the U.S. cruise missile attacks against Sudan and Afghanistan in 1998 in retaliation for al Qaeda's bombing of the American embassies in Kenya and Tanzania; and Israel's repeated air strikes against Palestinian refugee camps in Lebanon during the 1970s and 1980s in response to attacks by PLO guerrillas on Israeli villages, as well as Israel's military assaults against Palestinian villages in the West Bank and Gaza in response to terrorist homicide bombers who attacked Israel throughout 2002–2003. Claims of self-defense aside, the generally accepted view is that article 2 (4) outlaws armed reprisals, particularly since the Charter aims to provide more effective means of, and greater opportunities for, the peaceful settlement of disputes. For contemporary international law, the modern rule for reprisals becomes plain. Resort to armed reprisals is not legal, even when the unlawful act of provocation committed by another state involves the use of armed force. An armed reprisal is essentially an unlawful act of aggression and should be withheld in preference to nonviolent forms of civil response. In situations where a state's national security is perceived to be at risk, this conclusion is all too easy to posit, but far more difficult to prove.

Economic Coercion

The failure to achieve compliance with international legal rules through normal means for the peaceful settlement of disputes can lead to the imposition of economic coercion, or sanctions, against an offending state. Such sanctions may have various objectives. They may compel a state to halt an offensive or unlawful practice, or they may punish a state for an offense committed—or they may do both. Among the most common sanctions are economic measures, such as trade embargoes and boycotts; financial restrictions; prohibitions on the shipment of arms; and interdictive efforts on land, sea, and air to block the transportation of sanctioned goods to a targeted state. Economic sanctions may be imposed by a single state, a group of states, or by a regional or universal organization. States have frequently imposed such sanctions during the past thirty years, though only with modest results. Economic sanctions are usually ineffective and often serve to unify public opinion behind the government in the targeted country. The Security Council may order the mandatory imposition of sanctions under articles 10, 39, 41, 42, 45, and 94 (2) of the Charter and has done so on at least fourteen occasions. Among those states targeted were Southern Rhodesia (1968), South Africa (1977–1994), Libya (1993–1999), Haiti (1993–1994), the former Yugoslavia/Serbia (1993–2001), Kuwait (1990–1991), Iraq (1990–2003), Sierra Leone (1997–), Liberia (1992, 2001–), Angola/UNITA (1993, 1997, 1998-2002), Ethiopia and Eritrea (2000–2001), and Afghanistan (1999, 2000–).

A technique commonly used by states to impose economic coercion is the *trade embargo*. An embargo involves a government's decision to suspend trade to another state, completely prohibiting its export of goods to the target state. Numerous examples have occurred in recent years, though none has produced notable changes in the targeted state's policies. Embargoes are often placed on the export of arms, war materiel, or munitions to states engaged in armed conflict. Following the Arab–Israeli Six Days' War of June 1967, France imposed an arms embargo on all Middle Eastern countries. Similarly, the UN Security Council imposes arms embargoes on states embroiled in conflict with their neighbors or on parties to a civil war, to lessen access to weapons. Recent cases where the Security Council has placed an arms embargo include Iraq in 1990; Yugoslavia, 1991 and 1998; Somalia, 1992; Libya, 1992; Liberia, 1992 and 2002; Haiti, 1993; Angola, 1993; Rwanda, 1994; Sierra Leone, 1997; Ethiopia and Eritrea, 2000; and Afghanistan in 2000. Perhaps the best-known embargo is the Arab oil embargo imposed during 1973–1974 against those states who supported Israel during the 1973 October war—namely, the United States, Netherlands, Portugal, and South Africa. Yet, while these countries' economies were temporarily disrupted, the embargo did not compel Israel to withdraw from the occupied Arab territories seized during the 1967 June war, nor did the targeted states renounce their support for Israel.

The United States frequently uses embargoes as instruments of transnational economic coercion. For instance, during the Cold War years, the United States adopted special legislation that imposed "strategic embargoes" on sensitive or defense-related technologies that American corporations might sell to countries in the Soviet-dominated Warsaw Pact, as well as China, North Korea, Vietnam, and Cambodia. To demonstrate its displeasure over the Soviet invasion and takeover of Afghanistan in late 1979, the Carter administration in early 1980 placed an embargo on the sale of grain by American farmers to the Soviet Union. Although it depressed grain prices at home, the embargo had no impact on persuading the Soviets to leave Afghanistan. Perhaps most impressive, the United States—within a week following Saddam Hussein's invasion and conquest of Kuwait in August 1990—assumed the lead role in persuading the UN Security Council to adopt economic sanctions in the form of a trade embargo on goods shipped to Iraq. These UN sanctions against Iraq remained in effect until 2003 but produced little noticeable change in the Iraqi government's willingness to comply with UN resolutions.

Another form of economic coercion is the *boycott*. In general, a boycott involves a retaliatory action in which the citizens of an injured state suspend business and refuse to purchase goods from the citizens of the offending state. When a government becomes involved and officially institutes a boycott operation, that state adopts legislation to prohibit its citizens or corporations from purchasing any goods or from receiving any imports from the offending state. In that case the government of the injured state must assume state responsibility, and the boycott thus becomes a means of coercive self-help. A well-known example of the modern civilian boycott was the widespread refusal by the Chinese people to buy Japanese goods following Japan's conquest of Manchuria in 1931. Interestingly enough, during the forty years beforehand, the Chinese people actually boycotted Japanese goods on eight other occasions. Perhaps forming the most pervasive modern multilateral boycott are the sanctions imposed against Israel by the twenty-two-member League of Arab States. The Arab boycott, which actually began against Zionist businesses in Palestine in 1947 and continues as of 2004, involves all Arab states except Egypt, Jordan, and Kuwait and has attracted support from several non-Arab Islamic countries. A special Arab boycott office in Damascus, Syria, coordinates boycott operations among the Arab states, including a blacklist of foreign corporations that fail to comply with the boycott. The Western economies first felt the influence of the Arab boycott operation when oil prices were quadrupled by the Organization of Petroleum Exporting Countries in 1973, which became aggravated by the concomitant Arab oil embargo. These economic conditions allowed the Arab boycott to bite sharply into business opportunities of U.S. corporations and their subsidiaries operating abroad. Many U.S. firms felt compelled to avoid trading directly or indirectly with Israel to secure new petrodollar-fueled market outlets in the Arab world. The United States government, however, viewed such corporate compliance as an antireligious discriminatory practice that unlawfully restrained trade and in 1977 passed special antiboycott legislation that banned such corporate behavior.[30]

Enacting a *naval blockade* furnishes another means of coercive self-help just short of armed conflict. A hostile blockade involves a belligerent state's warships blocking access to the enemy's coast during wartime for the purpose of preventing entry or exit by vessels and aircraft of all states. A belligerent blockade is distinguished from a pacific blockade in that the latter occurs during peacetime, while the former occurs during ongoing hostilities. According to classic international law, imposition of a naval blockade was deemed a necessary element in effecting a condition of belligerency between two states. The Declaration of Paris of 1856 stipulated that for a blockade to be legal and binding on neutral states, it had to be declared and effective—that is, formal notification had to be given to all states, and naval forces had to actually enforce the blockade. Throughout the 19th and 20th centuries, blockades were instituted along the enemy's coasts, usually just beyond port facilities. In the years between the First and Second World Wars, changes and conditions in the means of modern naval warfare compelled blocking states to move their blockades further out into the high seas. At the same time, governments decreasingly relied on formal declarations of war as preconditions for engaging in international hostilities. Consequently, since the Second World War, resort to blockades has fallen into disuse as a legal perquisite for recognizing the onset of a formal condition of belligerency. Instead, imposition of a blockade—and other forms of naval interdiction, such as exclusionary zones—is now motivated by the need to increase diplomatic pressure against targeted states, usually to enforce measures of economic coercion adopted by the UN Security Council against a transgressor state. These pacific forms of blockade are not declared during wartime hostilities between belligerent governments. Rather, the Security Council employs them as enforcement measures, as ships from various states—namely, the United States, United Kingdom, France, and Russia—are used to inspect and search foreign vessels bound for a targeted country's ports to determine if contraband goods are being carried. Recent examples of these interdictive measures include blockades in the Persian Gulf imposed against vessels bound for Iraq (1991–2003), around Haiti (1993–1994), and offshore Serbia and Bosnia (1993–1995).

THE SECURITY COUNCIL AND THE USE OF FORCE

Under UN Charter law, the Security Council is responsible for maintaining international peace and security. The Council is given specific power under Chapter VII of the charter to act on behalf of all member states, even if doing so means using armed force. The Security Council is presumed to be the international peacekeeper and peace enforcer. Unfortunately, Cold War rivalries between the United States and the Soviet Union, political antagonisms between the developing world and the Great Powers, and the actual course of international events since 1945 have severely encumbered the Security Council's ability to exercise this function consistently and effectively.

Under article 39 of the Charter, if the Security Council determines that there exists a ''threat to the peace, breach of the peace, or act of aggression,'' it may take measures to deal with situation as specified in articles 41 and 42. While the General Assembly's 1974 Definition of Aggression supplies some assistance, it is not entirely clear about what kind of action should constitute a threat to international peace and security. Unquestionably, armed military actions such as Iraq's invasion of Kuwait, the violence in Bosnia, or al Qaeda's attack on the United States fall under article 39. But what about unstable domestic conditions in a state that produce massive violence or involve social conditions unacceptable to most of the international community? Is the United Nations legally bound under article 2(7) to respect the sovereignty of that state and the authority of its government to manage its own internal affairs? Or does the United Nations have the lawful authority to use sanctions to pressure that government to improve or change those conditions? The Security Council has tended to opt for the latter interpretation. As indicated by cases of South Africa, Southern Rhodesia, Liberia, Haiti, Rwanda, and East Timor, "threats to the peace" are not limited to transnational military situations. In these cases, internal conditions in these polities gave rise to actions under Chapter VII of the Charter. Similarly, in the case of Libya its connection to the infamous bombing of Pan Am flight 103 in December 1988 produced Security Council resolutions under Chapter VII for its government's alleged promotion of international terrorism. The point here is that the Security Council holds primary responsibility for the maintenance of international peace and security and is expected to act on that accountability.

The measures envisioned in article 41 involve nonmilitary sanctions, such as the imposition by the United Nations of a trade boycott—for example, against Haiti in 1993 and Southern Rhodesia in 1968; or an arms embargo—for example, against Liberia in 1993, Rwanda in 1994, and the former Yugoslavia in 1994; or even an embargo on international air flights—for example, against Libya in 1993 and Afghanistan in 1998. Such measures may also include total interruptions of economic and diplomatic relations. It is important to understand that decisions taken under article 41 are legally binding on all member states, the governments of which are generally required to report to the secretary-general for guidance on what actions they should take to further compliance with a resolution. To comply with Security Council–mandated economic sanctions, governments usually must implement domestic legislation that prohibits their own nationals from trading with the offending state.

The UN Charter recognizes that some acts of aggression may be so grave as to require the collective use of armed force. Under article 42, the Council is authorized to take military action "as may be necessary to maintain or restore international peace and security." This is the thrust of the collective security system as envisioned by the founders of the UN. The Council is given the power to authorize the use of armed force against a deviant state. Importantly, though, this authority is not stipulated for redressing breaches of international law as such. Rather, the Council acts to restore international peace and stability. It is supposed to authorize the use of armed force against an aggressor state to halt the violence being perpetrated against a victim state. It does not impose sanctions to punish a government for some act or to compel amends by a government for its perceived unlawful activities.

As emphasized earlier, the Charter explicitly provides for only two exceptions to the prohibition on the use of force: first, force may be undertaken if it is done in self-defense; and, second, force is permissible if the Security Council authorizes it. Article 51 asserts that states "maintain an inherent right of individual and collective self-defense if an armed attack occurs" against them, at least "until the Security Council has taken measures necessary to maintain international peace and security." Hence, if one state commits an armed attack against another state, the targeted state may use force to repel the attack until the Security Council acts. Moreover, the victim state may call on other states to assist it in an act of collective self-defense. Second, under article 39, the Security Council is empowered to determine if there exists a "threat to the peace, breach of the peace, or act of aggression." If so determined, the Council is permitted to authorize the use of military force or otherwise against an offending state. Finally, it should be noted that under Chapter VIII of the Charter, regional organizations are allowed to deal with "matters relating to the maintenance of international peace and security," but those organizations cannot undertake an "enforcement action" without authorization of the Security Council.[31]

According to the scheme originally envisioned in the Charter, the use of armed force by the Security Council under article 42 depended on satisfactory agreements being concluded under article 43, which would provide for an organized military force to be put permanently at the Council's disposal. Significantly, no such agreements were ever negotiated, nor are any expected in the future. As a consequence, the Charter is not likely to function as a pure form of collective security in the ways that its drafters had hoped. Yet, this does not mean that the Security Council lacks the capability to authorize or mobilize enforcement action. Indeed, it possesses the authority and the power to act under Chapter VII and has done so on a number of occasions.

In June 1950, the Security Council acted (in the absence of the Soviet delegate) to repel the invasion by North Korea of South Korea by voting to give assistance to the South. The United States provided the commander of the unified UN command and subsequently took overall control of military activities until the formal cessation of hostilities in 1954. More than a decade later, following the unilateral declaration of independence by Southern Rhodesia in November 1965, the Security Council passed a resolution calling on all states to refrain from any action that might assist and encourage the illegal regime. The Council asserted in particular that states should refrain from providing arms, materiel, and military equipment to the minority white government and should break economic relations with Southern Rhodesia, especially by embargoing oil and petroleum products. In April 1966, the Security Council determined that the situation in Southern Rhodesia constituted a threat to the peace and declared that mandatory sanctions should be instigated under article 41.

The next serious international situation confronted by the Security Council in the post–Cold War era was Iraq's invasion and occupation of Kuwait. On August 2, 1990, Iraq invaded Kuwait and swiftly overran the small Gulf state. That very day, the Security Council passed resolution 660, which condemned the invasion and asserted that the situation constituted a breach of international peace and security. Following Iraq's refusal to withdraw, the Council adopted resolution 661, which imposed comprehensive economic sanctions against Iraq. To provide for the collective self-defense of Kuwait, the United States and the United Kingdom pressed the Security Council to adopt resolution 678 on November 20, 1990. This measure authorized member states of the United Nations "to use all necessary means" to compel Iraq's withdrawal from Kuwait if it had not done so by January 15, 1991. Resolution 678 can be properly construed as an enforcement action authorized by the Council.

Chapter VII procedures were also used in Somalia and Bosnia, although in both instances, questions arose regarding the lawfulness of humanitarian intervention by the United Nations. In late 1992, the Security Council determined that famine conditions in Somalia constituted a threat to peace and security and in reaction authorized sending in UN troops to protect humanitarian aid workers who were distributing food to rural areas. The mission radically changed in June 1993 when the Security Council authorized in its resolution 837 that member states could use "all necessary means" in response to a Somali warlord's killing twenty-seven Pakistani UN peacekeepers engaged in the humanitarian relief operation in Somalia. In the same vein, the Council authorized in June 1993 a UN force in Yugoslavia to take "all necessary means" to protect the civilian population in Bosnia. Bosnian Serbs, through the horrific practice of ethnic cleansing, were exterminating Bosnian Muslims and other non-Serbs, and the Security Council intervened to halt such genocidal atrocities. However, the frustration and inability of UN forces to deal successfully with the Bosnian mission prompted the Security Council in September 1995 to delegate the effort to NATO armed forces through resolution 1031—the first time the UN had ever handed off a peacekeeping mission to a regional organization. Unlike previous situations, the principal concern in Somalia and Bosnia focused on provision of humanitarian relief to the local population, rather than a response to external military aggression by another state. The Security Council authorized the use of force in both instances, even though both cases are usually regarded as failed UN peacekeeping operations.

In June 1999 the Security Council continued this pattern of intervention to protect civilian lives as it adopted resolution 1246—to permit the use of all necessary measures by states to support the people of East Timor in their quest for self-determination—and authorized the establishment of the United Nations Mission in East Timor. In the aftermath of elections in August 1999 that overwhelmingly supported independence, pro-Indonesian militants launched a campaign of violence throughout the entire territory, which prompted the Security Council to authorize a multinational force under a unified command structure headed by Australia to restore peace and security in East Timor. In October 1999 the Security Council adopted resolution 1272, which established the United Nations Transitional Administration in East Timor as an integrated, multidimensional peacekeeping operation fully responsible for the administration of East Timor during its transition to independence.

The terrorist attacks of September 11, 2001, on the United States also triggered Security Council action justifying the use of military force as a lawful response. On September 12, 2001, the Security Council adopted resolution 1368, which strongly condemned the terrorist attacks and expressed the Council's "readiness to take all necessary steps" toward authorizing the use of force when U.S. military plans were ready. More significantly, the council acted under Chapter VII of the Charter in resolution 1373 of September 28, 2001, and decided that all states "shall take the necessary steps to prevent the commission of terrorist acts." Interestingly enough, the language used here is legally paradoxical. While the wording does not explicitly authorize the use of force, it may well intimate a broad, practically unlimited mandate to use force whenever and wherever a government decides that, for political reasons, armed force is necessary "to prevent the commission of terrorist acts." Moreover, the language is universal. It is not only directed to a response by the United States but is applied to all states. Consequently, any state—China or Russia, for example—might invoke resolution 1373 as a legal instrument to justify cracking down on dissidents ("terrorists") who are rebelling within their territory.

The case of Iraq well illustrates the complicated situation in which the use of force law now finds itself. In October 2002, the United States vigorously prompted the Security Council to once again consider the international threat posed by Iraq. The core issue was Iraq's refusal to comply with some sixteen Security Council resolutions since 1991 that mandate Iraq's disarmament of weapons of mass destruction and the insertion of UN inspectors to confirm that no chemical, biological, or nuclear weapons are being produced, stored, or stockpiled. Moreover, the Bush administration contended that Iraq might well give weapons of mass destruction to terrorist groups who might then use them against Western societies—in particular, the United States. In November 2002, the UN Security

Council unanimously adopted resolution 1441 under Chapter VII authorization, which asserted that Iraq had one last chance to cease its material breach of obligations or "face serious consequences."

Resolution 1441 may have been intended by most members of the Security Council to be a warning to Iraq, but it was interpreted by the United States to be the vehicle for legitimizing the use of force against Saddam Hussein's regime. In March 2003, after the UN Security Council refused to adopt a resolution authorizing the use of force, or "all necessary means," against Iraq, the United States proceeded with its military invasion under the legal umbrella of a multilateral, forty-nine-member "coalition of the willing." In actuality, the invasion of Iraq amounted to a U.S. operation. The military victory and overthrow of Saddam's government was accomplished in three weeks, with a minimum loss of American lives.

While many allied states and legal commentators believe that this use of armed force by the United States contravened modern international legal rules,[32] some contend that the ends justified the means: an evil tyrannical regime was removed, and a chance for democratic government was brought to the Iraqi people.[33] But for the future of international legal rules, the upshot is problematic. No single state—not even the world's lone superpower—possesses a unilateral right to function as the world's police officer unless authorized by the Security Council. Such authorization was not given in the case of the 2003 invasion of Iraq. If UN Charter law, especially the prohibition against the use of force contained in article 2 (4), can be so readily discounted, then of what proscriptive value is it? Has the relevance and legal authority of article 2 (4) been eroded so extensively by contemporary state practice that the normative power of the restriction is now at risk of failing entirely? That critical question is left hanging in the aftermath of the 2003 United States–Iraq war.

Notwithstanding the many UN actions taken under chapter 7, no pure collective security operation has yet been performed by the Security Council. Relatively few member states of the United Nations contribute troops or materiel to actions authorized by the Security Council. Nor does the Military Staff Committee convene and direct military operations as provided for in article 43. The UN operation in Korea in 1950 and actions taken to oust Iraq from Kuwait in the 1991 Gulf War were not collective security operations as envisioned in the Charter. They were peace enforcement actions that assumed the form of UN-approved coalitions acting in collective self-defense of an attacked state. In both instances, the United States government supplied nearly all of the soldiers and equipment and directed the military campaigns throughout the conflict. Neither the Secretary-General nor any other national government assumed the commanding role, and the Military Staff Committee played no part whatsoever. Directives came from the President of the United States, and an American military commander carried out operations on the ground. An armed attack had occurred against a sovereign state, and request for assistance from a legitimate government was made. The United Nations was properly used as the instrument to legitimize a coalition-based self-defense operation but not to implement it. In the absence of article 43 agreements that would allow the Security Council to directly use military force to perform its collective security function, the Council in recent years has recommended or authorized a variety of measures aimed at maintaining international peace and security.

As discussed earlier, the UN Security Council can adopt legally binding resolutions intended to mandate for all UN members specific economic sanctions against certain targeted states. Taken under Chapter VII by the Council, these economic measures are aimed to pressure those governments into halting violent actions that threaten international peace and security and to compel them to seek peaceful resolution of their conflict. Since 1989, Security Council sanctioned operations have been targeted against twelve states, most recently against Afghanistan.

PEACE OPERATIONS

Perhaps the best-known types of UN-sponsored security measures are peacekeeping operations authorized under Chapter VI ("Pacific Settlement of Disputes") or Chapter VII ("Action with Respect to Threats to the Peace, Breaches of the Peace, and Acts of Aggression") of the UN Charter. Since 1948, the Security Council has authorized the creation of fifty-six peacekeeping missions, with forty-five created since 1989. The cost of these operations has exceeded $25 billion over the life of the UN—equivalent to about one-sixteenth of the U.S. military budget for 2004. Sixteen UN peacekeeping missions were operating in late 2004. Given this not insignificant commitment of troops and financial resources, it is interesting to note that neither the term *peacekeeping* nor the phrase *peacekeeping operation* appears in Chapter VI, Chapter VII, or any other part of the UN Charter. The practice of peacekeeping evolved out of UN experience, beginning with the first deployment of military observers in the UN Truce Supervision Organization in 1948. During the ensuing five decades, the Security Council adapted UN peacekeeping to meet the unique demands of different kinds of conflicts in a changing geopolitical landscape. Consequently, peacekeeping has emerged as a routine means for controlling interstate and subnational conflict in a tension-filled world.

United Nations peacekeeping is based on the principle that an impartial UN presence on the ground can ease tensions and permit nonviolent solutions to violent situations. The first step in peacekeeping often involves intense diplomatic efforts by the UN Secretary-General to secure—before peacekeepers are deployed—a cease-fire to the fighting and the parties' consent for deployment. UN peacekeeping operations traditionally fall into two categories: first, military observer missions composed of relatively small numbers of unarmed officers, charged with such tasks as monitoring cease-fires, verifying troop withdrawals, and patrolling borders or demilitarized zones; and, second, peacekeeping forces composed of national contingents of troops, deployed to carry out tasks similar to those of military observers and often to act as a buffer between hostile parties. Over the past decade, however, a third category of UN peacekeeping mission has emerged. This mission is composed of military troops, civilian police, and other civilian personnel who are mandated to help create political institutions and provide emergency relief; demobilize former fighters and reintegrate them into society; clear landmines; and organize, conduct, and monitor national elections.[34]

Difficult challenges to UN peacekeeping arise when the disputant parties fail to live up to their commitments and resume fighting or when they purposely thwart efforts by peacekeepers. Much to their credit, UN peacekeepers often seek to stabilize such situations and to minimize the suffering of civilians—mainly through persuasion and negotiation and usually at significant personal risk, despite unclear mandates and insufficient resources. At times, however, a situation will be all but impossible. The conflicts in Bosnia and Somalia between 1992 and 1995 demonstrate the limits of UN peacekeeping in areas with no peace to be kept, complicated by the dilemmas created when force must be used by UN peacekeepers.[35]

THE GENERAL ASSEMBLY

Cold War competition between the United States and the Soviet Union paralyzed the collective security system in the early decades of the United Nations. The frequent use of superpower vetoes in the Security Council prompted the General Assembly to assume a more active role in the maintenance of international peace and security. In 1950, the General Assembly passed the Uniting for Peace Resolution, an initiative proposed by the United States to deal with Korea.[36] This measure resolved that if the Security Council was unable to discharge its primary responsibility owing to the use of a veto by a permanent member, the assembly will be called into a special emergency session to "consider the matter immediately with a view to making appropriate recommendations to members for collective measures, including in the case of a breach of the peace or act of aggression, the use of armed force when necessary, to restore international peace and security." The Assembly has invoked this resolution on several occasions to justify consideration of various cases where force has been used unlawfully against a state, such as in Korea in 1950 and Afghanistan in 1980. While these General Assembly actions cannot authorize the use of force against an aggressor state—this remains the sole preserve of the Security Council—the Uniting for Peace Resolution has been used as the basis for the formulation of a chapter 6 peacekeeping force, the UN Emergency Force, which operated on Egyptian soil with government consent after the Suez crisis in 1956. As was subsequently affirmed by the International Court of Justice in the Certain Expenses Case, the deployment of such a force did not constitute an enforcement action, since it operated with the consent of the territorial sovereign and therefore did not require Security Council authorization.[37] Nine special General Assembly sessions have been convened under the Uniting for Peace Resolution to deal with international crises: the Suez and Hungary cases in 1956, the Lebanon situation in 1958, the Congo crisis in 1960, the Arab–Israeli Six Days' War in 1967, Afghanistan in 1980, the question of Palestine in 1980 and 1982, Namibia in 1981, and the Occupied Arab Territories in 1981. Since the end of the Cold War, however, the reinvigoration of a functioning Security Council has deflated the General Assembly's ambitions in this area. The Uniting for Peace Resolution now serves more as a vehicle for bringing a matter before the Assembly for debate rather than as the legal instrument for instigating specific measures of collective UN action.

REGIONAL ORGANIZATIONS

Regional organizations also play a role in regulating the use of force by states. The Security Council under article 53 of the Charter may use regional organizations such as the Organization of American States, the Organization of African Unity, and the North Atlantic Treaty Organization to engage in "enforcement actions." In essence this amounts to a delegation function by the Council to regional organizations, although the lawfulness of authority remains with the Council. As article 53 asserts, "No enforcement shall be undertaken under regional arrangements or by regional agencies without the authorization of the Security Council." While this does not infringe on the right of collective self-defense by these organizations, it does mean that they lack the right to use force against a state without the express authorization of the Security Council. Three cases illustrate this point.

In December 1995, the council authorized member states acting in concert with NATO to take "all necessary measures" to supervise the General Framework Agreement in Bosnia and Herzegovina.[38] The resolution also transferred the authority and responsibilities of the UN force to the NATO force, including the functions stipulated in previous Council resolutions. This marked the first time that the Security Council had ever delegated a specific regional agency to fulfill the Council's primary responsibility to maintaining peace and international security.

By way of contrast, when it became clear in 1999 that the Security Council would not grant formal approval for NATO to intervene militarily (due to a likely Russian veto) to suppress Serbian ethnic-cleansing activities in the majority ethnic Albanian Kosovo province of Serbia, the United States led NATO in an intense bombing campaign. Although legitimacy for this action might be argued on grounds of humanitarian intervention, it breached the letter of UN Charter law: United States–NATO action against the Milosevic regime was taken neither in self-defense nor with the permission of the Security Council. Thus, the absence of formal UN approval became the critical ingredient for legitimacy missing from NATO action against Serbia in Kosovo.

The third illustrative case is international reaction to the civilian aircraft strikes against the World Trade Center and the Pentagon on September 11, 2001, as two regional organizations mobilized to condemn and respond to these attacks. Both NATO and the Organization of American States (OAS) identified the events of September 11 as constituting an "armed attack" against the United States and therefore legitimized the right to use force in collective self-defense against al Qaeda, the presumed aggressor. NATO invoked article 5 of the 1949 North Atlantic Treaty and the OAS invoked article 3 (1) of the 1947 Inter-American Treaty of Reciprocal Assistance (the Rio Treaty), both of which legitimized the legal conclusion that an attack on the United States was an attack on the entire alliance, thus making collective self-defense lawful as a response. What makes this situation particularly interesting is that for the first time regional organizations (as well as the Security Council) decided to invoke the legitimacy of exercising self-defense against a nonstate actor (the al Qaeda group) who resided in a state (Afghanistan) that provided the group with safe haven. International legal rules in the past held that self-defense could be undertaken only against states. In this instance, however, al Qaeda's terrorist attack was so massive and destructive that the assault rose to the level of "an armed attack" against the United States, legitimizing the use of self-defense by members of the regional alliances. Yet, it is worth noting that the Security Council subsequently adopted no explicit resolution authorizing the use of force by either NATO or the OAS. Even so, Security Council resolution 1368 (2001) of September 12 obviated the need for such a mandate, as it condemned the "horrifying terrorist attacks," regarded such terrorist acts as a threat to international peace and security, and stressed that those responsible for the attacks "will be held accountable."[39] The clear suggestion is that regional organizations such as NATO and the OAS could assist the United States in bringing the perpetrators to accountability under the principles of collective self-defense.

WEAPONS OF MASS DESTRUCTION

The development of nuclear weapons signaled the potential of destruction on a vast scale, even the end of human civilization as we know it. The dropping of atomic bombs in August 1945 by the United States on the Japanese cities of Hiroshima and Nagasaki demonstrated the horrific destructive power of such weapons as well as the gruesome effects of radiation fallout on those victims who survived the initial blast. It took three centuries to devise international legal rules for regulating the use of conventional weapons in interstate wars; the need to manage the spread of the new nuclear weapons of mass destruction demanded urgent attention.

The international response to this need—led mainly by the United States since 1960—has been the effort to limit the production and proliferation of nuclear warheads, as well as chemical and biological weapons, through the promulgation of a series of bilateral and multilateral agreements. Nevertheless, it is important to realize that the intention of none of these agreements has been disarmament—that is, the elimination of all these weapons. Rather, the fundamental process has been arms control, or seeking to stabilize the status quo and reduce the risk of nuclear war. Governments participating in arms control initiatives do so by imposing significant restrictions and limitations on their own acquisition and use of such weapons. Arms control regimes accept the existence of such weapons but strive to reduce the potential for armed conflict through peaceful settlement of disputes before they escalate to nuclear exchanges. The means for instituting arms control are codified in legally binding international agreements.

In this regard, the strategies for effecting arms control agreements fall into four categories of treaties and conventions: ones that mandate the reduction of such weapons; ones that limit the spread of such weapons; ones that declare certain areas of the world free of such weapons; and ones that prohibit the testing of such weapons.

Weapons Reduction

Many of the international agreements that reduce the inventory levels or limit development or production of certain types of weapons technology are bilateral between the United States and former Soviet Union (now Russia) and focus on nuclear arms. The first of these, the Strategic Arms Limitation Talks (SALT) Agreements, were precedent setting. Signed in 1972, SALT I provides for a five-year interim accord that restricts intercontinental ballistic-missile launchers as well as those based on submarines.[40] Negotiated in 1979 but never ratified, SALT II places a general ceiling of 2,250 on the number of intercontinental ballistic missile launchers, submarine launchers, heavy bombers, and surface-to-air ballistic missile launchers that the United States and the Soviet Union could deploy.[41]

During the 1980s, the United States and the Soviet Union undertook a second round of negotiations, the Strategic Arms Reduction Talks (START). The resultant two treaties reduced the superpowers' nuclear arsenals by 30 percent by cutting deployed U.S. and Soviet strategic nuclear warheads down to three thousand by 2003. START II also bans land-based multiple-warhead missiles. The most recent agreement, the 2002 Moscow Treaty on Strategic Offensive Reductions, reduces U.S. and Russian strategic nuclear warheads to a level of between seventeen hundred and twenty-two hundred by December 31, 2012, nearly two-thirds below 2002 inventories.[42]

In 1987 the two superpowers negotiated the Intermediate Range Nuclear Forces (INF) Treaty, which eliminates all nuclear-armed ground-launched ballistic and cruise missiles with ranges between five hundred and fifty-five hundred kilometers (about three hundred to thirty-four hundred miles) and their infrastructure. The INF Treaty is the first nuclear arms control agreement to actually remove categories of nuclear weapons already deployed with U.S. and Soviet forces, rather than merely establish ceilings for various categories of weapons. In total, the INF Treaty eliminated 846 long- and short-range American INF missile systems and 1,846 Soviet INF missile systems, all of which included the modernized U.S. Pershing II and Soviet SS-20 missiles.

Weapons Nonproliferation

The 1968 Treaty on the Nonproliferation of Nuclear Weapons, also known as the Nuclear Nonproliferation Treaty,[43] obligates the five acknowledged nuclear-weapons-possessing states—the United States, Russia, United Kingdom, France, and China—not to transfer nuclear weapons, other nuclear explosive devices, or nuclear weapons technology to any non-nuclear-weapons-possessing state. Non-nuclear-weapons states who are parties to the treaty are obliged not to acquire or produce nuclear weapons or nuclear explosive devices. Such parties are also required to accept safeguards to detect diversions of nuclear materials from peaceful activities, such as power generation, to the production of nuclear weapons or other nuclear explosive devices. This must be done in accordance with an individual safeguards agreement concluded between each non-nuclear-weapon state party and the International Atomic Energy Agency.

A number of multilateral instruments limit the spread of other types of weapons of mass destruction while also banning their use entirely. One early agreement that remains in force is the Protocol for the Prohibition of the Use in War of Asphyxiating, Poisonous, or Other Gases, and of Bacteriological Methods of Warfare, signed in Geneva on June 17, 1925.[44] The Geneva Gas Protocol restated the prohibition on the use of poisonous gases previously asserted in the Versailles Treaty and added a ban on bacteriological warfare. Some states, on ratifying or acceding to the protocol (including the United Kingdom, France, and the Soviet Union), declared that the provisions of the Geneva Gas Protocol would cease to be binding on them if their enemies or the allies of their enemies failed to respect its prohibitions.

A progeny of the 1925 Geneva Gas Protocol is the 1972 Convention on the Prohibition of the Development, Production, and Stockpiling of Bacteriological (Biological) and Toxin Weapons and on Their Destruction (the Biological Weapons Convention).[45] Under this instrument, parties agree not to develop, produce, stockpile, or acquire biological agents or toxins "of types and in quantities that have no justification for prophylactic, protective, and other peaceful purposes," as well as weapons and means of delivery.

The 1967 Treaty on Principles Governing the Activities of States in the Exploration and Use of Outer Space, including the Moon and Other Celestial Bodies (the Outer Space Treaty)[46] contains an obligation for states not to place nuclear or any other weapons of mass destruction in orbit around the earth, on the moon or on any other celestial body, or anywhere else in outer space. It limits the use of the moon and other celestial bodies exclusively to peaceful purposes and expressly prohibits their use for establishing military bases, installation, or fortifications; for testing weapons of any kind; or for conducting military maneuvers.

In 1977, the Convention on the Prohibition of Military or Any Other Hostile Use of Environmental Modification Techniques was negotiated.[47] This instrument defines environmental modification techniques as altering through the deliberate manipulation of natural processes the dynamics, composition, or structure of outer space or the earth, including its biota, lithosphere, hydrosphere, and atmosphere. The framers of this convention were concerned that the disruption of a region's ecological balance—or that the changes in weather or climate patterns, ocean currents, or the ozone layer or ionosphere—might stem from the use of such environmental modification techniques. Accordingly, parties to the Environmental Modification Convention undertake not to engage in military or any other hostile use of environmental modification techniques having widespread, long-lasting, or severe effects as the means of destruction, damage, or injury to any other state party.

The 1971 Seabed Arms Control Treaty prohibits parties from emplacing nuclear weapons or weapons of mass destruction on the seabed beyond a twelve-mile coastal zone.[48] The Seabed Treaty aims to prevent the introduction of international conflict and nuclear weapons into areas of ocean space.

The 1993 Chemical Weapons Convention (CWC) bans the production, acquisition, stockpiling, transfer, and use of chemical weapons.[49] Each state party is obligated to destroy any chemical weapons and production facilities it owns or possesses. The CWC penalizes nonmember states by inhibiting their access to certain treaty-controlled chemicals. The CWC regime monitors commercial facilities that produce, process, or consume dual-use chemicals to ensure they are not diverted for prohibited purposes. Importantly, the CWC contains a mechanism that is unprecedented in scope and in the stringency of its verification regime for verifying that states comply with the convention's provisions. The CWC is the first multilateral disarmament agreement that provides for the elimination of an entire category of weapons of mass destruction under universally applied international control.

Nuclear-Free Zones

A number of special arms control agreements have been negotiated expressly for the purposes of prohibiting the introduction of nuclear weapons into a particular region of the world. The first of these, the 1959 Antarctic Treaty, internationalizes and demilitarizes the Antarctic continent and circumpolar oceans out to 60 degrees south latitude.[50] Nuclear weapons tests and disposal of radioactive wastes are also prohibited within the region.

The 1967 Treaty for the Prohibition of Nuclear Weapons in Latin America (also known as the Treaty of Tlatelolco) obligates Latin American parties not to acquire or possess nuclear weapons nor to permit the storage or deployment of nuclear weapons on their territories by other countries.[51]

In 1985 the thirteen members of the South Pacific Forum adopted the Treaty on the South Pacific Nuclear Free Zone (Treaty of Rarotonga).[52] This agreement bans the manufacture, possession, stationing, and testing of any nuclear explosive device in treaty territories for which the parties are internationally responsible. It also bans the dumping of radioactive waste at sea.

The 1993 Treaty on the Southeast Asia Nuclear Weapon Free Zone (Treaty of Bangkok) commits parties not to conduct or receive or give assistance in the research, development, manufacture, stockpiling, acquisition, possession, or control over any nuclear explosive device by any means.[53] State parties also undertake not to dump at sea or discharge into the atmosphere anywhere within the zone any radioactive material or wastes.

Finally, there is the 1996 African Nuclear Weapon Free Zone Treaty (Treaty of Pelindaba).[54] Though not yet in force, this instrument will commit parties not to conduct, receive, or give assistance in the research, development, manufacture, stockpiling, acquisition, possession, or control over any nuclear explosive device by any means anywhere.

Testing

Agreements that limit or ban testing of weapons of mass destruction include the Test Ban Treaty of 1963, which prohibits nuclear weapons tests "or any other nuclear explosion" in the atmosphere, in outer space, and under water.[55] While not banning tests underground, this treaty does prohibit underground nuclear explosions if they cause "radioactive debris to be present outside the territorial limits of the State under whose jurisdiction or control" the explosions were conducted.

The 1996 Comprehensive Nuclear-Test-Ban Treaty prohibits any nuclear explosion, either for weapons or peaceful purposes.[56] The treaty establishes an organization to ensure implementation, including a conference of states parties, an executive council, and a technical secretariat, which contains the International Data Center. It also provides for onsite inspections.

It is worth noting that certain multilateral institutions have been instrumental in fostering international legal materials aimed at mitigating problems of arms control. Preeminent among these is the Conference on Disarmament (CD), set up in 1979 as the core multilateral disarmament negotiating forum of the international community. It succeeded three other Geneva-based negotiating fora—namely, the Ten-Nation Committee on Disarmament (1960), the Eighteen-Nation Committee on Disarmament (1962–1968), and the Conference of the Committee on Disarmament (1969–1978). The CD has focused on practically every multilateral arms control and disarmament problem, although its current attention is directed primarily at the following issues: halting the nuclear arms race and promoting nuclear disarmament; preventing nuclear war; preventing an arms race in outer space; negotiating effective international arrangements to assure non-nuclear-weapon states against the use or threat of use of nuclear weapons; monitoring the development of new types of weapons of mass destruction, including radiological weapons; and fostering a comprehensive program for disarmament and transparency in armaments. Of considerable significance is that the CD and its predecessors negotiated several major multilateral arms limitation and disarmament agreements, among them the Nuclear Nonproliferation Treaty, the Convention on Environmental Modification Techniques, the seabed treaties, the Biological Weapons Convention, the Chemical Weapons Convention, and the Comprehensive Nuclear-Test-Ban Treaty. There is no question that today these instruments form the essence of multilateral legal rules that regulate the national production and acquisition of weapons of mass destruction.

The Legality of Nuclear Weapons

In 1994, General Assembly resolution 49/75K requested the International Court of Justice to render an advisory opinion on the question "Is the threat or use of nuclear weapons in any circumstance permitted under international law?"[57] The court decided that neither customary nor conventional international law provides any specific authorization of the threat or use of nuclear weapons and that neither customary nor conventional international law provides for any comprehensive and universal prohibition of the threat or use of nuclear weapons as such. By a vote of 7–7, the Court decided that the threat or use of nuclear weapons would be generally contrary to the rules of international law applicable in armed conflict—in particular, the principles and rules of humanitarian law. However, given the current state of international law and of the elements of fact at its disposal, the Court asserted that it was unable to conclude definitively whether the threat or use of nuclear weapons would be lawful in an extreme circumstance of self-defense, in which the very survival of a state would be at stake.[58]

CONCLUSION

International legal rules prescribe the conduct for states within the international society and strive to make order out of anarchy. International law seeks to lessen the possibilities for conflict and works to promote international exchange and cooperation. In the 21st century, international legal rules still stem from specific sources. They also provide that self-help by governments is necessary to punish states. This occurs when dispute settlement fails under international law for whatever reason and when governments then seek restitution from other states. In resorting to self-help through the use of force, there is no centralized agency to approve or disapprove of a state's actions. Therefore, when the use of force is made part of the sanctioning process to obtain restitution, it takes the form of self-imposed sanctions. States therefore take the law into their own hands to enforce international legal rules and protect their legal rights. In making an assessment of how international legal rules treat the use of force, the principle of self-help emerges as the primitive form of law enforcement. But in this connection, the exercise of self-help through armed force may be viewed as the primary limitation on the effectiveness of international law. As a manifestation of the decentralized primitive international legal order, self-help remains a necessary but limiting compromise of the sanctioning process to punish state offenders, as governments insist on remaining sovereign and independent from any form of global police force.

International legal rules are not a panacea for outlawing war or for putting a brake on incorrigible governments who use force in their international relations. International law must change, adapt, and stay flexible to meet evolving needs. That said, international legal rules provide formally agreed-on ways and means to control violence between and among states. During the past century, the rules and norms for a government's right to use armed force have been severely restricted by UN Charter law, although in recent years terrorist groups have blurred the legal lines separating organization networks, individuals, and states. Yet, further complications on regulating the use of force today arise from the development of weapons of mass destruction—nuclear, chemical, and biological weapons—that dramatically escalate the stakes of international violence. It is significant that international legal rules have been formulated to regulate the development, production, stockpiling, and distribution of these weapons. However, such rules—while necessary—are not sufficient. Governments must make these rules work in their international relations, not only through obligations, but also by actual policy deeds. Such weapons render it imperative that all governments cooperate to that end. Traditionally, it could be said that governments make international legal rules, breach international legal rules, and enforce international legal rules. In the 21st century, acknowledging that formula is not longer adequate. In an age of terrorism and weapons of mass destruction, nonstate actors pose new threats that governments must confront. If the law is to work the way it is intended, and if international violence is to be controlled, more governments will have to cooperate more often to deal with more complicated issues than have ever been demonstrated before. The corpus of legal rules to accomplish this feat is amply available. It remains for governments to demonstrate the political will to make these rules function and to regulate the ways and means that armed force is used in international relations.

9

International Environmental Law

@ Formulation of Environmental Law
@ Legal Sources of Environmental Protection
@ Pollution Control Regimes
@ Natural Resource Management
@ The Changing Nature of International Environmental Law
@ Conclusion

On March 22, 2004, in a statement marking the ten-year anniversary of the UN Framework Convention on Climate Change (UNFCCC), the United Nations' chief environmental official strongly advocated the need for global reduction of greenhouse gas emissions. Moreover, he avowed that the long-range economic benefits of doing so far outweighed the short-term costs, and he asserted that regulation of polluting industries need not be viewed as "economic suicide." Citing recent estimates that climate-related disasters cost the global economy $65 billion in 2003 and that air pollution from automobile traffic may cost the United Kingdom alone $5 billion a year in health problems, UN Environment Program executive director Klaus Toepfer called for rapid ratification of the Kyoto Protocol. This addendum to the UNFCCC specifies how state parties should cut their greenhouse gas emissions to meet the convention's objective of attaining "stabilization of greenhouse gas concentrations." Two days later, on March 24, scientists at the 11,141-foot Mauna Loa Observatory in Hawaii issued a major report that posited that the level of carbon dioxide in the atmosphere had reached record-high levels after increasing at an accelerated rate during the past year. This report indicated that carbon dioxide, the gas believed largely responsible for global warming, had increased from 376 parts per million in 2003 to 379 in 2004. The increase of 3 parts is significantly higher than the average yearly increase of 1.8 parts over the past decade. Global temperatures increased by about 1 degree Fahrenheit during the 20th century, and scientists have mainly concluded that most of the warming is attributable to greenhouse gas emissions. Carbon dioxide that is emitted from burning coal, gasoline, and other fossil fuels traps heat that would otherwise radiate out to space. The UN-sponsored Intergovernmental Panel on Climate Change projects that, if left unchecked, atmospheric carbon dioxide levels will range from 650 to 970 parts per million by 2100. As a result, the panel estimates that between 1990 and 2100, average global temperatures may climb 2.7– 10.4 degrees Fahrenheit. Climatologists believe that this increase in temperatures *could cause sea levels to rise and produce other unpredictable consequences. Aggravating the greenhouse gas problem is rapid industrial growth in Asia. China is experiencing surging economic growth and burning a lot of fuel, mostly coal; likewise, India's rapid population explosion compounds its need for more fossil fuels. The 1997 Kyoto Protocol would obligate ratifying countries to reduce carbon dioxide emissions. The agreement so far has attracted an insufficient number of ratifying states to enter into effect. The United States, the world's greatest emitter of carbon dioxide, signed the agreement in 1997, but President George W. Bush withdrew U.S. support when he took office in 2001. Instead, Bush has called for U.S. industries to voluntarily reduce emissions and for scientists to conduct more research into climate change. Since U.S. withdrawal from the Protocol in 2001, its fate has rested on Russia, which is responsible for 17 percent of the world's carbon dioxide emissions. The protocol is backed by nations that account for 44 percent of emissions, but it must have the support of countries responsible for 55 percent of emissions to take effect. Notably, the United States discharges 36 percent of the world's carbon dioxide emissions.*

H uman activities have caused the earth's environment to deteriorate at an alarming rate during the last century. To arrest these destructive processes, legal strategies were formulated for managing environmental concerns—namely, transboundary pollution, commons resource conservation, global climate change, biological diversity, ozone depletion, and endangered species. Attention shifted to the enforcement of legal provisions that restrict acts thought to be injurious to the world environment. Consequently, since 1970, international law for protecting the global environment has evolved as an increasingly complex set of rules, emphasizing state responsibility for dealing with national activities that adversely affect the earth's ecosystem.

Two reasons account for the accelerated progress in developing international environmental legal rules during the past three decades. First, there has been a pronounced increase in sensational accidents with serious international pollution ramifications—in particular, the *Torrey Canyon* tanker disaster in 1967; the *Amoco Cadiz* oil spill in 1978; the Ixtoc I oil-well blowout in Mexico's Bay of Campeche in 1979; the Chernobyl nuclear power plant accident in 1986; the Union Carbide plant in Bopal, India; and the *Exxon Valdez* oil disaster offshore Alaska in 1989. These incidents spotlight the reality of anthropogenic pollutants and the visibly profound threats they pose for the environment. Worldwide media coverage has increased global consciousness and concern, which have become substantiated through the adoption of new national legislation and additional international instruments for regulating environmental concerns. Second, environmental issues have assumed greater saliency in multilateral fora since the 1970s. Especially significant is the 1972 UN Conference on Human Environment (the Stockholm Conference), which became the diplomatic foundation and catalyst for stimulating multiple multilateral negotiations and widespread rulemaking on international environmental issues. More so than any international gathering since World War II, the Stockholm Conference not only crystallized specific norms and principles on environmental concerns but also established the modern threshold for treating rules that regulate activities affecting the global environment as a distinct field of international law.

FORMULATION OF ENVIRONMENTAL LAW

Fundamental to the formulation of international environmental law is the consent of sovereign states. Consent manifests itself in two ways, by custom and by treaty. Customary principles of environmental law depend on the practice of states in their international relations, coupled with evidence that the practice is regarded as binding (*opinio juris*). While custom can mirror strong and widely held international social values, the development of customary law is slow and uneven, and the outcome may be uncertain and open-ended. For instance, the gradual evolution of customary rules would seem incapable of meeting the threats of greenhouse gases, global warming, and depletion of the ozone layer. The customary law of atmospheric pollution has been bolstered by the adoption of important treaties. As a consequence, customs and treaties may overlie one another—that is, one treaty may be used as evidence of an underlying custom, thereby binding states who are not party to the treaty. International agreements also elaborate customary environmental law by developing practices in great detail and by furnishing regulatory machinery. As with international law in general, breach of an environmental legal obligation is an internationally wrongful act that gives rise to state responsibility. A state incurs responsibility when it violates an international duty, which is often designated a primary rule of international law. Transgression of that primary rule by a state triggers secondary rules, which specify the content, forms, and degrees of international responsibility. In this regard, the consequences arising from the breach of an environmental law become new obligations of the delict state by virtue of its breach of the primary rule. Such new obligations generally entail the duty to make reparation for the injury caused to the other state or states. By so doing, the delict state is able to satisfy obligations in the form of an appropriate remedy and preclude itself from having to make future restitution. The concept of state responsibility supplies the legal foundation for compliance, accountability, and fault finding in international environmental law.[1] The responsibility devolves to governments of states—acting through international conferences, commissions, and other international bodies—to coordinate the establishment of environmental measures that can ensure an integrated approach to environmental protection, conservation, and sustainable development. To this end, the United Nations and its specialized agencies assume leading roles for creating framework strategies and special international legal rules, as well as the institutions necessary to promote them.

International organizations provide essential fora for environmental policymaking and the development of global environmental law. International institutions, mainly through the promulgation of multilateral treaties, elaborate specific, detailed rules for national activities affecting the world environment. Themes common in these agreements are the prevention of environmental harm and the conservation or sustainable development of natural resources and ecosystems.

Generally, multilateral environmental institutions take decisions by member votes, with the number of votes required for adopting a binding decision determined by the constituent instrument. Modern fishery conventions and pollution-control mechanisms often provide that amendments to the substantive convention be made by unanimous vote. Nonbinding recommendations are commonly made by a more flexible vote, usually a two-thirds or three-quarters majority. Many organizations within the United Nations system and even some external to it, such as the International Whaling Commission or the Antarctic Treaty Consultative Parties, strive to take decisions without formal votes, through consensus. This involves a negotiation process that seeks to arrive at a compromise agreeable to all, or at least not disagreeable to any one government. The aim here is to produce decisions that eschew formal votes, attract consensus, and express terms broadly and constructively. Such decisions are more likely to be accepted and practiced by all states concerned than if adopted by a divisive vote.

The UN Environmental Programme

The United Nations significantly affects the evolution of international environmental law by mobilizing and guiding the development of new legal instruments, especially through the UN Environmental Programme (UNEP). The UNEP was established in 1974 to help coordinate international responses to environmental concerns, particularly in developing countries. The organization has since become notably important in the evolution of several conventions and instruments for environmental protection, as well as in the creation of numerous nonbinding legal instruments, such as declarations, recommendations, guidelines, and codes.[2]

UNEP's rule-making approach follows a general pattern. First, scientific positions on an issue are formulated, then legal strategies are designed and promoted. During this process political support among governments is generated through the adoption of nonbinding normative documents—such as guidelines, codes, or principles—especially for rights and duties pertaining to more controversial issues. These nonbinding "soft" instruments may give rise to legally binding "hard" law in the form of international conventions. In the support-building process, multiple compromises often must be secured, which can create constructive ambiguities in definitions, terms, and obligations in the legally binding documents.

The UNEP is expected to do the following: develop and codify a new corpus of international law to meet new challenges generated by environmental concerns; contribute to the development of legal rules at national and regional levels; protect the global commons and promote regulation of activities that affect the commons environment or its natural resources; devise new institutional mechanisms for managing and coordinating environmental policies; and facilitate international cooperation in developing the law on state responsibility. Though lacking a founding treaty or charter, the UNEP exists as a semiautonomous structure within the UN system and consists of a governing council of fifty-eight members elected by the UN General Assembly and serviced by a small headquarters secretariat in Nairobi, Kenya.[3]

The UNEP Programme for the Development and Periodic Review of Environmental Law, adopted in 1982, endeavors to accomplish three goals. First, it seeks to conclude international legal agreements, an objective with which it has had marked success. Among the many legal instruments promulgated by UNEP are fourteen regional seas conventions; the 1979 Bonn Convention on the Conservation of Migratory Species;[4] the 1985 Vienna Convention for the Protection of the Ozone Layer;[5] the 1987 Montreal Protocol to the Vienna Convention (as amended);[6] the 1989 Basel Convention on the Control of Transboundary Movements of Hazardous Wastes and Their Disposal;[7] and the 1992 Convention on Biological Diversity.[8] Second, the UNEP seeks to develop international principles, guidelines, and standards that might be transformed into legal rules. Though not hard law, these instruments can shape the conduct of state practice and give rise to the acceptance of concepts and principles as expected behavior. Numerous such instruments have been adopted, among them are the 1978 Guidelines on the Use of Shared Resources and the 1987 Guidelines on Environmental Impact Assessment. Finally, the UNEP provides assistance for the design and oversight of national environmental legislation in developing countries. UNEP furnishes information and monitoring services under its Earthwatch Programme, including the Global Monitoring Systems and the International Referral System for Sources of Environmental Information.

These attributes notwithstanding, UNEP remains encumbered by weaknesses, both of commission and of omission. The agency remains hamstrung by severe financial constraints, as its funding remains tied to the UN budget and serviced by voluntary contributions. The UN's chronic economic crisis, aggravated by unpaid UN dues, adversely affects the UNEP. Another deficiency is UNEP's lack of executive power. Although UNEP can implement institutions in a variety of legal settings as well as encourage governments to adopt policies, it cannot compel them to do so.

Other Concerned Organizations

To some extent, nearly every UN specialized agency is involved in the development of international environmental law, but some are more salient than others. The International Maritime Organization (IMO) actively works at drafting international agreements aimed at maritime safety and the protection of the marine environment. Among the legal instruments it has sponsored are the 1972 Convention on the Prevention of Marine Pollution by Dumping of Wastes and Other Matter;[9] the 1973 International Convention for the Prevention of Pollution by Ships (and its 1978 protocol);[10] the 1974 International Convention for the Safety of Life at Sea;[11] and the 1972 Convention on the International Regulation for Preventing Collisions at Sea.[12] IMO also contributes to the raft of nonbinding norms, especially in its promulgation of important international codes. Exemplary among these is the International Maritime Dangerous Drug Code.[13] This code has been constantly updated and amended to keep pace with changing technologies and developments in the international shipping and chemical industries, with special attention on the classification of dangerous goods as well as on labeling, marking, packaging, and documentation requirements.

The International Labor Organisation (ILO) works to improve working conditions and to promote the economic and social welfare of workers through labor standard codes that affect the environment. The ILO is especially important for promoting safe, efficient working conditions on ships and for the training of seafarers, two objectives that contribute to making maritime accidents less likely and that indirectly protect the marine environment from collisions and from oil or chemical discharges. The ILO also promotes the role of trade unions in formulating environmental and sustainable development policies at the national level.[14]

The Food and Agriculture Organization (FAO) strives to counter poverty, malnutrition, and hunger, a mission that involves issues pertaining to agriculture, desertification, deforestation, and especially the conservation and management of international fisheries. In October 1995, FAO elaborated a nonbinding Code of Conduct for Responsible Fisheries, which sets out international principles and standards of conduct with a view to ensuring the effective conservation, management, and development of aquatic living resources.[15] To implement the code, FAO prepared a series of technical guidelines, involving issues such as fishery operations, the precautionary principle, coastal management, inland fisheries, responsible fish usage, and aquaculture. FAO actively promotes institution building in the form of eleven regional fishery bodies, among them the General Fisheries Commission for the Mediterranean, the Indian Ocean Tuna Commission, the Asia-Pacific Fisheries Commission, the South-Western Indian Ocean Fisheries Commission, and the South Pacific Fisheries Commission. FAO remains the principal global institution responsible for compiling statistics on fishery resources, and its Committee on Fisheries examines and recommends strategies to governments and to its regional fisheries organizations.[16]

Environmental law inevitably assumes economic and developmental facets. The substantive policies of environmental legislation require funding, which often generates tensions with developmental policies. Consequently, legal efforts to protect the environment in developing countries must be understood within the context of development agency projects that may produce significant environmental consequences. The International Bank for Reconstruction and Development—or the World Bank, as it is commonly known—is the largest, most influential development agency. The World Bank is legally responsible to the UN General Assembly through the Economic and Social Council, though it operates at arm's length from other UN institutions. Historically, the Bank has been criticized for its poor environmental record. Critics assert that World Bank projects exert more pressure to exploit natural resources by targeting development with the potential to generate foreign exchange for repayments, which tends to exacerbate poverty by further increasing overall national debt. The Bank responded to these criticisms by introducing a set of environmental guidelines to govern procedures of the Bank's project cycle, by creating an environmental department, and by establishing regional environmental units for the Bank's operational divisions. Furthermore, since 1990, the bank requires that all proposed projects come with preliminary assessments of environmental consequences; and in 1994, the Bank created an inspection panel to supervise the Bank's performance in implementing environmental projects.[17]

Regional organizations beyond the United Nations, in particular the European Union (EU), have addressed environmental issues within their ambit of legal concerns. The EU functions as a unique legal entity, since it possesses the organs and powers to create a strict environmental protection regime if its membership so desires. The EU's principal decision-making body, the Council of Ministers, can resort to various legislative measures to institute means for environmental protection, such as regulations, which have direct legal impact on all member states; directives, which bind member governments toward implementation within their own territory, in the appropriate situation; and decisions, which bind only states or persons to whom they are addressed. The Council may also adopt nonbinding recommendations.

Of note is the European Environment Agency (EEA), which was established by regulation 1210/90 and which entered into force on October 30, 1993 (later amended by regulation 933/1999 of April 29, 1999). Among the Agency's key functions are coordinating activities of the European Environment Information and Observation Network; providing EU and member states with information for framing and implementing environmental policies; recording, assessing, and disseminating data for member states; and stimulating forecasting and preventative techniques for member governments. The role of the EEA is weakened in that it has no direct policing or enforcement powers among EU institutions or member states.[18]

Since 1972, the EU has adopted some two hundred pieces of environmentally related legislation, thus accounting for an impressive package of environmental regulations throughout the region. Most of these measures pertain to limiting pollution by agreement on minimum standards, notably for waste management, water pollution, and air pollution. The EU takes an active role in participating in the negotiation and drafting of regional and international conventions, and it is a contacting party to several environmental instruments. Among these are the Paris Convention for the Protection of the Marine Environment in the North-East Atlantic,[19] the Basel Convention for the Control of Transboundary Movements of Hazardous Wastes and Their Disposal,[20] the Barcelona Convention for the Protection of the Mediterranean Sea against Pollution,[21] the Helsinki Convention on the Protection and Use of Transboundary Watercourses and International Lakes,[22] the Geneva Convention on Long Range Transboundary Air Pollution,[23] the Bern Convention on the Conservation of European Wildlife and Natural Habitats,[24] and the Bonn Convention on the Conservation of Migratory Species.[25]

The Organization for Economic Cooperation and Development (OECD) has twenty-four member states, which include not only European countries but also Canada, Japan, and the United States. The OECD functions to promote economic growth, assist developing states, and encourage the expansion of world trade. In the area of environment, the OECD examines and analyzes recent trends to signal forces driving environmental changes and pressures on the environment. As an organization, OECD commissions studies to examine common environmental problems and processes and to make recommendations for national action. OECD does not make legally binding policy for its member states; it remains for the governments of member states to implement policy suggestions suggested by OECD study findings.[26]

Though mainly a military alliance, the North Atlantic Treaty Organization established in 1969 the Committee on the Challenges of Modern Society. This special body examines ways to improve cooperation among the nineteen allies and twenty-seven other Euro-Atlantic partnership Council members to better environmental conditions in their states. While no regional legal rules or binding environmental strategies have emerged, the Committee has produced more than fifty pilot studies, including a number of environmental reports on coastal and inland water pollution, air pollution, and urban planning. Such activities and numerous seminars, conferences, and symposia enhance awareness among European governments about regional environmental problems and possible remedies.[27]

Conference Diplomacy

Worldwide discussion of the need for environmental legal rules has been generated over the past three decades through intensive international conference diplomacy. Beginning in 1972 with the Stockholm Conference on the Human Environment, a series of major UN-sponsored international conferences convened to discuss and formulate action plans to remedy vital environmental issues. In late 1973, the Third United Nations Conference on the Law of the Sea began its preparatory deliberations in New York, and its substantive negotiating sessions continued until late 1982; in 1974 the World Population Conference convened in Bucharest, Rumania, and a World Food Conference convened in Rome. In 1975, the First Conference on Women convened in Mexico City, and the First Conference on Human Habitat (urban areas) convened in Vancouver, Canada; in 1976, the World Conference on Water convened in Mar del Plata, Argentina. In 1977, the International Conference on Desertification convened in Nairobi, Kenya. In 1978, an international conference on science and technology convened in Vienna, Austria. Of these, the Stockholm Conference remains most critical, since it served to concentrate worldwide recognition of the need to address issues affecting the health of the planet. This global gathering, which convened June 5–16, 1972, to address the condition of the world environment, attracted 113 states and 13 UN specialized agencies as participants. Participant governments agreed by acclamation on the Declaration on the Human Environment (Stockholm Declaration), a nonbinding document that articulates a set of twenty-six principles intended to guide future activities affecting the environment—including human rights, natural resource management, institutional arrangements, and economic development. While the Stockholm Declaration does not codify these principles as legal obligations, they set constructive precedents that facilitate the emergence of environmental legal rules. Thus, the Stockholm Declaration serves as a catalyst for creating new international environmental cooperation and law.[28]

Twenty years after Stockholm, in June 1992, the United Nations Conference on Environment and Development (UNCED) convened in Rio de Janeiro to spur governments to rethink economic development and to find ways to halt the destruction of irreplaceable natural resources and the pollution of the planet. The attendance at UNCED was truly impressive. At least 100 heads of state attended, and some 178 states sent official representatives. In addition, more than a thousand nongovernmental organizations were present, as were some 10,000 journalists. The Rio Summit sought to create strategies that would facilitate the integration of environment and development with the consideration of present and future global conditions. While not meeting all of its goals, UNCED made notable strides in promoting international environmental legal rules. Three advancements stood out. First, the conference adopted the 1992 Convention on Biological Diversity, which has as its objectives "conservation of biodiversity and the sustainable use of its components and the fair and equitable sharing of the benefits arising out of the utilization of genetic resources." To accomplish these goals, contracting states are obligated to conservation and to sustainable use of resources, including national identification and monitoring of biological diversity, an environmental impact assessment, and a set of explicit conservation measures. Second, the 1992 United Nations Framework Convention on Climate Change was completed.[29] This instrument seeks to promote the "stabilization of greenhouse gas concentrations in the atmosphere at a level that would prevent dangerous anthropogenic interferences with the climate system." Guided by several principles, contracting parties agree to develop national inventories of human-made emissions and sinks of greenhouse gases, to develop regional programs to mitigate climate change, and to promote and cooperate in the transfer of technology to combat climate change. The main objective of the Climate Change Convention was to return the anthropogenic emissions of carbon dioxide and other greenhouse gases not controlled by the 1987 Montreal Protocol to 1990 levels by the year 2000. Finally, the conference drafted and adopted by consensus the Declaration of the UN Conference on Environment and Development (the Rio Declaration). The twenty-seven principles of the Rio Declaration were originally envisioned as forming a so-called Earth Charter, having the moral and political authority equivalent to the Universal Declaration of Human Rights—however, the declaration fell well short of its ambition. What emerged from Rio was weaker and mainly reinforced principles of the Stockholm Conference. More significant, the Rio Declaration emphasizes the importance for governments to recognize in their policies the need for sustainable development to protect the environment through a precautionary approach and to establish environmental assessment as a part of national policy—all critical elements of the corpus of modern international environmental legal rules.[30]

Another instrument agreed on and adopted by the Rio Conference is *Agenda 21*, an eight-hundred-page document that outlines a common international approach to major environmental and developmental priorities at the close of the 20th century. Agenda 21 presents a blueprint for state action that builds on existing laws and serves to initiate new ones. One initiative is the Commission on Sustainable Development (CSD), which stands as the primary institutional product of UNCED. The CSD was established in 1993 as a functional commission of the Economic and Social Council by General Assembly resolution 47/191. Comprising fifty-three members elected from the member states of the United Nations, the CSD is charged expressly with ensuring effective follow-up of the Rio Conference. In this regard, the commission "reviews progress" in the implementation of recommendations and commitments contained in the final documents of the UNCED. The CSD is also mandated to elaborate policy guidance and suggestions for future activities on how to best achieve sustainable development and how to promote dialogue and partnerships among governments and international institutions toward these ends.[31] While not a policymaking body, the CSD is designed to "facilitate, monitor, and evaluate implementation of the general commitments made by states at UNCED." The commission depends on governments to volunteer such information, but increasing numbers of states are now issuing annual reports to the CSD.

LEGAL SOURCES OF ENVIRONMENTAL PROTECTION

Certain core principles, or general rules adopted for policy action, have emerged as norms of international environmental law. These principles confirm the general obligation of all states to protect the environment and conserve natural resources. The principles are found in traditional sources of international law and are adapted by governments to bolster the normative framework for guiding interstate relations on matters affecting the environment. Interestingly, in establishing normative principles for world environmental law, the norm-creation process appears reversed. Traditionally in international law, state practice determines the reality of customary norms. In the case of contemporary environmental law, not only do non-precedent-setting judicial decisions involving bilateral disputes between states produce reasonable remedies based on fairness and equity for the disputants, but other states widely adopt the principles underlying the court's reasoning for those remedies as legally binding norms in international relations. Over time these norms become principles underpinning the general corpus of international environmental legal rules.

Judicial Cases

Modern international environmental law has its origins in important court rulings. Three major cases furnish the principal sources of a common law for dealing with world environmental issues. Preeminent among them was the Trail Smelter Arbitration Case in 1941 between the United States and Canada. The United States alleged that sulphur dioxide emissions from a smelter in British Columbia polluted the air over Washington State, causing harm to its citizens and private timber lands. Absent comprehensive international environmental legal rules on which to rely, the United States and Canada first submitted the problem in 1928 to the International Joint Commission. The report and recommendations of the commission were unacceptable to the United States, leading to subsequent negotiations that produced a convention in 1935 in which the parties agreed to submit the matter to an arbitral panel.[32] In 1941, the arbitral tribunal reached its decision using general principles of international law as well as principles of American law.[33] The arbitration panel concluded that Canada was responsible for the past and future conduct of the smelter, since "no nation state had the right to use or permit the use of its territory such that emissions cause injury in or to the territory of another state or properties or persons therein." The Trail Smelter Arbitration Case advances principles of state responsibility for pollution across state boundaries but does not specify how far such principles could extend. Even so, it remains the critical decision of an international tribunal specifically dealing with transfrontier pollution.[34]

A second jurisprudential source of environmental law stems from the Corfu Channel Case in 1947. Here the International Court of Justice was asked to determine whether Albania should be held liable for damage done to two British warships, resulting in the deaths of forty-four British seamen and in personal injuries to many more, caused by naval mines placed in the channel during World War II—even though Albania did not put them there nor admit knowing of their existence.[35] The Court reasoned that Albania must have known of the mines' presence, a decision that implied a degree of responsibility of the Albanian government for the placement of mines in the straits. It was thus a duty of the Albanian government to notify the world, including the approaching British naval units, of the existence of the mine field, not only on grounds of freedom of maritime communication, but also because of the obligation to disallow its territory from being used for acts contrary to the rights of other states. This legal reasoning formed the basis for the environmental protection principle, which asserts that a state is obligated to prevent its intraborder activities from causing transfrontier pollution and that it must willfully disclose harmful activities from within its purview or else be held liable to those states that suffer damage. This latter point suggests the procedural duty of a state to notify other states of known dangers, particularly if they lie within the former's territory. Such a duty assumes obvious relevance for international environmental law given the variety of problems that can stem from oil, toxic, or chemical spills as well as other transnational operations that involve substantial risk to another state's territory.[36]

As with the Trail Smelter and Corfu Channel cases, broad significance attaches to the Lake Lanoux Arbitration Case of 1957.[37] This dispute involved a French plan to divert water from Lake Lanoux, which in its natural course flows into Spain. The Spanish government claimed that this plan violated the 1866 Treaty and Additional Act between the two states and that the French project, even though located wholly within French territory, could not be carried out without prior agreement of both parties. The arbitral decision held that France was obligated to consult with Spain to safeguard the latter's rights in the watercourse, even though the diversion was being carried out entirely within French territory. The sovereignty of a state over rivers within its borders is qualified by recognition of equal and correlative rights of other riparian states. Consideration must be given to all interests affected by a proposed human-made alteration of the natural environment. This decision fundamentally rejected the so-called Harmon doctrine, which asserts the principle of absolute sovereignty over the use of rivers and other resources within a state's territory, regardless of the effects that resource use might have on neighboring states. In essence, the Lake Lanoux Arbitration Case illustrates the concept of "shared resources" as entailing equitable division between competing users of the waterway. Notable also, the tribunal elaborated on principles of general international law relating to the dispute, as was the obligation to negotiate an agreement.[38]

Normative Principles

Fundamental substantive principles have emerged as legal rules that establish rights and obligations pertaining to the environment. Preeminent among them is the principle of *harm prevention*—that is, the duty to prevent, reduce, and control environmental damage. This preventive principle entails the obligation not to cause transboundary environmental harm. Clearly, contemporary international legal rules require states to take steps to regulate sources of serious pollution that emanate from their territory and are thus subject to their jurisdiction. This preventive principle, a keystone to modern environmental law, draws its origins from the Trail Smelter Case and more directly from the Declaration of Principles adopted in 1972 at the Stockholm Conference on the Human Environment. Principle 21 of the declaration asserts that:

States have, in accordance with the Charter of the United Nations and the principles of international law, the sovereign right to exploit their own resources pursuant to their own environmental policies, and the responsibility to ensure that activities within their jurisdiction or control do not cause damage to the environment of other States or of areas beyond the limits of national jurisdiction.[39]

Principle 21 seeks to balance the right of a state to control matters within its own territory with its responsibility to ensure that what is done within that territory does not cause damage beyond its borders. This principle makes clear that rules of responsibility apply not only to damage caused to the environment of other states but also to any injury inflicted on global commons regions beyond the limits of national jurisdiction. While mandating the responsibility of states to prevent transfrontier environmental harm, principle 21 does not specify what legal consequences flow from the failure of a state to prevent harm. Likewise, principle 22 encourages continued efforts by states to cooperate in creating international law regarding liability and compensation for environmental damage but does not expressly assert the liability of a state for damages caused to some other state or to areas beyond that state's jurisdiction. This preventive principle stresses that states need to concern themselves with the condition of the environment and the potential damage to it that may result from new activities whose environmental impact may not have been initially known.

Governments are expected to exercise due diligence through national legislation and administrative control to ensure that no harm comes to the environment. In this regard, some form of prior assessment must be made to permit appropriate measures to prevent or mitigate pollution. This approach, widely known as the *precautionary principle,* concerns the decision making regarding an activity and its potential environmental effects in the face of scientific uncertainty. The precautionary principle posits that some types of activities pose environmental risks that may be more serious than others and that governments should therefore prejudice their actions to avoid them. Decision makers should err on the side of the environment or caution—or both. A modern interpretation of the precautionary principle is provided in principle 15 of the 1992 Rio Declaration, which declares,

> In order to protect the environment, the precautionary approach shall be widely applied by States according to their capabilities. Where there are threats of serious or irreversible damage, lack of full scientific certainty should not be used as a reason for postponing cost-effective measures to prevent environmental degradation.[40]

The principle of precautionary action may already be accepted as an international legal rule, albeit considerable disagreement still surrounds its meaning and limits. What specifically are the contents and functions of the principle of precautionary action? To that end, what specific regulatory instruments and approaches are necessary for implementation of the precautionary principle? As a regulatory standard embracing a legal rule, the precautionary principle remains problematic for its vagueness. It provides no objective criteria for determining what levels of risk warrant its application or what levels of precaution should be applied in which circumstances and at what costs. The 1985 Vienna Ozone Convention may be the best example of this approach, which has been applied to dumping at sea, transboundary movement of wastes, and efforts to control land-based sources of marine pollution.[41]

A critical point regarding the precautionary principle concerns how well governments can foresee environmental damage. Should states be obligated to protect the environment from all dangers (foreseeable and otherwise)? Or should there exist a set of legal standards that outline foreseeability? The precautionary approach must be distinguished from the preventative principle. The precautionary approach asserts that precautions should be taken to protect human health and the environment even in the absence of clear scientific evidence. Central to the precautionary approach is the assertion that action to protect the environment should be taken even if it precedes full scientific certainty of environmental damage. Such preclusive anticipation is to be carried out through systematic means of investigation and environmental impact assessment. The preventive principle, which is far more widely accepted, requires that environmental damage should be prevented in advance rather than have to be restored or compensated for after the event.

A third principle spotlights *sustainable use*, which means that resources may be used unless such use exhausts a resource or injures the environment. The principle of sustainable use comes from various sources. It can be seen in resource management conventions at the national and the international level; in such initiatives as the Framework Convention on Climate Change and the Convention on Biological Diversity; and in the 1985 ASEAN (Association of South East Asian Nations) Agreement on the Conservation of Nature and Natural Resources, which provides for "sustainable utilization of harvested natural resources" in accordance with scientific principles and with a view to attaining the goal of sustainable development.[42] In tandem with this comes the principle of equitable use, which calls for states to consider interstate concerns, such as resource sharing or exploitation. This principle is outlined in law regarding the management of shared natural resources, such as international rivers, as well as in the 1992 Convention on Biological Diversity.

A final normative principle of environmental law pertains to the duty to future generations. The concept of *intergenerational equity* concerns the notion that the present generation is responsible for protecting the environment for future generations. Governments share a basic obligation to manage resources and conserve the environment to present the greatest sustainable benefit to the present generation while also sustaining the potential to meet the needs and wants of future generations.[43]

Substantive principles must be implemented. Consequently, the need exists for international cooperation to protect and conserve the environment, within and beyond areas of national jurisdiction. International law imposes a general obligation on states to cooperate in their use of transboundary natural resources.[44] States are also mandated to cooperate with one another in mitigating transboundary environmental risks, a principle that flowed from the Lake Lanoux Arbitration Case. While the notion of shared resource integral to the decision remains polemical, the case's fundamental principle—that states must cooperate in averting adverse effects on their neighbors through impact assessment, notification, consultation, and negotiation—appears endorsed by state practice and international jurisprudence. Toward this end, certain procedural principles pertain to international environmental law.

In environmental matters, *prior notification* and *consultation* are twin duties of states. International law generally holds that governments—if they intend to use areas under their jurisdiction/control to engage in activities that might cause significant transfrontier pollution—are under a duty to give prior notification to states which might be harmed. Governments are also obliged to consult with, and to supply and exchange further information with, states who may be in harm's way. This duty for states to notify other states of potential environmental hazards grew out of the Corfu Channel Case. To avoid the risk of significant adverse effects on the environment beyond their national jurisdiction, states are obligated to give prior notification and engage in consultation before proceeding with activities that might cause damage to the environment. This duty is reaffirmed in principle 19 of the 1992 Rio Declaration, which asserts that

States shall provide prior and timely notification and relevant information to potentially affected States on activities that may have a significant adverse transboundary environmental effect and shall consult with those States at an early stage and in good faith.[45]

The clear language in which principle 19 is formulated suggests that the requirements of prior notification and consultation are legal obligations. This conclusion is reinforced by the fact that other international instruments reproduce these principles as evident duties of contemporary international environmental law.[46]

Still another key principle for implementing environmental legal rules obliges states to assess and monitor their activities for potential environmental effects and for actual environmental impact within their own territorial jurisdiction as well as in the areas beyond it. Fundamental to this process is the *environmental impact assessment*. Human activities have an impact on terrestrial, aquatic, and atmospheric ecosystems, which can indirectly affect human health. Environmental impact assessments entail measures or estimates of environmental consequences deriving from human activities. These impact assessments, complemented by monitoring to ensure verification, furnish the means for determining whether and how much harm might be inflicted by a human activity on some environment. Such a process appears to be emerging as a normative precondition for human activities in areas where environmental damage might be easily inflicted, such as in commons regions. It also serves as a means for encouraging compliance with environmental norms, principles, and rules, as well as for establishing liability in the event that some harm is done to the environment. Without liability—the requirement that blame be assigned and that amends be made for some misdeed that results in harm or injury to the environment—the failure to comply with existing norms and procedures may result merely in administrative or penal actions. If liability is attached to regulation, potential polluters confront the prospect of having to pay restoration or compensation for the damage they caused.

Finally, international environmental law adopts a principle of economic policy for allocating the costs of pollution to the juridical persons responsible for it. Though not a legal construct, the "polluter pays" principle holds that the polluter should bear the expenses of carrying out measures decided by public authorities to ensure that in the aftermath of a pollution incident, the environment is restored to and maintained in an acceptable condition. The "polluter pays" principle remedies environmental damage through the establishment of liability, which requires the polluter to be identified, the damage to be concrete and quantifiable, and the causal link to be established between the pollution and the polluter. Implicit in this notion are obligatory facets as well as the deterrent effects posed by the potential consequences of its application. In 1972 the Organization for Economic Cooperation and Development Council adopted as policy the "polluter pays" principle, although it was not made legally binding on member states.[47] In apt summary, the European Community Treaty in article 174 (2) asserts that the community policy on the environment shall be "based on the precautionary principle and on the principles that preventive action should be taken, that environmental damage should as a priority be rectified at source and that the polluter should pay." The European Union thus integrates the "polluter pays" principle as a cardinal ingredient into its regional environmental policy.[48]

International Agreements

As sources of rules for the global environment, multilateral agreements furnish hard content to customary norms. Treaties and conventions identify the primary obligations of states with greater clarity and in more practical ways through diplomatic conferences and international commissions. International agreements permit intense international supervision of standards of environmental protection and conservation, which customary law cannot provide. In this way, the system of international agreements facilitates protection of community interests, not merely the interests of states acting in their own capacity. What has emerged over the past four decades is an interstate system of environmental rights and obligations owed to the world community, highlighted by numerous agreements protecting states from transnational pollution activities as well as by efforts to regulate spaces of worldwide concern, such as the oceans, tropical forests, the ozone layer, and the global climate.

In environmental legal matters, treaties have the advantages of flexibility and detail and can include administrative and regulatory machinery. For instance, treaties often contain compliance mechanisms in the form of monitoring arrangements, financial incentives, arbitration, mediation, and so forth. But to produce workable enforcement provisions, a treaty may be deliberately couched in vague or ambiguous language not only to satisfy a broad range of political opinion but to obtain sufficient common ground between governments. Moreover, an important player may opt out of becoming a contracting party to a treaty because aspects of the agreement are seen to clash with its self-interest. The attitude of the United States toward the Kyoto Protocol in 2003 exemplifies this point.

Today, in the early 21st century, more than 500 multilateral treaties relating to the environment furnish international legal obligations for governments—325 of which are regional in scope and 302 of which were promulgated in the three decades since the Stockholm Conference convened in 1972.[49] During this period, intergovernmental bodies promoting regional integration, especially in Central America and in Europe, contributed considerably to this trend. Of substantial impact is the family of UNEP regional seas agreements and action plans, embracing forty-six conventions, protocols, and related agreements. Indeed, the greatest cluster of these agreements relates to the marine environment and accounts for 40 percent of the total. Among these, the most notable are the 1982 United Nations Convention on the Law of the Sea,[50] the recent International Maritime Organization marine pollution conventions and protocols, and the regional fisheries conventions and protocols.[51]

Multilateral agreements adopted since 1972 generically have similar institutional elements: a conference of the parties, which serves as the ultimate decision-making body responsible for implementation of each instrument as well as for the potential negotiation and adoption of further protocols or annexes; a secretariat, which assists, monitors, and evaluates governments' implementation of the agreement and which usually contains a clearinghouse mechanism that promotes technical and scientific cooperation and facilitates the exchange of scientific, technical, environmental, and legal information; advisory committees; and a financial agency.

The proliferation of environmental agreements is singularly impressive in expanding the regulatory scope and reach of substantive legal rules. Yet, this array of legal instruments imposes an increasing burden on contracting states to meet collective obligations and individual responsibilities for implementing the conventions and their related agreements.

The core environmental conventions can be categorized into five groups. First, there are biodiversity-related conventions, which aim to preserve and protect the existence and habitat of various species thought to be endangered or at risk. These agreements are broad in scope, ranging from the protection of individual species, as in the Polar Bears Convention,[52] the Convention on International Trade in Endangered Species of Wild Fauna and

Flora (CITES),[53] Conservation of Migratory Species,[54] the Agreement on the Conservation of Bats in Europe,[55] the Agreement on the Conservation of Small Cetaceans of the Baltic and North Sea,[56] to the protection of whole ecosystems, as in the Convention on Biological Diversity, the Convention on Wetlands, the International Coral Reef Initiative,[57] and the World Heritage Convention.[58] All these instruments strive to protect species and ecosystems, but several also promote sustainable use—in particular, the Convention on Biological Diversity, CITES, the Wetlands Convention, and International Coral Reef Initiative.

A second group of conventions concerns the *atmosphere*, and aims to protect the commons environment by eliminating or stabilizing anthropogenic emissions of substances that threaten to interfere with the atmosphere. Included in this group are the Vienna Convention on the Protection of the Ozone Layer, its Montreal Protocol, the UN Framework Convention on Climate Change, and its Kyoto Protocol, which in tandem furnish the contemporary legal regime for atmospheric space.

Land conventions constitute a third group, though only one major agreement is included—the United Nations Convention to Combat Desertification.[59] The chief aim of this convention is to counter desert spread and mitigate the effects of drought, particularly in Africa. Given the process of desertification—and its implicit linkages to climate change, drought, and the loss of biodiversity—the convention is strongly associated with the United Nations Framework Convention on Climate Change and the Convention on Biological Diversity. A fourth group consists of conventions concerned with chemical and hazardous wastes, the overriding objective of which is the protection of human health and the environment. Such protection is to be accomplished by controlling trade in selected dangerous chemicals through informed consent via the 1998 Rotterdam Convention on the Prior Informed Consent Procedure for Certain Hazardous Chemicals and Pesticides in International Trade;[60] by phasing out, reducing, and restricting the production and use of certain chemicals through the 2001 Stockholm Convention on Persistent Organic Pollutants;[61] and by reducing the production of hazardous wastes and their transboundary movements as provided for in the 1989 Basel Convention on the Control of Transboundary Movements of Hazardous Wastes and Their Disposal.

A fifth group of global environmental conventions deals with conditions within regional seas. Seventeen regional seas conventions and action plans constitute a web of agreements that have as their common objective the protection and sustainable use of marine and coastal resources. All these agreements address integrated coastal management, especially with a view to managing freshwater basins, monitoring land-based sources of pollution, conserving living marine resources, and minimizing the environmental impacts associated with the offshore exploration and exploitation of oil and natural gas. Since these agreements form essential elements of the legal regime for ocean space, they are discussed more fully in the following chapter.

Soft Law

Legal principles and multilateral agreements supply binding, hard law for international environmental protection and conservation strategies. International organizations—such as various UN specialized agencies, the United Nations Environmental Programme, regional fishery commissions and associations, wildlife protection bodies, and international conferences—produce a variety of nonbinding instruments: codes of practice, recommendations, guidelines, standards, and declarations of principles. These instruments are often referred to as soft law, an obvious misnomer since they are not legal rules per se. Legal rules are authoritative and prescriptive and hence binding on states. Soft law is voluntary and suggestive and thus not perforce obligatory for states. Even so, these legally nonbinding norms are recognized as being useful in areas as rapidly developing as international environmental law, for a number of reasons. Given the social, political, cultural, and religious diversity of contemporary world society, it is increasingly difficult to obtain widespread consent on new legal rules whether through treaty or custom. Securing agreement in the negotiation of new hard law instruments often leads to compromises and ambiguities in a completed text and makes even more difficult the establishment of universal standards for environmental protection. In addition, agreement on hard law for particular environmental issues—such as depletion of natural resources, acid rain, and climate change—may require a high degree of scientific certainty, which is difficult to attain. Furthermore, the evolution of state practice into customary rules may take too long to achieve.

Environmental soft law is normally articulated in written form, as legal or nonlegal documents that incorporate the norms either confirmed by states or adopted by international organizations. Such halfway normative measures enable governments to assume uncustomary obligations because such obligations are usually too ambiguously articulated to be deemed acceptable hard law. Such nonbinding norms might also permit governments to formulate quasi obligations in a precise and constrictive form that would not be acceptable under a binding treaty. While governments retain control over their degree of commitment, the very availability of a nonbinding normative instrument signals the direction in which legal rules are headed. In that way, soft law contributes to solidifying the international legal order. At the same time, resort to nonbinding norms permits states to address a problematic issue collectively, without confining their freedom of action. It may be that scientific evidence is not conclusive but that a cautionary approach is still warranted, or it may be that economic costs are unknown or too onerous. In any event, nonbinding norms fill in gaps or clarify concepts created by uncertainties during the lawmaking process.

The United Nations Environmental Programme is central for sponsoring global soft law instruments, often expressed as principles or special guidelines. Notable among UNEP soft law instruments are the Cairo Guidelines and the Principles for the Environmentally Sound Management of Hazardous Wastes;[62] Provisions for Cooperation between States in Weather Modification;[63] Conclusions on Offshore Mining and Drilling;[64] the Provisional Notification Scheme for Banned and Severely Restricted Chemicals;[65] Montreal Guidelines for the Protection of the Marine Environment against Pollution from Land-Based Sources;[66] Goals and Principles of Environmental Impact Assessment;[67] and the London Guidelines for the Exchange of Information on Chemicals in International Trade.[68]

POLLUTION CONTROL REGIMES

Rules and norms regarding pollution control vary widely and can be quite complex. While it is generally recognized that states have the obligation to cooperate to prevent pollution, this norm is neither simple nor straightforward. The obligation to cooperate has substantive and procedural facets and relates to several phases of pollution prevention: the conduct of environmental impact assessments of proposed activities; interstate notification prior to undertaking projects with potential environmental risks; timely consultation with other states on planned activities; engaging in monitoring activities; regular exchange of environmentally pertinent data and information; warning affected states of past polluting accidents; and providing assistance to states when such accidents occur.

What types of legal and policy issues are actually raised by international pollution? What particular actions concern the affected state and its population as well as the international community? Different norms have evolved related to whether the situation has to do with preventing pollution, mitigating the effects of pollution, or compensating for damage as a result of pollution. Indeed, special pollution control regimes have evolved through international agreement to fend off particular pollution threats and to protect certain resources from contamination. Each conventional regime contains specific principles and rules relating to prevention, mitigation, and compensation circumstances affected by pollution activity, as well as rules on other salient issues, such as how to deal with pollution management in the face of scientific uncertainty, how to regard developing countries as polluters, and how to regard the impact of the pollution activity on future generations. Some general norms have evolved common to all these regimes.

Riparian Law

Not only have states adopted general legal rules for the global environment, but they have also established special regimes to remedy discrete transnational environmental concerns. Some of these merit mention. First, a regime has emerged for regulating pollution that affects international watercourses, which are rivers and lakes shared by two or more states, such as the Senegal River basin, the Zambezi River basin, the Amazon River basin, the Rhine River, the Great Lakes, and Lake Victoria. For international watercourses, the most widely recognized principle treats these bodies as shared resources, subject to equitable utilization by the riparian states. The precept of shared resources, drawn from the 1957 Lake Lanoux Arbitration, implies equality of rights and shared sovereignty over a water body and its natural resources. It does not mean the equal division of resources. State experience demonstrates the desirability of formally instituting common management of watercourse basins, usually through a treaty arrangement. Notable examples of these arrangements include the River Niger Commission, the Permanent Joint Technical Commission for Nile Waters, the Zambezi Intergovernmental Monitoring and Coordinating Committee, the Danube Commission, the International Commission for the Protection of the Rhine, the Lake Chad Commission, and the U.S.–Canadian International Joint Commission. No question exists that transboundary cooperation is essential to ensure equitable utilization and pollution control for riparian states.

As regards riparian rights and duties, two international documents stand out. First, in 1966 the International Law Association meeting in Finland drafted the Helsinki Rules,[69] which at the time provided the most significant codification of international legal principles for transboundary water resources. The foundation for these river rules rests on practicality. Each state with an international drainage basin may rightfully participate in the reasonable and equitable sharing of those basin waters and their beneficial uses. While the Helsinki Rules are often cited as authoritative, their legal credibility suffers because they stem from the deliberations of a nongovernmental organization, not by a treaty agreement. The second document of note is the 1997 UN Convention on the Law of the Nonnavigational Uses of International Watercourses.[70] This agreement, adopted by the UN General Assembly on May 21, 1997, was negotiated by government delegations to the United Nations on the basis of a set of draft articles prepared over two decades by the International Law Commission of the United Nations. Though not yet in force, the convention remains the only universal agreement on nonnavigational uses of international waterways and retains salience as an instrument containing norms for cooperation over critical uses of international watercourses.

The Law of the Sea

A special subregime within the modern law of the sea regulates activities that produce marine pollution. As the world's largest expanse of commons space, the oceans become disposal areas for much of humankind's waste products. Consequently, the high seas are subjected to pollution by oil, chemicals, nuclear wastes, and effluents of industrial and urban society. The 1982 UN Convention on the Law of the Sea, in articles 192–195, strongly expresses the obligation of states to protect the marine environment—not only in their territorial waters and offshore jurisdictional zones but also in the ocean space as a whole, inclusive of the high seas. The Convention's protective scope is comprehensive in treating sources of pollution as it applies to wastes from land-based sources (the most serious threat to the oceans), offshore drilling, dumping wastes and toxic substances, vessel-source discharges, atmospheric fallout, and seabed operations. Of these, vessel-source pollution attracts the most legal action on the global level. The International Convention of 1954 for the Prevention of Pollution of the Sea by Oil marked the first effort of global regulation but sought only to combat deliberate discharges in special ocean zones.[71] It was later complemented by the 1969 Convention Relating to the Intervention on the High Sea in Cases of Pollution Casualties,[72] the Convention of 1969 on Civil Liability for Oil Pollution Damage,[73] and the 1971 Convention for the Establishment of an International Fund for the Compensation for Oil Pollution Damage.[74] In the 21st century, the major global instrument regulating vessel-source pollution is the International Convention for the Prevention of Pollution from Ships, with its 1978 protocol. Today ocean dumping is regulated globally by the 1972 Convention on the Prevention of Marine Pollution by Dumping Waste and Other Matter (the London Convention), with its 1996 protocol.[75]

Regional Agreements

Much of the international law regulating marine pollution stems from regional agreements. The UN regional seas conventions and action plans provide framework approaches that speil out general principles of pollution control, leaving detailed regulation to later protocols to fix specific policies for regional states. Several ad hoc pollution control arrangements have been negotiated in which specific types of marine pollution are treated. Among these, for example, are the 1969 Bonn Agreement for Cooperation in Dealing with Pollution of the North Sea by Oil,[76] the 1972 Oslo Convention for the Prevention of Marine Pollution by Dumping from Ships and Aircraft,[77] and the 1974 Paris Convention for the Prevention of Marine Pollution from Land-Based Sources.[78]

By way of integration, the 1982 Convention on the Law of the Sea provides for global and regional treaties on pollution threats and by implication affirms the duties contained in the 1972 London Convention and the 1973 International Convention for the Prevention of Pollution from Ships as primary obligations of states to prevent marine pollution. The 1982 UN Convention on the Law of the Sea, in concert with the raft of ancillary international agreements negotiated since 1970 on ocean law, converts pollution of ocean space from a matter of being a high seas freedom tempered by reasonable use into a fundamental legal obligation of all states to protect the marine environment.

Dumping of Hazardous Wastes

Control of hazardous waste presents another area of global environmental concern. Since 1980, international anxiety has mounted about hazardous materials—nuclear wastes, toxic chemicals, heavy metals, and pesticides—that are stored or used within countries. International environmental concern arises when these wastes move in trade across national borders, because their use and release may produce harmful environmental consequences.[79] Although most wastes are land based, they can generate legal implications for marine pollution, ocean dumping, and the transport of hazardous wastes for transboundary disposal. Sewage, industrial waste, and agricultural runoff are the most common effluents that enter the oceans from land, mainly through rivers. International law generally defers to national governments the responsibility for regulating their land-based pollution. Yet, the 1982 UN Convention on the Law of the Sea, in article 207, requires coastal states to take measures, including laws and regulations, to prevent, reduce, and control pollution from land-based sources. Each state is left to determine what measures it will enact, although national laws are expected to minimize "to the fullest extent possible" the release of toxic, noxious, or persistent substances into ocean space. Prominent regional-seas conventions for the northeast Atlantic, the Baltic, and the Mediterranean have special provisions for arresting land-based sources of marine pollution.

The dumping of hazardous waste at sea remains subject to the same legal restraints as those for the discharge of pollutants from land. The obligation exists to avoid unreasonable interference with other uses of the seas and, concomitantly, duties to prevent harming other states and polluting the marine environment. The 1972 London Convention provides the legal regime for these regulations on a global basis as well as the mandate for compelling all contracting states to attain minimal international standards for preventing potentially risky marine environment dumping. To this end, the convention distinguishes between different categories of pollutants and, for more hazardous substances, absolutely prohibits their discharge into the sea, save for emergencies and for warships (on account of sovereign immunity).

The first international attempt to regulate hazardous waste commerce was the 1989 Basel Convention on the Control of Transboundary Movements of Hazardous Wastes and Their Disposal. This instrument, the central multilateral agreement and the prevailing legal regime for trade in hazardous wastes, strongly confirms the receiving state's sovereign prerogative to determine what impacts it will accept on its territory. The Basel Convention affirms the broad agreement that transnational trade in hazardous substances may occur, but it also mandates that illegal trade must be prevented, with illegally imported waste remaining subject to return and with conditions of transport and disposal posing no threat to human health, the integrity of the environment, and the prevention of pollution. The essence of the Basel Convention's system of international control is the principle of prior consent from both the transit and the importing state. This requirement of informed written consent makes clear that a redirection has occurred in environmental legal rules: No longer can it be assumed that disposal of hazardous waste is permissible unless shown to be harmful. Rather, the precautionary approach to pollution control is being applied, even when scientific evidence is wanting. Now the hazardous waste transporter must demonstrate that no significant risk to the environment will result. In this way, the primary obligation imposed by the convention becomes evident—namely, to make the movement of waste across international boundary environmentally safe.

Modern nuclear technology creates risks for all states, irrespective of whether they use nuclear energy. The nuclear reactor accidents at Three Mile Island in the United States (1979) and Chernobyl in the former Soviet Union (1986) reveal the gravity of risks to health, agriculture, and the environment. The ultrahazardous threat of radioactive contamination, the spread of toxic substances produced from nuclear energy production, and the long-term health dangers from exposure to radiation make clear the need for international regulation of nuclear power activities. To deal with issues and standards for regulating nuclear energy and safety, the *International Atomic Energy Agency (IAEA)* was established in 1956. The IAEA actively promotes legally binding instruments to temper the dangers of using nuclear power. Among these are the 1986 Convention on Early Notification of a Nuclear Accident,[80] the Convention on Physical Protection of Nuclear Material,[81] and the Convention on Civil Liability for Nuclear Damage.[82] Moreover, the IAEA derives special inspection authority from the 1968 Treaty on the Nonproliferation of Nuclear Weapons and from regional agreements.[83] The effect of the Nonproliferation Treaty makes obligatory the acceptance of nonproliferation safeguards through bilateral agreements with the agency and permits compulsory periodic inspections for the purpose of verification. Some 224 safeguard agreements are in force between the IAEA and all 132 member states, with 2,467 safeguard inspections performed in 2000.[84] In addition, the IAEA actively sponsors the development of soft law instruments to articulate IAEA health and safety standards. Their nonbinding nature aside, these IAEA health and safety standards contribute to monitoring risks associated with nuclear energy. Standards reflect substantial expert and technical consensus and thus carry considerable influence among IAEA member states. Examples of IAEA soft law instruments include the 1981 Basic Safety Standards for Radiation Protection, the 1984 Regulations on Safe Transport for Radioactive Materials, the 1985 Principles for Establishing Intervention Levels for the Protection of the Public in the Event of a Nuclear Accident, the 1985 Code of Practice for the Management of Radioactive Waste from Nuclear Power Plants, and the 1990 Code of Practice on the International Transboundary Movement of Radioactive Waste. Yet, no special organ in the IAEA evaluates environmental risks or damage, nor does the IAEA possess authority to enforce its safety and health regulations directly on member states or impose sanctions on governments that violate those standards.

NATURAL RESOURCE MANAGEMENT

Modern international environmental law strives to protect and conserve the world's natural resources. The term *natural resources* encompasses all living resources, inclusive of plants and animals as well as water, soil, and nonrenewable resources such as petroleum, natural gas, coal, and other minerals. To accomplish this protection–conservation strategy, specialized transnational regimes have evolved since 1970. Similarly, three wildlife conservation strategies have emerged since 1980: the World Conservation Strategy;[85] the World Charter for Nature;[86] and the Report of the World Commission on Environment and Development (Brundtland Report).[87]

The World Charter for Nature asserts that humankind is responsible for all wildlife and must therefore fulfill that responsibility as the steward of the planet. The global community shares a moral obligation to respect nature and to safeguard all life forms. The World Charter for Nature enjoys the status of a General Assembly resolution and as a legally nonbinding declaration, albeit one with moral and political force. The World Conservation Strategy highlights priorities and actions at the national, the regional, and the international level and is necessary for maintaining the ecological processes and life-support systems, for protecting genetic diversity, and for ensuring the sustainable use of species and ecosystems. The document stresses the need for integrating conservation and development; for dealing with environmental threats posed by resource exploitation, trade in animal species, and deforestation; and for legal action to enforce protection measures. As such, this strategy supplies a blueprint for global conservation needs. While making no pretense of constituting a legal instrument, this document headlines issues and strategies required to develop international legal rules for the protection of wildlife.

The 1986 Brundtland Report strongly endorses and promotes sustainable development to preserve habitats and protect species. It emphasizes the protection of biological diversity and asserts collective responsibility for species as "a common heritage." The commission had recommended the creation of an international instrument to aid in the implementation of sustainable development. Developed by the Commission on Environmental Law of the International Union for Conservation of Nature and Natural Resources, the instrument is known as the International Covenant on Environment and Development. It is a document that aspires to provide a legal framework for such implementation, though it has no formal legal status. The draft covenant is designed to "establish integrated obligations to achieve the environmental conservation and sustainable development necessary for humans to enjoy a healthy and productive life within nature." In it are nine principles recommended as guidelines for state action:

1. respect for all life forms;
2. the concept of a common concern for humanity;
3. interdependence of peace, development, environmental protection, and respect for human rights;
4. the concept of intergenerational equity;
5. the principle of prevention;
6. the precautionary principle;
7. recognition of the right to development;
8. the eradication of poverty; and
9. the need to balance obligations relating to consumption patterns with those relating to demographic policies.

Specialized regimes for natural resource management aim to protect natural ecosystems as well as flora and fauna. Two worldwide conservation agreements adopt and promote international standards that contracting parties are expected to implement and enforce. The World Heritage Convention was adopted in 1972 to protect cultural and natural properties as world heritage sites and preserve them for present and future generations. The convention seeks to conserve important natural and cultural sites through use of the World Heritage List. As of late 2004, 177 states are contracting parties to the convention. Of these, 129 countries have designated 754 properties for inclusion on the World Heritage List, including 582 cultural sites, 149 natural sites, and 23 mixed sites.[88]

A second convention seeks to protect wetland sites in contracting states. Wetlands, which include swamps, marshes, and coastal waters less than twenty feet deep, are among the earth's most important ecosystems for protecting wildlife habitats and for controlling floods. Critical to wetlands is the quality and quantity of water resources, which are rapidly being depleted by drainage and pollution. In response to the worrisome loss of the wetlands area, the Convention on Wetlands of International Importance especially as Waterfowl Habitat (the Ramsar Convention) was adopted in 1971—the first major global wildlife convention that protects habitat, particularly wetlands, from human destruction. Governments must formally designate their state-protected wetlands on a national list, and they must meet every three years to review policies, activities, and plans. Though the convention contains no strict enforcement or oversight provisions, it spotlights the need for wetlands protection and permits international monitoring of protected areas by convention secretariat officials who conduct onsite visits. As of late 2004 at least 140 states are contracting parties to the Ramsar Convention, with some 1,374 sites covering 121.4 million hectares (303.5 million acres) on its protected list.[89]

Concern has long focused on the need to protect particular species of fauna and flora. That concern has broadened to the conservation of the biological diversity of natural systems, which means that protection efforts not only fall on endangered species but rather on the health of entire ecosystems. The case of tropical forests exemplifies the situation. The depletion of forests and their resources has proceeded apace the past five decades. National forests are being cut down to make way for development projects and to earn foreign exchange. Approximately forty thousand square miles of forests disappear every year, with reforestation replacing only about 10 percent of the loss. Tropical deforestation is particularly devastating. In a four-square-mile section of the Amazon basin rain forest, there are 750 species of trees, 125 kinds of mammals, 400 types of birds, 160 varieties of reptiles and amphibians, and as many as 300,000 insect species. The loss of biodiversity has pragmatic repercussions, leading to the loss of potentially beneficial pharmaceutical products derived from forest plants, soil erosion, and eventual desertification of the landscape. Deforestation, urbanization, and pollution destroy wildlife habitat, whereas development and economic incentives foster trade in endangered species. What has become clear is that forest, wildlife, and biodiversity resources must be conserved globally through legal means of protection.

The 1992 Convention on Biological Diversity was negotiated under the auspices of the UNEP and opened for signature at the UN Conference on Environment and Development in Rio de Janeiro in June 1992.[90] The convention serves as a framework agreement that treats biological diversity comprehensively by addressing biological and genetic resources, access to and transfer of biotechnology, and the provision of financial resources. It provides for the monitoring of biological diversity; the promotion of national plans and strategies to protect biological diversity; and the submission of reports by parties who must inventory plant and animal species, evaluate implementation of convention measures, and assess the effectiveness of national programs. The Biodiversity Convention entered into force on December 29, 1993, and by 2005 had attracted 184 contracting states. The United States has not ratified this instrument, mainly due to concerns that the intellectual property rights of its biotech industry would be unfairly penalized under the convention's provisions.

International trade in endangered species is lucrative and pernicious. Vast expansion of this commerce since 1950 to meet immense demand for ornamental flowers, pets, furskins, leather, ivory, and other animal products results in overexploitation of certain animal and plant resources worldwide and the serious depletion of particular species. To counter these efforts, the Convention on International Trade in Endangered Species of Wild Fauna and Flora (CITES) was adopted in 1973 to regulate commercial trade in endangered species and their products. In so doing, CITES indirectly contributes to the preservation of wildlife habitats. The convention operates through a national import/export permit system and an international management system. The permit system is keyed to regulating trade in species as enumerated in three appendixes: those threatened with extinction; those facing extinction if their trade is not governed; and those facing overexploitation. The convention is criticized for its lack of enforcement provisions, the nonbinding character of its conference resolutions, and loopholes that allow governments to take special exemptions to trade in endangered species listed in the appendixes.[91] Nevertheless, CITES contributes substantially to world environmental law by providing a global mechanism that regulates the taking of specified species and that underscores the need to protect endangered species. The fact remains that the success or failure of CITES, as with any international agreement, rests on the 166 governments currently contracted to the convention and how willing they are to implement and enforce its provisions, which cover more than eight hundred species categorized as seriously endangered, and five thousand animals and twenty-eight thousand plants on its threatened species list.[92]

As with international law in general, legal rules for managing transnational environmental activities suffer from less-than-effective enforcement. To enforce legal rules for the international environment, several techniques are used, including the establishment of convention secretariats to oversee the implementation of international environmental conventions and to promote the subsequent cooperation of states. Some conventions, such as CITES, have been able to promote enforcement by relying on existing mechanisms from other areas of the law—in this case, trade and customs law. The majority of international environment conventions contain provisions for dispute resolution, but not all of these mechanisms are compulsory. It is often difficult for a government to compel an offending state to accept dispute resolution, even if one state's act against the environment amounts to an international crime.[93]

Implementation of international environmental law may also result in the protection of certain locations in states through conventional obligation, as in the cases of the 1971 Wetlands Convention and the 1972 Convention Concerning the Protection of the World Cultural and Natural Heritage. Implementation and enforcement are connected in that states are often required to implement the convention to give effect to their international obligations. If they do not, they may be in violation of the convention. As a result, the conference of parties has emerged as means to facilitate discussion on implementation and enforcement. Such conferences of parties are now common in many international environmental conventions—for instance, in the Climate Change Convention, the Wetlands Convention, the Biodiversity Convention, and the Convention on Migratory Species of Wild Animals.

THE CHANGING NATURE OF INTERNATIONAL ENVIRONMENTAL LAW

In addition to legal principles, the rise of international environmental rules may also be attributed to other related developments. International environmental law and human rights are now recognized as sharing a close relationship. Modern legal rules affirm that a fundamental human right is the right to live in a clean environment. A polluted, degraded, or desecrated environment violates that fundamental human right. So too does poverty and human degradation, which demonstrate the linkage between concern over international environmental law and the need for sustainable development. International legal rules often emerge in response to perceived social problems by restraining the exercise of power and by establishing agreed norms for public conduct. Rules protecting human rights respond to threats to human dignity and existence by upholding fundamental foundations of human rights as recognized international instruments.[94] In addition, the rights of indigenous peoples have also played a role in the development of international environmental law, addressing such sensitive issues as indigenous peoples' fishing rights where endangered species are involved.[95] There is also the emerging notion of "environmental refugees." These are persons who are forced to leave their traditional homelands because of serious environmental disruptions, whether natural or anthropocentric, that affect their quality of life and put their existence at risk.[96] Such situations seem likely to become more prevalent as global environmental conditions continue to deteriorate. The plight of peoples forced to migrate on account of massive environmental degradation may worsen in future years given the threat of global warming. If sea level does rise approximately one meter over the next half-century, some 15–20 million environmental refugees could be created in the Pacific and Indian ocean island states as well as in coastal areas of Bangladesh, China, and Egypt.[97]

Better understanding now characterizes the relationship between the environment and international trade—specifically, the need to regulate and control certain trade practices that harm the environment. The first example of such legislation is the 1973 CITES convention that protects endangered species by controlling the international market for such species. More recently there has evolved a closer connection between international and regional trade laws and the environment—as seen on the regional level, in trading regimes in North America and Europe; and on the international level, in the formation of the World Trade Organization. Two recent arbitral decisions before the organization boldly underscore the conflict between environmental prerogatives and national commercial ambitions (and form a subject more fully addressed in chapter 11, concerning economic law):[98] one case involves the United States over disputes with Mexico concerning the latter's uncontrolled taking of dolphins in tuna nets;[99] and the other involves India, Malaysia, Pakistan, and Thailand over the incidental taking of endangered sea turtles in their shrimp nets.[100]

CONCLUSION

The global environment must be protected from harm, and prevention is key to that objective. Dolphins killed in purse seine tuna nets cannot be revived; the biodiversity lost when tropical forests are exploited for timber resources cannot be replaced; extinct species cannot be renewed; and the marine environment can take years, if ever, to recover from the pernicious impacts of a massive oil spill. A preventive approach to environmental protection can anticipate and avoid problems, but the effort to constrain the conduct of governments cannot be achieved so easily. State sovereignty remains the most formidable obstacle to that end, since governments are generally reluctant to give up their freedom of action, specifically regarding policies concerning economic development and the exploitation of their natural resources. Moreover, international environmental law lacks a coherent system. The body of law consists of a patchwork of rules, principles, and concepts that have been formulated in response to particular transnational problems. There are no central bodies for policymaking, dispute resolution, or enforcement.

Even so, since 1970 norms and obligations of environmental protection have emerged as international customary law and various treaty provisions, and the legal direction of their evolution is being forecast in a raft of nonbinding instruments, such as international declarations, resolutions, action plans, and expert guidelines. Normative principles are codified through international agreements into legal rules for state behavior. States are obligated in their activities to prevent harm to the environment. They must take precautionary measures before engaging in potentially harmful activities. Procedural rules to implement these norms assume various forms, such as requiring prior notification of planned activities; environmental impact assessment; sharing of data and information; and consultations, negotiations, and fact-finding.[101]

Some rules forming contemporary international environmental law function through nonbinding instruments rather than as hard law obligations. Such nonbinding norms serve international environmental law well in several ways: they allow states to accommodate their interests with emerging norms and principles of state conduct; they give rise to new hard law in the form of multilateral environmental conventions; and they have been able to develop more quickly than through traditional hard law instruments. Significantly, most governments adopt and mind these nonbinding instruments for a selfish, pragmatic reason: the standards, principles, and recommendations for action best serve the national interests of those states conducting the relevant activities. When formal legal commitment is not given, adherence is often evidenced in state practice.

International environmental law today is a distinct body of international legal rules, norms, and principles having as many facets as domestic environmental law. While municipal and international environmental law overlap in areas such as pollution, species protection, and resource conservation, the latter law directly extends to issues such as the respect for the natural common heritage of humankind, exploitation of global fisheries, and the rights of indigenous peoples regarding resource use and abuse. The current task for national governments is to promote the integration of domestic environmental statutes and international legal rules, with a view toward enhancing protection and toward strengthening conservation and international legal rights.

10

Global Commons Law

-   Regime Formation in the Global Commons
-   Common Space Resource Regimes
-   Regime Compliance and Enforcement
-   Conclusion

As the world's greatest common-space region, the oceans cover 71 percent of the earth's surface and provide numerous critical human needs, among them mineral and petroleum resources, fisheries, transportation, communication, interstate boundaries, and even the production of 80 percent of the earth's available oxygen. The UN Convention on the Law of the Sea, which was adopted in 1982 and entered into force in 1994, serves as the new constitution for regulating these and many other human activities that affect the use of oceans. In 2005 at least 145 states are as parties to the convention. Conspicuously absent, however, is the United States, although it has signed an attendant instrument, the Agreement Relating to the Implementation of Part XI of the United Nations Convention on the Law of the Sea of December 10, 1982, which modifies certain provisions in the 1982 instrument that relate to deep seabed mining. In October 2003 the Senate Foreign Relations Committee held two days of hearings on the treaty and in February 2004, through the leadership of Senator Richard Lugar, unanimously approved the interim agreement out of committee. Treaty backers believed that the United States needed to join the convention to maintain a role in international oceans policy. They wanted quick Senate approval so that the United States could participate in a review conference set for late 2004, when the treaty would be open for amendment. Backers viewed the 1982 treaty as an attempt to balance nations' interests in their own coasts with international interest in maintaining freedom to use the oceans. Issues covered include navigation, overflight, protection of the marine environment, exploitation and conservation of resources, and scientific marine research. Since 1994, support in the United States for the Law of the Sea Convention grew remarkably. The Bush administration publicly supported it, and Secretary of State Colin Powell formally endorsed it. The navy and the chief of naval operations strongly supported U.S. accession, owing to its value in helping to assure U.S. access to the sea, its protection of military mobility by codifying favorable transit rights, and its protection of the environment while preserving operational freedoms. The assistant secretary of state for oceans and international environmental and scientific affairs testified to the Foreign Relations Committee in October 2003 that as "the world's leading maritime power with the longest coastline and the largest exclusive economic zone in the world," the United States "benefits more than any other nation from this convention." He later told the Environment and Public Works Committee that "far from taking away our sovereignty," the agreement "affirms and extends U.S. sovereignty over vast resources." Industry groups in support of the convention include the American Petroleum Institute, the International Association of Drilling Contractors, the National Ocean Industries Association, the U.S. Tuna Foundation, the Chamber of Shipping, and the National Marine Manufacturers Association. Numerous environmental groups—such as the Ocean Conservancy, Natural Resources Defense Council, and League of Conservation Voters—also publicly expressed support for the treaty. Even so, a coordinated upsurge in conservative opposition sank U.S. Senate approval of the agreement in 2004, despite its broad endorsement by the Bush administration as well as by many Republicans, Democrats, environmentalists, and industry associations. Opponents argued that the treaty would sacrifice U.S. sovereignty and thus surrender too much power to the United Nations and to other international organizations. Led by Frank Gaffney, president of the Center for Security Policy, criticism focused on the creation of the International Seabed Authority as an organization staffed by "unelected and unaccountable international bureaucrats." He also asserted that the agency would operate "without the benefit of what amounts to 'adult supervision' provided by the [UN] Security Council," and he alleged that the United States would be unable to vote on decisions, due to membership rotation. In addition, Gaffney asserted that rulings by the convention's tribunal could "effectively supplant the constitutional arrangements that govern this nation." Other conservatives avowed that the convention established "a symbolic and dangerous precedent by creating a supranational regulatory and taxing organization with its own judicial process and unconstrained enforcement potential." They contend that the creation of yet another international court where "the United States and our citizens can be dragged before politically motivated foreign jurists to adjudicate and set penalties is not a pleasant prospect." On March 29, 2004, the Wall Street Journal, *which derided the treaty as an attempt to set up "an oceanic Great Society," called on the Senate to reject the accord, alleging that it was not in the best interests of the United States "to have its maritime activities—military or economic—subject to the control of a highly politicized UN bureaucracy." In an election year, it seemed that only real pressure from the White House could ensure full Senate consideration of what became an increasingly controversial treaty. The White House opted not to exert that pressure. Accordingly, no action was taken by the Senate to bring the ocean law instrument to the Senate floor for approval of its advice and consent.*

G lobal common spaces are those domains that lie beyond the exclusive jurisdiction of any state but which may be used by states or their nationals for their own purposes, such as resource extraction, waste disposal, or scientific research. Among areas traditionally considered to be global common spaces are the world's oceans, the Antarctic, the atmosphere, and outer space. Each region can be broken down into various aspects of commons use. For instance, the oceans contain numerous commons features—such as high seas fisheries, outer-continental-shelf energy resources, deep seabed manganese nodules, and ocean-floor geothermal energy—and they also act as a global sink for waste disposal. In the Antarctic, superabundant marine life swims in the circumpolar seas, which surround a vast ice-clad continent with unknown mineral and hydrocarbon potential. The atmosphere, the blanket of gases that surrounds the planet, contains carbon dioxide, which plants need for photosynthesis—a process that in turn generates oxygen, which living creatures need to survive. Beyond the atmosphere, there is the limitless void of space, in which are located countless celestial bodies with unknown resource potential. Admittedly, the *commons* character of such resource considerations is controversial and can produce ambivalent economic and political interpretations for both user and conservationist.

International law recognizes the right of all peoples to use common spaces. In the early 21st century, however, this right of access to the global commons is not unqualified. Norms and rules now require governments to undertake this right with reasonable regard to the interests of other states in the exercise of such freedoms. For example, while the contemporary law for the oceans ensures that nationals of all states may engage in fishing and other uses of the high seas, these rights are made subject to several rules, including treaty obligations assumed by a state, the rights of coastal states, and the rights of other seafaring states. Government activities in the Antarctic, on the continent and in the circumpolar waters, are restricted to preserve the unique environment and to ensure demilitarization of the area. Likewise, although outer space is free and open to all states for exploration and use, activities must be carried out exclusively for peaceful purposes to the benefit of all humankind.

The potential damaging effects of failing to manage commons spaces properly are profound in nature and global in scope. Unregulated exploitation of world fisheries will lead to their inevitable depletion and produce greater starvation throughout the world. Increasing ozone depletion will result in more people being exposed to greater ultraviolet radiation, thus exacerbating the greater onset of skin cancer in higher latitudes. Persistent emissions of greenhouse gases will pollute the atmosphere with higher levels of toxic gases and thus contribute to greater global warming. Aggravated global warming may cause the polar ice caps to melt, thereby increasing the sea level and thus the flooding of island states and low-lying coastal areas. It is no exaggeration to assert that at the beginning of the 21st century, the stakes in failing to manage global common spaces are worldwide in scope and life-threatening in severity. Governments are unable to manage, protect, and conserve global common spaces. Accordingly, they have opted to establish special multilateral regimes to attain those ends. These regimes comprise international agreements, normative principles, legal rules, and, at times, decision-making institutions. These means form a legal nexus that allows members to plan strategies, implement policies, and formulate regulations that protect the commons area.

REGIME FORMATION IN THE GLOBAL COMMONS

Motivations for formulating special multilateral legal agreements to coordinate and regulate activities of states in the global commons lie in the rise of new politico-economic ideologies, new technologies, and the desire by countries—both developing and developed—to exploit living and nonliving resources in the global commons for economic growth. The collapse of the Bretton Woods System in the early 1970s—compounded by the oil price shocks later in the decade—became the catalyst for developing countries' seeking to create a so-called *New International Economic Order* (NIEO), which included an attempt to reformulate the legal status of global common-space areas. This international movement, propelled by developing countries' desire for rapid development, argued for the exploitation of natural resources in the commons and the use of revenues derived from those exploitation efforts to subsidize development programs and opportunities. Central to these efforts was the common heritage of mankind principle (CHMP).[1] Relevant here is the CHMP's view that the commons area is not subject to state appropriation but rather owned by all humankind (*res communis*) and that economic benefits from a CHMP regime must be shared with all peoples and not just certain persons, corporations, or governments. In this context, economic demands of developing countries suggest a certain redistributive justice implicit in the CHMP, by which benefits might be allocated to poor countries. The CHMP concept also considers a commons area to be held in trust for future use and not only as a region to be exploited for present needs.[2]

The common heritage concept purports to embrace all humankind, not simply states. The inference follows that a common heritage management regime cannot rely on the goodwill of governments. Instead, the CHMP requires permanent international administration over a commons area, theoretically done by all peoples but performed practically through a supranational management and monitoring agency. Typical of such an institution is the International Seabed Authority, created under the 1982 UN Law of the Sea Convention to oversee and regulate international mining of mineral resources on the deep ocean floor.[3] Regardless of structure, the management regime would regulate the particular commons area beyond the limits of national jurisdiction.

Also driven by NIEO motivations were efforts by developing countries to apply the CHMP to outer space and the moon during the 1970s and to Antarctica in the 1980s, but with few appreciable legal impacts.[4] In this context, the common heritage concept was used to legitimize the exploitation of common-space resources, principally to benefit the development of poorer states. Such exploitation was fundamentally necessary if NIEO were to redistribute global wealth successfully. Arguments for common heritage emphasized the immediate political and economic returns rather than the legal propriety or ethical considerations for future generations.

The concept of common heritage became an integral feature of NIEO during the late 1970s. While NIEO aspirations and the common heritage concept remain linked philosophically, the prospects for realizing either have dimmed markedly over the past three decades. It is true that CHMP has emerged as a legitimate treaty-based principle of international law. That the UN Law of the Sea Convention entered into force in 1994 attests to as much.[5] Even so, the CHMP still lacks acceptance as a customary legal norm sustained and substantiated by state practice.

The emergence of the NIEO and its concomitant call by developing countries to create CHMP for resource exploitation paradoxically contributes to the desire among developed states to establish stronger regimes dedicated to management of the global common spaces. The NIEO movement demonstrates how developed states view structured commons management as a low-cost way to accommodate developing countries' economic dissatisfaction. Moreover, the NIEO clearly illustrates the intentions of developing states to exploit living and nonliving resources in the global commons. Legally based regime structures could supply strengthened internationally approved conservation rules and preservation norms to protect those resources in the long term.

Legal regimes are not merely created; they constantly evolve. Legal rules for global commons regimes must develop, adapt, and adjust to deal with new problems, new political realities, and new scientific discoveries. Thus, the negotiation of international instruments for managing states' activities in global common spaces experienced a progressive approach. The "convention with additional protocols" method of treaty making has become a vehicle for managing global areas, including as notable examples the core agreements for the Antarctic, the law of the sea, global climate change, and ozone depletion. While such instruments often proscribe conduct in commons regions, they usually do not require that causal links be substantiated between action and injury. Sanctions or specific provisions for fixing liability are not always incorporated into international environmental agreements for the commons area. Moreover, the costs of deviance from such accords are set comparatively low.

In the "convention cum protocol" approach, first comes the articulation of key principles in defining the problem and how to address it. The subsequent protocols are intended to operationalize these principles into meaningful regulatory action. Yet, the process of adding protocols invites the risk of politicizing issues. Developed states might be tempted to use relevant scientific information for their own negotiating advantage. Technologically advanced states are adept at reaping the remedial benefits of technology. Science is power. Science generates public and state action and can form the basis of agreement on an issue. Most international negotiations on the global commons area are reluctant to proceed without a scientific consensus on the core problem and without an agreement on the most appropriate means to resolve it. Whereas technology may assist in solving a problem, science increases understanding about it. The need for scientific consensus is demonstrated by the United States' paralysis over the Kyoto Protocol after a well-funded media assault by industry undermined public confidence in the facts of global warming and solidified domestic opposition to binding emissions cuts. Absent U.S. participation, the prospects for obtaining significant emissions reductions are greatly dimmed.

One means that governments use to develop and expand the jurisdiction of global commons regimes is so-called soft law—that is, the concept that certain hortatory instruments, while not obligatory, still denote the preferred permissible conduct by states. The resort to soft law invites criticism for an issue's being mushy and irresolute. Yet, these nonbinding norms remain beneficial for negotiating general precepts, for promulgating principles, and for reinforcing customary international law.[6] Use of soft law provides interim measures that indicate where the law appears to be headed. It is precisely because international resolutions and declarations containing broad normative statements lack binding enforcement authority that governments can be attracted to ratify an agreement. Such nonbinding legal accords are often negotiated for global commons issues that affect many states, particularly when scientific consensus is lacking on critical issues. The logic of pragmatism dictates such normative notions as a suitable, if only temporary, first remedy. The critical factor here remains the conduct of states and the willingness of governments to adopt legal principles in practice that they were unwilling to adopt as explicit binding policy.

COMMON-SPACE RESOURCE REGIMES

International response to managing the global commons has been significant but ad hoc. Over the past four decades, distinct and sophisticated regimes were established to regulate national activities on the high seas and in the Antarctic, the atmosphere, and outer space. For the oceans and the Antarctic, efforts to govern these commons cooperatively produced highly institutionalized regimes that incorporate strongly rooted norms and overlapping treaties. In the cases of the air and outer space, the governance regimes are treaty based but less developed. In all four areas, regime development has been driven by technological change and by a perceived grave threat to the commons area. The active involvement of powerful states remains essential for regime growth in each area. Significantly, abdication of leadership by powerful states can frustrate or block regime development and the progressive change favored by the majority of states.

The Oceans

The oldest recognized commons are the oceans—or, more accurately, the high seas. Ocean space covers 71 percent of the earth's surface, touches more than 150 states, and serves as a main conduit for international trade and commerce. The ocean commons contain a storehouse of food, mineral, and energy resources, the potential of which has yet to be fully realized. Even so, because of their vastness, the oceans have been used by humans principally as a sink for waste materials, whether via intentional discharge into rivers that empty into the sea, via land-based effluents, or via accidental oil spills by tankers. Accordingly, since the 1950s, ocean space became divided into legal zones, each designating special jurisdiction over various activities affecting the health of the high seas—among them shipping, fishing, dumping, transporting toxic wastes, mining the deep seabed, and vessel-source pollution. International agreements for regulating high seas activities were negotiated by special UN conferences as well as by ad hoc multilateral regional arrangements. Nonetheless, governance regimes for managing the high seas and its resources proved slow to develop, largely because various states' economic interests in exploiting high seas resources generated a patchwork of rules, principles, and treaty law. At the same time, serious problems were left unresolved.[7]

The modern law of the sea has evolved for over four hundred years, dating back to Hugo Grotius and the publication of his pamphlet *Mare Liberum* (The Free Sea, 1609), in which he asserts the notion of freedom of the sea. State practice gradually adopted the right of a coastal state to claim a zone of ocean space offshore as its *territorial sea,* though how far seaward remained controversial. Most governments accepted a distance of three nautical miles, based on the Dutch publicist Cornelius von Bynkershoek's suggestion in the early 1700s that a state's territorial waters should extend seaward as far as cannon on shore could fire into the ocean. Those principles—freedom of the sea and the three-mile territorial sea—remained the twin pillars of customary ocean law until 1945, when President Truman issued two special proclamations. The first dealt with fisheries in the high seas contiguous to the U.S. territorial sea. The second concerned natural resources of the seabed and subsoil of the continental shelf adjacent to the United States. It was the latter that proved especially problematic, as the United States asserted jurisdiction and control over all natural resources on its continental shelf, which protruded far beyond the three miles of ocean space claimed as U.S. territorial waters.[8]

The emergence of distant-water fishing fleets during the late 1940s prompted Latin American states, most notably Chile and Peru, to assert national territorial claims out to two hundred nautical miles. In 1952, Chile, Ecuador, and Peru issued the Santiago Declaration, which proclaimed their "sole sovereignty and jurisdiction" out to two hundred nautical miles from their coasts for the purpose of conserving, protecting, and regulating the use of natural resources. By the late 1950s, increasing disputes between fishing fleets and coastal states prompted the United Nations to convene the first United Nations Conference on the Law of the Sea (known as UNCLOS I) in Geneva to address issues pertaining to the high seas, the continental shelf, fisheries conservation, and territorial waters. UNCLOS I adopted for each issue a special convention that codified customary norms into treaty law.

Four conventions were adopted at UNCLOS I—all derived from drafts prepared by the

International Law Commission. The Convention on the Territorial Sea and Contiguous Zone affirms the right of the coastal state to claim a belt of ocean space offshore—the territorial sea—over which it has complete sovereign jurisdiction to the water column, to the seabed and subsoil below, and to the air space above.[9] Foreign vessels entering this zone have the right of *innocent passage,* defined as passage that is not prejudicial to the peace, good order, or security of the coastal state. Also defined is a special contiguous zone of twelve nautical miles in which the coastal state enjoys the right to protect its waters from impending "prejudicial activities" such as infringements on customs as well as fiscal, immigration, and sanitary regulations as applied to its territorial sea. These achievements aside, the convention fails to define a universally accepted breadth for the territorial sea, leaving the construct susceptible to international conjecture and to a creeping national jurisdiction seaward.

The Convention on Fishing and Conservation of Living Resources of the High Seas asserts that peoples of all states enjoy the right to fish on the high seas subject to certain interests and rights of coastal states.[10] The convention also requires contracting states to agree to measures to conserve the fishery resources of the high seas in accord with the undefined standard of "maximum sustainable yield." The convention, however, has made little legal difference, as many major fishing states have not ratified it, as coastal states have viewed it as not reflecting their interests, and as the standard for exercising "conservation" has lacked scientific precision and meaning.

The Convention on the High Seas codifies for all state parties—coastal and land-locked—certain freedoms of the high seas, including the freedoms of navigation, fishing, laying submarine cables and pipelines, and overseas flying.[11] Even states without a seacoast have the right of free access to the sea, and freedom of transit should be granted by coastal states to inland states. Under the convention, a state has the right to register ships under its flag, provided that a genuine link exists between the ship and the state. The convention affirms a coastal state's right to engage in hot pursuit—via air or water—of a private foreign vessel on the high seas whose passengers include those suspected of violating state law while in the coastal state's internal waters or territorial sea. Finally, the instrument calls for the suppression and punishment of acts of piracy and slave trading on the high seas.

The Convention on the Continental Shelf provides, for the first time, a legal definition of the *continental shelf*—the gentle slope of submarine land that extends from the edge of the coastline seaward to the point where there is a sudden drop-off to the sea floor below.[12] The key contribution of this 1958 convention comes in its recognition of the coastal state's exclusive rights to the seabed and subsoil resources of the continental shelf to a depth of two hundred meters or, beyond that limit, to where the depth of superjacent waters permits the exploitation of the natural resources of the shelf.[13] The critical problem with this convention was that technological progress soon overwhelmed the relevance of the provision. Certain industrialized states, in particular the United States, already possessed the technological wherewithal to explore and exploit far beyond the two-hundred-meter-depth criterion. Moreover, by the early 1960s, new technologies were already being developed for mining the ocean floor far beyond the limits of national jurisdiction. The Continental Shelf Convention became practically anachronistic before its entry into force in 1964.

It is significant that the Geneva Conference of 1958 produced the first major hard codification of the law of the sea. Yet, this conference failed to reach agreement on a number of pivotal issues: a standardized breadth for the territorial sea; the related question of coastal states' fishing rights in high seas areas adjacent to their territorial seas; a scientifi-

cally quantifiable definition of *conservation* for high seas fisheries; and a universally satisfactory definition of the continental shelf. More important is that the work of the
conference was soon overtaken by technological, economic, and political developments.

In 1960, a second Geneva conference was convened (UNCLOS II) to deal with the issues
of territorial sea breadth and the right of states to fish in high seas areas adjacent to their
territorial seas. Although eighty-seven states attended, the conference failed to achieve its
objectives, an outcome attributable mainly to increasing tensions between developed
states and developing Third World states over the latter's desire for greater national access
to ocean space and resources. The failure of UNCLOS II and the concurrent breakdown
of customary restraint in maritime claims meant that no reliable legal means were available for preventing states from making increasingly diverse and conflicting claims about
the use and control of the seas.

During the 1960s, new harvesting technologies for high seas fishing and deep seabed
mining created concern that developed states, which already possessed these technologies, would exploit ocean resources before the developing states could secure their share.
In November 1967, Arvid Pardo, ambassador from Malta to the United Nations, vigorously articulated these concerns in a dramatic three-hour speech before the UN General
Assembly. His plea to stop the race against ocean chaos catalyzed the United Nations to
establish in 1968 the Committee on the Peaceful Uses of the Seabed, which became the
bureaucratic vehicle for preparing the third United Nations Conference on the Law of the
Sea (UNCLOS III). This conference, which convened in eleven substantive sessions in New
York and Geneva from 1973 to 1982, produced the 1982 UN Convention on the Law of the
Sea (1982 LOS Convention), which was opened for signature on December 17, 1982, and
entered into force on November 16, 1994.

For the 21st century the 1982 UN Convention on the Law of the Sea is the framework
instrument for managing the ocean commons.[14] Its 440 provisions incorporate generally
accepted principles—variously identified as rules, standards, regulations, procedures, and
practices—relating to activities on, over, and under the world's oceans. Not to be underes-
timated is the heavy extent to which the UNCLOS III negotiators drew from the 1958
Geneva Conventions in drafting this new constitution for the world's oceans. Six main
areas form the focus of the Convention and its contributions to modern ocean law.

The first issue concerns *territorial limits*. International law has long debated the extent
of coastal states' offshore rights, and since 1950 coastal states have asserted a broad range
of territorial sea claims, from some claiming three nautical miles (Australia, Germany,
Qatar, United Kingdom, and the United States), twelve nautical miles (Algeria, Cuba,
India, Indonesia, and Soviet Union), fifty nautical miles (Cameroon, Gambia, Madagascar,
and Tanzania), and two hundred nautical miles (Argentina, Equator, Peru, Nicaragua, and
Sierra Leone). The lack of a standard breadth for national claims to territorial seas and
offshore fishery zones became increasingly problematic for fishers and navigators
throughout the 1960s and 1970s. The 1982 LOS Convention ameliorates this situation as it
adopts a twelve-mile territorial sea limit as the universal standard, over which the coastal
state enjoys all rights of sovereignty to the water column, to the seabed and subsoil, and
to the airspace above. In navigating these territorial waters, foreign vessels enjoy the right
of "innocent passage," so long as their passage is continuous, expeditious, and nonpreju-
dicial to the security of the coastal state, as determined by the coastal state. Warships
enjoy the same right of innocent passage, though submarines are required to navigate on
the surface and show their flags. The coastal state owns the ocean space in the territorial
sea as well as the living and nonliving resources therein. The Convention also creates a
twenty-four-mile *contiguous zone*, which gives the coastal state an additional regulatory

cushion between its territorial waters and harmful activities such as pollution, smuggling, and illegal immigration.

The Convention creates a novel legal notion, the *exclusive economic zone* (EEZ), to establish offshore jurisdiction over natural resources. Each coastal state may claim a two-hundred-nautical-mile offshore EEZ, throughout which it has sovereign rights to explore, exploit, conserve, and manage the living and nonliving natural resources of waters superjacent to the seabed and subsoil. Within the EEZ, the coastal state retains jurisdiction to regulate construction and use of structures for economic purposes, for scientific marine research, and for the protection of the environment. Importantly, while the coastal state is given sovereign rights over resource jurisdiction within the EEZ, it does not own those waters or resources. Within the EEZ but beyond the territorial sea, the freedoms of international navigation—including military activities and overflight—are preserved, as is the right to lay pipelines and cables.

Under the contemporary conventional law of the sea, islands may generate their own territorial seas, contiguous zones, and exclusive economic zones.[15] For states formed solely of islands—such as the Philippines, Indonesia, Maldives, and Seychelles—the convention establishes a new category of polity called the *archipelagic state*. Straight baselines connect the archipelago's outermost point of the outermost islands into a coherent whole, from which territorial seas and exclusive economic zones may then extend seaward. This scheme does not apply to groups of islands owned by a coastal state, such as Hawaii, but only to archipelagoes that are in and of themselves states. Although waters within the straight baselines of an archipelagic state are legally transformed into internal waters, the convention establishes the regime of archipelagic sea-lanes passage, which permits transit by foreign vessels.

The 1982 LOS Convention provides for the first time objective criteria for delineating the outer limits of the continental shelf. Under the agreement, the continental shelf extends seaward to the outer edge of the continental margin or to the 200-mile limit of the EEZ, whichever is greater, to a maximum of 350 miles. Notwithstanding the 1958 Convention on the Continental Shelf, no clear objective means were put into practice for demarcating the outer limit of the shelf, which left considerable ambiguity over its legal status. As a prospective remedy, the 1982 ocean law instrument creates a body of experts, the Continental Shelf Commission, to whom states are expected to submit reports and data that justify universally binding outer limits for their continental shelves.

The *high seas* refers to the ocean space beyond the zones of national jurisdiction and not within a state's *internal waters* (rivers, lakes, bays, and gulfs). The 1982 convention reaffirms a number of freedoms of the high seas that all states enjoy, whether coastal or landlocked. Every state has the freedom of navigation on the high seas—that is, the right to sail a ship flying its own state flag. However, ships are expected to observe rules relating to the safety of navigation, the protection of life at sea, and the prevention and control of polluting the marine environment. Warships and state-owned vessels are subject to *flag state jurisdiction* on the high seas but have complete immunity from the jurisdiction of any other state. All civilian and military aircraft have the right to overfly the high seas. All states have the right to fish on the high seas subject to their treaty obligations and to the rights and duties of coastal states. States are also obligated to conserve the ocean's living resources and to enforce such laws on their nationals. All states have the right to lay pipelines and cables on the ocean floor and on the continental shelf, subject to any special rules relating to the continental shelf. Finally, all states retain the right to conduct scientific research in the water column beyond the limits of the exclusive economic zones of coastal states, so long as it is done for peaceful purposes and does not obstruct international navigation in the process.

A second critical issue in the Convention pertains to the passage of vessels through international straits, which became a sensitive security concern for governments who wanted to maintain worldwide naval mobility during the Cold War. Major maritime powers—especially the United States, the United Kingdom, and the Soviet Union—wanted to preserve and secure unimpeded passage through international straits. States bordering on straits—in particular, Spain and Morocco (Strait of Gibraltar), Turkey (Bosporus and Dardanelles), Iran and Oman (Strait of Hormuz), and Indonesia and Malaysia (Strait of Malacca)—argued that the doctrine of innocent passage should be applied to the strait, a rule that would permit them the right to deny passage to ships they believed might threaten their interests. The Convention compromises these positions and adopts an innovative concept—*transit passage*—to regulate passage through straits used for international navigation. Today, at least 135 strategic international straits less than twenty-four miles wide are open to unimpeded transit. All ships and aircraft may navigate or overfly these straits for the purpose of continuous and expeditious transit, and submarines may pass through such straits submerged. As a trade-off, states bordering straits received new entitlements—namely, the right to designate traffic-separation schemes to promote safe passage of ships, as well as the right to regulate pollution standards and control resource exploitation of ships passing through the strait.

Environmental protection embodies the third broad area treated by the 1982 LOS Convention. Of all issues in the law of the sea negotiations, agreement dovetailed most on the need to protect ocean space from human-made pollution. The oceans cover nearly three-fourths of the earth's surface; they contain 97 percent of the world's water; and they produce nearly one-half of the global oxygen supply. Under article 194 of the 1982 LOS Convention, states are obliged to take measures for dealing with all pollution sources that affect the marine environment—that is, from land-based sources, dumping, atmospheric fallout, vessels, seabed activities, and maritime installations. For land-based sources, which account for some 80 percent of marine pollution, contracting states are required to adopt laws and regulations to prevent, reduce, and control such pollution. The bulk of attention on marine pollution in the 1982 LOS Convention, however, focuses on vessel-source pollution—most particularly, pollution of the sea by oil. Oil pollution from ballast tank flushing, spillage, and accidents account for less than 10 percent of anthropogenic ocean contamination. Rather than merely rely on flag states to enforce vessel-source pollution rules, the Convention charges coastal states, port states, and flag states to act against vessels suspected of breaching antipollution regulations within territorial or EEZ waters. Coastal state regulations, particularly within the EEZ, must be in accord with generally accepted international standards.

The conservation of living marine resources reflects a fourth area of concern in the 1982 LOS Convention. All states have the right to fish on the high seas subject to their treaty obligations. But the Convention also obligates parties to cooperate with other states in taking measures necessary for the conservation and management of living resources of the high seas and to ensure that their nationals comply with these measures. Coastal states are assigned two chief duties: first, to ensure—through proper conservation and management—that living resources in the EEZ are not endangered by overexploitation; and, second, to promote the objective of "optimum utilization" of the living resources within its EEZ by determining allowable catch and its own capacity to harvest that catch. The Convention also provides for the conservation of straddling stocks—fishery populations whose range includes areas of the EEZ and the high seas—and highly migratory species and marine mammals, such as whales.

Scientific marine research evolved into a fifth prominent issue dealt with in UNCLOS III. The debate focused on the right of free scientific research with notification of intent, favored by Western states; versus the obligation to obtain a coastal state's formal permission before performing any scientific research in an EEZ, favored by developing countries. Though unpopular to Western governments, the convention grants jurisdiction to the coastal state over foreign scientific marine research conducted within its EEZ or on its continental shelf, and it requires the consent of the coastal state for the conduct of such research. Such consent may not be denied or delayed unreasonably. Scientific research must be conducted exclusively for peaceful purposes and must not interfere with other legitimate uses of the sea.

The final and most vexatious issue among the UNCLOS III negotiations was *deep seabed mining*. The key question became, "Who has the lawful right to explore and exploit mineral resources on the deep ocean floor—called the Area in the Convention—those states with the technology and industry capable of doing so, or an international regime who ensures that mining operation revenues are shared with the states who need the most developmental assistance?" The resources at stake here are manganese nodules on the deep seabed, which could be a lucrative potential source of copper, nickel, cobalt, and manganese. The 1982 LOS Convention, in part XI, sets forth a regime and international organization structure to regulate future exploitation of this area of the ocean floor beyond the continental shelf and the limits of national jurisdiction. Underlying the regime is the common heritage principle, a concept used in the Convention to describe the deep seabed and its resources. Under this notion, no state may claim or exercise sovereignty or sovereign rights over any part of the Area or its resources; and all rights to the resources are vested in humankind as a whole.[16] The Convention intended for the International Seabed Authority, composed of all states party to the Convention, to administer the seabed mining regime. The Convention establishes four principal organs of the authority—namely, an assembly, a council, an enterprise, and a secretariat. As the plenary body, the assembly is composed of all authority members. It elects the council and secretary-general, assesses contributions, approves the budget, gives final approval to rules and regulations of the Authority, and decides on how mining revenues received by the Authority should be shared. The council, formed by thirty-six members, is the executive body and retains primary responsibility for administering the Authority. The enterprise, when functional, will serve as the mining arm of the Authority and will operate either alone or in joint venture arrangements with contracted private companies. The secretariat, headquartered in Kingston, Jamaica, functions as the record keeper and forum for decision making.

The United States and other Western states—preferring private, free enterprise capitalism as the philosophical principle for mining the ocean floor—perceived the Convention's common heritage translation of the deep seabed as international socialism. They strongly objected to the Authority regime's constituting a de facto world cartel over the exploitation of seabed minerals. Accordingly, most developed states, especially the United States, were slow to accept the 1982 LOS Convention as authoritative international law. To respond to objections asserted by the industrialized states, UN Secretary-General Perez de Cuellar initiated consultations with interested governments in 1990 that led to an agreement four years later. The 1994 Agreement Relating to the Implementation of Part XI of the United Nations Convention on the Law of the Sea and its accompanying annex were made integral parts of the 1982 LOS Convention and entered into force on November 16, 1994. The Implementation Agreement goes far in mollifying particular U.S. concerns, as it provides not only for the United States to have a guaranteed seat on the council but also for procedures that would allow industrialized states on the council to orchestrate votes to block decisions, if necessary. New language revises the prospects for a review conference, such that any amendments by a group would be difficult to approve without support from industrialized states. Other changes are also notable: provisions for mandatory transfer of seabed mining technology to the enterprise are eliminated, as are production limits on seabed minerals, which would have favored producers of copper, manganese, nickel, and cobalt from land-based developing countries; a set of principles replaces the expensive fees ($1 million annually) for corporate contracts to mine the deep seabed; and the original $500,000 application fee for a mining site is reduced to $250,000. As a consequence, most industrialized states over the past decade have reversed course and ratified the Convention. In August 2001, the 1982 LOS Convention—as modified by the 1994 Implementation Agreement—counts 136 states as contracting parties. Among major marine powers, only the United States remains a nonparty.

Linked to the 1982 LOS Convention are ad hoc subsidiary regimes created in response to various maritime needs and problems. The key institutional forum for regulating international shipping and navigation is the *International Maritime Organization* (IMO), a functional agency of the United Nations. The IMO's assembly, the organization's governing body, is formed by all 156 member states. The assembly meets every two years to approve the IMO's work program and budget, and to make recommendations to member governments for the adoption of regulations and guidelines on maritime safety and pollution control. As the executive organ of IMO, a thirty-two-member council coordinates the activities of IMO bodies and supervises work of the organization. Elected by the assembly, the council includes the eight states with the largest interest in international shipping. Two main committees—the Maritime Safety Committee and the Marine Environment Protection Committee—draft new rules and standards, whereas the Legal Committee considers shipping issues regarding the legal responsibility of states and shipowners. IMO also has special committees dealing with marine environmental protection, technical cooperation, and the facilitation of maritime traffic.

The IMO sets standards for ocean shipping to ensure vessel safety and universal navigation practices. IMO takes a leading role in preparing legally binding measures to prevent oil-tanker accidents and vessel-source pollution,[17] and it has negotiated more than forty conventions and protocols dealing with the efficiency of maritime services, safety standards, and marine environmental protection. The most prominent among these concern the dumping of wastes by ocean-going vessels, safety matters in commercial traffic, and the hijacking of ships at sea.[18] In addition fourteen regional seas conventions were negotiated during the 1980s and 1990s under the auspices of the UN Environmental Programme. These conventions address problems particular to their various regions, principally by promoting antipollution norms and conservation measures among littoral states.[19] Two other prominent international agreements complement the IMO's work by enhancing obligations of governments to enact international ship safety standards and to take measures to prevent maritime casualties—the 1974 International Convention for the Safety of Life at Sea[20] and the 1972 Convention on the International Regulations for Preventing Collisions at Sea.[21] Finally, IMO sponsors international instruments designed to curtail vessel-source marine pollution. As mentioned earlier, the principal products of IMO efforts are realized in the global regime to ban vessel-source pollution by dumping, through the 1972 Convention on the Prevention of Marine Pollution by Dumping of Wastes and Other Matter;[22] and by unlawful discharge of wastes into the oceans, through the 1973 International Convention for the Prevention of Pollution by Ships, with its 1978 protocol.[23]

Examples of soft law abound among internationally negotiated efforts to manage the world oceans. There are special IMO codes containing detailed standards for maritime navigation and commerce. Though formally nonbinding instruments, among these are the Construction and Equipment of Ships Carrying Dangerous Chemicals in Bulk (1971) and International Bulk Chemicals (1983); the Code for the Safety of Nuclear Merchant Ships (1981), which aims to minimize chances of nuclear accidents at sea; the IMO International Maritime Dangerous Goods Code (1965), which aims at prohibiting the carriage at sea of harmful substances in packaged form; and the International Gas Carrier Code (1983), which sets out minimum standards for the construction and equipment of liquified natural gas carriers. These codes and recommendations provide guidance for governments in framing national regulations for maritime safety and marine pollution control. IMO soft laws have been integrated into more than forty nonmandatory instruments, with some evolving into regulatory hard law. For example, after securing sufficient commitments based on carrier states' shipping tonnage, the International Safety Management Code became mandatory on July 1, 1998, for all oil tankers, chemical tankers, bulk carriers, gas carriers, and passenger ships on international voyages. The code's origins stem from concerns about poor management in the shipping industry. The requirements, which for a number of years were adoped by states on a voluntary basis, mainly address safety and environmental protection policies as well as procedures for reporting accidents, responding to emergencies, and performing internal audits. In 2004, this code covered 85 percent of merchant ships.

As a framework agreement, the 1982 LOS Convention provides general rules for ocean governance. Certain facets in the convention require refined legal regulation. In recent years, particular consideration was given to creating special regimes for managing fisheries and other living resources in the high seas. Central among these are the 1993 Food and Agriculture Organization Compliance Agreement to regulate the reflagging of fishing vessels;[24] the 1995 Fish Stocks Agreement[25] to deal with the problem of straddling stocks; and the increased prominence of regional fishery arrangements, among them the Northwest Atlantic Fisheries Organization, the Commission for the Conservation of Atlantic Tunas, and the Indian Ocean Tuna Commission.

Separate but integral to ocean resource management are two special regimes for overseeing the conservation of whales and seals. Motivated by the long history of overexploitation of whales, the International Whaling Commission was established in 1946 by the International Convention for the Regulation of Whaling, which sets quotas for how many whales can be taken and which has implemented among its member states voluntary moratoria intended to prevent the taking of certain whale species.[26] In 1994 the commission established a long-term ban on whale taking—in effect, a global whale sanctuary—in seas below 40 degrees south latitude.[27] The conservation of seals in the high seas also received particular management attention. Concern about overexploitation of seals in southern polar waters led to the negotiation in 1972 of the Convention on the Conservation of Antarctic Seals. Six species of seals were specifically protected, and commercial harvesting of seals in seas below 60 degrees south latitude was prohibited for state parties, including those nations most engaged in seal hunts throughout the 19th and 20th centuries—namely, Canada, Japan, Norway, Russia, the United States, and the United Kingdom.

Antarctica

The Antarctic commons region encompasses the massive ice-covered continent surrounded by the open Southern Ocean. Antarctica approximates the combined size of the United States and Mexico (5.4 million square miles). Antarctica is the world's largest desert (in terms of precipitation) yet paradoxically contains 70 percent of the world's fresh water, frozen in its massive ice cap. While the land surface of the continent is severely depressed by a massive ice sheet, the three-mile thickness of the ice makes Antarctica the highest continent above sea level. Antarctica is the most isolated and inhospitable of continents. There are no trees, grasses, reptiles, land mammals, or amphibians; and Antarctica is the only continent without an indigenous population.

Seven countries—Argentina, Australia, Chile, France, New Zealand, Norway, and the United Kingdom—claim territory in the Antarctic, and three of these claims overlap one another (those by Argentina, Chile, and the United Kingdom). In 1957–1958, twelve states participated in a project called the International Geophysical Year (IGY): the seven original claimants plus Belgium, Japan, South Africa, the Soviet Union, and the United States. Modeled on the International Polar Years of 1882–1883 and 1932–1933, the IGY scientific endeavor was overseen by the International Council of Scientific Unions. This body functioned as an apolitical, nonnationalistic, scientifically oriented agency from July 1957 to December 1958 to allow scientists from around the world to participate in a series of coordinated observations of various geophysical phenomena in the Antarctic and outer space. Special attention, however, fell on the Antarctic. The project scientists agreed that preserving international cooperation in the Antarctic region was necessary and appropriate and that the territorial disputes should be set aside to further that goal. During 1959, these governments negotiated the Antarctic Treaty, which entered into force in 1961.[28] The Antarctic Treaty regime represents an unprecedented example of conservation and research values codifying national interests and, in the process, forging sophisticated cooperation between erstwhile international rivals.

The 1959 instrument totally demilitarizes the continent and pledges the peaceful use of the treaty area, which includes the circumpolar ocean space below 60 degrees south latitude. Prohibited are nuclear explosions and radioactive waste disposal. The claims are set aside by the treaty's article 4, which in effect permits claimant and nonclaimant states to agree to disagree over the claims' legal status. The freedom of scientific investigation, exchange, and cooperation are guaranteed, and parties have the right to conduct unannounced inspection of other countries' stations and facilities on and around the continent. Thus, security and science form the core values of the 1959 Antarctic Treaty agreement.

Decisions to effect law and policy are taken by the Antarctic Treaty Consultative Parties (ATCPs), those governments contracting to the agreement who assert special national interests in the polar south and who undertake scientific activities to support those interests. While no formal organization or secretariat functions per se, representatives of ATCP states meet in annual meetings to discuss and decide policy for their nationals in the Antarctic. The ATCP group includes the twelve original members of the treaty, plus fifteen other states whose status has been approved over the years by consensus among the member ATCPs. A second group to the 1959 Antarctic Treaty—eighteen parties forming the so-called nonconsultative group—opts not to apply for ATCP status and is content to attend meetings as observers while still being legally bound to regime policies generated by ATCP decisions under Antarctic Treaty.

The Antarctic Treaty System (ATS) emanated from the rise of conservation and environmental protection concerns that made necessary new legal rules to regulate activities in the region. These new concerns and the successful experience of cooperation lent by the 1959 agreement facilitated the Antarctic Treaty's evolution into a sophisticated commons regime. The resultant constellation of Antarctic Treaty agreements was negotiated and implemented by the ATCPs and has matured into the ATS. The first element came in 1964 as the Agreed Measures for the Conservation of the Antarctic Fauna and Flora.[29] These measures fill in gaps from the 1959 treaty, specifically for environmental protection and conservation: they protect the continent's mammals, birds, and plant life, and they prohibit the introduction of nonindigenous flora and fauna. The instrument applies to the area below 60 degrees south latitude, including all ice shelves.

Reports of an impending Soviet sealing expedition led to the second prominent piece in the ATS, the aforementioned 1972 Convention for the Conservation of Antarctic Seals.[30] The Seals Convention, which entered into force in 1978, applies to all seal species below 60 degrees south latitude. Under the instrument, seals are considered a marine resource, and principles of sustainable yield are applied to prevent their being overharvested.

During the 1970s, certain fishing states—especially the Soviet Union, Japan, and Poland—began taking krill from Antarctic seas. A small, shrimplike crustacean, krill is the prey of whales, seals, and many sea birds in the Southern Ocean. Excessive harvesting of krill could disrupt the food chain throughout the circumpolar marine ecosystem. The ATCPs, alarmed by this possibility, completed negotiations on the Convention for the Conservation of Antarctic Marine Living Resources in 1980.[31] This instrument, which entered into force in 1982, seeks to prevent the overharvesting of living ocean resources—in particular, krill stocks. Given this broad imperative, this convention is the most comprehensive among ATS instruments in jurisdictional scope, extending as far north as 50 to 62 degrees south latitude. The agreement creates, first, a special commission headquartered in Hobart, Tasmania, who manages affairs and makes decisions affecting marine resources in the Southern Ocean; and, second, a scientific committee, which serves in an advisory capacity.

This convention aspires to preserve Antarctic marine life, such as fish, crustaceans (krill), creatures on the continental shelf, and birds. Importantly, conservation is to be performed through a holistic "ecosystemic approach"; that is, living resources are managed by scientific assessment of the ecological interrelationships between species and their physical environment. The commission, in addition to approving some one hundred special fishery conservation measures over the past two decades, adopted in 1991 a "precautionary ceiling" on krill harvesting for various conservation zones in the Southern Ocean. Finally, since 1990 an official convention-sponsored inspection system operates throughout the region to check vessels fishing in Antarctic waters.

From 1982 through 1988, the ATCPs negotiated a special regime to regulate the prospecting, exploration, and development of mineral resources in the Antarctic. In November 1988, the Convention on the Regulation of Antarctic Mineral Resource Activities was opened for signature in Wellington, New Zealand.[32] But the Wellington Convention was never legally consummated as part of the ATS. By mid-1989, political circumstances—especially campaigns by environmentalist critics, as well as the defection of Australia and France from being state parties to the convention—rendered stillborn the mineral convention's entry into legal force.

The demise of the Wellington Convention opened the diplomatic door for the ATCPs to reverse course and negotiate an instrument for comprehensive environmental protection of the Antarctic environment. On October 4, 1991, the Protocol on Environmental Protection to the Antarctic Treaty was adopted and opened for signature by the ATCPs in Madrid, Spain.[33] The Environmental Protection Protocol obligates parties to consider the

Antarctic—that is, the area below 60 degrees south latitude, inclusive of ocean space—as a "natural reserve devoted to science" and commits them to comprehensive protection of the region's environment.[34] Most important, it commits ATCP governments to policies aimed at preserving and protecting Antarctica's fragile ecosystem, on land and at sea.

Article 3 of the Protocol is pivotal for furnishing four legally binding principles aimed at protecting the Antarctic ecosystem. These principles take the form of duties and include the following party obligations:

1. to meet specific environmental standards and to limit, insofar as possible, adverse impacts on the environment;
2. to give priority to scientific research in Antarctica and to preserve Antarctica for global research;
3. to ensure that human activities are planned and carried out on the basis of information sufficient to permit prior assessments of their possible impacts; and
4. to conduct environmental monitoring.[35]

The Environmental Protection Protocol flatly prohibits all mining activity in Antarctica and presumably ensures that no mineral development can lawfully take place on Antarctica or in its circumpolar waters within the foreseeable future. This prohibition means that degradation of Antarctica is not likely to occur from mineral or hydrocarbon development or from transportation activities on or around the continent. Nor are natural habitats of Antarctic-living marine resources likely to be disrupted or destroyed by such activities for at least fifty years.

The Environmental Protection Protocol creates a new institutional body, the Committee for Environmental Protection, which is supposed to oversee compliance with the protocol but lacks independent capabilities and the power of compulsory enforcement sanctions. The committee possesses no decision-making authority, and its chief function is to provide advice and formulate recommendations to ATCP meetings concerning implementation of the Protocol and its annexes.

Five annexes are attached to the Environmental Protection Protocol. The first annex marks a major achievement of the Protocol, as it sets procedures for environmental impact assessment. The second annex restates the need for conservation of Antarctic fauna and flora and updates the aforementioned agreed measures. The third annex pertains to waste disposal and waste management, with stronger emphasis on retrograding waste and other materials from the continent. The fourth annex concerns the prevention of marine pollution and is directly linked to the International Convention for the Prevention on Pollution from Ships, as amended by its 1978 protocol. The fourth annex deals with discharges from ships—in particular, oil, noxious liquids, garbage, and sewage. Certain provisions also highlight needs for vessel-retention capacity as well as emergency response and preparedness. In October 1991 a fifth annex to the Protocol was adopted to expand the scope of the Antarctic-protected area system.

For the polar south, the ATCPs produced a network of legal rules and binding norms for their parties' activities in Antarctica. The Antarctic Treaty process is all consensual, yet more than two hundred recommended measures were adopted between 1961 and 1995, most of which ATCP national governments approved as legally binding for their own nationals. The others are still regarded as a body of soft law for the ATCPs. These recommended measures pertain to a range of activities, from international telecommunications, postage regulations, and meteorology to logistics, tourism, and the designation of specially protected areas and scientific sites.[36]

The Antarctic Treaty regime is highly developed and highly institutionalized, and it operates smoothly to address a range of environmental, scientific, commercial, and military issues surrounding the polar south. Even in the face of key states' overlapping sovereignty claims and despite the absence of a formal secretariat body until 2004, the ATS functioned well, largely due to the leadership of the United States, the United Kingdom, Australia, New Zealand, and Russia in developing the regime and to the relatively small numbers of states with tangible stakes in Antarctic management. However, the number of states participating in the ATS has steadily expanded, from twelve in 1961, when the Antarctic Treaty entered into force, to forty-five in 2004. With the growing number of participants came complications in decision making. In addition, growing numbers of shipborne tourists pose renewed concerns about degradation of the circumpolar environment, while advances in technology are making commercial exploitation of Antarctic mineral resources more realistic. Such intensifying pressures will test the ATS regime's flexibility and the extent to which norms and the "habits of compliance" among Antarctic Treaty states have taken root.

In the early 21st century, the gravest problems confronting the Antarctic Treaty regime include the need to supervise and regulate increasing shipborne tourism visiting the region, the worrisome depletion of fisheries in circumpolar seas,[37] and the need to agree on a formal liability regime that covers regional accidents from vessel-source pollution or operator mismanagement.[38]

The Atmosphere

The atmosphere includes the troposphere above the earth (where weather patterns begin) as well as the stratosphere (where the ozone layer is located), the mesophere, and beyond. While international law places no universally agreed ceiling on how high national air space extends, an upper limit of between fifty and one hundred miles is often suggested in legal treatises.

Life could not survive without the earth's atmosphere since it provides virtually limitless sources of oxygen, carbon dioxide, and nitrogen essential for plants and animals. The atmosphere provides the water needed for living resources and dissipates through its circumglobal reach many of the waste products of biological life and human industry. The atmosphere transmits the radiation from the sun that is essential for photosynthesis. At the same time it shields the earth from ultraviolet radiation as well as from cosmic rays and meteors that shower the planet. Moreover, the atmosphere acts as a blanket to maintain a higher temperature on Earth than would otherwise exist; it also moderates the planet's climate, warming the polar regions and cooling the tropical areas. The atmosphere is essential for communications. Air readily transmits sound and electromagnetic waves (light and radio waves), and an electroconductive layer in the upper atmosphere reflects radio waves, thus permitting communication beyond the horizon.[39]

Three specific human-made threats affecting the atmosphere have led to the development of three principal regimes for managing this commons space. The legal principle underpinning each regime is state responsibility to do no harm. Simply put, a state is duty bound to ensure that activities within its national jurisdiction or control do not cause damage to the environment of other states or to areas beyond the limits of national jurisdiction.[40]

The first threat manifests itself in the stratosphere and concerns the human-induced chemical changes that allow an ever-broadening range of solar radiation to penetrate the upper atmosphere, creating what is widely regarded as the ozone hole. The release of chlorofluorocarbons (CFCs) into the upper atmosphere causes a photochemical reaction and results in substantial ozone reduction, thus allowing increased exposure of the earth's surface to intense ultraviolet radiation and greatly amplifying the risk of skin cancer for a growing number of people in the Southern Hemisphere. In reaction to growing scientific information and popular concern about this threat, the Vienna Convention for the Protection of the Ozone Layer was negotiated in 1985.[41] The Vienna Convention does not contain specifics on how to combat ozone depletion; instead, it serves as a framework instrument that provides the basis for substantive future action by confirming the existence of a serious worldwide problem, and it calls for information exchange, monitoring, and research. As such, the Vienna Convention enables quick acknowledgment of a problem caused by many states, even while the implications for state policies are being debated. The Vienna Convention establishes a regular conference of the parties and a secretariat. As the executive body, the conference reviews implementation of the Convention, receives reports from parties, adopts policies, and establishes necessary programs. In September 1987, the Montreal Protocol on Substances That Deplete the Ozone Layer was concluded, which establishes a progressive phaseout of CFCs.[42] The Montreal Protocol, though not wholly satisfactory, furnishes an important precedent for rapid, positive remedial action to address a pressing problem of global commons preservation. Industrialized states pledged to reduce their CFC production to 50 percent of 1986 levels by 1999, though developing countries were permitted to increase their use of CFCs throughout the first decade, up to 0.66 pounds per capita annually. During the 1990s, several developments dovetailed to strengthen the regime: the ozone hole over Antarctica persistently grew each year; a new ozone hole was discovered over the Arctic, in the northern hemisphere; the European Community coalesced to take remedial action on its own; and new chemicals were added to the substances banned as potential threats to the ozone layer.

The key to the Montreal Protocol's flexible development and enforcement lies in its institutional provisions. The powers enjoyed by the Meeting of States Party are unique. If a consensus cannot be reached, certain decisions may be taken by a two-thirds majority that binds all members of the Protocol, including those that voted against the decision. Such decisions must be supported by a complement of developed and developing states. Second, the Protocol provides for a formal noncompliance procedure through which an implementation committee hears complaints and reports to the Meeting of States Party, which makes a decision on the most appropriate action. One measure of the Vienna Convention's and the Montreal Protocol's success is that the Convention, as of 2005, had 189 contracting parties, including Russia, the United States, the United Kingdom, Germany, and the European Economic Community. Substantial progress on the level of global adherence suggests that the Protocol should be even more effective.

The second atmospheric threat is global climate change, which, though no one is certain about its severity or future effects, is recognized as putting humanity at risk. In 1995, the UN Intergovernmental Panel on Climate Change issued a report that asserted that notable increases in carbon dioxide emissions had occurred since 1750 and would thus lead to increased concentrations over the next century.[43] It is now known that human activities—most important, deforestation and the burning of fossil fuels, such as coal, oil, and natural gas—are altering the atmosphere's composition and contributing to climate change. The results of global warming could cause the melting of glaciers and polar ice caps, thus raising sea levels and threatening islands and low-lying coastal areas. Other likely effects include shifts in regional rain patterns and agricultural zones, leading to famines and population displacements.[44]

The international response to the global warming threat comes in the UN Framework

Convention on Climate Change (UNFCCC), negotiated at the Rio Summit in 1992.[45] This instrument, which in 2004 had 189 contracting states, establishes a framework for international action and a process for agreement on policy action. The UNFCCC commits governments to voluntarily reduce greenhouse gases and to enhance greenhouse gas sinks (areas of the earth's surface, such as tropical forests, that absorb such gases). Directed at developed countries, these actions required greenhouse gas producers to reduce their emissions to 1990 levels by the year 2000. Even so, developing countries must accept increasing responsibility for emissions as their industrialization programs advance and thereby raise their share of greenhouse gas production. Industrialized countries are expected to render fiscal and technological assistance to economically developing countries to facilitate their control of indigenous greenhouse gases; and all parties are encouraged to exchange information about sources and sinks of greenhouse gases and what measures are being taken to control any local emissions.

Several principles guide the parties toward fulfilling the UNFCCC's objectives. Parties are obligated to protect the climate system for present and future generations. Developing countries should be accorded appropriate assistance to enable them to fulfill the convention's terms. Parties are expected to cooperate to maximize benefits from initiatives in controlling the climate system. In addition, certain commitments are assumed under the Convention. Parties are obliged to prepare national inventories on greenhouse gas emissions and to outline the actions taken to reduce such emissions; to formulate and implement programs for the control of climate change; to assume technological cooperation to control the climate change; to incorporate suitable national policies for the control of climate change; and to undertake education and training policies that will enhance public awareness about climate change. Developing-country parties and other states listed in the Convention's first annex commit themselves to take special measures to limit their anthropogenic emissions of greenhouse gases and to enhance the capacity of national sinks and reservoirs for the stabilization of such gases. Developed state parties and other states listed in second annex pledge to provide financial support to developing-country parties to enable the latter to comply effectively with provisions in the agreement.

Parties are expected to cooperate in the establishment and promotion of networks and programs for research into and systematic observation of climate change. The UNFCCC creates three institutions to assist efforts to monitor and minimize climate change. Its supreme body, the Conference of the Parties, meets regularly to promote and review implementation of the treaty and, if appropriate, to strengthen it. The UNFCCC also establishes a subsidiary body to provide scientific and technological advice on policy alternatives for governments, as well as a financial mechanism to provide resources and grants to fulfill objectives of the Convention. Finally, the Convention provides for a procedure for the settlement of disputes.

The action plan in the UNFCCC, though notable, suffers from being more of a pledge to principle than a hard, legally binding commitment. Moreover, the growing scientific consensus over global warming made it apparent that major greenhouse gas producers such as the United States and Japan would not meet their voluntary stabilization targets by 2000. The upshot was the negotiation in December 1997 of a special protocol in Kyoto, Japan, that committed industrialized states to legally binding reductions in greenhouse gas emissions of an average of 6–8 percent below 1990 levels between the years 2008 and 2012. Subsequent negotiations modified the Protocol such that on July 24, 2001, in Bonn, Germany, a compromise agreement was reached by 178 states that formally requires industrialized states to cut emissions of gases linked to global warming. The agreement permits industrial states with the greatest emissions of greenhouse gases, principally carbon dioxide, to achieve their cuts with greater flexibility. The 2001 revised Kyoto accord obligates the thirty-eight industrialized countries to reduce their combined annual gas emissions to 5.2 percent below 1990 levels by 2012. To this end, the negotiations clarified the design of the first global system for buying and selling credits earned by reducing carbon dioxide emissions. Developing countries do not have to do anything to reduce their emissions. Perhaps most notably, the greatest producer of greenhouse gases, the United States, repudiated the Kyoto Protocol in 2001 and refused to ratify the agreement.[46]

The third threat to the atmosphere as a common space is that it functions as a conduit for substances and hence permits *airborne pollution*. The air serves as a medium for many forms of pollutants, though much attention since the 1970s has focused on the transnational acid precipitation generated by the burning of fossil fuels. Emissions from the United Kingdom and northern Germany are carried across the sea and fall over Scandinavia; and transnational acid rain from industrial centers in the midwestern United States has caused serious degradation of forests and lakes in southeastern Canada.[47]

An early attempt to redress such forms of air pollution was the 1979 Convention on Long-Range Transboundary Air Pollution, which entered into force in 1983 and, as of late 2004, has forty-nine parties, among them the United States, Canada, and Russia.[48] This agreement is the first and only major transnational agreement devoted to the regulation and control of transboundary air pollution. The European air mass is treated as a shared resource, and parties are required to coordinate pollution control measures and common emission standards. In sum, the 1979 Treaty on Air Pollution aims to protect the earth's environment by limiting, reducing, and preventing air pollution, especially that traveling transnationally. The agreement intends to accomplish its objective by promoting ways and means to exchange information, to foster research and assessment, and to institute policies and strategies to combat the discharge of air pollutants. Of particular concern is the need to promote cooperation to reduce emissions of sulphur compounds and other major air pollutants. The Convention emphasizes research and monitoring for measuring emission rates and ambient concentrations of air pollutants. The Convention encourages parties to study the transmission of long-range transboundary air pollutants to determine their impact on human health and the environment—including agriculture, forestry, aquatic, and other natural ecosystems—to provide governments with sufficient scientific data to institute antipollution laws and policies. However, the instrument does not contain liability provisions for air pollution damage nor tangible commitments requiring specific reductions in air pollution. Parties are pledged instead to broad principles and objectives for pollution control policy. There are provisions on notification and consultation in cases of significant risk, but no multilateral tools of implementation or enforcement are institutionalized or required. In effect, the 1979 agreement contains an obligation not to pollute the atmosphere, absent means of implementation or enforcement.

The 1979 Treaty on Air Pollution and its series of eight protocols operate under the aegis of the UN Economic Commission for Europe, with an objective to coordinating nationals efforts aimed at curbing air pollution.[49] It has a secretariat and as its principal institution an executive committee formed by environmental advisers of the commission's governments, who meet annually. These institutions evaluate the convention's implementation via the effectiveness of national policies; they collect information on emissions and their dispersal; and they enable parties to make informed decisions regarding where to implement remedial measures. It is important to realize that none of these institutions for managing the atmospheric commons has either the authority to determine whether a state is violating a convention or the wherewithal to enforce sanctions against a state for detected violations. The ultimate agents for implementing the convention's provisions and for acting as arbiters for compliance and enforcement remain national governments.[50]

Outer Space

Though extending far beyond Earth, outer space may be regarded as global commons because of its "global" effects on those who are earthbound and because humans use outer space. In this regard, distinct commons regimes have been suggested for the moon and other celestial bodies, for outer space itself, for the geostationary orbit, and even for the broadcast frequency spectrum.

The need for international law to regulate activities in outer space came with the launching of *Sputnik* by the Soviet Union in 1957. For nearly two decades into the age of space exploration, launch vehicles and satellites were the property of national governments. But beginning in the 1970s, private corporations and institutions began not only developing their own satellites and experiment packages but also financing their own launches from government facilities. This became most notable in the field of communication satellites, but considerable attention has also focused on remote sensing and manufacturing possibilities. The increasing number of activities by state and private actors in the commercial exploration of outer space, especially in launching vehicles and in stationing orbital satellites, made necessary the creation of a special regime of international outer space law.[51]

Five international agreements form the legal regime for managing the outer space commons. Of these, four stand as fundamental pillars on which international space law rests. The keystone agreement is the 1967 Treaty on Principles Governing the Activities of States in the Exploration and Use of Outer Space.[52] This accord, generally referred to as the Outer Space Treaty, sets out the core freedoms and duties of states in using outer space. The need for such an instrument was considered by the General Assembly in 1966, and agreement on a text was reached that same year. The treaty is based on the Declaration of Legal Principles Governing the Activities of States in the Exploration and Use of Outer Space, adopted by the General Assembly in its resolution 1962(XVIII) in 1963, with some new provisions added. Opened for signature in January 1967, the Outer Space Treaty entered into force ten months later. It provides the basic framework on international space law, in which certain norms are crystalized. Among them are the following: the exploration and use of outer space shall be carried out for the benefit of, and in the interests of, all countries and shall be the province of all humankind; outer space shall be free for exploration and use by all states; outer space is not subject to national appropriation by claim of sovereignty, by means of use, occupation, or any other means; states shall not place nuclear weapons or other weapons of mass destruction in orbit or on celestial bodies or station them in outer space in any other manner; the moon and other celestial bodies shall be used exclusively for peaceful purposes; astronauts shall be regarded as the envoys of humankind; states shall be responsible for national space activities, whether carried out by governmental or nongovernmental activities; states shall be liable for damage caused by their space objects; and states shall avoid harmful contamination of space and celestial bodies. Enforcement of these normative principles is left to the states themselves. Certain freedoms have also emerged for activities in outer space. States are free to explore and use outer space without interference by other states or international organizations. States are free to use space in any manner, so long as activities are peaceful, do not establish claim to title, and do not seek to evade state responsibility.

A second space law instrument is the 1968 Convention on the Rescue and Return of Astronauts and the Return of Objects Launched into Space.[53] This multilateral agreement is designed to secure international cooperation in rescuing and returning home astronauts and objects launched into space. The Rescue Agreement develops the general principle on this subject and spells out in great detail the rights and duties of states with respect to the rescue of astronauts who land in the territory of a foreign country and to the return of space objects to the country of launch.

Third, the 1972 Liability for Damage Caused by Space Objects Convention articulates the rules for damage caused by objects launched into space.[54] Under this international agreement, the launching state is absolutely liable to pay compensation for damage caused by space objects to persons or property on the earth's surface or to aircraft in flight. Claims are brought by national governments, and if diplomatic negotiations prove unsuccessful, claims are to be resolved through a mixed claims commission. Compensation is to be determined on international legal principles of equity and justice, with the intent of restoration to that of prior condition. Thus, state responsibility has evolved as a principle of outer space law. The launching state is liable for harm and is responsible for activities of its nationals, even if its nationals act privately. In 1978, for example, *Cosmos 954* fell from orbit and crashed, scattering radioactive debris in a remote part of Canada. Canada thus became the first state to invoke the Liability Convention. To recover the remnants of its satellite, the Soviet Union eventually paid Canada $3 million in compensation for cleanup.[55]

A fourth outer space agreement, the Convention on Registration of Objects Launched into Outer Space, was negotiated in 1975.[56] This multilateral accord, which entered into force in 1976, introduced the duty of the launching state to register its satellites and other space objects in a national register and to furnish to the UN Secretary-General, as soon as practicable, detailed information about each space object—such as its registration number; date and territory or location of launch; basic orbital parameters, such as its nodal period, apogee, and perigee; and the space object's general function. This information is recorded in a central register of the United Nations to which full and open access is available. At least forty-four states are contracting parties to this convention.

A fifth instrument, the Agreement Governing the Activities of States on the Moon and Other Celestial Bodies (the Moon Treaty), was considered and elaborated by the Legal Subcommittee of the Committee on the Peaceful Uses of Outer Space (COPUOS) from 1972 to 1979.[57] The agreement was adopted by the General Assembly in 1979 in its resolution 34/68, though not until June 1984 did a fifth country, Austria, ratify the agreement, which allowed it to enter into force in July 1984. The agreement reaffirms and elaborates on many of the provisions of the Outer Space Treaty as applied to the moon and other celestial bodies, providing that those bodies be used exclusively for peaceful purposes, that their environments not be disrupted, that the United Nations be informed of the location and purpose of any station established on those bodies. In addition, the agreement provides that the moon and its natural resources are the common heritage of mankind and that an international regime should be established to govern the exploitation of such resources when such exploitation is to become feasible. It is this last provision that has deflected support for this agreement from any space-faring state. In late 2004, the Moon Treaty counts only eleven states as contracting parties.[58]

The use of outer space has traditionally been dominated by two states, the United States and Russia. The participation of these governments in any extraterrestrial legal regime is thus fundamental for ensuring a regime's success. Institutionally, the UN Committee on Peaceful Uses of Outer Space (COPUOS) remains the principal body for articulating international space law, even though it has neither lawmaking nor administrative authority. Since its establishment in 1959, COPUOS has been the central forum for discussing legal and technical outer space issues. Dominated during the 1960s through the 1980s by the United States and the Soviet Union, COPUOS drafted all five major space treaties and at times proposed certain guidelines in the absence of treaties. COPUOS drafted each agreement after the committee's deliberations had identified a prevalent issue of concern and articulated principles for resolving it.

COPUOS usually drafted, negotiated, and adopted these treaties and principles for outer space by consensus. The consensus procedure aims to promote compromise on issues while fostering willingness to ratify and respect treaties. While attaining consensus might be desirable, problems can arise from the process. The quest for consensus can exacerbate negotiations, dilute the legal strength and scope of an agreement, and render the product prosaic yet vague as a set of legally binding obligations.

Outer space is also exploited through Earth-orbiting satellites used for communications, broadcasting, and remote sensing. The operation of satellites relies on the use of radio frequencies; hence, consideration of outer space as a global commons becomes linked to use of the radio spectrum. One outer space orbit has emerged as paramount—the *geostationary orbit* (GSO). Located 22,300 miles (36,000 kilometers) above the earth's equator, a satellite that is placed in this orbit travels in the same direction as the earth's rotation, and thus appears stationary relative to points on the earth's surface. The GSO has become critically important for satellite television and for making cost-effective telephone and data communication links.

For telecommunications technologies to operate effectively and efficiently, a high level of technical international cooperation is required. Governments must establish transnational networks for standardizing technology for broadcast and reception. Throughout this century, governments have used the International Telecommunications Union (ITU), originally the International Telegraphic Union, as the principal forum for standardizing and regulating international telecommunications technologies.[59]

The role of the ITU has been notably expanded by the satellite system. Since radio signals are fundamental to satellite activities, states have enabled the ITU to require advance notification of satellite system plans. Further, while the ITU produces the laws, regulations, agreements, procedures, and practices for ensuring the operation of international telecommunications, it is also the forum in which use of the geostationary orbit is internationally regulated. The ITU sets technical standards for GSO use, many of which are found in its radio regulations, which guide worldwide frequency use. In this regard, the precise location of the satellite link is critical, and the GSO is suitable for various forms of telecommunications. The ITU strives to fix the actual location of transmitters and receivers to minimize mutual interference between systems, and it allocates frequencies through special administrative conferences. The ITU's Plenipotentiary Conference is the institution's supreme organ and consists of all members. The conference convenes every four years to determine the budget and general ITU policies.

Implementation of legal rules for managing outer space as extraterrestrial global commons remains encumbered by two prominent unresolved concerns: first, remote sensing of Earth from outer space; and, second, the regulation of direct broadcasts from satellites. Toward these ends, the ITU, operating under its 1973 convention, has since dealt with two limited natural resources critical to space telecommunications: the GSO and the radio frequency spectrum. Given its legally binding standard-setting authority, the ITU, rather than COPUOS, became the natural vehicle for bringing legal order to space telecommunications, including the regimes for managing remote sensing and direct satellite broadcasts.

World Administrative Radio Conferences (WARCs), to which all ITU members are invited, are critical means of devising and setting uniform international standards. Regulations adopted by these conferences are legally binding on members and have the same juridical status as the ITU Convention. These conferences discuss and set standards for operating telecommunications equipment—in particular, international telephone systems, radio spectrum use, and satellite orbit allocation.

Nonbinding norms help overcome interstate disputes in outer space law that otherwise could inhibit the development of an outer space regime. For instance, remote sensing, often from the geostationary orbit, allows satellite technology to gather detailed information about conditions on the earth's surface, including the location and condition of natural resources. Since the 1970s, remotely sensed high-resolution data, particularly photographic images, make this use of space controversial. In fact, the use of remote sensing came under direct challenge in the mid-1970s by equatorial developing countries as being an invasion of their national privacy, an encroachment on national security, and an intrusion into national economic sovereignty and the disposition of natural resources.[60]

Tensions arose in international negotiations during the 1980s over whether remote sensing should be considered a freedom of the use of outer space or whether the legal principle of sovereignty gives a sensed state the right of prior consent. In late 1986, following consensus approval in the COPUOS, the General Assembly adopted fifteen principles relating to the remote sensing of Earth from space. Remote sensing should be carried out for the "benefit and in the interests of all countries, irrespective of their degree of economic, social, or scientific development," with particular consideration given the needs of the developing states. In addition, remote sensing must be conducted in accordance with international law, and sensing states should promote international cooperation and environmental protection of Earth.[61] There remains, however, no principle of law that requires prior consent for remote sensing, thus leaving the issue open to controversy.

The debate over direct broadcast satellites (DBS) produced additional soft law for the space commons. Efforts to establish a prior consent regime began in the 1970s when COPUOS debated the relative merits of DBS transmissions originating beyond national boundaries as opposed to the free flow of information. In 1982, a nonbinding General Assembly resolution concerning principles governing the use of artificial earth satellites for international direct television broadcasting was adopted over the vehement objections of Western states. Although these states looked to the ITU as an alternative forum for developing a DBS regime, the outcome there proved no more successful. Discussions in ITU fora during the 1970s, 1980s, and 1990s failed to produce a regime for the space commons that regulates broadcast information or permits the complete freedom to broadcast directly across national borders. National policies and regulations exist, but these are not coordinated in the international realm. Thus, while no legally binding norm requires a government engaged in DBS to obtain prior consent from other states, nonbinding resolutions and decisions asserting such intent have been adopted by most states in the General Assembly. Some contend that these resolutions reflect an emerging body of soft law, though they are rejected by all states that own and operate the technology.

REGIME COMPLIANCE AND ENFORCEMENT

Governments implement and comply with international rules for regulating use of the commons area because such behavior is perceived to enhance their national interests. National governments remain the principal actors for negotiating, implementing, and enforcing international rules for global common spaces. Each national government decides for itself whether a particular multilateral global commons agreement is in its interest and whether to subscribe to it. Similarly, each government ultimately decides whether to become affiliated with a particular international institution or with a body created to make decisions affecting activities in a particular global commons. Nonetheless, once created, international institutions can become powerful shapers of state behavior with respect to the global commons.

Notwithstanding the establishment of legal regimes for regulating activities in common spaces, concerns over sovereignty and national interests make states reluctant to transfer exclusive or even substantial enforcement authority to international bodies. This reluctance has prompted nongovernmental organizations to become advocates for conservation and protection in the global commons area. Although lacking full-fledged international legal personality, environmental organizations are watchdogs involved in monitoring the implementation and enforcement of rules to conserve resources in the commons area. Prominent among nongovernmental organizations concerned about world fisheries are Greenpeace International, International Wildlife Management Consortium, the World Conservation Union, and the World Wide Fund for Nature; for Antarctica, Greenpeace International and the Antarctic and Southern Ocean Coalition; and for global warming, the Global Warming International Center, World Wildlife Federation, and Friends of the Earth International, who are engaged in campaigns to educate people on climate change.

Global commons regimes constitute a form of interstate governance. Governments enter into legal agreements to coordinate their behavior by abiding by certain rules. But for these regime elements to be meaningful, governments must deliver on their commitments. Governments must undertake the ways and means to make their laws, policies, and nationals comply with those rules. The extent to which multilateral regime norms and rules work to modify national foreign policies is difficult to ascertain, much less assess. Quantifiable criteria and objective targets are available in only a few instruments—for example, the ozone regime and the climate change convention; and even then, those are not without controversy between developed and developing states. Moreover, global common space regimes are not designed to monitor activities or verify parties' compliance. Determination of a regime's effectiveness may well hinge on the extent that state compliance can be verified or that national conduct can be independently assessed. The problem becomes compounded by the need to obtain reliable data to evaluate compliance.

Governments might comply with a global commons agreement simply because it requires little or no change in their behavior, which is undoubtedly the case for most states contracting to the 1967 Outer Space Treaty and its family of three other agreements, since they have no space-faring capabilities. Similarly, this is the case for most nonconsultative parties to the Antarctic Treaty, who are not engaged in any activities in the polar south. Conversely, compliance might be expected when agreements affecting a global commons area proscribe undesirable actions that no government presently wishes to undertake, in anticipation of restraining future economic, political, or technological incentives to take such actions. Such is the case for the Antarctic Environmental Protection Protocol, which prohibits drilling or mining activities in the Antarctic, though neither is viewed as being desirable or commercially profitable in the foreseeable future. Likewise with the case of deep seabed mining, which is not expected to be commercially attractive until the mid-21st century, if then.

If legal rules for managing common space regimes are to be enforced, governments of member states must be willing to enforce them on their own nationals as well as on other state parties. For instance, responsibility to enforce rules in the law of the sea devolves to national governments. But many opportunities for failure exist within the web of enforcement by flag states, port states, and coastal states. Enforcement by individual governments is often weak; reports are not always submitted; and when they are presented, they are not always accurate or complete. Violations might not be committed in willful disregard of norms or regulations but could result from the inability of governments to comply owing to lack of expertise or funds for enforcement. The names of vessels reported as being in noncompliance with standards are publicized in International Maritime Organization (IMO) lists. The IMO attempts to mobilize international opinion to shame governments that are not only delinquent in submitting reports but are also delinquent in correcting alleged deficiencies in their ships and facilities. In addition, the IMO maintains technical assistance programs to help states comply by providing assistance in running competent maritime administration, formulating maritime legislation, upgrading merchant shipping and facilities, and training qualified maritime personnel.

The IMO has no enforcement powers designated over such maritime conventions as the International Convention for the Prevention of Pollution by Ships, the International Convention for the Safety of Life at Sea, and the Convention on the International Regulation for Preventing Collisions at Sea. Formal enforcement authority under those conventions is allocated as appropriate to flag states, port states, and nonport coastal states. States are required to report to the IMO matters relating to application of conventions, including violations or alleged violations. IMO committees make efforts to see that reports are submitted and to follow up on possible violations of norms.

Responsibility for enforcing compliance with the formal legal agreements, recommended measures, and special norms adopted under the Antarctic Treaty System (ATS) falls to governments who are party to the Antarctic Treaty. The obligation to abide by these regulations accrues only to parties of the ATS instruments. While third-party states are not legally obligated to comply with ATS norms, the harsh Antarctic conditions have made this concern irrelevant, since nonparty states have little incentive, revenues, or interests to pursue Antarctic activities. If they do, it is usually by ''piggybacking'' their programs with an agreeable Antarctic Treaty Consultative Party.

Multilateral enforcement of Antarctic agreements has not occurred. There are no provisions in any ATS instrument for formal sanctions, although political and diplomatic suasion can be used by the more powerful Antarctic Treaty states to persuade other parties on a particular course of action. There are various provisions in each ATS instrument that call for resolving disputes over treaty provisions through negotiation, inquiry, mediation, conciliation, arbitration, judicial settlement, or other peaceful means. Importantly, as of 2005, no dispute concerning any ATS agreement has been reported that is sufficiently severe to require resort to any dispute settlement technique.

Enforcement of outer space law is done by national governments via their own space agencies or private space industries. Neither COPUOS nor the ITU has any real powers to sanction or punish governments or private actors who violate legal principles or legal agreements. The critical aspect of enforcement comes in the willingness of states to abide by norms of space law and to punish private actors whose activities transgress those norms. The key here is to produce norms that are clearly defined and universally agreed. A body of outer space law does exist, and certain norms and regulations have been consummated internationally. But consolidating management of the space commons has proved difficult. Disagreement persists between developing and developed states over how best to regulate space-based technologies—in particular, geostationary satellites that can sense the earth's surface remotely and broadcast directly across national frontiers.

The ITU does not have effective enforcement or policing mechanisms for its decisions.

Essentially, international telecommunications management and enforcement depends on member states' recognizing that the effects of failure to conduct their policies responsibly can harm everyone, including themselves. To ignore decisions of ITU Administrative Radio Conferences and other broadcast coordinating agencies would increase mutual radio signal interference, thus creating negative effects for all states.

Monitoring and reporting are crucial to detecting possible violations of rules. Governments are usually expected to report measures adopted for the implementation of their legal obligations to the appropriate institutions under various management regimes. Typically, this requires that statistical information be furnished on catch limits or harvests taken, on licenses and permits given, on scientific information regarding pollutant production and distribution, and on evidence of breaches or violations by nationals of a state party. In addition, governments are required to submit to a regional arrangement's central body (a headquarters or a commission) copies of national laws relating to resource exploitation and waste disposal, annual reports detailing breaches of such laws, and what sanctions were taken in response to those breaches.[62] These reports provide the means by which an institutional body in a global commons regime can assess the extent to which parties are complying with their obligations under the relevant agreement. In the case of the south polar commons, for example, the Scientific Committee on Antarctic Research provides essential, long-term impartial assessment and monitoring functions for the Antarctic Treaty regime. For the Southern Ocean, a special scientific committee conducts studies and furnishes data critical for the decisions made on fishing and conservation policies considered annually by the commission of the 1980 Convention on the Conservation of Antarctic Living Marine Resources. One model of effective monitoring can be found in the 1959 Antarctic Treaty, in which unannounced, onsite inspection of any scientific station is permitted. Requiring that specified data be collected and submitted to a central authority can also influence government behavior. Similarly, satellite surveillance of the commons area enhances global monitoring of harmful activities—for example, ocean dumping, pollution output, ozone depletion, and drift-netting activities.

It should be evident that key to effecting compliance is the availability of adequate scientific information on the condition of a commons area or its resources, such as the availability of fishing stocks, the pollutants being emitted into the atmosphere, and the impact of ozone depletion. This information can be used to monitor resource exploitation, perform surveillance, and trigger enforcement against offenders. For example, two general techniques have been used to foster national compliance with international fishery management in the high seas and in the circumpolar Southern Ocean. One involves putting controls on fishing efforts, including restrictions on the type of gear and size of mesh; limits on vessels, including vessel type, length, and horsepower; and restrictions on fishing seasons and areas.[63] The other is to impose controls on fishing catches or by catch quotas. It remains for governments, however, to decide whether to manage fishery resources by effort controls or through catch quotas.

The 1982 LOS Convention mandates compulsory, binding procedures for dispute settlement in most cases. Settlement is compulsory in that either party may submit dispute for arbitration or adjudication and that the other party is bound by the convention to comply with that option. Both parties are expected to comply with the decision rendered by a court or an arbitral tribunal.

For the atmosphere, the 1987 Montreal Protocol on ozone depletion provides for an unusual noncompliance procedure. An implementation committee was devised in 1990 to hear complaints and receive submissions from the parties concerned. The committee reports to the Meeting of the Parties, which can decide what measures should be taken to bring about full compliance. It is not clear that parties will be legally bound to comply with these decisions. In addition, the 1985 Vienna Convention provides, in article 11, for optional acceptance of compulsory arbitration or judicial settlement in the event of a dispute between parties. Alternatively, parties are required to negotiate a solution, ostensibly through good offices or mediation. Even so, these are not strong dispute settlement stipulations, since the multilateral noncompliance procedure emphasizes greater collective control and multilateral negotiation than that by reliance on bilateral resolution or formal adjudication. The Climate Change Convention in article 14 mandates dispute settlement between parties through negotiation or any other ''peaceful technique of their own choice,'' including resort to the International Court of Justice, arbitration, and a conciliation commission. The key sticking point remains the political will of the parties to compromise on an agreed-on solution.

The experience in creating, adapting, sustaining, and enforcing regimes for managing common spaces clearly demonstrates that leadership from the technologically developed world—most notably, from the United States—is necessary. The United States not only has the technological wherewithal but also the political presence and diplomatic clout. Multilateral regimes for global common spaces evolve because Great Powers recognize that a problem affects their mutual interests or constituencies; therefore, they take action to deal with that concern. Once global commons regimes are established, power configurations tend to be issue specific. Given the close association between international economics, communications, maritime, and environmental matters, the dominant players are likely to be developed states. But salient exceptions occur. As a major space power, Russia figured importantly in direct broadcast frequency and remote sensing negotiations. In the Antarctic Treaty meetings, Chile and Argentina played exceptional roles by their virtue of being claimant states and being geographically closest to the Antarctic continent. In the ozone negotiations, not only did the European Community, United States, Japan, and the Soviet Union have important parts but so did China and India. In sum, the active presence of Great Powers remains vital as the ingredient for making the regime happen.

CONCLUSION

The unique problems of the global common spaces led to the establishment by states of near-universal legal regimes that provide ways and means for governments to work closely together for managing activities in those regions. Participation in common space regimes develops habits of compliance and implicit expectations concerning mutual rights and obligations. Habitual patterns of compliance and expectations furnish a foundation for trust and credibility among governments in dealings with one another. Habits of compliance give rise to a sense of stability in intergovernmental relationships, and they contribute to regime cohesion. Practice suggests that an association of states can maintain a greater degree of order, predictability, and activity through regime cohesion than they could otherwise. Regime cohesion thus becomes a process through which states via an international association are linked by common norms, values, rules, and principles. The conformity to a commons regime means compliance with its rules, which in turn promotes cohesion and conformity to rules. The operation of a regime becomes a self-regenerative process, guided by norms and rules and substantiated by state practice through sustained behavior.

Management of the commons is driven by a utilitarian rationale—namely, to establish means for self-interested cooperation. The use of global common spaces remains earmarked by interdependence among users. Interdependence aggravates the possibilities for conflict and dissonance among users, which can spark instability and disorder in international relations. Regimes for managing common spaces coordinate the avoidance of mutually harmful conduct among parties; that is, securing mutual gains through institutional mechanisms in a commons regime is less a motivation than managing shared vulnerabilities arising from unregulated activities. The motivation aims to secure the protection of mutual welfare through jointly agreed rules and norms. Mutual vulnerability necessitates mutual management for mutual protection. Such a highly pragmatic motive explains in large measure why regimes have been created to manage problems affecting the global commons.

In a world of sovereign states and limited resources, questions of ownership and jurisdiction are likely to become prominent in the 21st century. Immediate issues of national sovereignty challenge policymakers more readily than do common space concerns. For the coming century, policies of restraint will be essential if the various regimes created for managing common spaces are to be respected and if the political and legal accommodations over sovereignty temptations in the global commons are to be upheld.

At the same time, it must be remembered that international legal regimes are dynamic creatures. The 1982 LOS Convention is a framework agreement, not a panacea for contemporary matters regarding the law of the sea. New issues surface that generate international concerns about managing the oceans. Similarly, in the polar south, new concerns over possible abuses of the area's resources create new needs for law and policy regulation. For the air commons, the agenda to create legal regimes was set by the realization that human activities are adversely affecting the atmosphere through depletion of the stratospheric ozone layer and through exacerbation of the greenhouse effect, thereby producing global warming, possible climate change, and widespread environmental degradation from acid precipitation. Outer space remains largely an arcane legal consideration. Even so, as more governments develop the technological capability to send more and more vehicles into orbit and beyond, rules to govern those activities will be needed.

That legal regimes have been fashioned for managing international activities in the oceans, the Antarctic, the atmosphere, and in outer space highlights a critical realization by governments: no state or group of states can satisfactorily deal with these global problems alone. If human-made threats to global common areas are to be seriously redressed, or at least curbed, a concerted international effort is required. There is international safety in numbers when the behavior of all parties is guided by one set of rules and guidelines. Only through such common legal means can these threats to the commons be minimized.

The key lesson for success is not the recurrent need to negotiate rules or attract state parties. The critical factor remains the ability to galvanize the requisite political will of governments to adhere to those rules and laws already created for various global commons regimes. This ability to influence the political will of states will largely be determined by the extent to which these regimes are seen as enhancing each state's national interests at costs perceived to be fair and not disadvantageous when compared to that state's being outside the regime. Governments must be willing to comply with and enforce these regulatory regimes to ensure that the oceans, polar regions, and atmosphere survive humankind's abuse. This is clearly an ambitious challenge that must be met if an acceptable quality of life on our planet is to be preserved and protected for future generations.

11

International Economic Law

  ❖ Bretton Woods System
  ❖ Regional Organizations
  ❖ International Commodity Agreements
  ❖ Conclusion

Domestic economic and political considerations can affect a state's respect for international legal rules. In March 2002, the Bush administration imposed high tariffs on steel to protect the domestic steel industry. The three-year, 30 percent tax on foreign steel would ostensibly allow U.S. companies to adjust to import competition, to restructure, and to consolidate so that they might become more competitive internationally. Such actions, referred to as safeguard measures, are permitted under article 5 of the Agreement on Safeguards and under article 6 of the General Agreement on Tariffs and Trade (GATT), which detail the conditions to be met before such a measure is considered justified. Yet, while the Bush administration generally supports free trade, domestic political considerations concomitantly became a prominent incentive for this reversal in U.S. trade policy. The Bush administration calculated that imposing these tariffs would please voters and labor unions in steel-producing, presidential-election swing states, such as Ohio, Pennsylvania, and West Virginia, as well as aid Republicans during the 2002 midterm elections in those key states. The international reaction was, predictably, anger and resentment, which resulted in the European Union (EU), Japan, South Korea, Norway, Switzerland, China, New Zealand, and Brazil jointly filing a case alleging trade discrimination before the World Trade Organization (WTO). In March 2003 the WTO ruled that the U.S. tariffs were unjustified. According to the WTO panel report, the United States did not meet the safeguard conditions and, in particular, had failed to show an increase in imports—in fact, according to the complainants, there had been a decrease in steel imports in the material period. Moreover, the United States also failed to adequately establish the link between imports and injury to its domestic steel industry, and it had included import figures from North American Free Trade Agreement countries in its injury investigation, even though it excused Canada and Mexico from application of the safeguard measures. A second WTO panel reaffirmed these conclusions in July 2003. In November 2003, a final WTO appeals panel confirmed the earlier panels' decision that the safeguard measures introduced by the United States in 2002 were unlawful *and that the EU and the other seven complainants had the right of retaliation, with sanctions of their own against U.S. goods. Toward this end, the EU threatened to impose $2.2 billion of retaliatory levies on U.S. products, including textiles, cigarettes, steel, fruits, and vegetables. The EU hit list was calculated to hurt Bush politically, as it would effectively price fruit and vegetables from Florida as well as textiles from the Carolinas out of European markets. In early December 2003, the Bush administration rescinded the controversial steel tariffs. Important to realize, however, is that this decision was not motivated by a desire to adhere to the international legal findings made repeatedly by the WTO. Rather, it rested more on the pragmatic calculation that it was better for the U.S. economy to avoid a trade war with the EU and Japan, whose retaliatory sanctions against U.S. products would be more politically costly than gains made in protecting the U.S. domestic steel industry. The alienation of the auto industry in Michigan (a major consumer of imported steel) as well as citrus producers in Florida and California and textile-manufacturing states such as North Carolina eventually proved less politically acceptable than protecting U.S. steel, especially in light of the adverse impacts such a trade war could have on voters in those key states during the 2004 presidential election.*

Alll states conduct international trade to varying degrees. No country is so self-sufficient that it can afford to erect protective barriers and economically ignore the rest of the world. The eventual aim of trade is to profit. For goods to sell, they must be better than rival products, which not only becomes a matter of price and quality but also reflects the efficiency of delivery and service. Buyer confidence is critical since it fosters the constant purchase of goods from sellers. Throughout the international commercial transaction process, legal rules operate to make trade happen. This international economic law may be broadly defined as the loosely connected body of legal rules, norms, customs, domestic legislation, treaties, and conventions that govern the conduct of international trade and business transactions between states and other international actors. Unlike international law in general, international economic law includes domestic commercial law as an essential component.

The body of rules for transnational trade in the 21st century derives from medieval commercial laws called the *lex mercatoria* and *lex maritima*—respectively, "the law for merchants on land" and "the law for merchants on sea." These rules stemmed from necessity and expediency, as merchants needed a degree of certainty in conducting their business transactions across national frontiers. The same desire is no less true today, as global interdependence has made international trade commonplace and increasingly complex. To facilitate opportunities for the growing volume of transnational transactions, international legal rules for commerce in the 21st century are being refined through public institutions—in particular, the United Nations Commission on International Trade Law, the Hague Conference on Private International Law, and the Rome International Institute for the Unification of Private International Law.[1] Yet, while international trade is often said to engage the governments of states, multinational corporations (MNCs) do most of the process of transnational commercial exchange. Today nearly 500,000 MNCs and their foreign affiliates remain at the forefront of the international movement of investment capital and private loans among countries operating worldwide. MNCs conduct international business that supplies services such as banking, insurance, and transportation. MNCs contribute enormous wealth and power to the economically developed countries. About 95 percent of the top five hundred MNCs operate in Northern countries, especially in the

United States, Europe, and Japan. In substantial part, the legal rules that regulate multinational corporate transactions today are the products of events during the last five decades and the evolution of a sophisticated system for governing the conduct of international economic relations.

THE BRETTON WOODS SYSTEM

The contemporary system for international trade evolved out of developments during the Second World War, as the Allied governments prepared for the postwar international economic order. During July 1–22, 1944, international economists and finance experts from forty-four governments of the Allied powers convened in the United Nations Monetary and Financial Conference at Bretton Woods, New Hampshire. The conference resulted in the creation of the International Monetary Fund (IMF), to promote international monetary cooperation, and the International Bank for Reconstruction and Development (World Bank), for development aid. By December 1945 the treaties creating the two organizations had entered into force, and by mid-1946 they began operation. In an effort to coordinate the world monetary system, member states contributed to the IMF, from which they could draw funds to overcome temporary exchange deficits, and each state was required to declare a par value of its currency in terms of the gold value of the American dollar. Added to these agreements was the General Agreement on Tariffs and Trade (GATT), which was negotiated in Geneva in 1947 to reduce international trade barriers and eliminate discriminatory treatment in international commerce.[2] These three instruments served as pillars for the Bretton Woods System, under which the post–World War II reconstruction of Europe and international economic relations functioned for two decades.

During the late 1950s and early 1960s, the dissolution of colonial empires created dozens of newly independent states, mostly in Africa and Asia, to form a southern tier of developing countries. To pursue their common interests, countries in the developing South began organizing themselves into political blocs and economic coalitions. In 1955 the Nonaligned Movement was founded at the Bandung Conference, and the Group of 77 was created in 1964 when developing countries created the United Nations Conference on Trade and Development. In that forum they argued for fair terms of trade and liberal terms for financing development. This conference was set up as a direct organ of the UN General Assembly and designed to promote the economic well-being of the newly independent and developing nations. Its work involved creation of a generalized system of preferences, a system of reduced tariffs and quotas for developing countries, and a system of primary commodity price supports. These supports were to nurture the developing countries' economies, whose main source of foreign exchange lay in the export of primary commodities. The developed Northern states responded with adamant insistence that the proper fora for any economic changes were the Bretton Woods institutions, in which they held the balance of power.

New International Economic Order

The collapse of the Bretton Woods System in the early 1970s, compounded by profound worldwide economic repercussions generated by the oil price shocks of 1973–1974, created severe global economic disruptions. In response, developing-country governments called on the UN General Assembly to convene a special session in May 1974 to discuss the international economic situation. There, the members of the Group of 77 declared the need for a systematic approach to integrating their needs into the global economy. This came as a proposal called the New International Economic Order (NIEO), which was embodied in two documents, passed over the objections of Western developed states: the Declaration on the Establishment of New International Economic Order[3] and the Programme of Action on the Establishment of a New International Economic Order.[4] This new global economic system would be based on equity, sovereign equality, interdependence, common interest, and cooperation among all states, irrespective of their economic and social systems. The aims of the NIEO were lofty indeed: to correct inequalities, redress existing injustices, eliminate the widening gap between the developed and the developing countries, and ensure steadily accelerating economic and social development as well as peace and justice for present and future generations. The legal parameters of the NIEO took shape in December 1974, when the General Assembly adopted the Charter of Economic Rights and Duties of States.[5] This charter called for redistribution of wealth and political power to promote international justice based on the duties of developed countries and the rights of developing countries. Moreover, it asserted the right of a government to expropriate foreign owners, and it advocated the right to form monopoly producer associations among the commodity-exporting countries—ventures such as the Organization of Petroleum Exporting Countries, the famous oil cartel. While these notions alarmed many developed-country governments during the late 1970s, the NIEO never happened. Over the next two decades it became clear that the NIEO concept was politically and commercially bankrupt. It was not possible to regulate international business through resolutions adopted at international conferences. Nor did protectionism, as advocated by Third World dependencia theorists, prove a workable strategy for developing countries. Societies closed to international trade and investment could not prosper; they suffered serious stagnation of their productive capabilities. Finally, the notion of investment through state-owned enterprises evaporated in the late 1980s with the worldwide failure of international communism, the collapse of socialist economies, and the rise of free enterprise capitalism. At the same time, Western-controlled institutions—especially the World Bank, IMF, and the GATT—emerged as key international incentives for constructively contributing to the economic development of Third World countries, a process that is underscored by completion of the Uruguay round of GATT negotiations in 1994.

World Trade Organization

The creation of the World Trade Organization (WTO) signals the rise of international economic law for the 21st century. The origins of the WTO trace back to 1947 when twenty-three states met in Geneva and drew up the General Agreement on Tariffs and Trade (GATT). This agreement was originally part of a draft charter for the International Trade Organization (ITO), the third leg of the Bretton Woods post–World War II economic order, as well as the International Monetary Fund and World Bank. The so-called Havana Charter of the ITO contained the GATT as well as provisions relating to employment, commodity agreements, restrictive business practices, international investment, and services. Entered into force on January 1, 1948, the 1947 GATT consisted of negotiated trade concessions and rules of conduct, but the rest of the Havana Charter never was ratified, primarily because of opposition in the U.S. Congress. For forty-seven years, the everexpanding group of contracting parties to the GATT—128 states when the WTO was created in 1994—treated the instrument as if it were a permanent commitment, though it was actually merely a provisional legal agreement. The small secretariat associated with the stillborn Havana Charter served as the secretariat for the GATT. Eight rounds of negotiations reduced tariffs and produced in piecemeal rules to govern international trade. Nontariff barriers were dealt with after 1965, among them antidumping measures, subsidies, countervailing duties, import licensing procedures, and selective government procurement. These agreements were contracted by only a few of the GATT members, mainly those who were members of the Organization for Economic Cooperation and Development.

The final GATT round, the Uruguay round, proved to be the most prolonged and most comprehensive. It lasted seven years and established a legal institution—the World Trade Organization—to replace the GATT of 1947, with all its amendments. Established by the Marrakesh Protocol on January 1, 1995, the WTO is a multilateral institution charged with administering rules of trade among member countries. Legally, it embodies an international intergovernmental organization, possessing international personality and competence in its own right independent of its member governments. Consequently, the WTO enjoys legal privileges and immunities necessary for the exercise of its mandate. As a body of legal rules, the WTO contains the GATT of 1994 and other non-goods-related agreements.

The WTO represents the preeminent international body dealing with the rules of trade between states. As of 2005, the 148 members of the WTO account for more than 97 percent of world trade, and its decisions affect nearly all the goods and services moving in international commerce. At its core are the WTO agreements, which serve as the ground rules for international commerce and trade policy. The main objectives of the WTO agreements are to assist trade to flow freely, achieve liberalization through negotiation, act as a forum for trade negotiations, and ensure impartial settlement of disputes. Succinctly put, the WTO's aim is to facilitate, with consistent policies, the free and fair flow of trade for its member states.

The WTO provides a code of rules and a forum for governments to discuss and resolve trade disputes and to continue negotiations toward expanding world trade opportunities. The WTO includes all GATT provisions for trade in goods, plus rules developed for trade in services and intellectual property, as well as rules and procedures governing the settlement of disputes. It operates as the principal international instrument body concerned with multilateral negotiations on the reduction of trade barriers and other measures that distort competition. In this regard, the WTO instills five fundamental principles that establish the foundation of the present multilateral commercial system: nondiscrimination through *most-favored-nation* treatment; free fair trade; consistent trade policies; open and fair competition; and concessionary treatment for developing countries.

The WTO's rules (called agreements) were negotiated during the Uruguay round. These rules run some thirty thousand pages of sixty agreements and separate commitments (called schedules) and set out acceptable procedures for customs duties and opening markets. Through these agreements, WTO members operate in a nondiscriminatory trading system that upholds their rights and obligations. Each state is guaranteed that its exports will be treated fairly and consistently by other members of the WTO. The Uruguay round produced 22,500 pages of text that list individual countries' commitments to cut and bind customs duty rates on imports of goods. The WTO agreements cover goods, services, and intellectual property; they articulate principles of liberalization and permissible exceptions; they prescribe special treatment for developing countries; and they require governments to make their trade policies transparent.

The November 2001 Declaration of the Fourth Ministerial Conference in Doha, Qatar, provides the mandate for negotiations on a range of subjects and other work, including issues relating to the implementation of the present agreements. The negotiations, which began in early 2000, include those on agriculture and services. A number of other issues have now been added. The declaration sets January 1, 2005, as the date for completing nearly all the negotiations, which will go forward in the Trade Negotiations Committee and its subsidiaries.

The legal structure of the WTO treaty breaks down into five parts. The main text of the WTO agreement, which establishes the organization, is informally called the Charter. It is the Charter that is concerned with institutional and procedural matters and asserts the key principles that undergird the benefits of the WTO for member states. Four substantive treaty texts of obligations are appended as annexes to the Charter. Annex 1 contains the large texts that impose binding obligations on parties. As parts of this, annex 1A contains the revised GATT agreement, related codes, and the vast schedules of concessions that form the bulk of the twenty-six thousand pages in the official treaty document. Annex 1B provides for the General Agreement on Trade in Services, and annex 1C sets out the provisions for the Agreement on Trade-Related Intellectual Property. Annex 2 contains the rules for dispute settlement, referred to as the Dispute Settlement Understanding, which are obligatory for all members and which form an integrated, uniform dispute mechanism. Annex 3 contains the Trade Policy Review Mechanism, through which the WTO reviews the general trade policies of each member on a periodic and regular basis and reports on these policies. The focus here does not fall on legal questions of compliance with obligations in the treaty but rather on transparency and overall impact of trade policies. Annex 4 contains optional agreements more hortatory in nature, which concern only a relatively few states. Among subjects treated by these agreements are civil aircraft, government procurement, dairy products, and bovine products. The importance of this fourth annex lies in its flexibility to permit the organization to evolve so that future agreements may be added as new salient issues emerge in the coming decades.

As an intergovernmental body, decisions in the WTO are based on consensus of the entire membership. The highest decision-making body is the Ministerial Conference, which meets every two years. In the interim, the General Council convenes several times per year and serves as the Trade Policy Review Body and Dispute Settlement Body. Also included are the Goods Council, the Services Council, and the Intellectual Property Council, all of which report to the General Council. A secretariat, headquartered in Geneva, furnishes technical support for committees and the councils and provides technical assistance to developing countries.

The General Agreement on Trade in Services furnishes a set of enforceable multilateral legal rules covering international trade in services. Consequently, all internationally operating banks, insurance firms, telecommunication companies, hotel chains, and transport companies enjoy the same principles of free and fair trade under the WTO that originally applied to trade in goods. The agreement operates on three levels—namely, the main text, which articulates the general principles and obligations; annexes dealing with rules for specific sectors; and individual state's particular commitments to provide access to their markets. All WTO members are legally obligated to stipulate which of their service sectors are open to foreign competition and how open those markets will be. Even so, this obligation does not alleviate contemporary disparities in national regulations. Some states still opt to retain financial controls over their insurance, banking, and brokerage service industries, which restrict the international interchange that might occur.

The *Agreement on Trade-Related Aspects of Intellectual Property Rights* (TRIPS) integrates intellectual property rights (copyrights, trademarks, and patents) under common international rules (GATT and WTO rules). The new agreement requires WTO member governments to adhere to minimum standards for the protection of intellectual property rights—essentially the standards spelled out in the main conventions of the World Intellectual Property Organizations, the Paris Convention for the Protection of Industrial Property, and the Bern Convention for the Protection of Literary and Artistic Works. The agreement applies national and most-favored-nation treatment to intellectual property rights and sets up provisions on how best to protect and enforce those rights as well as repress counterfeiting and piracy. Finally, the TRIPS makes conflicts between WTO members subject to the WTO's dispute settlement procedures. The TRIPS confirms that computer programs are protected as literary works under the copyright regime and not under that of trademarks and patents. It grants authors of computer programs and producers of sound recordings (phonograms) the right to authorize or prohibit the commercial rental of their work to the public. Provisions in TRIPS relate to industrial property as well and include the protection of trademarks, service marks, geographical indications, industrial designs and patents, integrated-circuit layout designs, and trade secrets.

Absent means for settling disputes, a rules-based commercial system would mean little if the rules could not be enforced. The WTO procedure underscores the rule of law and in this way makes the trading system secure and consistent. The system is predicated on clearly defined rules, with timetables for completion of a case. Resolving disputes is the responsibility of WTO's Dispute Settlement Body. This organ has sole authority to establish panels to consider the case and to accept or reject the panel's findings or the results of an appeal. In addition, the Dispute Settlement Body has the power to authorize retaliation when a government fails to comply with a ruling.

A dispute typically arises when a WTO member adopts a trade policy measure or takes some action that one or more WTO members consider to be a breach of the WTO agreements or a failure to live up to trade obligations. A case could then ensue, proceeding in three stages. The first stage is consultation, which can last up to sixty days and which allows the disputants to settle their differences by themselves. They may ask the WTO Director-General to mediate or assist in the negotiations. If these consultations fail, then the complainant can initiate the second stage, the WTO panel process, by requesting panel appointment. It can take forty-five days for a panel to be appointed and up to six months for the panel to conclude its deliberations. Panels resemble tribunals, but unlike a normal tribunal, panelists are usually chosen in consultation with disputant states. Only if the two sides cannot agree does the WTO Director-General appoint the panelists, which rarely occurs. Panels consist of three (but sometimes five) international experts, who examine the evidence and render a decision. The panel's report must be based on the agreements cited. It is then passed on to the Dispute Settlement Body, which can reject the report only by consensus. Panelists are chosen from lists of experts and serve in their own personal capacities. They may not receive instructions from any government.

The dispute settlement procedure is a structured process with clearly defined stages. For the WTO to function effectively, prompt settlement of a case is essential. Annex 2 of the WTO agreement sets out in detail the procedures and timetable to be followed in resolving disputes. If a case runs full course, its resolution should not take more than a year or, if appealed, fifteen months. Under the 1994 GATT procedure, a government that loses a case cannot block adoption of the ruling. Rulings are automatically adopted unless a consensus exists to reject it. That is, any state desiring to block a ruling must persuade all other WTO members, including its adversary, to share its view—a task that can be quite difficult. In the end, while the procedure may resemble a court or tribunal, the preferred solution is for governments to discuss their problems and negotiate a diplomatic solution between themselves, which explains why mediation remains possible even as the dispute settlement process continues to unfold.

The WTO has no specific agreement dealing with the environment, though some WTO agreements include provisions with environmental concerns. While the preamble to the agreement establishing the WTO states the objectives of sustainable development and environmental protection, much attention has focused on the perceived incompatibility between the WTO rules and the GATT rules as the protector of free trade and the objective of protecting living resources in the environment. Two cases in particular highlight these concerns, sparking great concern about the WTO among environmentalists.

The first case is the Tuna-Dolphin Case of 1991 in which a panel under the 1947 GATT dealt with the issue of territoriality.[6] In this case, the U.S. government passed a law, the Marine Mammal Protection Act,[7] which imposed a ban on all tuna caught by countries using nets that incidentally killed dolphins at a rate 1.25 times higher than the rate of American vessels operating in the same waters at the same time. If a country could not prove to the satisfaction of U.S. authorities that it met this protection standard, the U.S. government would embargo all imports of fish from that country. The government of Mexico challenged this measure as being an import ban contrary to articles 11 and 20 of the 1947 GATT. Mexico also protested the measure as an extraterritorial regulation of its fishing industry, imposed by the United States.

The Tuna-Dolphin Case turned on two key issues. First, can one government tell another government what its environmental regulations should be? Second, do trade rules permit one government to take action against another government regarding the means used to produce goods as opposed to the quality of goods themselves? The answer to both questions is no. The GATT panel hearing this case agreed with Mexico in that the United States attempted to impose American law outside its jurisdiction. The panel held that the exception per GATT, article 20 (b), could not be used to protect the environment outside U.S. territory. Furthermore, the panel also ruled on the "necessary" requirement of the article 20 exceptions. They held that the measure had to be necessary to the product and not to its production process. In other words, the United States could ban all tuna, but not tuna captured by a certain method. The ruling was due in part to the discriminatory manner in which the United States implemented the measure and in part to GATT's resistance to cases where a major factor is the process of production. The panel also decided that the labeling of "dolphin free" tuna did not conform to GATT standards. In the end, however, the GATT ruling was never applied. Due to political implications from negotiations with Mexico over the North American Free Trade Agreement, Mexico decided in 1993 not to pursue the case.

A similar case was brought against the United States in 1994 by the European Union, on grounds that these U.S. sanctions involved unlawful extraterritorial application of national measures for conservation reasons. While the GATT panel did not question or impugn the legitimacy of U.S. conservation motives, it did agree that the U.S. embargoes were intended to force other states to change their policies and, as such, were not permissible under the GATT instrument. Thus, the U.S. action was in violation of its commitment to free trade under GATT.[8]

The second dispute involves shrimp and sea turtles and may arguably be the most important environment-related case to come before the trade body tribunal. Thousands of sea turtles drown every year when they are caught in shrimp nets. The United States requires domestic shrimpers to use a protective technology called "turtle excluder devices," which are like trap doors through which turtles can escape from shrimp nets. In 1989, the U.S. Congress adopted section 609 of the Endangered Species Act and essentially banned the importation of shrimp caught by foreign shrimpers who do not use such devices. This United States–imposed trade embargo was expanded in May 1996 to include all shrimp-exporting countries, eventually affecting some forty states. In early 1997, India, Pakistan, Malaysia, and Thailand lodged complaints at the WTO, claiming that section 609 violated WTO rules.[9] On April 6, 1998, a dispute settlement panel ruled against the U.S. shrimp embargo, arguing that it represented the kind of unilateral measure that could jeopardize the multilateral trading system and thus could not be covered by article 20 of the GATT, which allows measures inconsistent with the WTO to be taken for environmental and health reasons. Moreover, the United States was acting in a discriminatory manner by giving Asian countries only four months to comply with the turtle-shrimp law while giving the Caribbean basin nations three years. In the Shrimp-Turtle Case, the panel found against U.S. legislation, because it was applied in a discriminatory fashion, not because of its environmental content.[10]

At first blush, these WTO rulings might appear to be anti-environmental. But they are not. The WTO/GATT rules do not permit one state to take trade action for the purposes of enforcing trade action in another country, even to protect the health of living creatures or exhaustible natural resources. If such national measures were lawful, then any state could assert trade restriction actions unilaterally on similar grounds, thereby producing confusion and inconsistent legal rules. Moreover, WTO dispute settlement panels cannot actually strike down national legislation; they can find laws to be inconsistent with WTO rules, and they can authorize compensatory retaliation by the complaining parties. Furthermore, the GATT panels did not pass judgment on whether U.S. laws were environmentally correct. Their sole task was to ascertain how GATT rules applied to the issue and whether U.S. laws were being applied with discrimination.

In rendering their decisions, the GATT dispute settlement panels were guided in the way they perceived economic actions and commercial agreements by two fundamental principles. First, the WTO is competent to deal only with trade. Second, regarding environmental issues, the WTO is solely concerned with questions that arise when national environmental policies affect international trade relations. In terms of environmental problems, arbitral solutions strive to uphold the principles of the WTO trading system. That is, an open, transparent, equitable, and nondiscriminatory multilateral trading system is vital to international and national efforts to protect and conserve environmental resources and promote sustainable development for all states.

International Financial Regulation

In the early 21st century, money is being globalized as increased trade, investment, and other factors launch torrents of funds into international channels. Worldwide currency flows likely exceed $1.5 trillion each day, or $550 trillion every year, two-thirds of which moves through four states—the United States, Germany, Japan, and the United Kingdom. Central banks use monetary reserves (foreign exchange and gold) to try to control exchange rates and reduce fluctuations. To accommodate the globalization of money, a parallel globalization of banking and financial services has occurred. Commercial banks hold more than $10 trillion in foreign deposits, with nearly the same amount in outstanding international loans. While no such thing truly exists as an international banking and finance system—since banks operate under the laws of the state in which they conduct their banking and financial business—international financial institutions assist in coordinating and facilitating this massive flow of money between states.

Banks play a central role in virtually all international commercial transactions. Payments between banks are the means by which a person in one country transfers value for goods purchased to a person in another country. Banks therefore supply the channels through which international commerce is conducted and consummated. Banks also contribute to the management of international commerce by providing customers with credit, settlement, and venture capital, mainly through loans and other financial services provided for international investments.

The present system of international banking and financing consists of two main sets of elements. First are private banks and financial institutions that operate internationally, and second are international financial institutions and organizations that are established under legal agreements concluded by sovereign states. The latter type of agency is not privately owned; rather, its funds are contributed by the member states in accord with their legal obligations to the organization. Though less extensive than private banks, international financial institutions and organizations still play an important role in international banking and financing. They may invest in international financial markets as private banks do, but their main function is to facilitate and support the economic development of member states. Preeminent among such international financial institutions is the International Monetary Fund (IMF).

The need for an organization such as the IMF became evident during the 1930s as the Great Depression ravaged the world economy. Thousands of banks failed worldwide; currencies became worthless; and unemployment numbers soared. International finance and world monetary exchange were also savaged. The lack of confidence in paper money precipitated a demand for gold, such that some states (such as the United Kingdom) were compelled to abandon the gold standard, a move that produced even greater uncertainty over the value of currencies. It became apparent to economists and government officials that only through an international mechanism could stability in global monetary affairs and the expansion of international trade be successfully achieved. Following much negotiation, the IMF was established at the Bretton Woods conference in 1944.

The Fund's legal authority rests on an international treaty called the Articles of Agreement of the International Monetary Fund, which entered into force in December 1945.[11] The IMF began financial operations in March 1947, with twenty-nine states as members. As of 2005, the IMF functions as an international organization with 184 member states. It promotes international monetary cooperation, exchange rate stability, and orderly exchange arrangements. In so doing, the IMF provides a forum for discussing international monetary concerns and gives temporary financial and technical assistance to governments to ease their balance of payments and adjustments. The Fund is not a development bank, nor a world central bank, nor an agency that can coerce its members. It is a cooperative institution in which members voluntarily join because they see the advantage of consulting with one another to maintain a mutual, stable system of buying and selling currencies.

Membership in the IMF is open to every state that conducts its own foreign policy and is willing to adhere to the Fund's charter of rights and obligations. Members give the IMF some authority over their payment policies, as these policies critically affect the flow of money between states. The exchange of money is the central point of financial contact between governments involved in the international trade process. Purchasing foreign currency is essential for importers, banks, governments, and any other institutions that need foreign currency to do business abroad. Widespread convertibility now permits easy exchange among most of the world's major currencies, which has allowed for virtually unrestricted travel, trade, and investment since 1970. The Fund operates to ensure that this remains the case.

The IMF exercises no effective authority over the domestic economic policies of its member states. Member states determine what policies the institution will follow. The

IMF can urge members to refrain from military expenditures and can allocate more revenues to public education and health needs. What authority the Fund does exercise comes in requiring members to disclose information on monetary and fiscal policies and to avoid putting restrictions on the exchange of domestic for foreign currencies.

Each member state contributes to the Fund a sum of money called a quota subscription. Quotas form a pool of funds from which the IMF can draw to lend to members in financial difficulty. Quotas also serve as the basis for determining how much the contributing states can borrow or receive from the IMF in periodic allocations of special assets, called special drawing rights (SDRs). In late 2004, the IMF operated with 212.7 billion SDRs, which was the equivalent to about $316 billion.[12] The more funds a member contributes, the more it can borrow in times of need. Finally, the quotas provide the means for determining the voting power of the member government. The richer the contributing state, the larger its quota, the heavier its weighted vote. For example, the United States, with the world's largest economy, contributes most to the IMF. In August 2003, the United States provided about 17.5 percent of the total quotas and has 371,743 votes (37,149 SDRs from a total of 212,794). Seychelles, with the world's smallest quota, contributes 0.004 percent and receives 338 votes. The most recent state to join the IMF is Timor-Leste on July 23, 2002. It contributes 8.2 million SDRs (0.004 percent of the total), totaling 332 votes.[13]

Specific policy decisions are taken by the IMF's Board of Governors, with one governor coming from each member state. Twenty-four executive directors meet three times per week to supervise implementation of the policies made by the Board of Governors. The executive board usually operates through the formation of consensus among its members, a practice that minimizes confrontation on sensitive issues and promotes acceptance of final decisions.

The main purpose of the IMF is to provide loans to countries experiencing balance-of-payment difficulties to enable such countries to restore conditions for sustainable economic growth. Countries in difficulty obtain foreign currency from the IMF in exchange for their own, which they must repay within three to five years. Such financial assistance provided by the IMF allows governments to rebuild their international reserves, stabilize their currencies, and continue paying for imports without having to impose trade restrictions or capital controls. Unlike development banks, the IMF does not lend for specific projects. IMF loans are normally provided under a so-called arrangement, which stipulates what conditions the country must meet to secure the loan. Arrangements are based on economic programs formulated by governments of states seeking loans in consultation with the IMF. If approved by the executive board, loans are then released in phased installments as the program is carried out. Each loan agreement made between the IMF and recipient member governments constitutes a specific set of legally binding obligations between parties.

The 1990s presented the IMF with daunting challenges and stimulated interest in ensuring that the IMF's mechanisms were able to comport with an interdependent world of integrated global markets for goods, services, and capital. Early in the decade, the IMF began a massive campaign to assist the countries of Central Europe, the Baltic states, Russia, and other new states formerly part of the Soviet Union in shifting from centrally planned economies to market economies. In early 1995, a financial crisis in Mexico necessitated that the IMF allocate a package of $17.8 billion in assistance to bolster international monetary confidence and stop contagion from spreading to other countries. The outbreak of the Asian financial crisis in late 1997 prompted the IMF to give record loans of $20.9 billion to Korea, $11.2 billion to Indonesia, and $4.0 billion to Thailand. In July 1998, serious economic and financial disruptions in Russia led to its receiving an $11.2 billion loan, which augmented a previous $9.2 billion IMF loan extended in March 1996. In the wake of these financial crises, the IMF is currently engaged in strengthening surveillance of members' financial policies, with a view to ensuring that financial data of member governments are accurate, timely, and transparent.

The International Bank for Reconstruction and Development—the World Bank—is a United Nations specialized agency created in 1944 at the Bretton Woods conference. It was set up to finance projects that further economic development of member states, and it began operation in 1946. In the postwar era, the Bank made loans for the reconstruction of Western Europe, though in the late 1950s its attention shifted to loans for economic development in Africa, Asia, the Middle East, and Latin America.

The World Bank has 184 member states, each of which must first join the International Monetary Fund. Member governments become shareholders in the Bank, though they do not hold equal decision-making weight within the organization. The Bank is self-sustaining and maintains a profit on its lending activities. It is controlled by its Board of Governors, one governor from each member state. Votes are allocated according to capital subscription. Ordinary dealings are conducted by the Bank's Executive Board of Directors, who constitute the chief decision makers for the Bank's work. The executive board comprises twenty-two members, five of which are appointed by the five leading contributors to the Bank—the United States, Japan, Germany, France, and the United Kingdom. They hold the most authority. The other seventeen board members are nominated and elected by the remaining member states.

The World Bank receives its money from subscriptions paid by member countries, from bond revenues of world financial markets, and from net earnings on the bank's assets. The ethos of the Bank is straightforward. States that are open to international trade, practice diversification, attract foreign investment, and adhere to free market principles are most likely to sustain growth. By encouraging governments to pursue capitalist economic management and by attracting private investment, national economies will grow and poverty will be eradicated. Much of the Bank's loan revenue therefore goes to efforts that strengthen national banks and capital markets and to projects intended to create efficient, corruption-free public institutions. In addition, funds are allocated to projects in states where private investors are unwilling to invest in infrastructure, especially in service sectors such as water supply and sanitation that have a heavy impact on the lives of the poor. Criticism that World Bank–financed projects were environmentally destructive led the Bank to establish in 1990 an environmental fund that provides low interest rates for developing countries. In addition the Bank created an environmental inspection panel to ensure, first, that projects will meet minimum environmental standards and, second, that the borrowing government will conduct environmental assessments to verify that bank-financed projects are environmentally sound and sustainable. These environmental assessments evaluate the risks and benefits of a project and consider the project's impact on local air, water, and land; on human health and safety; on social aspects, such as involuntary resettlement, indigenous peoples, and cultural property; and possible transboundary environmental repercussions. This policy is considered key to the Bank's polices for protecting the lives and culture of the peoples in a potential recipient state.

In 2003 the World Bank lent $18.5 billion to client states. It is no less important to realize that the World Bank is the product of an international legal instrument, the Articles of Agreement of the International Bank for Reconstruction and Development,[14] to which all member governments must formally commit themselves. Legal obligations flow reciprocally from this relationship. Moreover, each loan that the Bank makes to a member government constitutes an international legal transaction, with obligatory rights and duties appertaining to the lending institution and the recipient government.

In 1996 the IMF and the World Bank launched a special assistance program, the Initiative for the Heavily Indebted Poor Countries, for those states most seriously indebted and for whom traditional debt relief mechanisms are insufficient. In 2000 the IMF and the World Bank approved debt reduction measures for twenty-three states, nineteen of them in Africa. These packages lift $34 billion in debt—about one-half of what these countries owe. Underpinning these debt reduction packages are legal obligations that assert the rights and duties of the lending institution and the borrowing government.

Closely associated with the IMF and the World Bank is the International Finance Corporation (IFC), which was established in 1956 to invest in private enterprises without government guarantee. The IFC is the largest multilateral source of loan and equity financing for private-sector projects in the developing world. It provides advice and technical assistance to private companies, and it helps to mobilize financing in international financial markets. In addition, the Bank organized the International Development Association (IDA) in 1960 to extend long-term loans at zero interest to the poorest developing countries. The IDA seeks to support programs that reduce poverty and improve the quality of life in these most destitute countries. The IDA lends only to countries that have a per capita annual income of less than $885 and that lack the financial ability to borrow from the World Bank. In late 2004, eighty-one states are eligible to borrow from the IDA—a constituency that comprises 2.5 billion people, of whom 1.5 billion survive earning less than two dollars per day.

These institutions—the World Bank, the International Monetary Fund, the International Finance Corporation, and the International Development Association—form the World Bank Group, which through international legal agreements provides loans and development opportunities to reduce economic disparities across and within countries.

International Sale of Goods

More than $8.1 trillion worth of goods and services are involved in international commercial transactions each year.[15] Not surprisingly, the international sale of goods presents difficulties that must be resolved through legal means. To avoid problems in advance, the parties must have between them a valid contract that articulates their respective rights and obligations, the goods involved (quantities and qualities), and a clearly stipulated price. Since the transacting parties are in different states, a contract for an international sale of goods often involves more than one legal system. Indeed, persons located in different states are usually subject to different legal systems. When a trade contract is made between parties so situated, the application of respective domestic laws of the two states may produce significantly different solutions, resulting in a conflict of laws. Similarly, if disputes arise, one party may prefer that the question be judged under its own domestic laws in its own courts, which will likely be unacceptable to the other party. Many parties prefer to determine the applicable law and competent court in advance and so articulate those terms into the contract of sale. These practices have led to the development of disparate, often inconsistent rules relating to the sale of international goods. In an effort to ameliorate these problems, the United Nations sponsored the negotiation and adoption of its 1980 Convention on Contracts for the International Sale of Goods to provide consistency in international trade law.[16]

This convention grew out of frustration arising during the 1970s from the lack of a uniform law for the international sale of goods. The two key instruments at that time were the Hague uniform laws, known more specifically as the Convention on the International Sale of Goods[17] and the Convention on the Formation of Contracts for the International Sale of Goods,[18] both of which were formulated at a Hague Conference in 1964. Though these conventions entered into force, they soon became internationally unpopular. Strong criticism was leveled at their exclusive focus on Eurocentric commercial traditions as well as their complex legalisms and broad application, which failed to deal with considerations affecting overseas shipments that seriously disadvantaged developing states. In 1966, the UN Commission on International Trade Law (UNCITRAL) was established by the UN General Assembly to promote the progressive harmonization and unification of international trade law.[19] In establishing UNCITRAL, the General Assembly recognized that globalization of international trade was occurring and that disparities in national laws concerning international trade created obstacles to the free flow of commerce. The commission became viewed as the vehicle by which these obstacles might be removed or reduced. The 1980 Sale of Goods Convention came as the product of its deliberations to negotiate a practical, uniform law that would command wide acceptance. The instrument establishes a comprehensive code of legal rules governing the formation of contracts for international sale of goods, the obligations of buyer and seller, remedies for breach of contract, and other facets of the contract relationship.

UNCITRAL has contributed other legal instruments for the regulation of international business transactions, of which five stand out. The 1974 Convention on the Limitation Period in the International Sale of Goods, which entered into force in 1988, establishes uniform rules governing the period within which legal proceedings arising from international sales contracted can be commenced.[20] The 1978 UN Convention on the Carriage of Goods by Sea (the Hamburg Rules) entered into force in 1992 and sets out a uniform legal regime that regulates the rights and obligations of shippers, carriers, and consignees under a contract of carriage of goods by sea.[21] Though not yet in force, the Convention on the Liability of Operators of Transport Terminals in International Trade was promulgated in 1991.[22] This instrument provides a set of legal rules regarding the liability of a terminal operator for loss of, or damage to, goods being internationally carried while they are in a transport terminal and for delay by the terminal operator in delivering the goods. In December 1988, the General Assembly adopted and opened for signature the Convention on International Bills of Exchange and International Promissory Notes.[23] This convention, though not yet in force, provides a code of legal rules for regulating new international instruments for optional use by parties to international commercial transactions, with the specific intention of overcoming major disparities and uncertainties that currently exist for instruments used for international payments. UNCITRAL Arbitration Rules, which were adopted in 1976, provide a comprehensive set of procedures on which parties may agree for the conduct of arbitral proceedings arising out of their commercial relations.[24] These rules are widely used in ad hoc and administered arbitrations.

Carriage of Goods

International sales of goods usually involve the transport of goods from one state to another by sea, air, or land. The carriage of goods by sea is governed by two major international agreements. First, the 1924 International Convention for the Unification of Certain Rules Relating to Bills of Lading (formerly the Hague Rules, now popularly known as the Hague-Visby Rules) has more than eighty states as contracting parties and seeks to unify rules governing liability of a carrier.[25] Second, the 1978 UN Convention on the Carriage of

Goods by Sea (the Hamburg Rules) currently counts twenty-eight states as parties and imposes wide liabilities on the carrier.[26]

The carriage of goods by air is subject to the 1929 Warsaw Convention for the Unification of Certain Rules Relating to International Carriage by Air, as supplemented and amended by five subsequent protocols.[27] There are currently 151 states contracted to this convention, which sets out procedures for processing documents of carriage (called air waybills) and the liability of a carrier according to fault or neglect. The carriage of goods by land is subject to two key instruments: the 1980 Convention Concerning International Carriage by Rail[28] and the 1956 Geneva Convention on the Contract of International Carriage of Goods by Road.[29] The former entered into force on May 1, 1980, and provides rules for delivery of goods and liability of the carrier when goods are transported on railroads between states. The latter instrument, which pertains to carriage of goods by vehicles traveling on highways between two states, defines procedures for consignment notes, liability, and redress in the event of damage. There are also instruments for regulating multimodal transport—that is, the carriage of goods involving more than one means of transportation. The UN Convention on International Multimodal Transport of Goods was adopted in Geneva on May 24, 1980, to unify rules governing the liability of a multimodal transport operator in the international carriage of goods involving at least two different modes of transport.[30] It is not yet in force. Noncompulsory guidelines for parties to define liabilities to each other are provided in the United Nations Conference on Trade and Development/International Criminal Court Rules for Multimodal Transport, which became effective on January 1, 1992, but are merely guidelines (unless included in the terms of an international contract between the parties).

Intellectual Property Rights

When the GATT was concluded in 1947, its drafters' attention focused exclusively on the sale of goods across international borders. Sale of goods was considered the most important, if not the only, form of international trade. Since then, international trade and commerce have experienced tremendous changes. The establishment of the WTO in 1995 marked a response to those changes, as the WTO agreement includes dozens of subagreements covering many new areas not treated by the original GATT—especially intellectual property, services, investment, and the transfer of technology. Governments have negotiated new legal rules to deal with the new commercial activities and arrangements that fall outside the conventional mode of trade—in particular, the sale of goods.

Intellectual property refers to creations of the mind: inventions; literary and artistic works; and symbols, names, images, and designs used in commerce. Intellectual property is divided into two categories: first, industrial property, which includes inventions (to which patents are applied), trademarks, industrial designs, and geographic indications of sources; second, copyrights, which include literary and artistic works, such as novels, poems, plays, films, music, drawings, paintings, photographs, sculptures, and architectural designs.

There is no such thing as an international copyright that automatically protects a creator's materials throughout the world. Copyright is territorial. Protection against unauthorized use in a particular country depends on the national laws of that country. International copyright protection can only be secured by obtaining separate and independent copyright protection in each of the states where copyright protection is sought or through international treaties and conventions that provide the mutual recognition and protection of the intellectual property of the citizens of those states party to such treaties or conventions. Most governments offer protection to foreign works under conditions stipulated in international copyright treaties and conventions—in particular, the 1886 Berne Convention for the Protection of Literary and Artistic Property[31] and the Universal Copyright Convention.[32] Administered by the World Intellectual Property Organization (WIPO), the Berne Convention remains the keystone among international copyright agreements. Though revised numerous times over the past century, the Berne Convention establishes rules for the protection of works, including the right of copyright owners to authorize reproduction, translation, public performance, communication, and adaptation of their works. The negotiation of the WTO and its Agreement on Trade-Related Aspects of Intellectual Property Rights (TRIPS) in 1995 substantially improved the international legal protection for phonograms and musical compositions. All WTO members are obligated to protect sound recordings for fifty years and to protect all recording released within the past fifty years. TRIPS extends copyright protection to computer programs, compilations of data, and cinematographic works; and performers have the right to prevent their performances from being recorded, reproduced, or broadcast without their authorization. TRIPS further establishes that, through the WTO, governments can bring actions against other states for infringement. Finally, the 1996 WIPO Copyright Treaty[33] improves protection for copyright owners over the exclusive distribution rights and commercial rental of digital fixed copies, as does the 1996 WIPO Performances and Phonograms Treaty for the distribution, rental, and importation of digital sound recordings or their broadcast for commercial purposes.

As the process of globalization intensifies and the international community grows increasingly interdependent, opportunities likewise expand for licensing and franchising corporate businesses between states. These arrangements are concluded through international contractual agreements, which are regulated transnationally by contract law and intellectual property law. For example, fast-food outlets—McDonald's, Kentucky Fried Chicken, Burger King, Pizza Hut—that operate in foreign countries are all franchise business operations subject to franchising laws, licensing agreements, and distribution requirements. These contractual arrangements involve transfer-of-technology agreements, in which the party who owns a proprietary right over the technology concerned transfers certain rights to use or own the technology to another party under agreed upon terms and conditions. While no formal international convention exists on the transfer of technology, several international instruments set out an international legal framework for the transfer of such technology. Among these are the 1883 Paris Convention for the Protection of Industry Property,[34] the 1886 Berne Convention, the 1891 Madrid Agreement Concerning the International Registration of Marks,[35] the 1952 Universal Copyright Convention, the 1967 Convention Establishing the WIPO,[36] the 1970 Patent Cooperation Treaty,[37] the 1989 Treaty on Intellectual Property in Respect to Integrated Circuits, and the 1993 TRIPS.

No international legally binding code of conduct for the transfer of technology has been concluded, although during the 1980s United Nations Conference on Trade and Development did prepare an informal instrument for that purpose. The conference's International Code of Conduct on the Transfer of Technology defines technology transfer; sets out principles for guiding its national regulation; provides criteria for regulating restrictive trade practices; outlines rights and obligations of parties; and articulates special provisions for developing countries, including moral principles that should be taken into account by a developed state when making its domestic law on technology transfer. The code is not legally binding on any state or corporate entity, largely because of the disadvantageous position in which they might be placed.

A new area for international legal concern arises in the regulation of electronic commerce (or e-commerce)—that is, the production, advertisement, sale, and distribution of products through telecommunications networks. Stock trading and banking constantly occur on the Internet, with trillions of dollars being electronically transferred worldwide each day between corporations, banks, governments, and individuals. E-commerce represents a new dimension of trade, based on telecommunications networks carrying commercial activities. E-commerce, particularly through the Internet, operates as a commercial enterprise. These developments challenge traditional international commercial law, especially within the realm of jurisdictional issues. For example, electronic transactions might require electronic contracts and electronic signatures, the lawfulness of which might not have been articulated in the contract laws of many states. If a service or product is sold internationally over the Internet, in which geographical location can the transaction be said to have taken place? Regarding consumer protection and jurisdiction, whose laws apply where? As is often the case, international law lags behind the development of technology, but some instruments are available to guide the regulation of e-commerce. Four soft law documents in particular contribute to the evolving development of the international regulation of e-commerce: the 1985 UNCITRAL Recommendations on the Legal Value of Computer Records; the 1996 UNCITRAL Model Law on Electronic Commerce; the draft UNCITRAL Uniform Rules on Electronic Signature, done in 1999; and the United Nations Rules for Electronic Data Interchange for Administration, Commerce, and Transport. While these instruments suggest rules and assistance in the use of e-commerce in international commerce, none is binding on any government. Consequently, for the foreseeable future, international regulation of e-commerce will come through national legislation and through the courts of individual states.

Foreign Investment

The international flow of goods and services remains a vital concern for all states. In 1913, the entire of flow of goods in world commerce totaled $20 billion. Since then, world trade and investment has created a web of financial interdependency, with total world foreign direct investment involving major stakes in foreign companies or real estate now well over $2 trillion, including $650 billion in direct investments in the United States. Like most international economic processes, worldwide movement of investment is not evenly distributed. Few investors are from Southern countries, and the flow of profits from investment mostly benefits Northern companies and states. About two-thirds of foreign direct investment capital derives from economically developed countries.

Increased international trade, financial arrangements, and monetary exchange have led to the intermeshing of national economic health and international economics. Domestic economics, employment, inflation, and overall national growth are dependent on foreign markets, imports of resources, currency exchange rates, capital flows, and other international economic factors. This situation has fostered increased degrees of global economic interdependence, governed by the expansion of international commercial law. It has also made necessary the creation of near-universal institutions to facilitate the regulation of international commercial transactions.

A significant area of international economic law arose for foreign investment after World War II, when many countries gained independence and drastically needed capital, technology, and managerial skills to develop their own economies. As a result of foreign investment, local companies and industries came under the control of foreign owners, and economic conflicts and tensions invariably flared up among foreign investors, owners, workers, and governments. During the 1950s and 1960s, *nationalization* and *expropriation*, which involve the seizure of foreign-held properties, became common practice in many host countries, especially in newly independent states in Africa, Asia, and Latin America. These seizures highlighted the need for, and the role of, international law to furnish investment protection for foreign investors.

The normal agents of foreign investment are multinational corporations (MNCs), which control assets (mines, factories, offices) in two or more states. In any case, the distinguishing feature of an MNC is its ability to control its subsidiaries in various countries. Since foreign investment aims to infiltrate foreign markets and use foreign resources, the MNC becomes ideal as a vehicle to attain such purposes. The MNC can not only provide needed capital and technology to establish a competitive position in a market, but it can also secure tax advantages by moving capital and resources to countries where the foreign investment climate is more favorable.

When an MNC invests in foreign states, it accepts the political risk that a host government might want to take over the invested property and refuse to provide "proper" compensation. For compensation to be proper, it must be paid with sufficient promptness, in an adequate amount, and in an effective form—that is, in dollars or some other form of exchangeable currency. The United States holds to the standard of prompt, adequate, and effective compensation, although the international view suggests that "just" or "appropriate" are more accepted as indicators of compensation.

The terms *nationalization* and *expropriation* are often used interchangeably to mean a taking, followed by some form of compensation. Foreign takings of property may be compared to common law practices of eminent domain. A government takes property for some special use in the public good. More specifically, expropriation involves taking property in the host state owned by an investor, ostensibly for "a public purpose." The government accomplishes the taking by declaring that the investor is no longer the owner of the property being expropriated and that the act will be imposed by use of force against the investor if necessary. International law does not provide a remedy for domestic claimants in cases where expropriation of their property is done by their own government.[38]

Expropriation conflicts were frequent during the 1960s, beginning with the rather extensive takings by Cuba in 1960 and progressing through the 1970s in African, Asian, and Latin American states. Some takings were more selective, such as the Mexican expropriation of oil in 1938 and the Egyptian expropriation of the Suez Canal Company in 1956. In Chile, International Telephone and Telegraph operations were expropriated in 1971, the same year that Libya decreed its takeover of Bunker Hunt oil interests.[39]

Nationalization is generally distinguished from expropriation. Nationalization involves the taking by a host country of all the foreign investment of a particular industry—such as oil, insurance, banking, or mining—for the purpose of social or economic reform. Examples of nationalizations are seen in the seizure and takeover by Iran in June 1979 following the Islamic revolution of banking and insurance industries and the Chilean government's takeover of Kennecott Copper Corporation and Anaconda Copper Company in 1971. The lawfulness of nationalization can be complicated by differences in what governments perceive as constituting a public purpose and what should be required as compensation. This distinction holds true whether the property belongs to the state's own nationals or to foreigners. Regardless, the taking must be for a public purpose or in the public interest. Finally, an act of confiscation refers to a government's seizure of property without providing compensation, an act often done to punish an owner for personal reasons or for supposed deeds done to the state. Confiscation is normally viewed as a violation of international legal rules. Typical of such a case is Libya's taking of British Petroleum's holdings in 1973.

The purchase of investment insurance presents a simple direct option available to investors to reduce exposure to political risk. Available from various sources, political risk insurance typically provides coverage against such contingencies as currency inconvertibility, expropriation, and political violence. For example, some states provide government-sponsored insurance through agencies such as the United States' Overseas Private Investment Corporation (OPIC). As a self-sustaining U.S. government agency, OPIC sells political risk insurance for foreign direct investment, finances projects directly through loans, and furnishes other services to U.S. investors. Established in 1969, OPIC's chief objective is to promote American overseas private investment in sound business projects (and thereby improve U.S. global competitiveness abroad), create American jobs, and increase U.S. exports. Most other Western states have national insurance programs similar to OPIC—for example, the Export-Import Insurance Division of the Ministry of International Trade in Japan, the Treuarbeit AG in Germany, and the Export Credits Guarantee Department in the United Kingdom. Private insurance companies, such as Lloyd's of London, also compete with government-subsidized programs. Other private insurance companies offering political risk insurance include the Chubb Group, Citicorp International Trade Indemnity, Pan Financial, and the American International Group. Finally, a prominent multilateral agency, the World Bank's Multilateral Investment Guaranty Agency (MIGA), is actively involved with investment protection. Founded in 1988, MIGA aims to encourage the flow of investment to developing countries, with the objective being to provide a degree of security and incentive for what may be perceived as high-risk investments. An investor seeking coverage must be a national from a participating member state of MIGA.

Before investing in any country, an investor should carefully measure all risks associated with the proposed investment, including those political. One factor to be considered is the existence of special treaties in force between the host state and the investor's home state. Known as *bilateral investment treaties*, these instruments cover the circumstances under which each government will allow an investor from a foreign state to establish enterprises; the conditions under which the government may expropriate holdings from the other state; how compensation will be paid; and the methods of settling investment disputes between a state and the investors from the other state. That such treaties exist provides substantive evidence that a government intends to treat foreign investment fairly. Investors should also consider the host state's political and economic stability as well as its legal and regulatory framework, including domestic tax codes, investment laws, property laws, and intellectual property rights.

International law acknowledges the right of a sovereign state to retain full and permanent sovereignty over its natural resources and economic activities. Under the modern law of expropriation, a government may always expropriate the property of investors within its borders. For such expropriation to be lawful, that government must not discriminate against an investor; the taking must be for a public purpose; and the expropriation must be accompanied by full compensation, which should be prompt, adequate, and effective. To be sure, the law of state responsibility mandates the accountability of governments for violations of international legal rules and the requirements that they make reparation for such violations. When a state acts in violation of international law, the injured party may pursue remedies available to it under international law.[40] Acts of expropriation and nationalization necessitate compensation. Refusal by a host government to do so adequately constitutes a breach of international foreign investment law.

Following expropriation or breach of contract by a host government, an investor has the right to institute arbitral proceedings against the host state. Arbitration usually remains the only recourse for an investor to pursue remedies directly against the host state. Judicial proceedings are often not viable between a sovereign state and a national of another state, and litigation against the host state in the courts of the investor's state is unappealing since the host state's government is not likely to submit to another state's jurisdiction. The process of arbitration may also be less costly, more confidential, and more efficient than litigation before courts. This option reflects the international trend, as suggested in the World Bank's 1992 Guidelines on the Treatment of Foreign Direct Investment.

Two major forms of arbitration have proven to be of particular interest to investors conducting business with foreign governments: ad hoc arbitration under the rules of the United Nations Commission on International Trade (UNCITRAL)[41] and arbitration pursuant to the Convention on the Settlement of Investment Disputes between States and Nationals of Other States (the ICSID Convention).[42] The UNCITRAL rules have broad application in developed and developing states and are used, in modified form, in the United States–Iran Claims Tribunal, established in 1981 to resolve those disputes between U.S. nationals and the government of Iran arising over expropriations of U.S. investments in Iran. More than two thousand claims have been settled since the tribunal began its work.

To help cope with the rash of expropriations in the 1950s and early 1960s, the Washington Convention on the Settlement of Investment Disputes between States and Nationals of Other States was established in 1965 and entered into force the next year. At least 154 states in 2005 are contracting parties to this instrument. This convention establishes the International Centre for Settlement of Foreign Investment Disputes to deal with disputes arising out of nationalization or expropriation of foreign investment by local governments. Pursuant to the convention, the center provides facilities for conciliation and for arbitration of disputes between member states and investors who qualify as nationals of member states. Recourse to ICSID conciliation is wholly voluntary; however, once the disputants have consented to arbitration under the ICSID Convention, neither can unilaterally withdraw. All ICSID contracting states, irrespective of whether they are parties to the dispute, are required by the convention to recognize and enforce ICSID arbitral awards. Provisions on ICSID arbitration are commonly found in investment contracts between member governments and investors from other member states. Advance consent by governments to submit investment disputes to ICSID arbitration is stipulated in some twenty national investment laws and in over nine hundred bilateral investment treaties. Arbitration under the auspices of ICSID supplies a principal dispute settlement mechanism in four recent multilateral trade and investment treaties—namely, the North American Free Trade Agreement, the Energy Charter Treaty, the Cartagena Free Trade Agreement, and the Colonia Investment Protocol of Mercosur.

It is clear that the rapid development of foreign investment opportunities worldwide demands the availability of an adequate set of legal rules governing international foreign investment. A number of international organizations—among them the Organization for Economic Cooperation and Development (OECD), the United Nations Conference on Trade and Development, the International Monetary Fund, and the World Trade Organization—have engaged in developing universal rules for foreign investment as well as fundamental principles that might provide the foundation for a universal investment law. For instance, the OECD Declaration on International Investment and Multinational Enterprises was adopted in 1976. While it carries no formal legally binding weight, it remains the only formally adopted instrument concerning multinational corporate enterprises that carries sway, largely because most multinational corporations are from member states in the OECD.

Notwithstanding these risks, foreign investment grew rapidly in the 1990s, particularly after 1995, when the WTO began operation. The collapse of the Eastern bloc and the adoption of economic reforms by the Chinese government offered tremendous opportunities for foreign investors from industrialized countries. Within the WTO framework, members are obligated to abolish the use of trade-related investment measures (TRIMs), which offered more opportunities for foreign investment within the WTO. The TRIMS agreement in the WTO applies to investment measures related to trade in goods only; it does not apply to services. Since TRIMS concerns only existing GATT disciplines on trade in goods, the agreement does not deal with the regulation of foreign investment. Rather, it deals with discriminatory treatment of imported and exported products.

REGIONAL ORGANIZATIONS

Multilateral regional organizations play important roles in developing modern international economic law. Such multilateral actors and international conventions are inseparable, largely because every intraregional organization is founded by an international agreement.

A regional trade organization embodies an arrangement among states within a region for the purpose of fostering and strengthening economic and commercial relationships. The common bond of such an organization lies in the states' geographical connections and in the likelihood of heavy transborder trade. Regional trade organizations, such as the European Union (EU), the North American Free Trade Agreement (NAFTA), and the Association of South East Asian Nations (ASEAN), make important contributions to contemporary international commercial law.

The European Union

The European Union (EU), consisting of twenty-five states—Austria, Belgium, Cyprus, Czech Republic, Denmark, Estonia, Finland, France, Germany, Greece, Hungary, Ireland, Italy, Latvia, Lithuania, Luxembourg, Malta, Netherlands, Poland, Portugal, Slovakia, Slovenia, Spain, Sweden, and the United Kingdom—represents the most powerful and legally sophisticated regional trade organization functioning today. The history of the EU traces back a half century, with the establishment in 1952 of the European Coal and Steel Community among six countries: Belgium, France, Germany, Italy, Luxembourg, and the Netherlands. In 1957, these same six states concluded the European Economic Community Treaty[43] and the European Atomic Energy Community Treaty (Euratom Treaty),[44] together known as the Treaties of Rome. The evolution of the EU continued throughout the 1960s. Acknowledging a need for more uniform policies, these same states concluded the Merger Treaty in 1965 to form the European Economic Community.[45] The Merger Treaty integrated the three communities through four common institutions: the Council of Ministers, the Commission, the European Parliament, and the European Court of Justice. In 1986 the Single European Act was adopted to promote the concept of a European Union and thereby signal wider cooperation among the member governments.[46] During the 1990s, the Treaty on European Union (or Maastricht Treaty) was concluded, entering into force on November 1, 1993.[47] This agreement substantially amended the Merger Treaty to strengthen integration within the organization and streamline its legal framework. From this new legal arrangement, the European Economic Community became the European Community, as the word *economic* was dropped to indicate the broader scope of cooperation among its members, inclusive of monetary and fiscal considerations. With the move during the 1990s toward coordinating national policies on political, social, and economic issues, the European Community evolved into its present form: the European Union.

In 2005, the European Union contains an aggregate population of over 455 million citizens and produces a gross regional product exceeding $7 trillion. It remains the largest market for exports from the United States. No other regional legal regime can rival the EU in detail of legal rule making and in the extent to which its members have achieved economic and political integration. The tasks of the Union currently involve creation of an economic and monetary union, with an emphasis on price stability.

The EU seeks to enhance economic development of its member states, an objective being accomplished through a series of strategies that include

1. the pursuit of trade and economic growth, a common customs tariff and commercial policy toward non-EU countries, and the elimination of tariffs and quotas within the community;
2. the abolition of internal obstacles to the free movement of persons, services, and capital;
3. the adoption of common agricultural, fisheries, and transport policies; and
4. the harmonization of laws of member states to ensure proper functioning of the Common Market.

Specific areas of EU policy are manifold and include competition, taxation, government contracts, state monopolies, free movement, transportation, agriculture, dumping practices, state subsidies, regional development, commercial policy, trade relations, social policy, and promotion of the European Investment Bank.

As the principal organ of the EU, the Council of Ministers has ultimate decision-making power. The Council functions as a plenary body that consists of representatives from the ruling governments of all member states. It primarily coordinates economic policies of member states to fulfill the 1957 Treaties of Rome and exercises important authority in approving legislation and international agreements. Since enactment of the Maastricht Treaty, the council's role has been extended to foreign, security, and home affairs.

The Commission, the executive organ of the EU, has twenty commissioners appointed by the Council for five-year terms. Commissioners neither represent their states nor take orders from the governments of member states. Their allegiance is supposed to be to the Commission. The Commission exercises considerable power in running the daily operation of the EU. It has sole authority for administering the single market, supervises the execution of EC legislation, formulates EC competition policy, brings proceedings before the European Court of Justice, and serves as guardian of the treaties. In this regard, the Commission retains authority to render law enforcement decisions, formulate legislative proposals for the council, and act in situations that involve overriding public interest. The Merger Treaty enables the Commission to enforce, through the European Court of Justice, observance of treaty provisions and secondary law by other EU institutions, member governments, and even individuals. In this way, the Commission acts as an aggressive prosecutor of European Union law. The Commission remains the only European body that proposes and drafts EU legislation. Proposed legislation is submitted to the Council for adoption and can be amended only with unanimous Council consent. The Council is obligated to consult and cooperate with the European Parliament before enacting legislation.

The European Parliament represents an institution in evolution. The Parliament has historically played an advisory and supervisory role, rather than a legislative one, though it reflects the kaleidoscope of European politics. Since 1979, its seven hundred members have been elected by direct vote of the citizens of the member states, with the number of members apportioned roughly to the population of each country. Since enactment of the Maastricht Treaty, the European Parliament has shared decision-making power with the Council in that both bodies must agree, or at least agree to compromise, on a draft law. This gives to the Parliament real legislative authority tantamount to a veto. In addition, the Commission, its president, and all commissioners must secure approval by the parliament before taking office. The Parliament also exercises substantive budgetary authority, and it must endorse any international agreement having budgetary implications for the EU.

The European Court of Justice (ECJ) embodies the supreme judicial authority and final arbiter of EU legal matters and may exercise full jurisdiction over all member states, their citizens, and corporations within those territories. The Court is expected to observe law, through its interpretation and application of the Merger Treaty, an objective that has been construed by the ECJ to include enforcement of international and customary law as well as regional law. The Court is composed of twenty-five judges, one from each member state, who are appointed for six-year terms. For efficiency, the Court now operates through a grand chamber of eleven judges. There are also nine advocates-general, who evaluate and render advice on cases as opinions to the court. The Court operates independent of other European Union institutions and of the member states on matters concerning civil, administrative, and constitutional legal dimensions, exercising jurisdiction throughout the member states. The Court is given authoritative voice in the interpretation of EU law. National courts must observe and enforce EU law, but the ECJ remains the ultimate authority. National courts and law enforcement institutions are responsible for implementing judgments of the ECJ, such as the collection of fines or the prosecution of penalties against private enterprises. If a conflict arises between EU law and the domestic law of a member state, the ECJ has ruled that EU law is supreme.[48] National courts generally uphold this interpretation, though several national decisions have asserted that conflicts between EU law and national constitutional rights should be resolved in favor of the latter. In the end, EU law and domestic law coexist in that they are both enforced through national courts. Finally, as authorized by the 1986 Single European Act, a Court of First Instance is attached to the ECJ. Jurisdiction of this court is limited to actions by individuals and legal persons, with its main intention being to relieve the ECJ of some of its caseload.

The treaties establishing the European communities are more than international treaties among sovereign contracting states. They transfer sovereign rights concerning legislative, administrative, and judicial power from member governments to regional institutions. The Merger Treaty, for instance, allocates to the EU authority to make its own international agreements and treaties. In areas where member states have transferred "competence" to the EU, international agreements may be made only by the EU.[49] Since more transfers of competence are occurring each year, this amounts to a considerable transfer of sovereignty. European Union law includes the Merger Treaty, the European Economic Community Treaty, the European Atomic Energy Community Treaty, the Treaty on European Union, and all subordinate legislation. The remarkable fact is that member states accept union law as national law and apply it accordingly through their domestic statutes.

EU institutions normally legislate through regulations and directives. The Merger Treaty empowers both the Council of Ministers and the Commission to create such law for most regional policy. A regulation has general application; it is binding in its entirety; and it is applicable directly in all member states. Usually, a regulation is self-executing and creates rights and obligations for member governments and for their citizens as well. Most regulations concern agricultural policy, but some pertain to competition law. In contrast, a directive binds the member state to which it is addressed but leaves to that government the form and means of implementation. Thus, member states must often enact or amend their domestic laws or regulations to carry out EU directives. Such legislative instruments are used to harmonize national policies with common market concerns, such as tax systems, customs procedures, investment controls, labor mobility, products liability, environmental law, and so forth.

The Merger Treaty aims to achieve free movement of goods by the establishment of a customs union that eliminates intermember customs duties and other barriers to transnational trade. A common customs tariff for the outside world has also been established for EU members. The combined effect of removing internal duties and of creating a common external tariff has increased trade among member states while reducing trade with nonmember states.

The European Union has fostered certain freedoms and rights that portend considerable economic implications for its members. For one, workers have free movement from job to job within EU states, without discrimination based on nationality, type of employment, or other working conditions. Foreign workers from EU members are guaranteed access to the same social services as workers from the host member state. It is unlawful for an EU government to institute quotas or to require work permits for workers from other member states. "The right of establishment" permits an individual from an EU member state to take up business activities in any other EU state under the same conditions set down for its nationals. A third freedom concerns removal of restrictions from providing services across borders. To this end, the Council has adopted directives that free the transborder services of travel agents, tour operators, air and ship brokers, freight forwarders, and shipping agents, as well as some professions such as medicine and accounting. The Merger Treaty requires the removal of national restrictions on the free movement of personal and investment capital belonging to persons in member states. In addition, the EU has created the Common Agricultural Policy, which aims to increase productivity while ensuring a fair standard of living for farmers and stable markets, a common valued-added tax system, and a common commercial policy toward nonmember states. Included in the latter are uniform principles regarding tariff and trade agreements, fishing rights, export policy, and commodity support preferences for developing countries (many of which are former colonial territories).

North American Free Trade Agreement

The North American Free Trade Agreement (NAFTA) establishes the North American Free Trade Zone between Canada, Mexico, and the United States.[50] Concluded in December 1992, NAFTA entered into force on January 1, 1994. The agreement embodies a comprehensive 3,755-page document that contains specific rules on nine thousand categories of goods exchanged among the three states and on legal particulars for the free trade zone. As a legal instrument, NAFTA is permitted under article 24 of the GATT, which deals with customs union within the 1994 GATT. NAFTA remains consistent with the 1994 GATT so long as the three NAFTA states comply with their obligations under the WTO agreements. Unlike the European Union or Association of South East Asian Nations, NAFTA is a trade agreement rather than an organization. It intends to increase trade and investment among its partners through an ambitious schedule of tariff elimination and through a reduction of nontariff barriers, as well as by comprehensive provisions on the conduct of business in the free trade area. These include disciplines on the regulation of investment, services, intellectual property competition, and the temporary entry of business persons.

The North American trading bloc had its genesis in a free trade agreement in 1988 between the United States and Canada that produced the world's largest bilateral trade relationship. In August 1992, Canada, the United States, and Mexico announced their intention to create a free trade zone that would stretch from the Arctic Circle to Mexico's borders with Guatemala and Belize, forming the largest trilateral trade relationship in the world. NAFTA assumes profound economic and social consequence since it encompasses a trading bloc the size, wealth, and potential of which are unknown in history. The 420 million people in the NAFTA states produce more than $11 trillion worth of goods and services, and the dismantling of trade barriers and the opening of markets have fostered impressive economic growth in all three countries. By lowering trade barriers and by developing clear rules for commerce, NAFTA has expanded trade investment opportunities in the United States, Canada, and Mexico. From 1994 to 2000, the total volume of trade among the three NAFTA parties expanded from $297 billion to $676 billion, an increase of 128 percent. As the three economies grew, North America concomitantly became a magnet for foreign direct investment from around the world—a level that reached $12.3 trillion in 2000, or about 28 percent of the world's total.

The creation of NAFTA did not affect the phaseout of tariffs between Canada and the United States under the Canada–United States Free Trade Agreement. This agreement was completed by January 1, 1998, and by then virtually all tariffs on Canada–United States trade in originating goods were eliminated. Some tariffs remain in place for certain goods in each country's agricultural sector—for example, dairy and poultry for Canada; and sugar, dairy, peanuts, and cotton for the United States. NAFTA provided that nearly all tariffs be eliminated on trade in originating goods between Canada and Mexico by January 1, 2003.

As set out in article 102, NAFTA's objectives are clear. The agreement seeks to eliminate trade barriers, facilitate transborder movement of goods and services, promote conditions of fair competition, increase investment opportunities, provide adequate and effective protection of intellectual property rights, and implement and apply its rules effectively. Three fundamental principles are considered key for attaining these objectives through the operation of NAFTA's free trade zone. First is the national treatment principle, which ensures that a party accords to the nationals of other parties no less-favorable treatment than its own nationals and that it strives to ensure market access to, and equal protection of, goods, services, and investments within the NAFTA zone. Second is the most-favored-nation principle, which requires NAFTA states to grant one another equal status—that is, if one state offers a deal, privilege, concession, or benefit to another state, it has to do so for the remaining state. This principle operates as one of nondiscrimination within the context of NAFTA. Third is the broad principle of transparency regarding national laws and regulations, which guarantees a state's access to information concerning another state's select services, lawmaking, and management operations. While not setting out standards for the substance of law and regulations, the requirement of transparency does compel a government to consider its policies and the relevant law to ensure consistency with its obligations under NAFTA.

NAFTA's provisions liberalize trade in several ways. Tariffs are either eliminated or phased out over periods of up to fifteen years. Limits on investments are removed. Investors from any of the three countries are treated equally; currency is freely transferred at market rates; and performance requirements, such as maintaining export levels and trade balancing, are eliminated. Additionally, financial service institutions are permitted to establish foreign-owned institutions. Transportation regulations are liberalized such that today truck and bus operators have near unlimited access to the NAFTA countries. Finally, protection of intellectual properties is strengthened. This includes the protection of literary works, recordings, computer programs, and product and process patents. NAFTA also provides various means to enhance the flow of trade among the three countries, and special provisions are included to resolve disputes.

For implementing its provisions, NAFTA uses the Free Trade Commission (FTC), with a secretariat for administration and enforcement, as well as with several committees and ad hoc working groups. Formed by cabinet-level representatives of the three states, the FTC supervises implementation of NAFTA, resolves disputes concerning its interpretation or application, and oversees work of the committees and working groups. In these ways, the FTC establishes rules and procedures for NAFTA. Decisions are normally arrived at via consensus, and the FTC operates as a tripartite ministerial conference.

Established by the FTC to oversee NAFTA's operation, its secretariat is divided into Canadian, American, and Mexican sections and is primarily responsible for administering NAFTA's dispute settlement provisions. Even though nearly all trade in North America takes place in accord with the rules of NAFTA and the World Trade Organization, disputes are likely to emerge, given such a large trading area. When conflicts arise, NAFTA encourages the concerned governments to resolve their differences amicably either through NAFTA's committees and working groups or through other consultations. If no mutually acceptable solution comes about, NAFTA furnishes a variety of dispute settlement procedures. Under chapter 19, NAFTA provides for a system of binational panel review to deal with antidumping and countervailing duty matters. Chapter 20 relates to the avoidance or settlement of all disputes concerning the interpretation or application of NAFTA, through panel procedures similar to those in the WTO agreement. This ensures that free trade relations among the three parties are based on an established set of rules, as opposed to economic or political power. Chapter 11 also has special rules for dispute settlement via arbitration. A NAFTA investor who alleges that a host government has breached its investment obligations may seek recourse under various arbitral mechanisms, among them the World Bank's International Center for the Settlement of Investment Disputes (ICSID), the ICSID's additional facility rules, and the rules of the UN Commission for International Trade Law. Finally, disputes over financial services are handled under chapter 14, in which case their resolution is done by panels chosen from a roster of experts on financial services.

The Andean Group

The Andean Group, or Andean Common Market (ANCOM), was established in 1969 by the Cartagena Agreement to counter the economic clout of Argentina, Brazil, and Mexico and to reduce dependency on foreign capital. Members include Bolivia, Colombia, Ecuador, Peru, and Venezuela. Four ANCOM bodies exist today: the Commission, the Junta, the Andean Court of Justice, and the Parliament. The supreme organ is the Commission, which comprises one representative from each member state. The Commission is empowered to formulate regional policies; coordinate member states' developmental plans; and approve, amend, or veto legislative proposals by the Junta. The Junta functions as the administrative organ of ANCOM and is formed by three representatives.

While conflicts in national interests have blunted success of the Andean Group, the organization still adopts low tariffs and nontariffs on certain goods sold and manufactured within the membership and attempts to coordinate the economic policies of member states. Since 1989, members have cooperated extensively in formulating joint policies concerning trade relations, finance, technological assistance, investment, and multinational enterprises.

Association of South East Asian Nations

The Association of South East Asian Nations (ASEAN) was established through the Bangkok Declaration of 1967 by Indonesia, Malaysia, the Philippines, Singapore, and Thailand, promoting peace, stability, progress, and prosperity in Southeast Asia.[51] In January 1984, Brunei Darussalam was admitted as a member, as were Vietnam in July 1995, Laos and Myanmar in July 1997, and Cambodia in April 1999. With its Secretariat in Jakarta, ASEAN is a regional trade organization of ten countries and a population of five hundred million. Its organization takes the shape of the functions it wishes to perform. Meetings and committees are organized to implement various agreements reached by governments of the member states. The present structure of ASEAN assumes three levels of organization: government meetings, functional committees, and the Secretariat. Decisions are made by meetings at the government level and are implemented through the committees and the Secretariat.

When officials from ASEAN states convene to decide policy, they do so as well for their own governments. The highest authority in ASEAN resides in the meeting of ASEAN heads of government, known as the ASEAN Summit. These summits meet formally every three years and at least once informally during the interim to set initiatives for future ASEAN activities. Several functional committees convene within ASEAN and are supposed to implement specific decisions of ASEAN members.

To set out directions for economic cooperation and integration, the economic ministers of ASEAN states convene annually. Meetings of ministers in other fields—such as health, environment, labor, social welfare, education, science and technology, and justice and law—are held as necessary to draw up cooperative programs. Support for these ministerial bodies comes from 29 committees and 122 technical working groups.

Among tasks critical to these committees is the negotiation and drafting of new legal agreements for ASEAN. Included among those promulgated are the 1976 Treaty on Amity and Cooperation in Southeast Asia, the 1992 ASEAN Agreement on the Common Effective Preferential Tariff Scheme for the ASEAN Free Trade Area, the 1992 Framework Agreement on Enhancing ASEAN Economic Cooperation, the 1995 ASEAN Framework Agreement on Intellectual Property Cooperation, the 1995 Treaty on the Southeast Asian Nuclear Weapon-Free Zone, the 1995 ASEAN Framework Agreement on Services (and its 1997 and 1998 protocols), the 1998 ASEAN Framework Agreement on the Facilitation of Goods in Transit, the 1998 ASEAN Framework Agreement on Mutual Recognition Arrangements, and the 2000 e-ASEAN Framework Agreement regarding information and communications technology.

ASEAN's Secretariat, established at the 1976 Bali Summit by an agreement among the member states' foreign ministers, functions to enhance coordination and implementation of policies, projects, and activities of ASEAN bodies. The Secretariat's structure was revised in 1992 such that it now has four bureaus: one dealing with trade, investment, industry, tourism, and infrastructure; one with economic and functional cooperation; one with finance; and one with program coordination and external relations.

The member states of ASEAN do not seek to transform the organization into a political union under a central supranational authority. Each ASEAN member still continues to function as a sovereign state in accord with its national identity. ASEAN aspires to promote regional economic integration through binding its members into a liberal trading framework, as it eliminates intraregional tariffs and nontariff trade barriers, banishes restrictions on services, and binds its member states through an energy, transport, and communications infrastructure. Three long-term projects highlight the infrastructure aspiration: the ASEAN Power Grid, the Trans-ASEAN Gas Pipeline Network, the ASEAN Highway Network, and the Singapore–Kunming Rail Link. In telecommunications, ASEAN is working on integrating regional broadband interconnectivity and the creation of a comprehensive action plan for developing an ASEAN e-space for electronic commerce. ASEAN is more than merely an economic organization. Its members are expected to cooperate in areas of regional security and stability and to foster international relationships with other multilateral organizations and states.

INTERNATIONAL COMMODITY AGREEMENTS

Producers of at least ten natural commodities have sought to unite into producer organizations through special legal agreements. Briefly, these commodities include the following:

Petroleum. The Organization of Petroleum Exporting Countries (OPEC) was established in 1960 pursuant to an agreement by Iran, Iraq, Kuwait, Saudi Arabia, and Venezuela. Presently consisting of thirteen oil-exporting countries—the five original members plus Algeria, Ecuador, Gabon, Indonesia, Libya, Nigeria, Qatar, and the United Arab Emirates—OPEC acts internationally as an oil cartel. At its headquarters in Vienna, Austria, OPEC members meet in regular sessions and decide national production quotas and the prices of oil produced by its members. A sister organization, the Organization of Arab Petroleum Exporting Countries (OAPEC), was established at the Second Arab Oil Congress in 1968. It consists exclusively of oil-exporting Arab countries and counts as founding members Libya, Kuwait, and Saudi Arabia. Headquartered in Kuwait, the organization later extended membership to Algeria, Abu Dhabi, Bahrain, Dubai, the United Arab Republic, Iraq, Egypt, and Syria. It was OAPEC that was responsible for imposing the Arab oil embargo against the United States, the Netherlands, Portugal, South Africa, and Israel during the October 1973 war in the Middle East.[52]

Natural rubber. The International Rubber Organization, headquartered in Kuala Lumpur, Malaysia, was established in 1980 as the intergovernmental body to administer provisions in, and to supervise operation of, the 1979 International Rubber Agreement as subsequently renewed in 1987 and 1995.[53] The 1995 instrument, which entered into force on February 14, 1997, seeks to achieve a balance growth between the demand for and supply of natural rubber.[54]

Cocoa. The International Cocoa Organization was established in 1973 to administer the first International Cocoa Agreement as well as its successor agreements of 1975, 1980, 1986, and 1993.[55] These agreements, concluded among forty-two governments of cocoa-producing and cocoa-consuming countries, aim to balance cocoa supply and demand and thereby contribute to stabilizing prices in the cocoa economy. The 2001 International Cocoa Agreement was concluded and provisionally entered into force in 2002.[56]

Coffee. The International Coffee Organization, formed by member states who export and import coffee, administers the 2001 International Coffee Agreement, the most recent coffee instrument.[57] The first coffee agreement, promulgated in 1962, was designed to halt the decline in coffee prices by fixing import quotas for each producing country. The International Coffee Organization was thus set up in London in 1963 because of the tremendous international economic importance of coffee. At least sixty countries produce coffee, an industry that employs millions of people and, for some, can account for as much as 80 percent of total export earnings. The forty-five exporting members of the organization account for 97 percent of world coffee production, and the twenty importing members consume nearly 70 percent of the coffee produced.[58]

Wheat and grains. The International Grains Agreement, with twenty-three states in 2004 contracting as parties, consists of the 1994 Grains Trade Convention and the 1994 Food Aid Convention. It entered into force on July 1, 1995.[59] The International Grains Agreement is administered by the International Grains Council, an intergovernmental forum for cooperation on wheat and coarse grain matters. The Grains Trade Convention provides for information sharing, analyses, and consultations on grain market and policy developments. Under the Food Aid Convention, eleven donor countries pledge to provide, every year, either specified amounts of food aid to developing countries in the form of grain suitable for human consumption or cash to buy suitable grains in recipient countries. The International Grains Council's Secretariat, based in London since 1949, also administers the Food Aid Committee, created under a 1999 Food Aid Convention. The Grains Trade Convention applies to trade in wheat, coarse grains, and related products. It also seeks to further international cooperation in all aspects of grain trade; to promote expansion, openness, and fairness in the grains sector; to contribute to grain market stability; and to enhance world food security. These objectives are sought by improving market transparency through information sharing, analysis, and consultation on grain market and policy developments.

Jute. The International Jute Organization was responsible for administering the 1989 International Agreement on Jute and Jute Products, which expired on April 11, 2000.[60] At its end, the organization had twenty-five members, including the three largest exporting countries (Bangladesh, India, and Nepal) and twenty-two importing countries. On March 13, 2001, the Agreement Establishing the Terms of Reference of the International Jute Study Group was adopted by the UN Conference on Jute and Jute Products, though in late 2004 only four parties (Bangladesh, the European Community, India, and Switzerland) have contracted to it.[61]

Tin, lead, and zinc. The first International Tin Agreement was negotiated in 1956 as a price stabilization agreement.[62] It created a buffer stock of tin and sought to sustain price levels through the International Tin Council, which bought and sold tin on the world market. The sixth tin agreement failed in 1985 when the Council's resources were insufficient to halt the fall in tin prices. It was replaced by the Association of Tin Producing Countries, which operates an export quota system. The International Lead and Zinc Study Group is an intergovernmental organization created by the United Nations in 1959. With twenty-eight members, the group provides opportunities for regular consultations on the international trade of lead and zinc, especially that regarding supplies of concentrates and refined metals, world market conditions, and analyses of foreign trade difficulties.[63]

Olive oil. The International Olive Oil Council, with twenty-three members (including the European Union), is the intergovernmental organization responsible for administering the 1956 International Agreement on Olive Oil and Table Olives and was set up under the agreement's article 21.[64] Subsequent agreements on olives were negotiated in 1963 and 1979, with the most recent version coming in 1986. Known as the International Agreement on Olive Oil and Table Olives, it entered into force on December 1, 1988. Extended by the Council four times since then, its most recent expiration came in December 2002.

Sugar. The first International Sugar Agreement was negotiated in 1968, and successor agreements followed in 1973, 1977, 1984, and 1987. The instrument's most recent version, the 1992 International Sugar Agreement, entered into force in December 1996 and presently counts forty-four states as contracting parties.[65] Created by the 1968 sugar instrument and based in London, the International Sugar Organization is the intergovernmental body responsible for administering the International Sugar Agreement and for improving conditions on the world sugar market, through debate, analysis, special studies, and transparent statistics. Today the fifty-eight member states of the organization represent 75 percent of world sugar production, 55 percent of world sugar consumption, 90 percent of world exports, and nearly 60 percent of imports.[66]

Tropical timber. The International Tropical Timber Agreement, adopted in Geneva in January 1994 by the United Nations Conference on Tropical Timber, entered into force in January 1997.[67] With sixty states in 2004 as contracting parties, it is the successor agreement to the 1983 International Tropical Timber Agreement, which expired on March 31, 1994. The 1994 Timber Agreement has been extended through December 31, 2006, and aims, first, to promote among its members international cooperation and policy development on the use and sustainability of timber resources; and, second, to contribute to the expansion and diversification of international trade in tropical timber by improving conditions in international markets. The International Tropical Timber Organization, created by the 1983 International Tropical Timber Agreement, is headquartered in Yokohama, Japan. It administers the 1994 Timber Agreement and provides opportunities for consultation among producer and consumer member countries on all aspects of the world timber economy within its mandate. The International Tropical Timber Council, which consists of all International Tropical Timber Organization members, is the highest decision-making authority in the organization.[68]

CONCLUSION

Rapid and profound changes in the world system make international economic institutions critical players in international relations and produce, as a consequence, legal and political repercussions. For one, the Cold War masked the march of globalization, a process that accelerated during the 1990s and early 21st century. Today, there is no alternative to the open, competitive economic system that encourages globalization, to a great extent through the processes of international economic organizations. Second, contemporary economic issues have acquired policy weight for most states equal to military security concerns. Governments seem prepared to push economic disputes and are not so concerned about the need for coalition unity against an external enemy, as was the case during the Cold War. Third, most governments recognize and embrace the benefits of globalization, particularly in terms of growth and investment. At the same time, governments are wary about the loss of their own power and freedom in the process. The shield of national sovereignty is being eroded and displaced by processes of globalization, through the authority of legal commitments to international institutions, as well as by the force of economic globalization itself. These changes translate into a profound realization at the beginning of the 21st century. For one, the IMF and World Bank today represent truly global organizations, with 184 members, such as the United Nations itself. Though still young, the WTO is rising in stature as a mechanism for governing international trade and commerce. Membership in the WTO has increased steadily—it now has 148 states as members, with more than twenty others aspiring to join. The WTO is evolving into a salient multilateral organization and could become the most significant body for governing global economic affairs in the 21st century.

International trade of goods and services between states and multinational corporations expands every year. For this vast nexus of complicated business transactions to occur with regularity, uniform rules of international economic law must be in place and must be observed by the participant actors. These rules have evolved in large part since 1970, although the continued development of new technologies makes necessary the constant production of new legal rules. The protracted nature of this process is well illustrated in the need for international economic law for regulating the myriad international financial transactions that occur through the Internet every day. International law is caught up in a constant race to keep pace with the development of new technologies that produce transnational impacts. While international interdependence and financial globalization are drawing peoples in different countries into close commercial ties and intimate economic relationships with one another, these same forces make it essential that rules guide those processes. This need highlights the fundamental purpose of modern international economic law—namely, to sort out and provide universal rules of the road for the increasingly heavy traffic of world commercial interactions that earmark global economic life the early 21st century.

IV
Conclusion

12

Looking Back to See Ahead: Globalization and Challenges to the International Legal Order

      Q The Process of Globalization
      Q Conclusion

In a CBS news report on April 28, 2004, 60 Minutes II revealed several photographs of Iraqi detainees being physically abused by members of the 372nd U.S. Military Police Company at Abu Ghraib prison in Baghdad. This public revelation unleashed a huge human rights scandal that called into question the willingness of American military personnel to abide by the protections afforded to detainees under the 1949 Geneva Convention on Prisoners of War. Moreover, it was revealed that as early as May 2003, the International Committee of the Red Cross as well as Amnesty International had issued reports to American military commanders that outlined more than two hundred allegations of abuse and mistreatment of Iraqi prisoners. Restraining detainees in painful positions, hooding, threatening them with guard dogs, and prolonged sleep deprivation violate the prohibition on torture and cruel, inhuman, or degrading treatment. Yet, no formal action was taken by U.S. government officials or military commanders to halt this mistreatment. The CBS revelations followed a classified March 3, 2004, military investigative report prepared by Major General Antonio Taguba alleging that "numerous incidents of sadistic, blatant and wanton criminal abuses were inflicted on several detainees" at Abu Ghraib between October and December 2003. The Pentagon later revealed that twenty-five prisoners had died in U.S. custody in Iraq and Afghanistan, including two who were believed to have been killed by U.S. captors. Six U.S. soldiers faced criminal charges over alleged abuse at the prison, and six others were given letters of reprimand that are expected to end their military careers. The commander of the prison at the time of the alleged incidents, Brigadier General Janis Karpinski, was suspended from duty. The political damage was considerable, in terms of undermining Iraqis' respect for Americans in the U.S. occupation of Iraq as well as for deflating U.S. claims of championing human rights and abiding by the laws of war. But the scandal could not be contained domestically. Within minutes after CBS revealed the incriminating photographs (thanks to the globalized network of media and telecommunications technology), the entire world knew of these humiliating abuses.

Iternational legal rules in the 21st century govern relations among transnational actors—states in particular but also intergovernmental organizations, multinational corporations, and even individuals. These rules, which for the most part are considered legally binding, have as their chief objectives to maintain peace, protect human rights, and promote societal betterment through international cooperation. It is important to realize that international legal rules function on three levels. At base, they are intended to operate as constraints on the actions of states; that is, states are expected to adhere to these rules lest they be considered as acting unlawfully. Second, such legal rules operate somewhat as an international barometer in that they provide governments with majority views of what kinds of conduct are acceptable and appropriate in relations between states; coincidentally, they serve as guidelines for acting on these viewpoints. Finally, the composition of international legal rules unites states and other transnational actors into an international system that permits vast numbers of contacts and interconnections, while also providing individual governments opportunities to pursue their own foreign policy agendas under the protective guise of national sovereignty.

THE PROCESS OF GLOBALIZATION

But the world today is caught up in a revolutionary transformation. We live in a rapidly globalizing world. At the roots of this pervasive globalization lie forces of change, especially the profound alteration of societal mores and norms that challenge traditional state sovereignty and the nature of the international state system.[1] Globalization refers to the ongoing worldwide integration of capital, currency, goods, people, advanced technologies, and ideas that are moving across national borders at an accelerating pace. Globalization makes the world ever more interconnected and interdependent and, in doing so, transforms foreign affairs. In multifaceted ways, globalization affects the people, goods, information, norms, and institutions of all states, for good and for ill. As technology continues to advance and as the world becomes increasingly economically interdependent, the forces of globalization will penetrate into societies in increasingly profound ways. It is here that international legal rules must be shaped and implemented if various dimensions of globalization have any chance to be regulated, or at least directed, in manageable ways.

The Economic Dimension

With respect to the need for international legal rules, globalization assumes different dimensions in differing contexts. First is the economic dimension, in which globalization is earmarked by revolutionary developments in trade, markets, foreign investment, and transnational business practices. The principal actors are corporations, investors, and private service industries, as well as the governments of states and multilateral intergovernmental organizations. While economic globalization permits multinational firms to organize and concentrate their efforts to accumulate wealth efficiently, it fails to promote social justice and thus contributes to economic inequities.[2]

The globalization of finance transnationalizes and centralizes financial markets through the integration of capital flows. This worldwide concentration of financial arrangements is producing a unified global economic system. The volume of transnational capital flows has grown dramatically, from $18 billion per day in the early 1970s to well over $1.5 trillion in 2004. At the same time, financial globalization is further expedited through private currency transactions, in which as much as $2 trillion may be exchanged daily to make profits through arbitrage. The international sale of stocks, bonds, options, and commodity futures through online trading has further accelerated the volume of transborder financial exchanges. The upshot of these developments in the quickening mobility of capital flows is that financial markets are less able to be centered in states and regulated by national governments. The globalized market system is becoming less susceptible to regulation by any one state or group of states in particular, as most states are unable to retain control over these international financial transactions. As the state's ability to control its international financial activities continues to be undermined, the global marketplace is becoming increasingly dominated by the power of private multinational corporations. At the same time, the developing countries are being adversely affected, since their incoming capital flows are in decline as the globalization of finance rises.

Within the economic realm of intellectual property considerations, globalization facilitates the conduct of various illicit activities, such as the trafficking of pirated movies, music, computer software, and medical drugs to the tune of $10 billion each year. New technologies boost the supply and demand for illegally copied products, as well as the spread of products bearing illicit labels of famous brand names. Counterfeit technologies and products sell for a mere fraction of the original, a practice that obviously depreciates the market share available to the legitimate company.

International legal rules are available to deal with this bootlegging boom, principally through the World Trade Organization's Agreement on Trade-Related Aspects of Intellectual Property Rights (TRIPS) and through international organizations such as the UN's World Intellectual Property Organization, the World Customs Union, and Interpol. The critical factor, however, rests with national governments and their willingness to enforce these rules on their own nationals and to permit these agencies to work as they are intended.[3]

The Cultural Dimension

A second dimension of globalization pertains to its impact on culture. This aspect derives from the technological revolution, with direct spin-offs from economic globalization. The impacts can be socially profound. Driven by Western values, these new technologies take on the character of so-called Americanization, at the cost of challenging or transforming a traditional society's cultural norms and social mores. This form of globalization is not welcome and usually breeds strong resentment against Western culture, especially among conservative people in traditional society.

A number of activities of globalization generate severe social and cultural repercussions on societies, especially in developing countries. Rapid and unrestrained flow of communication is a hallmark of worldwide globalization. Cellular phones, computers, and the Internet reflect salient symbols of globalization. No area of economics, politics, or culture is immune from the impacts of computer technologies. Increasingly pervasive use of personal computers and the Internet have produced a massive, global electronic web of people, ideas, and interactions through cyberspace—unfettered by national borders. The Internet has become an enormous generator for conducting business and for the transferring of wealth through e-commerce across borders. At the same time, it has also encouraged people around the world to rethink their cultural values and personal attitudes in the debate over maintaining a traditional society versus questing for wealth and modernization. While national legislation for regulating the content of information flow by computers on the Internet might exist in some developed states, there is at present no overarching multilateral agreement that purports to set universal standards for regulating these transnational electronic transmissions between and among all national societies.

If the 21st century can be described as the Information Age, it is due in great part to the pervasive and powerful role of the media, which is controlled by only a few corporate telecommunication giants. Most of these powerful media sources are concentrated in the Northern tier of wealthy states, and their broadcasts disseminate the influence of Western values and culture worldwide. It is the $800 billion telecommunications industry that serves as the vehicle for rapidly spreading information, ideas, and images worldwide. Neither national governments nor their states' borders can inhibit these telecommunications, although a prominent multilateral legal agreement does create a regime intended to end both government and private telecommunications monopolies in many states. The World Trade Organization's World Telecom Pact seeks to liberalize telecommunications services. This agreement, negotiated in 1997 and endorsed today by nearly seventy states, aims to create an international regime that opens the industry to the free market and fosters international cooperation to conduct such global transactions by legal rules.

Still another issue impinging on national societies and their cultures is the transnational transmission of fatal diseases. Public health is currently a greater priority than ever before, simply because so many of the challenges exert global impacts and require global responses to attain global solutions. Importantly, globalization not only intensifies—through information and media services—the awareness of health risks and the outbreak of pandemics, but it also deprives the world of health sanctuaries. In an interdependent, globalizing world, bacteria and viruses travel practically as fast as e-mail transmissions and money. The processes of globalization—through rapid, extensive transportation networks—link people around the world. More than two million people cross international borders each day, about one-tenth of humankind every year. Of these, one million people travel from developing countries to industrialized countries each week. Diseases often travel with them, unrestrained by national borders and customs officials. The instruments of globalization, particularly transportation services, enhance the potential for the speedy spread of highly infectious communicable diseases, especially the SARS virus, HIV/AIDS, malaria, and tuberculosis. Growing numbers of transnational migrations and refugees, the huge rise in interstate truck transportation to carry goods across borders, spreading urbanization, and the travel of millions of airline passengers make the proliferation of potentially fatal diseases swift, frequent, and difficult to control. In a profoundly real sense, the need to protect human health has emerged as a critical issue of national security for all states.[4]

The lead international agency for combating the negative impacts of globalization on human health is the World Health Organization (WHO). Since 1995, WHO has collaborated with governments and other international agencies to promote a comprehensive, global approach to health, with special focus on three diseases—HIV/AIDS, tuberculosis, and malaria. WHO estimates that more than ninety million healthy life-years are lost to HIV/AIDS each year, forty million to malaria, and about thirty-six million to tuberculosis. Nearly six million people worldwide die each year from these diseases.[5] To determine the drain of disease on national societies, a WHO study released in 2001 advocates harnessing the forces of globalization to reduce suffering and promote human well-being through investment in health as a contribution to economic development.[6] WHO has also organized alliances and partnerships between developing and developed countries to generate developmental assistance. Prominent among these cooperative enterprises are the Global Fund to Fight AIDS, Tuberculosis, and Malaria and the Global Alliance for Vaccines and Immunization.

The Political Dimension

Finally, globalization assumes a political dimension, which is influenced considerably by the rise of the United States as the sole preponderant superpower that seeks to transform authoritarian governments into peace-loving democratic states. The vast numbers of international and regional organizations, as well as the upsurge in transnational nongovernmental organizations, also contribute to positive political globalization as they function to promote international peace and cooperation. But there is a deeply negative side to political globalization, personified in the rise of transnational crime and terrorism. Globalization facilitates the conduct of various international criminal activities and transnational terror through sophisticated instruments of communication and transportation as well as by the exorbitant levels of potential destruction through the use of weapons of mass destruction. The devastation of the World Trade Center on September 11, 2001, highlights the stark reality of this threat.

Several other illicit international activities having political ramifications prosper from the accelerating processes of globalization. For one, the forces and technologies of globalization facilitate the annual trade in illicit drugs The global supply chain uses numerous means to transport drugs transnationally, from passenger jets that can carry shipments of cocaine worth $500 million in a single trip to specially constructed submarines that ferry drugs from Colombia throughout the Caribbean. To foil intelligence gathering, drug traffickers communicate by special cell phones and sophisticated financial structures that blend legitimate and illegitimate enterprises to facilitate money laundering and currency smuggling.

Another area in which the processes of globalization expedite transnational violence is the unlawful trafficking of weapons. Technologies of globalization empower the abilities of arms traffickers to sell small arms and munitions illegally around the world. The illicit arms trade accounts for more than $1 billion each year and during the past decade has fueled forty-six of the forty-nine most grave internal conflicts. In 2001, illegal small arms accounted for some four hundred thousand deaths, more than 80 percent of whom were women and children. No less of a concern is the illegal market for military technologies, including tanks, radar systems, and weapons of mass destruction. The collapse of the Soviet Union in 1989, the unlawful smuggling activities of Pakistani nuclear scientists during the 1990s, coupled with the rise of rogue governments (such as North Korea and Iran) who seek to acquire destructive weapons underscore the gravity of the proliferation of weapons of mass destruction.

The mushrooming of money-laundering activities has profited greatly from intensified globalization. The world economic system has a gross national product of some $400 trillion. In 2004, estimates of global money-laundering activities range between $800 billion and $2 trillion. Smuggling money, gold coins, and other valuables has accelerated markedly over the past decade, due in no small part to technological changes associated with globalization. The vast amount of electronic transborder currency transfers—coupled with the progressive sophistication of computers, the Internet, intricate financial schemes, and the integration of dirty money with legitimate funds—makes national and international regulation of international money flows increasingly difficult. Within the secretariat of the Organization of Economic Cooperation and Development, the G-7 Summit in 1989 in Paris established the Financial Action Task Force on money laundering to coordinate policies and laws among its thirty-one member governments. The list of forty recommendations establishes a multifaceted framework for anti-money-laundering efforts that is intended to be universally applied. These suggested policies provide a comprehensive set of measures to counter money laundering within the criminal justice system and law enforcement, the financial system and its regulation, and international cooperation. Once again, the policies and rules are available; the critical consideration is for national governments to implement them effectively and efficiently.[7]

States will undoubtedly encounter serious obstacles in attempting to thwart these criminal activities, thanks largely to the forces of globalization. Criminal networks are likely to exploit new technologies more quickly and effectively than governments are able to cope with tight budgets, bureaucracies, media scrutiny, and domestic constituencies. With international trade and commerce continuing to grow, more opportunities for concealment are being created for illicit activities.

The forces associated with globalization penetrate national borders through new information and communication technologies. The implications of this process are huge. The protective shield known as national sovereignty is eroding and becoming increasingly porous, a condition that allows external influences to penetrate and affect the societal character of states. National laws are not enough to control these forces. International legal rules for various activities associated with globalization must also be negotiated, adopted, and implemented if the impacts of these forces are to be managed in national societies.

Moreover, as globalization has expanded the range of financial, commercial, cultural, and social interactions among foreign countries and nationals, so too has it increased the opportunities for discord and friction among them. Globalization adds further complexity to the policymaking in areas that are clouded by moral ambiguity, regular uncertainty, and rapid scientific advance. The forces of globalization, among them the rapid dissemination of scientific knowledge and the international nature of technology, suggest that the world community should, as much as possible, coordinate the regulatory policy. That is far more easily said than done, given competing powerful interests and constituencies in various states.

With certain technologies, globalization creates an apparent need for a high degree of international cooperation. More so than ever, technologies and information can easily move across borders. Thus, if the regulatory goals are to contain or ensure the safe application of a given technology, some level of agreement between governments will be needed to control the development and flow of such technologies. In fact, globalization increases the need for an international approach to policymaking.

CONCLUSION

The early 21st century reveals an age of important change—legally, economically, and politically—and thus necessitates new chapters in the development of international legal rules. The pervasive forces of globalization may be pushing state governments toward a "Grotian moment," which calls for a new conceptualization of, or at least a revitalized respect for, international legal rules.[8] The state as an international actor is clearly not dead. Even so, the archaic notion of absolute state sovereignty—a concept that embraced the state as a singular and impenetrable player, free to act as it chooses on the international scene—no longer goes unchallenged. The forces of globalization and interdependence combine to make absolute state sovereignty in the 21st century more fiction than fact, if for no other reason than the economic and political impracticability of operating in foreign relations among thousands of other international actors.[9]

The specific changes in international law that occurred at an accelerating pace over the past half-century appear earmarked by three general developments. First, the scope of international legal rules expanded to encompass international organizations. Not only are the current 193 states subject to international law, but so too are the thousands of intergovernmental organizations and multinational corporations that operate throughout the international system. Most of these organizations, whether public or private, possess international legal personality, just as states do. They have international legal rights and responsibilities. Second, the breadth of international legal rules has grown in another way in that individuals are now included as being subject to particular legal constraints. The massive body of human rights law that developed since the Second World War supplies a testament to the efforts to impose on governments and their agents international legal obligations concerning their treatment of persons within their own borders. The international criminal tribunals for the former Yugoslavia and Rwanda, as well as the International Criminal Court, clearly highlight this development. Third, it must be realized that the sources for making and rethinking international law are expanding. Traditionally, it was the state that made international legal rules. Today this is no longer the case. The major engine for generating international legal rules in the early 21st century has become the intergovernmental organization—the United Nations, the European Union, and other regional organizations that operate on behalf of their member states. Not only do these agreed-on rules govern the conduct of organizations' member states, but they also regulate the internal operation of these organizations, their administrative procedures, and the terms and conditions by which they function internationally.

Generally speaking, international legal rules function to preserve order. That is, international law embodies a system of sanctioned regularity, a certain order in itself, which conveys expectations to the members of international society. International legal rules provide for the regularity of activities that can be discerned, forecast, and anticipated within the international community. Through international law, the attempt is made to regulate behavior to ensure harmony and to maintain international society's values and institutions.

To qualify as law, it is generally recognized that the system of international legal rules must possess certain fundamental characteristics. For one, a statement of a prescribed pattern of behavior must be evident. Second, an obligational basis approved by international society must be present. Third, some process for punishing unlawful conduct in international relations must be available. As essential facets, the measure of how well these elements interact in the modern context in large part determines the effectiveness of the international legal system as well as the extent of its actual existence and performance. As demonstrated throughout this study, international law does indeed qualify as a legal system—albeit a primitive, decentralized, and imperfect one. The body of international legal rules consists of a set of norms that prescribe international behavior, accrued from interstate treaties and conventions, customary state practice, general principles of law, and to a lesser extent judicial decisions and the writing of scholars and jurists. There are reasons why governments obey international legal rules—namely, to protect their national interests, to ensure reciprocity among the interactions of governments, and to maintain their prestige as respectable law-abiding members of the international community. Finally, the process of self-help exists as a means to enforce international legal rules and to punish unlawful behavior in the international community. Not only must governments know when their rights have been violated, but they also must confront the state that allegedly committed that illegal act and must compel it to make restitution for its wrongdoing.

International law prescribes the conduct for members of the international community and makes coexistence and survival of that community possible. Not surprisingly, then, international legal rules are pervasive and fundamental. They seek to regulate or lessen opportunities for conflict and confrontation, and they work to promote international collaboration and cooperation on a multifaceted scale. International legal rules are human-made. Governments of states in the international society in great part determine the nature of that society and formulate rules to meet those ends. Hence, the ingredients of international law are neither preordained nor immutable.

International legal rules do constitute a system of law. These rules are not a means for diplomatic maneuvering or rhetorical camouflage. International legal rules have form and substance, and they have been generally accepted by states in their dealings with one another. In this regard, international law is neither apolitical nor wholly formed by normativity or legalism. The fact is that international legal rules are the products of the international political process as conducted by governments—which are, of course, highly politicized actors.

International legal rules are crafted carefully and intentionally by national governments. As demonstrated over the past five decades, this legal system is a product of the times and of the national governments that operate in the international milieu. They can adapt, change, and evolve. Thus, international legal rules are not static; they involve a dynamic evolutionary process that is shaped by events and that actively influences events. Contemporary international legal rules reflect the nature of the changing world because they must respond to it. Flexibility therefore remains a chief strength of international law. Yet, paradoxically, this quality is often blamed for fostering one of international law's greatest weaknesses—namely, the lack of a formal centralized structure for codifying international norms.

In the end, however, the system of contemporary international legal rules must not be regarded as a panacea for prohibiting international conduct or as a brake on incorrigible governments. Rather, these rules provide internationally acceptable ways and means for dealing with global problems and conflictive situations. International law in the 21st century may not satisfy all national governments all of the time, nor can it supply every answer for ills of the world community. Nonetheless, it remains far preferable to the alternative of having no law at all. Likewise, it is far wiser for national governments to appreciate the functions of this international legal system than to overlook or disregard the mutual advantages that it provides. International law remains the best touchstone and the only consistent guide for state conduct in an increasingly complex, multicultural, globalizing world.

In the early 21st century, grave global problems have produced serious international concern. The crisis of economic development within Third World countries, the disintegration of states through ethnoseparatism and civil wars, forced migrations and millions of displaced refugees, transnational terrorism, overpopulation, transboundary air and water pollution, global warming, the spread of HIV/AIDS, depletion of the ozone layer, drug trafficking, the proliferation of weapons of mass destruction—none of these issues is amenable to domestic or unilateral resolution. If politically viable solutions are to be reached, international cooperation is essential. International legal rules supply proven ways and means to facilitate these collaborative international efforts. Indeed, in the search for global solutions to global problems, the system of international legal rules furnishes the best opportunities for accommodating national interests with international priorities.

In the final analysis, international legal rules do not fail in contemporary world society. Instead, it is the governments of states who fail the law whenever they disregard their legal obligations. Thus, the need to overcome the fundamental obstacle of self-serving sovereign-state interests remains the preeminent challenge for enhancing the effectiveness of international law in this new century. Given the evidence and profound lessons of state conduct in the past, this will not be an easy task.

Notes

CHAPTER 1

1. In his introduction to the *Principles of Morals and Legislation* (1789), Jeremy Bentham coined the term *international law,* although the phrase *law of nations* is often used as a synonym (from a translation of Emmerich de Vattel's famous work *Droit des Gens,* 1758). See Jeremy Bentham, "Principles of International Law," in *The Works of Jeremy Bentham,* ed. John Bowring (New York: Russell & Russell, 1962), 2:535–60. While convenient, the term *international law* is technically incorrect. *Interstate law* or *law among states* would be more accurate since world community rules and norms are made primarily by states for states—and not by nations, which refer to groups of people bound together by a common history, culture, language, and religion. In keeping with conventional usage, however, this work still will use *international,* with the understanding that it refers mainly to states. See also Thomas Barclay, "International Law," in *The Encyclopedia Britannica,* 13th ed. (1926), 14:694–701.

2. This is the argument put forward by the arch critic of international law in the 19th century, John Austin, in his convincing work *The Province of Jurisprudence Determined and the Uses of the Study of Jurisprudence* (London: John Murray, 1832; reprinted ed., New York: Noonday Press, 1954). See also W. Jethro Brown, *The Austinian Theory of Law* (London: John Murray 1906), 50–53. For thoughtful counterarguments to Austin's views, see Anthony D'Amato, "Is International Law 'Law'?" *Northwestern University of Law Review* 79 (1984): 1293.

3. See Morton A. Kaplan and Nicholas de B. Katzenbach, *The Political Foundations of International Law* (New York: Wiley, 1961), 31–35.

4. For an insightful theoretical examination of international legal rules, see Anthony Clark Arend, *Legal Rules and International Society* (New York: Oxford University Press, 1999).

5. See generally Anthony D'Amato, *The Concept of Custom in International Law* (Ithaca, N.Y.: Cornell University Press, 1971).

6. Often cited to illustrate reliance on custom is the case of the *Pacquette Habana.* In this case, the U.S. Supreme Court ruled that the United States was liable for the capture of Cuban fishing boats sailing under the Spanish flag, and it based its decision on customary law that coastal fishing boats and their crews are exempt as prizes of war. See 175 US 677, 44 L. Ed. 320, 20 S. Ct. 290 (1899). This practice was subsequently codified in article 3 of the Hague Convention XI of 1907, 1 Bevans 711, signed at The Hague on October 18, 1907.

7. To reject or undermine this principle is to invite chaos and anarchy. Treaties must be made in good faith. But special circumstances might arise that make performance impossible—for example, the outbreak of war. A mere change in international conditions is not sufficient to require the change in treaty agreements or the release of a party from its treaty obligations.

8. In the practice of states, it bears noting that the difficulty comes not in the principle of third-party intercession but in seeking binding remedies, such as arbitration and adjudication. States are reluctant to accept *compulsory jurisdiction* of international tribunals and are unwilling to submit to the court many disputes that are considered to hold high stakes for their national interests.

9. See J. Ralston, *International Arbitration from Athens to Locarno* (Palo Alto, Calif.: Stanford University Press, 1929); and M. Tod, *Greek International Arbitration* (Oxford: Oxford University Press, 1913).

10. See Sir Henry Maine, *International Law* (London: John Murray, 1890), 26–35; and Sir Henry Maine, *Ancient Law: Its Connection with Early History of Society and Its Relations to Modern Ideas*, 4th ed. (London: John Murray, 1870), 8–14, 49–53.

11. See *De Indis et De jure belli relectiones* by *Franciscis de Victoria*, Classics of International Law, ed. James Brown Scott (Washington, D.C.: Carnegie Institution, 1917); and Francisco de Victoria, *The Law of War Made by the Spaniards on the Barbarians* (1532).

12. Francisco Suarez, *De legibus ac Deo legislatore* (Treatise on Laws and God as Legislator; 1612), trans. James Brown Scott, Classics of International Law (Oxford: Claredon Press, 1944).

13. Pufendorf's major studies are contained in *Elementorum jurisprudentiae universalis libri duo* (Two Books on the Elements of Universal Jurisprudence; 1660) and in *De jure naturae et gentium libri octo* (Eight Books on the Law of Nature and Nations; 1672), each translated in Classics of International Law (Oxford: Clarendon Press, 1931).

14. Hugo Grotius, *De juri belli ac pacis libri tres, in quibus jus naturae et gentium; item juris publicae praecipua explicantur* (1625), trans. James Brown Scott, Classics of International Law 3 (Washington, D.C.: Carnegie Institution, 1925).

15. Peace Treaty between the Holy Roman Emperor and the King of France and their respective allies, at Westphalia, October 26, 1648. The texts of both agreements forming the Peace of Westphalia can be found in the Yale Law School's Avalon Project, at www.yale.edu/lawweb/avalon/westphal .htm (accessed March 1, 2004). See also Leo Gross, "The Peace of Westphalia, 1648–1948," *American Journal of International Law* 42 (1948): 20–41.

16. Hugo Grotius, *Mare liberum sive de jure quod Bataavis competit ad Indicama commercia dissertatio* (1609), translated in Classics of International Law (Washington, D.C.: Carnegie Institution, 1916).

17. See Christian von Wolff, *Institutiones Juris Naturae et Gentium* (Institutes of the Law of Nature and of Nations; 1750).

18. See Emmerich de Vattel, *Le droit des gens, ou principe de la loi Naturelle* (The Law of Nations; or, Principles of Natural Law Applied to the Conduct and Affairs of Nations and of Sovereigns; 1758), trans. C. G. Fenwick, Classics of International Law (Washington, D.C.: Carnegie Institution, 1916).

19. A more modern variety of this distinction between primary and secondary rules is provided by H. L. A. Hart, *The Concept of Law* (New York: Oxford University Press, 1961), 89–93.

20. See Alberico Gentilis, *De jure belli commenatatio* (The Law of War; 1598), trans. Coleman Phillipson, Classics of International Law (Washington, D.C.: Carnegie Institution, 1926).

21. To challenge Grotius, the English crown commissioned a British scholar, John Selden, to write a rebuttal. His product, *Mare Clausum sive de dominio maris* (The Closed Seas; or, the Dominion of the Seas), appeared in 1618 and was published in 1635. In this work, Selden contends that portions of the sea were lawfully appropriated by England. This remained the official British doctrine for a century, although freedom of the seas prevailed with governments and courts.

22. Richard Zouche, *Juris et judicii feciale, sive juris inter gentes et quaestionum de eodem explicatio* (Explanation of the Jus Feciale and of the Questions Concerning It, 1650).

23. Van Bynkershoek's major works are *De foro legatorum* (Jurisdiction over Ambassadors (1721) and *Quaestionum juris publici libri duo* (Two Books on Questions of Public Law; 1737), trans. Tenney Frank, Classics of International Law (Oxford: Clarendon Press, 1930).

24. *De dominio maris dissertatio* (Dominion of the Sea; 1702), translated in Classics of International Law (New York: Oxford University Press, 1923).

25. John Jacob Moser, *Volkerrecht* (The Law of States), 5 vols. (1778–1781).

26. Georg Friedrich von Martens, *Precis du droit des gens moderne de l'Europe fonde sur les traits et l'usage* (An Essay on the Law of Modern European Nations; 1789).

27. In sum, positivism provides substance for the status, source, and sanctions of legal rules. See Nicholas G. Onuf, "Global Law-Making and Legal Thought," in *Law-Making in the Global Community*, ed. Nicholas G. Onuf (Durham, N.C.: Carolina Academic Press, 1982), 6–9.

CHAPTER 2

1. Montevideo Convention on the Rights and Duties of States, 1933, article 1, 49 Stat. 3097, TS no. 881, 165 LNTS 19.

2. Union of International Associations, "Statistics," in *Yearbook of International Organizations, 1909–1999* (Munich: Verlag, 2000).

3. Union of International Associations, "Statistics," in *Yearbook of International Organizations, 1909–1999* (Munich: Verlag, 2000).

4. U.S. Department of State, *Patterns of Global Terrorism 2003* (Washington, D.C.: April 2004, revised June 22, 2004), vi, 101.

5. Russell D. Howard, "Understanding al Qaeda's Application of the New Terrorism—the Key to Victory in the Current Campaign," in *Terrorism and Counterterrorism: Understanding the New Security Environment*, ed. Russell D. Howard and Reid L. Sawyer (Guilford, Conn.: McGraw-Hill, 2004), 75, 77.

6. Stephen D. Krasner, "Structural Causes and Regime Consequences: Regimes as Intervening Variables," in *International Regimes*, ed. Stephen D. Krasner (Ithaca, N.Y.: Cornell University Press, 1983), 1. John Ruggie considers a regime to be a set of mutual expectations, rules, and regulations; plans, organizational energies, and financial commitments that have been accepted by a group of states. See John Gerard Ruggie, "International Responses to Technology: Concepts and Trends," *International Organization* 29 (1975): 570.

7. Some members of the Commonwealth (e.g., Malaysia, India, and Pakistan) no longer regard the British monarch as their head of state but instead consider that sovereign as the symbol of a voluntary association.

8. Four states today have self-proclaimed their permanent neutral status: Cambodia, Sweden, Finland, and Costa Rica. For a historical discussion on neutrality, see Cyril E. Black et al., *Neutralization and World Politics* (Princeton, N.J.: Princeton University Press, 1968).

9. See Robert Clute, *The International Legal Status of Austria, 1938–1955* (The Hague: M. Nijhoff, 1962).

10. Treaty on the Final Settlement with Respect to the Germanys, reprinted in *International Legal Materials* 26 (1990): 1186. In addition to the Germanys, other parties to this agreement included the United States, France, the Soviet Union, and United Kingdom.

11. For the texts of the "covenants" made with the United States as the "principal" state, see *International Legal Materials* 14 (1975): 344.

12. UN Charter, article 2(1).

13. UN Charter, article 2(7).

14. See generally Hedley Bull, *The Anarchical Society: A Study of Order in World Politics* (New York: Columbia University Press, 1977).

15. See R. Y. Jennings and A. D. Watts, *Oppenheim's International Law*, 9th ed. (London: Longmans, Green, 1992), 1:52.

16. Among the leading advocates of the monist school is Hans Kelsen. See his *Principles of International Law*, 2nd ed. (New York: Rinehart, 1966), 290–94.

17. In *West Rand Central Gold Mining Co. v. The King*, Lord Alverstone agreed with the proposition averred by Lord Robert Cecil that "international Law is part of the law of England." [1905] KB 391. In the United States, the same doctrine was underscored by Justice Gray when he asserted that "international law is part of our law and must be ascertained and administered by the courts of justice of appropriate jurisdiction, as often as questions of right depending upon it are duly presented for their determination." *Paquete Habana* and *The Lola* 175 US 677 (1900).

CHAPTER 3

1. See R. Y. Jennings, *The Acquisition of Territory in International Law* (Manchester: University of Manchester Press, 1963).

2. *Legal Status of Eastern Greenland Case*, PCIJ ser. A/B, no. 53 (1933).

3. *The Anna*, Great Britain, High Court of Admiralty, 5 C. Robinson 373 (1805).

4. D. H. Thomas, "Acquisitive Prescription in International Law," *British Year Book of International Law* 27 (1950): 332.

5. See Julius Goebel Jr., *The Struggle for the Falkland Islands*, rev. ed. (New Haven, Conn.: Yale University Press, 1982); Lowell Gustafson, *The Sovereignty Dispute over the Falkland (Malvinas) Islands* (New York: Oxford University Press, 1988).

6. The Island of Palmas Arbitration involved a U.S. claim of sovereignty over an island in the Philippine archipelago that had been improperly ceded by Spain to the United States in 1898. United States–The Netherlands, 1928 Permanent Court of Arbitration, *United Nations Reports of International Arbitration Awards* 2, no. 19 (1928): 829. The decision in the Island of Palmas Arbitration produced the principle that continuous and peaceful display of the functions of state within a given region is a constituent element of territorial sovereignty and is a recognized principle of modern international law.

7. See Lawrence T. Farley, *Plebiscites and Sovereignty: The Crisis of Political Illegitimacy* (Boulder, Colo.: Westview Press, 1986).

8. See the treaty for the cession to the United States of any and all islands of the Philippine Archipelago lying outside of the lines described in article 3 of the treaty of peace of December 10, 1898, signed November 7, 1900, entered into force March 23, 1901, 31 Stat. 1942, TS 345, 11 Bevans 623.

9. Treaty of Versailles, Covenant of the League of Nations, article 10 (1919).

10. The Pact of Paris, signed August 27, 1928, entered into force July 24, 1929, 94 LNTS 57.

11. See Harvard Research in International Law, "Draft Convention on the Rights and Duties of States in Case of Aggression," *American Journal of International Law* (special suppl. 33): 889.

12. Robert Langer, *Seizure of Territory, the Stimson Doctrine, and Related Principles in Legal Theory and Diplomatic Practice* (Princeton, N.J.: Princeton University Press, 1947).

13. UN Charter, article 2 (4). See also 1970 Declaration on Principles of International Law Concerning Friendly Relations and Co-operation among States in Accordance with the Charter of the United Nations, GA res. 2625, UN GAOR, supp. 28, 25th sess. (1970).

14. Compare the views of Sharon Korman, *The Right of Conquest: The Acquisition of Territory by Force in International Law and Practice* (New York: Oxford University Press, 1996).

15. In the early 1900s, floods and accretion affected six hundred acres of the Chamizal Tract area along the Rio Grande, leading to a territorial land dispute in the border region between the United States and Mexico. An arbitration panel settled the dispute on rules of accretion. See Award by the United States–Mexico International Commission Constituted by the Treaty of June 24, 1911, *United Nations Reports of International Arbitration Awards* 11 (1962): 309.

16. See summary of the Indo-Pakistan Western Boundary (Ram of Kutch Case) (*India v. Pakistan*) Award of February 19, 1968, 17 UN Rep. International Arbitral Awards (1980), 1968 *International Law Reports* (1976): 2; reprinted in *International Legal Materials* 7 (1968): 635.

17. See S. Shauna, *Territorial Acquisition, Disputes, and International Law* (The Hague: Martinus Nijhoff, 1997).

18. See Hurst Hannum, *Autonomy, Sovereignty, and Self-Determination: The Accommodation of Conflicting Rights* (Philadelphia: University of Pennsylvania Press, 1996).

19. Frederic Kirgis, "Degrees of Self-Determination in the United Nations Era," *American Journal of International Law* 88 (1994): 304, 306–7.

20. Both the International Covenant on Civil and Political Rights and the International Covenant on Economic, Social, and Cultural Rights have as their article 1 a provision that asserts, "All peoples have the right of self-determination. By virtue of that right they freely determine their political status and freely pursue their economic, social, and cultural development." See also article 27, which provides that similar opportunities should be accorded to ethnic, religious, and linguistic minorities to enjoy their own culture, religion, or language.

21. Advisory Opinion on the Western Sahara, *International Court of Justice Reports* 1975 (advisory opinion of October 16, 1975): 12, 33; reprinted in *International Legal Materials* 14 (1975): 1355.

22. See Lea Brilmayer, "Secession and Self-Determination: A Territorial Interpretation," *Yale Journal of International Law* 16 (1991): 177.

23. See Jorri Duursma, *Fragmentation and the International Relations of Micro-states: Self-Determination and Statehood* (Cambridge: Cambridge University Press, 1996); Christian Tomuschat, ed., *Modern Law of Self-Determination* (Boston: Martinus Nijhoff, 1993); and W. Ofuatey-Kodjoe, *The Principle of Self-Determination in International Law* (New York: Nellen, 1977).

24. See Thomas D. Grant, *The Recognition of States: Law and Practice in Debate and Evolution* (Westport, Conn.: Praeger, 1999).

25. See Robert Clute, *The International Legal Status of Austria, 1938–1955* (The Hague: Martinus Nijhoff, 1962).

26. See Scott Pegg, *International Society and the De Facto State* (Brookfield, Vt.: Ashgate, 1998).

27. See Charles L. Cochran, "De Facto and De Jure Recognition: Is There a Difference?" *American Journal of International Law* 62 (1968): 457–64.

28. Estrada Doctrine of Recognition (September 27, 1930), reprinted in Marjorie M. Whiteman, ed., *Digest of United States Practice in International Law* (Washington, D.C.: U.S. Department of State, 1963), 2:85. See also Phillip Jessup, "The Estrada Doctrine," *American Journal of International Law* 25 (1931): 719.

29. James L. Brierly, *The Law of Nations*, rev. by Humphrey Waldock, 6th ed. (Oxford: Oxford University Press, 1963), 138–40; and James Crawford, *The Creation of New States in International Law* (New York: Oxford University Press, 1979), 15–19.

30. Hersh Lauterpacht, *Recognition in International Law* (Cambridge: Cambridge University Press, 1947), 23–24. Importantly, however, some commentators have argued that states are entitled to democracy as a form of government. See Thomas M. Franck, "The Emerging Right to Democratic Government," *American Journal of International Law* 86 (1992): 46. See also Sean Murphy, "Democracy, Legitimacy and Recognition of States and Governments," *International and Comparative Law Quarterly* 48 (1999): 545–48.

31. Convention on the Rights and Duties of States, done at Montevideo December 26, 1933, entered into force December 26, 1934, 49 Stat. 3097, TS no. 881, 3 Bevans 145, 165 LNTS 19.

32. See Thomas M. Franck, "Is Personal Freedom a Western Value?" *American Journal of International Law* 91 (1997): 593.

33. UN Charter, articles 2 (1) and 78. See also the declaration in note 13, which respects that sovereignty of other states rises to the level of an affirmative duty for all governments.

34. See Gamal Badr, *State Immunity: An Analytical and Prognostic View* (The Hague: Martinus Nijhoff, 1984).

35. Regarding governmental property abroad, only the title to such property can be subject to the courts of another state. *The Schooner Exchange v. MacFaddon*, 11 U.S. (7 Cranch) 116, 137 (1812).

36. See the case *Underhill v. Hernandez*, 168 US 250 (1897).

37. *Banco Nacional de Cuba v. Sabbatino*, 376 US 398, 421 (1964).

38. Foreign Assistance Act of 1964, section 301 (2), *Statutes at Large* 78: 1009, 1013 (1964).

39. See *Vavasseur v. Krupp*, Great Britain, Court of Appeal, 9 Ch. Div. 351 (1978); Ex Parte Republic of Peru (The Ucaydi), 318 US 578 (1943).

40. See Richard B. Lillich, ed., *International Law of State Responsibility for Injuries to Aliens* (Charlottesville: University of Virginia Press, 1983); and Ian Brownlie, *State Responsibility* (New York: Oxford University Press, 1983).

41. See text in *Department of State Bulletin* 26 (June 23, 1952): 984; and in Marjorie M. Whiteman, ed., *Digest of United States Practice in International Law* (Washington, D.C.: U.S. Department of State, 1971), 4:569.

42. 90 Stat. 2891, 28 USC secs. 1330, 1332 (a)(2)(3)(4), 1391 (f), 1441 (d), 1602–11.

43. See Report of the Committee of the Whole House on the State of the Union, "Jurisdiction of the United States Courts against Foreign States, Sept. 9, 1976," reprinted in *International Legal Materials* 15 (1976): 1398; and G. R. Delaume, "Public Debt and Sovereign Immunity: The Foreign Sovereign Immunity Act of 1976," *American Journal of International Law* 71 (1977): 399.

44. 28 USC sec. 1605 (a)(7). In March 1998, a U.S. court rendered an initial judgment under this

revision to FSIA, as Iran was ordered to pay $247.5 million to the parents of an American woman killed in a 1995 suicide bombing in Gaza, for which Iran's Islamic jihad claimed responsibility. *Flatow v. Iran*, 999 Fed. Supp. 1 (D.C. Dist., 1998).

45. See Advisory Opinion of the International Court of Justice on Reparations for Injuries Suffered in the Service of the United Nations, *International Court of Justice Reports* 1949:174; reprinted in *American Journal of International Law* 43 (1949): 590.

46. See *Sei Fujii v. State of California*, 38 Cal. 2d 718, 242 P. 2d 617 (1952); reprinted in *American Journal of International Law* 46 (1952): 559.

47. Article 2 (4) of the UN Charter prohibits the use of force "against the territorial integrity or political independence of any state, or in any other manner inconsistent with the purposes and principles of the United Nations." See also the Case Concerning Military and Paramilitary Activities in and against Nicaragua (*Nicaragua v. United States, International Court of Justice Reports* 1986:14, 106); The Declaration on the Inadmissibility of Intervention into the Domestic Affairs of States, UN GA res. 2131 (20) (1965); and the Declaration on Principles of International Law, UN GA res. 2625 (25) (1970).

48. Marjorie M. Whiteman, ed., *Digest of United States Practice in International Law* (Washington, D.C.: U.S. Department of State, 1971), 4:268.

49. Articles 2(3) and 33 in the UN Charter highlight the duty of the need to resort to peaceful settlement of disputes.

50. Principle 21 of the 1972 Stockholm Declaration serves as a pillar for contemporary international environment law.

51. See Philippe Sands, *Principles of International Environmental Law: Frameworks, Standards, and Implementation,* 2nd ed. (Cambridge: Cambridge University Press, 2003); and Patricia W. Birnie and Alan E. Boyle, *International Law and the Environment,* 2nd ed. (Oxford: Clarendon Press, 2002).

52. See D. P. O'Connell, *The Law of State Succession* (Cambridge: Cambridge University Press, 1956).

53. See the Treaty of Versailles, section 4 (Saar Basin) and section 5 (Alsace-Lorraine).

54. Treaty on the Establishment of German Unity, August 31, 1990, FRG-GDR, 30 *International Legal Materials* 457 (1991). For discussion, see Marian J. Gibbon, A. Kathryn, S. Mack, and A. Bradley Shingleton, eds., *Dimensions of German Unification: Economic, Social, and Legal Analyses* (Boulder, Colo.: Westview Press, 1995); Charlotte Kahn, *Ten Years of German Unification: One State, Two Peoples* (Westport, Conn.: Praeger, 2000).

55. See Vienna Convention on the Succession of States in Respect of Treaties, signed August 22, 1978, entered into force November 6, 1996, 1946 UNTS 3; reprinted in *International Legal Materials* 17 (1978): 1488; and Vienna Convention on the Succession of States in Respect of Property, Archives, and Debts, done April 8, 1983, UN doc. A/CONF. 117/14 (not yet in force).

CHAPTER 4

1. The terms *national* and *citizen* are not necessarily synonymous. A national is a person who owes permanent allegiance to a state, though may not qualify as a citizen. A citizen enjoys special rights and duties that are allocated by law. A citizen of any country is at the same time a national of that state. For example, the people who live in Puerto Rico and American Samoa are U.S. nationals but are not U.S. citizens. They reside in U.S. territory and enjoy U.S protection but may not vote in presidential elections nor hold federal elective offices.

2. See Nottenbaum Case (*Liechtenstein v. Guatemala*), International Court of Justice, Preliminary Objection, *International Court of Justice Reports* 1953:111; second phase, *International Court of Justice Reports* 1955:4. See H. F. van Panhuys, *The Role of Nationality in International Law* (Leiden, Neth.: A. W. Sythoff, 1959).

3. See *Tomasicchio v. Acheson*, 98 F. Supp. 166 (U.S. Dist. Court, D.C. 1951). Even so, certain international obligations can impinge on the state's right to enact its own nationality laws. See *Nationality Degrees Issued in Tunis and Morocco*, PCIJ ser. B, no. 4. (1923).

4. In the United States, the Fourteenth Amendment of the Constitution provides the rule for applying *jus soli* in the United States. See *United States* v. *Wong Kim Ark*, 169 US 649 (1989).

5. Such a process was applied to the people in territories acquired by the United States throughout the 19th century, as well as to Lithuania, Latvia, and Estonia by the Soviet Union following their annexation by the Soviet Union in 1940. See Decree of September 7, 1940, Records of the Supreme Soviet of the USSR, 1940, no. 31.

6. UN GA res. 217A (3). See Nehemia Robinson, *Universal Declaration of Human Rights: Its Origin, Significance, Application, and Interpretation* (New York: Institute of Jewish Affairs, World Jewish Congress, 1950).

7. Done July 28, 1951, entered into force April 22, 1954, 189 UNTS 150. There are today 142 parties to this instrument.

8. Done September 28, 1954, entered into force June 6, 1960, 360 UNTS 117. Only fifty-seven states are today contracting parties to this convention.

9. Done August 30, 1961, entered into force December 13, 1975, 989 UNTS 175. Only twenty-nine states today are parties to this convention.

10. This situation of mass statelessness occurred in Germany and in the Soviet Union after the First World War.

11. See capitulations granted by the Ottoman Porte to England since 1675, renewing those of 1580, *British & Foreign State Papers* 1 (1812–1814): 747; supplementary treaty between Great Britain and China of October 8, 1843, *British & Foreign State Papers* 31 (1842–1843): 132; Abolition of the Capitulations and the Establishment of Tariff Autonomy in Iran, 1927–1928, *Documents on International Affairs* (1928): 200–209; and Montreux Convention for the Abolition of Capitulations in Egypt, May 8, 1937, British Cmd. Paper 5630 (1937).

12. For representative cases involving territorial asylum, see *INS v. Doherty*, 112 S. Ct. 719 (1992); *Haitian Centers Council, Inc. v. McNary*, 969 F. 2d, 1350 (1992); and *Sale v. Haitian Centers Council, Inc.*, 113 S. Ct. 2549, 125 L. Ed. 2d 128 (1993).

13. Declaration on Territorial Asylum, UN GA res. 2312 (22), 22 UN GAOR (supp. no. 16), at 81, UN doc. A/6716 (1967).

14. See M. Cherif Bassiouni, *International Extradition: United States Law and Practice,* 3rd ed. (Dobbs Ferry, N.Y.: Oceana, 1996).

15. To counter these abuses, the United States and the United Kingdom sought to curtail blanket protection afforded by the principle of nonextradition of political criminals. This was done in 1985 through the negotiation of a new bilateral extradition treaty between the two states. See Supplementary Extradition Treaty, June 25, 1985, United States–United Kingdom, reprinted in *International Legal Materials* 24 (1985): 1105; and M. Cherif Bassiouni, "The 'Political Offense Exception' Revisited: Extradition Between the U.S. and the U.K.—a Choice between Friendly Cooperation among Allies and Sound Law and Policy," *Denver Journal of International Law & Policy* 15 (1987): 255.

16. For the indictment (*Auto de procesamiento*; in Spanish), see http://puntofinal.cl/especial/justicia/justicia.html. For edited excerpts of the indictment (in English), see "They Drove Augusto Pinochet to Face Justice Yesterday: This Is Why," *Independent*, December 12, 1998, 1. For an unofficial English translation of Order no. 1/98, see Reed Brody and Michael Ratner, eds., *The Pinochet Papers: The Case of Augusto Pinochet in Spain and Britain* (2000), 95. For the request for extradition from England to Spain, see *Regina v. Bartle & Commissioner of Police*, Ex Parte Pinochet, (1998) 3 WLR 1456 (HL), reprinted in *International Legal Materials* 37 (1998): 1302; aff'd and rev'd in part, (1999) 2 WLR 827 (HL); reprinted in *International Legal Materials* 38 (1999): 581.

17. See M. Cherif Bassiouni and Edward M. Wise, *Aut Dedere Aut Judicare: The Duty to Extradite or Prosecute in International Law* (Dordrecht: M. Nijoff, 1995).

18. See Alona Evans, "The Apprehension and Prosecution of Offenders: Some Current Problems," in *Legal Aspects of International Terrorism*, ed. Alona Evans and John Murphy (1978), 493–503.

19. Done December 16, 1970, entered into force October 14, 1971; 22 UST 1641; 860 UNTS 105.

20. Entered into force January 26, 1973, 24 UST 564, TIAS no. 7570, ICAO doc. 8966.

21. Adopted December 10, 1984, entered into force June 26, 1987, 1465 UNTS 85.

22. Done March 10, 1988, entered into force March 1, 1992, 1678 UNTS 222.

23. Done December 9, 1999, entered into force April 10, 2002, Sen. Treaty doc. no. 106-49.

24. See Christopher C. Joyner, "International Extradition and Global Terrorism: Bringing International Criminals to Justice," *Loyola of Los Angeles International & Comparative Law Review* 25 (2003): 493.

25. See Mary Gardiner Jones, "National Minorities: A Case Study of International Protection," *Law & Contemporary Problems* 14 (1949): 599, 604–5.

26. See PCIJ Advisory Opinion relating to German Settlers in Poland, ser. B, no. 6 (September 10, 1923); PCIJ Advisory Opinion on the Treatment of Polish Nationals in Danzig, ser. A/B, no. 44 (1932); and PCIJ Advisory Opinion on Minority School in Albania, ser. A/B, no. 64 (1935).

27. See M. Cherif Bassiouni, "The Sources and Content of International Criminal Law: A Theoretical Framework," in *International Criminal Law*, ed. M. Cherif Bassiouni, 2nd ed. (Ardsley, N.Y.: Transnational Publishers, 1999), 1:3–125.

28. UN Charter, preamble, paragraph 2 and article 1 (3).

29. UN Charter, article 1 (3).

30. See, for example, Richard B. Lillich, *International Human Rights: Problems of Law, Policy, and Practice,* 2nd ed. (Boston: Little, Brown 1991), 86–163.

31. Done December 16, 1966, entered into force March 23, 1976, 999 UNTS 171, TIAS no. 14668. Today at least 153 states are parties to the Covenant on Civil and Political Rights.

32. Opened for signature December 19, 1966, 993 UNTS 3, entered into force January 3, 1976. TIAS no. 14531. By 2005, at least 150 states are parties to the Covenant of Economic, Social, and Cultural Rights.

33. See generally David P. Forsythe, *Human Rights in International Relations* (Cambridge: Cambridge University Press, 2002); and Louis Henkin, ed., *The International Bill of Human Rights: The Covenant on Civil and Political Rights* (New York: Columbia University Press, 1981).

34. Done December 7, 1948, entered into force January 12, 1951, 78 UNTS 277. At least 136 states are now parties to the Genocide Convention.

35. Genocide Convention, article 2.

36. Genocide Convention, article 6.

37. A. Bayesfy, "The Principle of Equality of Non-discrimination in International Law," *Human Rights Law Journal* 11 (1990): 1.

38. Opened for signature March 7, 1966, entered into force January 4, 1969, 660 UNTS 195. At least 170 states are today party to the Racial Discrimination Convention.

39. Slavery Convention, done September 25, 1926, entered into force March 9, 1927, TIAS no. 1414, 60 LNTS 253; and the Supplementary Convention on the Abolition of Slavery, the Slave Trade, and Institutions and Practices Similar to Slavery, done September 7, 1956, TIAS no. 3822, 266 UNTS 3. There are presently 119 parties to this more modern supplementary antislavery convention.

40. Opened for signature on November 30, 1973, UN GA res. 3068 (28), UN GAOR, 28th sess. (supp. no. 30) 75, UN doc. A/9030 (1973), 1015 UNTS 243, entered into force July 18, 1976, TIAS no. 14861. Today the Apartheid Convention counts at least 101 states as parties.

41. Apartheid Convention, article 1.

42. Apartheid Convention, article 3.

43. Done March 31, 1953, UN GA res. 640 (7), GAOR 7th sess. (supp. no. 20), 27, entered into force July 7, 1954, 193 UNTS 135 (1953). In 2004 at least 118 states have contracted as parties to this instrument.

44. Done December 18, 1979, UN GAOR, 34th sess. (supp. no. 21) 193, UN doc. A/Res/34/180, entered into force September 3, 1981, 1249 UNTS 13, TIAS no. 20378. Today at least 179 states are parties to the CEDAW.

45. "Discrimination against women" is defined as "any distinction, exclusion, or restriction made on the basis of sex" that impairs the enjoyment by women of "the human rights and fundamental freedoms in the political, economic, cultural, civil or any other field." CEDAW, article 1.

46. CEDAW, article 2.

47. See Rebecca J. Cook, "Women," in *The United Nations and International Law*, ed. Christopher C. Joyner (Cambridge: Cambridge University Press, 1997), 181–207.

48. Done November 20, 1989, UN GA res. 4425, UN GAOR 44th sess., suppl. no. 49 (1989), at 166, entered into force September 2, 1990, 577 UNTS 3, TIAS no. 27531. Today 192 states are contracted as parties to this convention to protect children.

49. Opened for signature February 4, 1985, GA res. 39/46, UN doc. A/RES/39/708 (1984), entered into force June 26, 1987. In late 2004 at least 138 states are parties to the Convention to Prevent and Punish Torture.

50. Convention to Prevent and Punish Torture, article 1 (1).

51. Convention to Prevent and Punish Torture, article 2 (1).

52. See David M. Trubek, "Economic, Social and Cultural Rights in the Third World: Human Rights and Human Needs," in *Human Rights in International Law: Legal and Policy Issues,* ed. Theodore Meron (Oxford: Clarendon Press 1984), 205, 213–22.

53. See K. J. Partsch, "The Committee on the Elimination of Racial Discrimination," in *The United Nations and Human Rights, 1945–1995* (New York: UN Department of Public Information, 1995), 339.

54. Opened for signature December 19, 1966, entered into force March 23, 1976, 999 UNTS 171. For discussion, see Dinah Shelton, "Individual Complaint Machinery under the United Nations 1503 Procedure and the Optimal Protocol to the International Covenant on Civil and Political Rights," in *Guide to International Human Rights Practice,* ed. Hurst Hannum (Philadelphia: University of Pennsylvania Press, 1984), 59, 67–73. Today at least 104 states are party to the protocol.

55. The Inter-American Commission of Human Rights chronicled many of these cases. See, for example, *Masacre Las Hojas v. El Salvador,* case 10.287, report no. 26/92, Inter-Am. CHR, OEA/Ser.L/V/II.83 doc. 14, 83 (1993); *Consuelo et al. v. Argentina,* case 10.147, 10.181, 10.240, 10.262, 10.309, 10.311, report no. 28/92, Inter-Am. CHR, OEA/Ser.L/V/II.83 doc. 14, 41 (1993); and *Meneses Reyes, Lagos Salinas, Alsina Hurtos and Vegara Inostroza v. Chile,* case 11.228, 11.229, 11.231, and 11.182, report no. 34/96, Inter-Am. CHR, OEA/Ser.L/V/II.95 doc. 7, rev. at 196 (1997). The cases heard by the Commission are provided at www1.umn.edu/humanrts/cases/commissn.htm (accessed April 29, 2004). Also see the Committee against Torture's website at www.unhchr.ch/html/menu2/6/cat/ (accessed April 29, 2004).

56. Done at Rome, November 4, 1950, entered into force September 3, 1953, 213 UNTS 221, European Treaty ser. no. 5.

57. See David P. Forsythe, *Human Rights in International Relations* (Cambridge: Cambridge University Press, 2000), 117.

58. Done January 7, 1970, OAS Official Records OEA/Ser. K/XVI/1.1. doc. 65, rev. 1, corr. 1.

59. Statistics are drawn from the University of Minnesota's Human Rights Library, "Inter-American Court of Human Rights" on the web (accessed March 1, 2004) at www1.umn.edu/humanrts/iachr/iachr.html.

60. See the Amnesty International website at www.amnesty.org.

61. See the website for Lawyers Committee for Human Rights at www.lchr.org; Human Rights Watch at www.hrw.org; and International Human Rights Law Group at www.hrlawgroup.org.

62. The ICRC website is located at www.icrc.org.

63. See the International Court of Justice's website at www.icj.org.

CHAPTER 5

1. Before May 1, 2004, the member states of the European Union were Austria, Belgium, Denmark, Finland, France, Germany, Greece, Ireland, Italy, Luxembourg, the Netherlands, Portugal, Spain, Sweden, and the United Kingdom. On April 9, 2003, in separate votes for each of ten acceding nations, the 626-member EU Assembly overwhelmingly supported the expansion scheduled for May 1, 2004. The ten new members of the EU are Poland, Lithuania, Estonia, Latvia, Hungary, the Czech Republic, Slovenia, Slovakia, Malta, and Cyprus. "EU Approves Expansion for 10 New Members," *New York Times,* April 9, 2003, online at www.nytimes.com/aponline/international/AP-EU-Expansion.html?pagewanted = print &position = top (accessed April 10, 2003).

2. Charter of the United Nations with the Statute of the International Court of Justice annexed

thereto. Signed at San Francisco, June 26, 1945; entered into force October 24, 1945, 59 Stat. 1031, TS 993, 3 Bevans 1153. As of 2005, there are 191 state parties to the UN Charter. As a unique actor, the United Nations organization enjoys certain special privileges and immunities under international law. See Convention on the Privileges and Immunities of the United Nations, done at New York, February 13, 1946, entered into force September 17, 1946, 21 UST 1418, TIAS no. 6900, 1 UNTS 16, 90 UNTS 327 (corrigendum). Available at www.un.org/Depts/Treaty/bible/Part_I_E/III_III_I.html (accessed August 14, 2003).

3. See UN Charter, article 7, chapters 4–5, 10, 13–15.

4. The United Nations, "United Nations Member States," at www.un.org/members/index .html (accessed April 29, 2004).

5. Interestingly enough, more governments have subscribed to obligations under the Statute of the ICJ than to the UN Charter itself.

6. "International Court of Justice—the Court at a Glance," February 10, 2003, available online at www.icj-cij.org/icjwww/igeneralinformation/icjgnnot.html (accessed March 25, 2003).

7. See online at www.icj-cij.org/icjwww/idocket.htm (accessed March 25, 2003).

8. UN doc. S/RES/808, paragraph 1 (1993). For discussion, see Christopher C. Joyner, "Enforcing Human Rights Standards in the former Yugoslavia: The Case for an International War Crimes Tribunal," *Denver Journal of International Law and Policy* 22 (1994): 235.

9. UN doc. S/RES/955, annex (1994).

10. See the discussion at the EU website, at www.eca.eu.int/EN/menu.htm (accessed August 24, 2003).

11. In full, article 24, paragraph 1, of the Charter provides that "in order to ensure prompt and effective action by the United Nations, its Members confer on the Security Council primary responsibility for the maintenance of international peace and security, and agree that in carrying out its duties under this responsibility the Security Council acts on their behalf."

12. See Christopher C. Joyner, "Collective Sanctions as Peaceful Coercion: Lessons from the United Nations Experience," *1995 Australian Year Book of International Law* (1996): 241–70; and Christopher C. Joyner, "United Nations Sanctions after Iraq: Looking Back to See Ahead," *Chicago Journal of International Law* 4 (2003): 329.

13. This figure is from the UN website at www.un.org/Docs/sc/unsc_resolutions.html (accessed March 1, 2004).

14. UN Charter, article 10. The right of the General Assembly to make recommendations is explicitly circumscribed if those recommendations concern disputes then being considered by the Security Council, unless the Council so requests. UN Charter, article 12(1).

15. UN Charter, article 3(1)(b).

16. Convention on the Prevention and Punishment of the Crime of Genocide, done December 9, 1948, entered into force January 12, 1951, 78 UNTS 277.

17. For commentary on recent ILC activities, see Robert Rosenstock, "The Forty-sixth Session of the International Law Commission," *American Society of International Law Proceedings* 89 (1995): 390.

18. See International Law Commission, "Draft Articles on the Origin of State Responsibility," *International Law Commission Yearbook* 2 (1980): 30–34.

19. In 1991 the Commission adopted a Draft Code of Offenses on its first reading. See Twelfth Report on the Draft Code of Crimes against the Peace and Security of Mankind, submitted by Doudou Thiam, UN doc. A/CN.4/460 (1994). For an insightful assessment, see M. Cherif Bassiouni, *Commentaries on the International Law Commission's 1991 Draft Code of Crimes against the Peace and Security of Mankind,* Nouvelles Etudes Penales 11 (Toulouse, Fr.: Erès, 1993). Also compare Draft Code of Offences against the Peace and Security of Mankind, UN GAOR, 9th sess., 504th plen. mtg., supp. no. 7, UN doc. 898 (9) (1954).

20. International Law Commission Revised Report of the Working Group on the Draft Statute for an International Criminal Court, UN doc. A/CN.4/L.490 (1993). For an appraisal, see James Crawford, "The ILC's Draft Statute for an International Criminal Court," *American Journal of International Law* 88 (1994): 140. A statute for the International Criminal Court was adopted by an international conference in Rome in July 1998, and the court actually came into being in July 2002.

21. Convention on the High Seas, done at Geneva April 29, 1958, entered into force September 30, 1962, 13 UST 2312, TIAS 5200, 450 UNTS 82; Convention on the Continental Shelf, done at Geneva April 29, 1958, entered into force June 10, 1964, 15 UST 471, TIAS 5578, 499 UNTS 471; Convention on the Territorial Sea and the Contiguous Zone, done at Geneva April 29, 1958, entered into force September 10, 1964, 15 UST 1606 516, TIAS 5639, UNTS 205; and Convention on Fishing and Conservation of Living Resources of the High Seas, done at Geneva April 29, 1958, entered into force March 20, 1966, 17 UST 138, TIAS 5969, 559 UNTS 285.

22. Done April 18, 1961, entered into force April 24, 1964, 500 UNTS 95, 23 UST 3227.

23. Adopted May 22, 1969; opened for signature May 23, 1969; entered into force January 27, 1990. UN Conference on the Law of Treaties, 1st and 2nd sess., UN doc. A/CONF. 39/27 (1969), 289.

24. TIAS no. 8532, reprinted in *International Legal Materials* 13 (1977): 41; adopted December 14, 1973, by GA res. 3166 (annex), 28 GAOR, supp. 30, UN doc. A/9030, entered into force February 20, 1977.

25. Done August 23, 1978, entered into force November 6, 1978. See text at www.un.org/law/ilc/texts/treasucc.htm (accessed August 14, 2003).

26. Adopted April 7, 1983; opened for signature April 8, 1983. UN doc. A/CONF.117/14, 36 UN GAOR, supp. no. 51, 243. Available at http://untreaty.un.org/ENGLISH/bible/ (accessed August 13, 2003).

27. This figure was compiled by comprehensively searching the *UN General Assembly Official Records,* dating 1945–2004. See the UN website at www.un.org/Depts/dhl/resguide/gares1.htm.

28. Done January 27, 1967, entered into force October 10, 1967, 18 UST 2410, TIAS 6347, 610 UNTS 205. See Declaration of Legal Principles Governing the Activities of States in the Exploration and Use of Outer Space, GA res. 1962 (XVIII), December 13, 1963, 18 UN GAOR supp. no. 15, 15–16, UN doc. A/5515 (1963); Resolution Regarding Weapons of Mass Destruction in Outer Space, October 17, 1963, UN GA res. 1884 (XVIII), 18 UN GAOR supp. no. 15, 13, UN doc. A/5515 (1964).

29. Done July 1, 1968, entered into force March 5, 1970, 21 UST 483, TIAS 6839, 729 UNTS 161.

30. Treaty on the Prohibition of the Emplacement of Nuclear Weapons and Other Weapons of Mass Destruction on the Seabed and Ocean Floor and in the Subsoil Thereof, 23 UST 701, TIAS no. 7337, reprinted in *International Legal Materials* 10 (1971): 146.

31. Other basic instruments pertaining to activities in outer space include the Agreement on the Rescue and Return of Astronauts and the Return of Objects Launched into Space, done April 22, 1968, entered into force December 3, 1968, 19 UST 7570, TIAS no. 6599, 672 UNTS 119; Convention on International Liability for Damage Caused by Space Objects, done March 29, 1972, entered into force September 1, 1972, 24 UST 2389, TIAS no. 7762, 961 UNTS 1187; Convention on Registration of Objects Launched into Space, done January 14, 1975, entered into force September 15, 1976, 28 UST 695, TIAS no. 8480, 1023 UNTS 15.

32. GA res. 217 (III), December 10, 1948. 3 UN GAOR, res. UN doc. A/810, at 71.

33. Opened for signature December 10, 1966, entered into force March 23, 1976, 999 UNTS 171. See also GA res. 2200 (XXI), 21 UN GAOR, supp. no. 16, 52, UN doc. A/6316 (1967).

34. Opened for signature December 19, 1966, entered into force January 3, 1976, 993 UNTS 3. See also UNGA res. 2200 (XXI), 21 UN GAOR, supp. no. 16, 49, UN doc. A/6316 (1967).

35. Convention on the Elimination of All Forms of Racial Discrimination, opened for signature March 7, 1966; entered into force January 4, 1969, 660 UNTS 195; reprinted in *International Legal Materials* 5 (1966): 352.

36. International Convention on the Suppression and Punishment of the Crime of Apartheid, done November 30, 1973, entered into force July 18, 1976, GA res. 3068 (28). This convention was promoted by GA res. 3068 (XXVIII), 28 UN GAOR, supp. no. 30, 75, UN doc. A/9030 (1974), reprinted in *International Legal Materials* 13 (1974): 50.

37. Convention on the Elimination of All Forms of Discrimination against Women, GA res. 280 (34), opened for signature December 18, 1979, entered into force September 3, 1980, reprinted in *International Legal Materials* 19 (1980): 33. See Declaration on the Elimination of Discrimination against Women, November 7, 1967, GA res. 2263 (XII), 22 UN GAOR supp. no. 16, 35, UN doc. A/6880 (1968).

38. Convention on the Rights of the Child, opened for signature November 20, 1989, entered into force September 2, 1990. See GA res. 1386, 14 GAOR, supp. no. 16, 19–20, UN doc. A/4354 (1989). Today 192 states are parties to the Rights of the Child Convention.

39. International Convention against the Taking of Hostages, adopted by the General Assembly on December 17, 1979, GA res. 34/14b (34), entered into force June 3, 1983, reprinted in *International Legal Materials* 18 (1979): 1456. TIAS 11081, 1316 UNTS 205. At least 144 states are parties to this instrument.

40. Convention against Torture and Other Cruel, Inhuman, or Degrading Treatment or Punishment, adopted by GA res. 39/46/Annex, December 10, 1984, 39 UN GAOR supp. no. 51, 197, UN doc. A/39/51, entered into force June 26, 1987. At least 138 states are parties to the Convention against Torture. See also, Declaration on the Protection of All Persons from Being Subjected to Torture and Other Cruel, Inhuman, or Degrading Treatment or Punishment, GA res. 3452 (29) (December 9, 1975).

41. Declaration of Principles of Law Concerning Friendly Relations and Cooperation among States in Accordance with the charter of the United Nations, GA res. 2625 (XXV), October 24, 1970, 25 UN GAOR (supp. 28), UN doc. A/8028, at 121 (1970).

42. See GA res. 2749, 25 UN GAOR, supp. no. 27, 24, UN doc. A/8027 (1970). Significantly, this resolution was adopted 108–0, with fourteen abstentions.

43. Adopted by UN GA res. 3068 (XXVIII), 28 UN GAOR, supp. no. 30, 75, UN doc. A/9030 (1974).

44. See GA res. 1803 (XXVII), 17 UN GAOR, supp. no. 17, 15, UN doc. A/5217 (1963).

45. For example, at the 1992 UN Conference on the Environment and Development, international conventions were produced on climate change and biodiversity. See United Nations Framework Convention on Climate Change, done May 9, 1992, entered into force March 21, 1994, 1771 UNTS 107. There are 189 parties to the Climate Change Convention. See Convention on Biological Diversity, done June 5, 1992, entered into force December 29, 1993, 1760 UNTS 79. In 2004, 188 states are party to the Biodiversity Convention.

46. For example, Agenda 21 (an eight-hundred-page action plan), the Statement on Forestry Principles, and the Declaration on the Environment and Development, which came out of the 1992 United Nations Conference on the Environment and Development.

47. See UN Charter, chapters 12 and 13.

48. As a special "strategic" trust territory, Palau was actually placed under the administrative aegis of the Security Council, which cooperated with the Trusteeship Council in overseeing the area. See UN Charter, article 83.

49. The ECOSOC website is located at www.un.org/esa/coordination/ecosoc.

50. Constitution of the United Nations Food and Agriculture Organization, done at Quebec October 16, 1945, entered into force October 1945, 12 UST 980, TIAS no. 4803, online at www.fao.org/DOCREP/003/X8700E/x8700e01.htm#P8_10 (accessed August 11, 2003).

51. Articles of Agreement of the International Bank for Reconstruction and Development, done at the Bretton Woods Conference July 1–22, 1994; opened for signature December 27, 1945; entered into force December 27, 1945, 60 Stat. 1440, TIAS no. 1502; 3 Bevans 1390, 2 UNTS 134.

52. See the World Bank website at www.worldbank.org.

53. Articles of Agreement of the International Development Association, done at Washington, D.C., on January 26, 1960, entered into force September 24, 1960, 12 UST 2284, TIAS 4607, 439 UNTS 249. At least 164 states are members of the IDA.

54. Articles of Agreement of the International Finance Corporation, done in Washington, D.C., on May 25, 1955, entered into force July 20, 1956, 7 UST 2197, TIAS 3620, 264 UNTS 117. Today at least 176 states are party to the IFC. See the IFC website at http://ifcln1.ifc.org/ifcext/about.nsf.

55. Convention on Civil Aviation, done in Chicago on December 7, 1944, entered into force April 4, 1947, 61 Stat. 1180, TIAS 1591, 3 Bevans 944, 15 UNTS 295.

56. See ICAO Treaty Collection at www.icao.int/icao/en/leb/ (accessed August 14, 2003).

57. Agreement Establishing the International Fund for Agricultural Development, done at Rome June 13, 1976, entered into force November 30, 1977, 28 UST 8435, TIAS 8765, 1059 UNTS 191.

58. See the International Fund for Agricultural Development website at www.ifad.org.

59. Instrument for the Amendment of the Constitution of the International Labor Organization, dated October 9, 1946, entered into force April 20, 1948, 62 Stat. 3485, 4 Bevans 188, 15 UNTS 35.

60. See the ILO website at www.ilo.org.

61. Convention on the Intergovernmental Maritime Consultative Organization, done March 6, 1948, entered into force March 17, 1958, 9 UST 621, TIAS no. 4044, 289 UNTS 48. The title of the convention was changed to the Convention on the International Maritime Organization, by amendment on November 14, 1975, effective May 22, 1982.

62. See the IMO's list of conventions at www.imo.org/home.asp?topic_id = 161 (accessed August 13, 2003).

63. Articles of Agreement of the International Monetary Fund, formulated at the Bretton Woods Conference, July 1–22, 1944; opened for signature at Washington, D.C., December 27, 1945; entered into force December 27, 1945, 60 Stat. 1401, TIAS 1501, 3 Bevans 1351, 2 UNTS 39.

64. See International Monetary Fund website at www.imf.org.

65. International Telecommunications Convention, with annexes and protocols, done at Nairobi on November 6, 1982, entered into force January 1, 1984, replacing International Telecommunications Convention, with annexes and protocols, adopted at Malaga-Torremolinos on October 25, 1973, entered into force January 1, 1975, 28 UST 2495, TIAS 8572.

66. See the ITU website at www.itu.int/home.

67. See the UNESCO website at www.unesco.org.

68. Convention of the United Nations Industrial Development Organization, with annexes, adopted at Vienna April 8, 1979, entered into force June 21, 1985, TIAS 23432, 1401 UNTS 3.

69. Constitution of the United Nations Industrial Development Organization, done April 8, 1979, entered into force June 21, 1985, 1401 UNTS 3, at www.org/Depts/Treaty/bible/Part_I_E/X_/X_9.html (accessed April 14, 2003). See the UNIDO website at www.unido.org.

70. Constitution of the Universal Postal Union, with final protocol, done at Vienna July 10, 1964, entered into force January 1, 1966, 16 UST 1291, TIAS 5881, 611 UNTS 7.

71. See the UPU website at www.upu.int.

72. Constitution of the World Health Organization, done at New York on July 22, 1946, entered into force April 7, 1948, 62 Stat. 2679, TIAS 1808, 4 Bevans 119, 14 UNTS 185.

73. See the WHO website at www.who.int/en.

74. See the draft text at www.who.int/tobacco/fctc/text/final/en.

75. Convention establishing the World Intellectual Property Organization, done at Stockholm July 14, 1967, entered into force April 26, 1970, 21 UST 1749, TIAS 6932, 828 UNTS 3.

76. See the WIPO website at www.wipo.org.

77. Convention of the World Meteorological Organization, with related protocol. Done at Washington, D.C., on October 11, 1947, entered into force March 23, 1950, 1 UST 281, TIAS 2052, 77 UNTS 143.

78. See the WMO website at www.wmo.org.ch/index-en.html.

79. Statute of the International Atomic Energy Agency, done at New York on October 26, 1956, entered into force July 29, 1957, 8 UST 1093, TIAS 3873, 276 UNTS 3.

80. See the IAEA website at www.iaea.org/worldatom. It was IAEA inspections that were used during the 1990s to monitor nuclear activities in Iraq and North Korea.

81. General Agreement on Tariffs and Trade, with annexes and schedules attached to the final act of the United Nations Conference on Trade and Employment, signed in Geneva October 30, 1947, entered into force January 1, 1948, 61 Stat. (5) (6), TIAS 1700, 4 Bevans 639, 55–61 UNTS.

82. The GATT's functions have been subsumed by the WTO. See the WTO website at www.wto.org.

CHAPTER 6

1. Vienna Convention on the Law of Treaties, UN doc. A/Conf. 39/27 (1969), opened for signature on May 23, 1969, entered into force Janury 27, 1980, 1155 UNTS 331, article 2. At least ninety-

eight states are currently contracting parties to this treaty on the law of treaties. Online at http://fletcher.tufts.edu/multi/texts/BH538.txt (accessed April 24, 2004).

2. UN Charter, article 2 (4).

3. *Legal Status of Greenland (Norway v. Denmark)* PCIJ Ser. A/B, no. 53 (1933), at 194.

4. Reprinted in *International Legal Materials* 25 (1986): 543.

5. See James H. Breasted, *History of Egypt* (New York: MacMillian, 1905), 437–38.

6. A valid and binding international agreement may come from an official conversation between a foreign minister and a diplomatic agent of another state. *Eastern Greenland Case (Denmark v. Norway)*, PCIJ 1933, Ser. A/B, no. 53.

7. Vienna Convention on Treaties, article 18.

8. Each state has its own municipal law for determining the procedure through which a treaty is made binding on that state. In the United States, for example, the executive branch negotiates and signs the treaty. When the text is agreed on, the treaty is presented to the Senate for its advice and consent. After advice and consent is given, the treaty is returned to the president for ratification, which may be completed or refused per presidential discretion. U.S. Constitution, article 2, section 2.

9. See *Treatment of Polish Nationals in Danzig*, PCIJ 24 Ser. A/B, no. 44 (1932).

10. Treaty of Versailles (1919), available online at www.yale.edu/lawweb/avalon/imt/parti.htm.

11. Comprehensive Test Ban Treaty, opened for signature, September 24, 1996, not yet in force. Text available online at www.state.gov/www/global/arms/treaties/ctb.html.

12. See Vienna Convention on Treaties, articles 19–23.

13. Reservations to multilateral agreements can pose complex problems for states parties, a subject addressed by the International Court of Justice in an advisory opinion: "Reservations to the Convention on the Prevention and Punishment of the Crime of Genocide," *International Court of Justice Reports* (1951): 15.

14. Article 31 of the 1969 Vienna Convention furnishes the rule of interpreting the treaty in accordance with its ordinary meaning but within the context of the treaty's overall objective.

15. In the Case Concerning the Temple of Preah Vihear *(Cambodia v. Thailand)*, Thailand claimed that the map used for the border agreement with Cambodia had contained an error. The court rejected that argument because members of the Thai Border Commission had seen and approved use of the map during the course of the boundary negotiations. *International Court of Justice Reports* (1962): 6 (judgment of June 15, 1962).

16. As codified in article 53 of the Vienna Convention on Treaties.

17. See Lauri Hannikainen, *Peremptory Norms (Jus Cogens) in International Law: Historical Development, Criteria, and Present Status* (Helsinki: Finnish Lawyers Pubishing, 1988).

18. This method was used by President Carter in 1978 when he authorized withdrawal from the 1954 Mutual Defense Treaty with the Republic of China (Taiwan).

19. See Opinion of Acting Attorney General Biddle of the United States with respect to International Load Line Convention, *Opinions of the Attorney General* 4 (1941): 119. This convention aimed to prevent competition in merchant shipping by overloading merchant vessels such that life and property were jeopardized at sea. In view of drastic changes in World War II in 1941, when merchant ships became essential to the allied war effort, restrictive limitations imposed by Load Line Convention were deemed not applicable to wartime shipment of men and materiel.

20. While the term *dispute* has no precise connotation in international law, it was defined by the Permanent Court of International Justice in the Mavrommatis Palestine Concessions Case *(Greece vs. Great Britain, 1924)*, and it usually refers to "a disagreement on a point of law or fact, a conflict of legal views or of interests between [the parties]." PCIJ, ser. A, no. 2 (1924), reported in *International Law Reports* 2:27.

21. American Law Institute, *Restatement of the Foreign Relations Law of the United States*, 3rd ed. (St. Paul, Minn.: American Law Institute, 1987), section 902.

22. See the Manila Declaration on the Peaceful Settlement of International Disputes, formulated by the UN General Assembly's Special Committee on the Charter of the United Nations and on Strengthening the Role of the Organization, approved by the Assembly in A/RES/37/10 (November 15, 1982).

23. See U.S. Department of State, "Statement on the U.S. Withdrawal from the Proceedings Initiated by Nicaragua in the International Court of Justice, January 18, 1985," reprinted in *Dept. State Bull.* 64 (March 1985), which asserted that "the Conflict in Central America, therefore, is not a narrow legal dispute; it is an inherently political problem that is not appropriate for judicial resolution. The conflict will be solved only by political and diplomatic means—not through a judicial tribunal. The International Court of Justice was never intended to resolve issues of collective security and self-defense and it is patently unsuited for such a role."

24. GA res. A/RES/46/ (Dec. 9, 1991), annex.

25. See J. G. Wetter, *The International Arbitral Process Public and Private,* 5 vols. (Dobbs Ferry, N.Y.: Oceana, 1979); Fred Soons, ed., *International Arbitration* (The Hague: Dordrecht, 1990); and Andreas Lowenfeld, *International Litigation and Arbitration* (The Hague: Martinus Nijhoff, 1996).

26. John Bassett Moore, *International Arbitrations* (New York: 1898), 1:495.

27. See S. Rosenne, ed., *The Hague Peace Conferences of 1899 and 1907 and International Arbitration: International Litigation and Arbitration* (The Hague: Kluwer Law International, 2001), and the Permanent Court of Arbitration's website: www.pca-cpa.org/ENGLISH/GI/.

28. *International Law Reports* 50 (1971): 2.

29. *International Law Reports* 54 (1978): 6.

30. See, respectively, *International Legal Materials* 24 (1978): 738; and *International Legal Materials* 31 (1985): 1.

31. See *Iran–United States Claims Tribunal Reports* (1981–present); George H. Aldrich, ed., *The Jurisprudence of the Iran–United States Claims Tribunal* (Oxford: Oxford University Press, 1996); and W. Mapp, *The Iran–United States Claims Tribunal: The First Ten Years 1981–1991* (Manchester: Manchester University Press, 1993). Statistics are from the tribunal's website, at www.iusct.org.

32. See United Nations Compensation Commission at www.unog.ch/uncc/start.htm. Statistics drawn from www.unog.ch/uncc/status.htm (accessed March 1, 2004).

33. For example, as was done by the ICJ in the North Sea Continental Shelf Case *(Fed. Rep. of Germany v. Denmark; Fed. Rep. of Germany v. Netherlands), International Court of Justice Reports* (1969): 10 (judgment of February 20); and in the Continental Shelf Tunisia/Libyan Arab Jamahiriya Case *(Tunisia v. Libyan Arab Jamahiriya), International Court of Justice Reports* 1982 (1982): 18 (judgment of February 24).

34. Legality of the Threat or Use of Nuclear Weapons (advisory opinion of July 8, 1996), *International Court of Justice Reports* (1996): 226, online at www.icj-cij.org/icjwww/idecisions.htm.

35. While the Central American Court of Justice was revived as a juridical instruction in 1965, it has yet to render any decisions.

36. This case involved the "interim measures of protection" decision in the *Anglo-Iranian Oil Company Case.* Great Britain brought the case before the Security Council, but when the ICJ declined to hear the case on grounds of lacking jurisdiction, the order for measures of protection lapsed, and the question of Security Council enforcement became moot.

CHAPTER 7

1. See, for example, articles 20, 23, and 24, Statute of the International Criminal Court, UN doc. A/CONF.183/9 of 17 July 1998, available at www.un.org/law/icc/statute/romefra.htm.

2. See Lauri Hannikainean, *Peremptory Norms (Jus Cogens) in International Law: Historical Development, Criteria, Present Status* (Helsinki: Finnish Lawyers Pubishing, 1988).

3. See Advisory Opinion on Reservations to the Convention on the Prevention and Punishment of Genocide, *International Court of Justice Reports* 1951 (May 28, 1951): 15; and South West Africa Cases (Preliminary Objections) *(Ethiopia v. S. Africa; Liberia v. S. Africa), International Court of Justice Reports* 1963 (December 21, 1963): 319.

4. Slavery Convention, signed at Geneva on September 25, 1926, and amended by the protocol, done December 7, 1953, entered into force July 7, 1955, 212 UNTS 17; Supplementary Convention

on the Abolition of Slavery, the Slave Trade, and Institutions and Practices Similar to Slavery, done September 7, 1956, entered into force April 30, 1957, 266 UNTS 3.

5. See John B. Duff and Larry A. Green, *Slavery: Its Origin and Legacy* (New York: Crowell 1975); M. Cherif Bassiouni, "Enslavement as an International Crime," *New York University Journal of International Law & Politics* 23 (1991): 445.

6. The U.S. government estimates that as many as 800,000–900,000 people are annually trafficked across international borders worldwide, while UN calculations indicate that trafficking in persons generates $7–10 billion per year for traffickers. Among the most egregious offenders ("tier 3" countries) are Bosnia, Burma, Cuba, Dominican Republic, Georgia, Kazakhstan, Suriname, Haiti, Liberia, North Korea, Sudan, Turkey, and Uzbekistan. See U.S. Dept. State, *Victims of Trafficking and Violence Protection Act of 2000: Trafficking in Persons Report* (June 11, 2003), available at www.state .gov/g/tip/rls/tiprpt/2003/21277.htm (accessed August 24, 2003), and John Miller, "Slavery in 2004," *Washington Post,* January 1, 2004, A-24.

7. The dramatic increase in the traffic of women and children for sexual exploitation that has occurred during the past two decades has become the subject of a special convention, the Protocol on International Traffic in Women and Children, which is part of the Convention on Organized Crime of December 2000, UN draft doc. A/AC.254/4/Add.3/Rev.6 (2000).

8. According to Oppenheim's traditional definition, piracy is "every unauthorized act of violence committed by a private vessel on the high seas against another vessel with the intent to plunder (*animo furandi*)." Hersch Lauterpacht, *Oppenheim's International Law,* 8th ed. (London: Longmans, Green, 1955), 1:608. For an authoritative treatment, see Alfred Rubin, *The Law of Piracy* (Newport, R.I.: Naval War College Press, 1988). Authorized acts of piracy called privateering once were permissible but were abolished and declared unlawful by the Declaration of Paris of 1856.

9. As provided for in article 101 of the 1982 United Nations Convention on the Law of the Sea, UN doc. A/CONF.62/122 (1982), reprinted as United Nations, *Official Text of the United Nations Convention on the Law of the Sea with Annexes and Index,* UN sales no. E.83.V.5 (1983). While critical to the legal definition, the phrase "committed for private ends" remains problematic due to its lack of formal definition. Does this phrase mean that there must be the intention to rob a vessel, or might it also include feelings of hatred or revenge as a motivation? Though unclear in either event, the act must be committed for private ends to be regarded in law as piratical.

10. Samuel Pyeatt Menefee, "Foreign Naval Intervention in Cases of Piracy: Problems of Strategy," *International Journal of Marine & Coastal Law* 14 (1999): 254.

11. See Christopher C. Joyner, "The 1988 IMO Convention on the Safety of Maritime Navigation: Toward a Legal Remedy for Terrorism at Sea," *German Year Book of International Law* 31 (1989): 230.

12. See the Convention for the Suppression of Unlawful Acts against the Safety of Maritime Navigation, done March 10, 1988, entered into force March 1, 1992, IMO doc. SUA/CON/15 (1988), and the Protocol for the Suppression of Unlawful Acts against the Safety of Fixed Platforms Located on the Continental Shelf, done March 10, 1988, entered into force March 1, 1992, at www.imo.org/home.asp.

13. Malvina Halberstam, "International Maritime Navigation on the High Seas," in *International Criminal Law,* ed. M. Cherif Bassiouni, 2nd ed. (Ardsley, N.Y.: Transnational Publishers, 1999), 1:819–37.

14. Done September 14, 1963, TIAS no. 6768, 704 UNTS 219, entered into force December 4, 1969, available at www.icao.int/cgi/eshop_conv.pl?GUESTguest#Conventions.

15. Opened for signature December 16, 1970, TIAS no. 7192, ICAO doc. no. 8920 (1971), entered into force October 16, 1971, available at www.icao.int/cgi/eshop_conv.pl?GUESTguest#Conventions.

16. Opened for signature September 23, 1971, TIAS no. 7570, ICAO doc. 8966, entered into force January 26, 1973, available at www.icao.int/cgi/eshop_conv.pl?GUESTguest#Conventions.

17. See Christopher C. Joyner and Robert A. Friedlander, "International Civil Aviation," in Bassiouni, *International Criminal Law,* 1:837–57.

18. See Joseph J. Lambert, *Terrorism and Hostages in International Law* (Cambridge, Eng.: Grotius Publications, 1990).

19. See *International Legal Materials* 18 (1979): 1464, 1482.

20. Case Concerning United States Diplomatic and Consular Staff in Teheran *(United States of America v. Iran), International Court of Justice Reports* 1980:3, reprinted in *International Legal Materials* 19 (1980): 553.

21. International Convention against the taking of Hostages, done December 17, 1979, GA res. 34/146 (34), 34 UN GAOR supp. (no. 46), 245, UN doc. A/34/46 (1979), TIAS no. 11081, entered into force June 3, 1983.

22. Opened for signature December 14, 1973, GA res. 3166 (28), 28 UN GAOR Supplement (no. 30), 146, UN doc. A/9030 (1974), 28 UST 1975, 1035 UNTS 167, entered into force February 20, 1977.

23. UN doc. E/CONF.82/15 corr. and corr. 2, reprinted in *International Legal Materials* 28 (1989): 497.

24. For discussion on the role of the Universal Postal Union, see www.upu.int.

25. Signed on April 20, 1929, 112 LNTS 371, entered into force February 22, 1931.

26. See the discussion in chapter 10.

27. See the *SIPRI Yearbooks, 1975–1996* and A. J. Jongman and A. P. Schmid, "Contemporary Conflicts: A Global Survey of Higher and Lower Intensity Conflict and Serious Disputes," *PIOOM Newsletter and Progress Report* 7 (Winter 1995): 14; and "Study," *PIOOM Newsletter* 6 (1994): 17. Compare Rudolph Rummel, *Death by Government* (New Brunswick, N.J.: Transactions Publishers, 1994), who estimates 72.5 million deaths. Rummel's webpage puts his "democide" estimate of the number of persons murdered by their own governments at "nearly 170 million." See www.hawaii.edu/powerkills/20TH.HTM (accessed August 24, 2003).

28. Opened for signature March 7, 1966, 660 UNTS 195, entered into force January 4, 1969, available at www.hrcr.org/docs/CERD/cerd2.html.

29. Opened for signature November 30, 1973, UN GA res. 3068 (28), UN GAOR 28th sess., supp. no. 30, 75, UN doc. A/9030 (1973), 1015 UNTS 243, available at www.unhchr.ch/html/menu3/b/11.htm.

30. See Roger S. Clark, "Apartheid," in Bassiouni, *International Criminal Law*, 1:643–62.

31. Resolution on the Definition of Aggression, GA res. 3314, UN GAOR, 29th sess. (supp. no. 31), 142.

32. Resolution on the Definition of Aggression, article 5.

33. Agreement for the Prosecution and Punishment of Major War Criminals of the European Axis, Charter of the International Tribunal, August 8, 1945, 59 Stat. 1544, EAS no. 472, 82 UNTS 279.

34. Key among the Nuremberg Charter's central provisions is its article 6, which defines the jurisdiction of the court in these terms: "The following acts, or any of them, are crimes coming within the jurisdiction of the Tribunal for which there shall be individual responsibility: (a) Crimes against the Peace: Namely, planning, preparation, initiation, or waging of a war of aggression, or a war in violation of international treaties, agreements or assurances, or participation in a common plan or conspiracy for the accomplishment of any of the foregoing; (b) War crimes: Namely, violations of the laws or customs of war. Such violations shall include, but shall not be limited to, murder, ill-treatment or deportation to slave labor or from any other purpose of civilian population of or in occupied territory, murder or ill-treatment of prisoners of war or persons on the seas, killing of hostages, plunder of public or private property, wanton destruction of cities, town or villages, or devastation not justified by military necessity; (c) Crimes against Humanity: Namely, murder, extermination, enslavement, deportation, and other inhumane acts committed against any civilian population before or during the war, or persecutions on political, racial or religious grounds in execution of or in connection with any crime within the jurisdiction of the Tribunal, whether or not in violation of the domestic law of the country where perpetrated. Leaders, organizers, instigators and accomplices participating in the formulation or execution of a common plan or conspiracy to commit any of the foregoing crimes are responsible for all acts performed by any persons in the execution of such plan."

35. See Christopher C. Joyner, "Enforcing Human Rights Standards in the Former Yugoslavia: The Case for an International War Crimes Tribunal," *Denver Journal of International Law & Policy* 22 (1994): 235.

36. The four Geneva Conventions of August 12, 1949, are the Convention for the Amelioration

of the Condition of the Wounded and the Sick in Armed Forces in the Field (Geneva Convention I), August 12, 1949, 6 UST 3114, 75 UNTS 31; Convention for the Amelioration of the Condition of Wounded, Sick, and Shipwrecked Members of Armed Forces at Sea (Geneva Convention II), August 12, 1949, 6 UST 3217, 75 UNTS 85; Convention Relative to the Treatment of Prisoners of War (Geneva Convention III), August 12, 1949, 6 UST 3316, 75 UNTS 135; Convention Relative to the Protection of Civilian Persons in Times of War (Geneva Convention IV), August 12, 1949, 6 UST 3516, 75 UNTS 28.

37. Convention on the Prevention and Punishment of the Crime of Genocide, December 9, 1948, 1 UN GAOR res. 96 (December 11, 1946) 78 UNTS 277.

38. See Agreement for the Prosecution and Punishment of Major War Criminals of the European Axis (London Charter), signed at London August 8, 1945, 59 Stat. 1544, 82 UNTS 279, 3 Bevans 1238, entered into force August 8, 1945; International Military Tribunal for the Far East, proclaimed at Tokyo, January 19, 1946, and amended April 26, 1946, TIAS no. 1589, 4 Bevans 20; Affirmation of the Principles of International Law Recognized by the Charter of the Nuremberg Tribunal (United Nations General Assembly Resolution), adopted at New York, December 11, 1946, UN GA res. 95 (1), UN doc. A/64/Add.1 (1946); Principles of International Law Recognized in the Charter of the Nuremberg Tribunal and in the Judgment of the Tribunal, adopted at Geneva, July 29, 1950, 5 UN GAOR supp. no. 12, 11, UN doc. A/1316 (1950), *American Journal of International Law* 44 (1950): 126; Code of Crimes against the Peace and Security of Mankind: titles and texts of articles on the Draft Code of Crimes against the Peace and Security of Mankind adopted by the International Law Commission at its forty-eighth session (1996), UN GAOR International Law Commission, 48th sess. UN doc. A/CN.4/L.532 (1996), July 15, 1996, revised by UN doc. A/CN.4/L.532/corr.1, UN Document A/CN.4/L.532/corr.3; Convention on the Nonapplicability of Statutory Limitations to War Crimes and Crimes against Humanity, opened for signature at New York, November 26, 1968, GA res. 2391, UN GAOR, 23d sess., supp. no. 18, 40, UN doc. A/RES/2391 (1968), 754 UNTS 73, entered into force November 1970, reprinted in *International Legal Materials* 8 (1969): 68; and European Convention on the Nonapplicability of Statutory Limitations to Crimes against Humanity and War Crimes (Inter-European), signed at Strasbourg, January 25, 1974, Europe TS no. 82, reprinted in *International Legal Materials* 13 (1974): 540; not yet in force.

39. As defined in the four Geneva Conventions, certain "grave breaches" are crimes committed against persons or property protected by the conventions and include "(i) Willful killing, torture or inhuman treatment of protected persons; (ii) Willfully causing great suffering or serious injury to body or health of protected persons; (iii) Taking of hostages and extensive destruction and appropriation of property not justified by military necessity and carried out unlawfully and wantonly; (iv) Unlawful deportation or transfer or unlawful confinement of a protected person; (v) Compelling a prisoner of war or other protected person to serve in the forces of a hostile power; and, (vi) Willfully depriving a prisoner of war or other protected person of the rights of fair and regular trial prescribed in the Geneva Conventions."

40. International Criminal Tribunal for Rwanda Statute, article 4.

41. Hague Convention 4, Respecting the Laws and Customs of War on Land, October 18, 1907, 36 Stat. 2277.

42. See Diane F. Orentlicher, "Responsibilities of States Participating in Multilateral Operations with Respect to Persons Indicted for War Crimes," in *Reigning in Impunity for International Crimes and Serious Violations of Fundamental Human Rights,* ed. Christopher C. Joyner, Nouvelles Etudes Penales 14 (Toulouse, Fr.: Erès, 1998), 193.

43. Genocide Convention, articles 4, 5, 6.

44. GA res. 96, 1 UN GAOR, UN doc. A/64, (1946), 188.

45. This is provided for in the Convention on the Nonapplicability of Statutory Limitations to War Crimes and Crimes against Humanity, entered into force November 11, 1970, 754 UNTS 73, reprinted in *International Legal Materials* 8 (1969): 68. See M. Cherif Bassiouni, *Crimes against Humanity in International Criminal Law* (Boston: M. Nijhoff, 1992).

46. See Treaty on European Convention for the Prevention of Torture and Inhuman or Degrading Treatment or Punishment (Inter-European), opened for signature at Strasbourg, November 26,

1987, European TS no. 126, in *International Legal Materials* 27 (1989): 1152, entered into force February 1, 1989; Inter-American Convention to Prevent and Punish Torture, done at Cartagena de Indias, December 9, 1985, AG/Resolution 783 (25-0/85), OAS General Assembly, 15th sess. IEA/Ser.P. AG/Document 22023/85 rev. 1, 46–54 (1986), OAS Treaty Series, no. 67, *International Legal Materials* 25 (1986): 519, entered into force February 28, 1987.

47. See the discussion in *Final Report of the Commission of Experts*, 55–60. In late 1992–early 1993, the European Community sent a special mission headed by Dame Ann Warburton to investigate the treatment of Muslim women in the former Yugoslavia. This mission found that the number of women raped ranged from ten thousand to sixty thousand and that rape was used by the Serbs as a premeditated strategy to terrorize Muslim populations and to force them to leave their homes. See *European Community Investigative Mission into the Treatment of Muslim Women in the Former Yugoslavia: Report to European Community Foreign Ministers*, UN Document S/25240 (February 3, 1993), annex 1, 2; and M. Cherif Bassiouni and Marcia McCormick, *Sexual Violence: An Invisible Weapon of War in the Former Yugoslavia*, Occasional Paper 1 (Chicago: DePaul International Human Rights Law Institute, 1996).

48. See Draft Code of Crimes against the Peace and Security of Mankind: titles and texts of articles on the Draft Code of Crimes against the Peace and Security of Mankind adopted by the International Law Commission at its forty-eighth session (1996), UN GAOR International Law Commission 48th sess. UN doc. A/CN.4L.532 (1996), article 2. See also the Rome Statute of the International Criminal Court, A/Conf. 183/9 (1998), article 25.

49. Indeed, as set by the Nuremberg precedent and resurrected for modern humanitarian law, the ICTY and ICTR Statutes assert that "2. The official position of any accused person, whether as Head of State or Government or as a responsible Government official, shall not relieve such person of criminal responsibility nor mitigate punishment. 3. The fact that any of the [criminal] acts . . . of the present Statute were committed by a subordinate does not relieve his superior of criminal responsibility if he knew or had reason to know that the subordinate was about to commit such acts or had done so and the superior failed to take the necessary and reasonable measures to prevent such acts or to punish the perpetrators thereof." ICTY Statute, article 7, paragraphs 2–3; ICTR Statute, article 6, paragraphs 2–3.

50. American Law Institute, *Restatement on the Foreign Relations Law of the United States*, 3rd ed. (St. Paul, Minn.: American Law Institute, 1987), sec. 402 (1). See also *United States v. Aluminum Company of America*, 148 F. 2d 416 (2d Cir. 1945).

51. See M. Cherif Bassiouni, "Universal Jurisdiction for International Crimes: Historical Perspectives and Contemporary Practice," *Virginia Journal of International Law* 42 (2001): 81; Christopher C. Joyner, "Arresting Impunity: The Case for Universal Jurisdiction in Bringing War Criminals to Accountability," *Law & Contempory Problems* 59 (1996): 148; and Kenneth C. Randall, "Universal Jurisdiction under International Law," *Texas Law Review* 66 (1988): 785. In addition, a special set of principles on universal jurisdiction was developed in 2001 from a project on universal jurisdiction convened at Princeton University. See *Princeton Project on Universal Jurisdiction* (Princeton University Program in Law and Public Affairs, 2001).

52. Kellogg-Briand Pact, at www.yale.edu/lawweb/avalon/imt/kbpact.htm.

53. See R. John Pritchard, ed., *The Tokyo Major War Crimes Trial* (Lewiston, N.Y.: E. Mellen Press, 1998–2004).

54. The statistics are drawn from the ICTY's webpage at www.un.org/icty/glance/index.htm. See also Virginia Morris and Michael Scharf, *An Insider's Guide to the International Criminal Tribunal for the Former Yugoslavia* (Irvington-on-Hudson, N.Y.: Transnational Publishers 1995), 64–65; and Megan Kaszubinski, "The International Criminal Court for the Former Yugoslavia," in *Post-conflict Justice*, ed. M. Cherif Bassiouni (Ardsley, N.Y.: Transnational Pub., 2002), 459.

55. See Roman Boed, "The International Criminal Tribunal for Rwanda," in Bassiouni, *Post-conflict Justice*, 487. Indictment statistics are taken from the ICTR's webpage at www.ictr.org/ENGLISH/factsheets/detainee.htm.

56. In Rome, votes against the ICC Statute were cast by the United States, Iran, China, Iraq, Yemen, Qatar, and Libya.

57. Rome Statute of the International Criminal Court, UN doc. A/CONF.183/9 of July 17, 1998, depositary notifications at http://untreaty.un.org/ENGLISH/bible/englishinternetbible/partI/ chapterXVIII/t reaty10.asp (accessed March 1, 2004).

58. As a compromise, article 5 provides that the court will exercise jurisdiction over aggression once an amendment is adopted that resolves those issues. Under the terms of the Rome Statute, the amendment cannot be made sooner than seven years after the treaty comes into force.

59. In relevant part, article 29 of the Yugoslavia Tribunal Statute and article 28 of the Rwanda Tribunal Statute assert that "1. States shall cooperate with the International Tribunal in the investigation and prosecution of persons accused of committing serious violations of international humanitarian law. 2. State shall comply without undue delay with any request for assistance or an order issued by a Trials Chamber, including, but not limited to: . . . (d) the arrest or detention of persons; (e) the surrender or the transfer of the accused to the International Tribunal." ICTY Statute, article 29; ICTR Statute, article 28.

60. See Priscilla B. Hayner, *Unspeakable Truths: Confronting State Terror and Atrocity* (New York: Routledge, 2001); and Robert I. Rotberg and Dennis Thompson, eds., *Truth v. Justice: The Morality of Truth Commissions* (Princeton, N.J. : Princeton University Press, 2000).

61. See Alex Boraine, *A Country Unmasked: Inside South Africa's Truth and Reconciliation Commission* (New York: Oxford University Press, 2000); and Kader Asmal, Louise Asmal, and Ronald Suresh Roberts, *Reconciliation through Truth: A Reckoning of Apartheid's Criminal Governance,* 2nd ed. (New York: St. Martin's Press 1997).

62. See Steven Ratner and Jason Abrams, *Accountability for Human Rights Atrocities in International Law* (Oxford: Clarendon Press, 1997).

63. See M. Cherif Bassiouni, "Accountability for Violations of International Humanitarian Law and Other Serious Violations of Human Rights," in Bassiouni, *Post-conflict Justice,* 3–54; and Christopher C. Joyner, ed., *Reigning in Impunity for International Crimes and Serious Violations of Fundamental Human Rights,* Nouvelles Etudes Penales 14 (Toulouse, Fr.: Erès, 1998).

CHAPTER 8

1. Ruth Ann Sivard, *World Military and Social Expenditures* (Washington, D.C.: World Priorities, 1996), 7.

2. For an insightful account, see William V. O'Brien, *The Conduct of Just and Limited War* (New York: Praeger, 1981) and Michael Waltzer, *Just and Unjust Wars,* 3rd ed. (New York: Basic Books, 2002).

3. League of Nations Covenant, available online at Yale University's Avalon Project: www .yale.edu/lawweb/avalaon/league/league.htm.

4. Treaty for the Renunciation of War as an Instrument of National Policy, signed August 27, 1928, entered into force July 24, 1929, 2 Bevans 732, 94 LNTS 57.

5. The Kellogg-Briand Pact served as the legal genesis for codifying the concept of "crimes against the peace," which became one of four principal charges against defendants at the Nuremberg Tribunal proceedings in 1945.

6. See, for example, Thomas M. Franck, *Recourse to Force: State Action against Threats and Attacks* (Cambridge: Cambridge University Press, 2002), 76–96.

7. See the Declaration on the Inadmissibility of Intervention in the Domestic Affairs of States, GA res. 2131 (XX) (1965); the Declaration of the Principles of International Law, GA res. 2625 (XXV) (1970); and the Definition of Aggression, GA res. 3314 (XXIX) (1974).

8. Case Concerning Military and Paramilitary Activities in and against Nicaragua (*Nicaragua v. United States*), *International Court of Justice Reports* 1986:14.

9. See the Corfu Channel Case (*U.K. v. Albania*), *International Court of Justice Reports* 1949:4; and D. W. Bowett, *Self-Defense in International Law* (Manchester: Manchester University Press, 1958).

10. Appended to the definition are six offenses that are stipulated as qualifying as acts of aggression: "(1) The invasion or attack by the armed forces of a State of the territory of another State, or

any military occupation, however temporary, resulting from such invasion or attack, or any annexation by the use of force of the territory of another State or part thereof; (2) Bombardment by the armed forces of a State against the territory of another State or the use of any weapons by a State against the territory of another State; (3) The blockade of the ports or coasts of a State by the armed forces of another State; (4) An attack by the armed forces of a State on the land, sea or air forces, or marine and air fleets of another State; (5) The use of armed forces of one State which are within the territory of another State with the agreement of the receiving State, in contravention of the conditions provided for in the agreement or any extension of their presence in such territory beyond the termination of the agreement; and (6) The action of a State in allowing its territory, which it places at the disposal of another State, to be used by that other State for perpetrating an act of aggression against a third State." For the discussions and debate in the Special Committee, see Reports of the Special Committee on the Question of Defining Aggression, 23 UN GAOR, 6th comm., UN doc. A/7185/Rev.11 (1968); 24 UN GAOR, 6th comm., UN doc.A/7620 (1969); 25 UN GAOR, 6th comm., UN doc. A/8090 (1970); 26 UN GAOR, 6th comm., UN doc. A/8419 (1971); 27 UN GAOR, 6th comm., UN doc. A/8719 (1972); 28 UN GAOR, 6th comm., UN doc. A/9019 (1973); and 29 UN GAOR, 6th comm., UN doc. A/9619 (1974).

11. For a thoughtful analysis of the 1974 Definition of Aggression, see Yehuda Melzer, *Concepts of Just War* (Leiden, Neth.: Sijthoff, 1975).

12. For discussions on the ambiguity and varying interpretations of article 2(4) of the UN Charter, see Oscar Schachter, "The Right of States to Use Armed Force," *Michigan Law Review* 82 (1984): 1620, 1624–28; Louis Henkin et al., *International Law: Cases and Materials,* 3rd ed. (St. Paul, Minn.: West Pub., 1993), 892–93.

13. There are some scholars who argue that the UN Charter does not have this sweeping effect. Michael Glennon argues that because article 1 (4) and article 51 are in irremediable conflict, nothing in the UN Charter impairs a state's sovereign right to use force to defend itself as it deems necessary. Glennon, "The Fog of Law: Self-Defense, Inherence, and Incoherence in Article 51 of the United Nations Charter," *Harvard Journal of Law & Public Policy* 25 (2002): 539–58. See also Ian Brownlie, *International Law and the Use of Force by States* (Oxford: Clarendon Press, 1963), 279, 370 (commenting on the inapplicability of article 51 to indirect forms of aggression); Louis Henkin, *How Nations Behave: Law and Foreign Policy,* 2nd ed. (New York: Columbia University Press 1979), 295 (asserting that article 51 attempts to outlaw any form of anticipatory self-defense).

14. See, for example, Oscar Schachter, *International Law in Theory and Practice* (Boston: M. Nijhoff Publishers, 1991), 1001–113; Hedley Bull, *Intervention in World Politics* (New York: Oxford University Press, 1984), 184–87; Franck, *Recourse to Force,* 1–19.

15. The entire series of six dispatches and letters exchanged by Daniel Webster and Lord Ashburton are available through Yale's Avalon Project at www.yale.edu/lawweb/ avalon/diplomacy/britian/br-1842d.htm.

16. "Letter from Daniel Webster," cited in John Bassett Moore, "The Destruction of the Caroline," *Digest of International Law* 2 (1906): 412. See also "Letter from Mr. Webster to Mr. Fox," April 24, 1841, *British & Foreign State Papers* (1857): 1129, 1138; and Timothy Kearley, "Raising the Caroline," *Wisconsin International Law Journal* 17 (1999): 325.

17. The issue of whether nuclear weapons can be used lawfully as a defensive measure to respond to a conventional or nuclear attack remains unclear, however. That question was not satisfactorily resolved by the International Court of Justice in its Advisory Opinion on the Legality of the Threat or Use of Nuclear Weapons, ICJ General List no. 95 (Advisory Opinion of July 8, 1996). See also C. Moxley Jr., *Nuclear Weapons and International Law in the Post Cold War World* (Lanham, Md.: Austin & Winfield 2000).

18. See Oscar Schachter, "Self-Defense and the Rule of Law," *American Journal of International Law* 83 (1989): 259.

19. The invasion by the United States of Iraq in March 2003 to preempt the latter's prospective use of weapons of mass destruction, the proven or demonstrated existence of which was not known at the time, can be cited as a case in point.

20. See Yoram Dinstein, *War, Aggression, and Self-Defence* (Cambridge, Eng.: Grotius, 1988), 172–

75. Professor Dinstein makes no distinction between the terms *preventive* and *anticipatory* self-defense, holding that article 51 does not allow for preemptive self-defense.

21. See UN Charter, article 53.

22. *International Court of Justice Reports* 1986. See also, the General Asssembly's 1987 Declaration on the Enhancement of the Effectiveness of the Principle of Refraining from the Use of Force in International Relations, GA res. 42/22 (1987), reprinted in *International Legal Materials* (1988): 1672.

23. See Franck, *Recourse to Force,* 76–96; Schachter, "The Right of States," 1629–33.

24. See, for example, Julius Stone, *Aggression and World Order* (London: Stevens, 1963), 43, 95–96; Derek W. Bowett, "The Use of Force for the Protection of Nationals Abroad," in *The Current Legal Regulation of the Use of Force,* ed. A. Cassesse (Boston: M. Nijhoff, 1986); and Natalino Ronzitti, *Rescuing Nationals Abroad* (Boston: M. Nijhoff, 1985).

25. See Bruno Simma, "The UN, Kosovo and the Use of Force: Legal Force?" *European Journal of International Law* 10 (1999): 23; Editorial Comments, "NATO's Kosovo Intervention," *American Journal of International Law* 93 (1999): 824–62; and Ved Nanda, "NATO's Armed Intervention in Kosovo and International Law," *Journal of Legal Studies* 10 (1999–2000): 1–26.

26. Discussion of the lawfulness of humanitarian intervention has recurred periodically since at least the 19th century. The issue of intervening to protect the Christian Bulgarians from oppression by the Ottoman Turks was a contentious campaign issue in Britain between William Gladstone's Liberals and Benjamin Disraeli's Conservatives in the second half of the 19th century. See, for example, Myres S. McDougal and Florentino P. Feliciano, *The International Law of War* (Boston: M. Nijhoff, 1994), 18.

27. This refers to the notion of anticipatory humanitarian intervention. See Christopher C. Joyner and Anthony Clarke Arend, "Anticipatory Humanitarian Intervention: An Emerging Legal Norm?" *Journal of Legal Studies* 10 (1999–2000): 27–60.

28. Article 51 of the UN Charter conditions the right to individual and collective self-defense despite the Security Council's not as yet having taken action.

29. Naulilaa Incident Arbitration, *UN Reports of International Arbitral Awards* (1928): 1012.

30. The 1977 Amendments to the Export Administration Act of 1969, Act of June 22, 1977, Public Law 95-52, 91 Stat. 235 (1977). See the discussion in Christopher C. Joyner, "The Transnational Boycott as Economic Coercion in International Law: Policy, Place, and Practice," *Vanderbilt Journal of Transnational Law* 17 (1984): 205, 268.

31. See UN Charter, article 53.

32. See, for example, Richard Falk, "What Future for the UN Charter System of War Prevention?" *American Journal of International Law* 97 (2003): 590–98; Richard N. Gardner, "Neither Bush for the 'Jurisprudes,'" *American Journal of International Law* 97 (2003): 585–90; Miriam Sapiro, "Iraq: The Shifting Sands of Preemptive Self-Defense," *American Journal of International Law* 97 (2003): 599–607.

33. See, for example, William H. Taft IV and Todd F. Buchwald, "Preemption, Iraq, and International Law," *American Journal of International Law* 97 (2003): 557–63 (Taft served as the State Department's Legal Advisor during the 2003 invasion of Iraq); John Yoo, "International Law and the War in Iraq," *American Journal of International Law* 97 (2003): 563–76; Ruth Wedgwood, "The Fall of Saddam Hussein: Security Council Mandates and Preemptive Self-Defense," *American Journal of International Law* 97 (2003): 576–85.

34. See William J. Durch, ed., *UN Peacekeeping: American Politics and the Uncivil Wars of the 1990s* (New York: St. Martin's Press, 1996).

35. All UN member states share the risk of maintaining peace and security. Since 1948, some 130 governments have contributed military and civilian police personnel. In late 2004, at least 102 states are contributing 62,307 military personnel and civilian police to the current UN missions. Of these states, the top five were Pakistan (8,936 troops), Bangladesh (8,219 troops), Nigeria (3,588 troops), India (3,044 troops), and Ghana (3,320 troops). The small island state of Fiji has participated in every UN peacekeeping operation, as has Canada. Since 1948, 1,946 peacekeepers have been killed in the line of UN duty. See the UN's website at www.un.org/Depts/dpko/dpko/ques.htm (accessed February 15, 2004).

36. GA res. 377 (V) (1950), UN GAOR 5th sess. (1950), supp. no. 20, UN doc. A/1775, 10.

37. Certain Expenses of the United Nations Case, *International Court of Justice Reports* 1962:15, sec. 1.

38. SC res. 1031, UN doc. (1995).

39. SC res. 1368, UN doc. SC/7143 (2001).

40. Interim Agreement between the United States of America and the Union of Soviet Socialist Republics on Certain Measures with Respect to the Limitation of Strategic Offensive Weapons, UST, signed May 26, 1972, entered into force October 3, 1972, at www.fas.org/nuke/control/salt1/text/salt1.htm (accessed June 15, 2003).

41. Treaty between the United States of America and the Union of Soviet Socialist Republics on the Limitation of Strategic Offensive Arms Together with Agreed Statements and Common Understandings Regarding the Treaty, signed June 18, 1979, S. Exec. Doc., 96th Cong., 1st sess. (1979) (not in force), at www.fas.org/nuke/control/salt2/text/salt2-2.htm (accessed June 15, 2003).

42. Done May 24, 2002, at www.whitehouse.gov/news/releases/2002/05/20020524-3.html (accessed June 25, 2003).

43. 21 UST 483, TIAS no. 6839, 729 UNTS 161, entered into force March 5, 1970, at http://disarmament.un.org/TreatyStatus.nsf (accessed June 25, 2003). At least 189 states are parties to the Nuclear Nonproliferation Treaty.

44. 94 LNTS 65, 26 UST 571, TIAS no. 8061, signed June 17, 1925, entered into force February 8, 1928, at www.lib.byu.edu/~rdh/wwi/hague/hague13.html (accessed June 15, 2003).

45. 26 UST 583, TIAS no. 8062, signed April 10, 1972, entered into force March 26, 1975, at www.fas.org/nuke/control/bwc/text/bwc.htm (accessed June 15, 2003). In late 2004 at least 151 states are party to this convention.

46. 610 UNTS 205, 18 UST 2410, TIAS no. 6347, signed January 27, 1967, entered into force October 10, 1967, at www.iaea.or.at/worldatom/Documents/Legal/bginf179.shtml (reproduced from UN doc. A/6663) (accessed June 15, 2003). At least 125 states today are parties to this treaty.

47. 1108 UNTS 151, entered into force October 5, 1978, at www.state.gov/t/ac/trt/4783.htm (accessed June 15, 2003). At least sixty-nine states are now party to this convention.

48. Treaty on the Emplacement of Nuclear Weapons and Other Weapons of Mass Destruction on the Seabed and the Ocean Floor and in the Subsoil Thereof, 23 UST 01, TIAS no. 7337, 955 UNTS 115, done February 11, 1971, entered into force May 18, 1972, available at www.state.gov/t/ac/trt/5187.htm (accessed August 26, 2003). At least ninety-four states are party to the Seabed Arms Control Treaty.

49. UN GAOR, 47th sess., supp. no. 27, UN doc. A/47/27, app. 1 (1992), opened for signature January 13, 1993, entered into force April 29, 1997, at www.cwc.gov/treaty/treatytext_html (accessed March 1, 2004). As of September 2004, 167 states are party to the CWC.

50. 402 UNTS 71, 12 UST 794, TIAS no. 4780, signed December 1, 1959, entered into force June 23, 1961, at www.nsf.gov/od/opp/antarct/anttrty.htm (accessed June 15, 2003). In late 2004, forty-five states are party to the Antarctic Treaty.

51. 634 UNTS 281, 22 UST 762, opened for signature February 14, 1967 (not yet in force), at www.state.gov/t/ac/trt/4796.htm#treaty (accessed June 15, 2003). In 2004 at least 33 states in the Americas are party and individually obliged to this agreement.

52. Adopted August 6, 1985, entered into force December 11, 1986, at www.iaea.or.at/worldatom/Documents/Infcircs/Others/inf331.shtml (accessed June 15, 2003). The following states are party to this agreement: Australia, the Cook Islands, Fiji, Kiribati, Nauru, New Zealand, Nieu, Papua New Guinea, the Solomon Islands, Tonga, Tuvalu, Vanuatu, and Western Samoa, all of whom are members of the South Pacific Forum.

53. Signed December 15, 1995, entered into force March 27, 1997, at www.iaea.or.at/worldatom/Documents/Infcircs/1998/infcirc548.pdf (accessed June 15, 2003).

54. Opened for signature April 11, 1996, at www.iaea.or.at/GC/gc40/documents/pelindab.html (reproduced from UN GA doc. A/50/426) (accessed June 15, 2003).

55. Treaty Banning Nuclear Weapons in the Atmosphere, in Outer Space, and Under Water, 480 UNTS 43, 14 UST 1313, TIAS no. 5433, signed August 5, 1963, entered into force October 10, 1963, at www.fas.org/nuke/control/ltbt/text/ltbt2.htm (accessed June 15, 2003).

56. GA res. 245, UN GAOR, 50th sess., annex, agenda items 8 and 65, UN doc. A/50/1027 (1996), opened for signature September 24, 1996 (not yet in force), at http://pws.ctbto.org/ (accessed June 15, 2003).

57. In May 1993 the World Health Organization requested the Court to give an advisory opinion on the question "In view of the health and environmental effects, would the use of nuclear weapons by a State in war or other armed conflict be a breach of its obligations under international law including the WHO Constitution?" By a vote of 11–3, the court concluded that it was not able to give the advisory opinion that was requested of it under World Health Assembly Resolution WHA46.40 of May 14, 1993, but it could address the issue concerning the lawfulness of nuclear weapons.

58. Legality of the Threat or Use of Nuclear Weapons, *International Court of Justice Reports* 1996:226 (advisory opinion).

CHAPTER 9

1. See the discussion in P. M. Dupuy, "Overview of the Existing Customary Legal Regime Regarding International Pollution," in *International Law and Pollution,* ed. Dan Magraw (Philadelphia: University of Pennsylvania Press 1991), 61–68.

2. UNEP conventions tend to be of the framework type, establishing general principles but leaving detailed and substantive elements to be set by protocols later.

3. See the UNEP website at www.unep.org.

4. See the Conservation of Migratory Species website at www.wcmc.org.uk/cms.

5. Vienna Convention for the Protection of the Ozone Layer, entered into force September 22, 1988, reg. no. 26264, 1513 UNTS 293. Today, there are 189 parties to this agreement.

6. Montreal Protocol on Substances That Deplete the Ozone Layer, entered into force January 1, 1989, reg. no. 26369, 1522 UNTS 3. As of 2005, there are at least 188 parties to the Montreal Protocol.

7. Basel Convention on the Control of Transboundary Movements of Hazardous Wastes and Their Disposal, entered into force May 5, 1992, reg. no. 28911, 1673 UNTS 57. At least 163 states are contracting parties to this agreement.

8. Convention on Biological Diversity, done June 5, 1992, entered into force December 23, 1993, UNEP/Bio.Div/N7-INC.5/4 (June 5, 1992), reg. no. 30619.

9. Convention on the Prevention of Marine Pollution by Dumping of Wastes and Other Matter, done December 29, 1972, entered into force August 30, 1975, 26 UST 2403, 1046 UNTS 120, TIAS no. 8165.

10. International Convention for the Prevention of Pollution from Ships, done November 2, 1973, IMO doc. MP/CPNF.WP.35/ (1973); and Protocol of 1978 Relating to the International Convention for the Prevention of Pollution from Ships, done February 17, 1978, entered into force October 2, 1983, IMO doc. TSSP/CONF/11 (1978).

11. International Convention for the Safety of Life at Sea, 1974, entered into force May 25, 1980, 1184 UNTS 2, TIAS no. 9700.

12. Convention on the International Regulations for Preventing Collisions at Sea, entered into force July 15, 1977, 28 UST 3459, TIAS no. 8587.

13. IMO doc. MSC/Cr. 497, July 26, 1988.

14. See the ILO website at wwww.ilo.org, especially under workers' activities related to sustainable development.

15. See FAO doc. COFI/93/10 (February 1993), FAO Fisheries Department: Code of Conduct for Responsible Fisheries, at www.fao.org/fi/agreem/codecond/ficonde.asp.

16. See the FAO website at www.fao.org.

17. See the World Bank website at www.worldbank.org, especially its "New Environment Strategy."

18. For further information on the European Environmental Agency, see http://europa.eu.int/ pol/env/index_eu.htm.

19. Done September 22, 1992, entered into force March 25, 1998. See www.ospar.org.

20. Done March 22, 1989, entered into force May 5, 1992, available at www.basel.int. As of 2005 there are 163 parties to this agreement.

21. Done February 16, 1976, entered into force February 12, 1978. Text reprinted at www .unep.ch/seas/main/med/medconvi.html. For the Barcelona Convention's website, see www .rempec.org/barcelona.html.

22. Adopted March 17, 1992, entered into force October 6, 1996. doc. ENVWA/R.53 and Add. 1. reg. no. 33207. For the Helsinki Convention's website, see www.waterland.net. At least thirty-five states are party to this agreement.

23. Done November 13, 1979, entered into force March 16, 1983, reg. no. 21623, 1302 UNTS 217.

24. Done September 19, 1979, entered into force June 1, 1982, reg. no. 21159.

25. Done at Bonn on June 23, 1979, available at www.wcmc.org.uk/cms/cms_conv.htm.

26. Organisation for Economic Cooperation and Development, *OECD Environmental Strategy for the First Decade of the 21st Century*, adopted by the OECD Environmental Ministers, May 16, 2001, available at www.oecd.org.env.

27. See www.nato.int/ccms.

28. See Louis B. Sohn, "The Stockholm Declaration on the Human Environment," *Harvard International Law Journal* 14 (1973): 423–89.

29. United Nations Framework Convention on Climate Change, done May 9, 1992, entered into force March 21, 1994, 1771 UNTS 107, reg. no. 30822. At least 189 states are party to this agreement. The Kyoto Protocol implements the framework. Done December 11, 1997, December 1/CP. of the Conference of States parties to the convention at the third session. Though not yet in force, in late 2004 this protocol has 126 states as parties.

30. See David A. Wirth, "The Rio Declaration on Environment and Development: Two Steps Forward and One Back, or Vice Versa?" *Georgia Law Review* 29 (1995): 599–653.

31. See the Commission on Development website at www.un.org/esa/sustdev/csd.htm.

32. Convention for the Final Settlement of the Difficulties Arising through Complaints of Damage Done in the State of Washington for Fumes Discharged from the Smelter of the Consolidated Mining and Smelting Company, Trail, British Columbia, April 15, 1935, 49 Stat. 3245 (1935), TS no. 893, 162 LNTS 74 (effective August 3, 1935).

33. Trail Smelter Arbitration (*United States v. Canada*), Ad Hoc International Arbitral Tribunal, 1941, *UN Reports of International Arbitral Awards* 4 (1941): 1991, 1938.

34. See J. Read, "The Trail Smelter Dispute," *Canadian Year Book of International Law* (1963): 213.

35. *International Court of Justice Reports* 1949:3.

36. See L. F. E. Goldie, "Liability for Damage and the Progressive Development of International Law," 14 *International & Comparative Law Quarterly* 14 (1965): 1189, 1229–31.

37. Lake Lanoux Arbitration (*France v. Spain*), Ad Hoc International Arbitral Tribunal, 1957, *UN Reports of International Arbitral Awards* 12 (1957): 281.

38. See Samuel Bleicher, "An Overview of International Environmental Regulation," *Ecology Law Quarterly* 2 (1972): 1, 27–29.

39. Stockholm Declaration of the United Nations Conference on the Human Environment, principle 21 in *Report of the UN Conference of the Human Environment*, adopted June 16, 1972, UN doc. A/CONF. 48/14 (1972).

40. See Rio Declaration on Environment and Development, principle 15, adopted by the United Nations Conference on Environment and Development, June 14, 1992, UN doc. A/CONF.151/5/Rev. 1, June 13, 1992.

41. See Lothar Gundling, "The Status in International Law of the Principle of Precautionary Action," *International Journal of Estuarine & Coastal Law* 5 (1990): 23–30; O. McIntyre and T. Mosdale, "The Precautionary Principle as a Norm of Customary International Law," *Journal of Environmental Law* 9 (1997): 221–41; David Freestone and Ellen Hey, eds., *The Precautionary Principle and International Law: The Challenge of Implementation* (The Hague: Kluwer Law International, 1996).

42. ASEAN Agreement on the Conservation of Nature and Natural Resources, done at Kuala Lumpur on July 9, 1985, fundamental principle 1.

43. Intragenerational equity means that people within a single generation may enjoy a clean, healthy environment and its resources at the national and the international level. See generally Edith Brown Weiss, *In Fairness to Future Generations: International Law, Common Patrimony, and Future Generations* (Dobbs Ferry, N.Y.: Oceana, 1989).

44. See GA res. 2995 (XXVII); GA res. 3129 (28); OECD Recommendation C (74) 224 of November 14, 1974, on Principles Concerning Transfrontier Pollution; and principles 1, 7, 9, and 12 of the UNEP draft Principles of Conduct.

45. Rio Declaration on Environment and Development, principle 15.

46. See General Principles Concerning Natural Resources and Environmental Inferences, articles 15, 16, and 17, Final Report of the Experts Group on Environmental Law on Legal Principles for Environmental Protection and Sustainable Development, Experts Group on Environmental Law of the World Commission on Environment and Development (Brundtland Commission), *Environmental Protection and Sustainable Development* (1987): 29–30; Rules of International Law Applicable to Transfrontier Pollution, articles 7 and 8, International Law Association, *Report of the Sixtieth Conference, Montreal* (1982): 158, 171, 175; United Nations Convention on the Law of the Nonnavigational Uses of International Watercourses, UN doc. A/RES/51/229, July 8, 1997, articles 11–19.

47. OECD, Guiding Principles Concerning International Economic Aspects of Environmental Policies, Recommendation C (72), 128, paragraph 4, reprinted in *International Legal Materials* 11 (1972): 1172.

48. See European Commission, *White Paper on Environmental Liability* (February 2000), available at http://europa.eu.int/comm/environment/liability/index.htm.

49. United Nations Environmental Programme, Multilateral Environmental Agreements: A Summary (background paper prepared by the secretariat), Open-Ended Intergovernmental Group of Ministers or Their Representatives on International Environmental Governance, 1st meeting, April 18, 2001, UN doc. UNEP/IGM/I/INF/1, 3 (March 30, 2001).

50. UN doc. A/CONF./62/122, done December 10, 1982, entered into force November 16, 1994, available at UN Division for Ocean Affairs and the Law of the Sea, www.un.org/Depts/los/losdocs .htm.

51. For discussion of these developments, see Christopher C. Joyner, "The International Ocean Regime at the New Millennium: A Survey of the Contemporary Legal Order," *Ocean & Coastal Management* 43 (2000): 163–203.

52. Adopted November 15, 1973, entered into force May 26, 1976, 27 UST 3918, TIAS no. 8409. Parties to the Polar Bear Convention include Canada, Denmark, Norway, the Soviet Union (now Russia), and the United States.

53. Done March 3, 1973, entered into force July 1, 1975, 27 UST 1087, TIAS no. 8249, 993 UNTS 243. At least 166 states are party to the CITES agreement. See www.cites.org/eng/disc/parties/ chronolo.sthml.

54. Convention on the Conservation of Migratory Species of Wild Animals (Bonn), 1979 reprinted in *International Legal Materials* 19 (1980): 15.

55. Agreement on the Conservation of Bats in Europe, done September 10, 1981, entered into force January 16, 1994, reg. no. 31714, reprinted at http://ww.wcmc.org.uk/cms.

56. Agreement on the Conservation of Small Cetaceans of the Baltic and North Sea, done March 17, 1992, entered into force March 29, 1994, reg. no. 30865.

57. The International Coral Reef Initiative seeks to coordinate efforts among some eighty states with the aim of ensuring sustainable use and conservation of coral reefs for future generations. The initiative provides an informal mechanism, as opposed to a formal treaty structure, that allows representatives of coastal states with coral reefs to sit in equal partnership with major donor states and development banks, international environmental and development agencies, scientific associations, the private sector, and NGOs to decide what strategies might best conserve the world's coral reef resources.

58. UNESCO Convention Concerning Protection of the World Cultural and Natural Heritage, adopted November 16, 1972, entered into force December 17, 1975, 27 UST 37, TIAS 8225, 1037 UNTS 151, reprinted in *International Legal Materials* 11 (1972): 1358.

59. Convention to Combat Desertification in Those Countries Experiencing Serious Drought and/or Desertification, particularly in Africa, done October 14, 1994, entered into force December 26, 1996, 1954 UNTS 3, reg. no. 33480. As of 2005, 191 states contracted to this instrument.

60. Rotterdam Convention on the Prior Informed Consent Procedure for Certain Hazardous Chemicals and Pesticides in International Trade, done at Rotterdam, September 10, 1998, UN doc. UNEP/FAO/PIC/CONF/5 (not yet in force). In late 2004 at least 77 states are party to this agreement.

61. Stockholm Convention on Persistent Organic Pollutants, done at Stockholm, May 22, 2001 (not yet in force). In late 2004 83 states are parties to this agreement.

62. UNEP Environmental Law Guidelines and Principles, Decision 14/30 of the General Council of UNEP, June 17, 1987.

63. Decision 8/7 of the Governing Council of UNEP, April 29, 1980.

64. Decision 10/14/VI of the Governing Council of UNEP, May 31, 1982.

65. Decision 12/14, adopted by the Governing Council of UNEP, May 28, 1984.

66. Decision 13/18/II of the Governing Council of UNEP, June 17, 1987.

67. Decision 14/25 of the Governing Council of UNEP, June 17, 1987.

68. Decision 14/27 of the Governing Council of UNEP, June 17, 1987.

69. International Law Association, Helsinki Rules, *Report of the Fifty-Second Conference: Helsinki* (1967): 477, 485.

70. Convention on the Law of the Nonnavigational Uses of International Watercourses, done in New York, May 21, 1997, UN doc. A/51/869 (not yet in force).

71. Done May 12, 1954, entered into force July 26, 1958, 12 UST 2989, TIAS no. 4900, 327 UNTS 3.

72. Adopted November 29, 1969, entered into force May 6, 1975, 26 UST 765, TIAS no. 8068.

73. Adopted November 29, 1969, entered into force July 16, 1975. The Liability Convention was negotiated to update and replace the 1954 antipollution agreement.

74. Adopted December 18, 1971, entered into force October 16, 1978.

75. Convention on the Prevention of Marine Pollution by Dumping of Wastes and Other Matter, done December 29, 1972, entered into force August 30, 1975, 26 UST 2403, 1046 UNTS 120, TIAS no. 8165; Protocol Amending Convention on the Prevention of Marine Pollution by Dumping of Wastes and Other Matter, IMO doc. A/52/487, paras. 288–95.

76. Adopted 1969, entered into force August 9, 1969, 704 UNTS 3.

77. Done February 15, 1972, entered into force April 6, 1974, 932 UNTS 3, reprinted in *International Legal Materials* 11 (1972): 262, at http://sedac.ciesin.org/pidb/texts/marine.pollution.dumping.ships.aircraft.197 2.html (accessed April 21, 2004).

78. Done June 4, 1974, entered into force May 6, 1978, reprinted in *International Legal Materials* 13 (1974): 352, amended by protocol of 1986, in force February 1, 1990, reprinted in *International Legal Materials* 27 (1988): 625, at http://sedac.ciesin.org/pidb/texts/marine.pollution.land.based.sources.1974.ht ml.

79. See Katharina Kummer, *The International Management of Hazardous Wastes* (Oxford: Clarendon Press, 1995).

80. Entered into force October 27, 1986, IAEA reg. no. 1532.

81. Entered into force February 8, 1987, IAEA reg. no. 1533.

82. Entered into force November 12, 1977, IAEA reg. no. 1277.

83. Treaty on the Nonproliferation of Nuclear Weapons, signed July 1, 1968, entered into force March 5, 1970, 21 UST 483, TIAS no. 6839, 729 UNTS 161, reprinted at *International Legal Materials* 7 (1968): 811.

84. See the IAEA's website at www.iaea.org/worldatom/About/numbers.html.

85. International Union for Conservation of Nature and Natural Resources, *Caring for the Earth: A Strategy for Sustainable Living* (Gland, Switz.: Author, 1991).

86. *Consideration and Adoption of the Revised Draft World Charter for Nature: Report of the Secretary-General*, 37/UN GAOR (Agenda Item 21), UN doc. A/398 (1982), GA res. 37/7, October 28, 1982.

87. Final Report of the Experts Group on Environmental Law on Legal Principles for Environmental Protection and Sustainable Development, Experts Group on Environmental Law of the

World Commission on Environment and Development (Brundtland Commission), *Environmental Protection and Sustainable Development* (1987).

88. Data is from the World Heritage List website: http://whc.unesco.org/heritage.htm (accessed April 21, 2004).

89. Data is from the Ramsar Convention website at www.ramsar.org (accessed April 21, 2004).

90. See the Biological Diversity Convention website at www.biodiv.org.

91. See the discussions in Simon Lyster, *International Wildlife Law: An Analysis of International Treaties Concerned with the Conservation of Wildlife* (Cambridge: Cambridge University Press, 1985); Michael J. Glennon, "Has International Law Failed the Elephant?" *American Journal of International Law* 84 (1990): 1–4; John B. Heppes and Eric J. McFadden, "The Convention on International Trade in Endangered Species of Wild Fauna and Flora: Improving of the Prospects for Preserving Our Biological Heritage," *Boston University International Law Journal* 5 (1987): 229–45.

92. Data is from the CITES webpage at www.cites.org.

93. See Stephen McCaffrey, "Crimes against the Environment," in *International Criminal Law*, ed. Cherif Bassiouni (Ardsley, N.Y.: Transnational Pub., 2001), 1:943–1004.

94. See the discussion in Dinah Shelton, "Human Rights, Environmental Rights, and the Right to Environment," *Stanford Journal of International Law* 28 (1991): 103–33; Philip Alston, "Making Space for New Human Rights: The Case for the Right to Development," *Harvard Human Rights Journal* 1 (1988): 3; and Noralee Gibson, "The Right to a Clean Environment," *Saskatchewan Law Review* (1990): 5.

95. See Hurst Hannum, "New Developments in Indigenous Rights," *Virginia Journal of International Law* 28 (1988): 649–78.

96. See Michelle Leighton Schwartz, "International Legal Protection for Victims of Environmental Abuse," *Yale Journal of International Law* 18 (1993): 335.

97. Paul Kennedy, *Preparing for the Twenty-First Century* (New York: Random House, 1993), 109–10.

98. See Christopher C. Joyner and Zachary Tyler, "Marine Conservation versus International Free Trade: Reconciling Dolphins with Tuna and Sea Turtles with Shrimp," *Ocean Development & International Law* 31 (2000): 127–15.

99. GATT: Dispute Settlement Panel Report on United States Restrictions on Imports of Tuna, August 16, 1991, reprinted in *International Legal Materials* 30 (1991): 1594; GATT: Dispute Settlement Panel Report on United States Restrictions on Imports of Tuna, May 20, 1994, reprinted in *International Legal Materials* 33 (1994): 839 (appellate brief).

100. WTO Report of the Panel Concerning the United States—Import Prohibition of Certain Shrimp and Shrimp Products, May 15, 1998, 1998 WL 256632; WTO Report of the Panel Concerning the United States—Import Prohibition of Certain Shrimp and Shrimp Products, October 12, 1998, 1998 WL 720123 (appellate brief).

101. See Francisco Francioni and Tullio Scovazzi, eds., *International Responsibility for Environmental Harm* (Gaithersburg, Md.: Aspen, 1991); Kamen Sachariew, "Promoting Compliance with International Environmental Legal Standards: Reflections on Monitoring and Reporting Mechanisms," *1991 Year Book of International Environmental Law* (1992): 31; Edith Brown Weiss, "Strengthening National Compliance with International Environmental Agreements," *Environmental Policy & Law* 27 (1997): 297.

CHAPTER 10

1. For an authoritative and provocative study, see Kemal Baslar, *The Concept of the Common Heritage of Mankind in International Law* (The Hague: Martinus Nijhoff, 1998). Compare the views in Christopher C. Joyner, "Legal Implications of Common Heritage of Mankind," *International & Comparative Law Quarterly* 35 (1986): 190–99.

2. See Edith Brown Weiss, *In Fairness to Future Generations: International Law, Common Patrimony, and Intergenerational Equity* (Dobbs Ferry, N.Y.: Transnational Press, 1989).

3. For the powers and functions of the International Seabed Authority, see United Nations Convention on the Law of the Sea, opened for signature December 10, 1982, entered into force November 16, 1994, 1833 UNTS 3, articles 156–83 (hereinafter 1982 LOS Convention). For text, see UN Division for Ocean Affairs and the Law of the Sea, at http://ww.un.org/Depts/los/index.htm. Controversy over the nature of the Authority led to the eventual modification of its structure, powers, and functions to make the convention acceptable to developed states as a whole. See Christopher C. Joyner, "The United States and the New Law of the Sea," *Ocean Development & International Law* 27 (1996): 41–58.

4. See article 11 in the Agreement Governing the Activities of States on the Moon and Other Celestial Bodies, UN doc. A/34/664 (1979). During the 1980s the United Nations became the forum wherein international politics over Antarctica were concentrated. Led by Malaysia in the General Assembly, developing countries contended that Antarctica should be declared part of the common heritage of mankind, as had already been done for the deep seabed and for the moon and its resources. Other political criticisms by the developing countries asserted that the Antarctic Treaty parties formed an exclusive, secretive "club," that the inclusion of the white minority government of South Africa should not be considered a legitimate Antarctic Treaty Consultative Party and, most profoundly, that the negotiation of a mineral regime, if consummated, would benefit only those states in the Antarctic Treaty regime at the expense of the majority of humankind. Interestingly, on every issue except South Africa, the Antarctic Treaty Consultative Parties (inclusive of China, India, Brazil, Argentina, and Chile) stood fast as a group of "not participating" states in several votes taken between 1983 and 1988 on General Assembly resolutions on the Antarctic question. The demise of the Antarctic Treaty minerals regime by 1990 prompted Malaysia to abandon its perennial call for Antarctica to be made part of the common heritage, leaving the Antarctic Treaty system as the implicitly lawful regime for administering activities of states interested in the polar south. See the discussion in Christopher C. Joyner, *Governing the Frozen Commons: The Antarctic Regime and Environmental Protection* (Columbia: University of South Carolina Press, 1998), 220–58.

5. Article 136 of the 1982 LOS Convention flatly asserts that the deep seabed and "its resources are the common heritage of mankind." By late 2004, at least 157 states had signed, and 145 had ratified the 1982 LOS Convention, thereby becoming legally obligated to treating the deep seabed as the common heritage of mankind.

6. See Edith Brown Weiss, ed., *International Compliance with Nonbinding Accords* (Washington, D.C.: American Society of International Law, 1997); and Dinah Shelton, ed., *Commitment and Compliance: The Role of Non-Binding Norms in the International Legal System* (New York: Oxford University Press, 2000).

7. See *The Ocean Our Future: Report of the Independent World Commission on the Oceans* (Cambridge: Cambridge University Press, 1998); Anne Platt McGinn, *Safeguarding the Health of Oceans*, Worldwatch Paper 145 (Washington, D.C.: Worldwatch Institute, March 1999); and Elisabeth Mann Borgese, *The Oceanic Circle: Governing the Seas as a Global Resource* (Tokyo: United Nations University Press, 1998).

8. 10 Fed. Reg. 12, 303 (1945), reprinted in Marjorie Whiteman, *Digest of International Law* 4 (1965): 756.

9. Done at Geneva April 29, 1958, entered into force September 10, 1964, 15 UST 1606, TIAS no. 5639, 516 UNTS 205.

10. Done April 29, 1958, entered into force March 20, 1966, 17 UST 138, TIAS no. 5969, 559 UNTS 285.

11. Done April 29, 1958, entered into force September 30, 1962, 13 UST 2312, TIAS no. 5200, 450 UNTS 82.

12. Done April 29, 1958, entered into force June 10, 1964, 15 UST 471, TIAS no. 5578, 499 UNTS 311.

13. Convention on the Continental Shelf, article 1.

14. United Nations Convention on the Law of the Sea, opened for signature December 10, 1982, entered into force November 16, 1994, 1833 UNTS 3., reg. no. 31363.

15. An island is "a naturally formed area of land, surrounded by water, which is above water at high tide." 1982 LOS Convention, article 121.

16. See 1982 LOS Convention, article 136.

17. For contemporary information on the structure and functions of IMO, see the IMO website at www.imo.org.

18. Outstanding among these IMO instruments are the 1965 Convention on the Facilitation of International Maritime Traffic; the 1972 Convention on the Prevention of Marine Pollution by Dumping of Wastes and Other Matter; the 1973 International Convention for the Prevention of Pollution by Ships; the 1974 International Convention for the Safety of Life at Sea; the 1972 Convention on the International Regulation for Preventing Collisions at Sea; and the 1988 Convention on the Suppression of Unlawful Acts Threatening the Safety of International Navigation.

19. These regional conventions cover the following areas of the ocean commons: The Mediterranean Sea, the Persian/Arabian Gulf, West African coast, South-East Pacific, Red Sea and Gulf of Aden, Caribbean Sea, East African region, and South-West Pacific. See Christopher C. Joyner, "Biodiversity in the Marine Environment: Resource Implications for the Law of the Sea," 28 *Vanderbilt Journal of Transnational Law* 672–79 (1995), and Peter H. Sand, *Marine Environment Law in the United Nations Environmental Programme* (New York: Tycooly, 1988). Outside the United Nations system, other special regional seas agreements have been negotiated for the Baltic Sea and the circumpolar Antarctic waters.

20. Adopted November 1, 1974, entered into force May 25, 1980, 1184 UNTS 2, TIAS no. 9700.

21. Adopted October 20, 1972, entered into force July 15, 1977, 28 UST 3459, TIAS no. 8587.

22. Convention on the Prevention of Marine Pollution by Dumping of Wastes and Other Matter, done December 29, 1972, entered into force August 30, 1975, 1046 UNTS 120, TIAS no. 8165, available at www.londonconvention.org/main.htm (accessed August 26, 2004).

23. International Convention for the Prevention of Pollution from Ships, done November 2, 1973, IMCO doc. MP/CPNF.WP.35/ (1973); and Protocol of 1978 Relating to the International Convention for the Prevention of Pollution from Ships, done February 17, 1978, entered into force October 2, 1983, IMCO doc. TSSP/CONF/11 (1978), available at www.londonconvention.org/main.htm (accessed August 26, 2004).

24. Agreement to Promote Compliance with International Conservation and Management Measures by Fishing Vessels on the High Seas, adopted November 1993, entered into force on April 24, 2003, reprinted in *International Legal Materials* 33 (1994): 969, at www.fao.org/legal/treaties/012t-e .htm (accessed August 26, 2003). Today at least twenty-nine states are party to this instrument.

25. Agreement for the Implementation of the Provisions of the United Nations Convention on the Law of the Sea of December 10, 1982, relating to the Conservation and Management of Straddling Fish Stocks and Highly Migratory Fish Stocks, opened for signature December 4, 1995, entered into force December 11, 2001, reprinted in *International Legal Materials* 34 (1995): 1542, at www .un.org/Depts/los/convention_agreements/convention_overview_fish_st ocks.htm (accessed August 26, 2003). At least fifty-two states are parties in 2005 to this agreement.

26. International Convention for the Regulation of Whaling, December 2, 1946, entered into force November 10, 1948, TIAS no. 1849, 161 UNTS 72, available at www.iwcoffice.org/Convention.htm (accessed August 26, 2003). At least fifty-seven states are now members of the International Whaling Commission.

27. Even today, Japan, Norway, and Iceland persist in taking minke whales for "scientific" purposes, despite the IWC ban.

28. Antarctic Treaty, opened for signature December 1, 1959, entered into force June 23, 1961, 12 UST 794, 402 UNTS 71, at www.scar.org/Treaty/Treaty_Text.htm (accessed August 26, 2004). In 2005 forty-five states are parties to the Antarctic Treaty.

29. Done at Brussels June 2–13, 1964, 17 UST 996, 998, TIAS no. 6058, modified in 24 UST 1802, TIAS no. 7693 (1973).

30. Done at London June 1, 1972, entered into force March 11, 1978, 27 UST 441, TIAS no. 8826.

31. Done May 20, 1980, 33 UST 3476, TIAS no. 10,240.

32. Done at Wellington June 2, 1988, opened for signature November 25, 1988. Document AMR/SCM/88/78 (June 2, 1988), reprinted in *International Legal Materials* 27 (1988): 859. For discussion of the negotiations that produced this agreement, see Christopher C. Joyner, "The Antarctic Minerals Negotiating Process," *American Journal of International Law* 81 (1987): 888.

33. Protocol on Environmental Protection to the Antarctic Treaty, Eleventh Special Consultative Meeting in Madrid, doc. 11 ATSCM/2, June 21, 1991, adopted October 4, 1991.

34. Protocol on Environmental Protection to the Antarctic Treaty, article 2.

35. Importantly, much of the substance of article 3 in the Madrid Protocol is borrowed from article 4 in the Wellington Minerals Convention, save for the significant difference that article 3 in the protocol strives to apply comprehensive uniform standards for all human activities in the Antarctic, not just those that might be related to minerals development.

36. See Christopher C. Joyner, "Recommended Measures under the Antarctic Treaty: Hardening Compliance with Soft International Law," *Michigan Journal of International Law* 19 (1998): 401–43.

37. See Christopher C. Joyner, "Managing Common-Pool Marine Living Resources: Lessons from the Southern Ocean Experience," in *Anarchy and the Environment: The International Relations of Common Pool Resources,* ed. J. Samuel Barkin and George E. Shambaugh (Albany: State University of New York Press, 1999), 70–96.

38. See Christopher C. Joyner, *Governing the Frozen Commons: The Antarctic Regime and Environmental Protection* (Columbia: University of South Carolina Press, 1998), 220–58.

39. See Marvin S. Soroos, *The Changing Atmosphere: The Quest for Global Environmental Security* (Columbia: University of South Carolina Press, 1997).

40. Importantly, this reflects the cardinal notion of international environmental law found in principle 21 of the 1972 Declaration of the United Nations Conference on the Human Environment at Stockholm, UN doc. A/CONF.48/14/REV.1.

41. Convention for the Protection of the Ozone Layer, in force September 22, 1988, reprinted in *International Legal Materials* 25 (1987): 707, at www.unep.org/ozone/viennaconvention2002.pdf (accessed August 26, 2004).

42. Protocol on Substances that Deplete the Ozone Layer, done at Montreal September 16, 1987, entered into force January 1, 1989, reprinted in *International Legal Materials* 26 (1987): 154, at www.unep.org/ozone/pdf/Montreal-Protocol2000.pdf (accessed August 26, 2003).

43. Intergovernmental Panel on Climate Change, "Climate Change 1995: Second Assessment" (Geneva, Switz.: IPCC, 1996).

44. See Wayne A. Morrissey and John R. Justus, "89005: Global Climate Change," *CRS Issue Brief for Congress,* January 11, 1999, at www.cnie.org/nle/clim-2.html#_1_4; G. O. P. Obasi, "The Atmosphere: Global Commons to Protect," *Our Planet* 7 (February 1996): 5, at www.ourplanet.com/imgversn/75/obasi.html; and the website prepared by the Intergovernmental Panel on Climate Change entitled "Common Questions about Climate Change," at www.gcrio.org/ippc/qa/11.html.

45. United Nations Framework Convention on Climate Change, done May 9, 1992, entered into force March 24, 1994, UN doc. A/AC.237/18 (Part II)/Add.1, at www.unfccc.de, reprinted in *International Legal Materials* 31 (1992): 849.

46. Andrew C. Revkin, "178 Nations Reach Climate Accord; U.S. Only Looks On," *New York Times,* July 24, 2001, 1.

47. See Gareth Porter, Janet Welsh Brown, and Pamela S. Chasek, *Global Environmental Politics,* 3rd ed. (Boulder, Colo.: Westview Press, 2000), 69–72; John McCormack, *Acid Earth: The Global Threat of Acid Pollution* (Washington, D.C.: Earthscan, 1985); and Lynton Keith Caldwell, *International Environmental Policy: From the Twentieth to the Twenty-First Century,* 3rd ed. (Durham, N.C.: Duke University Press, 1996), 209–10.

48. Convention on Long-Range Transboundary Air Pollution, done in Geneva on November 13, 1979, entered into force March 16, 1983, reprinted in *International Legal Materials* 18 (1979): 1442, at www.unece.org/env/lrtap/lrtap_h1.htm (accessed August 26, 2004).

49. By 2005, at least eight protocols have been negotiated to augment the LRTAP, and five of them have entered into force. The first of these, the Protocol on the Reduction of Sulphur Emissions or Their Transboundary Fluxes, entered into force in 1987 and required parties to reduce sulphur emissions by 30 percent by 1993. The other protocols in force deal with financing the program for monitoring and evaluation to facilitate the prevention of transboundary air pollution, the reduction of nitrous oxide emissions, the further reduction of sulphur emissions, and the need to control transboundary transmission of volatile organic compounds. The remaining protocols call for reductions

in persistent organic pollutants, acidification, eutrophication and ground-level ozone, and heavy metals.

50. For more detailed treatment, see ECE's website at www.unece.org/env/lrtap.

51. See Ralph G. Steinhardt, "Outer Space," in *The United Nations and International Law*, ed. Christopher C. Joyner (Cambridge: Cambridge University Press, 1997), 336–61; and N. Jasentuli-yana, ed., *Space Law: Development and Scope* (Greenwood, Conn.: Praeger, 1992). The United Nations Office for Outer Space Affairs is the Secretariat for the Legal Subcommittee of the United Nations Committee on the Peaceful Uses of Outer Space, the primary multilateral forum for the development of laws and principles governing outer space. See www.oosa.unvienna.org/SpaceLaw/space law.htm.

52. Treaty on Principles Governing the Exploration and Use of Outer Space Including the Moon and Other Celestial Bodies, article 1, 18 UST 2410, TIAS 6347, 610 UNTS 205. Ninety-five states are parties.

53. Agreement on the Rescue of Astronauts, the Return of Astronauts, and the Return of Objects Launched into Outer Space, entered into force December 3, 1968, 19 UST 7570, TIAS 6599; 672 UNTS 119. At least eighty-eight states are party to this agreement. At www.oosa.unvienna.org/SpaceLaw/rescuetxt.htm.

54. Convention on International Liability for Damage Caused by Space Objects, entered into force September 1, 1972, 24 UST 2389, TIAS no. 7762, 961 UNTS 187, available at www.oosa.un vienna.org/SpaceLaw/liability.htm. Eighty-eight states are party in 2005 to the Liability Convention.

55. The diplomatic exchanges between Canada and the former Soviet Union are reproduced in *International Legal Materials* 18 (1979): 899. Also see Carl Cristol, "International Liability for Damage Caused by Space Objects, *American Journal of International Law* 74 (1980): 346.

56. Convention on the Registration of Objects Launched into Outer Space, entered into force September 15, 1976, 28 UST 695, TIAS 8480, 1023 UNTS 15, available at www.oosa.unvienna.org/SORegister/regist.html. At least forty-five states are party to this convention.

57. Agreement Governing the Activities of States on the Moon and Other Celestial Bodies, entered into force July 11, 1984, UN doc. A/34/664, reprinted in *International Legal Materials* 18 (1979): 1434, at www.oosa.unvienna.org/SpaceLaw/moon.html. There are only eleven parties to this convention, none of which is a space-faring state.

58. Namely, Australia, Austria, Chile, Morocco, Netherlands, Pakistan, Philippines, Uruguay, Kazakhstan, and Mexico.

59. There are also important external organizations. The International Telecommunications Satellite Organization was established in 1964 to create a global satellite telecommunications system on commercial basis. This organization provides public international telecommunications services and is the world's largest satellite organization. Other satellite organizations have also been established, among them the International Maritime Satellite Organization in 1979 and INTERSPUTNIK, the Soviet/Russian effort established to rival INTELSAT. For the Middle East and Europe, respectively, ARABSAT and EUTELSAT provide more limited regional coverage.

60. This was the so-called Bogota Declaration. See Carl Q. Cristol, *The Modern International Law of Outer Space* (New York: Pergamon Press, 1982), 891–96.

61. GA res. 41/65, UN doc. A/RES/41/65, 95th plen. mtg., December 3, 1986.

62. Regional fishery organizations usually have as part of their arrangement a secretariat with headquarters to serve as a clearinghouse for managing national reports and scientific information concerning the fishery area. For example, the Asia-Pacific Fishery Commission has its headquarters in Bangkok, the Indian Ocean Fishery Commission has headquarters in Rome, the Indian Tuna Commission's headquarters is in the Seychelles, the Western Central Atlantic Fishery Commission is headquartered in Barbados, and the headquarters for the Commission for Antarctic Marine Living Resources is located in Hobart, Tasmania, Australia. See Food and Agriculture Organization, Fisheries Department, "Regional and Other Bodies," at www.fao.org/WAICENT/FAOINFO/FISHERY/body/bodyf.htm.

63. See UN Division for Ocean Affairs and the Law of the Sea, Office of Legal Affairs, *The Law of the Sea: The Regime for High Seas Fisheries; Status and Prospects* (1992), 33.

CHAPTER 11

1. International Institute for the Unification of Private Law, Principles of International Commercial Contracts (1994) available at www.unidroit.org/english/publications/principles/main.htm (accessed August 27, 2004). The Principles of International Commercial Contracts are available in fifteen languages: Arabic, Chinese, Czech, Dutch, English, Farsi, French, German, Hungarian, Italian, Portuguese, Russian, Slovak, Spanish, and Vietnamese.

2. See John H. Jackson, William J. Davey, and Alan O. Sykes, *Legal Problems of International Economic Relations: Cases, Materials and Text on the National and International Regulation of Transnational Economic Relations*, 4th ed. (St. Paul, Minn.: West Group, 1995), 559.

3. Declaration on the Establishment of a New International Economic Order, adopted by GA res. 3201 (S-VI), 2,229th plen. mtg. (May 1, 1974).

4. Programme of Action on the Establishment of a New International Economic Order, adopted by GA res. 3202 (S-VI), 2,229th plen. mtg. (May 1, 1974).

5. Charter of Economic Rights and Duties of States, adopted by GA res. 3281 (29), UN GAOR, 29th sess., supp. no. 31, 50 (1974) (December 12, 1974).

6. GATT: Dispute Settlement Panel Report on United States Restrictions on Imports of Tuna, August 16 1991, reprinted in *International Legal Materials* 30 (1991): 1594.

7. 16 USC, secs. 1361–1421h (1994).

8. GATT: Dispute Settlement Panel Report on United States Restrictions on Imports of Tuna, May 20, 1994, 33 *International Legal Materials* 839, para. 5.42 (1994).

9. WTO Report of the Panel concerning the United States—Import Prohibition of Certain Shrimp and Shrimp Products, May 15, 1998, 1998 WL 256632.

10. See the discussion in Stephen L. Kass and Sean M. McCarroll, "Sea Turtles and World Trade," *New York Law Journal*, April 24, 1998; and Paul Stanton Kiebel, "Justice for the Sea Turtle: Marine Conservation and the Court of International Trade," *UCLA Journal of Enviromental Law & Policy* 15 (1996/1997): 57.

11. Opened for signature December 1945, entered into force December 27, 1947; 60 Stat. 1401, TIAS no. 1501, 3 Bevans 1351, 2 UNTS 39.

12. "IMF at a Glance," at www.imf.org/external/np/exr/facts/quotas.htm (accessed April 22, 2004).

13. "IMF Members' Quotas and Voting Power, and IMF Board of Governors," at www.imf.org/external/np/sec/memdir/members.htm#t (accessed April 22, 2004).

14. Articles of Agreement of the International Bank for Reconstruction and Development (as amended effective February 16, 1989), at www.worldbank.org/html/extdr/arttoc.htm (accessed August 27, 2004).

15. "World Trade Slows Sharply in 2001 amid the Uncertain International Situation," WTO press release, October 19, 2001, at www.wto.org/english/news_e/pres01_e/pr249_e.htm#table1.7 (accessed August 27, 2004).

16. See United Nations Conference on Contracts for the International Sale of Goods, done April 11, 1980, entered into force January 1, 1988, UN doc. A/CONF.97/18, reprinted in *International Legal Materials* 19 (1988): 668. See Amy H. Kastely, "Reflections on the International Unification of Sales Law: Unification and Community; A Rhetorical Analysis of the United Nations Sales Convention," *Journal of International Law and Business* 8 (1988): 574, 576–77. In 2005, there were at least sixty-two contracting states, among them Argentina, Australia, Canada, China, France, Germany, Israel, Iraq, Italy, Mexico, Russia, Spain, and the United States.

17. Hague Uniform Laws, known more specifically as the Convention on the International Sale of Goods.

18. Available at www.uncitral.org/english/texts/sales/CISG.htm (accessed April 21, 2004).

19. United Nations General Assembly, United Nations Commission on International Trade Law, at www.uncitral.org/en-index.htm (accessed August 27, 2004). Developments through UNCITRAL and the Hague Conference on Private International Law represent developments that are more congruent with specialized areas of law than the general categories of "international" or "comparative"

law. To illustrate, the legal instruments developed through the Hague Conference include conventions covering areas such as the form of testimony dispositions (1961), recognition of adoption decrees (1965), foreign service of documents in civil and commercial issues (1965), recognition of foreign judgments (1971), taking evidence abroad (1970), recognition of divorces (1970), traffic accidents (1971), product liability (1973), recognition of marriages (1978), marital property (1978), trusts (1985), child abductions (1980), agency (1978), and so on. Further examples include UNCITRAL's conventions, such as the UN Convention on the Carriage of Goods by Sea (1978), the UN Convention on Contracts for the Sale of Goods (1980), the UN Convention on International Bills of Exchange and International Promissory Notes (1994), the UN Convention on the Liability of Operators of Transport Terminals in International Trade (1991), and the UN Convention on Independent Guarantees and Standby Letters of Credit (1998). In addition, UNCITRAL's model codes—covering International Commercial Arbitration (1985); International Credit Transfers (1992); Procurement of Goods, Construction, and Services (1995); Cross Border Insolvency (1999); and Electronic Commerce (1991)—indicate the breadth of topics relating to international commercial transactions that UNCITRAL studies.

20. Convention on the Limitation Period in the International Sale of Goods, done June 14, 1974, entered into force August 1, 1988. A Protocol to the 1974 Limitation Convention was concluded at Vienna on April 11, 1980, entered into force August 1, 1988. Texts available at www.uncitral.org/english/texts/sales/limit-conv.htm (accessed August 27, 2004).

21. United Nations Convention on the Carriage of Goods by Sea, Hamburg, done March 30, 1978, at www.jus.uio.no/lm/un.sea.carriage.hamburg.rules.1978/doc.html (accessed August 27, 2004). Also see United Nations Conference on the Carriage of Goods by Sea, UN doc. A/CONF.89/14 (1981); Erling Selvig, "The Hamburg Rules, the Hague Rules and Marine Insurance Practice," *Journal of Maritime Law & Commerce* 12 (1981): 299, 311; and Rolf Herber, "The UN Convention on the Carriage of Goods by Sea, 1978: Hamburg Rules, Its Future and the Demands of Developing Countries," *Year Book of Maritime Law* (1984): 81.

22. Convention on the Liability of Operators of Transport Terminals in International Trade, done April 17, 1991, not yet in force, online at www.uncitral.org/english/transport/transport.htm (accessed April 12, 2004).

23. Done December 9, 1988, not yet in force, at http://untreaty.un.org/ENGLISH/bible/englishinternetbible/partI/chapterX/treat y24.asp (accessed April 22, 2004).

24. GA res. 31/98 (December 15, 1976), at www.pca-cpa.org/ENGLISH/BD/uncitralrules.htm (accessed April 21, 2004).

25. The new name resulted from the convention's being amended in 1968 and 1979 by two Brussels protocols. Hague-Visby Rules (1924–1968–1979), International Convention for the Unification of Certain Rules Relating to Bills of Lading (Hague Rules), as amended by the Brussels Protocol of 1968 and the Brussels Protocol of 1979, at atw.jus.uio.no/lm/sea.carriage.hague.visby.rules.1968/doc.html (accessed April 21, 2004).

26. Entered into force November 2, 1992. See United Nations Convention on the Carriage of Goods by Sea, 1978 (Hamburg), at www.jus.uio.no/lm/un.sea.carriage.hamburg.rules.1978/ (accessed April 21, 2004).

27. Done October 12, 1929, entered into force February 13, 1933, at www.jus.uio.no/lm/air.carriage.warsaw.convention.1929/index.html (accessed April 21, 2004).

28. Consolidated Text of the Convention Concerning International Carriage by Rail, done May 9, 1980, entered into force May 1, 1985, at www.unece.org/trade/cotif/Welcome.html (accessed April 21, 2004).

29. Geneva Convention on the Contract of International Carriage of Goods by Road, done May 19, 1956 as amended by protocol to the convention, Geneva, July 5, 1978, entered into force, at www.jus.uio.no/lm/un.cmr.road.carriage.contract.convention.1956.amended.protocol.1978/toc.html (accessed April 21, 2004).

30. Done May 24, 1980, not yet in force, at www.jus.uio.no/lm/un.multimodal.transport.1980/doc.html (accessed April 21, 2004).

31. Done September 9, 1886, entered into force with amendments, September 28, 1979, 828

UNTS 221, at www.wipo.int/clea/docs/en/wo/wo001en.htm (accessed April 21, 2004). At least 156 states are now party to the Berne Convention.

32. Done September 6, 1952, as revised July 24, 1971, 943 UNTS 178, reg. no. 13444, at www.unesco.org/culture/laws/copyright/html_eng/page1.shtml (accessed April 21, 2004).

33. Adopted in Geneva on December 20, 1996, at www.wipo.int/clea/docs/en/wo/wo033en .htm (accessed September 7, 2004). Thirty-eight states are parties to this agreement.

34. Signed on March 20, 1883, as amended and revised through September 28, 1979, at www .wipo.int/clea/docs/en/wo/wo020en.htm (accessed April 21, 2004). There are 168 state parties to this agreement in 2004.

35. Madrid Agreement for the Repression of False or Deceptive Indications of Source on Goods, signed April 14, 1891, periodically revised through July 14, 1967, at www.wipo.int/clea/docs/en/ wo/wo032en.htm (accessed April 21, 2004).

36. Convention establishing the World Intellectual Property Organization, done July 14, 1967, amended September 28, 1979, at www.wipo.int/clea/docs/en/wo/wo029en.htm (accessed April 21, 2004). WPO now has 181 member states.

37. Patent Cooperation Treaty, done 1970, entered into force April 1, 2001, at www.wipo.org/ pct/en/ (accessed April 21, 2004). In 2004, 123 states are parties to this convention.

38. *Banco Nacional de Cuba v. Sabbatino*, 307 F. 2d 845, 861 (2d Cir. 1962), rev. on other grounds, 376 US 398 (1964).

39. Reprinted in *International Legal Materials* 13 (1974): 58.

40. Factory at Chorzow (*Ger. V. Pol.*), 1928 PCIJ, ser. A, no. 17 (1928).

41. United Nations Commission on International Trade, 31 UN GAOR, suppl. no. 17, 35, UN doc. A/31/17 (1976).

42. Done March 18, 1965, 17 UST 1270, 575 UNTS 159, reprinted in *International Legal Materials* 4 (1965): 532.

43. Done in Rome March 25, 1957, entered into force January 1, 1958, at http://europa.eu.int/ abc/obj/treaties/en/entoc05.htm (accessed April 21, 2004).

44. Done in Rome March 25, 1957, entered into force on January 1, 1958, at http://europa.eu.int/ abc/obj/treaties/en/entoc38.htm (accessed April 21, 2004).

45. Also called the EC Treaty. Established the Single Council and the Single Commission of the European Communities, done April 8, 1965, entered into force July 13, 1967, OJ 152 (July 13, 1967), at http://europa.eu.int/abc/obj/treaties/en/entr13a.htm#B__Treaty_establishing_a_Single_ Council (accessed April 21, 2004).

46. Done February 17, 1986, entered into force July 1, 1987, OJL 169 (June 29, 1987).

47. Treaty on European Union, signed at Maastricht February 7, 1992, entered into force, November 1, 1993, at http://europa.eu.int/en/record/mt/top.html.

48. *Costa v. ENEL* (211964) Eur. Comm. Rep. 585.

49. *Commission v. Council* (1971) Eur. Comm. Rep. 263 (the ERTA decision).

50. Done December 17, 1992, entered into force January 1, 1994, at www.nafta-sec-alena.org/ DefaultSite/home/index_e.aspx (accessed April 21, 2004).

51. For more details see ASEAN's website at www.aseansec.org.

52. See International Monetary Fund website at www.imf.org/external/index.htm (accessed April 21, 2004).

53. Original agreement at Australian Treaty Series 26 (1980), done in Geneva on October 6, 1979, entered into force April 15, 1982. Following the withdrawal of Malaysia, Thailand, and Sri Lanka, the members decided in December 1999 to liquidate the organization.

54. For more details on world rubber trade, see the International Rubber Organization's website at www3.jaring.my/inro.

55. The original 1972 International Cocoa Agreement, 882 UNTS 67, entered into force June 3, 1973, and expired by its own terms September 30, 1976. Since then four subsequent cocoa agreements were negotiated and entered into force, the most recent in 2001.

56. International Cocoa Agreement, adopted March 2, 2001, entered into force October 1, 2003, doc.TD/COCOA.9/7 (2001) at www.icco.org (accessed April 21, 2004). Thirteen states are parties to the 1991 Cocoa Agreement.

57. Done September 28, 2000, entered into force October 1, 2001, reg. no. 37769, at http://216.239.37.104/search?q = cache:_A3BB9vyFGcJ:untreaty.un.org/English/notpubl/xix-43E.doc + international + coffee + agreement&hl = en&ie = UTF-8. The text of a new International Coffee Agreement was agreed by the sixty-three member governments of the International Coffee Council, adopted in Council resolution 393. The six-year agreement will strengthen international cooperation among producing and consuming countries.

58. See the International Coffee Organization's website at www.ico.org.

59. UN reg. no. 32022.

60. Done November 3, 1989, entered into force April 12, 1991, reg. no. 28026, 1605 UNTS 211.

61. Done March 13, 2001, UN doc. TD/JUTE.4/6 (March 13, 2001), at http://untreaty.un.org/English/notpubl/19-45E.pdf (accessed April 21, 2004).

62. Available at Australian Treaty Series (1956), no. 15, done in London March 1, 1954, entered into force July 1, 1956.

63. See www.ilmc.org.

64. UN Publication 1956, II.D.1 (E/CONF.19/5), done at New York November 15, 1955. This olive oil agreement never formally entered into effect.

65. Done March 20, 1992, entered into force provisionally on January 20, 1993, and definitively on December 10, 1996, reg. no. 29467, 1703 UNTS 203. The agreement has been extended three times, most recently until December 31, 2003.

66. See www.isosugar.org/frameset.htm.

67. UN doc. TD/TIMBER.2/L.8, entered into force provisionally January 1, 1997, reg. no. 33484.

68. See the International Tropical Timber Organization website at www.itto.or.jp/Index.html.

CHAPTER 12

1. See Lester Thurow, "Globalization: The Product of a Knowledge-Based Economy," *Annals of the American Academy of Political and Social Science* 570 (2000): 19.

2. See, for example, John Dunning, "Whither Global Capitalism?" *Global Focus* 12 (2000): 117; "Globalization and Its Critics: A Survey of Globalization," *Economist*, September 29, 2001, at www.economist.com/surveys/displayStory.cfm?Storyid = 795995; "Symposium: Globalization, Accountability and the Future of Administrative Law," *Indiana Journal of Global Legal Studies* (Fall 2000).

3. See Keith Aoki, "Sovereignty and the Globalization of Intellectual Property," Indiana Journal of Global Legal Studies 6 (1998): 11.

4. Andrew Price Smith, *The Health of Nations: Infectious Diseases, Environmental Change, and Their Effects on National Security and Development* (Cambridge, Mass.: MIT Press, 2002); Jonathan Ban, "Health as a Global Security Challenge," Seton Hall Journal of Diplomacy and International Relations 4 (Summer/Fall 2003): 19–28.

5. Gro Harlem Brundtland, "The Globalization of Health," *Seton Hall Journal of Diplomacy and International Relations* 4 (Summer/Fall 2003): 11.

6. World Health Organization, Macroeconomics and Health: Investing in Health for Economic Development, report of the Commission on Macroeconomics and Health, December 20, 2001.

7. See www1.oecd.org/fatf/MLaundering_en.htm (accessed June 4, 2004).

8. See Richard Falk, "The Grotian Quest," in *International Law: A Contemporary Perspective*, ed. Richard Falk, Friedrich Kratochwil, and Saul H. Mendlovitz (Boulder, Colo.: Westview Press, 1985): 36–42.

9. See, for example, Ali Khan, "The Extinction of Nation-States," *American University Journal of International Law & Policy* 7 (1992): 197; and John O. McGinnis, "The Decline of the Western Nation State and the Rise of the Regime of International Federalism," *Cardozo Law Review* 18 (1996): 903.

Glossary

absolute sovereign immunity   The historical preclusion of one government to permit lawsuits to be filed in its courts against the government of another state, usually on the basis of mutual respect.

accession   The formal acceptance of a treaty or convention by a state that did not participate in its negotiation and signing.

accretion   The slow, almost imperceptible process of creating land (and legal title to it) through the natural action of water, such as river currents and ocean tides.

act of state doctrine   The practice in the United States whereby its federal courts will not sit in judgment of another state that has allegedly violated international law. However, under the Hickenlooper Amendment of the U.S. Foreign Assistance Act, courts are expected to hear such cases unless the president through the Department of State intervenes to request that the case be dismissed for political reasons.

adjudication   A means of dispute resolution through special courts or established tribunals.

adoption   The second stage of the treaty-making process in which government agents affirm the draft text.

Agenda 21   The eight-hundred-page comprehensive blueprint for managing all sectors of the environment in the 21st century, established at the United Nations' 1992 Rio Conference. Agenda 21 is the most extensive statement of environmental priorities encouraging the worldwide review and assessment of international environmental law, the development of implementation and compliance measures, and the effective participation by all states in lawmaking and dispute-resolution processes.

aggression   The use of armed force by a state against the sovereignty, territorial integrity or political independence of another state, or in any other manner inconsistent with the Charter of the United Nations.

Agreement on Trade-Related Aspects of Intellectual Property Rights   Integrated into the World Trade Organization, an agreement that includes intellectual property rights—copyrights, trademarks, and patents—under common international rules.

anticipatory self-defense   Rather than wait to be attacked by armed force (as required in article 51 of the UN Charter), a state undertakes preemptive defensive action to avoid some impending aggression by another state.

apartheid   The intentional separation of peoples in a society on the basis of race.

arbitration   A legally binding method of international dispute resolution whereby governments choose and appoint an experienced arbitrator or panel of jurists to decide the merits of their dispute.

archipelagic state   An independent state created by the 1982 UN Law of the Sea Convention that comprises islands, parts of islands, and interconnecting waters that are reconsidered so closely interrelated that they are historically regarded as an intrinsic geographical, economic, and political entity.

Area, the   Under the 1982 UN Law of the Sea Convention, the Area is the ocean floor and its subsoil beyond the limits of national jurisdiction. This is the deep seabed area under the oceans that does not otherwise fall within any other coastal zone. Its resources, mainly manganese modules, are declared the common heritage of all mankind.

associated state   A state that delegates special government functions to a "principal state" while retaining its independent status.

avulsion   A rapid change in the course of rivers or water bodies caused by natural events such as floods, tidal waves, or earthquakes that does not alter the prior legal boundaries of the affected territory.

baseline   The low-water line along the coast as marked on charts officially recognized by the coastal state that demarcates the inner-most boundary of various sea zones that extend seaward from the coastline.

bilateral investment treaty   An agreement that sets out conditions and circumstances under which a government will permit foreign investors to operate within that state.

boycott   A form of coercive self-help in which a government or citizens of an aggrieved state undertake retaliatory action by suspending the import of goods from the offending state.

capitulation   The system of unequal extraterritorial jurisdictions in the late 19th and early 20th centuries imposed by Western governments on Asian and African countries.

cession   The conveyance of territory by one state to another state done by international agreement, usually a treaty of sale. The grantee state's right to title stems from the treaty between the states involved in the transfer.

City State of the Vatican   The sovereign independent state (since 1929) of the Vatican in Rome headed by the Pope.

collective self-defense   The collective response by a group of states under article 2(4) of the UN Charter in response to an attack against a state by an aggressor state.

collective use of force (or collective security)   The system of international rules embodied in articles 39–44 in Chapter VII of the UN Charter, which governs the collective resort to force under the authority of the United Nations for the purpose of maintaining or restoring international peace and security.

compulsory jurisdiction   Also referred to as mandatory jurisdiction, this is ability of an international tribunal to require a defendant state to litigate a dispute before the court.

conciliation   A commission of select persons, appointed with the disputant parties' agreement, who impartially clarify the facts of a dispute, typically through a non-binding report that contains a settlement proposal.

conditional state   A state that is admitted into the international community under formal agreement to fulfill a special obligation imposed by other states as the price for admission.

condominium   The status of jurisdiction over a shared territory that is shared by two or more states.

confederation   A formal association of states loosely tied by a treaty, often having a central government with certain powers over the member polities but not directly over the citizens in those polities.

conquest   The acquisition of another state's territory through force, which no longer is considered a lawful basis for acquiring title to territory under contemporary international law.

constitutive theory of recognition   The notion that holds other governments must recognize an entity's statehood before it is entitled to de jure status as an international legal person.

consultation   The principle in environmental law that affirms the duty of governments to consult with one another in the event of environmental risks.

contiguous zone   The zone of water twenty-four nautical miles seaward from the coastal state in which the state exercises extrajurisdictional authority over such activities as unlawful immigration, pollution, customs, and smuggling.

continental shelf   The coastal state's seabed and subsoil of the submarine areas extending beyond its territorial sea throughout the natural underwater prolongation of its land territory. Its range varies, from 200 nautical miles from the coastal baseline to 350 nautical miles, depending on the natural extension of the coastal state's underwater land mass.

Convention   Generally, a multilateral lawmaking agreement. The multiparty international convention is a principal source for constructing the content of contemporary international law.

Council of the European Union   The main decision-making body of the European Union.

Court of Auditors   The tribunal that functions to investigate and prevent fraud against the European Community budget.

Court of Justice of the European Community   The juridical arm of the European Union that interprets community law.

customary international law   The facet of international law comprised of state practices and their related expectations and which is predicated upon what governments do and what they consider legally binding in their mutual relations.

deep seabed mining   The extractive process for exploiting ferromanganese nodules from the deep ocean floor (the Area).

de facto recognition   Provisional recognition by the government of one state acknowledging that another state exercises authoritative control over its respective territory and people.

de jure recognition   Formal recognition by a government of the legal status of another state's government as being the valid authority to speak and act for the latter state.

denaturalization   The process by which a government deprives a person of his or her nationality.

deposit of ratification   The formal registration of an international agreement.

diplomacy   The aims and means of national policy and the conduct by governments of their foreign affairs.

diplomatic asylum   Sanctuary from arrest or extradition, typically given to a host state's political refugee by a foreign government's embassy in that host state.

diplomatic immunity   General treaty-based protection from host state laws, lawsuits, seizure, or censure. A diplomatic pouch is thus immune from search and seizure, as are the premises of the mission, key diplomatic personnel and communications from that embassy.

discovery   A means of acquiring territory by claiming land previously unclaimed (*terra nullius*).

dualists   Those who hold the view the legal relationship between national and international law is that each is a distinct legal system representing two separate legal orders—one which binds the individual and other which binds the state.

Economic and Social Committee (ESC) of the European Union   The European Community advisory body for ensuring that various economic and social interests are represented in the European Union.

effects doctrine   Application of territorial jurisdiction whereby a state may regulate conduct that occurs abroad when that conduct has the requisite effect within the state.

embargo   A form of coercive self help in which a government suspends trade with another state by prohibiting exports to that state.

entry into force   The point at which the binding force of an international treaty or convention begins.

environmental impact statement (or assessment)   The requirement that government agencies must prepare a report that considers the potential effects of proposed agency action on a local environment or the global commons.

Estrada Doctrine   The doctrine asserting that a government should not apply subjective consideration to extending recognition of a new government, but rather accept the existence of that government.

European Commission   The main executive body of the European Union that implements European legislation and the budget.

European Community law   The body of rules and regulations that govern the European Union's legal relations on an intra-regional basis. The 25 sovereign members have given EU organs the power to require state compliance with community law.

exclusive economic zone   The jurisdictional zone that overlaps the territorial sea and the contiguous zones. The exclusive economic zone extends a limited degree of coastal state authority—as far out as two hundred nautical miles from the baseline—over a foreign state's economic activities in the zone, especially those regarding fishing and mineral resource exploitation.

executive agreement   A special domestic instrument that performs treaty-like functions but does not require formal approval by a state's municipal legislature.

expatriation   The act by which a person renounces his or her nationality and acquires the nationality of a new state.

expropriation   The lawful seizure of foreign-held property for public purposes through transfer to the expropriating state or third parties in return for just compensation, meaning that it is prompt, adequate, and effective.

extradition   The investigation, arrest, and transfer of an accused fugitive from one state to another that is typically based on a bilateral treaty that contains a schedule of extraditable crimes.

extraterritorial jurisdiction   The state's legal ability to prohibit or regulate conduct beyond its territorial borders, or a state's unlawful exercise of sovereign power beyond its internationally sanctioned limits.

federal state   A merger or union of previously autonomous or independent polities into a single state, with a government exercising direct powers over its citizens and functioning as a single, independent legal person.

flag state jurisdiction   A fundamental principle of jurisdiction whereby a vessel on the high seas (or an aircraft in the high skies) is subject only to the jurisdiction of the state under whose flag it flies.

force   A broad term that encompasses an array of unacceptable state behavior as prohibited by UN Charter principles. Examples include disproportional military, economic, and political use of force that is not exercised in self defense.

General Agreement on Tariffs and Trade   The 1947 international agreement to promote free, nondiscriminatory trade and lower import tariffs. Now one of several agreements on services and other matters within the new and more formalized World Trade Organization, it contains thousands of tariff concessions and negotiated tariff schedules.

General Assembly   The deliberative body, with many associated agencies, that consists of all 191 UN member states. The General Assembly issues studies, reports, and nonbinding resolutions designed to further the UN Charter's objectives.

general principle of international law   A norm in the internal law of states that becomes commonly used in the international legal system. When such a norm attains the perceived necessary degree of acceptance, it may evolve into a source for a substantive international legal rule.

genocide   Acts that are perpetrated with the intent to destroy in whole or in part a national, ethnical, racial, or religious group.

geostationary orbit   The orbit 22,300 miles above the equator in which a satellite circles the earth at a rate of speed synchronized with that of the earth's rotation and thus appears to be stationary.

good offices   A nonbinding technique of peaceful dispute settlement in which a third party, acting with the consent of the disputing parties, serves as an intermediary to facilitate communication and to persuade the states to return to negotiating between themselves to resolve the dispute.

harm prevention   The duty in environmental law to prevent, reduce, and control environmental damage.

high seas   The portion of ocean space that is beyond the limits of national jurisdiction.

humanitarian intervention   A purported basis for legitimizing territorial intrusion, often abused by governments to unilaterally intervene in the affairs of another state. Express purposes include rescuing the people at large, certain political figures, or nationals of the intervening state who are being held hostage.

human rights   Those rights possessed by an individual that cannot be deprived by the state. Most of these rights are contained in the International Bill of Human Rights, which embraces the composite regime for human rights treaties.

innocent passage   Passage through territorial waters that does not disturb the peace, good order, or security of the coastal state.

inquiry   A nonbinding dispute settlement technique that involves establishment of an impartial commission to objectively assess the facts of the case for consideration by the disputing parties.

intellectual property   Materials protected by the internal copyright, patent, or trademark laws of a state.

Inter-American Agency for Cooperation   The development body in the Organization of American States that promotes cooperation among Organization of American States member states.

intergenerational equity   A principle in environmental law that asserts the present generation should be responsible for protecting the environment from harm for the benefit of future generations.

intergovernmental organization   A multilateral organization created by states to accomplish treaty-based objectives. Some organizations, including the European Union, have the juridical power to effectively ensure state compliance with their decisions.

internal waters   Lakes, rivers, bays, and waters on the landward side of the baseline that demarcates the inner edge of the coastal state's territorial sea.

International Atomic Energy Agency   The United Nations body responsible for inspecting states' nuclear facilities and for promoting binding international legal agreements to regulate and control the use of nuclear power.

International Bill of Human Rights   The three major human rights documents since World War II that constitute the general foundation for numerous issue-specific treaties. These human rights pillars are the Universal Declaration of Human Rights, the International Covenant on Civil and Political Rights, and the International Covenant on Economic, Social, and Cultural Rights.

international comity   International rules of courtesy and goodwill that should be observed by governments in their mutual dealings on grounds of convenience, honor, and reciprocity.

International Court of Justice   The judicial arm of the United Nations, headquartered in The Hague, Netherlands. Its fifteen judges resolve contentious disputes between states that arise under international law in legally binding decisions and issue advisory opinions when requested from certain UN organs and agencies.

International Criminal Court   The international tribunal negotiated in 1998 and activated in 2002 that tries individuals accused of committing war crimes, genocide, or crimes against humanity.

international ethics   International moral principles that are concerned with governing international relations from the higher reaches of conscience, justice, or humanity.

international law   The body of rules that international persons (such as states and intergovernmental organizations) recognize as binding in their mutual relations. Its major sources derive from treaties and conventions and from custom and general principles of law.

International Law Commission   The United Nations' body that facilitates codification of international law by discussing and drafting international legal agreements.

international legal personality   A juridical term signifying that an entity has legal standing as a member of the community of states and possesses certain rights and obligations as a subject of international law.

International Maritime Organization   The functional agency in the United Nations dedicated to regulating international shipping, navigation, and ocean pollution.

International Seabed Authority   Under the 1982 UN Law of the Sea Convention, the International Seabed Authority is charged with the responsibility to manage deep seabed mining in the Area.

Intervention   Dictatorial interference by a state or group of states into the affairs of another state, usually involving the threat or use of armed force, for the purpose of maintaining or altering existing conditions in the target state.

intervention by right   A permissible exception to the rule of nonintervention, for reasons that include the rescue of nationals abroad, the use of force by an international organization, and for reasons as authorized by a former treaty agreement.

jurisdiction   The state's right to regulate conduct of individuals and organizations and to punish violations of international norms. Such misconduct may occur within the state's borders or may have the requisite effect within its borders.

jus cogens   Compulsory law that is a peremptory norm from which states cannot escape and that is accepted and recognized by the international community as a whole.

jus gentium   The law of nations, or the Roman-based notion that certain norms and legal principles are common to peoples everywhere.

jus naturale   The norms and principles that derive from natural law by which man and states are bound.

jus sanguinis   The nationality of an individual that depends on the blood (nationality) of the parents.

jus sol   Individual nationality based on the soil and the place of birth.

lawmaking treaty   A multilateral agreement that creates new norms designed to transform existing state practices.

laws of war   The rules in the four 1949 Geneva Conventions sponsored by the International Committee of the Red Cross that protect private citizens and foreign soldiers during times of warfare.

liberal interpretationists   The school of thought that holds armed force may be used by a state under certain extraordinary circumstances to right unjust wrongs or protect innocent lives in another state.

mandate   A region administered by Great Britain, France, or South Africa under the League of Nations after World War I.

mediation   A nonbinding technique of international dispute settlement in which a third party, acting with the agreement of the disputing parties, actively participates in the negotiating process by offering substantive suggestions and by attempting to resolve contentious points between the disputants.

ministates or microstates   The small, thinly populated polities, mostly from island groups, that became independent during the 1960s and 1970s.

monists   A theoretical school of thought that asserts the relationship between international law to municipal law upholds the unity of all law and declares each body of law is a segment of a unified system that binds both the state and the individual.

most-favored-nation treatment   The condition under which a state promises to trade with a particular partner on the most favorable tariff terms available for like goods and thus taxes the latter's imported goods at the lowest amount that the taxing state charges any state with which it trades.

municipal law   The historic term that refers to the domestic law of a state, as opposed to the international law applied by the community of states.

nation   A group of people having a common culture, language, and historical background (and often a common religion).

nationality   A legal bond based on individual or corporate allegiance to a state, which rests on the existence of reciprocal rights and duties between a state and its nationals.

nationality principle   The notion that a state's jurisdiction extends to its nationals and their actions beyond the territorial jurisdiction of the state.

nationalization   The taking by a host government of all the foreign investment of an industry in that state for social or economic reform.

naturalist school of thought   The school of thought during the classical period through the 18th century that believed the origin and authority of international law derived from the law of nature.

naturalization   The legal process through which a foreign national acquires the nationality of another state.

negotiation   The process though which parties to a dispute communicate and bargain with one another to work out an acceptable solution. Also, the first step in the treaty-making process carried out by government agents to produce a satisfactory draft text.

neutralized state   A state that accepts the status of neutrality imposed on it by a group of other states.

New International Economic Order   An ambition contained in a 1974 UN General Assembly resolution that sought to assert a Charter of Economic Rights and Duties of States that promoted economic advantages in international commercial dealings for developing countries.

nongovernmental organization   A private association not comprised of states that pursues special interest objectives.

occupation   An original means of acquiring title to territory unclaimed by any state (*terra nullius*) by demonstrating real, effective permanent settlement of that territory.

opinio juris   The short term of *opinio juris sive necessitatis* that asserts a norm of customary international law is predicated on the consistent acceptance by states that a practice is legally binding.

pacta sunt servanda   A Latin phase meaning that treaties made in good faith shall be binding. Regarded as the fundamental principle of the customary law of treaties.

passive personality principle   The notion that acts committed by an alien against a state's nationals abroad convey jurisdiction to the host state.

Permanent Council of the Organization of American States   The principal OAS organ responsible for peaceful settlement of disputes.

personal immunity   A national leader's historical immunity from prosecution by another state or by an international tribunal for acts undertaken while in office.

personal union   An arrangement in which several states share a single head of state, although each state retains its own sovereignty and separate legal personality.

positivist school of thought   The school of thought on the nature and origin of international law that maintains international legal rules consists of those norms that states voluntarily consent to obey.

precautionary principle   The notion that asserts when certain human activities pose possible environmental risks, governments should prejudice policy actions to avoid them.

prescription   The acquisition of title to territory originally owned by another state through uncontested exercise of sovereignty over an extended (albeit undefined) period.

prior notification   The principle of environmental law that asserts a duty for states to notify other governments that their activities could pose possible harm to the local environment.

private international law   The body of rules pertaining to transnational commercial activities between governments and multinational corporations.

protective principle   The notion that a state's jurisdiction can be applied in cases where the action of an individual takes place outside the territorial jurisdiction of the state, but is viewed as prejudicial to its security interests.

protectorate   A legal status whereby a dependent state retains control over its internal affairs while transferring responsibility for its external affairs to another state.

publicist   A prominent legal scholar whose writings are considered a subsidiary source for determining the content and significance of international legal rules.

ratification   The final step in the treaty-making process whereby an individual state expressly establishes its definitive consent to be bound by an international agreement.

real union   A treaty arrangement in which two or more states form a union, making them a single, composite international legal person.

rebus sic stantibus   A fundamental change in circumstances whereby a state seeks to avoid or renegotiate its treaty obligations because the objective of the agreement is rendered difficult or impossible to perform.

recognition   The discretionary function exercised unilaterally by the government of a state that officially acknowledges the existence of another state or government. Recognition carries with it entitlement to certain rights and privileges as well as duties and obligations under international law.

reprisal   An unlawful coercive measure short of war, directed by a state against another state in retaliation for alleged unlawful acts. Reprisal serves as a means for obtaining reparation or satisfaction for such wrongful acts.

res communis   Space not subject to legal ownership by any state, such as the oceans and outer space.

reservation   A unilateral assertion that is submitted at the time of a multilateral treaty's acceptance and that excludes or modifies the legal effect of certain provisions in their application to the reserving state.

restrictive theory of sovereign immunity   Under this modern theory, a foreign state may be subjected to suit in another state's courts when it is engaged in a local commercial enterprise.

retorsion   A lawful but intentionally unfriendly act directed by a state against another state in retaliation for an equally unfriendly but lawful act. Done for the purpose of compelling that state to alter its unfriendly conduct.

satellite state   A category of states usually associated with Eastern European states during the Cold War that were legally independent of external control but were actually oppressed by the Soviet Union in foreign affairs.

sector theory A mechanical basis for national claims to sovereignty over the polar regions that involves drawing meridian lines from the farthest extremities of the contiguous state's land mass to the pole.

self-determination The right of a people to choose their own legal and political institutions and status in the community of states.

signature The official affixing of names to the text of a treaty by representatives of negotiating states indicating provisional acceptance of that agreement subject to ratification by those states' municipal processes.

Sixth (Legal) Committee of the General Assembly The body under the UN General Assembly that is responsible for considering and elaborating legal issues.

slavery The condition of a person over whom the power of ownership by another person is exercised.

sources of international law As enumerated in article 38 of the Statute of the International Court of Justice, the recognized sources of international law are treaties and conventions, customary state practice, general principles of law, and judicial opinions and the teachings (writings) of highly qualified publicists.

sovereign immunity Deriving from a state's sovereignty, the immunity from suit enjoyed by states and certain international organizations in the courts of other states.

sovereignty A fundamental principle in international law denoting the supreme indivisible authority possessed by a state to enact and enforce its law with respect to all persons, property, and events within its territory.

State Historically, the only actor that possesses the capacity to act on the international level. A state normally consists of a permanent territory with recognized borders, a defined people, a government capable of participating in international relations, and the qualities of sovereignty and independence.

statelessness The deprivation of an individual's nationality whereby that person becomes a refugee who lacks the international protection afforded by the legal connection with any particular state.

state responsibility The obligation of the state to make reparation arising from a failure to comply with an obligation under international law. It is predicated on an act of omission in violation of an international legal obligation resulting in injury to the claimant state.

Stimson doctrine of nonrecognition The principle, named after U.S. Secretary of State Henry Stimson, that proclaims that territory secured through conquest or forcible annexation will not be recognized as lawfully acquired.

strict interpretationists The school of thought that construes UN Charter provisions on the use of force strictly such that no use of unilateral armed force is permitted except in self-defense.

succession The process of one or more states legally taking the place of a former state. The new entity thus succeeds to the sovereign attributes of the predecessor state, which no longer exists because of this transfer of sovereignty.

sustainable use A principle in environmental law that asserts resources may be used unless such use exhausts a resource or harms the environment.

terra nullius Territory that is susceptible to ownership because it is not yet claimed or under sovereign control. The land is characterized as belonging to no one and thus capable of ownership through some act of occupation or control.

territorial sea A strip of water adjacent to the coast—twelve nautical miles in breadth—wherein the coastal state exercises total sovereignty to the same degree it exercises such sovereignty within its territory.

thalweg The main navigable channel in a river, which is used to delineate boundaries between riparian states.

transit passage The type of passage adopted by the Third Conference on the Law of the Sea to regulate transit through international straits.

treaty An international agreement concluded between two states or international organizations, typically in written form.

trusteeship system The arrangement after World War II in which territories were administered by countries under the supervision of the United Nations.

union A composite international actor created when two or more independent states become linked such that they act internationally as a single actor.

United Nations Treaty Series The authoritative UN registry published by the Secretariat containing some fifty thousand international legal agreements.

universal jurisdiction The international legal obligation that affirms that when a person's conduct is so heinous that it offends the conscience of humankind and constitutes a crime against all states, each member of the international community of states may prosecute or extradite the individual criminal for trial, regardless of where the conduct occurred.

vassal state The condition of certain polities during the Ottoman Empire that were granted domestic rights and privileges by a suzerain state.

World Trade Organization The global trade entity based in Geneva, Switzerland, and created in 1995 that oversees all facets of the General Agreement on Tariffs and Trade and its related agreements that cover goods, services, and intellectual property.

Index

Abu Ghraib prison, Baghdad, 144, 287–88
accession to treaties, 110
accountability for state criminal offenses, 148–49
accretion, acquisition of territory through, 44
Achille Lauro (ship), 138
act of state doctrine, 52
actors. *See* international actors
adjectival law, 13
adjudication, 127
administrative law, international organizations and, 87, 96–98, 103–4
adoption of treaties, 109
aerial hijacking, 138–39
Afghanistan, 28, 169, 171, 174, 179, 181, 182
African Nuclear Weapon Free Zone Treaty (1996), 193
Agenda 21, 204
aggression: definition of, 166; as international crime, 142–43, 151; types of, 316n10
Agreed Measures for the Conservation of the Antarctic Fauna and Flora (1964), 237
Agreement Governing the Activities of States on the Moon and Other Celestial Bodies, 244
Agreement on Trade-Related Aspects of Intellectual Property Rights (TRIPS), 258–59, 268, 289
agreements, 105–19; bilateral, 108; environmental, 209–11; formulation of, 109–13; influence of, 108; interpretation of, 113–15; lawmaking treaties, 108; legal rules for, 113; multilateral, 108; termination of, 116–18; terms for, 107; validity of, 115–16. *See also* treaties
AIDS, 23
airborne pollution, 242
Alabama (ship), 125
Alaska Purchase (1867), 44
Albania, 205–6

aliens: asylum for, 65–66; extradition of, 66–69; immigration laws, 64–65; and political offenses, 67–69; state responsibility regarding, 56
Alsace Lorraine, 57
American Convention on Human Rights (1978), 79–80
Americanization, 289
Amin, Idi, 177
Amnesty International (AI), 80–81, 287
Amoco Cadiz oil spill, 198
Anaconda Copper Corporation, 270
ANCOM. *See* Andean Group
Andean Court of Justice, 129
Andean Group, 278–79
Andorra, 31
Annan, Kofi, 85, 105
Antarctic Treaty (1959), 193, 236–39, 249
Antarctic Treaty Consultative Parties (ATCPs), 236–38
Antarctic Treaty System, 236–39, 248
Antarctica, 236–39, 325n4
Antiballistic Missile Treaty, 117
apartheid, 73–74, 142
arbitration, 125–26, 271–72
archipelagic state, 231
Argentina: and Antarctic Treaty, 250; arbitration involving, 126; good offices negotiations involving, 124; territory dispute involving, 46
Arias, Oscar, 124
Aristide, Henri, 49
Armenia, 46
ASEAN. *See* Association of South East Asian Nations
Ashburton, Lord, 168
associated states, 31
Association of South East Asian Nations (ASEAN), 279–80

Association of Tin Producing Countries, 281
Assyrians, 15
asylum, 65–66
atmosphere, 211, 239–43, 249–50
Augustine, Saint, 162
Austria, 29, 30
aut dedere aut judicare, 68–69
avulsion of territory, 45–46
Azerbaijan, 46

Babylonians, 15
Baker, James, III, 4
Banco Nacional de Cuba v. Sabbatino (1964), 52
Bangkok Declaration (1967), 279
Bangladesh, 175, 177
banking, 261–62, 269
Basel Convention on the Control of Transbound-
    ary Movements of Hazardous Wastes and
    Their Disposal (1989), 215
baseline, coastal, 43
Beagle Channel dispute, 126
Belgium: commission of conciliation involving,
    125; as neutralized state, 30; and personal
    union, 29; protection of nationals abroad by,
    176
bellum justum. See just war
Bentham, Jeremy, 297n1
Berne Convention for the Protection of Literary
    and Artistic Property (1886), 268
Berne Union, 101
Biafra, 177
bilateral investment treaties, 271
bilateral treaties, 108
bin Laden, Osama, 171
biodiversity, 210–11, 218
Biological Weapons Convention (1972), 192
birth control, 23, 24, 31
Blix, Hans, 85
blockades, 183
bombing, as tactic of war, 8
Bormann, Martin, 152
Bosnia-Herzegovina: commission of inquiry
    involving, 125; peacekeeping in, 188; rape in,
    147; Security Council action on, 186; self-
    determination movement in, 175; UN-NATO
    action on, 189–90; war crimes tribunal for, 90
Bowett, D. W., 176
boycotts, 182–83
Brazil, 29
Bretton Woods System, 225, 255
Britain. *See* Great Britain
British Commonwealth of Nations, 29
British Petroleum, 270

Brundtland Report, 217
Brunei, 46
Bulgaria, 32
Bunch, Ralph, 124
Bunker Hunt, 270
Bush, George W.: and anticipatory self-defense,
    169–70; on international law, 4; and Iraq war,
    3–4, 161, 186; and Kyoto Protocol, 198; and
    steel tariffs, 253–54
Bush, George H. W., 181
Butler, Richard, 85
Bynkershoek, Cornelius van, 18

Cambodia, 33, 49, 156, 177–78
Canada, 29, 205
Canada–United States Free Trade Agreement
    (1998), 277
cannon shot rule, 13, 18, 228
capitulations, 65
Caroline (ship), 168
carriage of goods, 266–67
Cartagena Agreement (1969), 278
Carter, Jimmy, 124, 139–40, 182
CEDAW. *See* Convention on the Elimination of
    All Forms of Discrimination against Women
Central American Court of Justice, 128
Certain Expenses Case, 189
cession of territory, 44–45
changing circumstances, doctrine of, 117
Charter of Economic Rights and Duties of States
    (1974), 256
charters, of international organizations, 88
chemical and hazardous wastes, treaties on, 211
Chemical Weapons Convention (CWC) (1993),
    193
Chernobyl nuclear power plant accident, 198,
    215
children: international criminal law concerning,
    158; rights of, 74–75, 78
Chile: and Antarctic Treaty, 250; arbitration
    involving, 126; expropriation by, 270; nation-
    alization by, 270
China: boycott of Japan by, 182; as divided state,
    30; early international law in, 15; recognition
    of, 49; territory dispute involving, 46
Chvalkovsky, Frantiek, 115
citizenship, 63–64, 302n1
civil war, 174
classification of states, 28–33; associated states,
    31; City State of the Vatican, 30–31; condi-
    tional states, 30; condominia, 33; divided
    states, 30; dwarf states, 31; federal states, 29;
    ministates, 31; neutralized states, 30; nonsov-

ereign entities, 31; protectorates, 33; real unions, 28–29; satellite states, 31; semisovereign states, 32–33; subservient states, 32; vassal states, 32–33

Climate Change Convention (1992), 72

Clinton, William, 124

coalitions of the willing, 173

cocoa, 280

Code of Conduct for Responsible Fisheries, 201

coercion short of war, 180–83; economic, 181–83; reprisals, 180–81; retorsion, 180

coffee, 280–81

Cold War, 20

collective security, 163, 179, 184–85

collective self-defense, 173, 179

colonialism: and apartheid, 73–74; and capitulations, 65; De Vitoria's criticism of, 16; protectorates and, 33; and self-determination movements, 174–75; spread of, 20

Commission on Sustainable Development (CSD), 204–5

commerce. *See* trade

Commission of European Union, 274

commissions of conciliation, 125

commissions of inquiry, 124–25

Committee against Torture, 77–78

Committee on Economic, Social, and Cultural Rights (1985), 76

Committee on the Challenges of Modern Society, NATO, 203

Committee on the Elimination of Discrimination against Women, 77

Committee on the Elimination of Racial Discrimination, 76

commodity agreements, 280–82

Common Agricultural Policy of EU, 276

common heritage of mankind principle (CHMP), 226, 233

communication satellites, 245–46

Comprehensive Nuclear-Test-Ban Treaty (1996), 111, 194

conditional states, 30

condominia, 33

confederations, 29

Conference on Disarmament (CD), 194

confiscation, 270

conflict of interests, 120

conflict of rights, 120

Congo, 82, 176

Congo Free State, 29

Congress of Vienna (1815), 19

Connally Amendment (1946), 128

conquest of territory, 45

consensus, 199, 245

constitutional law, international organizations and, 87, 88–90, 102–3

constitutive theory of recognition, 48

consultation, environmental action and, 208–9

Contadora Framework, 124

contiguous zone, 230–31

continental shelf, 228, 229, 231

contraception. *See* birth control

Convention against Illicit Traffic in Narcotic Drugs and Psychotropic Substances (1988), 140

Convention against Torture (1979), 69

Convention against Torture and Other Cruel, Inhuman or Degrading Treatment (1984), 75, 146

Convention Concerning International Carriage by Rail (1980), 267

Convention for the Conservation of Antarctic Marine Living Resources (1980), 237

Convention for the Conservation of Antarctic Seals (1972), 237

Convention for the Pacific Settlement of International Disputes (1899), 126

Convention for the Protection of Cultural Property in the Event of Armed Conflict (1954), 101

Convention for the Protection of Literary and Artistic Works, 101

Convention for the Suppression of Unlawful Seizure of Aircraft (1970), 100, 139

Convention of Early Notification of a Nuclear Accident, 102

Convention of Saint-Germain-en-Laye (1919), 136

Convention on Assistance in the Case of a Nuclear Accident or Radiological Emergency, 102

Convention on Biological Diversity (1992), 72, 204, 218

Convention on Contracts for the International Sale of Goods (1980), 265

Convention on Fishing and Conservation of Living Resources of the High Seas, 229

Convention on International Bills of Exchange and International Promissory Notes (1988), 266

Convention on International Multimodal Transport of Goods (1980), 267

Convention on International Trade in Endangered Species of Wild Fauna and Flora (CITES), 218–19

Convention on Long-Range Transboundary Air Pollution (1979), 242

Convention on Offences and Certain Other Acts Committed on Board Aircraft (1963), 100

Convention on Physical Protection of Nuclear Material, 102

Convention on Registration of Objects Launched into Outer Space, 244

Convention on Suppression of Financing Terrorism, UN (1999), 69

Convention on the Carriage of Goods by Sea (Hamburg Rules) (1978), 266–67

Convention on the Conservation of Antarctic Seals (1972), 235

Convention on the Continental Shelf, 229

Convention on the Elimination of All Forms of Discrimination against Women (CEDAW, 1979), 74

Convention on the High Seas (1958), 137, 229

Convention on the Law of the Nonnavigational Uses of International Watercourses (1997), 213

Convention on the Law of the Sea (1982), 72, 136, 137, 214, 215, 223–24, 230–34, 249

Convention on the Liability of Operators of Transport Terminals in International Trade (1991), 266

Convention on the Limitation Period in the International Sale of Goods (1974), 266

Convention on the Marking of Plastic Explosives for the Purpose of Detection (1991), 100

Convention on the Political Rights of Women (1953), 74

Convention on the Prevention and Punishment of Crimes against Internationally Protected Persons, Including Diplomatic Agents (1973), 94, 140

Convention on the Prevention and Punishment of the Crime of Genocide (1948), 72–73, 93, 145

Convention on the Privileges and Immunities of the United Nations (1946), 85

Convention on the Prohibition of Military or Any Other Hostile Use of Environmental Modification Techniques (1977), 192

Convention on the Prohibition of the Development, Production, and Stockpiling of Bacteriological and Toxin Weapons and on Their Destruction (1972), 192

Convention on the Protection of the Underwater Cultural Heritage (2001), 101

Convention on the Reduction of Statelessness (August 30, 1961), 64

Convention on the Regulation of Antarctic Mineral Resource Activities (1988), 237

Convention on the Rescue and Return of Astronauts and the Return of Objects Launched into Space (1968), 243–44

Convention on the Rights of the Child (1989), 74–75, 78

Convention on the Settlement of Investment Disputes between States and Nationals of Other States (1965), 127, 272

Convention on the Succession of States in Respect of State Property, Archives, and Debts (1978), 94

Convention on the Succession of States in Respect of Treaties (1978), 94

Convention on the Suppression of Unlawful Acts against the Safety of Maritime Navigation (1988), 69

Convention on the Suppression of Unlawful Seizure of Aircraft (1970), 69

Convention on the Territorial Sea and Contiguous Zone, 229

Convention on Wetlands of International Importance especially as Waterfowl Habitat (Ramsar Convention) (1971), 217–18

Convention Relating to the International Status of Refugees (1933), 64

Convention Relating to the Status of Refugees (1951), 64

Convention Relating to the Status of Stateless Persons (September 28, 1954), 64

Convention to Suppress the Slave-Trade and Slavery (1926), 136

conventions. *See* international conventions

Conventions on the Law of the Sea (1958), 94

copyrights, 267–68

Corfu Channel Case (1947), 205–6

Corps of the Political Leaders of the Nazi Party, 152

Costa Rica, 124

Council of European Union: and environmentalism, 202; role of, 92, 274

counterfeiting, 141

Court of Auditors, European Union, 90

Court of First Instance, European Union, 90

Court of Justice of the European Coal and Steel Community, 129

Court of Justice of the European Communities, 90

Covenants on Human Rights, UN (1966), 46

crime, transnational, 291–92

crimes against humanity: apartheid, 74; ICC jurisdiction over, 156–57; Nuremberg trials for, 152; Pinochet and, 68–69; UN special tribunals for, 90; as war crimes, 145–47

crimes against the peace, 143, 151
criminal law. *See* international criminal law
Croatia, 175
Cuba, 33, 270
culture, globalization and, 289–91
custom: difficulties pertaining to, 12–13; natural law and, 16; and persistent objector rule, 13; positivism and, 18, 19; as source for international legal rules, 11–13
Czech Republic, 57
Czechoslovakia: as conditional state, 30; partition of, 57; Soviet Union and, 174

De Groot, Huigh Cornets. *See* Grotius, Hugo
De Jure Belli ac Pacis Libri Tres (Three Books on the Law of War and Peace) (Grotius), 17
De Vitoria, Francisco, 16
Declaration of Paris (1856), 183
Declaration of Principles of International Law (1970), 176
Declaration of the UN Conference on Environment and Development (Rio Declaration), 204, 207, 208–9
Declaration on Principles of International Law Concerning Friendly Relations and Cooperation among States (1970), 95, 181
Declaration on the Granting of Independence to Colonial Countries (1960), 46
Declaration on the Human Environment (1972), 203, 206–7
Declaration on the Inadmissibility of Intervention in Domestic Affairs of States (1965), 176
declaratory theory of recognition, 48–49
deep seabed mining, 230, 233–34
delict, international, 55
Delimitation of the Continental Shelf arbitration, 126
democracy, and international law, 19
Democratic Republic of Germany, 49
Democratic Republic of Korea, 49
demographic projections, 23–24
denationalization, 64
Denmark, 29, 125
dependent states, 32–33
deposit of ratifications, 110
dereliction, loss of territory through, 46
developing countries: debt reduction for, 265; and global commons, 225–26, 230; and international economics, 255–56
diplomacy: communication of behavioral expectations through, 7; definition of, 5; and dispute negotiation, 123; severance of ties of, 180
diplomatic immunity, 68

discovery of territory, 43–44
disease, 290–91
dispute settlement, 119–30; "dispute" defined, 310n20; as duty of state, 55; Hague peace conferences on, 19; institutions for, 124–28; nature of disputes, 120–21; obligations regarding, 121–23; political versus legal concerns, 123; processes of, 123–24, 130; regional courts, 128–30; state relationships and, 123; UN secretary-general and, 97
divided states, 30
dolphins, 260
domestic law. *See* municipal law
Dominica, 31
Dominican Republic, 174
drug offenses, 140–41, 291
dual citizenship, 63
dualism, 38–39
due process, 13
duties of states, 53–55; abstention from intervention, 53–55; dispute settlement, 55; prevention of counterfeiting, 55; prevention of harm to other states, 55; refraining from fomenting civil war, 55
dwarf states, 31

Earthwatch Programme, 200
East Germany, 174
East Jerusalem, 46
East Timor: and cession of territory, 44; Security Council action on, 186; self-determination of, 174–75
eclectic school of legal thought, 17–18
Economic and Social Committee (ESC) of EU, 98–99
economics: economic coercion (*see* sanctions); environmentalism and, 203, 209; globalization and, 288–89; and international crime, 291–92; nineteenth century irrelevance of, 19. *See also* international economic law; trade
effects doctrine, 150
Egypt, ancient, 15
Egypt, modern, 124, 169
Eighteen-Nation Committee on Disarmament, 194
El Salvador, 124
electronic commerce, 268–69
endangered species, 218–19
enforcement of international law: global commons law, 246–50; through states, 5–6, 36, 147–51; through tribunals, 151–55
Entebbe, 171, 173, 176
entry into force of treaties, 111

environment: accidents threatening, 198; consultation as duty of state, 208–9; environmental refugees, 219–20; future issues regarding, 102; harm prevention principle, 206–7; impact assessment concerning, 209; intergenerational equity principle, 208; natural resource management, 216–19, 232–33, 235; pollution control regimes, 212–16; precautionary principle, 207–8; preventive principle, 208; prior notification as duty of state, 208–9; shared resources, 213; state duties regarding, 55; sustainable use of, 208, 217; trade in relation to, 220; unlawful acts against, 141; World Bank and, 202, 264; WTO and, 260–61. *See also* global commons law; international environmental law

Environmental Modification Convention (1977), 192

equality of states: as fundamental principle of international law, 17–18; real versus ideal, 34; right of, 51; sovereignty as basis of, 34

Eritrea, 46, 124

Estonia, 45

Estrada Doctrine, 48

Estrada, Genaro, 48

Ethiopia: conquest by Italy of, 45, 164; good offices negotiations involving, 124; territory dispute involving, 46

ethnic cleansing, 125, 153, 177, 186, 190

ethnicity: effect on international law of, 40; effect on sovereignty of, 50; protection of minority groups, 69–70. *See also* racial discrimination

Europe, as foundation of international law, 19

European Atomic Energy Community Treaty (1957), 273

European Coal and Steel Community, 273

European Commission: and contract awards after Iraq war, 3–4; role in EU of, 92

European Commission of Human Rights, 79

European Community (EC), 273

European Convention for the Protection of Human Rights and Fundamental Freedoms (1950), 78–79

European Court of Human Rights (ECHR), 79

European Court of Justice (ECJ): establishment of, 129; role of, 275

European Economic Community, 273

European Economic Community Treaty (1957), 273

European Environment Agency, 202

European Parliament, 95

European Union (EU), 273–76; administrative law for, 87; Commission of, 274; Council of,

92, 202, 274; directives of, 276; Economic and Social Committee (ESC), 98–99; and economics, 274, 276; European Commission, 3–4, 92; history in outline of, 273–74; judicial system of, 90; Parliament of, 95, 274–75; regulations of, 275–76; rights and authority of, 275; as sovereign polity, 36; and U.S. steel tariffs, 253–54

exclusive economic zone (EEZ), 231

executive agreements, 113

expatriation, 64

expropriation, 269–70, 271

extinction of states, 56–58

extradition, 66–69; Pinochet and, 68–69; political offenses, 67–69; process of, 67

extraterritorial jurisdiction, 149

Exxon Valdiz oil spill, 198

Falkland Islands, 44, 46, 124

Far Eastern Agreement (1945), 113

federal states, 29

financial regulation, 261–65, 288–89

fishing regulations, 229, 232–33, 235, 237

flag state jurisdiction, 231

Florida Purchase (1819), 44

Food Aid Convention (1994), 281

Food and Agriculture Organization (FAO), 99–100, 201

foreign investment, 269–73

Foreign Sovereign Immunities Act (FSIA) of 1976, 52

Fourteen Points, 46

France: arbitration involving, 126; commission of conciliation involving, 125; and Lake Lanoux Arbitration Case, 206

franchise businesses, 268

fraudulent documentation, 141

Free Trade Area of the Americas, 99

Free Trade Commission (FTC), 278

freedom of the seas, 17, 18, 228, 229

Gadsden Purchase (1853), 44

Gaffney, Frank, 224

Galvao (Portuguese captain), 137

Gambia, 29

Garzón, Baltasar, 68

General Agreement on Tariffs and Trade (GATT): and changing trade circumstances, 103–4; establishment of, 255, 256–57; overview of, 102; principles of, 53; safeguard measures in, 253; Uruguay round, 257. *See also* World Trade Organization

General Agreement on Trade in Services, 258

General Assembly, United Nations: Declaration on Asylum (1967), 66; declarations of, 94–95; and human rights, 75; International Law Commission, 93–94; on Israeli West Bank barrier, 41; legislative role of, 93–95; resolutions of, 14, 93, 94–95; Sixth (Legal) Committee, 93; studies and recommendations of, 93; and use of force, 189

general principles of law, 13–14

Geneva Convention on the Contract of International Carriage of Goods by Road (1956), 267

Geneva Convention on the Status of Refugees (1951), 66

Geneva Conventions (1949): grave breaches of, 143–44; on prisoners' rights, 287; Red Cross and, 80; Saddam Hussein and, 61–62

Geneva Gas Protocol (1925), 192

genocide, 73, 125, 145, 153–55, 157, 177, 186, 190

Gentilis, Alberico, 18

geography, and international law, 15

geostationary orbit, 245–46

Germany: as confederation, 29; and conquest of territory, 45; as divided state, 30; as federal state, 29; reunification of, 58. *See also* Democratic Republic of Germany

Gestapo, 152

Ghandi, Indira, 177

global commons law, 223–51; Antarctica, 236–39; atmosphere, 239–43; compliance and enforcement issues, 246–50; future issues regarding, 251; oceans, 228–35; outer space, 243–46; regime formation, 225–27. *See also* international environmental law

global warming, 197–98, 240–42

globalization: and culture, 289–91; and economics, 288–89; and politics, 291–92

Goering, Hermann, 115, 152

Golan Heights, 45, 46

good offices, 123–24

goods, international sale of, 265–67

government-owned enterprises, 52

grains, 281

Grains Trade Convention (1994), 281

grave breaches of Geneva Conventions of 1949, 143–44, 314n39

Great Britain: arbitration involving, 125; and Corfu Channel Case, 205–6; good offices negotiations involving, 124; and personal union, 29. *See also* United Kingdom

Greece, ancient, 15

Greece, modern, 125

greenhouse gas emissions, 197, 204, 240–42

Grenada, 31, 173, 174, 176, 179

Grotius, Hugo (Huigh Cornets De Groot), 17, 163, 228

Group of 77, 255

Group of Three (apartheid review), 74

Guam, 28

Guatemala, 124

Gulf of Acaba, 44–45

Gulf War (1991), 45, 126, 179

Gun, Katherine, 85

Hacha, Emil, 115

Hague Agreement Concerning the International Deposit of Industrial Designs, 101

Hague Conference on Private International Law, 254

Hague Convention Respecting the Laws and Customs of War on Land (1907), 144

Hague Peace Conference (1899), 125, 126

Hague Peace Conference (1907), 125

Hague peace conferences, 19

Hague-Visby Rules, 266

Haig, Alexander, 124

Haiti, 49, 178

Hanover, 29

harm prevention, principle of, 206–7

Harmon doctrine, 206

Havana Charter, 256

hazardous waste dumping, 214–16

Headquarters Agreement (1947), 85–86

health issues, 290–91

Hebrews, 15

Hegel, Georg Wilhelm Friedrich, 19

Helsinki Rules (1966), 213

Hickenlooper Amendment to Foreign Assistance Act of 1961, 52

high seas, 231. *See also* ocean law

hijacking, aerial, 138–39

Hindus, 15

Hiroshima, 190

Hitler, Adolf, 115

Holocaust, 72, 145, 151

Holy See, 30–31

Honduras, 124

hostage taking, 139–40

hosti humani generis, 150

human rights, 69–80; Abu Ghraib prison scandal, 144, 287–88; apartheid and, 73–74; children and, 74–75, 78; collective, 72–75; discrimination and, 73; General Assembly resolutions and, 94; implementation of, 75–78; and international environment law, 219; permissible intervention regarding, 54; regional systems regarding, 78–80; slavery

and, 73; three generations of, 71–72; and torture, 75; women's status and, 74, 77. *See also*
crimes against humanity; human rights law
Human Rights Committee, 71, 76–77
human rights law: development of, 70–71; ethics
and, 4; and individuals as subjects in international law, 28
humanitarian intervention, 176–78
Hungary, 29, 174
Hussein, Saddam, 61–62, 140, 161

ICC. *See* International Criminal Court
Iceland, 29
ICJ. *See* International Court of Justice
IGOs. *See* international organizations
Ile des Faisans, 33
immigration, 64–65
immunity: diplomatic, 68; personal, 51; sovereign, 51–52; state, 51–52
imputability, 56
incorporation, doctrine of, 39
independence (sovereignty) of states: concept of,
33–35; as fundamental in international relations, 19; as fundamental principle of international law, 17–18; globalization effect on, 292;
human rights and, 69; interdependence versus, 37; limits on external, 38; as obstacle to
international law, 33–35, 37–38; rights pursuant to, 50–51; states as political actors, 25; war
decisions and, 163
India: arbitration involving, 126; and Bangladesh, 175, 177; and dereliction regarding territory, 46
indigenous peoples, 219
individuals, 61–82; human rights of (*see* human
rights); as international actors, 28; international crime committed by, 136–41; jurisdiction over aliens, 64–69; nationality of, 63–64;
statelessness, 64; as subjects of international
law, 28, 39, 62, 70
Indonesia, 174–75
industrial property, 267
INGOs. *See* international nongovernmental
organizations
innocent passage, 229, 230
insurance for investments, 271
intellectual property, 101, 258–59, 267–69, 289
Inter-American Agency for Cooperation and
Development (IACD), 99
Inter-American Commission on Human Rights,
79
Inter-American Court of Human Rights
(IACHR), 79–80

Inter-American Development Bank, 99
Inter-American Treaty of Reciprocal Assistance
(1947), 190
interdependence of states, 35–36, 37
intergenerational equity, principle of, 208
intergovernmental organizations (IGOs). *See*
international organizations
Intermediate Range Nuclear Forces (INF) Treaty
(1987), 191
internal waters, 231
international actors: individuals as, 28; nonstate,
27; regimes, 27–28; sovereign states, 25, 33;
terrorist groups, 27; transnational, 25–26;
Trusteeship Council and preparation of new,
98
International Atomic Energy Agency (IAEA),
102, 216
International Bank for Reconstruction and
Development (World Bank): Center for the
Settlement of Investment Disputes, 127; and
environment, 202, 264; formation of, 255, 264;
operation of, 264; overview of, 100
International Bill of Human Rights, 72
International Bureau of Paris Union, 101
International Civil Aviation Organization
(ICAO), 100, 125, 138–39
International Cocoa Organization, 280
International Code of Conduct on the Transfer
of Technology, 268
International Coffee Agreement (2001), 280–81
international comity, 5
International Commission of Jurists, 80
International Committee of the Red Cross, 61,
80, 287
international commodity agreements, 280–82
International Convention against the Taking of
Hostages (1979), 140
International Convention for the Suppression of
Counterfeiting Currency (1929), 141
International Convention for the Unification of
Certain Rules Relating to Bills of Lading
(Hague-Visby Rules) (1924), 266
International Convention on the Elimination of
All Forms of Racial Discrimination (1965), 73,
142
International Convention on the Suppression
and Punishment of the Crime of Apartheid
(1973), 74, 142
international conventions, definition of, 11
International Council of Scientific Unions, 236
International Court of Arbitration of the Interna-
tional Chamber of Commerce, 126
International Court of Justice (ICJ): advantages

for dispute settlement of, 127–28; advisory opinions of, 128; Certain Expenses Case, 189; Corfu Channel Case, 205–6; decisions of, 14, 89; establishment of, 127; Iran hostage incident, 139–40; on Israeli West Bank barrier, 41–42; judge elections for, 127; and judicial sanction, 6; purpose of, 263; role of, 88–90, 155; and self-determination, 46

international courts, 88–90, 103. *See also* International Court of Justice

International Covenant on Civil and Political Rights (1976), 71, 72, 76, 94

International Covenant on Economic, Social, and Cultural Rights (1976), 72, 76, 94

International Covenant on Environment and Development, 217

International Criminal Court (ICC), 155–59; formation of, 81, 148, 156; jurisdiction of, 156–57; Ugandan rebel leaders case, 133

international criminal law, 133–60; governments as criminal perpetrators, 141–43; International Criminal Court and, 155–59; nature of, 134–36; private persons as criminal perpetrators, 136–41; special tribunals regarding, 151–55; state responsibility regarding, 147–51; truth commissions, 159; war crimes, 143–47

International Criminal Tribunal for Rwanda, 134, 144, 148, 154–55

International Criminal Tribunal for the Former Yugoslavia, 134, 144, 148, 153–54. *See* Nuremberg Charter (1945)

international delict, 55

International Development Association, 100, 265

international drug offenses, 140–41

international economic law, 253–83; Andean Group and, 278–79; Association of South East Asian Nations, 279–80; Bretton Woods System, 255; commodity agreements, 280–82; European Union and, 273–76; financial regulation, 261–65, 288–89; foreign investment, 269–73; intellectual property rights, 267–69, 289; municipal law and, 254; NAFTA and, 276–78; New International Economic Order, 255–56; regional organizations and, 273–80; sale of goods, 265–67; significance of, 282–83; World Trade Organization, 256–61

international environmental law, 197–221; changing nature of, 219–20; conference diplomacy concerning, 203–5; enforcement of, 219; formulation of, 198–205; human rights and, 219; international agreements, 209–11; international organizations and, 199–202; judicial

cases bearing on, 205–6; natural resource management, 216–19; normative principles of, 206–9; ocean law, 210, 211, 214, 232, 234–35; pollution control regimes, 212–16; soft law, 211–12; sources of, 205–12; state responsibility regarding, 199. *See also* environment; global commons law

international ethics, 4–5. *See also* international morality

International Finance Corporation, 100, 265

international financial regulation, 261–65, 288–89

International Fund for Agricultural Development, 100

International Geophyiscal Year, 236

International Grains Agreement (2004), 281

international interest, 112

International Jute Organization, 281

International Labor Organization, 100, 201

international law: coining of term, 297n1; concept of, 5–6; criticisms of, 5; definition of, 4, 297n1; diplomacy and, 5; doctrine of incorporation and, 39; dualism versus monism, 38–39; dynamic nature of, 36, 38; enforcement of, 5–6, 36; first manual of, 18; formulation of, 6; fundamental principles of, 17; future of, 287–92; Grotius as father of modern, 17; historical development of, 14–21; horizontal structure of, 24, 37; incentives for, 6–8, 10, 15; international comity and, 5; international ethics and, 4–5; municipal law versus, 19; national interests and, 9–10; national policy versus, 5; post–World War II developments in, 293; private, 32; state sovereignty as obstacle for, 33–35, 37–38; UN Secretariat and, 97. *See also* global commons law; international economic law; international environmental law; international legal rules

International Law Commission of UN General Assembly, 93–94

International Lead and Zinc Study Group, 281

international legal community, 23–40; actors in, 25–28; classification of states, 28–33; doctrine of incorporation, 39; dualism versus monism, 38–39; legal relations between states, 36–37; maintenance of, 37–38; state sovereignty, 33–35; territorial sovereignty, 35–36

international legal rules: creation of, 9–10; dynamic nature of, 21; functions of, 288; international organizations' role in, 86–88; nature of, 7–8; role in international criminal law of, 147; sources of, 10–14

International Load Line Convention, 117

international mail, unlawful use of, 141
International Maritime Dangerous Drug Code, 201
International Maritime Organization (IMO), 100, 138, 201, 234–35, 248
International Military Tribunal at Nuremberg, 143, 148, 151–52
International Military Tribunal for the Far East, 148, 152–53
International Monetary Fund (IMF): crises of 1990s, 263–64; and foreign investment, 272; formation of, 100–101, 255, 262; operation of, 101, 262–63
international morality: definition of, 4–5; difficulties with, 14
international nongovernmental organizations (INGOs), 26, 27
International Olive Oil Council, 281
international organizations (IOs), 85–104; and administrative law, 87, 96–98, 103–4; charters of, 88; and constitutional law, 87, 88–90, 102–3; and environmental law, 199–202; future trends of, 102–4; and prescriptive law, 87, 90–96, 103; resolutions of, as source for international legal rules, 14; rights of, 53; role in legal rules of, 86–88; and socioeconomic concerns, 98–102; as transnational actors, 25–26
international relations: increasing significance of, 7; nineteenth century assumptions about, 19
International Rubber Organization, 280
International Safety Management Code, 235
international sale of goods, 265–67
International Seabed Authority, 226, 233–34
International Sugar Organization, 282
International Telecommunication Union, 101, 245–46
International Telephone and Telegraph, 270
International Tin Council, 281
International Trade Organization (ITO), 256
International Tropical Timber Agreement (1994), 282
International Whaling Commission, 235
Internet, 269, 289–90
Interpol, 289
intervention in state affairs, 53–55
Iran: and Bosnia-Herzegovina, 175; commission of inquiry involving, 125; good offices negotiations involving, 124; hostage taking in, 139–40; nationalization by, 270; state-sponsored terrorism by, 27; territory dispute involving, 46

Iraq: good offices negotiations involving, 124; hostage taking by, 140; invasion of Kuwait by, 45, 126, 171, 179, 182, 185; and Israel, 170, 171; no-fly zones over, 178; sanctions against, 182; territory dispute involving, 46; U.S. reprisal against, 181; U.S.-Iraq war (2003), 3–4, 61–62, 105, 161–62, 169–70, 173, 186–87, 287–88
Iraq war (2003): Abu Ghraib prison scandal, 287–88; coalitions of the willing and, 173; contract bidding after, 3–4; preemptive self-defense and, 169–70; Saddam's capture after, 61–62; UN Security Council and, 105, 186–87; use of force concerns over, 161–62
Island of Palmas arbitration, 126
Islas Malvinas, 44, 46, 124
Israel: Arab boycott against, 182; and conquest of territory, 45; and Iraq, 170, 171; mediation involving, 124; and Palestinian conflict, 41–42, 181; and Six Days' War, 169; territory dispute involving, 46; and Uganda, 171, 173, 176
Italy: commission of conciliation involving, 125; invasion of Ethiopia by, 45, 164
Ixtoc I oil-well blowout, 198

Japan: Chinese boycott of, 182; and conquest of territory, 45; mediation involving, 124; territory dispute involving, 46
Jordan, 44–45
judicial decisions, as source for international legal rules, 14
jurisdiction: extent of state, 149–51; extraterritorial, 149; over aliens, 64–69; of states, 62–63; universal, 68, 74
jus cogens, 115, 135, 142
jus gentium (law of nations), 15, 16, 17
jus in bello, 163
jus sanguinis, 63
jus soli, 63
jus voluntarium. See voluntary law
just war: De Vitoria's denial of, 16; development of concept of, 162–64
jute, 281

Kambanda, Jean, 155
Kampuchea, 49
Karadzic, Radovan, 154
Karpinski, Janis, 287
Kashmir, 46
Kellogg-Briand Pact (1928), 45, 152, 164, 168
Kennecott Copper Corporation, 270
Khetasar, 107
Khmer Rouge, 156

kidnapping of diplomats, 140
Kiribati, 31
Kony, Joseph, 133
Korea, 30, 185. *See also* Democratic Republic of Korea
krill, 237
Kurile islands, 46
Kuwait, invasion by Iraq of, 45, 171, 179, 182, 185
Kyoto Protocol, 197–98, 227, 241–42

Lake Lanoux Arbitration Case (1957), 206, 213
lakes, 213
land conventions, treaties on, 211
Laos, 30
Lateran Treaty (1929), 30
Latvia, 45
law: adjectival, 13; definition of, 5; general principles of, 13–14; natural, 15, 16–18; schools of, 15–21; substantive, 13
law of nations, 297n1. *See also* international law; *jus gentium*
law of the sea. *See* Convention on the Law of the Sea (1982); ocean law
lawmaking treaties, 108
Lawyers Committee for Human Rights, 81
Le droit des gens (Vattel), 17
lead, 281
League of Arab States, 129, 182
League of Nations: and conquest of territory, 45; overview of, 20; on self-defense, 168; and subservient states, 32; U.S. Senate rejection of, 111; on use of force, 163–64
legal equality. *See* equality of states
lex maritima, 254
lex mercatoria, 254
Liability for Damage Caused by Space Objects Convention (1972), 244
Liberia, 176
Libya, 91, 181, 270
Liechtenstein, 31
Lithuania, 45
Lockerbie bombing, 91
London Charter (1945), 152
London Court of International Arbitration, 126
Lord's Resistance Army (LRA), 133
Louisiana Purchase (1803), 44
Lugar, Richard, 223

Maastricht Treaty (1993), 273
Malay states, 33
Malaysia, 46
Maldive Islands, 31
Manchuria, 45, 182

Manley, John, 3
maritime navigation, threats to, 138
Marrakesh Protocol (1995), 257
Marshall Islands, Republic of the, 31
Martens, Georg Friedrich von, 18
Mauritania, 46, 136
McDougal, Myers, 176
mediation, 124
Merger Treaty (1965), 273, 275–76
Mexico: expropriation by, 270; as federal state, 29; and tuna-dolphin regulations, 260
Micronesia, Federated States of, 31
microstates, 31
Middle Ages, legal developments during, 16
ministates, 31
minority groups, protection of, 69–70
Mladic, Ratko, 154
Monaco, 31
money-laundering, 291–92
monism, 38–39
Montenegro, 30
Montreal Convention for the Suppression of Unlawful Acts against the Safety of Civil Aviation (1971), 69
Montreal Convention to Discourage Acts of Violence against Civil Aviation (1971), 139
Montreal Protocol on Substances That Deplete the Ozone Layer (1987), 240, 249–50
Moon Treaty, 244
Moreno-Ocampo, Luis, 133
Morocco, 33, 46
Moscow Treaty on Strategic Offensive Reductions (2002), 191
Moser, John Jacob, 18
Multilateral Investment Guaranty Agency (MIGA), 271
multilateral treaties, 108, 111
multinational corporations (MNCs): as actors, 27; foreign investment by, 270; private international law and, 32; significant trade role of, 254–55
municipal law: dualism versus monism, 38–39; international economic law and, 254; international versus, 19; role in international criminal law of, 147
Museveni, Yoweri, 133

NAFTA. *See* North American Free Trade Agreement
Nagasaki, 190
Nagorno-Karabagh, 46
Namibia, 32
national interests, international law and, 9–10

national liberation movements, 174–75
nationalism: effect on international law of, 18, 19, 40; effect on sovereignty of, 50
nationality: acquisition of, 63–64; citizenship versus, 302n1; loss of, 64; statelessness and, 64
nationality principle of jurisdiction, 150
nationalization, 269–70
nations, versus states, 25. *See also* nationalism
natural law, 15, 16
natural resource management, 216–19, 232–33, 235
natural rubber, 280
naturalist school of legal thought, 15–17
naturalization, 63–64
Nauru, 31
naval blockades, 183
negotiation of disputes, 123
negotiation of treaties, 109
Netherlands, 126
neutralized states, 30
New Hebrides, 33
New International Economic Order (NIEO), 225–26, 255–56
new solidarity rights, 72
Nicaragua, 124
Nicaragua v United States, 165–66, 172
Nigeria, 177
Nonaligned Movement, 255
nongovernmental organizations (NGOs), human rights role of, 80–81. *See also* international nongovernmental organizations (INGOs)
nonproliferation, 192–93
nonstate actors, 27
Noriega, Manuel, 30
North American Free Trade Agreement (NAFTA), 276–78
North Atlantic Treaty Organization: and Afghanistan, 179; and Bosnia-Herzegovina, 189–90; and collective self-defense, 173; and environmentalism, 203; and Kosovo, 190; and September 11 terrorist attacks, 190
North Yemen, 29
Northern Marianas, Commonwealth of the, 31
Norway, 29
Nuclear Nonproliferation Treaty (1968), 192
nuclear power, 215–16
nuclear weapons. *See* weapons of mass destruction
nuclear-free zones, 193
Nuremberg Charter (1945), 146, 313n34
Nuremberg Trials. *See* International Military Tri-

bunal, Nuremberg; Nuremberg Charter (1945)
Nyerere, Julius, 177

obligatio erga omnes, 135
occupation of territory, 44
ocean law, 228–35; archipelagic state, 231; cannon shot rule (three-mile rule), 13, 18, 228; custom as origin of, 12; enforcement of, 248–49; environmentalism and, 210, 211, 214, 232, 234–35; exclusive economic zone (EEZ), 231; freedom of the seas, 17, 18, 228, 229; high seas, 231; innocent passage, 229; internal waters, 231; resource management, 232–33, 235; territorial sea, 13, 18, 43, 228–29, 230; transit passage, 232; United States and, 223–24. *See also* Convention on the Law of the Sea (1982)
October war (1973), 182, 280
oil embargo, 182
olive oil, 281
opinio juris (sive necessitatis), 12
Organization for Economic Cooperation and Development (OECD), 203, 209, 257, 272
Organization of African Unity, 129
Organization of American States (OAS): administrative law for, 87; Department of International Law, 96; establishment of, 125; and human rights, 79; Inter-American Juridical Committee, 96; legislative role of, 95–96; Permanent Council of, 92; Secretariat for Legal Affairs, 95; and September 11 terrorist attacks, 190; socioeconomic concerns of, 99
Organization of Arab Petroleum Exporting Countries (OAPEC), 280
Organization of Eastern Caribbean States, 179
Organization of Petroleum Exporting Countries (OPEC), 182–83, 256, 280
Ottoman Empire, 32
outer space, 243–46, 248
Outer Space Treaty (1967), 72, 74, 94, 192, 243
Overseas Private Investment Corporation (OPIC), 271
ozone layer, 239–40

Pact of Bogota (1948), 125
pacta sunt servanda, 17, 55, 108, 115
Pakistan: arbitration involving, 126; and Bangladesh, 175, 177; and dereliction regarding territory, 46
Palau, 31, 32, 97–98
Palestinians: *Achille Lauro* incident, 138; and Israeli conflict, 41–42, 181; mediation involv-

ing, 124; territory dispute involving, 46; U.S. diplomat kidnappings by, 140
Panama, 174, 176
Pardo, Arvid, 230
Paris Peace accords (1975), 113
Parliament of European Union, 95, 274–75
passive personality principle of jurisdiction, 150
Peace of Westphalia (1648). *See* Treaty of Westphalia (1648)
peacekeeping, 103, 188
People's Republic of China. *See* China
Perez de Cuellar, Javier, 124, 233
Permanent Council of the Organization of American States, 92
Permanent Court of Arbitration, 19, 126
persistent objector rule, 13
personal immunity, 51
personal unions, 29
petroleum, 280
Philippines, 46
Pinochet, Augusto, 68–69
piracy, 137–38
Pol Pot, 177–78
Poland, 30
political offense, 67–69
politics: asylum and, 66; globalization and, 291–92; political offenses, 67–69; recognition of states and, 48, 49
pollution control regimes, 212–16; air pollution, 242–43; hazardous waste dumping, 214–16; law of the sea, 214; regional agreements, 214; riparian law, 213
population projections, 23–24
positivist school of legal thought, 16, 18–19, 163
Powell, Colin, 223
precautionary principle for environment, 207–8
Precis du droit des gens moderne de l'Europe (Martens), 18
preemptive strikes, 169–70
prescription, acquisition of territory through, 44
prescriptive law, international organizations and, 87, 90–96, 103
preventive attacks, 170
preventive principle for environment, 208
prior notification, environmental action and, 208–9
private international law, 32
protectionism, 256
protective principle of jurisdiction, 150
protectorates, 33
Protocol for the Prohibition of the Use in War of Asphyxiating, Poisonous, or Other Gases, and of Bacteriological Methods of Warfare (1925), 192

Protocol for the Suppression of Unlawful Acts of Violence at Airports Serving International Civil Aviation (1988), 139
Protocol on Environmental Protection to the Antarctic Treaty (1991), 237–38
public health, 290–91
Puerto Rico, 28, 46
Pufendorf, Samuel, 16–17

al Qaeda, 27, 171, 179, 181, 190
Quadaffi, Muammar, 181

racial discrimination, 73
Ramsar Convention on Wetlands of International Importance Especially as Waterfowl Habitat (1971), 101
Ramses II, 107
Rann of Kutch arbitration (1968), 46, 126
rape, 147
ratification of treaties, 110
real unions, 28–29
realist school of legal thought, 34, 36, 37
rebus sic stantibus, 117
recognition of states, 47–49; constitutive theory of, 48; de facto versus de jure, 48; declaratory theory of, 48–49; political considerations and, 48, 49; tests for, 49
Red Cross. *See* International Committee of the Red Cross
refoulement, 65
refugees, 66, 219–20
regime cohesion, 250
regimes: as actors, 27–28; definition of, 27
regional organizations and institutions: for dispute settlement, 128–30; and environmentalism, 202; for human rights, 78–80; international economic law, 273–80; as transnational actors, 26; and use of force, 189–90
Reisman, Michael, 176
religion: effect on international law of, 40; natural law and, 16; terrorist groups and, 27
remote sensing, 245–46
reprisals, 180–81
research: in Antarctica, 236; regulations on marine, 233
reservations, on treaties, 111
resolutions: General Assembly, 93, 94–95; as source for international legal rules, 14, 95
respect, state right of, 51
restitution for unjustified harm, 13
restrictive theory of sovereign immunity, 52
retorsion, 180
Rhineland, 45

Ribbentrop, Joachim von, 115

rights of states, 50–53; commercial intercourse, 52–53; equality before law, 51; respect, 51–52; self-preservation, 50; sovereign decision-making, 50–51

Rio Declaration, 204, 207, 208–9

Rio Treaty (1947), 190

rivers, 43, 206, 213

Rome, early international law in, 15

Rome International Institute for the Unification of Private International Law, 254

Rome Statute, 156–58

Roosevelt, Theodore, 124

rubber, 280

Rumania, 32

Russia: and debt responsibility, 58; as federal state, 29; mediation involving, 124; and outer space, 244–45, 250; territory dispute involving, 46. *See also* Soviet Union

Rwanda, 90, 134, 143–44, 178

Saar Basin, 57

safeguard measures, 253

Salazar, Antonio, 137

San Marino, 31

sanctions: boycotts, 182–83; naval blockades, 183; as Security Council means, 91–92; trade embargoes, 181–82; for use of force, 164, 181–83

Santa Maria (ship), 137

Santiago Declaration (1952), 228

satellite states, 31

satellites, 245–46

Saudi Arabia, 44–45

scholarly writings, as source for international legal rules, 14

schools of legal thought, 15–21; eclecticism, 17–18; naturalism, 15–17; positivism, 16, 18–19, 163; realism, 34, 36, 37

Schroeder, Gerhard, 3–4

sea turtles, 260–61

seabed, 230, 233–34

Seabed Arms Control Treaty (1971), 94, 193

seals, 235, 237

Security Council, United Nations: legal authority of, 91–92; membership of, 102–3; power of, 34; and regional organizations, 189–90; and self-defense principle, 184–85; on self-determination, 174–75; and use of force, 183–88

Selden, John, 18

self-defense, 168–73; anticipatory, 169–71; collective, 173, 179; definition of, 168–69; legal constraints on, 13; Security Council and, 184–85

self-determination of states, 46–47, 174–75

semisovereign states, 32–33

Senegal, 29

Senegambia, 29

September 11, 2001 terrorist attacks, 169, 171, 179, 186, 190

Serbia: and Bosnia-Herzegovina, 175; humanitarian intervention in, 177; U.S.-NATO bombing of, 190; as vassal state, 32

services, trade in, 258

shared resources, 213

Sharon, Ariel, 42

"shock the conscience" standard, 135, 136

Short, Clare, 85

shrimp, 260–61

Shrimp-Turtle Case (1998), 260–61

signature of treaties, 109–10

Sihanouk, Prince, 49

Single European Act (1986), 273

Six Days' War (1967), 169

Sixth (Legal) Committee of UN General Assembly, 93

60 Minutes II, 287

skyjacking, 138–39

slavery, 73, 136–37

Slovakia, 57

social Darwinism, 69

socioeconomic concerns, 98–102

soft law, on environment, 211–12, 227, 235

Somalia, 28, 178, 185–86

South African Truth Commission, 159

South Pacific Forum, 193

South Yemen, 29

Southern Rhodesia, 185

sovereign immunity, 51–52

sovereigns, as subject to law, 13, 51–52

sovereignty. *See* independence (sovereignty) of states; territorial sovereignty

Soviet Union: and conquest of territory, 45; use of force by, 174. *See also* Russia

Spain, 46, 206

special drawing rights, 263

special international tribunals, 90

Spratlys group, South China Sea, 46

Sputnik, 243

SS (Nazi Germany), 152

stare decisis, 14, 89

state immunity, 51–52

state responsibility, 55–56

statelessness of individuals, 64

states, 41–59; as actors, 25; associated, 31; characteristics and conditions of, 25, 28; classification of, 28–33; conditional, 30; divided, 30; duties of, 53–55; dwarf, 31; extinction of, 56–58; international crime committed by, 141–43; jurisdiction of, 62–63, 149–51; legal relations between, 36–37; ministates, 31; nations versus, 25; neutralized, 30; recognition of, 47–49; responsibility for criminal offenses of, 147–55; rights of, 50–53; satellite, 31; self-determination of, 46–47; semisovereign, 32–33; sovereignty of, 33–35, 37–38; state responsibility, 55–56; subservient, 32; succession of, 56–58; territory of, 43–46. *See also* independence (sovereignty) of states; territorial sovereignty

steel tariffs, 253–54

Stimson doctrine of nonrecognition, 45

Stimson, Henry, 45

Stockholm Chamber of Commerce Arbitration, 126

Stockholm Conference on the Environment (1972), 55, 198, 203

Stockholm Declaration (1972), 203, 206–7

Stoicism, 15

straits, 232

Strasbourg Agreement Concerning the International Patent Classification, 101

Strategic Arms Limitation Talks (SALT) Agreements, 191

Strategic Arms Reduction Talks (START) Agreements, 191

Suarez, Francisco, 16

Subcommission on Prevention of Discrimination and Protection of Minorities (1947), 76

subservient states, 32

substantive law, 13

subversive intervention, 54–55

succession of states, 56–58

Sudan: as condominium, 33; slavery in, 136–37; U.S. missile attack on, 171, 181

Suez Canal, 66, 189, 270

sugar, 281–82

Supplementary Convention on the Abolition of Slavery, the Slave Trade, and Institutions and Practices Similar to Slavery (1956), 136

sustainable use principle, 208, 217

Sweden, 29

Switzerland, 29, 30, 125

Syria, 46

Taguba, Antonio, 287

Taiwan, 46

Taliban, 171

Tanganyika, 29

Tangier, 33

Tanzania, 29, 177

tariffs, Bush and steel, 253–54

Tate, Jack B., 52

technology: crime and, 291–92; electronic commerce, 268–69; globalization and, 289–92; as obstacle to custom as source of law, 12–13; transfer of, 268

telecommunications, 245–46, 269, 290

Ten-Nation Committee on Disarmament, 194

territorial sea, 228–29, 230

territorial sovereignty, 43–46; acquisition of territory, 43–45; establishment of borders, 43; as fundamental in international relations, 19; as fundamental principle of international law, 17–18; interdependence versus, 35–36; and loss of territory, 45–46; origin of concept of, 35; passive personality principle of jurisdiction versus, 150; self-determination versus, 47

territoriality principle of jurisdiction, 149–50

terrorist groups: as actors, 27; growth of, 291; self-defense and, 170–71. *See also* al Qaeda

Test Ban Treaty (1963), 193

thalweg, 43

Three Mile Island nuclear power plant accident, 215

timber, tropical, 282

tin, 281

Toepfer, Klaus, 197

Tojo, Hideki, 153

Tokyo Convention on Offenses and Certain Other Acts Committed on Board Aircraft (1963), 138

Tokyo War Crimes Trials. *See* International Military Tribunal for the Far East

Torrey Canyon oil spill, 198

torture, 69, 75, 77–78, 146

trade: electronic commerce, 269; environment in relation to, 220; European Union and, 276; international sale of goods, 265–67; NAFTA and, 277–78; state rights regarding, 52–53. *See also* international economic law

trade embargoes, 181–82

Trail Smelter Arbitration Case (1941), 205

transfer of technology, 268

transit passage, 232

transnational actors, 25–26

transnational business enterprises. *See* multinational corporations

travaux preparatoires, 114

treaties: accession to, 110; ancient, 15, 107; bilateral, 108; bilateral investment, 271; of cession,

44; contract, 11; contract-like nature of, 109; environmental, 209–11; as evidence of international law, 8; fomulation of, 109–13; interpretation of, 113–15; lawmaking, 108; legal rules for, 113; multilateral, 108, 111; obligations of, 13, 17, 55, 108, 113–14, 115; reasons for compliance with, 114–15; regimes organized around, 28; reservations on, 111; state succession and, 58; termination of, 116–18; *United Nations Treaty Series*, 97; U.S. procedures regarding, 310n8; U.S. Senate role in ratifying, 111; validity of, 115–16. *See also* agreements

Treaties of Rome (1957), 273

Treaty for the Prohibition of Nuclear Weapons in Latin America (1967), 193

Treaty of Bangkok (1993), 193

Treaty of Pelindaba (1996), 193

Treaty of Rarotonga (1985), 193

Treaty of Tlatelolco (1967), 193

Treaty of Westphalia (1648): fundamental principles of, 17; international legal rules grounded in, 11, 21; and just war authority, 162

Treaty on Antarctica (1959), 72

Treaty on European Union (1993), 273

Treaty on Principles Governing the Activities of States in the Exploration and Use of Outer Space, including the Moon and Other Celestial Bodies (1967). *See* Outer Space Treaty (1967)

Treaty on the Nonproliferation of Nuclear Weapons (1968), 94, 216

Treaty on the Southeast Asia Nuclear Weapon Free Zone (1993), 193

Treaty on the South Pacific Nuclear Free Zone (1985), 193

tribunals for enforcement of international criminal law, 151–55, 158–59

tropical timber, 282

Truman, Harry S., 228

truth commissions, 159

tuna, 260

Tuna-Dolphin Case (1991), 260

Tunis, 33

Tuvalu, 31

Uganda: and Israel, 171, 173, 176; as protectorate, 33; rebel crimes in, 133; and Tanzania, 177

Ukraine, 46

UNCLOS I, 228–29

UNCLOS II, 230

UNCLOS III, 230

Union Carbide plant accident, 198

Union of Soviet Socialist Republics. *See* Soviet Union

unions: confederations, 29; federal states, 29; personal, 29; pseudo-, 29; real, 28–29

United Arab Emirates (UAE), 29

United Kingdom: arbitration involving, 126; eavesdropping on UN by, 85–86; and no-fly zones, 178; territory dispute involving, 46. *See also* Great Britain

United Nations: administrative law for, 87; agencies of, 26; Charter of, 34, 45, 53, 70; Commission on Human Rights, 75; Commission on International Trade Law, 126, 254, 266, 272; Committee on Peaceful Uses of Outer Space, 244–46; Compensation Commission, 126; Conference on Trade and Development, 272; Conferences on the Law of the Sea, 228–30; eavesdropping on, 85–86; Economic and Social Council (ECOSOC), 98; Economic Commission for Latin America and the Caribbean, 99; Environmental Programme (UNEP), 200–201, 212; interventionist role of, 105–6; organs of, 88; Population Division, 24; Secretariat, 96–97; significance of, 20, 26, 70–71, 86; specialized agencies for socioeconomic concerns, 99–102; and subservient states, 32; Trusteeship Council, 97–98; World Intellectual Property Organization, 289. *See also* General Assembly, United Nations; Security Council, United Nations; Universal Declaration of Human Rights (1948)

United Nations Charter: on dispute settlement, 122; as fundamental constitutional law, 88; fundamental principles of international law in, 90–91; and international interest, 112; on self-defense, 168; significance as international agreement of, 106–7; on use of force, 91, 105–6, 164–65

United Nations Conference on Environment and Development (UNCED), 203–4

United Nations Educational, Scientific, and Cultural Organization (UNESCO), 101

United Nations Framework Convention on Climate Change (UNFCCC) (1992), 197, 204, 240–41

United Nations Industrial Development Organization (UNIDO), 101

United Nations Treaty Series, 97

United States: and Abu Ghraib prison scandal, 287–88; acquisition of territory by, 44; act of retorsion by, 180; and Afghanistan, 169, 171, 179, 181; arbitration involving, 125, 126; commission of inquiry involving, 125; as confederation, 29; continental shelf of, 228, 229; eavesdropping on UN by, 85–86; and environmentalism, 198, 205, 227, 241–42; as federal state, 29; and global commons law, 250; and Grenada, 173, 174, 176, 179; and IMF, 263; Iranian hostage incident, 139–40; and Iraq reprisal, 181; Iraq war (2003), 3–4, 61–62, 105, 161–62, 169–70, 173, 186–87, 287–88; and Libya, 181; and no-fly zones, 178; and ocean law, 223–24, 233–34; and outer space, 244–45; and Panama, 174, 176; recognition of states by, 49; and shrimp–sea turtle regulations, 260–61; treaty procedures of, 310n8; and tuna-dolphin regulations, 260; on UN role, 105–6; use of force by, 174, 176, 179

United States UN Strategic Trust Territory of the Pacific, 31

Uniting for Peace Resolution, 189

Universal Copyright Convention (1952), 101, 268

Universal Declaration of Human Rights (1948): and asylum, 66; codification of, 72; as fundamental to human rights law, 71; General Assembly and, 94; on right of nationality, 64; and self-determination, 46

universal jurisdiction, 68, 74, 150

Universal Postal Union, 101

Uruguay round of GATT, 257

U.S. Census Bureau, 23

use of force, 161–95; aggression as international crime, 142–43; coercion short of war, 180–83; for collective security, 179; definition of, 166; economic coercion, 181–83; General Assembly and, 189; for humanitarian intervention, 176–78; internal conflicts and, 173–75; liberal school concerning, 167; and peace operations, 188; pre–UN Charter law, 162–65; protection of nationals abroad and, 176; regional organizations and, 189–90; reprisals and, 180–81; restrictions on, 163–64; Security Council and, 183–88; strict interpretation concerning, 167; UN Charter on abstention from, 91, 105–6, 165–67; weapons of mass destruction and, 190–94. *See also* war

USSR. *See* Soviet Union

Vanuatu, 33

vassal states, 32–33

Vatican, City State of the, 30–31

Vattel, Emmerich de, 17–18

Versailles Peace Treaty (1919), 57, 111, 112

Vienna Convention for the Protection of the Ozone Layer (1985), 240

Vienna Convention on Civil Liability for Nuclear Damage, 102

Vienna Convention on Diplomatic Relations (1961), 86, 94

Vienna Convention on the Law of Treaties (1969), 94, 111, 113

Vienna Ozone Convention (1985), 207

Vietnam: and Cambodia, 177–78; as divided state, 30; piracy against boat people of, 137; recognition of, 49; territory dispute involving, 46

Virgin Islands, 28, 44

voluntary law, positivism and, 18

Waldheim, Kurt, 125

Wall Street Journal, 224

war: bombing as tactic of, 8; civil, 174; death toll from 20th century, 162; Hague peace conferences on, 19; Kellogg-Briand Pact and, 45; laws or customs of, 144–45; as national policy, 45; Pufendorf and natural law, 16–17; Red Cross and, 81. *See also* use of force

war crimes, 143–47; crimes against humanity, 146–47; genocide, 145; grave breaches, 143–44; ICC jurisdiction over, 157; Nuremberg trials for, 151–52; Saddam Hussein and, 61–62; UN special tribunals for, 90; violations of laws or customs of war, 144–45

Warsaw Convention for the Unification of Certain Rules Relating to International Carriage by Air (1929), 267

Warsaw Convention on International Civil Aviation (1944), 100

weapons of mass destruction, 190–94; future dangers of, 291; Iraq war and, 161; legality of, 194; nonproliferation, 192–93; nuclear-free zones, 193; testing of, 193–94; weapons reduction, 191

weapons reduction, 191

weapons trafficking, 291

Webster, Daniel, 168

West Bank, 41–42, 45

Western Sahara, 46

Westphalia. *See* Peace of Westphalia (1648)

wetlands, 217

whales, 235

wheat, 281

wildlife, 216–19, 237

Wilson, Woodrow, 46

Wolff, Christian von, 17

Wolfowitz, Paul, 3

women: international criminal law concerning, 158; and rape, 147; rights of, 74, 77

World Administrative Radio Conferences
(WARCs), 245–46
World Bank. *See* International Bank for Recon-
struction and Development
World Bank Group, 265
World Charter for Nature, 216
World Conservation Strategy, 216–17
World Court. *See* International Court of Justice
(ICJ)
World Customs Union, 289
world government, concept of, 17
World Health Organization (WHO), 101, 290–91
World Heritage Convention (1972), 217
World Intellectual Property Organization, 101,
268
World Meteorological Organization (WMO),
101–2
world politics. *See* international relations
World Telecom Pact (1997), 290

World Trade Organization (WTO), 256–61; and
arbitration, 126; components of, 258; dispute
process in, 259; and environment, 260–61;
and foreign investment, 272–73; formation of,
256, 257; objectives of, 257; principles of, 257;
procurement rules of, 3–4; trade agreements
under, 53; treaty sections of, 258; and U.S.
steel tariffs, 253
World War I, human rights and, 69–70
World War II, human rights and, 70

Yemen, Republic of, 29, 30
Yugoslavia, 30, 90, 134, 143–44, 146

Zanzibar, 29, 33
zinc, 281
Zinser, Adolfo Aguilar, 85
Zouche, Richard, 18

About the Author

Christopher C. Joyner is professor of government and foreign service at Georgetown University, where he teaches courses on international law, U.S. foreign policy, and global environmental law. Currently the director of Georgetown University's Institute for International Law and Politics, he received the Edmund A. Walsh medal for teaching excellence from Georgetown University's School of Foreign Service in 1997, 2001, and 2004.

He has been a professor of political science and international affairs at George Washington University, a visiting professor in the Department of Government and Foreign Affairs at the University of Virginia and Dartmouth College, senior editor of the *Virginia Journal of International Law* and co-director of the Center for Peace and Environmental Studies at Florida State University. He was a senior research fellow on ocean law issues with the Marine Policy Center at Woods Hole Oceanographic Institution, a visiting research fellow with the Institute of Antarctic and Southern Ocean Studies at the University of Tasmania, Australia, and a Visiting Canterbury Fellow with the Faculty of Law and Gateway Antarctica at the University of Canterbury in Christchurch, New Zealand.

Currently the national vice president of the International Studies Association, he is past vice chair of the Governing Council of the Academic Council on the United Nations (ACUNS). He has served as chair of the Committee on Antarctica for the International Law Association and as a member of the ILA's Committee on the Law of the Sea. He twice served on the Executive Council of the American Society of International Law and was elected to its Executive Committee. He directed the ASIL's Project on the United Nations and the International Legal Order, sponsored by the Ford Foundation. He is co-editor of *United Nations Legal Order* (Cambridge University Press, 1995), the two-volume product of that research effort involving 20 scholars worldwide and the editor of its revision, *The United Nations and International Law* (Cambridge University Press, 1997).

He has written extensively on the use of force in foreign policy, Middle East politics, economic sanctions, humanitarian law, and transnational terrorism, as well as global environmental problems affecting the oceans, outer space, and Antarctica. His recently authored books include *Governing the Frozen Commons: The Antarctic Regime and Environmental Protection* (1998), *Antarctica and the Law of the Sea* (1992), *Eagle Over the Ice: The U.S. in the Antarctic* (with Ethel Theis, 1997), and *Teaching International Law* (with John King Gamble, 1997). Among works he recently edited are *Reining in Impunity for International Crimes* (1998), *The Persian Gulf War* (1990), *The Antarctic Legal Regime* (1988) and five special issues of *Ocean Development and International Law Journal*.